THIRD
BOOK OF JUNIOR AUTHORS

THE AUTHORS SERIES

THIRD
BOOK OF
JUNIOR AUTHORS

EDITED BY
DORIS DE MONTREVILLE
AND
DONNA HILL

THE
H. W. WILSON COMPANY
NEW YORK   1972

THIRD BOOK OF JUNIOR AUTHORS

Copyright © 1972
By The H. W. Wilson Company
First Printing 1972
Second Printing 1973
Printed in the United States of America

Library of Congress Catalog Card Number 75-149381

International Standard Book Number 0-8242-0408-5

PREFACE

The THIRD BOOK OF JUNIOR AUTHORS continues the work of Stanley J. Kunitz and Howard Haycraft in THE JUNIOR BOOK OF AUTHORS, second edition, revised, 1951, and of Muriel Fuller in MORE JUNIOR AUTHORS, 1963.

This latest work includes 255 autobiographical or biographical sketches of authors and illustrators of books for children and young people. Most of these authors and illustrators have come into prominence since the publication of MORE JUNIOR AUTHORS, but a few are older authors of continuing or renewed popularity who were not in the previous books.

In a two-year study of the field the editors compiled a preliminary list of 1200 candidates for inclusion in this work from which a voting list of 800 names was drawn after careful review. In selecting names for the voting list the editors considered the authors and illustrators of works that have won national or international awards, have appeared in standard selection aids and on lists of outstanding books, and have received generally favorable reviews.

Final selection was made by the editors with an advisory committee comprising Helen R. Sattley, Director of School Library Service for New York City, Adeline Corrigan, Assistant to the Director of the Cleveland Public Library, and Della Thomas, formerly Director of the Oklahoma State University Curriculum Materials Laboratory, now Director, European Studytours in Children's Literature. The vote of at least two committee members was required for a candidate's inclusion in this work.

Arrangement. Sketches are in alphabetical order by the name appearing most frequently on title pages, whether pen name or actual name, with cross references. Phonetic pronunciations are given when useful and obtainable. When authors have omitted important information about themselves, such as honors and awards received, editorial additions have been made following their autobiographical sketches.

When research disclosed conflicting information, inquiry was made of the biographees, when possible, to avoid perpetuating errors. Caldecott and Newbery awards are cited for the years in which the awards were made. Others are cited as they appear in announcements or news reports.

Special Features. New to this volume in the junior authors series are the lists of selected works published in the United States which are appended to the sketches. The editors have tried to list books which have received outstanding notice and those which the biographees themselves preferred, but in most cases only a sampling was possible because of space limitations. Although many of the authors and illustrators included have done distinguished work for adults as well as for children, the listing of adult works is outside the scope of this volume. When feasible, however, the editors have mentioned the biographees' other accomplishments.

Also new to this volume are biographical references, drawn from generally available sources. Only the latest editions of reference works such as *Who's Who* are cited.

Other new features are the reproduction, when authorized, of autobiographees' signatures and an index of all the authors and illustrators included in this volume and its two predecessors.

PREFACE

The editors and the publisher are grateful to the many children's book editors in the United States and abroad who have supplied information and photographs and have traced sometimes elusive biographees; to the staffs of the Hunter College Library, the Graduate School of Library and Information Sciences, University of Pittsburgh, the Carnegie Library of Pittsburgh, and the New York Public Library, in particular the Central Children's Room; to Catherine Bourlett, Muriel Fuller, Alice Penrose, and John Polak; to translators Elisa Di Giorgio, Lovisa J. Jenkins, Rita Rosenfeld, Mary Hayes Somers, Jean T. Wilde, and George Zenaty; and to writers of third person sketches Judy-Lynn Benjamin, Carolyn Dudley, Sheila Dugan, Jessica Fitzgerald, Letty Grierson, and Marjorie Smith. The editors also appreciate the many helpful suggestions of the advisory committee and their careful consideration of the voting list. Most essential thanks, of course, go to the writers and illustrators for their autobiographical sketches, which are the substance of this work.

THE EDITORS

CONTENTS

THIRD BOOK OF JUNIOR AUTHORS

ADRIENNE ADAMS

February 8, 1906-

ILLUSTRATOR OF *The Day We Saw the Sun Come Up*, etc.

Autobiographical sketch of Adrienne Adams Anderson:

I GREW up in Indian territory, in Okmulgee, Oklahoma, the capital of the Creek nation. Children usually find this interesting; I did not realize just how interesting it was until long after I had left it. Didn't everyone grow up that way?

On the first day of each school year we answered the roll call with a statement of the percentage of Indian blood in our veins —one half, one thirty-second, one sixty-fourth. Unthinking, I did not know or question why this was done. Of course, Indians were school-tax exempt to the extent that they were Indian; this was merely a tax-status check. I was not Indian, but many of my peers were.

I always enjoyed working with my hands. In my early days girls played with paper dolls, and I made original ones for my sister and friends, with large wardrobes of costumes. And doll houses: I constructed and furnished several of those.

I cut designs in linoleum blocks and printed fabrics. I spent hot, drenching summer days in the garage stamping on the blocks with my feet. The fabrics we used for dresses and tablecloths.

I went to college in Missouri and returned to Oklahoma to teach school; but it was not for me. Finally I knew I must do something in the graphic arts, so I came to New York with no real training and tried several things —display, murals, textile designs, then book illustration. That *was* it, for me. It is a wonderful field, with the most appreciative audience possible.

I live in New Jersey with my husband, Lonzo Anderson, who has written a number of children's books. We did *Two Hundred*

Rabbits and *Bag of Smoke* (for older children) together; also *Ponies of Mykillengi*, for which we made a trip to Iceland to get personally acquainted with those wonderful long-haired animals, so large-eyed and beautiful. We saw the volcano, Hekla, and drove our car down part of the rift in the earth created by the earthquake that preceded its eruption long ago.

We live in a stone-and-log house on twenty-seven acres in the Hunterdon Hills of New Jersey. We have a creek where ducks gather. Pheasant, grouse, partridge live in our woods. Deer and raccoon pass through. We have a little winter house on St. John, one of the Virgin Islands; we swim in those turquoise waters and work, too.

We are very lucky.

———

Adrienne Adams attended Stephens College and was graduated from the University of Missouri. In New York she studied at the American School of Design for three months, before beginning to do free-lance designing, then illustrating. Twice she has been a runner-up for the Caldecott Medal, for *Houses from the Sea,* 1960, and *The Day We Saw the Sun Come Up,* 1962. She received the Alumnae Achievement Award from Stephens College in 1964. Her work has been exhibited by the American Institute of Graphic Arts and has received citations from the New York Society of Illustrators.

SELECTED WORKS ILLUSTRATED: Bag of Smoke, by Lonzo Anderson 1942, 1968; Houses from the Sea, by Alice E. Goudey, 1959; Thumbelina, by Hans Christian Andersen, 1961; The Day We Saw the Sun Come Up, by Alice E. Goudey, 1961; In the Middle of the Night, by Aileen Fisher, 1965; Ponies of Mykillengi, by Lonzo Anderson, 1966; The White Rat's Tale, by Barbara Schiller, 1967; Two Hundred Rabbits, by Lonzo Anderson, 1968; Jorinda and Joringel, by The Brothers Grimm, 1968; Summer's Coming In, by Natalia Maree Belting, 1970.

ABOUT: Hopkins, Lee Bennett. Books Are by People; Hürlimann, Bettina. Picture Book World; Kingman, Lee and others, comps. Illustrators of Children's Books: 1957-1966; Viguers, Ruth Hill and others, comps. Illustrators of Children's Books: 1946-1956; American Artist November 1965.

IRVING ADLER

April 27, 1913-

AUTHOR OF *The Reason Why* books

and

RUTH ADLER

April 20, 1915-March 30, 1968

AUTHOR AND ILLUSTRATOR OF *The Reason Why* books

Biographical sketch of Irving Adler (who writes under his own name and under the pen name of "Robert Irving") and Ruth Relis Adler by Irving Adler:

READERS of my books often ask me, "What made you begin writing books for young people?" The answer to this question is that there was once a book that grew up by itself in my head. When it was fully grown, it began pounding on my skull, shouting "Let me out of here!" It happened this way. In 1937, while I was a high school teacher of mathematics in New York City, I took a course in *atomic structure* at Columbia University. This course planted in my head two ideas:

First, that the main ideas that physicists have put together in their theories of atomic structure are so simple that it should be possible to explain them to children. Secondly, that it was fascinating that everything we know about the tiny atoms of which all things are made is based on coded light messages sent to us by the atoms. These ideas were watered and fertilized when, in 1946, I took a course in *star identification* at the planetarium in New York. I read some books about astrophysics, and became fascinated by the fact that everything we know about the distant stars is based on coded light messages sent to us by the stars. By this time there was a full-grown book in my head clamoring to be let out to explain to children how we learn about small things like atoms and big things like stars by studying the coded light messages that they send us. I knew I would have no peace until the book was written. So I wrote it. Later it was split into two parts. The first part, dealing with atomic structure, was published under the title, *The Secret of Light.* The second part, dealing with the stars, was published under the title, *The Stars: Steppingstones Into Space.*

Writing books is like eating peanuts. As soon as you finish one, you start on another. By this time I have written over fifty books, and shared with my late wife Ruth the work of writing about two dozen more. For seven of my books I used the pen name Robert Irving. I used my own name for all the rest.

I was born in New York City, the third of five children. I went to the New York public schools and to Townsend Harris High School, and then to City College, from which I received the bachelor of science degree in 1931.

I began work as a graduate student in mathematics at Columbia University in the fall of 1931, paying my fees with a YMHA scholarship. When these funds ran out, I began teaching in 1932, and became the chief breadwinner of my family during the depression years while my father was unemployed. Since teaching hours conflicted with the hours of most graduate courses at Columbia, my graduate study at this time did not go beyond obtaining a master of arts degree in 1938. In 1956, when my work

RUTH ADLER

as a writer permitted me to choose my own working hours, I returned to the study of mathematics at Columbia University. I received the Ph.D. degree in pure mathematics in October 1961.

I was a teacher in the New York City high schools from 1932 to 1952. Since 1952 I have devoted most of my time to writing, but I have also done some lecturing, and have taught at Columbia University and Bennington College.

In 1932, while I was a graduate student at Columbia, I met Ruth Relis, a seventeen-year-old sophomore at Barnard College. Ruth was born on a farm in Sullivan County, New York, the third of four children. She went first to a one-room schoolhouse, then to a two-room schoolhouse, and then to Liberty High School. At the age of sixteen she came to New York City to go to Barnard. We were married in 1935, one day before she received her bachelor of arts degree. After our children reached school age, Ruth did graduate work in mathematics and education at Hunter College, where she received the master of arts degree in 1959. She also taught in the New York City schools, in Rockville Centre, and at Bennington College.

Ruth began illustrating my books with the second book that I wrote, *Time in Your Life*. She also played an increasing role in the writing of the books. At first she helped me select the subjects, discussed my outlines with me, and read and criticized everything that I wrote. Then, when we started doing *The Reason Why* books, she began writing whole books herself. Of the first thirty books in this series, Ruth wrote twenty-three and she illustrated nearly all of them.

In 1960 we moved to Shaftsbury, Vermont, where we built a house out in the country.

Our children are Dr. Stephen L. Adler, a theoretical physicist, and Mrs. Peggy Walsh, who is an author and illustrator. She has illustrated several of our books.

During Ruth's final illness in 1968, she was corresponding with a long-time friend, Joyce Sparer, who was teaching literature at the University of Guyana in South America. When Ruth was too weak to write any more, she asked me to answer Joyce's last letter for her. As a result of writing this letter for Ruth, I found myself, after Ruth died, writing more letters to Joyce, then seeing her, and finally marrying her. We hope that there will some day be books written by "Irving and Joyce Adler" to join those written by "Irving and Ruth Adler."

———

Irving Adler was graduated *magna cum laude* from City College and is a member of Phi Beta Kappa and Kappa Delta Pi. He also belongs to the Mathematical Association of America and Authors League.

Ruth Adler received the mathematics prize at Barnard College and graduated with honors.

The Adlers received National Science Foundation Fellowships in 1959 and in 1961 shared an award for "outstanding contributions to children's literature" from the New York State Association for Supervision and Curriculum Development.

Besides her work on *The Reason Why* books, Mrs. Adler illustrated about thirty-five other books written by her husband.

Mrs. Adler died of cancer in New York City.

SELECTED WORKS BY IRVING ADLER: The Secret of Light, 1952; Hurricanes and Twisters, 1955; Time in Your Life, 1955; The Stars, 1956; Magic House of Numbers, 1957; Giant Golden Book of Mathematics, 1960.

SELECTED WORKS COAUTHORED AND ILLUSTRATED BY RUTH ADLER: Things That Spin, 1960; Your Eyes, 1963; Your Ears, 1963; The Earth's Crust, 1963; Logic for Beginners, 1964; Atoms and Molecules, 1966; The Calendar, 1967; Directions and Angles, 1969.

ABOUT IRVING ADLER: Author's and Writer's Who's Who, 1963; Contemporary Authors, Vol. 7-8; Something About the Author, Vol. 1.

ABOUT RUTH ADLER: Contemporary Authors Vol. 7-8; Something About the Author, Vol. 1.

JOAN AIKEN

September 4, 1924-

AUTHOR OF *The Wolves of Willoughby Chase*, etc.

Autobiographical sketch of Joan Aiken:

I WAS born in Rye, Sussex. My father, Conrad Aiken the poet, is American, my mother Canadian. They had met when he was at Harvard and she at Radcliffe. They had come to England a couple of years before my birth because they thought the education there would be better for my elder brother and sister. They forgot to register me at the United States Embassy, so I'm an English citizen. My mother, who is an M.A.,

taught me at home till I was twelve because we were hard up and lived in a very remote country village. My brother and sister, respectively twelve and seven years older, were away a lot of the time at boarding school and university, so I was pretty solitary; there were no playmates of my age round about. My main amusements were reading (we had an immense supply of books in the house, both adult and just about all the classic children's books) and going for walks. I used to make up stories about imaginary friends to amuse myself on these walks. Later, when my half brother, seven years younger, was old enough to come on walks with me, I used to make up stories to amuse him, and cheer him up when he was tired.

A tremendous lot of reading aloud went on in our family; when I was three or four I can vividly remember being gripped by dramatic scenes from *The Cloister and the Hearth*, which my mother was reading to the older ones. And in the vacations when my elder brother was at home he used to read funny books, Thurber and Mark Twain and Saki; also ghost stories. Then my mother used to read me aloud Scott and Dickens and so forth; we'd go for walks and picnics, taking books in baskets, and sit under trees and read. I now live once more in the same part of the country which isn't much changed since I was a child; I can still find the spot where David Copperfield first met Mr. Murdstone and the tree where the Knight of the Leopard had his picnic with Saladin.

When I was five I spent my month's pocket money on a large blue note pad and started filling it with stories and poems. I still have it, and about a dozen successors; I was always writing something from then on. When I was seventeen I wrote down some of the fairy tales I'd been telling my younger brother and sent them to the British Broadcasting Corporation, who broadcast some of them on their Children's Hour. I also wrote a full-length children's novel and entered it for a competition, which it didn't win.

By now it was World War II, so I had various jobs, in the BBC, at St. Thomas's Hospital, and with the United Nations; then I got married and presently left work to have two children, John and Liz. I'd been writing short stories at odd times all along. In 1953, when John was four, I had a collection of these published by Cape, *All You've Ever Wanted* and a second batch, *More Than You Bargained For*, in 1955. Abelard-Schuman did these in America the following year. Then I got out my children's novel and rewrote it, and Abelard-Schuman published that, *The Kingdom and the Cave*. Then I started on a book I really wanted to write—*The Wolves of Willoughby Chase*—but had to put it aside, as my husband fell ill. I had to leave it for a long time, while I did various jobs, on a magazine called *Argosy*, and with J. Walter Thompson, the advertising firm. Meanwhile I wrote some adult stories and thrillers, but all the time I went on wanting to get back to *Wolves*, and finally I did get back and finished it, and it did well, so that we didn't have to worry about money any more. Then I wrote two sequels to it, *Black Hearts in Battersea* and *Night Birds on Nantucket*. Now I'm planning another, to be called *The Cuckoo Tree*. But in the meantime various things happened—

John and Liz grew up, for one thing. I'd always read them my books in instalments as I wrote them. Now they are too old, or almost, but luckily I have a nephew and niece, children of that younger brother, who are still quite small, so I wrote a book for small children, *A Necklace of Raindrops*, for them. And I went to Wales and fell in love with it, and wrote a book set in Wales called *The Whispering Mountain*. Jan Pienkowski, who drew the beautiful pictures for *A Necklace of Raindrops*, said he'd like to illustrate some Eastern European fairy tales, so I collected some of those, which was a delicious task. That's about all for the moment. I am sorry this piece seems to be mostly book titles, but writing books seems to be mostly what I do.

———

Joan Aiken attended Wychwood School in Oxford. She is the widow of Ronald George Brown, whom she married in 1945, and the mother of John Sebastian and Elizabeth Delano. *The Wolves of Willoughby Chase* won a Lewis Carroll Shelf Award in 1965. *The Whispering Mountain,* published in England in 1968, won the Guardian Children's Book Award for 1969, and was runner-up for the Carnegie Medal, 1969.

SELECTED WORKS: The Kingdom and the Cave, 1959; The Wolves of Willoughby Chase, 1963; Black Hearts in Battersea, 1964; Night Birds on Nantucket, 1966; Armitage, Armitage, Fly Away Home, 1968; A Necklace of Raindrops, 1969; The Whispering Mountain, 1969; Smoke from Cromwell's Time, 1970.

ABOUT: Author's and Writer's Who's Who, 1963; Contemporary Authors, Vol. 9-10; Publishers' Weekly December 9, 1968.

"FLOYD AKENS"

See *Baum, L. Frank*

JOHN ALCORN
February 10, 1935-

ILLUSTRATOR OF *Books*, etc.

Biographical sketch of John Alcorn:

JOHN ALCORN was born and grew up on Long Island, New York. In 1955 he was mar-

JOHN ALCORN

ried and settled with his wife, Phyllis, in New York City. He studied graphic arts for three years at Cooper Union under the direction of Philip Grushkin and Jerome Kuhl, among others. Having worked for *Esquire,* the Push Pin Studios, and a pharmaceutical advertising agency, he joined the CBS art department in 1958, where he became interested in typography. After a year at CBS, he decided to free-lance.

In 1962 Alcorn designed and illustrated *Books,* written by Murray McCain. It was selected by the American Institute of Graphic Arts as one of the Fifty Books of the Year. *Books* delightfully describes how and why books are made. The eclectic type and brilliant fuchsias, golds, and umber give the almost-psychedelic look used in the avant-garde cartoon films of the fifties and early sixties. With this book Alcorn's reputation was established. That year he did illustrations for Ogden Nash's collection of verse entitled *Everyone But Thee and Me* and Al Hine's *Where in the World Do You Live?* In 1963 he illustrated another of Hine's books, *Money Round the World,* and designed several paperback covers and a number of book jackets.

The next year, in addition to fulfilling various commissions for more paperback covers, jackets, and promotion materials, Alcorn illustrated *La Petite Famille,* a book

in easy French for children by Sesyle Joslin, and a sequel to *Books* called *Writing.*

Another book by Sesyle Joslin, *La Fiesta,* a beginner's Spanish book, was illustrated by Alcorn in 1967. Again he used his fuchsia, gold, and umber style.

John Alcorn lives with his wife and four sons in Ossining, New York, commuting as seldom as possible to the city.

Alcorn has received awards from the New York Art Directors Club, the New York Type Directors Club, and the Society of Illustrators. He won first prize at the 1968 Bologna Children's Book Fair, and the Augustus St. Gaudens Medal from the Cooper Union, 1970. He was a participant in the Push Pin Studios Retrospective Show at the Louvre, March 1970.

SELECTED WORKS ILLUSTRATED: Books, by Murray McCain, 1962; Where in the World Do You Live?, by Al Hine, 1962; The Circus, by Mary Kay Phelan, 1963; Writing, by Murray McCain, 1964; La Petite Famille, by Sesyle Joslin, 1964; A Letter to Anywhere, by Al Hine, 1965; A Wonderful Time, by Phyllis McGinley, 1966; La Fiesta, by Sesyle Joslin, 1967.

ABOUT: Kingman, Lee and others, comps. Illustrators of Children's Books: 1957-1966; Publishers' Weekly June 1, 1964.

LLOYD ALEXANDER
January 30, 1924-

AUTHOR OF *The High King,* etc.

Autobiographical sketch of Lloyd Chudley Alexander:

EVERY writer, I suspect, must be painfully aware of the gap between what he has in mind to do, what he feels and wants to say —and what he finally sets down on the page. After a good many years of writing for adults, my happiest surprise came when I began writing for children. It has let me come closer to expressing the ideas, attitudes, and values that mean most to me. The gap between intention and achievement is still there (a good thing, for it keeps you constantly trying to improve). But it might have narrowed a little.

A surprise, for I had never imagined I'd find so much joy in writing for young people.

And certainly my own career began under unlikely circumstances. Born in Philadelphia, Pennsylvania, and hoping, from the age of fifteen, to become a poet, I was more inclined to believe I'd never be able to write anything at all. A reader—yes. I devoured every book I could get hold of: Dickens, Mark Twain, Shakespeare; Grimm, Andersen; King Arthur, Robin Hood; Greek mythology, Celtic mythology; all mixed in a compost indigestible to anyone but a child. At sixteen, when I graduated from high school and learned the distressing fact that my family couldn't afford sending me to college, I went despairingly to work as a bank messenger during the days; and, just as despairingly, studied and wrote during most of the nights. I did save up for a year at college but was disappointed, for I wanted to learn more than what was being taught. In World War II, I joined the Army—amazed that such a large organization should be at such a loss what to do with me. In quick succession I became an artilleryman, a cymbal player in the band, a first-aid man, a harmonium player in the post chapel; and after a tour of duty in Wales, a staff sergeant in combat intelligence in France and Germany; and finally was attached to a counter-intelligence unit in Paris.

After the war, I stayed in Paris and went to the Sorbonne. I began translating the poetry of Paul Éluard, some of the novels of Jean-Paul Sartre and other contemporary authors. I also married a Parisian girl, Janine Denni, in 1946, and we came back to the United States where I spent about seven years writing the worst novels ever perpetrated. Luckily, they weren't published. My fourth try did succeed, however, and for the next ten years I wrote a variety of books for adults. At the same time, I worked as an advertising writer, cartoonist, layout artist, associate editor for an industrial magazine.

My first fantasy for children, *Time Cat,* led me deeper into a much longer fantasy, an attempt to create my own mythical world in the five books of Prydain. These, I believe, somehow linked up my experiences in Wales, the hero tales of my childhood, and my own sense of at last discovering that writing for children was indeed what I loved best.

Are any aspects of my own life reflected in the books? Yes, certainly. I think that every creative work, on the deepest levels, is an aspect of the writer himself, and his own personal vision. This, really, is all that any writer can offer—along with the hope that he will offer it well.

———

Lloyd Alexander's book *The Black Cauldron* was a runner-up for the Newbery Medal for 1966. *The High King* won the Newbery Medal for 1969. *The Marvelous Misadventures of Sebastian* received the 1970 National Book Award for children's books.

SELECTED WORKS: Border Hawk, 1958; Time Cat, 1963; The Book of Three, 1964; The Black Cauldron, 1965; Coll and His White Pig, 1965; The Castle of Llyr, 1966; Taran Wanderer, 1967; The Truthful Harp, 1967; The High King, 1968; The Marvelous Misadventures of Sebastian, 1970.

ABOUT: Alexander, L. C. Janine Is French, 1959; Contemporary Authors, Vol. 1; Who's Who in America, 1970-71; Horn Book April 1965; August 1968; February 1970; Library Journal May 15, 1969; New York Times Book Review May 4, 1969; Publishers' Weekly February 17, 1969; Top of the News November 1968.

LECLAIRE GOWANS ALGER

See *"Nic Leodhas, Sorche"*

ALIKI

September 3, 1929-

AUTHOR AND ILLUSTRATOR OF *Keep Your Mouth Closed, Dear,* etc.

Autobiographical sketch of Aliki Liacouras Brandenberg:

ACKNOWLEDGING my place of birth always makes me uncomfortable, for it was accidental. I lived in (and later near) Philadelphia, but was born at the seashore (Wildwood Crest, New Jersey) while my family was still vacationing.

I don't know exactly when I first started drawing, but I remember vividly when two of my paintings were exhibited in kindergarten. They were both portraits of families with three girls and a boy named Peter. My own and Peter Rabbit's. Such a fuss was made over them that the course of my life was decided that day.

My first-grade teacher used any excuse to give me books on drawing. I even stopped biting my nails for a week for one such reward.

All through school I drew constantly, even when I wasn't supposed to, and took Saturday art classes. After high school in Yeadon, Pennsylvania, I attended the Philadelphia Museum College of Art.

Following graduation in 1951 I spent a year in New York working in the display department of the J. C. Penney Company, and the next five in Philadelphia. I freelanced in advertising art and display, painted murals, had a greeting card company, and taught art and ceramics.

In 1956 I went abroad, sketching and painting, mainly in Italy and Greece. The trip was memorable, for although my parents were born in Greece and I spoke Greek before English, it was then I discovered my background.

I also met Franz Brandenberg, whom I married a year later. We lived in Switzerland (in Berne and Zurich), where I continued my career. It was there I realized William Tell was Swiss. We visited the territory in which he lived, and the legend took on new meaning. I wrote and illustrated my first book, *The Story of William Tell,* which was published (by Faber and Faber, London) in 1960.

That year we moved to New York and among other things, I was asked to illustrate several books. One was for the T. Y. Crowell *Let's Read and Find Out* series. While I drew, another book was forming in my mind. One Friday evening I wrote the words and called it *My Five Senses.* I drew the dummy on Sunday and Monday, and on Tuesday it was accepted. Later, I found it is not quite that easy, but that most books do germinate in a hidden part of the mind, and are released by a pen and a clean sheet of paper.

I have illustrated about forty books, fifteen of which I have written, including *Keep Your Mouth Closed, Dear, The Story of Johnny Appleseed, A Weed Is a Flower—The Life of G. W. Carver,* and two Greek folk tales, *Three Gold Pieces* and *The Eggs.*

I have always felt close to children and books, and feel fortunate that I can direct what creativity I have to both. Besides, I have found myself, for in advertising, I was

Aliki: *ah LEE ki*

always asked, "What are you? Full color? Pen and ink? Gouache?" In books I can express a manuscript any way I choose, and still be myself.

We have two children, Jason (April 15, 1964) and Alexa (June 7, 1966), who are both picture-book age. They are finding a way in my books.

———

Aliki's work has been in exhibitions of the American Institute of Graphic Arts. Interested in many forms of arts and crafts, she makes dolls and has worked in silver, enamel, ceramics, papier-mâché, clay, and various forms of collage.

SELECTED WORKS WRITTEN AND ILLUSTRATED: My Five Senses, 1962; The Story of Johnny Appleseed, 1963; A Weed Is a Flower: The Life of George Washington Carver, 1965; Keep Your Mouth Closed, Dear, 1966; Three Gold Pieces, 1967; Hush Little Baby, 1968; The Eggs, 1969; Diogenes, 1969; My Visit to the Dinosaurs, 1969.

SELECTED WORKS ILLUSTRATED: Cathy Is Company, by Joan Lexau, 1961; This Is the House Where Jack Lives, by Joan Heilbroner, 1962; Bees and Beelines, by Judy Hawes, 1964; One Day It Rained Cats and Dogs, by Bernice Kohn, 1965; Oh, Lord, I Wish I Was a Buzzard, by Polly Greenberg, 1968; Five Dolls and Their Friends, by Helen Clare, 1968; At Home, by Esther Hautzig, 1968; I Once Knew a Man, by Franz Brandenberg, 1970.

ABOUT: Contemporary Authors, Vol. 4; Kingman, Lee and others, comps. Illustrators of Children's Books: 1957-1966.

E. M. Almedingen (signature)

E. M. ALMEDINGEN

July 21, 1898-March 5, 1971

AUTHOR OF *Young Mark*, etc.

Autobiographical sketch of Martha Edith von Almedingen:

I WAS born in St. Petersburg in the summer of 1898. Much later someone called the family "the League of Nations in little," because we were all bits and pieces, English, German, Austrian, Danish and Russian. I did not go to any school until I was fifteen. Literature was in my blood. On my mother's side there were Edmund Spenser and Robert Southey. On my father's side a great-aunt, Catherine Almedingen, (1829-1893) stood

in the forefront of children's authors. My earliest predilection was for history, and they made me Member of the Faculty (Petrograd University) in 1922. But that degree, however honourable, was not much use as a means of livelihood when I came to England in 1923. Writing could be, but it took me eighteen years to reach my first break with my autobiography *Tomorrow Will Come*, awarded the Atlantic Monthly best nonfiction book of the year prize in 1941.

In the early fifties I began writing for children—first fairy tales and historical stories which were followed by family chronicles.

It is rather difficult to answer the question "How do you write?" A friend's aunt was disgusted by my answer: "Well, I take up my pen and a sheet of paper." In reality, any book I have ever written had been lived with and walked with some time before the first sentence was shaped. Writing is at once a delight and an agony. I have always believed that were I ever to be pleased with anything I have written, I would put my pen down for good, and superlative reviews leave me with an odd sense of being plunged into an unbearably hot bath.

To write for "the young of all ages" is, however, more of a delight than an agony. Somehow, children seem to be the most discerning critics, and their attitude to any book makes it a *sine-qua-non* to be honest with them. Hence, instead of the dry bones of an adult bibliography I put a note sketching out the sources of my material and adding a paragraph or two about the treatment. Thus, *Katia* was based on my great-aunt's book *The Story of a Little Girl* (first published in 1878 and a best-seller until 1917). But my *Katia* was ruthlessly shortened: the original ran to nearly 400 pages, small print, demi octavo. Again, it had to be changed since usages and incidents familiar to a Russian child of more than a hundred years ago would be hardly intelligible to a Western reader today. *Young Mark*, the story of my great-great-grandfather, was based on very scrappy reminiscences, the manuscript once kept in the Emperor's private library.

When I reached England in 1923, the first county I came to know was Somerset. Now, after years of living in London and in other parts of England, I have returned to my "first love"—an exquisite seventeenth-century cottage, the gift of a generous fan—since become my closest friend, in 1962. She now shares it with me. The other tenants are two blue Persian cats, Alexander and Clovis. The cottage stands at the mouth of a valley, a trout stream running through the grounds.

An illness some three years ago left me a semi-demi-cripple, and the long "wanders" belong to the past. But it is possible to start on most entrancing journeys of the mind—rewarding companionship, books, music, correspondence and work. All these are so many stimuli urging one on and on—to give out as much as one can. Oh! and I must not forget the birds! To watch a heron fly over the water, to hear an owl in the night, to see a wagtail on the window-sill . . . Really, there is no end to the joys, and the five years (1917-1922) spent in Russia in an atmosphere of midnight house-searches, machine-gun snipers, beetroot doled out as a bread ration and all the rest of it, have certainly taught me to appreciate all I have found in my mother's country.

———

E. M. Almedingen was educated privately before she entered Xenia Nobility College in 1913, where she earned highest honors in literature and history. From 1916-1920 she was a doctoral student at the University of Petrograd and afterwards lectured there on English medieval history and literature. Later she lectured at Oxford University, England, on Russian history and literature, and in 1951 was elected a Fellow of the Royal Society of Literature.

Young Mark received a 1968 *Book World* Children's Spring Book Festival Award. *The Knights of Kiev* was on the Honor List, German Juvenile Book Prize, 1968.

SELECTED WORKS: Russian Folk and Fairy Tales, 1957, 1963; The Knights of the Golden Table, 1964; The Story of Gudrun, 1967; Katia (adapted from Catherine Almedingen), 1967; A Candle at Dusk, 1968; One Little Tree, 1968; Young Mark, 1968; Ellen, 1970.

ABOUT: Almedingen, E. M. The Almond Tree, 1947; Late Arrival, 1952; Tomorrow Will Come, 1941; Within the Harbour, 1950; Author's and Writer's Who's Who, 1963; Contemporary Authors, Vol. 2.

VICTOR G. AMBRUS

August 19, 1935-

AUTHOR AND ILLUSTRATOR OF *The Three Poor Tailors*, etc.

Autobiographical sketch of Victor G. Ambrus:

I WAS born in Budapest. Until I was nine years old I lived with my family in a small town on the outskirts of this city.

I had heard a lot about the war from my parents, but one day it arrived on our doorstep. Somehow we all survived it, and life began to return to normal and it was not long before the schools reopened.

My father, who is a chemical engineer, was often driven to despair over my total lack of understanding of mathematics and science. After trying to explain what he believed to be a simple mathematical problem for hours on end, he would finally give up, saying that he hoped some other hidden talent would come to light and save me from starvation when I eventually left school!

Victor G. Ambrus.

When I did leave grammar school, it was with a reasonable certificate of matriculation and a pile of drawings—mainly battle scenes consisting of twenty or more figures struggling on horseback. At that time I was very strongly influenced by nineteenth century romantic historical paintings in national museums and the collections of arms and armour in the Museum of Military History.

I considered myself very fortunate to gain entrance to the Hungarian Academy of Fine Art, which has a tradition of high academic standards with a strong emphasis on drawing. I studied graphics, etching, lithography, anatomy, and illustration which continued to interest me throughout my school years.

My elder twin brothers were training to be engineers at the University in true family tradition. The three of us had marvelous times together, which included getting lost in a hitherto undiscovered cave two hundred feet under the ground, going on long hikes around the mountains of Budapest or hunting for geological specimens with my brother John who had a passion for crystals and fossils.

After I spent three years at the Academy in truly Bohemian atmosphere, I left Hungary in 1956 and carried on as a student in London at the Royal College of Art and completed a diploma course in graphics. During my second year at college I was very fortu-

nate to be commissioned by Blackie & Sons, Ltd., to illustrate one of their books, *White Horses and Black Bulls.*

One of the drawings was published in the *Times Literary Supplement* and I was asked to illustrate books for other publishers. After finishing at college I started to work for Oxford University Press, under the expert art direction of Miss Mabel George.

Having illustrated a number of books, including a colour series, *The British Army, Royal Navy, The Royal Air Force,* and *The Merchant Navy,* I tried my hand at a picture book—*The Three Poor Tailors,* which was awarded the Kate Greenaway Medal by the Library Association of Great Britain. I feel very honoured by the award, even more so, because the story was based on a folk tale from Hungary. Since then I have illustrated several other picture books as well as a large number of black and white books.

I am married, with a ten-year-old son, and we live in Hampshire. My main interest, besides illustrating, is collecting old weapons.

———

Victor G. Ambrus is now a British subject, married to an English woman, the former Glenys Chapman, who is also a painter. Their son's name is Mark.

In 1959 Ambrus received the award of Royal Scholar from the Royal College of Art. He is an Associate of the Royal College and also of the Royal Society of Engravers. Twice he was a runner-up for the Kate Greenaway Medal before he received it in 1967 for *The Three Poor Tailors,* and other work the preceding year.

SELECTED WORKS WRITTEN AND ILLUSTRATED: The Three Poor Tailors, 1966; Brave Soldier Janosh, 1967; The Little Cockerel, 1968; Seven Skinny Goats, 1970.

SELECTED WORKS ILLUSTRATED: Time of Trial, by Hester Burton, 1964; The Maplin Bird, by K. M. Peyton, 1965; The Bushbabies, by William Stevenson, 1965; No Beat of Drum, by Hester Burton, 1967; The Pieces of Home, by Miska Miles, 1967.

ABOUT: Hürlimann, Bettina. Picture Book World; Kingman, Lee and others, comps. Illustrators of Children's Books: 1957-1966; Something About the Author, Vol. 1; Who's Who in Art, 1970; Library Association Record June 1966.

GERALD AMES
October 17, 1906-

and

ROSE WYLER
October 29, 1909-

AUTHORS OF *The New Golden Book of Astronomy*, etc.

Biographical sketch of Rose Wyler Ames (who writes as Rose Wyler and under the pen name of "Peter Thayer") and Gerald Ames by Gerald Ames:

OUR writing team began shortly after 1948 when I (with one daughter) and Rose (with two sons) merged our families and our debts, gave up our jobs, and risked becoming free-lance writers. The children were assets as captive readers and advisors. In addition, we had some professional preparation.

Rose was one of the pioneers in developing elementary science programs in New York State and elsewhere. She had taught and supervised the teaching of science in elementary schools, had given graduate courses in science education at several universities, including Teachers College of Columbia, and had directed the first successful elementary science program on radio. Farther back than that, Rose was steered toward nature study and science through the Girl Scouts and by haunting the American Museum of Natural History in New York. As for me, Gerald, I had some training in geology, biology, and anthropology, and had written on science subjects for popular magazines. So when my stepson Karl one day, at the age of five, looked up at me and asked, "Gerald, what do you want to be when you grow up?" I was able to answer, "A writer."

We began with projects that attempted to outline a whole scientific field (*The Golden Book of Astronomy* and *The Golden Book of Biology*) for the middle and higher grades. Later we got ambitious or foolhardy and tried to reach very young children, including beginning readers. Recently we have gone from science to magic (reversing history). The magic activities (*Magic Secrets* and *Spooky Tricks*) are meant to bewitch chil-

dren into reading by offering them the reward of learning how to fool their parents and friends.

We are reconciled to our home base, New York City, partly because, from our roost in a high rise, we can look up the Hudson River and the Palisades and sometimes see the wild

geese on their wonderful migratory flights.
We get away when we can to summer on
the Maine coast, snorkel in the Caribbean,
and motel up and down the West Coast.

As conservationists, we oppose the de-
struction of countries and people in wars,
and have been active in the movement to
bring peace in Viet Nam. We are also active
members of our professional association, the
Authors Guild. Along with our colleagues,
we try in whatever way we can to further
the civil rights movement and in particular
to integrate books in text and illustration.

Rose Wyler graduated from Barnard College in 1929 and in 1931 took an M.A. from
Teachers College, Columbia University, the
first ever given there in elementary science.

The children of Rose Wyler and Gerald
Ames are Eva Lee Baird, Joseph, and Karl.
Eva Lee Baird was the coauthor with Rose
Wyler of *Science Teasers*.

SELECTED WORKS BY GERALD AMES AND ROSE
WYLER: Story of the Ice Age, 1956; The First
People in the World, 1958; First Days of the
World, 1958; The Golden Book of Biology, 1961;
The New Golden Book of Astronomy, 1965;
Food and Life, 1966; Magic Secrets, 1967;
Spooky Tricks, 1968.

ABOUT GERALD AMES AND ROSE WYLER:
Hopkins, Lee Bennett. Books Are by People.

ABOUT ROSE WYLER: Who's Who of American Women, 1964-65.

KARIN ANCKARSVÄRD

August 10, 1915-January 16, 1969

AUTHOR OF *Bonifacius the Green*, etc.

Biographical sketch of Karin Inez Maria Olson Anckarsvärd by Cecile Anckarsvärd:

OUR mother, Karin Anckarsvärd, used
to tell us how she came to write children's
books.

When she was four or five, day after day
she asked people around her: "Read a story,
please! Read!" She wanted to learn how to
read and write as soon as possible. So she
was allowed to start school one year earlier
than usual.

Every day on her way to school she passed
a bookshop selling writing materials. She

Anckarsvärd: *ANG kahr svaird*

KARIN ANCKARSVÄRD

was excited by so many empty notebooks
with yellow, red, and black covers. Secretly
she emptied her moneybox containing two
kronor, quite a fortune for a child in those
days. And she bought a lot of notebooks.
Now she could fill page after page with the
thrills that she had missed in her own story-
books. She wrote about villains, thefts, house-
breaking, and several brave dogs. She and
her brother played the leading parts. Her
handwriting grew worse and worse. But that
didn't matter. The main point for her was
that the letters became words and the words
became stories.

About one year after her start she won
second prize in a fairy tale competition. She
was overwhelmed and proud when she got
twenty kronor for "Christmas of the Hares."
This of course inspired her to continue her
writing.

Karin Anckarsvärd was born in Stockholm.
She was the daughter of a county medical
officer. She often accompanied him on visits
to his patients. She wrote down the impressions she got from these visits in *Doctor's
Boy* and *Svenssons pojk*. *Doctor's Boy* received the Nils Holgersson plaquette, 1964,
which is given to the best children's books
of the year in Sweden.

In 1933 she qualified as a student, and
after that she studied literature, history, and
psychology at Oxford. She married in 1939.
When her first book came out in 1951 she

had five children, aged three, five, seven, nine, and eleven. Her first book was a fairy tale, *Bonifacius the Green,* which was about a lizard with a human character. She wrote ten pages at a time and then would read what she had written to us children. We always wanted more and more. When we were a bit older she started writing mystery books. She also wrote books for girls. *Aunt Vinnie's Invasion* and *Aunt Vinnie's Victorious Six* are about young people and their problems, something which she knew a lot about. We children often acted as models for the characters in the books.

In all she wrote fourteen books, which are read by children in Sweden, the United States, England, Germany, Switzerland, Denmark, Norway, and Finland.

———

Karin Anckarsvärd was the daughter of Oscar Emil and Iris (Forssling) Olson. After attending Oxford University, 1934-1935, she took a commercial college degree in Stockholm in 1936. She married Carl M. Cosswa Anckarsvärd and had five children, Marie Christine, Marie Cecile, Marie Madeleine, Mikael, and Carl Henrik. Mrs. Anckarsvärd served as secretary of Sveriges Yngre Lakares, 1936-1940. She was president of the Catholic Women's League of Sweden and a member of Association of Sweden's Authors of Children's Books, Association of Sweden's Authors, and Conservative Women's League. Her books have received honors and awards in Sweden as well as in the United States. She received a Swedish State Stipend in 1960. Two of her works have been Honor Books in New York *Herald Tribune* Children's Spring Book Festivals: *The Robber Ghost* in 1961, *Bonifacius the Green* in 1962.

SELECTED WORKS: The Mysterious Schoolmaster, 1959; Rider by Night, 1960; Bonifacius the Green, 1961; The Robber Ghost, 1961; Springtime for Eva, 1961; Aunt Vinnie's Invasion, 1962; Aunt Vinnie's Victorious Six, 1964; The Doctor's Boy, 1965; The Riddle of the Ring, 1966; Struggle at Soltuna (translation of Svenssons pojk), 1968.

ABOUT: Contemporary Authors, Vol. 9-10.

ADRIENNE ADAMS ANDERSON

See *Adams, Adrienne*

C. W. ANDERSON

April 12, 1891-March 26, 1971

AUTHOR AND ILLUSTRATOR OF *Billy and Blaze,* etc.

Autobiographical sketch of Clarence William Anderson:

I WAS born in Nebraska, in a small town with the improbable name of Wahoo. After finishing high school I taught country school for two years to earn money to go to the Art Institute of Chicago, where I studied for three years. Free-lancing in New York for some years starting with cartoons and such illustration as I could find, I finally began to concentrate on drawing horses. A friend of mine, then turf writer for a New York paper, Peter Burnaugh, took me to the track and I saw Crusader, son of Man O' War, come surging through the stretch to win going away, and I knew what I wanted to draw and paint from then on.

My first book was a picture book for beginners with full-page pictures that told the story and only a couple of lines of text on the opposite page. It was called *Billy and Blaze* and seemed to be liked, for it is selling much better now than when it was published in 1936. There are now ten of the Blaze books. I have done a number of books that were planned as adult books for horse enthusiasts but judging by the letters I receive, my readers in this case range from eight to thirteen or fourteen. When these youngsters not only read such books as *Big Red,* a biography of Man O' War, *The Smashers, Tomorrow's Champion,* and *Horses Are Folks* but ask such technical questions that I have to go to the record books for answers, I guard against ever "writing down" to children of any age.

All of my forty books have been in black and white. My publisher told me at first that books for very young children always called for color. I argued that if the drawings had enough reality children would not be aware that the pictures lacked color. I am glad that this proved to be the case for only with the most expensive color reproduction, such as was used in my six portfolios, can the subtle variation in tones be satisfactorily portrayed.

I strongly believe that the best judge of a child's book is a child. For that reason I feel very fortunate for the large amount of mail I receive from children about my books. Obviously the young horse enthusiast is not lukewarm in enthusiasm. Almost all of the letters begin "I love horses more than anything in the world." Then they tell just what they liked about a book and why. Nothing could be more helpful to an author. When a little girl writes, "I like your books although they are a little thin for my age," I ignore the possibility of subtle criticism and try to add another chapter or two to the next one.

Of course you must make allowance for youthful enthusiasm. I received a letter from a little girl, years ago, that read "You are the greatest artist in the world and I love you." Naturally this made a great impression on me and I kept the letter. Several years later I received another letter from the same girl. She wrote, "Your pictures are very nice," and signed it "Yours respectfully." She was growing up.

I try to make everything in my books possible even though limits of probability are pushed pretty far. Especially important to me is the idea that any information that a child may get about horses from the books must be correct and that a horseman could read them to his child without wincing.

C. W. Anderson followed horse breeding, racing, and hunter trials with great interest, was qualified as a judge of hunters and jumpers by the American Horse Shows Association, and judged in a number of shows. In addition to his many books of fiction for children and adults, he wrote nonfiction on horses and riding and on how to draw horses. He painted figures and landscapes, liked to sketch from nature and showed his work in galleries and museums throughout the United States. For his children's books he usually made lithographs, working directly on stone.

Anderson was married to Madeline Paltenghi, a poet. They had a country home in New Hampshire, where Anderson built a studio of native granite. Nearby are miles of trails in the woods through which the Andersons rode horseback almost daily for many years.

SELECTED WORKS WRITTEN AND ILLUSTRATED: Billy and Blaze, 1936, 1962; Blaze Finds the Trail, 1950; Horses of Hurricane Hill, 1956; Blaze and the Indian Cave, 1964; Twenty Gallant Horses, 1965; Another Man O' War, 1966; Blaze Finds Forgotten Roads, 1970; The Miracle of Greek Sculpture, 1970.

ABOUT: Hopkins, Lee Bennett. Books Are by People; Kingman, Lee and others, comps. Illustrators of Children's Books: 1957-1966; Mahony, Bertha E. and others, comps. Illustrators of Children's Books: 1744-1945; Viguers, Ruth Hill and others, comps. Illustrators of Children's Books: 1946-1956; Who's Who in American Art, 1962; New York Times March 28, 1971.

LONZO ANDERSON

March 1, 1905-

AUTHOR OF *Two Hundred Rabbits*, etc.

Autobiographical sketch of John Lonzo Anderson:

THE name I sign to letters and checks is John L. Anderson. The "L." stands for "Lonzo", my father's name. I use Lonzo Anderson for my writing because there are so many John Andersons who are or have been writers.

I was born in Georgia because my parents happened to be there at the time, but I haven't a single root or relative in that state.

It was in the happy horse-and-buggy days that I was born and raised. My father was a "circuit-rider"—a country preacher. He had four churches, one for each Sunday in the month, and he rode to them on horseback, making the "circuit"; in a month that had five Sundays he didn't have a thing to do on the fifth one!

Although he was a Northern Methodist preacher, he was preaching in the deep south, not as a "missionary," but because there was a pocket of Northern Methodism in that (what was then) backwoods area of North Georgia, in the foothills of the Appalachian chain of mountains.

During the week he was the principal of a country school. It was a busy life.

My mother was a teacher in the school. She and my father were newlyweds when they took these jobs, and before they had been married even one year he was drowned trying to cross a swollen stream on horseback after a storm, on his way to work. This was ten days before I was born, so I never knew him and had to grow up without him, and without any brothers or sisters.

My mother kept trying to get better teaching jobs, and so we moved about a lot; but almost always we were far out in the country, and I grew up rather like a rabbit, barefoot, with freedom to wander far and wide and learn about nature from being up to my chin in it. I like cities because I like all kinds of people, the more kinds the better; but for true living, give me the backwoods country with all its wild creatures and plants.

At the age of three I found out that stories didn't just grow, along with the paper they were on. I decided then and there to be a writer, and dictated my first story to my mother. It would be pretty embarrassing to read that story now.

It was a very long way from there to here. I eventually worked my way through college, graduated from Harvard, and went to New York, where I did all *sorts* of jobs in order to keep alive while I wrote and tried to sell stories. There I met a girl artist—I had always known I would—and we got married and lived through the depression in Greenwich Village.

My first published book was *Bag of Smoke* (Viking Press). My wife illustrated it, and that was the start of her delightful career as Adrienne Adams, children's illustrator.

She has since illustrated two picture books for me as well as *A Fifteenth Century Cookry Boke* (Scribner, 1962) for grownups. Also, she has reillustrated for me a rewritten *Bag of Smoke* that Knopf published in 1968.

Another young book of mine, *Zeb* (Knopf, 1966), about a pioneer boy surviving alone in the wilderness, was illustrated by a superb outdoor artist, Peter Burchard.

Believe it or not, I am a licensed real estate broker. I used to sell farms, country homes, and land out here in lovely Hunterdon County, New Jersey, where Adrienne and I have lived ever since we left New York in 1953. I am still very much interested in real estate, especially land—"the good green earth."

Adrienne and I have a second milieu—the little paradise island of St. John in the

Virgin Islands, which we have known since 1935; we have our second home there.

Our chief interest outside of our work—perhaps even more than our work—is the brotherhood of man.

SELECTED WORKS: Bag of Smoke, 1942, 1968; Ponies of Mykillengi, 1966; Zeb, 1966; Two Hundred Rabbits, 1968.

ABOUT: Hopkins, Lee Bennett. Books Are by People.

JOAN WALSH ANGLUND

January 3, 1926-

AUTHOR AND ILLUSTRATOR OF A *Friend Is Someone Who Likes You*, etc.

Autobiographical sketch of Joan Walsh Anglund:

WHEN I was a young girl, about eight or nine years old, I used to escape to the attic to read and draw for long, delicious hours. I read and reread all of *My Book House, The Lives of the Saints, The Book of Knowledge*, and all the Oz books. I would sit there in the dusty quiet and lightly draw pictures and write stories up and down the margins and then erase them, so as not to hurt the book, before I went down to dinner. I would repeat the process with a different story the next day.

Both my father and mother were artists, and so drawing seemed as natural to me as writing my name. We never just *wrote* a note, we designed it. We drew on everything: mirrors, tables—even the sandwiches in our lunches were made in the shape of faces. My father, Tom Walsh, was a commercial artist who died when I was ten. My mother, Mildred Pfiefer Walsh, was a painter in oils and watercolors. Our household was very warm and loving and volatile.

My books are the accumulated memories of my own childhood upon which are superimposed the newer, more freshly etched experiences of my own children's childhood. The two seem to fuse into one, not of any particular date but always of the "time" of childhood. It seems I have always been searching for the "essence" of things—the seed, the inner secret—"to see the world in

joan walsh anglund

a grain of sand and eternity in an hour." The possibility of this delights me. Especially with my drawings, a great deal of my work is elimination and focus. With the writing, this is done somewhere in my subconscious before the words come out. The words are always of primary importance to me. The drawings are made to "serve" the idea.

I never "decide" to write a book, it decides to write itself, and I must hurry to "catch" it as it comes. *Friend* was written as I stood on a playground with my young children. Todd was riding his tricycle round and round at my feet, and Joy and a friend were bouncing a large blue rubber ball back and forth above my head.

I wrote *Friend* after a long period of intense loneliness and deep homesickness. My husband and the children and I had left our small town in Illinois to move to New York City. We were no longer among old and comfortable friends. We walked on concrete instead of running across meadows and playing on lawns. Everyone seemed to be living in separate "boxes" of distrust. Then one day I realized that we were *not* alone—that there were friends everywhere—but often we shut ourselves away from the friendships that surrounded us just waiting for us to "notice" them . . . and that's when I jotted down those few words on a green steno-pad and put the crumpled sheets in the back of my drawer. That night my husband happened to find and read those lines. The next day he was leaving on a business trip and he asked me to finish the book before he came back. A week later he took it to the first publisher. It was presented to several publishers but Margaret McElderry of Harcourt, Brace decided to publish it, and that was the beginning, in 1958.

The children in my drawings are impressions of my own children. Todd was *The Brave Cowboy*. When he was three and four and five, he dressed in a big floppy black cowboy hat that someone had given him, and he refused to take it off even when he went to bed. He wore that same two-gun holster and those big cowboy boots. The toys and the bed and the cat and the general "confusion" were drawn in Todd's room. It is very precious to me now to open the cowboy books and "see" Todd just as he was, so stalwart, so brave, so full of imagination and yet so little and vulnerable.

The little red-headed girl with the ponytail in the green dress and white pinafore on the first page of *Friend* is Joy, just as *she* looked when she was seven. We still have that green dress and pinafore tucked away in our attic.

Many people have asked me why I do not put noses and mouths in my drawings. It is simply something that has evolved. Slowly the noses and mouths became smaller and less distinct until one day I realized I was drawing children as I do now. But to me the noses and mouths are still there. I still "see" different expressions on the faces. I think I am trying to get the "essence" of a child—of childhood itself, perhaps. This too may be why I find myself dressing the children in a timeless manner, but always with a vague sense of nostalgia.

Many of the backgrounds of the illustrations are drawn from life right here in my home in Westport, Connecticut. The well house on the cover of *Spring* is the well house just outside our dining-room window, and the large fireplace in *Nibble Nibble Mousekin* is the walk-in fireplace in our own living room. We live in a house built in 1754,

once an inn used by British soldiers during the Revolutionary War.

My studio is just above the old blacksmith's forge (which is now the center of our kitchen). I reach it by a little hidden staircase. My studio is tiny and cozy and cluttered, but "happily" so. Once there, I am up among the tree-tops with the birds which perch at my window and sometimes look in at me as I draw. It is here I sit, quietly working, creating my small designs, much as a spider weaves her web, slowly spinning a shape from her own inner substance.

––––––––

This sketch by Joan Walsh Anglund was originally written in somewhat different form for her niece in college, who wanted information for a paper she was writing for a class in children's literature.

Joan Walsh Anglund was born in Hinsdale, Illinois. She studied at the Chicago Art Institute and the American Academy of Art and became an apprentice to Adele Roth, a commercial artist. She married Robert Anglund in 1947. Their daughter Joy was born in 1949 and their son Todd in 1954.

A Friend Is Someone Who Likes You was named by the New York *Times* as one of the ten best-illustrated children's books of 1958.

Mrs. Anglund has said that she never expected her books to have universal appeal. Nevertheless, her work has been phenomenally popular. *A Friend Is Someone Who Likes You* has sold more than one million copies in the United States and has also been published in England, Denmark, Sweden, Norway, Finland, Holland, and Germany. Eleven of her other books have each sold more than 100,000 copies.

SELECTED WORKS: A Friend Is Someone Who Likes You, 1958; Love Is a Special Way of Feeling, 1960; In a Pumpkin Shell, 1960; Christmas Is a Time of Giving, 1961; Nibble Nibble Mousekin, 1962; Spring Is a New Beginning, 1963; What Color Is Love? 1966; A Cup of Sun; A Book of Poems, 1967.

ABOUT: Contemporary Authors, Vol. 7-8; Kingman, Lee and others, comps. Illustrators of Children's Books: 1957-1966; Who's Who in America, 1970-71; Who's Who of American Women, 1970-71; Publishers' Weekly July 8, 1963; January 11, 1971.

"BARBIE ARDEN"

See *Stoutenberg, Adrien*

RICHARD ARMSTRONG

June 18, 1903-

AUTHOR OF *Cold Hazard*, etc.

Autobiographical sketch of Richard Armstrong:

I WAS born in a village on Hadrian's Wall right in the heart of the coalfield that lies between the River Tyne and the Northumbrian moors. My father was a blacksmith and my mother a miner's daughter. I grew up among miners and steelworkers, was educated with their sons in the village school and went to work in the steel plant near my home just after my thirteenth birthday. The rest of my education I picked up along the way.

For four years I shovelled coal, drove cranes, and helped in various other ways to turn hunks of white hot steel into forgings weighing up to twenty tons; then I went to sea in the merchant service to knock about the world until I was into my thirties. For various good reasons I left the sea in 1936 and, settling in London, worked at a variety of jobs including a spell on a small newspaper.

I never made a conscious decision to become a writer. It was something that just happened. I learned the trade while still at sea but did not submit a manuscript to a publisher until 1941 and was staggered when it was immediately accepted. It was a book about my schooldays in Northumberland. After that I continued to write in my spare time for another twelve years or so and in 1949 had the good fortune to be awarded the Library Association Carnegie Medal for a book called *Sea Change* which never found an American publisher.

But life in London was becoming an increasing strain. My son had been launched on a career as a film maker and feeling the need for quiet and time to think, my wife and I began looking for a cottage in the country. We found it in the summer of 1954

and moved into it that autumn after which I began to unload my London commitments. It took me two years to get out from under but I made it and since the end of 1956 I have worked full time as a professional writer.

Our cottage is at least three hundred years old with walls up to three feet thick and not a square corner in it. It stands five hundred feet up on the northwest spur of the Quantock Hills and is only half a mile from the sea. Watching things is my hobby and this is a wonderful place in which to indulge it. From my window the horizon is thirty miles away and on a clear day I can watch the deep-water ships heading in from the Atlantic to Swansea, Cardiff, and Avonmouth.

The first of my books to be published in America was *Cold Hazard* which was brought out in 1956 by Houghton Mifflin and took first prize in the *Herald Tribune* Festival of Books. Others have followed and three of them—*Ship Afire!*, *The Big Sea*, and *The Mutineers*—have been Literary Guild choices. Translations of my work have been done in Japan, Germany, and Brazil and are contracted for in Denmark and Poland. I have also written novels for adults, a biography of Grace Darling, and have just completed a three-volume study of the history of seafaring.

Richard Armstrong and his wife Edith were married in 1926. They have one son, John.

SELECTED WORKS: Cold Hazard, 1956; Ship Afire! a Story of Adventure at Sea, 1961; The Big Sea, 1965; The Secret Sea, 1966; The Mutineers, 1968.

ABOUT: Author's and Writer's Who's Who, 1963; Library Association Record April 1949.

WILLIAM H. ARMSTRONG

September 14, 1914-

AUTHOR OF *Sounder*, etc.

Autobiographical sketch of William Howard Armstrong:

IN taking a measurement of my life I find a paradox which is probably responsible for the fact that my writing has been described as being "for all ages."

Born on a farm near Lexington, Virginia, in that most beautiful Shenandoah valley, I walked with history where General Lee had walked, and went to Sunday School in a Presbyterian Church where "Stonewall" Jackson had taught. It was in this Sunday School that I was moved from the world of my contemporaries into the adult world. At the age of twelve I listened while the Sunday School teacher opened all the stops in telling the story of Jesus, the carpenter of Nazareth, driving the demons out of the possessed persons and into the Gadarene swine.

When the swine ran down the hill and perished in the lake, it was too much for a farm boy, so I asked: "What about the poor man who owned the swine? Who paid for his loss?"

In a stern Scotch Presbyterian household, where God and discipline were real and working, and for which I am daily grateful even now, it was decided that I would be moved into the Men's Bible Class where I would not annoy the teacher. This was my entrance into the adult world, and here and later in school and college I found my friends among older people. After college I began

to teach thirteen- and fourteen-year-olds and have spent my life with them.

As in the Men's Bible Class I discovered that the questions of young and old were about the same, so in teaching I early became aware that the young will rise to mature stature, and if not given that challenge will become bored and indifferent to reading and learning.

Along the way, walking through this beautiful creation, which the Creator has given me to enjoy, I have managed to be a farmer, tending my sheep on a rocky hill farm overlooking the Housatonic River in Connecticut. I have also found time to become a carpenter and stone mason. I cleared my own land, built my own house. After teaching, building an uncoursed stone wall to stand as long as time, gives me greatest pleasure.

I have three children whose mother died when they were very young. We have grown up together. They were forced to help with the household chores, often having to be alone. Perhaps their greatest legacy came of necessity—an appreciation of work and the ability to endure their own company. One is a criminologist and the other two are artists—realists in a rather unreal age.

My formal education included Augusta Military Academy, Hampden-Sydney College, and the University of Virginia. In each school I found one or two great teachers to whom I am forever grateful.

William H. Armstrong received his A.B. (*cum laude*) from Hampden-Sydney College in 1936. He married Martha Stone Street Williams in 1942 and their children are Christopher, David, and Mary.

In 1945 Armstrong became a history master at Kent School in Kent, Connecticut. He still lives in the house built entirely by his own hands and raises purebred Coniedale sheep. He received the National School Bell Award of the National Association of School Administrators in 1963 for distinguished service in the interpretation of education. *Sounder*, a story of a dog and his devotion to his master, a black sharecropper, won the Newbery Medal for 1970. *Sounder* also won a Lewis Carroll Shelf Award for 1970.

SELECTED WORKS: Study is Hard Work, 1956; Through Troubled Waters, 1957; The Peoples of the Ancient World (with Joseph Ward Swain) 1959; The Tools of Thinking; a Self-help Workbook for Students in Grades 5-9, 1969; Sounder, 1969; Barefoot in the Grass, 1970; Sour Land, 1971.

ABOUT: Contemporary Authors, Vol. 19-20; Horn Book August 1970; Publishers' Weekly August 17, 1970; Top of the News April 1970.

ISAAC ASIMOV

January 2, 1920-

AUTHOR OF the *Foundation* trilogy, etc.

Autobiographical sketch of Isaac Asimov who also writes under the pen name "Paul French":

I WAS born in the Soviet Union. However, I remember nothing of my foreign experiences since before I was three years old my family set out on the road to the United States, carrying with them me and my younger sister. We arrived in New York in February 1923 and by September 1928 we

all were American citizens. (My younger brother, born in 1929, was a citizen to begin with.)

We all set about learning English at once. It never occurred to my parents that it might be useful for me, someday, to know Russian. The result is that I now know approximately 40,000 different words of English and about 12 different words of Russian. (Of *course*, I'm sorry.)

My youth was divided between studying in various public schools in New York and working in my parents' various candy stores. At the age of fifteen I was inserted into a niche in Columbia University.

By 1939, I had received my bachelor's degree, having majored in chemistry. Not wanting to break up a winning combination, I decided to continue onward for more of the same. Same school, same major, same working in the store outside school hours, and by 1941 I had an M.A. and kept right on going.

However, we all know what happened at the end of 1941. I left both school and store to do what seemed useful. I was a chemist at the Naval Air Experimental Station in

Philadelphia, and then served in the armed forces.

On February 14, 1942 (yes, Valentine's Day), I happened to meet a Miss Gertrude Blugerman, originally of Toronto but at that time of New York City. Filled with instant wild enthusiasm over this meeting, I laid violent siege to the young lady and, by shrewdly not giving her time to think things through, I found myself married to her on July 26 of that year. I am still married to her, and the fruits of the union include a boy with short brown hair and a girl with long blond hair. The boy, David, was born in 1951; the girl, Robyn Joan, in 1955.

World War II over, I picked up at Columbia University, passed the store on to my younger brother, and earned my Ph.D. in 1948. I stayed awake all night following my oral examination staring fatuously at the ceiling and periodically chuckling with delight (my wife informs me) at the thought that now I could refer to myself as "Dr. Asimov."

But another aspect of my life was assuming greater prominence. Back in 1929, while I was in charge of the magazine rack in my father's store, reams of fascinating blood and violence lay all about me and yet were kept from me by my father's stern notions about the degenerating influence of cheap literature. Then a science fiction magazine, *Amazing Stories*, passed under his eagle glance and received the august paternal nod. I was hooked.

I can't remember when I wasn't on fire to write. At the age of twelve (possibly earlier), I was filling a nickel notebook with scrawlings, divided into chapters, and entitled "The Greenville Chums at College." In 1936, my father dug into the almost invisible family savings and bought me a secondhand typewriter. I promptly taught myself to touch-type and began a rambling fantasy-novel.

By June 1938, I had actually completed a story and carried it to the offices of *Astounding Science Fiction*. The editor, John W. Campbell, Jr., rejected the story but kindly discussed with me, then and thereafter, all angles of the writing art. My father cooperated also by finding the funds, somehow, to buy me a spanking-*new* typewriter.

In October 1938, four months after my first submission and after twelve rejections from various magazines, I made my first sale, a story entitled "Marooned off Vesta," bought by *Amazing Stories*.

By the time I received my Ph.D., the atomic bomb had lent science fiction a new (and rather horrible) respectability and it was beginning to appear in hard covers by major publishers. My first book, the science fiction novel *Pebble in the Sky*, was published in January 1950.

In 1949, I had accepted a position on the faculty of the Boston University School of Medicine. I am still there, with the present rank of Associate Professor of Biochemistry. (I occasionally chuckle at the thought that I may now call myself "Professor Asimov.")

My academic career has affected my writing, too. In 1950 I began work (with two other members of our department) on a textbook for medical students. Little by little, my science writing swallowed up the rest of me. By 1958 I had given up first my research, then most teaching, and finally science fiction. Now I devote myself almost entirely to science-writing.

I live in a house in West Newton, Massachusetts. The rest of the family live on the main floor, which has the usual rooms, bathrooms, and so on. I live in the attic, equipped with a fairly large reference library, a record player, an FM radio, an air-conditioner, a globe, a large desk, numerous cubbyholes, and most important—two electric typewriters.

My father attributes my success to the stern fashion in which he kept me from worthless literature, allowing me only science fiction. I am grateful for that, yes; but I am even more grateful for his faith in me. He bought two typewriters for me when it was a fairly rocky business to find money for the next meal—and this before I had sold a single story.

————

Isaac Asimov was born in Petrovichi, the son of Judah and Anna Rachel (Berman) Asimov. His father died in 1969. Since 1965, he has, among other work, written several historical books for young people, including a general background book on the Bible.

Asimov is a member of American Chemical Society, Sigma Xi, and Mensa Club. In 1966 he received the Hugo Award of the World Science Fiction Convention for his *Foundation* trilogy. Asimov had published more than a hundred books by 1970, with others in process.

SELECTED WORKS: I, Robot, 1950; Foundation trilogy (Foundation, 1951; Foundation and Empire, 1952; Second Foundation, 1953); Words of Science and the History Behind Them, 1959; Breakthroughs in Science, 1960; Realm of Measure, 1960; Kingdom of the Sun, 1960; Building Blocks of the Universe, 1961; Inside the Atom, 1961; The Kite that Won the Revolution, 1963; The Greeks, 1965; The Roman Empire, 1967; Asimov's Guide to the Bible, 1968.

ABOUT: American Men of Science, 1965; Author's and Writer's Who's Who, 1963; Columbia Encyclopedia, 1963; Contemporary Authors, Vol. 2; Current Biography Yearbook, 1968; Moskowitz, Sam. Seekers of Tomorrow; Something About the Author, Vol. 1; Who's Who in America, 1970-71; Who's Who in Science, 1968; Chemical and Engineering News March 29, 1965; Fantasy and Science Fiction October 1966; New York Daily News October 4, 1967; New York Times Book Review August 3, 1969; Newsday March 18, 1967; Time July 7, 1967.

JACQUELINE AYER

May 2, 1930-

AUTHOR AND ILLUSTRATOR OF *Nu Dang and His Kite*, etc.

Autobiographical sketch of Jacqueline Brandford Ayer:

BORN in New York of Jamaican parentage, my early years were considered as "temporary residence" since preparations were always underway to return to Jamaica. Nonetheless, I spent my grade school years in New York, in the Bronx, in a predominantly Russian/Polish area, a very confining community. Home life was on one hand very much in the colonial Negro-Jamaican tradition, but in school and out on the streets I was as Russian/ Polish/ Jewish as the group I grew up with.

After graduating from high school—Music and Art—and a brief interim at the Art Students League, I attended Syracuse University for two years as a painting major. I continued my training in painting and fine arts at the École des Beaux Arts in Paris.

It was in Paris that I started a brief but hectic career as a fashion illustrator. After returning and spending a year in New York, I went again to Paris, ostensibly for a vacation. While there, I married an American from Akron, Ohio, and we set out for the East where he taught and did research at the University in Bangkok. Two daughters were born, Margot in 1956 and Elizabeth in 1958. The early years in Bangkok were full of the excitement and strangeness of being ten thousand miles away from home. This, of course, was mixed with trifling inconveniences and the intermittent boredom of a fairly solitary existence. Armed with sketch paper and pencil, I would roam through Bangkok by scooter or sampan.

I first met Margaret McElderry on a trip to New York in 1958, and it was she who convinced me and gave me the courage to try and put all these pictures and words together in the shape of books for children. *Nu Dang and His Kite* was the first product of these years. *A Wish for Little Sister*, and *The Paper-Flower Tree* followed.

In 1960 I joined IBEC—International Basic Economy Corporation—and started a small division called Design Thai. It mushroomed to disproportionate size rather quickly, and it was not until 1966 that I was able to extricate myself from being full-time Fabric and Fashion Designer and lady executive to return to the familiar West and live in London as Consultant and Head Fashion Designer.

My travels have been and still are extensive, and I know Thailand, Hong Kong, Japan and India fairly well. There have been frequent trips to spots in between, as well.

Though it's a long way from my days playing "Johnny on the Pony" in the Bronx and those nostalgic days in Bangkok on my scooter, when the air was still perfumed with the innocence of isolation, the world, and indeed my life, go at a faster and more complicated pace. There are still, fortunately for me, the joy and the opportunity to see things with the open eyes of a children's book artist and writer—all the delights and details of those faraway places—and to bring them home to share with others.

———

Jacqueline Ayer also studied at the École Paul Calin in Paris. She was married to Frederic Ayer and has two daughters, Margot and Elizabeth. A designer of books as well as an illustrator, she has received the Gold Medal from the Society of Illustrators and has been represented in exhibitions of the American Institute of Graphic Arts.

Nu Dang was inspired by the son of the boatman she hired to paddle her up and down the rivers and canals of Bangkok.

SELECTED WORKS WRITTEN AND ILLUSTRATED: Nu Dang and His Kite, 1959; A Wish for Little Sister, 1960; The Paper-Flower Tree, 1962.

SELECTED WORKS ILLUSTRATED: Humpy, by Peter Yershov, 1966; Rumpelstiltskin, by The Brothers Grimm, 1967; Princess September, by William Somerset Maugham, 1969.

ABOUT: Hürlimann, Bettina. Picture Book World; Kingman, Lee and others, comps. Illustrators of Children's Books: 1957-1966.

"ELEANOR BABBIS"

See *Friis-Baastad, Babbis*

BETTY BAKER

June 20, 1928-

AUTHOR OF *The Dunderhead War, etc.*

Autobiographical sketch of Betty Lou Baker:

AS a pre-schooler in Bloomsburg, Pennsylvania, my only playmate was a boy across the street who loved to play cowboy and Indian. I was the Indian. I must have been shot, trapped, massacred, and burned at the stake a hundred times. One Fourth of July I rebelled. I crept up behind the officious little cowboy, pointed my cap pistol and shouted, "Bang, bang! You're dead!"

He turned around and said with great disgust, "You can't do that. You're the Indian."

Which probably explains why I write about Indians. I'm still proving to that son of a dentist that Indians *can* do that.

Other than the cowboy across the street, my companions from age four to ten were books. I read myself out of the library's children's section and soon began on the adult books by courtesy of my mother's card and her willingness to smuggle them out for me. My favorite—*Beau Geste, Captain Blood, The Three Musketeers* and *The Border Legion*—indicate my taste for action writing.

As World War II threatened, I was uprooted from this introverted life and plunked down outside Newark, New Jersey. Oh, tragedy! No library in walking distance! In sheer boredom I looked about and discovered real people.

I was unaware that we were poor, disadvantaged (except for lack of a library which bothered no one but me) or that our neighbors were minority groups. I only knew that each apartment smelled of strange food, odd cadences altered the English language, and attitudes and customs were not what I'd been accustomed to. Real people, I discovered, were as interesting and even more puzzling than those in books. From this background stepped Uncle Fritz in *The*

Dunderhead War and Brother Solano in *Walk the World's Rim* as well as parts of many others.

Maturity began a few years later on visits back to the small Pennsylvania towns. I listened in astonishment to positive statements made of various nationalities and religions, statements I knew from experience to be blatantly false. They were all little cowboys, smugly convinced that Indians couldn't do that.

Now it's obvious that a writer was in the making, but I felt no urge until my son (now age sixteen) was in first grade and frustrated by beginning-to-read books that he could not possibly read. Later I was spurred by the boring sketchiness and occasional inaccuracies of his history books. But though I usually begin with an intriguing historical situation, people soon involve me and history is relegated to the background. But then, history *is* people.

Primarily, I write the sort of book I liked to read, about interesting people involved with lots of action and none of the boring stuff I skip when I read. But under all the

humor and thunder, I'm still battling the little cowboys, showing that Indians—or Negroes or Mexicans or you or I—*can* and *did* do that!

Betty Baker attended public schools in Orange, New Jersey. Her marriage to Robert George Venturo in 1949 was ended by divorce in 1964. She has one son, Christopher Patrick.

She has worked at many jobs and once owned a gift shop. In addition to her schedule of writing five thousand words a day, she lectures before local groups and edits the monthly *Western Writers of America*.

She received the Western Heritage Award for *Killer-of-Death* in 1963 and the Western Writers of America Golden Spur Award in 1967, for *The Dunderhead War*.

SELECTED WORKS: Little Runner of the Longhouse, 1962; The Shaman's Last Raid, 1963; Killer-of-Death, 1963; Walk the World's Rim, 1965; Blood of the Brave, 1966; The Dunderhead War, 1967; Do Not Annoy the Indians, 1968; And One Was a Wooden Indian, 1970.

ABOUT: Contemporary Authors, Vol. 4; Who's Who of American Women, 1970-71.

JAN BALET

July 20, 1913-

AUTHOR AND ILLUSTRATOR OF *Joanjo*, etc.

Autobiographical sketch of Jan Bernard Balet:

ONCE upon a time, when I was four years of age, I lived in the house of a very pleasant grandfather. He showed me how to draw a horse. I thought it was a terrible horse. So he bought more paper and more pencils and was also a patient audience to my first artistic excursions, on how to draw a better horse.

Later I went to school. After a summer vacation we had to write about something that had happened during our holiday. Four pages were required. I wrote one page and padded the essay with three pages of illustrations. It was a novel idea and I was a big success.

Many years later I wrote and illustrated

Jan Balet

a little book as a Christmas present for my four year old son (no horses!) A friend saw it, he showed it to another friend, who showed it to an agent, who took it to a publisher. The book was published and accepted among the fifty best books of the year (ten were children's books). More books were accepted by the fifty best books, a few got other prizes and several were translated into other languages. Now once a year I try to think up a new story about something amusing that has happened during the year.

Someday, maybe, my son Peter will have a son and I, the grandfather, will draw for him a "terrible horse."

———

Jan Balet was born in Bremen, Germany. His father, a museum director and art historian, was half French, half Dutch, and his mother was German. When Jan Balet was four he and his mother went to the south of Germany to live with her parents. As a teen-ager, Jan Balet worked as an apprentice with a painting and decorating firm in Munich, and then, at seventeen, was admitted to the Arts and Crafts School. He studied for several years at the Academy of Fine Arts in Munich, and also studied art in Berlin and supplemented his education with wide travel in Europe. In 1938 he came to the United States in protest against the Hit-

ler regime, lived in New York, and became an American citizen. He contributed illustrations to a number of magazines, did advertisements for New York department stores and for many national firms, became art director for *Mademoiselle* magazine and then for *Seventeen,* and was often represented in annual shows of the Art Directors Club, from which he has received two Gold Medals and fifteen Awards of Merit. In 1965, he returned to Europe and now lives and works in Munich. A painter as well as an illustrator, he attributes much of his early inspiration to Greek, Roman, and Egyptian art, and to primitive folk art. He has also illustrated about twenty books for other authors.

SELECTED WORKS WRITTEN AND ILLUSTRATED: Amos and the Moon, 1948; Ned & Ed & the Lion, 1949; What Makes an Orchestra, 1951; The Five Rollatinis, 1959; The Gift, 1967; Joanjo, 1967; The King and the Broommaker, 1968; The Fence, 1969.

SELECTED WORKS ILLUSTRATED: Alarcón, Tales from the Spanish, 1948; Rosalinde, by Helen Wing, 1952; Fair, Brown and Trembling; an Irish fairy tale adapted by Patricia Jones, 1957; Birthday Angel, by Martha Bennett King, 1959; Rumpelstiltskin; an adaptation from Grimms' Fairy Tales by Patricia Jones, 1955; The Snow Queen, retold from Hans Christian Andersen by Martha Bennett King, 1961; The Mice, the Monks and the Christmas Tree, by George Selden, pseud., 1963; Just One Me, by Aileen Brothers and Cora Holsclaw, 1967.

ABOUT: Viguers, Ruth Hill and others, comps. Illustrators of Children's Books: 1946-56; American Artist November 1946; January 1951; Graphis No. 51, 1954; Vogue August 1, 1959.

"LAURA BANCROFT"

See *Baum, L. Frank*

MICHEL-AIMÉ BAUDOUY

April 1, 1909-

AUTHOR OF *Bruno, King of the Mountain,* etc.

Autobiographical sketch of Michel-Aimé Baudouy:

I WROTE my first children's book in prison. Rather, it was in a cell in a prisoner of war camp in Germany, after the failure of an

Baudouy: *BO DOO EE*

M. A. Baudouy

attempted escape. This book tells of a young boy who raises eagles, tames them and succeeds in having them carry him in the air. I believe that being deprived of space and liberty inspired the writing of this tale which appeared in English under the title of *Noel and the Eagles.*

As a child I lived in the country, not far from the Pyrénées. Memories of adventures there and a taste for nature helped me in writing this story. The success of this first book naturally led me to write a second, then a third, et cetera, and thus I came to explore this fascinating and special field, children's literature.

My first readers and critics were of course my own children (two boys and one girl). However, as a teacher I was constantly in contact with young people. Some of my works were inspired by family characters and situations (*More Than Courage*) or events from real life (*Secret of the Hidden Painting*).

It was, I believe, my love of nature which led me to write *Bruno, King of the Mountain* and *Old One-Toe.* Of all my works these have been translated most often, along with *More Than Courage.*

Deception at St.-Nazaire and *The Boy Who Belonged to No One,* which take place respectively in a shipyard and a roadblock on a high mountain, required a great deal of research.

I do not believe that children's literature is an unimportant part of the field. Nor do I believe that the author is justified in writing any kind of unlikely adventures without the slightest concern for psychological truths, or in using a careless and silly style of writing under the pretext that his readers are mere children. On the contrary, it is precisely because the readers are children that the author must be more careful in his documentation and must (if he can) show even more talent than if he were writing a book for adults.

As for me, I feel that the technique which the children's author must use is the same as that of the novelist, that it deals with the same problems of creative writing and with some others which are even more difficult to solve.

I receive numerous letters, particularly from American readers, asking questions which are sometimes embarrassing, for they touch upon the essence of the trade of writer: "Why do you write? What leads you to write? How do you come by the idea of writing a book?" Is not that itself the mystery of creation?

In various schools throughout the United States, in Belgium, in Switzerland, in Japan, in a school in Africa, boys and girls have presented studies on my books to their friends and sometimes to radio and television audiences. On such occasions they have asked me a series of specific questions in order to document the account.

At present a growing number of "round-table discussions" between writers and young readers are organized by professors, librarians, associations of students' parents, and by cultural groups. These direct contacts are certainly of interest to the children, but they are very fruitful for the authors themselves, for they teach them sincerity and modesty. To see the seriousness and care with which the children read, to feel the trust they have in the author, to recognize from the originality of their questions what powers of poetic creativity they have must lead authors to conclude that the real "inventors of stories" are children.

Finally I believe that the truly great authors are those who have preserved the spirit of childhood.

To conclude this bio-bibliographic statement may I add that I have published in France a collection of short stories and five novels for adults, essays on the Spanish Mystics and the cultural unity of the Occident (*Europe, My Country*) three pieces for radio and a play given in Paris in 1957-58: *Pity for Heroes.*

———

Michel-Aimé Baudouy and his wife Yvonne have two sons, Jean-Paul, a doctor, and Jacques, a medical student, and one daughter, Michèle, who studied law and is married to an Ingénieur-Directeur of the Institute of Technology. Baudouy has seven grandchildren, Anne, Isabelle, Jean-Michel, Patrice, Philippe, Véronique, and Matthieu. Baudouy has won numerous literary prizes in France. He received certificates of distinction as a runner-up for the Hans Christian Andersen Award in 1960 and 1970.

SELECTED WORKS: Old One-Toe, 1959; Bruno, King of the Mountain, 1960; More Than Courage, 1961; Deception at St.-Nazaire, 1963; Secret of the Hidden Painting, 1965; The Boy Who Belonged to No One, 1967.

L. FRANK BAUM

May 15, 1856-May 6, 1919

AUTHOR OF *The Wonderful Wizard of Oz,* etc.

Biographical sketch of Lyman Frank Baum, who wrote under his own name and under the pen names of "Laura Bancroft," "Floyd Akens," "Edith Van Dyne," "John Estes Cook," "Suzanne Metcalf," "Schuyler Stanton" and "Captain Hugh Fitzgerald":

THE son of Benjamin Ward Baum, a prosperous oil dealer, and Cynthia Stanton Baum, Lyman Frank Baum was born and reared near Syracuse, New York. From birth Lyman Frank, or Frank, as he preferred to

L. FRANK BAUM

be called, had a heart condition which restricted his activities, causing him to turn to his imagination for adventure and companionship. Tutored at home, he briefly attended the Peekskill Military Academy, where he developed a lifelong distaste for the military. An indulgent father supported his hobbies, which included printing a monthly paper on his own printing press, stamp collecting, and, later, poultry breeding. He was also interested in the theater, and his earliest jobs were in the acting and newspaper professions. In 1880 he became the manager of a chain of small-town theaters owned by his father, for which he wrote a number of plays. One of them, *The Maid of Arran,* was such a popular success that he took it on tour in 1882. In the same year, on November 9, Baum married a Cornell student, Maud Gage, and the newlyweds toured with Baum's troupe for several months before settling in Syracuse, where Baum went to work in a family business and where their first son, Frank Joslyn, was born in December, 1883.

In the late 1880s the death of Baum's father and elder brother, the extended illness of his wife following the birth of their second son, Robert Stanton, in February, 1886, and the dishonesty of an employee depleted the family fortune. Urged by his wife, who had relatives in North Dakota, Baum moved to Aberdeen in 1888. There his last two sons were born—Harry Neal, in December 1889, and Kenneth Gage, in March 1891—while he tried operating a notions store and then a newspaper, both of which failed. In 1891 Baum moved to Chicago, where he held jobs as a newspaper reporter, crockery buyer, and traveling salesman before starting a successful trade magazine, *The Show Window,* which he published between 1897 and 1902.

At home, Baum amused his sons by making up stories based on Mother Goose characters. His mother-in-law persuaded him to write them down and submit them to a publisher, and in 1897 his first children's book, *Mother Goose in Prose,* appeared. The book sold well, and Baum's collection of jingles, *Father Goose, His Book,* published in 1899, sold even better. But neither approached the overwhelming popularity of *The Wonderful Wizard of Oz.* Published in 1900, it aroused childish appetites for more stories about the magical place Baum named after the letters O-Z on a label of his filing cabinet.

Baum wrote the book and lyrics for a musical comedy based on *The Wizard of Oz,* which opened in Chicago in 1903 and played in New York to capacity houses for a year and a half. *The Wizard of Oz* was also the basis for two silent movies and the musical color film starring Judy Garland.

Between 1900 and 1910 Baum turned out five more Oz books as well as an assortment of fantasies with other settings. Under his various pen names, he also produced adventure stories for teen-agers and several adult novels, some of which were inspired by a trip to Europe and Egypt which he made in the winter of 1905-06. By the time *The Emerald City of Oz* was published in 1910, he was determined to end the series and wrote that Oz had been cut off from the rest of the world. For four years Baum, who had moved from Chicago to Hollywood, resisted his readers' pleas for more Oz books. Finally, in 1914, he resumed the series, and thereafter wrote one Oz book a year. After his death in Hollywood, publishers employed others to continue the series, turning out twenty-six titles in addition to Baum's four-

teen. In total the Oz books have sold over seven million copies, have inspired radio, television, puppet shows, and movies, many Oz clubs, and even fan magazines. In 1956, Columbia University held an exhibition in Baum's honor. In 1968 *The Wizard of Oz* received a Lewis Carroll Shelf Award.

SELECTED WORKS: Father Goose, 1899; Wonderful Wizard of Oz, 1900; Dot and Tot of Merryland, 1901; Queen Zixi of Ix, 1905; Dorothy and the Wizard in Oz, 1908; Emerald City of Oz, 1910.

ABOUT: Dictionary of American Biography, 1929; Gardiner, Martin and Russell B. Nye. The Wizard of Oz and Who He Was; MacFall, Russell P. and Frank Joslyn Baum. To Please a Child; National Cyclopedia of American Biography, 1906; Wagenknecht, E. C. Utopia Americana; Who Was Who in America, 1897-1942; Who's Who in America, 1912-13; American Heritage December 1964; American Quarterly Spring 1964; Chicago Review, no. 2, 1965; Georgia Review Fall 1960; Hobbies September 1957; May 1959; Life December 28, 1953; The New Republic December 12, 1934; The New York Times Book Review May 13, 1956; May 2, 1971; Publishers' Weekly October 30, 1937; July 15, 1939; February 13, 1961; Reader's Digest June 1966; Saturday Review April 11, 1959; July 29, 1967; Top of the News November 1970.

HANS BAUMANN
April 22, 1914-

AUTHOR OF *Sons of the Steppe,* etc.

Autobiographical sketch of Hans Baumann:

WHEN I was seven years old, I was given a thick book as a present. All the pages were blank. Because I wanted to be a painter, I painted a picture on each page. Nothing more came of it. At ten, I began to play the violin and later the organ, although my legs weren't really long enough. My head was full of nothing but music, and I resolved to write symphonies and operas. But with the exception of some hundred songs, which I wrote later, I did no composing at all. I was twelve when I wrote "my first poem," and I stuck to writing. I filled a whole exercise-book with verse, all in rhyming couplets, and it was printed. Later I experimented with plays, which were put on in Berlin by some well-known people, such as Gustav

Gründgens. I don't enjoy seeing these plays
staged nowadays, and I don't like to have
the early poems reprinted. A few songs,
which I wrote as a young teacher in a village
school, have kept their freshness. I was a
teacher for a year when I was nineteen. Then
I studied in Berlin and traveled in the East
and in North Africa.

During the war I was a soldier in Russia,
and it was then that my affection for the
Russian people originated; since then I have
done translations from the Russian, especially poems and stories for children. And
I began to write books for children and
young people myself. In the winter of 1943,
near Novgorod, I decided to write the story
of two boys whose destiny was to be determined by a so-called "great man." I was
taken prisoner, and during my imprisonment
I began *Sons of the Steppe*, the book about
the two grandsons of Genghis Khan, one
of whom fell under the influence of the great
destroyer while the other became a con-
queror himself. It is not a historical book;
I tried to describe what I myself had experienced and I used a remote setting in order
to make everything clearer. The same ap-
plies to *I Marched with Hannibal, Son of
Columbus, The Barque of the Brothers*. An-

other series of books has early civilizations
for its subject. The first of these books was
The Caves of the Great Hunters. When I
learned that some children had discovered
the nine important caves with pictures dating
from the Iron Age, I set off on an expedition
and traced the footsteps of the young explorers. What I enjoy most, however, is
writing little stories for children—and poetry.
I like poetry so much that I have collected
poems for children written in seventy-five
languages and have translated many of
them. The book which contains these poems
is called *Ein Reigen um die Welt* (*A Dance
Around the World*). None of my other books
is so important to me.

I come from a modest background and I
grew up in the confines of a small town.
Early on I developed a longing to cross fron-
tiers. Today my books are at home in many
countries, and this more than anything en-
courages me in my work. My wife is a violinist; she too travels widely in many countries on her concert tours. Our daughter is
studying languages.

———

Hans Baumann was born in Amberg, Bavaria, and studied at the University of Berlin. He married Elisabeth Zolgmann in
1942. Their daughter is Eva Veronika. During World War II, Baumann served with
the German army in France as well as in
Russia and was taken prisoner in France.
He won the New York *Herald Tribune*
Spring Book Festival Award in 1958 for
*Sons of the Steppe. I Marched with Hanni-
bal* was named an Honors Book in 1962. He
has also won the Friedrich Gerstacker Prize,
(Germany), for best children's book of the
year 1956. *In the Land of Ur* won the Mildred Batchelder Award in 1971. His works
are available in more than 130 translations.

SELECTED WORKS: Sons of the Steppe, 1958;
The Barque of the Brothers, 1958; I Marched
with Hannibal, 1962; The Caves of the Great
Hunters, revised edition, 1962; Gold and Gods
of Peru, 1963; Lion Gate and Labyrinth, 1967;
Alexander's Great March, 1968; In the Land
of Ur, 1969; Gatalop the Wonderful Ball, 1971.

ABOUT: Author's and Writer's Who's Who,
1963; Contemporary Authors, Vol. 7-8; Who's
Who in America, 1968-69; Bookbird no. 3, 1965.

PAULINE BAYNES

September 9, 1922-

ILLUSTRATOR OF A *Dictionary of Chivalry*, etc.

Autobiographical sketch of Pauline Diana Baynes Gasch:

I HAVE always been, if not a book illustrator, a book embellisher. Born in Brighton, England, I was a spoilt and determined baby, used to getting my own way, by fair means or foul. I progressed through a destructive childhood in India, where my father was in the Indian Civil Service, scribbling all over my older sister's much-loved books, to a succession of boarding schools in England, where I continued to scribble, this time all over my textbooks, for which I was in endless trouble. I left school at fifteen, with no qualifications or aptitude, but with much relief and a strong determination to go on scribbling and become a book illustrator. My few terms at art school, first at Farnham, Surrey, and then at the Slade School, were interrupted by the start of World War II. I joined the war effort by making demonstration models at the Army Camouflage Centre, where, with all the other personnel, which included stage designers, etc., I scribbled over the walls of our hut. I went on to drawing charts at the Hydrographic Department of the Admiralty, which was rather more disciplined scribbling. By this time I had got my first illustrating commission, and I drew at week ends, at night, and whenever it could be managed. I have been drawing for books ever since.

Right at the beginning of my career, a helpful editor advised me always to be *accurate* in every detail. He used to say that an artist could get by with not-so-good drawings if he or she had a reputation for accuracy. I have always tried to remember this, and I hope that, through a succession of historical books, I have at least managed to acquire a reasonable knowledge of costume and "period" things in general, and that the scribbling has improved a little. I far prefer to do historical work and find modern things and people very difficult to draw. Some people feel a strong affinity with the past, and I am certainly greatly attracted by it. I feel I should have appreciated the slower tempo of days gone by, the beautiful buildings, the gorgeous costumes, the wonderful craftsmanship, all that courtesy, the wild life (now so fast disappearing)—not to mention the lack of complicated machinery and advanced education!

Somehow all the right sort of books, the ones I would have chosen for myself, seem to have come my way, and I have been incredibly fortunate in being able to work for many splendid authors and special people, like C. S. Lewis and J. R. R. Tolkien.

Today, my husband and I live, with our four dogs, in a tiny and remote country cottage in Surrey and I have become a *compulsive* scribbler, miserable and hideous to live with if a day goes by without some sort of drawing being done. In 1969 I was awarded the Kate Greenaway Medal for my work in Grant Uden's *Dictionary of Chivalry*. As you can imagine this seemed a most gratifying way of rewarding so much scribbling, and a life of doing exactly what I pleased.

Which all goes to show, maybe, that there is something to be said for starting as a determined baby.

————

Before attending art school, Pauline Baynes was educated at Beaufront School, Camberley, where she later taught art. At the age of sixteen she was elected to membership in the Women's International Art Club, from which she eventually resigned. She is now a member of the Society of Industrial Artists. In 1961 she married Fritz Otto Gasch. The illustrator of more than sixty books, she has been represented in several exhibitions of the American Institute of Graphic Arts.

SELECTED WORKS ILLUSTRATED: The Lion, the Witch and the Wardrobe, by Clive Staples Lewis, 1950; Farmer Giles of Ham, by John Ronald R. Tolkien, 1950; Miracle Plays, by Anne Malcolmson, 1959; A Family Book of Nursery Rhymes, by Iona and Peter Opie, comps., 1964; A Dictionary of Chivalry, by Grant A. Uden, 1969; Saint George and the Dragon, by Edmund Spenser, adapted by Sandol S. Warburg, 1969; The Most Wonderful Animals that Never Were, by Joseph Wood Krutch, 1969.

ABOUT: Kingman, Lee and others, comps. Illustrators of Children's Books: 1957-1966; Viguers, Ruth Hill and others, comps. Illustrators of Children's Books: 1946-1956.

"BB"

July 25, 1905-

AUTHOR AND ILLUSTRATOR OF *The Little Grey Men*, etc.

Autobiographical sketch of Denys James Watkins-Pitchford, who uses the pen name "BB":

IF I hadn't had appendicitis when I was seven years old it is highly probable I should never have written books or even painted pictures. My two brothers went off to prep school and then public school but I was educated at home and much of my time was spent alone, not really alone, for I was out in the woods and fields every free day, sometimes riding a little Shetland pony called Little Man.

D J Watkins-Pitchford ("BB")

Little Man had an uncertain temper; he bit me on my small behind and stood on my toe and once did his best to kill me. I hadn't secured the saddle girth and the saddle slipped. My foot was caught in the stirrup and I was dragged, luckily for me over soft grass, for about two hundred yards. It was a horrible experience until my foot came free. But I told nobody about this or it would have been the end of my expeditions on Little Man.

There was a stream near my home, the Folly Brook. It twisted and coiled through valley meadows, bushed in by ancient oaks and thorn thickets. It had little shingly bays and still brown pools. Blue kingfishers haunted it and I liked to think of it as the home of a race of diminutive men, clad in mouse skins who lived by hunting. These were *The Little Grey Men* and I wrote about them when I was teaching at Rugby School, fifteen years later.

Schoolmastering was irksome to me; I felt too much sympathy for young creatures whose whole day was spent under supervision or at lessons and I found that all the inspiration I had for stories was drained away by the time I could sit down to write.

I was born in Lamport, a tiny village in the centre of England. From both my parents I inherited a gift for drawing and from my maternal grandfather a passion for the countryside and wildlife. I studied art at the Royal College of Art under Rothenstein, taking my Diploma in the Painting School. I also studied in Paris for a short time and then went to teach at Rugby.

My story of the Little Grey Men won the Carnegie Medal and since then I have written over twenty-five books, six of them for adults. I illustrate all my own work in black and white and colour. This gives an author a great advantage. I have also illustrated many books for other people, mostly in black and white.

After teaching at Rugby for sixteen years I was able to break free and live by my own writing and illustrating which has meant a very satisfying life. I married in 1939 and had two children, first a daughter, Angela, then a boy, Robin, who died when he was seven. His death was the first dark shadow in my life, a shadow which has never entirely passed from me.

When I write for young people I do not "write for children," I write to please myself, which perhaps shows that I have, possibly, never reached full maturity. If this is so I hope I never do.

This world, the natural world of woods and fields, flowers, birds, and beasts, butterflies, and insects, scents and sounds, and the pageantry of the seasons, are entirely magical to a small child. Much of that magic still remains for me, though as one grows older the intensity fades and this is quite tragic.

My children's books have been published in Germany, Holland, the USA, Israel and Yugoslavia, and one was adapted for the Swiss TV programme.

The BBC also dramatized my book *Brendon Chase* for the radio and are now considering a TV version of *The Little Grey Men*.

———

"BB" is the son of Walter Watkins-Pitchford, a country parson, and Edith Elizabeth (Wilson) Watkins-Pitchford. He married Cecily Mary Adnitt. From 1925 to 1929 he served in the Royal Horse Artillery territorial army and received the King's Prize medal, 1928. During World War II he became a captain in the Home Guard. Besides doing numerous books for children and adults, he has contributed to *Country Life* and *Field*.

SELECTED WORKS WRITTEN AND ILLUSTRATED: Wild Lone, 1938; Manka, the Sky Gipsy, 1939; The Little Grey Men, 1949, 1962.

SELECTED WORKS ILLUSTRATED: Fairy Tales of Long Ago, edited by M. C. Carey, 1952; Prince Prigio and Prince Ricardo, by Andrew Lang, 1961; Granny's Wonderful Chair, by Frances Browne, 1963; The Lost Princess, by George Macdonald, 1966; Jungle Rescue, by A. R. Channel, 1968.

ABOUT: Author's and Writer's Who's Who, 1963; Contemporary Authors, Vol. 9-10; Higginson, Alexander Henry. British and American Sporting Authors; Viguers, Ruth Hill and others, comps. Illustrators of Children's Books: 1946-1956; Bookbird no. 3, 1967.

JOHN BEATTY

January 24, 1922-

and

PATRICIA BEATTY

August 26, 1922-

AUTHORS OF *At the Seven Stars*, etc.

Biographical sketch of John Louis Beatty and Patricia Robbins Beatty by Patricia Beatty:

WHEN I, Patricia Beatty, started writing a children's novel—largely as a resort from boredom—in 1956, I had no idea that writing was about to become first my avocation with a vengeance and then a full-time job. Nor did I have any idea that my long-suffering Ph.D. husband, John Beatty, was also to be snatched up before long into the wild wide world of authorship. It has all been a great surprise to us!

We were born in Portland, Oregon, in the same year and in the same hospital. To further the coincidence, our mothers knew each other slightly while we were small children. But we didn't become truly acquainted until twenty years later at Reed College where we both took B.A. degrees. And it was

twenty-eight years, 1950, before we finally got married. Our daughter, Ann Alexandria, was born in 1957.

Both of us are teachers. He is a professor at the University of California, Riverside, specializing in the history of England in the 16th, 17th and 18th centuries. I had been a high school teacher prior to our marriage—of history and English. As history teachers both, what is more natural than that we should collaborate on historical novels?

But this didn't come about all at once. For four years I wrote alone about Indians and pioneer life. Then in 1959 we went to England to live. There I began a novel (out of boredom) set in London in 1752 and there I acquired my sometimes coauthor by the simple expedient of telling him, "You have to help me with this book, Jack. After all, English history is your field, isn't it?"

So it was! And so he did! Six other novels of England's past have been written since that book, *At the Seven Stars.* Some of them are *Campion Towers, The Royal Dirk,* (both prize-winners) *The Queen's Wizard* and

Pirate Royal. We trust we still have more of this type of novel brewing inside us.

And in the interstices I've gone on alone writing eight others about the American West before the turn of the century, such as *The Nickel-Plated Beauty, The Queen's Own Grove, Me, California Perkins* and *Bonanza Girl.*

In all of our writing (mine and ours) we aim to teach history to young readers in what we conceive to be its most painless form, the historical novel. Once a teacher always a teacher! I have taken this motto so much to heart that I now also teach formally on a university level—currently a course in writing children's fiction through the University of California at Los Angeles' Extension Department.

———

John Beatty took his B.A. from Reed College in 1943, his M.A. from Stanford University in 1947 and his Ph.D. from the University of Washington, Seattle, in 1953. He served in the Army, 1943-45, became a staff sergeant and received the Silver Star, the Purple Heart, and a Presidential Unit Citation with Cluster. He had a Foundation for Economic Education fellowship in 1953 and an American Philosophical Society grant in 1959. He collaborated with Oliver A. Johnson on *Heritage of Western Civilization: Select Readings.*

Patricia Robbins Beatty took her B.A. from Reed College in 1944 and did graduate study at the University of Idaho and the University of Washington, Seattle. She taught high school English and history in Coeur d'Alene, Idaho, did technical library work in Wilmington, Delaware, and has been a business and science librarian in Riverside, California.

The Beattys received the Commonwealth Club of California Silver Medal for *Campion Towers* in 1965 and the Southern California Council on Children's and Young People's Literature Medal for *The Royal Dirk* in 1967.

SELECTED WORKS BY JOHN AND PATRICIA BEATTY: At the Seven Stars, 1963; Campion Towers, 1965; Donkey for the King, 1966; The Royal Dirk, 1966; The Queen's Wizard, 1967; Pirate Royal, 1969.

SELECTED WORKS BY PATRICIA BEATTY: Bonanza Girl, 1962; The Nickel-Plated Beauty, 1964; The Queen's Own Grove, 1966; Me, California Perkins, 1968; Hail Columbia, 1970.

ABOUT: JOHN AND PATRICIA BEATTY: Horn Book February 1967.

ABOUT JOHN BEATTY: Contemporary Authors, Vol. 7-8; Directory of American Scholars, Vol. 1, 5th Edition.

ABOUT PATRICIA ROBBINS BEATTY: Contemporary Authors, Vol. 4; Something About the Author, Vol. 1.

THELMA BELL

July 3, 1896-

and

CORYDON BELL

July 16, 1894-

AUTHORS AND ILLUSTRATOR OF *The Riddle of Time,* etc.

Biographical sketch of Thelma Harrington Bell and Corydon Whitten Bell by Thelma Bell:

WHEN I was a child, I was very glad that I wasn't a boy, because a boy grew up to be a man, and a man had to decide on his life work, and how was it possible to make such a decision. Also, if he ever hoped to get married, he had to propose in flowery terms— the way they did in books.

Times changed. When I left Western Reserve University in Cleveland with a B.A. degree—major in English, minor in psychology—clutched in my hand, I too was looking for a job. I found one in the advertising department of a large store. And Corydon never did propose. "Oh, to be in England, now that April's there," I quoted, one evening as we waited out a deluge of rain in someone's doorway. "Let's go," Corydon said. And so in 1921 we started out together.

Throughout high school, Corydon, who is an autodidact, had dipped avidly into every stream of endeavor: writing, composing, scientific experimentation. He had always sketched. He was in his last year of university, first as a pre-med, then as an English and

science major, when World War I set him down in a bacteriological laboratory at Camp Jackson, South Carolina, and kept him there.

His first postwar job was with a printing firm where the art offered to customers was so poor that he substituted his own efforts. And so, later, when our money gave out in England and we returned home, it seemed natural for us to brazenly open a free-lance art and copywriting studio.

Then came the children, two girls and a boy. Our first book, *Black Face,* was written for them: about a black-faced lamb and the locomotive that Corydon had built. Besides his free-lance advertising art, Corydon was now occasionally illustrating books for New York publishers.

When the children were grown and in college, quite suddenly we called a halt. Life had become a series of short-term deadlines, overrun by a feeling of stagnation. We pulled up stakes, burned bridges, and with what funds the depression had left us, started a new life in a large one-room studio cabin that we built on a mountainside in western North Carolina, among a handful of mountain neighbors who looked us over and figured that we "wouldn't build a winter."

We are still in the Blue Ridge, in love with the mountains, and with the state. Here, all the rest of our books have been written, beginning with *Mountain Boy*, about a small neighbor I taught to read. *Captain Ghost* won the Dorothy Canfield Fisher Award, voted by Vermont children.

Always fascinated by snow, we researched and experimented, even to producing plastic replicas of snow crystals from the original fragile forms. *Snow*, published in 1954, was reviewed by *Scientific American* as "the year's most distinguished science book for children." Corydon's more definitive book for all ages was *The Wonder of Snow*. More books on science subjects followed. And now we have just saluted our adopted state with a portrait of North Carolina today for junior high school age.

Besides illustrating our books, Corydon has designed and illustrated books by other authors as well. What do we do when not writing or illustrating? I paint the wild-flowers and mushrooms of this mountain region. Corydon's avocation is music, and he paints mountain characters in their habitat for pleasure.

Thelma Bell is a member of Authors Guild of the Authors League of America and of Phi Kappa Zeta.

Corydon Bell attended the University of Michigan, Western Reserve University and Army Medical School.

The Bells' children are Patricia Bell Liston, Nancy Bell Smithson, and Corydon Whitten Bell, Jr.

SELECTED WORKS BY THELMA AND CORYDON BELL: Black Face, 1931; Mountain Boy, 1947; Yaller-Eye, 1951; Snow, 1954; John Rattling-Gourd of Big Cove, 1955; Captain Ghost, 1959; Thunderstorm, 1960; The Two Worlds of Davy Blount, 1962; The Riddle of Time, 1963; A Dash of Pepper, 1965; North Carolina, 1971.

ABOUT THELMA AND CORYDON BELL: Walser, Richard Gaither. Picturebook of Tar Heel Authors; Elementary English December 1962.

ABOUT THELMA BELL: Contemporary Authors, Vol. 1; Who's Who of American Women, 1960-61.

ABOUT CORYDON BELL: Contemporary Authors, Vol. 7-8; Kingman, Lee and others, comps. Illustrators of Children's Books; 1957-1966; Viguers, Ruth Hill and others, comps. Illustrators of Children's Books: 1946-1956.

NATALIA MAREE BELTING

July 11, 1915-

AUTHOR OF *The Sun Is a Golden Earring*, etc.

Autobiographical sketch of Natalia Maree Belting:

I'VE not used a pen name, yet. I've a couple picked out. But since I still have trouble getting folks to pronounce my first name as it is spelled, Natalia, not Natalie, and nobody bothers to use my middle name, which I like very much, and my students insist on addressing me as "Mrs." as if Belting were my name only by marriage, maybe I've trouble enough.

I'm not married. I live in a house I built eleven years ago in the style the French evolved for their houses in southern Illinois in the eighteenth century because I wrote my doctoral dissertation in history on the French colonization of the Illinois country and uncovered the description of this unique blend of Norman and Caribbean architecture in the records I used.

The house stands on six acres across from

Natalia Maree Belting

an eighty-acre tract of virgin timber owned by the University of Illinois (I'm an assistant professor of history at the University), and as a result I not only share my living with some cats, dogs, goldfish, snails, toads, native turtles and Asian aquatic turtles, but also with whatever birds and animals decide to visit from the woods.

Anyone might suppose I'd write about animals. So far, I've just done two books about them, *Cat Tales* and *The Long-Tailed Bear*. Someday I may tell about my coyote who came to me one day completely wild and terrified of humans—he had a long gash over his eye from something somebody had thrown at him. Today he's a loving scamp, all one hundred pounds of him, who much prefers to be a house dog, and is, and gives in, on occasion, to the temptation to upset one of the other dogs, or me, into the fish-pond.

I don't remember ever deciding to be a writer, but I don't remember any time I've not been writing. I was brought up on reading and writing: we had all the good magazines and a couple thousand books in the house to read; my father wrote college text books and knew Shakespeare and Browning and the poetical books of the Bible by heart.

My first book was produced when I was six and, having read all the *Peter Rabbit* books, I wrote another to find out what happened next.

The first time I was paid for any of my writing was my senior year in journalism at the University of Illinois when I sold an article on a puzzle party to the now long-dead magazine, *Leisure*. But before that there were years of themes and articles and stories (mostly read only by the teacher who assigned them) and the class play my senior year in high school, and reams of poetry because my freshman English teacher in college was very much interested in what in those days was called "free verse."

After I received my B.S. in journalism in 1936, I was a proofreader and then a society reporter on the Champaign-Urbana *Courier;* then I went back to the University of Illinois for a master's and a doctor's degree in history, the latter in 1940. A year later the University hired me, and I've been teaching ever since. My first book, *Pierre of Kaskaskia,* and my third, *In Enemy Hands,* were both based on the material I had dug up for my Ph.D. thesis.

I was born in Oskaloosa, Iowa, where my father was high school principal. Like preachers, teachers move around quite a bit. We lived in New York City, while Father got his Ph.D. at Columbia; I went to grade school in Urbana, Illinois, and Iowa City, Iowa, and to high school in Cedar Rapids, Iowa. My freshman year I attended Coe College, Cedar Rapids. All the rest of my college years, indeed, all the years since, have been here in Urbana, at the University of Illinois.

Natalia Maree Belting has been a member of the board of governors of the Champaign County Historical Society and belongs, among other organizations, to the American Historical Society and to Delta Zeta Sorority. She has done occasional preaching in rural Presbyterian churches. *The Sun Is a Golden Earring*, with illustrations by Bernarda Bryson, was a runner-up for the Caldecott Medal for 1962. Miss Belting received the Recognition of Merit, Claremont Children's Book Center, 1965.

SELECTED WORKS: Pierre of Kaskaskia, 1951; In Enemy Hands, 1953; Cat Tales, 1959; The Long-Tailed Bear, 1961; The Sun Is a Golden Earring, 1962; Calendar Moon, 1964; Stars Are Silver Reindeer, 1966; Winter's Eve, 1969; Christmas Folk, 1969; Summer's Coming In, 1970.

ABOUT: Contemporary Authors, Vol. 1.

PAUL BERNA

February 21, 1910-

AUTHOR OF *The Secret of the Missing Boat*, etc.

Autobiographical sketch of Paul Berna:

THE magnificent natural landscape in which I spent the best years of my early childhood left a profound impression upon me. It was the Bay of Hyères near Toulon in the south of France, where Joseph Conrad spent some of the last days of his life, which was the background of his last novel *The Rover* and where a few years later Georges Simenon came to write, aboard his yacht, the first of the Inspector Maigret series. I have not, however, drawn any special aptitude for the craft of author from living here, although I love the seashore where I was born and the countryside has often served as background for my stories.

Life, however, is not easy. My father was a brilliant chemical engineer who managed a factory in the suburbs of Lyon. My most distinct memory of him was of a tall, thin officer wearing a red and black uniform, boarding an artillery train with his regiment. This occurred in September, 1914. I was four years old then and I never saw him again. One month later he was killed at the front in Aisne, leaving behind a wife and seven children of whom the eldest was only twelve.

The hardest job in the world is that of being a mother. I know, for I have seen my mother work, suffer, but remain cheerful in the midst of seven voracious and quarrelsome children. The worries which we caused her while growing up killed her before her time.

The last vision I have of her is that of a smiling, emaciated woman, leaning over the balcony of a Parisian apartment building, with her arm raised to say goodby. I never saw her again. This happened September 6, 1939: her seven children had taken the train to go to another war. Four returned.

Like all my brothers I studied at a French college in Fribourg in Switzerland. The pleasant life we spent there was devoted largely to winter sports and football. This period left me with many wonderful memories which, much later, became the inspiration for *Flood Warning*. Since writing cannot be learned in school, I learned in the streets of a large city while performing thousands of odd jobs for a salary which was often preposterously low. In fact, my first steps in life were far from brilliant. While I was still very young, I almost succeeded in becoming a trainee at the Observatory of Meudon, but my scientific knowledge was not extensive enough. The yearning which I felt after this lost chance would one day find expression in my two first books, *Threshold of the Stars* and *Continent in the Sky*.

I spent the years 1930 to 1936 as an unknown journalist on a small newspaper in the suburbs of Paris. My work did not bring any great glory to me, but my wanderings proved

profitable in the long run for they permitted
me to imagine the plots of *The Horse Without a Head, The Clue of the Black Cat* and
several other novels.

In 1950, twenty years after leaving my
native countryside, I had the good fortune
to return to it and this wonderful experience
found expression in *The Knights of King
Midas.* The child in me had forgotten nothing, not even the memory of a bright summer
I had spent in Brittany cruising on an old
yacht with red sails and piloted by Fanch,
the hero of *The Secret of the Missing Boat.*

Rather late in life (but it was worth waiting for a providential encounter), I married
a young woman who also writes novels for
young people, Jany Saint-Marcoux, well
known to European readers. Our partnership
has given us the most precious gift in the
world, two boys who are now eight and ten
years old and who, unknowingly, make us
young again. Our greatest reward is the
happiness we feel in working for them.

———

Paul Berna, who studied at Villa Saint-
Jean in Fribourg, has two sons named Bern-
ard and Philippe. The Mystery Writers of
America awarded Berna a scroll for *The
Secret of the Missing Boat,* as one of the top
four juvenile mysteries of 1967.

Selected Works: The Horse Without a
Head, 1958; Threshold of the Stars, 1960; The
Knights of King Midas, 1961; Flood Warning,
1963; Continent in the Sky, 1963; The Clue of
the Black Cat, 1965; The Secret of the Missing
Boat, 1967.

About: Author's and Writer's Who's Who,
1963.

ERIK BLEGVAD

March 3, 1923-

and

LENORE BLEGVAD

May 8, 1926-

Illustrator and Author of *The Great
Hamster Hunt,* etc.

Biographical sketch of Erik Blegvad and
Lenore Hochman Blegvad by Erik Blegvad:

DENMARK in the 1920s was a fine and quiet
place to be born. It still is, but in those days it

ERIK BLEGVAD

Lenore Blegvad

was like a peaceful backwater to the busy
stream of the rest of the world. I was born
in Copenhagen, which is today much as it
was then, and as it has been for hundreds
and hundreds of years. My childhood was
spent in the city or in the countryside or on
board the trawler my father used in his explorations as a marine biologist for the Danish
government. Our home was always filled
with books. My older sister and I were eager
readers. We read books by our own Hans

Christian Andersen, by other Scandinavian writers or by French and English authors. Some of them were beautifully illustrated.

I drew from the earliest age and as I drew with more enjoyment after I had read a good story it is not surprising to me to find myself an illustrator today, although then I had other ambitions. I wanted to fly aeroplanes. During the Second World War this dream was brought down to reality when Denmark was occupied by the Germans. Instead of aeronautical training I pursued my second ambition, to become an artist, and from 1941-1944 I was a student in the Copenhagen School of Applied Arts. In 1945, after Denmark was liberated, I had to do my military service and this I did in Germany as an interpreter with the British Forces.

When that was over, in 1947, I went to Paris where I worked as a free-lance artist for book and magazine publishers, and it is here that my wife Lenore enters my autobiography. She had come to Paris from New York to study painting. In 1950 we were married in Copenhagen. In 1951 we moved to New York where I began to illustrate the American children's books that you may have seen.

One of the first books I illustrated was *Bed-knob and Broomstick*, by Mary Norton and books by other writers followed. I also translated and illustrated two of Hans Christian Andersen's fairy tales, *The Swineherd* and *The Emperor's New Clothes*, but most exciting for me was when my wife began to write children's books. I have greatly enjoyed illustrating the three she has done so far.

But the list is too long to mention each title and author as there are now more than fifty books that I have illustrated. Each was a delight for me to work on. Most of them were done while we lived in Connecticut. When our two sons, Peter, who is now eighteen and Kristoffer, who is fifteen, were old enough to appreciate it, we moved to London where we now live. Both boys will soon be better artists than I ever dreamed of being.

My wife, Lenore, was born in New York City. She studied history of art at Vassar College before going to Paris to study paint-

ing. Now she divides her time equally between painting and writing.

As a young man, Erik Blegvad illustrated some of the books on fishing written by his father, Dr. Harald Blegvad.

In Paris, Erik Blegvad did work for *France Soir, Elle,* and *Femina,* and in the United States, for a number of periodicals, including *Esquire,* the *Saturday Evening Post* and *McCall's.* Among other assignments for *Woman's Day,* he did the pictures for its serialization of Mary Norton's *The Borrowers* and *The Magic Bed Knob.* He illustrated *The Margaret Rudkin Pepperidge Farm Cook Book.* Blegvad's work has been represented in several exhibitions of the American Institute of Graphic Arts.

SELECTED WORKS ILLUSTRATED BY ERIK BLEGVAD: Bed-knob and Broomstick, by Mary Norton, 1957; The Swineherd, by Hans Christian Andersen, 1958; The Emperor's New Clothes, by Hans Christian Andersen, 1959; Plenty of Fish, by Millicent Selsam, 1960; Diamond in the Window, by Jane Langton, 1962; Elizabeth the Bird Watcher, by Felice Holman, 1963; Mr. Jensen and Cat, by Lenore Blegvad, 1965; One Is for the Sun, by Lenore Blegvad, 1968; The Great Hamster Hunt, by Lenore Blegvad, 1969.

ABOUT ERIK BLEGVAD: Kingman, Lee and others, comps. Illustrators of Children's Books: 1957-1966; Viguers, Ruth Hill and others, comps. Illustrators of Children's Books: 1946-1956; American Artist September 1961.

MICHAEL BOND

January 13, 1926-

AUTHOR OF *A Bear Called Paddington,* etc.

Autobiographical sketch of Thomas Michael Bond:

I WAS born in Newbury, England. Six weeks later my parents left town—taking me with them fortunately—and settled in Reading, where I spent what is laughingly known as my formative years—catching newts, bringing up three guinea pigs and a dog called Binkie, cycling, reading *The Magnet* under the bedclothes (I was fortunate, too, in having parents who read to me), creeping like a snail unwillingly to school, and suffering from a chronic inability to take life too seriously.

michael Bond

At an early age felt a faint stirring deep down that I would like to *Create Something* so, glossing over the fact that I couldn't draw, I sent a cartoon to *Punch*. It was terrible! A man with two heads sitting at a desk. Caption: "I always say, Smithers, two heads are better than one!" But the editor did a very noble thing. He scribbled "better luck next time" on the rejection slip and didn't kill my yearnings stone dead.

In 1943 joined the Royal Air Force as a navigator. It was a love/hate affair. I loved moving around a lot and meeting a great many people from undreamed-of walks of life. But I hated flying because I was airsick and didn't give a damn where the plane was so long as we got down. (If you ever find yourself sitting alongside someone being ill before the plane takes off—that's me!)

In 1945 transferred to the Army. The news got around. Hitler threw in the sponge and I was sent to the Middle East. In between jobs like picking stones out of the desert "because they made it look untidy" wrote a short story which I sent to *London Opinion*. Two things remain in my mind. The unbelievable feeling of excitement when it was accepted and the fact that I couldn't cash the cheque. The army didn't want to know about it and the local Arabs thought it was all part of an imperialist plot and threw stones at me. British told to get out of Egypt.

But I was a writer, albeit a struggling one, and writers write, so I wrote and wrote and wrote. Short stories, articles, radio plays—they once bought six in Hong Kong! Ten years later I was still struggling. It was a good year if I made more than a hundred pounds. Come to think of it, it was a good year if I made less than a hundred pounds! Meantime I had left the Army, married Brenda Mary Johnson and became a television cameraman with the British Broadcasting Corporation.

Christmas 1957 I happened to come across a small toy bear which had been left on the shelf in a large London store. I felt sorry for him and bought him as a "stocking-filler" for my wife. Because we were living near Paddington Station in London at the time I christened him Paddington. The book *A Bear Called Paddington* was born and ten days later it was finished. Nowadays they take longer!

It was published in 1958—the year our daughter Karen was born.

In 1965 I gave up being a cameraman in order to write full time. There are now eight *Paddington* books. Three books about a mouse called *Thursday*. A television puppet series called *The Herbs*. And in the back of my mind an idea for an entirely new set of characters, plus the feeling that one day I would like to create an adult equivalent of Paddington. One day . . .

———

Michael Bond studied at Presentation College. Besides doing children's books, he has contributed to British periodicals and written television and radio plays produced in Europe, the United States, Canada, South Africa, Hong Kong, and Ceylon. His avocational interests include motoring, theater, and gardening.

SELECTED WORKS: A Bear Called Paddington, 1960; Paddington Helps Out, 1961; More About Paddington, 1962; Paddington at Large, 1962; Paddington Marches On, 1965; Paddington at Work, 1967; Here Comes Thursday, 1967; Thursday Rides Again, 1969.

ABOUT: Author's and Writer's Who's Who, 1963; Contemporary Authors, Vol. 5-6.

FRANK BONHAM
February 25, 1914-

AUTHOR OF *Durango Street*, etc.

Autobiographical sketch of Frank Bonham:

"A SHORT story a day" was my goal when I settled on a writing career, at age twenty, alone in a mountain cabin in Southern California. As to the quality of those short stories —well, I'd hate to come across one of them now. But if I learned nothing else in that cabin, I learned how to apply myself to the lonely art of fiction writing. Guilt, ambition, and anxiety were the fuel I burned; I had to drop out of college, and my father was sending me three dollars a week of depression money to subsist on. I felt indebted and anxious, and realizing I had better find a way to make a living speedily, I stayed pretty close to the typewriter. In addition to cutting my own wood for cooking and heating, carrying all my drinking water uphill, and performing the other tasks of a bachelor in a primitive area, I found time to write a hundred and seven stories in two years, of which I sold about ten.

That was thirty-five years ago, and I have now written over five hundred short stories, novelettes, and articles, plus a dozen television scripts and thirty-five novels.

As to vital statistics, I was born a third-generation Californian. I married a high-school sweetheart named Gloria Bailey. We now have three sons, David, Bruce and Keith, two of them grown.

While I have written more books for adults than for children, I now write exclusively for young people. The rewards and responsibilities of writing for children are great. One has a sense of writing for an eager audience, of not daring to bore this audience, and of not making rash statements one cannot back up—of adhering to sincerity always.

Children think in superlatives, and, like all writers for young readers, I receive mail telling me that not only am I the best writer my correspondents have ever read, but the first, in many cases. These letters naturally cheer me enormously. Often they come from minority youngsters who have found familiar

scenes and characters in my books for "inner-city" boys and girls; intrigued by the familiar wedded to the dramatic, they have finished the story—something many of them have never done before. Some of these readers have gone on in a short time to read adult books supposedly too old for them. If I ever lacked a sense of meaning in my work, this relationship with my audience has more than supplied it. A substantial part of my writing in the past few years has consisted of novels grounded in the complex problems of minority adolescents.

In addition to such work, I have written, and am writing, books about dolphins and submarines, jungle warfare and life in Baja California, Niseis and racing cars, samurai swords and tide pools. This is less of a tribute to my versatility than to the receptiveness of young minds that have not yet set like cement.

Authors feel a close—sometimes uncomfortably so—linkage between their work and their personal lives. This is most definitely the case with me. My story ideas struggle to become books, as I strive to become the kind of person I wish I were. I never will, and my books will never fulfill my yearnings for them. But at the heart of my discontent lies a seed of satisfaction. My job will never be taken by a computer, because in order to write you must be able to suffer, as well as to have fun.

———

Frank Bonham attended Glendale Junior College. He served in the Army during World War II. In addition to stories, novels, and articles, he has written extensively for television, including scripts for such well-known series as *Wells Fargo* and *Death Valley Days.* His work has appeared in the *Saturday Evening Post, McCall's* and other magazines. *Durango Street* received the Claremont Children's Book Center Recognition of Merit. Special Award of Mystery Writers of America was given to *Honor Bound, Mystery of the Red Tide,* and *Mystery of the Fat Cat.* Frank Bonham enjoys camping, classical music and skin diving and is vice president of Crash, Inc., an agency working in the field of juvenile delinquency.

SELECTED WORKS: Burma Rifles; a Story of Merrill's Marauders, 1960; War Beneath the Sea, 1962; Honor Bound, 1963; Speedway Contender, 1964; Durango Street, 1965; Mystery of the Red Tide, 1966; Mystery of the Fat Cat, 1968; The Nitty Gritty, 1968; The Vagabundos, 1969; Viva Chicano, 1970.

ABOUT: Contemporary Authors, Vol. 11-12; Something About the Author, Vol. 1.

CROSBY NEWELL BONSALL

January 2, 1921-

AUTHOR AND ILLUSTRATOR OF *The Case of the Cat's Meow,* etc.

Autobiographical sketch of Crosby Barbara Newell Bonsall:

"I WANT two fathers, one with red hair and one with no hair, and I need an extra mother because my sister stuck her chewing gum on my favorite one. And it did. Stick I mean."

That's the way it began a long time ago in Long Island where I was born. I spent every summer supplying the neighborhood with paper dolls. Endless rows of paper families who lived highly complicated lives and who were beautifully gowned for any emergency as long as it was exotic. Fathers toppled off pillow mountains outfitted for the Matterhorn and mothers in three-piece traveling ensembles fell under speeding Orient

CROSBY NEWELL BONSALL

Express milk bottles. Fires or shipwrecks were out. A seaside locale in the bathtub once lost an entire family tree.

Words and pictures in school papers continued to be my world but when I arrived at The American School of Design in New York, it was pictures only, commercial art, in which I specialized and brought no honor either to it or to me.

My first working years were spent in small advertising agencies doing layouts, writing copy, emptying waste baskets and answering the telephone. My messages may not have been accurate but they were illustrated.

It was a doodle that ushered me into writing for children. A doodle became a rag doll and a rag doll led to a book. I was back with my made-to-order families and I was happy.

But when I was asked to supply the text for Ylla's magnificent pictures of animals and to follow such illustrious writers as Margaret Wise Brown, it was such a long way from my paper dolls that I considered hurling myself under the nearest train. I couldn't find a milk bottle big enough so I hurled myself, instead, into the task. *Polar Bear Brothers* was the first, and *Here's Jellybean Reilly* and *Whose Eye Am I?* are the latest.

My husband, George Bonsall, an avid collector of rare books, old toys and games, is actively interested in libraries and publishing. *Tell Me Some More,* my first *I Can Read* book was a happy collaboration. It was his idea and I'm still grateful. *Who's a Pest?* followed and then I thought children might enjoy some very simple mystery stories and "The Case of the" books started with *Hungry Stranger*. I liked my cast of characters and used them in *Cat's Meow* and *Dumb Bells*.

All that commercial art, advertising copy, and the year I spent at New York University School of Architecture struggling with sculpting and design were not lost. Writing copy to space teaches you a discipline which I find handy in writing books for children just learning to read. I've never used a controlled vocabulary—I just keep the consumer in mind. Even those old paper dolls did not live in vain. Today I get my orders from so many children I've never seen, written in large block letters on lined paper. "Please write another mystery story about Tubby." "Please put a girl in your books, with long curls." I will. I will.

_____

Before her marriage, Crosby Bonsall published under her maiden name of Crosby Newell. Besides her own books she has illustrated a number by other writers and has written the text for six books featuring Ylla's photographs.

SELECTED WORKS WRITTEN: Polar Bear Brothers, 1960; Here's Jellybean Reilly, 1966; Whose Eye Am I? 1968.

SELECTED WORKS WRITTEN AND ILLUSTRATED: Hurry Up, Slowpoke, 1961; Who's a Pest? 1962; What Spot? 1963; The Case of the Cat's Meow, 1965.

ABOUT: Kingman, Lee and others, comps. Illustrators of Children's Books: 1957-1966.

ELIZABETH BORTON

See *Treviño, Elizabeth Borton de*

LUCY BOSTON

1892-

AUTHOR OF *A Stranger at Green Knowe*, etc.

Biographical sketch of Lucy Maria Wood Boston:

LUCY BOSTON was born Lucy Maria Wood in Southport, Lancashire, in the northwest

LUCY BOSTON

of England, one of the five children of James, an engineer, and Mary (Garrett) Wood. Her upbringing was strict, as her family, and especially her mother, was Victorian in the sense we now use the word, and repressive of all the things Lucy later learned to love—music, dance, drama, and art. Her father died when she was six. When she was eleven her mother's health required a milder climate and the family spent a year in the Lake District, where Lucy developed her love and understanding of natural beauty.

Lucy's formal education included Downs School in Sussex and a Quaker school in Surrey, a finishing school in France, and Somerville College, Oxford, where she read classics and distinguished herself at lacrosse. When World War I erupted she quit her studies, took brief training at St. Thomas's Hospital in London and went off to nurse in France, a disillusioning experience for which her previous life had hardly fitted her. However while there in 1917, she met and married a young English flying corps officer named Boston. She has one son, Peter.

When the war ended they returned to England and lived in Cheshire. During her years there she waged a continuous campaign against the industrial pollution which was destroying the beauties of the countryside, but her efforts were consistently rebuffed. In 1935, when her marriage ended, she left

England, she thought forever. Traveling in France, Italy, and Hungary and studying painting in Vienna, she indulged with zest all the artistic tastes that had been repressed in her childhood.

Having two Jewish grandmothers, she felt compelled by the political events of the late thirties to return to England, and she did so on the eve of World War II. When an old manor house at Hemingford Grey near Cambridge, which Lucy Boston had long known and admired, came on the market in 1939 she bought it. With the help of Peter and the advice of an architect, she began its restoration. As they stripped away the layers of plaster, the blocked windows, the false partitions that previous generations had superimposed; as they cleared the weeds and brambles that suffocated the gardens, they discovered the beauty and dignity of the original house and the way of life it revealed.

Mrs. Boston was past sixty when she began to write. There seems to have been no period of apprenticeship for her: from the start, her style was clear and felicitous; indeed her stories read aloud so well that they are regularly used on the BBC children's story-reading hour. Her first two novels, *Persephone* (published in the United States as *Stronghold*) and *Yew Hall* (1954 in England), are the only ones written for adults. In 1954 Mrs. Boston published the first of her series of juveniles using her house as background, *The Children of Green Knowe*, with illustrations by her son. The house itself is the only constant in the series, although in most of them the owner of the house, Mrs. Oldknow, and her great-grandson Tolly also appear. The other characters are often children from some period in the history of the house, not ghosts but friendly presences. But these novels are by no means historical; the past is used to illuminate the present. To give one example: the problem of the displaced child, with which no sensitive European of Mrs. Boston's time could be other than involved, is a recurrent theme in *The River at Green Knowe*, and *A Stranger at Green Knowe*.

In *An Enemy at Greene Knowe*, perhaps the most exciting of her stories, past and present are blended in the most subtle and convincing manner, and Miss Melanie D. Powers (Ph.D., Geneva) at once a psychology researcher and an evil spirit of medieval caliber, threatens the very existence of Green Knowe.

In 1961, Mrs. Boston received the Carnegie Medal for *A Stranger at Green Knowe*. *The Children of Green Knowe* received a Lewis Carroll Shelf Award in 1969.

SELECTED WORKS: The Children of Green Knowe, 1955; Treasure of Green Knowe, 1958; The River at Green Knowe, 1959; A Stranger at Green Knowe, 1961; An Enemy at Green Knowe, 1964; The Castle of Yew, 1965; The Sea Egg, 1967; Nothing Said, 1971.

ABOUT: Author's and Writer's Who's Who, 1963; Rose, Jasper. Lucy Boston; Junior Bookshelf December 1962; Library Association Record May 1962; Wilson Library Bulletin October 1962.

ALIKI LIACOURAS BRANDENBERG

See *Aliki*

RAYMOND BRIGGS

January 18, 1934-

ILLUSTRATOR OF *The Mother Goose Treasury*, etc.

Autobiographical sketch of Raymond Redvers Briggs:

I WAS born in London and evacuated to the country when the Blitz began. Although over a hundred miles from London, we were sometimes woken by loud machine gun fire as planes dived low overhead. Aunt Betty would cry, "Get the cases, Flo!" Flo was my other spinster aunt and the cases were always packed ready for an instant getaway if the Jerries came. Once, the small stone cottage was ringed by jettisoned German bombs, but no harm came except for the glass falling out of the grandfather clock.

In 1944 I went to a suburban grammar school of the usual English type, which tries to model itself on the famous, and even more dreadful, public schools. There was the usual vicious discipline by the prefects and everyone was expected to be dedicated to "The School" as if it was a religious institution.

R. R. Briggs

Sport and science were the holy subjects. Anyone interested in art or music was looked upon as hopeless. The school's only claim to fame is that one of the most famous murderers of this century went there. We were taught to enunciate our vowels properly in order to conceal our cockney accents and lowly origins. Even now I still speak an uneasy mixture of pompous pseudo-BBC and south suburban cockney. Neither accent feels natural.

Despite the school I became interested in cartoons and decided to become a cartoonist. (I realised just recently how almost all my favorite illustrators are cartoonists or near cartoonists—Gerard Hoffnung, Ralph Steadman, Quentin Blake, Steinberg, Thurber and Feiffer.)

So it was with great relief that I left in 1949 and went to the Wimbledon School of Art. Here we were trained in the nineteenth-century academic tradition. This ignored all that had happened in art since 1880—including the Impressionists. Everything since then was looked upon as mad and almost immoral. All this was accepted as gospel truth as we were only fifteen or sixteen and had no knowledge of art from the grammar school. At the art school cartoons were very despised so I decided to become a painter. We had four years of figure drawing, figure composition, life painting and still-life. No "basic design," no abstraction. Although this was insane as a training for a present-day painter, I now realise it was the perfect training for an illustrator.

After two years in the boring British Army, which was like a mild form of school, I went to the Slade School of Fine Art. Civilisation at last! There I slowly and painfully discovered what painting really was, and realised that I was not a painter and had never been one.

I had always wanted to illustrate as well as paint, so I began taking work round to the publishers. Then another slow realisation began to dawn. Virtually all book illustration was children's books! Ugh! Horrors! When one editor asked me how I felt about fairies I could scarcely manage a polite reply.

However it was not long before I realised that children's book illustration was a wonderful field to work in. Compared with advertising and magazine work—the illustrator's other main fields—it is much less commercial, more warm, human and free.

My wife Jean and I married in 1963, and as she trained as an illustrator then became a painter, and I trained as a painter then became an illustrator, this makes quite a good balance.

We have no children and do not particularly want any. I quite like some children—in small doses. They are interesting to draw, to watch, to photograph and to read about their customs and games. Pigs are interesting in the same way, too, but you don't want them charging round the house screaming and making messes in corners, though at the moment we have a young sheep doing just that.

———

Raymond Briggs designs many of the books he illustrates. His *Fee Fi Fo Fum* was a runner-up for the Kate Greenaway Medal in 1964, and his *The Mother Goose Treasury*, for which he did 897 illustrations, won the award in 1966.

SELECTED WORKS WRITTEN AND ILLUSTRATED: Ring-A-Ring O' Roses, 1962; The White Land, 1963; Fee Fi Fo Fum, 1964; The Mother Goose Treasury, 1966; Jim and the Beanstalk, 1970.

SELECTED WORKS ILLUSTRATED: Arches and
Spires, by Alfred Duggan, 1962; Whistling
Rufus, by William Mayne, 1965; Jimmy Murphy
and the White Duesenberg, by Bruce Carter,
1968.

ABOUT: Hopkins, Lee Bennett. Books Are by
People; Hürlimann, Bettina. Picture Book
World; Kingman, Lee and others, comps. Illus-
trators of Children's Books: 1957-1966; Ryder,
John. Artists of a Certain Line.

BERNARDA BRYSON

March 7, 1903-

AUTHOR AND ILLUSTRATOR OF *Gilgamesh*, etc.

Autobiographical sketch of Bernarda Bryson
Shahn:

Born: Athens, Ohio; mother taught Latin in
Ohio University, father owned and edited
two newspapers.

Schools: "Model School" to the 5th grade,
then no school until high school. Columbus
School for Girls then Ohio University for
three years, Ohio State University one year.
Have also attended Western Reserve College
and the New School for Social Research and
the Cleveland School of Art.

Worked: First at commercial art, then covered art news and wrote column, *The Ohio
State Journal,* edited a small weekly, taught
etching and lithography in the Columbus
Museum School of Art. New York, worked on
several depression-type projects. Washington,
did a series of lithographs for the Resettle-
ment Administration; New York, assisted my
husband on Bronx Post Office mural, worked
for CIO doing cartoons and various kinds of
drawings.

Illustration: For a number of years I made
drawings chiefly for *Fortune Magazine, Harper's* and *The Scientific American,* intermit-
tently for many others, *The Reporter, Life,*
etc. I illustrated a children's book for Houghton Mifflin—*The White Falcon,* then did
numerous others. I wrote and illustrated *The
Twenty Miracles of Saint Nicholas,* published
by Little Brown. This was chosen for
the AIGA Fifty Books. For Holt, Rinehart
and Winston, I illustrated *Calendar Moon,*
(which won a California award) and *The*

BERNARDA BRYSON

Sun Is a Golden Earring (which was runner-
up for the Caldecott award). I wrote and
illustrated for them, *Gilgamesh,* which was
chosen for the AIGA Fifty Books. For
Coward McCann, I illustrated *The Return of
the Twelves,* which received some sort of
Herald Tribune recognition. Almost all the
above books have had awards of some kind.
I'm not too familiar with the significance of
these large or small awards so I cannot give
them in detail, although they are very nice
to receive.

Married: Ben Shahn, painter; I have three
children, Susanna, Jonathan, a sculptor, post-
doctoral fellow, University of Illinois, Abigail Shahn Slamm, a painter.

Important influences: Undoubtedly the academic background of my family, the fact
that my mother read books both to and with
my sister and me, that much poetry was read
and said in our family, that my father read
plays with us, that there was a diverse family
library. In college, philosophy was most in-
fluential study for me.

———

Bernarda Bryson married the noted artist
Ben Shahn in 1935. Their daughter Susanna
died in 1967, and Shahn in 1969.

SELECTED WORKS WRITTEN AND ILLUSTRATED:
The Twenty Miracles of Saint Nicholas, 1960;
The Zoo of Zeus, 1964; Gilgamesh, 1967.

SELECTED WORKS ILLUSTRATED: White Falcon, by Charlton Ogburn, 1955; The Sun Is a Golden Earring, by Natalia Maree Belting, 1962; The Return of the Twelves, by Pauline Clarke, 1964; Calendar Moon, by Natalia Maree Belting, 1964.

ABOUT: Kingman, Lee and others, comps. Illustrators of Children's Books: 1957-1966; Viguers, Ruth Hill and others, comps. Illustrators of Children's Books: 1946-1956; New York Post January 29, 1970; Print September 1955.

WALTER BUEHR

May 14, 1897-January 2, 1971

AUTHOR AND ILLUSTRATOR OF *Knights and Castles and Feudal Life*, etc.

Autobiographical sketch of Walter Franklin Buehr:

I WAS born in Chicago, went to high schools and several art schools including the Art Students League of New York, where I later taught for eight years. I started as a commercial artist, later an illustrator, designer, architect and finally author. Since 1949 I have written and illustrated fifty-six books, mostly junior books for libraries and school libraries, but have also written four adult books, one of which, on weapons before gunpowder, was chosen by the American Library Association as one of the outstanding reference books of the year. The title was *Warriors' Weapons*.

I am married to a portrait artist, have three daughters, and five grandchildren, two of whom live in Paris and can't speak English, which is hard on their grandfather who speaks only Army French.

I have been a sailor for years, living on my boat every summer until recently, and have cruised the Atlantic coast and the Mediterranean, and my hobby led to the writing of my first book. I decided to write a book on ships and sailing and life at sea so that boys (and girls) living in the Middle West far from the sea, might be able to understand the terms used by writers of sea stories, how a ship was rigged and operated, the life of the sailor during windjammer days, and how a ship of the line or a frigate was fought during battle. This book, *Ships and Life Afloat*, now out of print, was forerunner of a series of historical, exploration, naval and military titles, as well as books on electricity, mining, plastics, lumbering etc. I have written a book on earthquakes, and will soon start on one about storms—hurricanes, typhoons, tornados and their causes, and some of the devastating ones.

I built a house overlooking the ocean on one of the Bahama Islands, where we spend about a third of our time, where the swimming, boating and fishing are super, and our harbor one of the loveliest along our southern coast.

———

Walter Buehr attended the Detroit School of Design and the Philadelphia School of Industrial Arts as well as the Art Students League, and also studied in Europe. In World War I he served with the first camouflage section of the United States Army Engineers, 1917-1919, became a first sergeant, and was awarded the active service medal with three battle clasps. He married Camilla Goodwyn in 1938 and their daughters are Joan, Cynthia, and Wendy. Buehr designed furniture, was interested in ceramics and high fidelity systems, belonged to the Norwalk Yacht Club, and contributed to yachting and architectural magazines. He received

Buehr: *BYOOR*

the Gold Medal of the Art Directors Club of New York.

SELECTED WORKS: Ships and Life Afloat, 1953; Harvest of the Sea, 1955; Knights and Castles and Feudal Life, 1957; Wonder Worker, the Story of Electricity, 1961; The Spanish Armada, 1962; Volcano! 1962; Plastics, the Man-Made Miracle, 1967; Salt, Sugar, and Spice, 1969.

ABOUT: Contemporary Authors, Vol. 5-6; Kingman, Lee and others, comps. Illustrators of Children's Books: 1957-1966; Viguers, Ruth Hill and others, comps. Illustrators of Children's Books: 1946-1956.

ROBERT BURCH

June 26, 1925-

AUTHOR OF *Queenie Peavy*, etc.

Autobiographical sketch of Robert Joseph Burch:

LIKE Brer Rabbit I was "born and bred in the briarpatch." Or maybe it was the cotton patch. In any event, it was in rural Georgia, where I grew up with seven brothers and sisters during the Great Depression, having so much fun that we didn't have time to worry about the hard times that had settled onto the country. Anyway, other things were more important to us than money—cousins, for instance, who knew how to dam up a small stream to make a "wash hole" big enough for swimming. When we weren't swimming in it, we were seining it, catching more crawfish and tadpoles than anything else.

We also had work to do. I cannot remember when I first began tending chickens, planting a garden, or hauling stovewood, and the milking job was mine from the year I was in the fifth grade until I went away to college. But it was possible to combine work with pleasure, and chores were turned into 4-H Club projects—participation in the county fair being a special attraction of the club to me. Most years I exhibited chickens (two hens and a rooster). They never won even a small award, but they entitled me to a free pass to the fair grounds! One year my entry was Pearlie, a scrub-Jersey calf, who won blue ribbons and top prize money, which pleased Pearlie and me but upset club

members who owned pedigreed stock and felt that aristocracy should have been rewarded.

At our house there were always pets—dogs, cats, farm animals, and wild creatures that we tamed. In addition to Pearlie, my favorites were a turkey that followed me everywhere, a racoon, a mocking bird that kept coming back for visits after I had set him free, and a mule named Kate (quite gentle and sweet, opposite to the cantankerous Twilight I was to use in a book, D.J.'s Worst Enemy, many years later.)

After one year of college in the Blue Ridge Mountains I joined the army, serving during World War II in the South Pacific. When the war was over, I entered the University of Georgia, graduating from its School of Agriculture in 1949. Later, I worked in the Orient, traveled around the world on a freighter, and settled in New York.

I never gave a thought to writing stories, even as a hobby, until I was thirty years old. It was then that Dr. William Lipkind (the "Will" of the Will & Nicholas picture book team), instructor in a writing course I had decided to take for the fun of it, encouraged me to think seriously about a writing career. A number of years later A Funny Place to Live was published. It was followed by

Tyler, Wilkin, and Skee, in which I first used incidents of my own boyhood. While working on it I discovered the real pleasure in writing books for young people.

Eventually I moved back to Georgia to the house in which I spent my youth. It's quieter now than it was then, and the only pets are two cats. One of them provided me with the idea for the story, *Joey's Cat*, and the other is one of Joey's cat's kittens, now quite grown up.

When Robert Burch circled the globe, the freighter on which he worked part of his way was Danish. Coincidentally, perhaps, several of his books have been published in Denmark—*Skinny, D. J.'s Worst Enemy* and *Queenie Peavy*. *Skinny* was an Honor Book in the New York *Herald Tribune* Children's Spring Book Festival, 1964. *Queenie Peavy* received the Children's Book Award of the Child Study Association in 1966 and the Jane Addams Children's Book Award in 1967.

SELECTED WORKS: A Funny Place to Live, 1962; Tyler, Wilkin, and Skee, 1963; Skinny, 1964; D. J.'s Worst Enemy, 1965; Queenie Peavy, 1966; Renfroe's Christmas, 1968; Joey's Cat, 1969; Simon and the Game of Chance, 1970.

ABOUT: Contemporary Authors, Vol. 5-6; Elementary English December 1965.

PETER BURCHARD

March 1, 1921-

AUTHOR AND ILLUSTRATOR OF *Jed*, etc.

Autobiographical sketch of Peter Duncan Burchard:

DURING World War II I enlisted in the United States Army and was sent to New Orleans where I illustrated training aids. I remember making pictures of amphibious landings, the kind of landings subsequently made in Normandy. New Orleans was all I'd ever heard it was. A misty moon hung over Jackson Square. There were checked table cloths at The Court of the Two Sisters where you could dance to the music of a three-piece band. But I'd quit my studies to join the battle so I asked to be transferred

PETER BURCHARD

to radio school. When I finished training I was assigned to a troopship which had just come off the ways in Mississippi. My ship was assigned to convoy duty in the North Atlantic and Mediterranean. We sailed to Africa, England and France. I made eighteen crossings of the Atlantic, lived on the sea in winter and summer, with its violence and serenity. The love affair continued after the war when I sailed small boats in all kinds of weather.

In 1947 I finished my studies at the Philadelphia College of Art and came to New York where I designed book jackets and illustrated books. I learned while I earned and some of my work was less than first-rate. I'd always wanted to write and in 1960 I started writing seriously. I'd done a little writing but I'd written in imagination all my life, telling stories to myself as I lay in bed at night, walked in the country or in city streets, crossing out words, rephrasing and striking out again, mostly in my head. I'm a skillful draftsman and a good illustrator but when I write my spirit takes wing. I'm in my forties now and feel I've no more than just begun. I've written picture books, two novelettes and two full-length novels, all for children of various ages, and one biography for adults. The biography won me a Guggenheim Fellowship, awarded in 1966. The novels are set against a background of American history. The biography was as true as intense research could make it. I've been especially interested in American slavery and the antislavery movement and, of course, in the Civil War. *Stranded: A Story of New York in 1875* is about an innocent Scottish boy caught in the toils of the wicked city. *Bimby* is set in 1859 and tells the story of a crucial day in the life of a young slave in the sea islands of Georgia. *Jed* was my first serious work of fiction. It is the short, simple story of an act of decency performed by a youthful Union soldier in Mississippi in 1862.

I'm still an active illustrator and expect to remain so but writing has become my primary interest. I am currently working on a fourth historical novel and two short contemporary urban stories.

I am the father of three, two girls and a boy. My children have gone their separate ways but we have wonderful times when we are together. My elder daughter Lee is a free-lance designer, my son Chip (Peter, Jr.) is a sophomore at Boston University and my second daughter Laura lives in California.

My personal life has been turbulent. I'm not a collector of serene landscapes. As a boy I was introspective and quite accustomed to being alone. I liked making things, drawing, painting and reading. As I pushed forward into my teens I became more gregarious. I loved sports, especially football which I found intensely exhilarating. I still play tennis, skate and swim and of course I sail whenever I can.

Peter Burchard has illustrated more than a hundred titles, mostly books for children. *Jed*, written and illustrated by him, won a Lewis Carroll Shelf Award in 1966.

SELECTED WORKS WRITTEN: North by Night, 1962; Stranded, 1967; Chito, 1969.

SELECTED WORKS WRITTEN AND ILLUSTRATED: Jed, 1960; Balloons; From Paper Bags to Skyhooks, 1960; Bimby, 1968.

SELECTED WORKS ILLUSTRATED: Roosevelt Grady, by Louisa R. Shotwell, 1963; Pirate Chase, by Earl Schenck Miers, 1965; Zeb, by Lonzo Anderson, 1966; The Street of the Flower Boxes, by Peggy Mann, 1966; Museum Adventures, by Herbert and Marjorie Katz, 1969.

ABOUT: Contemporary Authors, Vol. 5-6; Kingman, Lee and others, comps. Illustrators of Children's Books: 1957-1966; Viguers, Ruth Hill and others, comps. Illustrators of Children's Books: 1946-1956.

NANCY EKHOLM BURKERT

February 16, 1933-

ILLUSTRATOR OF *The Nightingale*, etc.

Autobiographical sketch of Nancy Ekholm Burkert:

MY family moved often while I was young —from Colorado, to Michigan, to Missouri, to Illinois and finally to Wisconsin. I earned a B.S. and M.S. in applied art at the University of Wisconsin in Madison and there, after my junior year, I married my fellow student, the artist Robert Burkert. We now have two children, Claire and Rand—who appear in my books wherever I can put them!

In ninth grade I wrote and illustrated a story for children, in high school I served as art editor of the yearbook and took painting classes at Western Museum, in Racine. During college I was art editor of the literary magazine, illustrated USAFI booklets and exhibited, as I continue to do, my watercolors and drawings in professional shows. Bob and I collaborated on a psychology textbook and in 1957 I illustrated a textbook for Scott, Foresman. In 1958 I wrote and illustrated a fantasy in rhyme—rhyme and fantasy being rare in juvenile publishing at the time! The poetry was terrible but the art work pleased Virginia Fowler at Knopf who gave me my first great opportunity—to illustrate Roald Dahl's *James and the Giant Peach*. Since then I have illustrated five books—each different from the other but with one thing in common—literary substance and a writer's skill that I respect.

I have been drawing all my life, filling the reams of paper my father brought to me, drawing many hours as I listened to the radio. Unlike television, radio did not supply the pictures and therefore in one way stimulated the visual imagination far more! As a child I did not see many magazines

Nancy Ekholm Burkert

and though I remember two or three Disney movies and the "funnies," my picture books provided my only source of visual art. I still have, as companions, the books of my childhood, among the most precious a collection of D'Aulnoy and Perrault, a Grimm's *Snow White*—the images of the illustrations like old friends in my mind. I am in love with books, the feeling, the nearness of them. I am in awe of what the printed word means to mankind—one certainty in this uncertain world.

If a story and I are meant for one another —I can "see" the illustrations in my mind immediately as I read it. I usually can "see" the whole book—the format, etc. At Harper and Row—with Ursula Nordstrom—a wonderful attitude exists—a respect for an individual's "vision" of a book and a receptivity to all ideas.

My favorite painters are the artists of the ancient Chinese scrolls, fifteenth-century Flemish artists (especially Hugo van der Goes's Portinari altarpiece) and Odilon Redon. My favorite illustrator is Arthur Rackham. My professors at the University instilled a lasting respect for fine draughtsmanship of all eras.

In my illustrations I try to project real rather than idealized or cliché faces, (using my children and friends' children as models),

a "sense of place" (as one would design a set for a play) and particularized forms in nature. Three-fourths of my time is spent in research. I try to suit the technique to the quality I feel in the text. For example— soft warm charcoal pencil for *Jean-Claude's Island*, matter-of-fact brush and inks for *A Child's Calendar*.

If my drawings illuminate and expand the story as the author intended, I am fulfilled. If my drawings please the children for whom the stories were written—I am joyful!

———

Nancy Ekholm married Robert Burkert in 1953. He is a printmaker and an Associate Professor of Art at the University of Wisconsin, Milwaukee. Their daughter, Claire Loren, was born in 1958 and their son, Randall Evan, in 1961.

Mrs. Burkert has exhibited her watercolors in New York and the Midwest. *The Nightingale* was an Honor Book in the New York *Herald Tribune* Spring Book Festival, 1965, and was awarded the Gold Medal of the Society of Illustrators in 1966. Her work has also been exhibited by the American Institute of Graphic Arts.

SELECTED WORKS ILLUSTRATED: James and the Giant Peach, by Roald Dahl, 1961; Jean-Claude's Island, by Natalie Savage Carlson, 1963; The Big Goose and the Little White Duck, by Meindert De Jong, 1963; The Nightingale, by Hans Christian Andersen, 1965; A Child's Calendar, by John Updike, 1965; The Scroobious Pip, by Edward Lear and Ogden Nash, 1968; The Fir Tree, by Hans Christian Andersen, 1970.

ABOUT: Kingman, Lee and others, comps. Illustrators of Children's Books: 1957-1966.

HELEN OXENBURY BURNINGHAM

See *Oxenbury, Helen*

JOHN BURNINGHAM
April 27, 1936-

AUTHOR AND ILLUSTRATOR OF *Borka*, etc.

Autobiographical sketch of John Macintosh Burningham:

AS a child I was brought up in the country and missed a considerable amount of

schooling as my parents moved about a lot during the war. I went to about ten different schools in all and as a consequence got rather far behind with my academic education. My final school years were spent at A.S. Neill's school Summerhill where I gave more time and energy to the art classes than to any other subject.

On leaving school, I was faced with military service and decided to become a conscientious objector. I spent two years working on farms doing forestry work, in hospitals and in many work camps, renovating slums, building schools, etc. I travelled and worked abroad a great deal, in Southern Italy, Yugoslavia and Israel. The experiences gained in this two-year period have proved invaluable in the work which I now do.

I now had to make a decision about some further training. Like many young people of that age I had no idea what I wanted to do and applied for admission to the Central School of Arts and Crafts in London simply because a friend of mine was a student there. I studied illustration and graphic design for three years.

When I left the Central School, I was a qualified book illustrator and graphic designer with a diploma (with distinction). But, as I was to discover, this did not help me to find work. I did the usual round of advertising agencies and publishers but could not persuade anyone to give me work. I managed to get a few poster commissions for London Transport, but publishers would give me nothing.

I worked for a year on an animated film, designing backgrounds and puppets, in the Middle East, then returned to England.

Out of desperation with publishers, I decided that the only way to get my drawings published was to write and illustrate my own book. *Borka* was the result. It was such a success, winning the Kate Greenaway Award, that I have continued writing and illustrating books for children ever since.

My other work includes murals, exhibitions, animated films and three-dimensional models. I have no fixed ambitions for the future except to continue to work for the amusement of children. I find getting down to work and concentrating very hard and spend months planning my books. I develop a story which works pictorially at first, then, when all the pictures are finished, I write the text.

I am married with two small children and live near Hampstead Heath in London. My wife is also a designer and now illustrates her own books.

———

John Burningham was born in Farnham, Surrey, England. He married Helen Oxenbury in 1964 and they have two children. Burningham has designed friezes for children's rooms and does advertising and magazine illustration. He won the Kate Greenaway Medal in 1963 for *Borka* and again in 1970 for *Mr. Gumpy's Outing*. His work has been exhibited by the American Institute of Graphic Arts.

SELECTED WORKS WRITTEN AND ILLUSTRATED: Borka: the Adventures of a Goose with No Feathers, 1964; John Burningham's ABC, 1967; Humbert, Mr. Firkin and the Lord Mayor of London, 1967; Cannonball Simp, 1967; Harquin: the Fox Who Went Down to the Valley, 1968.

SELECTED WORKS ILLUSTRATED: Chitty-Chitty-Bang-Bang, by Ian Fleming, 1964; The Extraordinary Tug of War, retold by Letta Schatz, 1968.

ABOUT: Hürlimann, Bettina. Picture Book World; Kingman, Lee and others, comps. Illustrators of Children's Books: 1957-1966; Library Association Record June 1964.

HESTER BURTON

December 6, 1913-

AUTHOR OF *Time of Trial*, etc.

Autobiographical sketch of Hester Burton:

I WAS born in the quiet market town of Beccles, Suffolk, England, where my father, a man of much humour and humanity, was the local family doctor. He was a wise man; he believed that since a daughter had only one childhood, she had better spend it in happiness. I went to school, of course, but no one bullied me to pass examinations. My early years unfolded in a peaceful dream of imagining myself a Red Indian, trying to write poetry, swimming in the River Waveney, and reading. Each children's book that I write is a kind of "thank-you" to my parents for this untroubled start in life.

At eighteen, I entered Oxford University where I took an honours degree in English Literature. Here, again, I was the most fortunate of mortals. My teacher in Anglo-Saxon was Professor Tolkien, the famous author of *The Hobbit* and *The Lord of the Rings*. The most brilliant lecturer in the Literature Faculty who, incidentally, taught me all I know about the Middle Ages, was C. S. Lewis, who later turned his gifts to writing the famous Narnia books. Oxford was a wonderful experience. For one thing, it gave me a sense of history. It still does, for immediately upon leaving the University I married an Oxford don and we have lived on the edge of this charmed city ever since. It is here, close to a quiet reach of the River Cherwell, opposite a mill which goes back to the eleventh century, that we have brought up our three daughters.

Looking back on the children's books I have written, I recognise that they are all of a piece with my life. I have chosen to write historical novels, I am sure, not only because of the sense of history I acquired at Oxford but also because an historical theme lends itself to the fast-paced stories, packed with incident, which I enjoyed so much as a child. As a writer, too, I am less shy of exploring the heights and depths of emotion felt by my characters if those characters lived a long time ago. In a curious way, history gives me a sense of release.

Perhaps this is because for one brief period, very early in our married life, we too found ourselves caught up in the pages of history. The summer months of 1940—Dunkirk, the Battle of Britain, the first bombing of London—were the most rousing and self-forgetting months I have ever known. Partly it was the peril we were all in; partly it was the voice of Churchill coming to us over the radio. What I learnt in those summer months has opened wide for me an understanding of other people living at other times who have also had to face seemingly hopeless odds. I have tried to recapture the amazing feeling of 1940 in *In Spite of All Terror*. This story is in no sense autobiographical, but—like a great many of my other books—is the result of a patient and careful putting together of incidents that really happened at that time.

Hester Burton married Reginald William Boteler Burton in 1937. Their daughters are Catharine Anne, Elizabeth Mary and Janet Hester. Her book, *Time of Trial,* won the Carnegie Medal for 1963, and received an Honorable Mention in the New York *Herald Tribune* Children's Spring Book Festival, 1964.

SELECTED WORKS: Castors Away! 1963; Time of Trial, 1964; No Beat of Drum, 1967; The Flood of Reedsmere, 1968; In Spite of All Terror, 1969; Beyond the Weir Bridge, 1970.

ABOUT: Library Association Record June 1964.

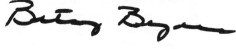

BETSY BYARS

August 7, 1928-

AUTHOR OF *The Summer of the Swans,* etc.

Autobiographical sketch of Betsy Cromer Byars:

I WAS born in Charlotte, North Carolina, and grew up there, living part of the time in the city and for a few years in a small mill community nearby. I was a happy carefree girl during my school years and not an outstanding student in any respect.

After graduating from Central High School I went to Furman University for two years and then returned to Charlotte where I earned a degree in English from Queens College in 1950. While at Queens I met Edward Byars who was teaching engineering at Clemson University, and we were married shortly after my graduation.

Although I had always been an avid reader, I had never thought of writing until my husband became a graduate student at the University of Illinois and I found myself with long hours to fill. At first I wrote magazine articles, funny ones, which were published in such magazines as *Saturday Evening Post, Look* and others. As my family grew, however, I became interested in writing books for children. The first, *Clementine,* was published in 1962.

Ed and I are the parents of four children— Laurie, Betsy Ann, Nan, and Guy, and they are my severest critics. "Mom, nobody would say *that,*" can be harsh criticism indeed.

I find many of the ideas for my books in things that happen around me—in newspaper stories, in things my children tell me happen in their schools, in magazine articles. The idea for *The Summer of the Swans* came from an article in my college alumni magazine telling about the swans on the University lake which persisted in flying away to other, less desirable ponds.

We now live in Morgantown, West Virginia, where my husband is a professor at West Virginia University. I do most of my writing during the winter months because we have a cabin on a nearby lake where I enjoy spending the summers, and I also share my husband's hobby, which is gliding.

There is no activity in my life, however, which has brought me more pleasure than my writing. And the moment of receiving a package in the mail, opening it, and seeing the finished book for the first time is beyond description.

———

Mrs. Byars won the Newbery Medal for *The Summer of the Swans* in 1971.

SELECTED WORKS: Clementine, 1962; The Dancing Camel, 1965; Rama, the Gypsy Cat, 1966; The Groober, 1967; The Midnight Fox, 1968; Trouble River, 1969; The Summer of the Swans, 1970; Go and Hush the Baby, 1971.

ABOUT: Horn Book August 1971; Top of the News April 1971.

MARY CALHOUN
August 3, 1926-

AUTHOR OF *Depend on Katie John*, etc.

Autobiographical sketch of Mary Huiskamp
Calhoun Wilkins:

IF authors are shaped by early gifts,
mine would be an imaginative, storytelling
mother and a musty, high-ceilinged public
library two blocks away. Being an only child
in a household of adults—mother, father,
grandmother and assorted renters—must
have helped with the shaping, too.

I was born Mary Huiskamp in Keokuk,
Iowa, a Mississippi River town. There I
grew up in a big brick house on a hill above
the river. My great-grandfather built the
house, and there were lots of rooms and
gardens to go to. When I was seven I discovered the delights of reading at the library and decided to become an author. Ro-
mantically sitting under a gooseberry bush
I composed a long fairy tale, burying the in-
stallments in a White Owl cigar box under
the bush between sessions. I still have the
box. The librarians were mostly spinster ladies, and they mothered me, bringing me
Oz books when I had the mumps, allowing
me into sacred, cobwebby back rooms where
the bound copies of *St. Nicholas* and *John
Martin's Magazine* were kept.

Keokuk was stimulating to the imagination, with its rivertown flavor of old houses
and the rich variety of people who lived in
them. And the river, The River, was inviting
to the imagination as it curved away and
carried towboats on down to New Orleans.
Of course I wanted to float down the river
on a raft.

Instead I worked in the library three summers in my late teens and went on to the
University of Iowa. After my first creative
writing course there I concluded I had no
talent for fiction and majored in journalism.
My first job out of college was writing wom-
en's features on the Omaha (Nebraska)
World-Herald. There I met Frank Calhoun,
a reporter-photographer. We were married
and lived in a number of towns in California,
Oregon and Washington.

Mary Calhoun

When our children, Michael and Gregory,
were born, I gave up newspaper work to be
with them. Presently I was telling them
story after story, in the tradition of my mother. I wrote down some of these, and after
a period of rejection slips, these began to
sell to children's magazines and then to a
book publisher.

My first book sale, however, was *Making
the Mississippi Shout*, written out of nostalgia for the river. The later *Katie John* books
resulted from happy memories of the big old
house in which I grew up. Although the
stories are not biography, many of the incidents are based on things I did as a girl, as
well as feelings and problems I had, so I
suppose Katie John has a good deal of me
in her.

Frank died of a heart attack in 1961. Now
I am married to Leon Wilkins, a friend from
high school days. In those days I introduced
him to the Episcopal Church and rather
shaped my own future, willy-nilly, for Leon
became an Episcopal minister, and we live
in a house connected to the church in Rangely, Colorado.

Being a minister's wife and mother of two
teenage boys keeps me busy. Still, weekday
mornings are set aside for writing, some

afternoons for walking in the hills with the dogs, and some evenings for sitting with a cat in lap. It's a good life.

———

Mary Huiskamp received her B.A. from the State University of Iowa in 1948. She served on the Mount Vernon (Washington) Library Board 1960-61 and was president of the Rangely (Colorado) Library Board in 1970.

SELECTED WORKS: Making the Mississippi Shout, 1957; The Sweet Patootie Doll, 1957; Wobble the Witch Cat, 1958; Katie John, 1960; Honestly, Katie John! 1963; The Witch of Hissing Hill, 1964; The Thieving Dwarfs, 1967; The Goblin Under the Stairs, 1968; White Witch of Kynance, 1970.

ABOUT: Contemporary Authors, Vol. 5-6; Who's Who of American Women, 1970-71.

ELEANOR CAMERON

March 23, 1912-

AUTHOR OF *The Wonderful Flight to the Mushroom Planet*, etc.

Autobiographical sketch of Eleanor Butler Cameron:

PERHAPS it was my mother's stories of her childhood in England that started me off on my long delight with English fantasies and fairy tales, and was the influence that led indirectly to fantasy when I began writing for children. Both my parents had been born in England and then came to Canada, where I was born. In 1915 we moved to the little town of South Charleston, Ohio, and then to Berkeley, California, three years later, where I fell in love with the old Carnegie Public Library (since torn down) and with the whole world of books. Here I went to Washington Grammar School, Garfield Junior High, and Berkeley High. At the age of twelve, when my first writings began to appear in the Children's Page of the Berkeley *Daily Gazette*, I decided, upon seeing my works in print, that someday I would be "a real writer," and that I would support myself meanwhile (for you cannot live on the earnings of writing alone, I was told) by being a librarian.

ELEANOR CAMERON

And so I did, though not in Berkeley. When I was sixteen, I underwent a terrible uprooting; the family moved to Los Angeles and so I found myself on the bare new campus of UCLA instead of the (then) beautiful wooded one of UC. Meanwhile I started my library career by working as a clerk in the Literature Department of the Los Angeles Public Library. It was an uprooting from which I think I never really recovered, for all my richest memories, the usable material of any writer's life, go back to my years in Berkeley from the ages of six to sixteen, and to vacations on the Monterey Peninsula.

Lately I have returned to the Peninsula for good with a husband who loves this country as much as I do. But long before this return I began writing books whose "place" was Berkeley, in the case of my one published novel, *The Unheard Music*, and the Peninsula, in the case of my children's books. *The Unheard Music* reflects a love of libraries; it was begun when my husband, Ian Stuart Cameron (whom I married in 1934), was in the army, and was continued during the first years of our son, David's, childhood. He was seven, and a reading animal like his parents, when he asked that I write a space story for him with magic in it. Already I was in my third phase of exploring the world of children's books; the first had taken place during my own childhood, and the second when I worked in the Los Angeles City Schools Library becoming thoroughly acquainted with what had been published since I was a child. The third phase was spent in exploring this engrossing world with David, and in finding joy in it through his reactions as well as my own.

Out of my love of astronomy and of fantasy and out of David's request for a story especially for him came the five Mr. Bass books that began with *The Wonderful Flight to the Mushroom Planet*, as well as four others: *The Terrible Churnadryne, The Mysterious Christmas Shell, The Beast with the Magical Horn* and *A Spell Is Cast*. Now I have entered a fourth phase of exploration, which draws on the other three and which has resulted in a collection of critical essays, *The Green and Burning Tree: On the Writing and Enjoyment of Children's Books*.

———

Eleanor Cameron won the Commonwealth Award and a scroll from the Mystery Writers of America, both in 1964, for *A Spell Is Cast*. In 1965 she received the annual award from the Southern California Council on Literature for Children and Young People. In 1970 she was given her second Commonwealth Award, for *The Green and Burning Tree: On the Writing and Enjoyment of Children's Books,* 1969.

SELECTED WORKS: The Wonderful Flight to the Mushroom Planet, 1954; Stowaway to the Mushroom Planet, 1956; The Terrible Churnadryne, 1959; A Mystery for Mr. Bass, 1960; The Beast with the Magical Horn, 1963; A Spell Is Cast, 1964; Time and Mr. Bass, 1967.

ABOUT: Contemporary Authors, Vol. 4; Something About the Author, Vol. 1; Wilson Library Bulletin October 1962.

ALOIS CARIGIET

August 1902-

AUTHOR AND ILLUSTRATOR OF *Anton the Goatherd*, etc.

Biographical sketch of Alois Carigiet:

ALOIS CARIGIET, the seventh of ten children, was born in the Alpine village of Truns, in the canton of Graubünden in east

Alois Carigiet: *al WAH cah ree JYAY*

ALOIS CARIGIET

Switzerland. His family, both on his father Alois's side and his mother Barbara's, were farmers. He has particularly happy memories of his childhood among the narrow valleys and steep slopes of the Grison Alps, a landscape of swift streams, pine woods, goat and chamois, and alpine wild flowers. His mother's memory he holds especially dear.

He spent ten years at school in Chur, the capital of the canton, followed by four years of apprenticeship as a decorative painter. While living in Chur he belonged to a boys' club and was active in its theatricals. In 1923 he moved to Zurich and worked in a studio for industrial design where he painted ads and posters and made shop displays. Then he broke away and began to work as a free lance. He made stage sets for the Zurich municipal theater, sets and costumes for a cabaret called the "Cornichon," and designs for the Swiss Tourist Office. In 1939 he did a great deal of work with the Swiss National Exposition which took place in Zurich on the eve of World War II.

It was in that same year, when he was home on a holiday, that he came upon and fell in love with the village of Platenga near his birthplace. He was overcome with longing to give up the city and commercial art. With the help of his brother Zarli he made the move, and then he began to paint as he pleased. His work gained increasingly in quality and intensity, and he began to be recognized as a leading Swiss artist.

In 1940 on a visit to Zurich he met a poet from his own canton, Selina Chönz, from Guarda in the Engadin. She showed him a book she was writing in verse about a little boy called Ursli, brought up like himself in the Alps. He began to work on illustrations for it and collaboration between artist and poet was initiated. It continued during many visits to the Chönz family in Guarda, where a pine-panelled attic was set aside as a studio for Carigiet. Three books came of this friendship: *A Bell for Ursli*, a companion piece, *Florina and the Wild Bird* about Ursli's sister, and another story about the two children, *The Snowstorm*. The verse was originally written in Romansh, the Graubünden dialect which in 1938 became the fourth official language of Switzerland. The books were translated into German and then into many other languages.

Carigiet has described how they collaborated. Together they worked on the layout of the books while he sketched and painted the scenes. Often the text was not written until after the illustrations had been made, so he has never regarded himself as purely an illustrator. The pictures are full-page color drawings in which the high, clear mountain air can almost be felt in the glowing alpine colors. The mountain children, slightly coltish but surefooted and utterly at home in their surroundings, go about their lives of work and play; the story often ends in a festival, such as the procession of the bell ringers in *Ursli*, or the contest for the best-decorated sled in *The Snowstorm*. Perhaps the most beautiful illustration is that showing the discovery by Florina, in *Florina and the Wild Bird*, of a magic jewel high among the alpine cliffs where only the edelweiss grows.

After six years at Platenga, Carigiet married and began to build a house in the village, next to the chapel. He was now getting many commissions, especially for the painting of murals in famous halls in Zurich and in his own canton. The problem of schooling for his two children finally forced him to give up the house and move back to Zurich. Luckily about the same time the house of his maternal relatives at Flutginas became available to him. This house, which he was able to use as a summer home, had a magnificent studio.

The response of children all over the world to his books was great, and greatly surprised him. Many requests to illustrate books by other writers came, but these he refused, saying he could only illustrate what he himself had experienced. He then attempted one for which he was both author and illustrator, *Anton the Goatherd*. It won the Swiss Juvenile Book Prize, 1966. In the same year, Carigiet won the Hans Christian Andersen Medal. This was the first of the Andersen awards to illustrators.

The Pear Tree, the Birch Tree and the Barberry Bush, which he also wrote and illustrated, was on the Honor List of the German Juvenile Book Prize in 1968.

Carigiet has said that his happy mountain childhood lingers in his memory "like an unforgotten tune" and has inspired him to make these books children have loved so much.

SELECTED WORKS WRITTEN AND ILLUSTRATED: Anton the Goatherd, 1966; The Pear Tree, the Birch Tree and the Barberry Bush, 1967; Anton and Anne, 1969.

SELECTED WORKS ILLUSTRATED: A Bell for Ursli, by Selina Chönz 1950; Florina and the Wild Bird, by Selina Chönz, 1953; The Snowstorm, by Selina Chönz, 1958.

ABOUT: Hürlimann, Bettina. Picture Book World; Kingman, Lee and others, comps. Illustrators of Children's Books: 1957-1966; Viguers, Ruth Hill and others, comps. Illustrators of Children's Books: 1946-1956; Bookbird no. 4, 1966; no. 2, 1967.

MARY CHALMERS
March 16, 1927-

AUTHOR AND ILLUSTRATOR OF *Come for a Walk with Me*, etc.

Autobiographical sketch of Mary Eileen Chalmers:

FOR me, childhood was a deep involvement with things of the earth. Flowers, weeds, trees; little white stones. Water. If there wasn't a stream or lake handy, you made

MARY CHALMERS

your own with a dishpan. The wonderful light, sandy soil of southern New Jersey. White sand. Animals. Music. Being read to. But, most of all, we seemed always to be in a woods or a field. My sister, Janice and I. She is two years older than I and we have always been very close. It was always We.

I don't remember any creative drawing on my part in the grammar school years. I was a constant copier, though, and spent hours copying detailed pen and ink drawings. I simply loved making lines. My creativity was my—our—daily life. It was a steady game of pretend, along with the awareness of surroundings that only children have.

When I was in the fifth grade Janice decided she would be an artist and so I decided to be one too. "When we grew up." That was that. It was all decided. There was still not much creativity, though, until, for some reason in high school Jan suddenly presented me with an oil painting set. I promptly started studies of fruits and violins. I don't know that they were especially creative but at least they were my own.

I was born in Camden, New Jersey, and grew up in one of its suburbs, Audubon. Except for two glorious years spent in an airport on the western edge of the New Jersey Pine Barrens. (They are not barren, by the way—anything but—early settlers called them that because they could not grow

grains there.) We lived in quarters attached to the side of the hangar, got rides in the lovely little yellow biplanes—thus the plane in *A Hat for Amy Jean*—and hunted for pink lady slippers in nearby woods. Just to look and count, understand.

I attended the School of Industrial Art—now the Philadelphia College of Art—and for two years attended lectures at the Barnes Foundation in Merion, Pennsylvania.

I didn't do my first children's book until Jan had her first baby. The experience of my first niece, Susan, was truly the inspiration I needed and, naturally, the book *Come for a Walk with Me* was about walking in fields and woods and picking flowers, although somehow my companion-sister was transformed into a rather odd-looking rabbit. *Throw a Kiss, Harry* was originally a six-page thank-you book to my editor, Ursula Nordstrom. And *A Christmas Story* was a Christmas card for her.

These days my time is divided between writing and illustrating, my own animals, and volunteer work for a humane organization. I'm currently director of humane education. I feel it is terribly important to teach children love and respect for animals and nature. Or as we say at the shelter, to teach people simply to be kind. I also scrub kennels and rescue cats from trees.

After art school, Mary Chalmers spent several years as a commercial artist. She is also a painter. Among a number of her works in private collections is a lithograph owned by the Barnes Foundation.

SELECTED WORKS WRITTEN AND ILLUSTRATED: Come for a Walk with Me, 1955; A Christmas Story, 1956; A Hat for Amy Jean, 1956; Kevin, 1957; Throw a Kiss, Harry, 1958; The Cat Who Liked to Pretend, 1959; Take a Nap, Harry, 1964; Be Good, Harry, 1967.

SELECTED WORKS ILLUSTRATED: The Secret Language, by Ursula Nordstrom, 1960; The Three Funny Friends, by Charlotte Zolotow, 1961; The Happy Birthday Present, by Joan Heilbroner, 1962; The Crystal Tree, by Jennie Dorothea Lindquist, 1966.

ABOUT: Contemporary Authors, Vol. 5-6; Kingman, Lee and others, comps. Illustrators of Children's Books: 1957-1966; Viguers, Ruth Hill and others, comps. Illustrators of Children's Books: 1946-1956.

"WALKER CHAPMAN"

See *Silverberg, Robert*

WARREN CHAPPELL

July 9, 1904-

AUTHOR AND ILLUSTRATOR OF *They Say Stories,* etc.

Autobiographical sketch of Warren Chappell:

IN 1915, when I was eleven years old, I was singled out by the art supervisor of the Richmond (Virginia) public schools and given a tub of good modelling clay. That same year I saw Boardman Robinson's outstanding drawings which were made to accompany the war reporting of John Reed from the Eastern Front. These two occurrences seem to have had major influences on my work. I have devoted my life to drawing, and have approached drawing and later the graphic arts in general with a strongly-developed plastic awareness.

My admiration for Robinson's work led finally to an association with him as both student and assistant. Meanwhile, after getting a liberal arts degree at the University of Richmond, I studied at the Art Students League, where I was also a member of the Board of Control and an instructor in graphic art. My art schooling was reinforced by practical work in a good print shop. In 1931 and 1932 I worked in Germany with Rudolf Koch, learning to cut type-punches in steel by hand. The latter experience automatically drew me more deeply into typographic designing as well as printmaking. It also led to the designing of two type faces: *Lydian* and *Trajanus.*

In 1937 I worked with the legendary librarian Anne Carroll Moore and her several editorial assistants on the design and illustration for a multi-volume collection of children's stories. The plan called for classic stories accompanied where possible by their classic illustrations. A few years later, in 1940, I began my association with Alfred Knopf which still continues. The *Don Quixote* for boys and girls, originally issued

under a different imprint, was taken over by Knopf in 1945. Among titles under the Borzoi imprint are *The Magic Flute, The Ring* and at present in progress *Bottom's Dream* from *A Midsummer Night's Dream,* in all of which I have been most fortunate in having a text supplied by John Updike.

I have done two collections: *The Borzoi Book of French Folk Tales* (and a shorter version of the same stories titled *French Fairy Tales*), and for Doubleday a remaking of the Kate Douglas Wiggins stories, a selection of just under fifty, titled *The Fairy Ring.*

Among the texts which have especially impressed me but failed to have their deserved commercial success were William McCleery's *Wolf Story* and Catherine Besterman's two *Johnny Longfoot* books. I hope both will be rediscovered.

In 1928 I married Lydia Anne Hatfield and for most of the following twenty-three years we lived in the center of New York. In 1951 we moved into our pre-Revolutionary house in Norwalk, Connecticut, where I have a studio adjacent.

Warren Chappell, a member of Phi Beta Kappa, graduated from the University of

Chappel: *CHAP el*

Richmond in 1926. After studying at the Art Students League, he worked with George Grady at the Strawberry Hill Press and for three years was promotional art director for *Liberty Magazine*. Following his study with Rudolf Koch at the Offenbacher Werkstatt in Germany, he went to the Colorado Springs Fine Arts Center and spent fifteen months, 1935-36, working with Boardman Robinson.

Chappell's type face *Lydian*, named for his wife and designed for American Type Founders, has been widely used in American advertising. Less well known here is his *Trajanus*, done for the Stempel Foundry in Frankfurt.

Chappell is the author of *The Anatomy of Lettering*, 1935, *A Short History of the Printed Word*, 1970, and of a number of articles on printing, illustrating, and book design. Many of the books he has illustrated have been exhibited by the American Institute of Graphic Arts and by libraries here and abroad.

In 1969, Chappell received an honorary Doctor of Fine Arts degree from the University of Richmond. In 1970, he was awarded the Goudy Medal of the Rochester Institute of Technology.

SELECTED WORKS ILLUSTRATED: Peter and the Wolf, 1940; Hansel and Gretel, by The Brothers Grimm, 1944; Quaint and Curious Quest of Johnny Longfoot, by Catherine Besterman, 1947; The Adventures of Don Quixote, retold by Leighton Barret, 1939, 1960; Wolf Story, by William McCleery, 1947, 1961; The Magic Flute, adapted by John Updike, 1962; The Ring, adapted by John Updike, 1964; Bottom's Dream, adapted by John Updike from A Midsummer Night's Dream, 1969.

SELECTED WORKS ADAPTED AND ILLUSTRATED: The Nutcracker, 1958; They Say Stories, 1960; The Sleeping Beauty, 1961; Coppelia, 1965.

ABOUT: Contemporary Authors, Vol. 19-20; Kingman, Lee and others, comps. Illustrators of Children's Books: 1957-1966; Mahony, Bertha E. and others, comps. Illustrators of Children's Books: 1744-1945; Viguers, Ruth Hill and others, comps. Illustrators of Children's Books: 1946-1956; Who's Who in American Art, 1970; Who's Who in Graphic Art, 1962; Who's Who in the East, 1964-65; American Artist October 1944; Publishers' Weekly September 10, 1949; October 1, 1955.

"NICHOLAS CHARLES"

See *Kuskin, Karla*

REMY CHARLIP
January 10, 1929-

AUTHOR AND ILLUSTRATOR OF *Arm in Arm,* etc.

Autobiographical sketch of Remy Charlip:

I REMEMBER when I was little wanting to be a clown, a farmer, an artist, and a violinist. My mother wouldn't buy me a violin because she said I would lose interest in it like everything else.

My first taste of glory in relation to art was in kindergarten when I filled up the blackboards with a drawing in colored chalks of an ocean liner with hundreds of portholes, and it was left up for Open School Week.

Two of my pictures were chosen by a gallery for a show of children's art. One was a version of a tropical scene I was fond of painting: green palms, purple mountains, orange sunset, blue water. The other was a copy of a charcoal drawing I found in the street of a tenement: stoop, window with sickly plant, garbage cans, lurking cats. It interests me now that the fantasy scene was in full color and I felt free to rearrange it whereas the slum scene I knew so well was in black and white and was a direct copy. I was amazed to overhear my father proudly showing his friend a newspaper clipping about the exhibition, for he never showed his pride or love to me. I see now where the confusion stems about receiving love for what I did, rather than what I was. This love was further confused by the fact that I felt both pictures were not really my own or original.

I got my first lesson in originality when a brilliant teacher in a settlement house plopped a lump of clay in front of me and said not to give it form until I had looked at it long enough for something to suggest itself. I poured my soul into that grey lump. When it was finished I brought it home to my family. I called it "The Dead Horse." It

Remy Charlip: *REH* [not *ray*] *mee SHAR lip*

Remy Charlip

was laughed about for weeks. Was it after incidences like this, where something deeply felt seemed funny to others, that I got the idea to be a clown?

When it came time to choose a high school, my mother came up to see my guidance teacher who was also my French teacher. I wanted to go to farming school. I had a plot of land in a small park and grew carrots, radishes, corn, lettuce and flowers. The Eiffel Tower on display that I had made out of toothpicks influenced the decision. "I think Remy should be an artist," my mother said. "It's more practical."

I graduated from the Fine Arts department of Cooper Union, but being a painter seemed hopeless to me. I thought I didn't have any meaningful ideas worth expressing. I didn't yet know how to use the lesson of the lump of clay, nor did I know how a work of art can grow from the seed of feeling, no matter how slight or delicate and that it could be "worthwhile" even when humorous and uncomplicated.

So I started to study dancing to try to get away from "ideas" by experiencing things more physically. I danced in Merce Cunningham's company for eleven years and was a founder of the Paper Bag Players, a

theater for children. Since we made little money performing I supported myself doing costume, set, poster, textile and book-jacket designs.

One day I had an appointment with May Garelick, editor at Young Scott. She forgot she had a wedding party that weekend and was at the hairdresser's. I waited and waited, finally asked for a blank dummy, filled it with pictures and text, and when she returned she bought it, my first children's book, *Dress Up and Let's Have a Party*.

I have just finished my nineteenth book, *Arm in Arm*, and it is my favorite. I have enjoyed collaborating on books with Margaret Wise Brown, Ruth Krauss, Judith Martin, Betty Miles, Sandol Stoddard Warburg and Burton Supree and I think all are good books. But *Arm in Arm* is special, a kind of culmination of all that I have been doing: painting, writing, dancing, choreographing, teaching, film-making, directing. And yet too, I feel it is only a beginning.

———

Remy Charlip is head of the Children's Theatre and Literature Department at Sarah Lawrence College. He is on the advisory panel of the Connecticut Commission on the Arts' "Project Create," the Brooklyn Children's Museum's "Muse" and the Judson Poets' Theatre and Dance Theatre. He has been consultant and lecturer at a number of educational institutions, including New York University, Bank Street School of Education, Mills College, The New School, and the School of Visual Arts. He received the Ingram Merrill award in 1961 and 1963 for the "experimentation, creation, and development of children's plays and children's literature." In 1966 he won the "Obie" (Off-Broadway) Award for the direction of *A Beautiful Day*, by Ruth Krauss, and he received a '68-'69 Yale-Joseph E. Levine Grant. He won a Boys' Clubs of America Junior Book Award in 1967 for *Mother, Mother, I Feel Sick.* . . . A number of his works have appeared in exhibitions of the American Institute of Graphic Arts.

The Remy Charlip Library of the Greenville (Delaware) Elementary School houses a collection of his paintings, drawings, dummies, manuscripts, and photographs and has a one-hundred-foot mural painted by him.

SELECTED WORKS WRITTEN AND ILLUSTRATED: Dress Up and Let's Have a Party, 1956; Where Is Everybody? 1957; The Tree Angel (with Judith Martin) 1961; Fortunately, 1964; Mother, Mother, I Feel Sick, Send for the Doctor, Quick, Quick, Quick (with Burton Supree) 1966; Arm in Arm, 1969.

SELECTED WORKS ILLUSTRATED: The Curious Little Kitten, by Bernadine Cook, 1956; David's Little Indian, by Margaret Wise Brown, 1956; A Moon or a Button, by Ruth Krauss, 1959; A Day of Summer, by Betty Miles, 1960; A Day of Winter, by Betty Miles, 1961; Four Fur Feet, by Margaret Wise Brown, 1961; My Very Own Special Particular Private and Personal Cat, by Sandol Stoddard Warburg, 1963; What a Fine Day for . . . , by Ruth Krauss, 1967.

ABOUT: Hürlimann, Bettina. Picture Book World; Kingman, Lee and others, comps. Illustrators of Children's Books: 1957-1966; Viguers, Ruth Hill and others, comps. Illustrators of Children's Books: 1946-1956; Print June 1966.

NAN CHAUNCY

May 28, 1900-May 1, 1970

AUTHOR OF *The Secret Friends*, etc.

Autobiographical sketch of Nan Masterman Chauncy:

IT sounds lucky to be born as a twin under the sign of Gemini, with a total eclipse of the moon thrown in for good measure. However in the year 1900 twins were not lucky. Our brothers and sister duly had their births heralded in *The Times*. Not so my twin brother and myself. No neat clipping in the family album. Years later my mother explained it: "I was so ashamed. My sisters were horrified. 'My dear Lilla,' they said. 'Twins! Such a thing has never happened in the family before!'"

But luck was with me. The early years followed the pattern of a fairly conventional well-to-do English family living in a large house about twenty miles from London. The six children inhabited the top floor and rarely ventured downstairs—as has been described in a book I wrote later called *Half a World Away*. Then the pattern shifted completely. My father, a consulting engineer, sold the

NAN CHAUNCY

house. Nursemaids, nurses and governesses vanished never to return—all except a well-loved governess who came with us to Tasmania and there was married. Could a landing on the moon have seemed stranger to us as children? I doubt it. We had been drilled in good manners—servant's manners—were called "Master" and "Miss" and must never soil our hands with anything menial. A servant was required to lace up our boots before the daily walk. Saturdays and Sundays were the splendid days because we saw Father then. He and Mother became "Mum" and "Dad" on the small steamer making her maiden voyage to Australia.

Most of my twelve books for children are based on this astonishing new life made at an impressionable age. For Dad bought acres of uncleared bush in a narrow valley where no other house existed. His plan was to build a home for us all and clear away enough land of gum trees to plant as an apple orchard. This and the farm he would create would provide for retirement. It was a miserable failure financially but a glorious success for us as children. We were free in an utterly different world where platypuses swam in the pools of the creek, wombats slept in caves and there was always a danger of snakes. We worked hard. Milking cows, driving the buggy and washing-up were children's chores. So was barking the green sappy bark from trees felled with the axe. There were also dull terms at boarding school, too uninteresting to dwell upon. The bush we loved of course.

What more to tell? I traveled the world a few times, married and came back to the valley which both my husband and I love. But it is a different world now, and quite a different valley to our daughter.

Imagination is only experience. I began to experience more true adventures in little-known parts of Tasmania. My last two books are of the lives of children whose fathers are lighthouse keepers living on rocky islands off the coast.

Meanwhile my husband and I live in the little house I once watched being built. No electricity, only the soft light of the oil lamp and the dogs snoring on the skin mat, the iron kettle singing in praise of simple things.

Col. P. H. Fawcett in his book on exploration says: "A man who has once sampled extreme simplicity of existence will seldom return to the artificial life of civilization. The burden of it is not realized until it has been laid aside."

Come to think of it, this is all my books for children are about.

After the Masterman children grew up, they went back to England, and Nan lived for a time with a brother on a houseboat, moored on the Thames below Windsor Castle. Returning to Australia in 1938, she met Antony Chauncy, a fellow-passenger on the boat, and married him the same year. They turned her father's land north of Hobart into a wildlife sanctuary. Here their daughter Heather grew up familiar with wallabys, kangaroos, and wombats.

Before her marriage, Nan Masterman taught English in the Spejderskolen, children's schools run by the Girl Scouts in Denmark. Later she founded a company of Girl Guides in Tasmania, and was Australian correspondent for Girl Guides and for the Girl Scouts international magazine, *The Council Fire*. She contributed to *Wild Life, Quadrant* and other Australian magazines, and wrote scripts for the Australian Broadcasting Commission.

Nan Chauncy won the Australian Book of the Year Award three times, for *Tiger in the Bush*, 1958, *Devil's Hill*, 1959, and *Tangara*, 1961 (published in the United States as *The Secret Friends*). She received the Boys' Clubs of America Award in 1961 for *Devil's Hill*, and was named to the Hans Christian Andersen Award Honors List for *Tangara*. Columbia Pictures filmed *They Found a Cave*, the first Australian picture in color for children, at her home, Chauncy Vale. Her work has been translated into seven languages and published in Braille.

Nan Chauncy served as president and vice-president of the Tasmanian branch of the Writers Fellowship of Australia.

SELECTED WORKS: Devil's Hill, 1960; They Found a Cave, 1961; Tiger in the Bush, 1961; The Secret Friends, 1962; The Roaring 40, 1963; High and Haunted Island, 1965.

ABOUT: Contemporary Authors, Vol. 3; Horn Book August 1969.

JOHN CIARDI

June 24, 1916-

AUTHOR OF *The Man Who Sang the Sillies*, etc.

Autobiographical sketch of John Anthony Ciardi:

I WAS born in Boston (I have an infant memory of the spire of the Old North Church rising outside our kitchen window) and brought up in Medford, Massachusetts, to which we moved when I was about three and a half. I remember returning often to the crowded tenements of the North End of Boston to visit relatives. Medford, on the other hand, was a semi-rural town marked by many pre-Revolutionary traces. In a sense I lived in two worlds and such a division must certainly have had an effect (so, too, the fact that I spoke Italian at home and English out-of-doors) but I don't really know how to say what that has to do with my writing, except that when one lives in two worlds each world tends to ask questions of the other, and writing is always a way of asking and working out experiences.

Ciardi: *CHAR-dee*

I wrote for many years before I turned to writing for children. I had gone off to World War II as an aerial gunner and returned to teach at Harvard. Apartments were scarce right after the war and for over a year my bride and I lived with my sister and mother in the big old house I had been brought up in. My sister had three small children, and it was the fact of having them around that started me writing children's poems. Poetry was a game we played.

A few years later we had children of our own. With a built-in reason and audience, therefore, I began to write children's poems once again. My happiest experience in writing for children came when I was asked to do a book of poems based on a first-grade reading vocabulary. My daughter Myra was then in kindergarten and it came to me that I would like to write the first book she read all the way through.

The result was *I Met a Man*. As I finished each poem, Myra would draw a crayon sketch to illustrate it. She seemed to memorize the poems instantly. Then, though she could not read, she could tell by her crayon drawings which poem was which. She kept the collection in a black notebook, and was forever pretending to read the poems to any-

one, child or adult, she could get to sit still, looking at the page as if reading while she recited from memory. Then suddenly I discovered she had in fact learned to read. It was a lovely bonus. I wrote ten or so other books for her and for my sons, Jonnel (John L.) and Benn.

As the children grew older, alas, they became less interested in poetry for children. They began to feel that my poems were "too young." They were in a hurry to grow up. I had to stop writing for them, therefore. But I am in no hurry to grow up. I am, in fact, trying to stretch my childhood for as long as possible. I can no longer pretend that I write for my children. I write for myself now. In ten years or so the children will all be in their early to mid twenties and may even have children of their own. At that time, I expect, they will be in less of a hurry to grow up and will probably be learning all over again the pleasures of poetry for boys and girls.

Vita: Medford Public Schools, Tufts University (B.A. '38) University of Michigan (M.A. '39). T. Sgt. USAAF, World War II. Taught at Kansas City University, Harvard, Rutgers. Resigned from Rutgers in 1961 to become a free lance. Poetry Editor, *Saturday Review*. Director, Bread Loaf Writers' Conference. Married Myra Judith Hostetter, 1946. Children: Myra Judith, John Lyle Pritchett, Benn Anthony.

————

John Ciardi, who has written some twenty-five volumes of poetry, both for children and adults, is a Fellow of the American Academy of Arts and Sciences, a member of the National Institute of Arts and Letters and of Phi Beta Kappa. Among his many awards are the Oscar Blumenthal Prize, 1943; the Eunice Tietjens Award, 1945; the Levinson Prize, 1947; and the Harriet Monroe Memorial Award, 1955. He held a Fellowship in Literature at the American Academy in Rome, 1956, and he has been awarded several honorary degrees, including a Litt.D., Tufts University, 1960, and a D.Hum., Wayne State University, 1963.

I Met a Man was an Honor Book in the New York *Herald Tribune* Children's Spring Book Festival, 1961, and *The Man Who*

Sang the Sillies won the Boys' Clubs of America Junior Book Award in 1962.

SELECTED WORKS: The Reason for the Pelican, 1959; Scrappy, the Pup, 1960; The Man Who Sang the Sillies, 1961; I Met a Man, 1961; John J. Plenty and Fiddler Dan, 1963; You Know Who, 1964; Monster Dan, or Look What Happened at My House, 1966.

ABOUT: Contemporary Authors, Vol. 7-8; Harte, Barbara and Carolyn Riley. 200 Contemporary Authors; Hopkins, Lee Bennett. Books Are by People; International Celebrity Register, 1963; Newquist, Roy. Counterpoint; Peragallo, O. Italian-American Authors and Their Contributions to American Literature; Twentieth Century Authors (First Supplement), 1955; Who's Who in America, 1970-71; Current Biography October 1967; Horn Book April 1964; Literary Cavalcade October 1965; Poetry June 1947; May 1948; Time February 18, 1957; Wilson Library Bulletin February 1964.

"HELEN CLARE"

See *Clarke, Pauline*

PAULINE CLARKE

1921-

AUTHOR OF *The Return of the Twelves*, etc.

Autobiographical sketch of Pauline Clarke Hunter Blair, who writes under her maiden name and under the pen name "Helen Clare."

I AM a graduate of Somerville College, Oxford. I lived for many years in Norfolk, which is therefore the background of many of my books: *The Boy with the Erpingham Hood, The Golden Collar,* and all the *James the Policeman* stories. In these years I worked closely with my illustrator, Cecil Leslie. In 1963 I won the Carnegie Medal for *The Twelve and the Genii* (called in America *The Return of the Twelves*), the German edition of which was awarded a Deutsche Jugend Buchpreis for 1968. Under the name Helen Clare I wrote the series which started with *Five Dolls in a House,* which were illustrated from the original house and some of its dolls by Cecil Leslie. In the American edition they were illustrated by Aliki Brandenberg. I am now married to

PAULINE CLARKE

a fellow of Emmanuel College and live in Cambridge.

———

Pauline Clarke was born in Nottinghamshire and went to school in London and Essex before studying English literature at Somerville College, Oxford. She has been a free-lance writer since about 1949 and has written stories, articles, and plays for adults, as well as books for children. In 1963 she ran a seminar for the British Council in Accra to teach Ghanaians how to write children's stories in English with African settings. A series of short plays about an African family, which she wrote for the BBC Overseas Educational Department, was recorded for use in teaching English to African children. She has also lectured on children's literature and reviewed books.

Besides the Carnegie Medal and the German award, *The Return of the Twelves* received a Lewis Carroll Shelf Award in 1965, was an honor book in the New York *Herald Tribune* Children's Spring Book Festival, 1964, and was on the Hans Christian Andersen Honor List, 1964.

SELECTED WORKS: The White Elephant, 1957; Hidden Gold, 1957; Silver Bells and Cockle Shells, 1962; The Return of the Twelves, 1963.

ABOUT: Author's and Writer's Who's Who, 1963; Library Association Record May 1963.

HILA COLMAN

AUTHOR OF *The Girl from Puerto Rico*, etc.

Autobiographical sketch of Hila Crayder Colman:

AS the younger of two sisters, the first words I learned to say were "Me too." It wasn't until I became an adolescent in my parents' summer home in Cedarhurst, Long Island, that I discovered that I could make it on my own: make my own friends, get invited to parties, go off on bike rides by myself (and enjoy it), and lead a life independent from my older sister. We had both gone to the Calhoun School in New York City, and when I left for Radcliffe College in Cambridge, Massachusetts, alone, I thought the "me too" was left behind.

Yet through all the years of two marriages, two sons, (and now four grandchildren), I have found that the conflicts and patterns and yearnings of adolescence never quite vanish, nor are forgotten—which makes the writing for and about teenagers to me the most fascinating occupation. I love teenagers. Their insane hair, their wild clothes, their extreme heights of gaiety and depths of depression, their marvelous humor and incessant music, their involvement with the world and with themselves all fascinate me. I am on their side because they are fluid, fermenting and rich with life and living. Few things give me greater pleasure than filling my house in Bridgewater, Connecticut, with young people and listening to their talk.

I did not grow up wanting to be a writer. As a matter of fact it all started accidentally when my two sons were very young, and I was working in New York and became embroiled in a great battle with my husband (and myself) about whether to stay home or to continue working. I vented my anger in an article that I called *Can a Man Have a Family and a Career?*, a spoof on all the trivia being written on the subject of whether women could. A writer friend of mine read it, was amused, gave it to an agent who promptly sold it to *The Saturday Evening Post*. That started me on a career of magazine writing that lasted several years,

Hila Colman [signature]

until I wrote my first book, *The Big Step*, published by William Morrow in 1957. I've been writing for older girls ever since, plus books for younger children, and recently career books for both sexes. I write under my own name of Hila (pronounced highla) Colman, but I do have a new series started (for reluctant readers) that will be published under the pen name of Teresa Crayder.

As to the biographical facts: I was born in New York City, lived there until 1948, when my second and present husband and our two sons moved to Bridgewater, Connecticut. My older son, Jonathan, is Director of City Planning in Hartford, Connecticut, and is the young father of the four grandchildren. My younger son, James, is also interested in urban affairs. My husband, Louis, a medical writer, and I still live in Bridgewater, but maintain a small apartment in Greenwich Village in New York.

———

Hila Colman attended Radcliffe College for two years. For several years after that she did publicity and promotion work in New York, and then she was executive director of the Labor Book Club, New York. She is a member of the Democratic Town Committee, Bridgewater, Connecticut, and

Hila: *HIGH la*

a former member of the Bridgewater Board of Education. Since 1949 she has been a free-lance writer, doing books for young people and stories and articles for adults, which have appeared in a number of magazines, including the *Saturday Evening Post*, *McCall's*, *Ingenue*, and *Redbook*. Her book for girls, *The Girl from Puerto Rico*, won the Child Study Association Children's Book Award in 1962. A number of her books have been republished in paperback.

SELECTED WORKS: The Big Step, 1957; The Girl from Puerto Rico, 1961; Peter's Brownstone House, 1963; Classmates by Request, 1964; Car-Crazy Girl, 1967; Claudia, Where Are You? 1969; Making Movies: Student Films to Features, 1969.

ABOUT: Contemporary Authors, Vol. 15-16; Something About the Author, Vol. 1.

MOLLY CONE

October 3, 1918-

AUTHOR OF *Mishmash*, etc.

Autobiographical sketch of Molly Lamken Cone:

"DEAR Aunt Fanny, How are you. I am fine."—I wrote when I was a child, belatedly, and with little zest.

My Aunt Fanny still can't understand how a person who can sit and write books for hours at a time can't sit down and write a letter. I'm not sure I can understand it myself. Anymore than I can understand why I always got a good mark for effort in penmanship but almost no one could ever read my writing.

My handwriting didn't improve when I grew up, either. One day my ten year old came home from school bringing a friend and found me busy at the typewriter. For some reason this astonished the friend and embarrassed my son. I heard him apologetically explaining behind the back of his hand, "Her handwriting isn't very good."

I was born, Molly Lamken, in the house in which I grew up, in Tacoma, Washington. Ahead of me in the family already were a sister and a brother, and two years later another sister followed, and then another.

With five children, we were the largest family in the neighborhood, we had the most visiting relatives, and my mother was sure that we had the loudest voices. Plus the fact that we didn't celebrate Christmas (Hanukah), we didn't go to Church (Synagogue), and our grandmother who lived with us spoke only Yiddish (we replied in English), was enough to make us feel different from our neighbors.

But I would have felt different anyway. No other girl I knew climbed trees so zealously, pounded with hammer and nails so joyfully, or blushed as easily as I did. I thought collecting pictures of Hollywood stars was silly, and telling secrets inexcusable, and felt with a passionate conviction that I could be anything I really wanted to be. I wanted to be a writer.

In my mind, I always was. But I expected to wait until I grew up for other people to recognize it. I was editor of my school newspaper in Stadium High School, and took a flurry at a number of things during my student days at the University of Washington. I sold advertising space and wrote the copy too. My first stories for children were published in children's magazines well after my marriage in 1939 to Gerald Cone. I didn't begin to write my first book until 1958. It was published, 1960.

". . . a lump in the throat"—that's what a living poem begins with, Robert Frost said. I sometimes found growing up a "lumpy" sort of process. Out of the feelings of my growing-up years began such books as *Only Jane, Too Many Girls, A Promise Is a Promise*, and *Reeney*.

Life with Jerry (he likes to cook, too), children (we have three—Susan, Gary, Ellen), pets (successively and unsuccessfully), friends and relatives (thirty-two of family last Thanksgiving), going places (Mexico and Europe, Greece and Israel, so far), gave me new feelings, new convictions and new dimensions. Out of them "happened" such books as the *Mishmash* series of four, *The Trouble With Toby, The Real Dream, Crazy Mary*, and others like the story-biography, *Hurry Henrietta*; and *The House in the Tree*, and *The Green Green Sea*.

I'm always forgetting people's names, and those important dates everyone is supposed to remember—but my historic memory seems to be growing and growing. Some of this interest has propelled me into the writing of the kind of stories which would have made my grandmother happy—*The Jewish Sabbath, The Jewish New Year*, and *Purim* in the Crowell Holiday Series. And for Jewish children particularly: *Stories of Jewish Symbols*, and *Who Knows Ten*.

———

Molly Cone received a Myrtle Wreath Achievement Award, Seattle Chapter Hadassah, in 1967, a Theta Sigma Phi Women of Achievement Matrix Table Honor Award in 1968 and a Literary Creativity Citation, Music and Art Foundation of Seattle, in 1968. Molly Cone collaborated with Margaret Pitcairn Strachan under the joint pseudonym of Caroline More on *A Batch of Trouble*, 1963.

SELECTED WORKS: Mishmash, 1962; Reeney, 1963; Stories of Jewish Symbols, 1963; A Promise Is a Promise, 1964; Hurry Henrietta, 1966; The Jewish New Year, 1966; The Other Side of the Fence, 1967; The Green Green Sea (Greece), 1968; Annie Annie, 1969.

ABOUT: Contemporary Authors, Vol. 4; Something About the Author, Vol. 1; Who's Who of American Women, 1964-65.

"JOHN ESTES COOK"

See *Baum, L. Frank*

MARY FRANCIS CRAIG

See *Shura, Mary Francis*

JULIA CUNNINGHAM
October 4, 1916-

AUTHOR OF *Dorp Dead*, etc.

Autobiographical sketch of Julia Woolfolk Cunningham:

I WAS not truly convinced I was a writer (though the lined notebooks began to fill earlier) until I was twelve when my first rejection arrived. It was a real letter from a real editor, something I was to find a glory later but not too frequently received. It started: "You are a writer but—" The "but" was to bar the entrance to publication until I reached the age Brahms did when his first symphony was performed, neither of us young. This statement, however, was the wedge, the first self-recognition of the truth. I was a writer, committed to the invention of images and to find a whole new landscape of character relationships.

Schools, many and different, then jobs, most of them in New York, in a bank, a music company, a museum, a publishing house, a company that reduced air to boredom, and, at last, a year and a half in France. There the craftsmanship and the stories began, together, to become form. But the subjects were fantasy and the market not friendly. Perhaps stubbornness accounted for the footlocker of rejection slips or just simple desire. It was not courage. That is needed, as is well known, to begin a story and to end it but not to send it out.

Then one day another letter came and there were no "but"s in it! Mary Cosgrave was the editor, Houghton Mifflin the publisher, the first book *The Vision of Francois the Fox*. The delight was mine. Mrs. Cosgrave, with faith and encouragement to give, offered life also to *Dear Rat* and, for Pantheon Books, *Macaroon*. Then my editor be-

Julia Cunningham [signature]

came Fabio Coen who first accepted *Candle Tales* and then he dared, because he liked it, the controversial *Dorp Dead* which was followed by *Viollet* and *Onion Journey*.

I have only two statements to make as a published writer. The first: it's a good road, a kind of pilgrim's progress lined by the trees of darkness and regeneration, and the way itself is dusty, thorned and paved with joy. And, second: a good editor is a gift, a source of refreshment (and I don't mean lunches), criticism and confidence. And I am very grateful both to be and to have.

———

Julia Cunningham was born in Spokane, Washington, and attended art school in Charlottesville, Virginia. She worked for G. Schirmer, Inc., publishers, and in the Metropolitan Museum of Art as a saleswoman in the book and art shop, was associate editor of *Screen Stories* and until recently was a buyer and bookseller in Santa Barbara, California. She has lived in Mexico as well as in France and her interests include music.

Dorp Dead won a New York *Herald Tribune* Children's Spring Book Festival Award in 1965 for age groups 8-12.

SELECTED WORKS: The Vision of Francois the Fox, 1960; Dear Rat, 1961; Macaroon, 1962; Candle Tales, 1964; Dorp Dead, 1965; Viollet,

1966; Onion Journey, 1967; Burnish Me Bright, 1970.

ABOUT: Contemporary Authors, Vol. 9-10; Something About the Author, Vol. 1; Who's Who in America, 1968-69; Who's Who of American Women, 1970-71; Horn Book April 1967; Publishers' Weekly July 8, 1968.

BORGHILD DAHL

February 5, 1890-

AUTHOR OF *Rikk of the Rendal Clan,* etc.

Biographical sketch of Borghild Margarethe Dahl:

BORGHILD DAHL was born in Minnesota of Norwegian immigrant parents, Peder M. and Ingeborg (Haugseth) Dahl. In infancy an illness impaired her eyesight, and she became almost blind. Her mother devoted herself to the task of bringing up the child to feel her handicap as little as possible. She taught the little girl all the things that were hard, such as finding her way around the house, by doing them alongside her. As Borghild grew older and could do her share of work in the house, her mother held her to standards as high as those for the other children. The fact that Borghild had her own eye doctor was made to seem a distinction. And it was during these early years that she heard from her mother the Norse myths she was to weave into her own stories for children later. At an early age she displayed a talent for writing, publishing her first story at the age of twelve in the *Minneapolis Journal Junior.*

Her father's influence grew as she grew older. An American by adoption, he had a deep respect for the institutions of this country. He was also a firm believer in education and, less typically, in women's suffrage, an important issue at the time Borghild was growing up. He taught her to work (not fight) for it. In high school, to her surprise she won a debate on the subject, taking the affirmative against a polished speaker. There is nothing of the rebel about Borghild Dahl; she has humor, however, and can comment wryly on the fact that she used her hard-won first vote to help elect Warren Harding.

BORGHILD DAHL

The effect of this upbringing on a child of a naturally happy disposition was to build a confidence that was to serve her well. Her school grades were above average although she had to hold the book she was studying close to her face. She graduated from the Minneapolis School of Music and Dramatic Art and earned her college tuition by teaching piano. She went on to the University of Minnesota and decided to become a teacher. One of her professors tried to discourage her, insisting that her handicap would make such a career impossible. For a time she was downhearted but her determination was not shaken. She took her A.B. in 1912 and fulfilled her ambition to become a high school teacher and principal, serving in South Dakota and Minnesota from 1912-1922. At the very start of her teaching career both her parents died, leaving her with three younger siblings to raise, the youngest eight. She managed, and all three graduated from college.

In 1923 Miss Dahl took time off to get her Master's degree at Columbia University, and while there she received a fellowship for study in Norway from the American-Scandinavian Foundation. She spent the year 1924-25 in Norway, the first woman of a foreign country to be made a Norsk Akademiker of the University of Oslo. During this year she also gained firsthand the knowledge of the Norwegian scene she later used in some of her stories. From 1926-39 Borghild Dahl was professor of literature and journalism at Augustana College, South Dakota.

The man who had discouraged her was not uninfluential in her success as a teacher. She worked out a system which disguised her blindness, memorizing the content of the lesson so that she did not have to peer at the book, and learned to recognize her pupils by voice, color of clothes, and even scent. Miss Dahl had only one-sixteenth vision in one eye and a cataract began to form over that when she was in mid-career as a teacher. In 1939 and 1940 she underwent a series of dangerous operations at the Mayo Clinic, to prevent total blindness. While recovering, she received a letter from Augustana College saying that the uncertainty of the operations made it impossible to renew her contract. This crushed her for a time but she rallied and recognized that a new life lay ahead. The operations were successful and for a time her vision was better than it had ever been (although in 1959 she was to suffer a detached retina and lose her sight completely). Encouraged by a fellow townsman, Marchette Chute (herself a successful writer), she moved to New York and began to write the story of her life (*I Wanted to See*, 1944). She continued to work as a freelance writer, at the same time tutoring students from Columbia University in languages and literature. Her love and understanding of children made it natural for her to write often for them. For the very young she has written stories based on Norse myths (*The Cloud Shoes*, etc.) and for teen-agers stories based on her own experience growing up in Minnesota (*Under This Roof*, etc.).

Miss Dahl is a member of Delta Phi Lambda and Kappa Delta. King Haakon of Norway has presented her with the Medal of St. Olaf for promoting good relations between Norway and the United States.

SELECTED WORKS: Karen, 1947, 1958; The Cloud Shoes, 1957; Stowaway to America, 1959; Under This Roof, 1961; This Precious Year, 1964; Good News, 1966; Rikk of the Rendal Clan, 1968.

ROALD DAHL

September 13, 1916-

AUTHOR OF *Charlie and the Chocolate Factory*, etc.

Autobiographical sketch of Roald Dahl:

I AM not much in favour of a biographical essay written by the subject himself. Facts are all right so long as they are bare and unembellished, but once the writer begins to indulge in reminiscence and prose, then there is bound to be trouble. There is hardly a writer in the world who is completely unaffected by his own brilliance, and when he sits down to write about himself the result is certain to be biased. The self-praise, oblique and sly, and often carefully concealed under a few self-deprecating phrases, will invariably come through in the end.

I myself would fall right into the same trap. I shall therefore confine myself to giving a few bare facts and then a list of my faults and bad habits.

Born in Llandaff, South Wales, to Norwegian parents. I had five sisters and one brother. One sister died at the age of seven. My father died when I was four. I went to boarding school in England when I was seven. My main schooling was at Repton, a famous "public school" where my headmaster was Geoffrey Fisher, later Archbishop of Canterbury. At eighteen, I turned down my mother's offer of going to Oxford. Instead, I joined the Eastern Staff of the Shell Oil Company. At twenty, Shell sent me to Dar-es-Salaam, Tanzania, where I remained until the war broke out in September 1939. I then drove up from Dar-es-Salaam to Nairobi and joined the Royal Air Force. I did initial flying training in Nairobi and advanced training at Habbaniya, Iraq. In 1940, I joined a fighter squadron in the western desert of Libya, and was promptly shot down by the Italians. I spent six months in hospital in Alexandria and rejoined my squadron in Greece, flying Hurricanes. When the Germans kicked us out of Greece, we flew against the Vichy French in Syria. Then my old injuries caught up with me and I was invalided home to England. In 1942, I was sent to Washington, D.C. as an Assistant Air Attaché, and that is when I started writing stories. My first children's story was called *The Gremlins*, (1943), a word I am supposed to have invented. I did not write another book for children until seventeen years later, (*James and the Giant Peach*), when I had children of my own. By then I had married a beautiful American actress, Patricia Neal (1953). We have had five children: Olivia, who died of measles when she was seven. Tessa, born 1957. Theo, born 1960. Ophelia, born 1964. Lucy, born 1965.

I wrote *Charlie and the Chocolate Factory* in 1964, and *The Magic Finger* in 1966. In 1969 I wrote a long book for four-, five- and six-year-olds. I have had published three books of adult short stories, *Over to You,*

Someone Like You and *Kiss Kiss*. I shall be fifty-three this year and am growing old.

My faults and foibles are legion. I become easily bored in the company of adults. I drink too much whisky and wine in the evenings. I eat far too much chocolate. I smoke too many cigarettes. I am bad-tempered when my back is hurting. I do not always clean my finger-nails. I no longer tell my children long long stories at bedtime. I bet on horses and lose money that way. I dislike Mother's Day and Father's Day and all other Days and all the cards that people buy and send out. I hate my own birthday. I am going bald.

Roald Dahl attained the rank of wing commander in the Royal Air Force. He has twice won the Edgar Allan Poe Award.

SELECTED WORKS: The Gremlins, 1943; James and the Giant Peach, 1961; Charlie and the Chocolate Factory, 1964; The Magic Finger, 1966; Fantastic Mr. Fox, 1970.

ABOUT: Author's and Writer's Who's Who, 1963; Contemporary Authors, Vol. 1; Farrell, Barry. Pat and Roald; Something About the Author, Vol. 1; New York Herald Tribune Book Review December 6, 1953; New York Times Book Review December 20, 1953; February 7, 1960; April 23, 1961; Wilson Library Bulletin February 1962.

LESTER DEL REY

June 2, 1915-

AUTHOR OF *Marooned on Mars*, etc.

Biographical sketch of Ramon Felipe San Juan Mario Silvo Enrico Álvarez-del Rey:

LESTER DEL REY was born in Clydesdale, Minnesota. His mother died shortly after he was born, leaving the infant and his older sister in the care of their father, a fifty-five-year-old carpenter and tenant farmer. Their father soon married the woman who had been taking care of them since their mother's death, but she was unable to establish any rapport with the boy as he grew older. By the time he was four, their relationship had deteriorated to the point where he looked only to his father for discipline, guidance, and affection.

LESTER DEL REY

Though not formally educated himself, del Rey's father read a great deal and kept a reasonably well-stocked library in the house, where his growing son found books in all fields of learning. "By the time I was ten," says del Rey, "I had been through the Bible three times—twice through the King James version and once through the Douay. The Bible is the greatest foundation a writer can have, and I have used it many times." Two of his best known novels, *The Eleventh Commandment* and *For I Am a Jealous People*, rely heavily on Biblical sources.

Del Rey finished grade school in Minnesota and in 1931 received a certificate of completion from high school, not formally graduating. In 1931 he moved to Washington, D.C., to live with an uncle while attending George Washington University on a scholarship. For two years he took general science courses and then left school permanently, picking up whatever jobs he could find to support himself. At this time he began writing verse and sold about twenty poems to various popular magazines before deciding he was not a poet and quitting that field completely.

During his school years he had read the works of Jules Verne and H. G. Wells and become fascinated with literature that speculated about the future. He came upon his first science-fiction magazine in 1920, discovering an interest in the field that would become a lifelong enthusiasm and the basis for his writing career. During the early thirties he read most of the science-fiction magazines and contributed letters of comment to them. Many of his letters were published, and his name soon became familiar to regular readers of the magazines.

Del Rey's first published story was written on a dare from a friend after he had made some disparaging remarks about the plot development of a story by a professional writer. His friend suggested that if he knew so much about writing he should submit a story. Having done some writing for a newspaper, del Rey took a day and wrote "The Faithful," not really expecting to sell it. According to the wager, he would win if he received a personal letter from the editor instead of the standard rejection slip. Eight days later an envelope arrived from the magazine's offices not with a letter, but with a check. The editor had accepted his story for publication. And del Rey has been writing and selling magazine stories, novels, and books of nonfiction ever since.

In 1951 he began writing a series for young readers, the first of these juveniles being *A Pirate Flag from Monterey*. His book, *Marooned on Mars*, received the first Boys' Clubs of America Science Fiction Award in 1953. Two weeks before the Russians launched Sputnik and started the space age, his *Rockets Through Space* was published. This nonfiction book which mentioned the Russian space efforts was a big seller. The Science Fiction Writers of America selected "Helen O'Loy," del Rey's classic short story for their Hall of Fame volume of the best stories ever published in the field. In 1967 del Rey was the Guest of Honor at the 25th World Science Fiction Convention.

Since the early 1950s del Rey has lived in Red Bank, New Jersey. When he hasn't been writing he has been editing a series of science-fiction and fantasy magazines for various publishers. He has been a frequent guest on radio talk shows and, on one all-night program, logged, according to his estimate, more than two thousand hours discussing everything from flying saucers to bug-eyed monsters.

SELECTED WORKS: Marooned on Mars, 1952; Mission to the Moon, 1956; Rockets through Space, 1960; Mysterious Earth, 1960; Mysterious Sky, 1964; Tunnel through Time, 1966; Prisoners of Space, 1968.

ABOUT: Moskowitz, S. Seekers of Tomorrow.

EILÍS DILLON
March 7, 1920-

AUTHOR OF *A Family of Foxes*, etc.

Autobiographical sketch of Eilís Dillon O'Cuilleanain:

I WAS born in Galway, Ireland, where my father was Professor of Chemistry at the University. The last two years of the Irish war of independence still lay ahead and both of my parents were heavily involved in it. My earliest memory is of a raid by Black and Tans—shouting, wrecking and finally taking my mother away to gaol. My father was already "on the run." When I was small, the story of his midnight escapes by way of the back garden, while my mother conversed derisively with the Black and Tans from an upstairs window to gain time, used to make me shiver with excitement. We lived in a terrace house then "because it could not be surrounded."

When the fighting was over we moved to a beautiful country house on the river Corrib. It was very remote, with a mile-long drive, and this among other considerations made us move again, this time to Barna, a tiny village on the west side of Galway.

Barna was Irish-speaking in those days and though it was only four miles from Galway, the lack of transport made it almost like an island. My two older sisters and my little brother and I went to the local elementary school where we made friends through the children with everyone in the village. My father already had us all talking Irish which he had learned in gaol in England. Irish political prisoners in English gaols always started classes in Irish among themselves, and it was this enthusiasm of my father's which opened up a whole world for me. From my knowledge of Irish I have always been able to understand and appreciate

Eilís: *el EESH*

Eilís Dillon [signature]

the real people of Ireland, the inheritors of the oldest language and literature in western Europe. I was able to understand their songs, their humour, their delicate, gentle but tough mentality and their essential goodness.

I began to write very early, at seven or eight years of age, and I think this is why I write so much for children. I never made a serious division between what was children's and adults' reading, since my parents read children's books with obvious enjoyment and when my father read aloud to us, it was Shakespeare's plays. I am sure that listening to these gave me my habit of hearing the sound of everything I write, especially the vowel sounds. My intensive study of music helped me also, and gave me a sense of form.

My high school was the Ursuline Convent in Sligo. My teachers there were all enthusiasts for Irish also, and I began to learn in depth about the poetry and literature of ancient Ireland. Sligo was W. B. Yeats's town and we were told that Mr. Yeats was a great poet, and that anyone about to be a writer would do well to follow his example and seek their inspiration at home.

For a time I thought of being a professional 'cellist. However in 1940 I married Cormac O'Cuilleanain, professor of Irish literature in the University of Cork, and later Warden. We lived in Cork for twenty-three years. We have three children: Eiléan who lectures in English at Trinity College, Dublin; Maire who is a violinist and Cormac who is in his second year at University College, Dublin.

In 1963 we moved to Rome for my husband's health, and are now happily back in Ireland again after more than five years' absence. Italy, and especially Rome, was an invaluable experience and will always be a part of me.

I have made three lecture tours in the United States, speaking at universities and colleges. Specially interesting was the discovery of the contribution made by Irish people who emigrated there over the last two hundred years.

I like to write in many different fields so as to keep a certain freshness in them all. I have written four novels, three mysteries, a play which was produced in the Abbey Theatre, some radio plays, about fifteen long novels for children and many shorter stories. I have also made a translation of the long Irish poem of the nineteenth century, "The Lament for Arthur O'Leary" which was published in the *University Review* of Summer 1968, and I have translated from Italian Ignazio Silone's play *As It Was in the Beginning*. At present I am engaged on a book for children about ancient Rome. My next work will be a novel.

———

Eilís Dillon speaks Gaelic, English, French, and Italian. Her books have been translated into French, German, Dutch, Swedish, and Norwegian.

The Singing Cave and *The Coriander* received Honorable Mention in the New York *Herald Tribune* Children's Spring Book Festivals, 1960 and 1964 respectively. *A Family of Foxes* was on the Honor List, German Juvenile Book Prize, 1968. *A Herd of Deer* received a Lewis Carroll Shelf Award, 1970.

SELECTED WORKS: The Singing Cave, 1960; The Fort of Gold, 1962; The Coriander, 1964;

A Family of Foxes, 1965; The Sea Wall, 1965; The Cruise of the Santa Maria, 1967; The Seals, 1969; A Herd of Deer, 1970.

ABOUT: Author's and Writer's Who's Who, 1963; Contemporary Authors, Vol. 9-10.

JANINA DOMANSKA

AUTHOR AND ILLUSTRATOR OF *Look There Is a Turtle Flying*, etc.

Autobiographical sketch of Janina Domanska Laskowski:

I WAS born in Warsaw, Poland. My father was an engineer, my mother a writer. My early childhood was spent in our country house near Warsaw. It was a secluded place, and other than my older brother there were few children around. I remember orchard trees and my favorite, a pink acacia, near the old well. I climbed the trees and made prints of the leaves on clay.

When I was five, my family returned to Warsaw. My mother had a great influence on my life and my art. I started to draw when I was very young. Often, to amuse fellow classmates, I would draw caricatures of my teachers. Expectedly, the drawings got me into trouble: I was even requested to change schools. Fortunately, my mother made peace with the school officials. I graduated from high school in Warsaw.

I attended the Academy of Fine Arts in Warsaw, where I studied painting and graphic arts. After the war I won first prize in an all-Poland exhibition, and the prize included a trip to Italy.

I spent five years in Italy, teaching art in a private school and drawing and painting. I was represented in the International Exposition in Genoa, and exhibited my work in the Roman Foundation of Fine Arts Show, in competition with major Italian artists. I had two personal exhibitions of my work in Rome, and two later in New York. A number of my paintings are in the Museum of Art in Warsaw and several are in private galleries in Rome. While I was in Italy I did illustrations for a children's magazine as well. In 1952 I came to America, and in 1954 I married Jerzy Laskowski, a journalist and writer.

When I arrived in New York I took a position as a textile designer. I could converse fluently in four languages, but not in English! As my English began to improve, I spent my lunch hours visiting publishers with a portfolio of my drawings.

I luckily met Susan Carr Hirschman at Harper! She encouraged me to write and illustrate children's books. I have now illustrated many books for children, doing both the words and the pictures for a number of them. *The Golden Seed* and *The Coconut Thieves* were translated from the Polish and adapted.

I am now an American citizen. My husband and I live in Connecticut with our beagle, Ringo. I am very happy doing what I like best—writing and illustrating books for children.

———

Janina Domanska has won a number of awards, including the New York *Herald Tribune* Children's Spring Book Festival Award for *The Coconut Thieves*, 1964. Besides illustrating *The Golden Seed* and *The Coconut Thieves*, Miss Domanska translated them from the Polish. Several of her books have been exhibited by the American Institute of Graphic Arts.

SELECTED WORKS WRITTEN AND ILLUSTRATED: Why So Much Noise? 1965; Palmiero and the Ogre, 1967; Look There Is a Turtle Flying, 1968; The Turnip, 1969; Marilka, 1970; If All the Seas Were One, 1971.

SELECTED WORKS ILLUSTRATED: The Golden Seed, by Maria Konopnicka, 1962; The Coconut Thieves, adapted by Catharine Fournier, 1964; Master of the Royal Cats, by Jerzy Laskowski, 1965; The Dragon Liked Smoked Fish, by Jerzy Laskowski, 1967.

ABOUT: Contemporary Authors, Vol. 17-18; Kingman, Lee and others, comps. Illustrators of Children's Books: 1957-1966; Who's Who of American Women, 1970-71; Who's Who in America, 1970-71.

V. H. DRUMMOND

July 30, 1911-

AUTHOR AND ILLUSTRATOR OF *Mrs. Easter and the Storks*, etc.

Autobiographical sketch of Violet Hilda Drummond:

I WAS born in London. When the first World War broke out my father rejoined his regiment, the Scots Guards, and was killed at Ypres in November, 1914. Soon after the war my mother and my two sisters and I went to live in a tall house in a London square. The houses in this square have now been pulled down and replaced by ugly blocks of flats, but the garden remains.

We led a quiet life. We seemed to go for a walk in Hyde Park or Kensington Gardens every day with our governess. In the Park and on the way to it we often used to see the same people and dogs and make up stories about them and give them imaginary names. In those days the Head Park Keeper used to wear a top hat with a cockade and a green coat with brass buttons.

I was very bad at my lessons and drove our governess crazy by scribbling and drawing all over my exercise books.

I was glad when we went to live in the country but somehow I never forgot those days in London, and many of the characters in my books are derived from the people I saw then—the cab drivers, policemen, ticket collectors, and Park Keepers.

When our governess left I went to a small private boarding school at the seaside, on the South Coast, and later to a finishing school in Paris.

I started to write children's books after I was married and had returned to live in London. I wanted to be a free-lance book illustrator. But none of the publishers seemed interested in my work, so I decided that, if nobody wanted me to illustrate his books, I had better write one myself.

I wrote about my son Julian, who was then about three, and his toys.

His favourite toy was a knitted woollen squirrel called Rufus. He could not pronounce the word Rufus so he called him Phewtus. So that is why my first book was called *Phewtus the Squirrel*. After that I wrote *Mrs. Easter's Parasol, Miss Anna Truly, Mr. Finch's Pet Shop* and others, but though I was writing for Julian and getting many of my ideas from him, I think I was always remembering my own childhood in the London parks.

Because of the bombing during the second World War we went to live in the country and then my books had a more rural background, such as *Lady Talavera* and *The Flying Postman*.

Now, once more I am living happily in London, with my second husband, in a house with a garden in St. John's Wood.

With the help of my family I produced a series of eighteen short cartoon films made with cutouts called *Little Laura*, which was shown on British television. I wrote the stories, painted the backgrounds and drew and cut out the characters. It was all very hard work but very enjoyable. I have also done a certain amount of book illustration both for children's writers and humorous adult books.

Some time ago I got tired of writing children's books so I took up painting watercolour pictures of London street scenes which I exhibit in a London gallery.

But now that I have three grandchildren I find it easier to write and draw for children and my new book, *Miss Anna and the Christmas Lights* is based on an adventure that we all had together in a London store.

So now sometimes I paint pictures and sometimes I make children's picture books.

Violet Drummond is a descendant of Andrew Drummond, founder of Drummond's Bank, one of the great banks of London. She attended The Links, Eastbourne, and Le Chateau Vitry-Sur-Seine, Paris. After her studies in Paris she was presented at Court to the late Queen Mary. She lived for a time in India and returned to London to study briefly at St. Martin's School of Art.

In 1948 she married Anthony Swetenham. Her son by a previous marriage is Julian Pardoe. Violet Drummond won the Kate Greenaway Medal for *Mrs. Easter and the Storks* in 1957.

SELECTED WORKS WRITTEN AND ILLUSTRATED: Mrs. Easter's Parasol, 1944; The Flying Postman, 1949, 1964; Miss Anna Truly, 1949, 1965; Mrs. Easter and the Storks, 1958, 1960; Phewtus the Squirrel, 1966.

ABOUT: Author's and Writer's Who's Who, 1963; Contemporary Authors, Vol. 13-14; Hürlimann, Bettina. Picture Book World; Kingman, Lee and others, comps. Illustrators of Children's Books: 1957-1966; Viguers, Ruth Hill and others, comps. Illustrators of Children's

Books: 1946-1956; Who's Who in Art, 1970; Horn Book January 1948; Junior Bookshelf October 1949; Library Association Record May 1958.

"WALTER DRUMMOND"

See *Silverberg, Robert*

ED EMBERLEY
October 19, 1931-

and

BARBARA EMBERLEY
December 12, 1932-

ILLUSTRATOR AND AUTHOR OF *Drummer Hoff*, etc.

Autobiographical sketch of Edward Randolph Emberley and Barbara Anne Collins Emberley, by Ed Emberley:

BARBARA and I were brought up in the greater Boston area, Barbara mostly in Lexington, Massachusetts and I mostly in Cambridge, Massachusetts. We met in school (the Massachusetts College of Art in Boston) where I studied painting and illustration and Barbara studied fashion design.

Our interest in children's books did not start until after I had finished school, two years in the Army as a sign painter, another year of school at the Rhode Island School of Design, and four years doing various commercial art chores, including a lot of cartooning.

I usually draw all the pictures (to date —Barbara is at work on her own book this year). Barbara and I work on all the other thousand and one things that go into turning pictures into books—research, finding and or adapting of material, preparation of art for the printer, type selection, ink selection, etc.

You will find some variety in the way our books are illustrated. A good comparison would be *London Bridge is Falling Down*, Little Brown, pencil line with pale color washes, and *Drummer Hoff*, Prentice-Hall, woodcuts with bright strong color. Both

books were done during the early spring of 1967 and were often on the drawing board at the same time.

Our shared outside interests other than books, art and related subjects include gardening, antiques, sailing and cross-country skiing. Variety is the spice of our life and work.

Ed and Barbara Emberley both took B.F.A. degrees from Massachusetts College of Art. They live in a seventeenth-century salt box house in Ipswich, Massachusetts, with their two children, Rebecca Anne and Michael Edward. Among their many interests are ceramics, weaving, carpentry, jewelry making, photography, and printing limited editions of children's books on their own hand press, under the imprint, Bird in the Bush Press. *The Wing on a Flea,* 1961, and *Punch and Judy,* 1965, were both on New York *Times* lists of best-illustrated books of the year. *One Wide River to Cross* was sole runner-up for the Caldecott Medal for 1967. *Drummer Hoff* won the Caldecott Medal for 1968 and a Lewis Carroll Shelf Award in 1968.

SELECTED WORKS WRITTEN AND ILLUSTRATED BY ED EMBERLEY: The Wing on a Flea, 1961; The Parade Book, 1962; Punch and Judy, 1965; London Bridge Is Falling Down, 1967; Ed Emberley's Drawing Book of Animals, 1970.

SELECTED WORKS WRITTEN BY BARBARA EMBERLEY AND ILLUSTRATED BY ED EMBERLEY: Night's Nice, 1963; The Story of Paul Bunyan, 1963; One Wide River to Cross, 1966; Drummer Hoff, 1967; Simon's Song, 1969.

SELECTED WORKS ILLUSTRATED BY ED EMBERLEY: The Big Dipper, by Franklyn Mansfield Branley, 1962; Yankee Doodle, by Richard Shackburg, 1965; Ladybug, Ladybug, Fly Away Home, by Judy Hawes, 1967.

ABOUT ED AND BARBARA EMBERLEY: Hopkins, Lee Bennett. Books Are by People; Publishers' Weekly February 26, 1968.

ABOUT ED EMBERLEY: Contemporary Authors, Vol. 5-6; Kingman, Lee and others, comps. Illustrators of Children's Books: 1957-1966; American Artist November 1966; Horn Book August 1968; PTA Magazine April 1968; School Library Journal October 15, 1963; Top of the News April 1968.

ABOUT BARBARA EMBERLEY: Contemporary Authors, Vol. 5-6.

TOM FEELINGS

May 19, 1933-

ILLUSTRATOR OF *To Be a Slave*, etc.

Autobiographical sketch of Tom Feelings:

I WAS born and raised in the Bedford-Stuyvesant section of Brooklyn, New York. Since a child I have been interested in drawing and painting.

I attended the George Westinghouse Vocational High School, where I majored in art, and received upon graduation a scholarship to the School of Visual Arts which I attended for two years before entering the U.S. Air Force, 1953.

I was stationed in London, England, where I worked those four years in the Graphics Division as staff illustrator. I returned to the United States in 1957 and resumed studies at the School of Visual Arts.

In 1958 I created a comic strip series, "Tommy Traveler in the World of Negro History," which I wrote and illustrated for the (now defunct) *New York Age* until 1959. I created this series from an old desire I had as a child to know more about the history of my people.

From 1959 to 1964 I worked as a freelance artist. My first subjects were the black people of my community whom I drew on the streets, in homes, bars, poolrooms—anywhere I found them. My first published works drawn from life appeared in *The Liberator*, a black monthly magazine, where my work received wide exposure to the black community; also in *Freedomways*, a black quarterly. I also received some exposure through *Look, Harper's, Pageant*. I was one of the illustrators for the Negro Heritage Library, its volumes *Profiles of Negro Womanhood* and *Reader for Young People*.

My field of graphic concentration has been the black peoples of the world, a subject that I feel deserves much fuller illustrative exploration than the neglect it has received.

In September, 1961, I went to the South where I drew the people of the black rural communities of New Orleans. Some of the drawings were used in *Look* magazine's feature article, "The Negro in the U.S.," and *The Reporter's* depiction of "Images of the South."

In 1964 I left the United States for Ghana, in West Africa, stopping in Dakar, Senegal, West Africa, for one month before going on to Ghana. There I put on a one-man show of works done of the black people of New York, the South, and of Senegal. I then went on to Ghana, where I worked for two years for the Ghana Government Publishing House, illustrating *The African Review*, a monthly magazine, and local newspapers. My life in Ghana was one of the most meaningful and rewarding experiences of my life. The warmth and pride of the people, and seeing real black power—living in a country where every facet of the nation's operations is manned by black people. The children I drew had the faces I had seen here, except that the Ghanaian children reflected a glow of happiness and security I had for so long wanted to see in the black children I drew in America.

I returned to the United States in 1966 to find that the black community all over the country was far more enlightened and demanding of change; among those changes was a demand for more representational literature and imagery of themselves. Because of the demands the various heads of media including the publishing world were pressed to produce more literature of relevance to the black public.

As I stated earlier, it had always been my desire that black children see images of themselves in books which were positive and honest, and then embarked on the field of children's book illustration. Though in the last three years a number of books have been published dealing with the black subject, I feel there still is a great need for more which are written and illustrated by those who live and therefore know first-hand the experience—black authors and illustrators. There is a world of talent in these and other fields, in the black community which has always been there, but left untapped, discouraged too long. Speaking from personal experience (which is also the experience of so many black artists), I met with great discouragement from the time I entered art school onward because I portrayed the thing I knew best—black subject. I regard the fact that I have been able to do the volume of work I have done since my return to the United States as no "success story," but merely a reflection of an outgrowth of change brought about by Black America.

The books for children which I have illustrated since 1966 deal with African and Afro-American themes.

My wife, Muriel, also has lived in Africa —Uganda in East Africa, where she taught art in a high school in Kampala, the capital. She is the author of *Zamani Goes to Market*, based on some of her impressions of rural life in East Africa.

We have a one-year old son, Zamani, after whom the book was named.

The Society of Illustrators has awarded me the Certificate of Merit for exhibition years 1961, 1962, 1967 and 1968.

I have exhibited drawings and paintings at Morgan State College, the Fulton Art Fair in Brooklyn, the 21st and 22nd Atlanta University Annual Negro Artists Exhibition, the Park Village Gallery, a one-man show at the Market Place Gallery in Harlem and the St. Marks Gallery, the Metropolitan Applied Research Center's Black Artists Exhibition, Black Artists Exhibit at the Community Room of the Brooklyn Museum, and a one-man show at the Ghana Cultural Center in Accra, Ghana.

Exhibits of children's books illustrated appeared at the Central Children's Room of the New York Public Library, Chatham Library in Milwaukee, Wisconsin, and Central Library in San Francisco, California.

Tom Feelings married Muriel Gray in 1968. He plays the guitar and collects recordings of African and Afro-American music. *To Be a Slave* was a runner-up for the Newbery Medal for 1969.

SELECTED WORKS ILLUSTRATED: Bola and the Oba's Drummers, by Letta Schatz, 1967; The Tuesday Elephant, by Nancy Garfield, 1968; When the Stones Were Soft, East African Fireside Tales, collected by Eleanor Heady, 1968; Song of the Empty Bottles, by Osmond Molarsky, 1968; To Be a Slave, by Julius Lester, 1968; Panther's Moon, by Ruskin Bond, 1969; Tales of Temba, by Kathleen Arnott, 1969; Zamani Goes to Market, by Muriel Feelings, 1970.

ABOUT: Hopkins, Lee Bennett. Books Are by People; Wilson Library Bulletin September 1969.

EDWARD FENTON

July 7, 1917-

AUTHOR OF *The Phantom of Walkaway Hill*, etc.

Autobiographical sketch of Edward Fenton:

I AM a third-generation New Yorker. When I was a boy I spent a lot of time roaming the streets of the city, my eyes wide open and my feet tireless. As a result, nothing I have ever seen in my travels subsequently has ever surprised me. My reaction has merely been, "Oh yes, this is the real thing." New York has changed since my boyhood, when for a few cents one could travel, as it were, all around the world without leaving Manhattan Island. I suspect, however, that today's young New Yorkers can, if they

have eyes to see, still explore the entire world in the course of a long Saturday.

Like so many New Yorkers, I have spent my life escaping that city which I love so much. I was a college dropout (Amherst), spent a year of my stormy adolescence literally on the bum in New Orleans, often subsisting for whole days on bananas, which in those depression days were the cheapest thing you could get. I worked for a while on the New York *Herald Tribune* (night shift), moved to Bucks County where on a dime and a combination of innocence and enthusiasm I opened a bookshop. With World War II, I joined the American Field Service, finally becoming a part of the British 8th Army and crossing North Africa behind Rommel's retreating forces. It was then that I first began to be published: poems and stories in the *New Yorker, Harper's Bazaar,* the *Atlantic Monthly,* etc.

Back from the war, I worked as an editor on a publication called *Young America,* where *Us and the Duchess* first appeared as a serial. In January of 1946 my love affair with Greece began, out of which came a novel for grown-ups and *Aleko's Island.* I have also been deeply involved with Italy (*The Golden Doors, A Matter of Miracles*).

Five years were spent at the Metropolitan Museum—a time of great pleasure for me. It was like going to college again. But eventually I felt that there was no time to write my books, and so I left to go back to writing full time. With the money from Disney's purchase of *The Golden Doors* (the film was disastrous and I have never seen it), I bought a large 143-acre farm in Duchess County, New York—the scene of *The Phantom of Walkaway Hill* and *The Riddle of the Red Whale.* When my house burned to the ground in 1960, I went back to Europe to live, taking my beagle, Kate, with me.

Home in Greece once again, I met and married Sophia Harvati, a Greek psychologist, who is now also writing books for children. We have a house in Washington, on Capitol Hill, and an apartment in Athens, and divide our time between our two homes.

I am often asked if I have children—people assume that if you write for children, you have to have them for inspiration. I always answer that I write children's books because that is simply the way the stories come out. I think the truth of the matter is that I have never unlearned to think as a child, so see the world with the wide-eyed wonder it deserves, and to keep an open heart.

———

Edward Fenton speaks fluent Greek, French, and Italian and says his German is so-so. His works have been translated into French, Italian, German, Dutch, Polish, Greek, and Spanish. *The Phantom of Walkaway Hill* won the Edgar Allan Poe Award in 1962, and *Wildcat Under Glass,* which he translated, received the Mildred L. Batchelder Award, 1970.

SELECTED WORKS: Us and the Duchess, 1947; Aleko's Island, 1948; The Golden Doors, 1957; Fierce John, 1959; The Phantom of Walkaway Hill, 1961; The Riddle of the Red Whale, 1966; The Big Yellow Balloon, 1967; A Matter of Miracles, 1967; Wildcat Under Glass, tr. from the Greek of Alki Zei, 1969; Penny Candy, 1970.

ABOUT: Author's and Writer's Who's Who, 1963; Contemporary Authors, Vol. 9-10; Horn Book June 1968.

HARVEY FISCHTROM

See *Zemach, Harve*

MARGOT ZEMACH FISCHTROM

See *Zemach, Margot*

LEONARD EVERETT FISHER

June 24, 1924-

AUTHOR AND ILLUSTRATOR OF *The Glass-makers,* etc.

Autobiographical sketch of Leonard Everett Fisher:

I WAS given the gift of life on June 24, 1924. My art career began five years later. Without warning I drew a faithful portrait of a willing uncle. No one seemed too surprised at the time, least of all my father. He was an amateur artist and the greatest engineering draftsman that ever lived. He could also recite *Caesar's Gallic Wars* from memory just to remind us all that he had a taste for literature and meaningful history. My mother filled in the gaps by reading to me from *Compton's Encyclopedia.* In any event, my father created for me a looseleaf "how to draw this and that" book. By the time I was ready for more formal schooling I already knew simple perspective, human figure proportions, what asteroids were, and all about howler monkeys. When I was seven I won my first award in the Wanamaker Art Competition for New York City School Children. I had submitted a picture of a Pilgrim shooting a turkey. The following year I was enrolled in the art classes of the Heckscher Foundation and began the long, hard process of more dispassionate instruction.

My apprenticeship continued through a variety of schools and artists. I went to war in 1942 and came out alive in 1946. This was my second gift of life and I made the most of it at the Yale Art School where I finally became an educated craftsman. Shortly thereafter I was sent to Europe as a Winchester and Pulitzer Fellow. I had spent the first twenty-six years of my life preparing for that trip. I remained spell-bound through it all. I knew what I had seen as no pleasure-bent tourist could imagine and as no casually trained artist or amateur could understand. It was a humbling artistic experience.

I needed a new perspective and reassurance. I experimented for a while and then, in 1951, I took a job in New York as an assistant to a muralist. My credentials were two murals painted during the war and Yale's long reputation for graduating wall painters. However, I quit at the end of the first week to accept an appointment as Dean of the Whitney Art School in New Haven. Several months later I found Margery Meskin. This was my third gift of life. We were married in December, 1952. Meanwhile I had had a one-man show in Manhattan and my paintings were beginning to turn up in various exhibitions. But by the time Julie, Susan and James were born I had left the school, put aside my paint brush and turned to the illustration of children's books. It seemed the natural way of celebrating their arrival. Now, some fourteen years later, I still think it was the natural thing to do.

Since 1955 I have illustrated countless books of all types. I even added a new dimension when I began to write in 1960.

This diversification is a reflection of my enthusiasm for everything that goes on in this world. I continue to paint, illustrate and write with ever-increasing zest. But more important, the images I produce stem from my passion for the miracle of life. Moreover, I am a participant in that miracle. And if my images seem to be uncompromising and nondecorative and bold it is because of my own unfaltering belief in the indomitable spirit of the human being. And I try to move my audiences that much closer to this conviction with honest rendering and simple arrangements rather than with complicated, vacant designs.

Leonard Everett Fisher received his B.F.A. in 1949 and his M.F.A. in 1950, both from Yale. He won a William W. Winchester Fellowship in 1949 and a Pulitzer Fellowship in Art in 1950, both of which he used for travel. His paintings have been exhibited in New York galleries and selected for national tours by the American Federation of Arts and by the Emily Lowe Foundation. He began illustrating books for children in 1954, and since then has done more than a hundred and seventy-five. Several of his works for children have been in exhibitions of the American Institute of Graphic Arts and some of his originals are in collections of the Library of Congress, University of Minnesota, and other institutions. The University of Oregon maintains an extensive collection of his works, papers, and correspondence.

Casey at the Bat was named one of the ten best-illustrated children's books of the year 1964 by the New York *Times Book Review*. In 1964, three of his works originally done for children's books were incorporated into a mural for the Washington Monument. The Fifth International Book Fair held in Bologna, Italy, awarded him its Graphics Prize for a Juvenile Book in 1968. In 1960, Fisher also began to write books for children. The series *The Colonial Craftsmen*, which he both writes and illustrates, expresses his respect for early American craftsmanship and colonial American perseverance.

SELECTED WORKS WRITTEN AND ILLUSTRATED: Pumpers, Boilers, Hooks and Ladders, 1961; The Colonial Americans, 17 volumes, 1964-1971; Picture Book of Revolutionary War Heroes, 1970; Two If by Sea, 1970.

SELECTED WORKS ILLUSTRATED: A Message to Garcia, by Elbert Hubbard, 1962; The Golden Frog, by Anico Surany, 1963; Casey at the Bat, by Ernest Lawrence Thayer, 1964; Ride the Cold Wind, by Anico Surany, 1964; Lora, Lorita, by Anico Surany, 1969; America: A History for Peter (3 volumes), by Gerald W. Johnson, 1959-1960.

ABOUT: Contemporary Authors, Vol. 3; Kingman, Lee and others, comps. Illustrators of Children's Books: 1957-1966; Viguers, Ruth Hill and others, comps. Illustrators of Children's Books: 1946-1956; Who's Who in American Art, 1970; Who's Who in the East, 1970; American Artist September 1966; The Christian Science Monitor, Section C13 May 3, 1962; Design November 1945; June-September 1952.

"CAPTAIN HUGH FITZGERALD"

See *Baum, L. Frank*

JOAN MARGARET FITZHARDINGE

See *"Phipson, Joan"*

LOUISE FITZHUGH

October 5, 1928-

AUTHOR AND ILLUSTRATOR OF *Harriet the Spy*, etc.

Biographical sketch of Louise Fitzhugh:

LOUISE FITZHUGH was born in Memphis, Tennessee, the daughter of Millsaps Fitzhugh, an attorney, and Louise Perkins Fitzhugh. She attended the Hutchison School and Southwestern College in Memphis, Florida Southern College in Lakeland, Florida, Bard College at Annandale-on-Hudson, New York, and the School of Education at New York University. She was a literature major when she stopped six months short of a degree.

Because her interest in art won out at this time, she enrolled at the Art Students League and later at Cooper Union. In May of 1963 a one-man show of her paintings at the Banfer Gallery in New York City was very well received.

Louise Fitzhugh has been writing ever

LOUISE FITZHUGH

since she was eleven, although her first work, *Suzuki Beane,* written in collaboration with Sandra Scoppettone, the playwright, was not published until 1961. It has Miss Fitzhugh's humorous illustrations.

Her second book, *Harriet the Spy,* a novel for young people which she wrote and illustrated, was selected by the New York *Times Book Review* as one of the sixteen "year's best juveniles," won the 1967 Sequoyah Children's Book Award of Oklahoma, and was among the eleven "most loved children's books" listed in *Family Circle* in July 1968.

Her third book, *The Long Secret,* is a sequel to *Harriet the Spy.* Miss Fitzhugh, whose fourth book, *Bang Bang You're Dead,* was also written in collaboration with Sandra Scoppettone, has illustrated all of her books.

Adult readers of Louise Fitzhugh's books divide into two camps. Those who find Harriet's spying on her classmates and adults unsuitable for children's books also disapprove of the "bloody" illustrations in *Bang Bang You're Dead.* On the other side are those who love Harriet and many of the other characters, and believe that today's child can accept their exploits and at the same time expand his horizons and learn sound principles from the morals intrinsic in the books.

Miss Fitzhugh spent six months in Europe in 1954, and a year in Italy in 1957. She

has lived in Washington, D.C., and now divides her time between New York City and the North Shore of Long Island. When she is not busy with her writing, illustrating, and painting, she enjoys tennis and plays the flute.

SELECTED WORKS WRITTEN AND ILLUSTRATED: Suzuki Beane (with Sandra Scoppettone) 1961; Harriet the Spy, 1964; The Long Secret, 1965; Bang Bang You're Dead (with Sandra Scoppettone) 1969.

ABOUT: Something About the Author, Vol. 1.

SID FLEISCHMAN

March 16, 1920-

AUTHOR OF *By the Great Horn Spoon!* etc.

Autobiographical sketch of Albert Sidney Fleischman:

NOTHING surprises me more than to discover myself a writer. I wanted to become a magician. I spent most of my school years mastering sleight-of-hand tricks. Once out of high school I performed in vaudeville and traveled throughout the United States with a magic show. At the same time I began writing a book of original feats of sleight-of-hand, for magicians only, which was published when I was seventeen.

But during those late depression years vaudeville and stage shows were virtually disappearing. When World War II came along I served in the U.S. Naval Reserve aboard a destroyer escort. If I went into the war a magician, I came out four years later—by some hocus-pocus—a writer.

My first novels were mystery and suspense stories. After being graduated from San Diego State College with a B.A. degree in 1949, I became a reporter and rewrite man on the now defunct San Diego *Daily Journal.*

When one of my novels was bought for motion pictures I wrote the screenplay; since then several of my novels have been made into motion pictures. I now divide my time between writing for the screen and writing books for young people.

It was natural that my first novel for children would be about a magician—*Mr. Mysterious.* While with a magic show years

earlier I had traveled through the California gold country and tried (unsuccessfully) to pan for gold. Out of that experience came *By the Great Horn Spoon! The Ghost in the Noonday Sun* arose from a chance encounter with a folklore belief that anyone born at the stroke of midnight has the power to see ghosts. In *Chancy and the Grand Rascal* I wanted to see what I could do with the tall tale and wrote the book for the sheer fun of it.

McBroom Tells the Truth was originally a one-page tall tale in *Chancy*. But I decided I had not fully explored its possibilities. I took it out and developed it into a complete story. While I don't usually write sequels (they so rarely maintain the freshness and spontaneity of the original) I couldn't resist—and wrote *McBroom and the Big Wind*, and a third, *McBroom's Ear*.

I suspect my magician's mind reveals itself in the way I plot my scenes and write my characters. I cannot resist mystery, surprise and heroes capable of a kind of sleight-of-mind in outwitting the villains.

I was born in Brooklyn, New York, but grew up in San Diego, California. My wife, Betty Taylor, and I were married on January 25, 1942. We have three children—Jane, Paul and Anne.

My full name is Albert Sidney Fleisch-

man, but I have always been called Sid, and that's the way I sign my books.

Sid Fleischman has won the 1964 Boys' Clubs of America Junior Book Award, the 1963 Spur Award, Western Writers of America, the 1964 Southern California Council on Literature for Children Award, the 1966 Commonwealth Club of California Award, and a 1969 Lewis Carroll Shelf Award.

SELECTED WORKS: Mr. Mysterious & Company, 1962; By the Great Horn Spoon! 1963; The Ghost in the Noonday Sun, 1965; Chancy and the Grand Rascal, 1966; McBroom Tells the Truth, 1966; McBroom and the Big Wind, 1967; Longbeard the Wizard, 1970; McBroom's Ear, 1970.

ABOUT: Contemporary Authors, Vol. 3; Dictionary of International Biography, 1967.

JAMES FLORA

January 25, 1914-

AUTHOR AND ILLUSTRATOR OF *Grandpa's Farm*, etc.

Autobiographical sketch of James Royer Flora:

MY father and grandfather were superb storytellers. They could whip up a story about anything from a one-eyed wombat to a three-legged ice baby at the South Pole. I naturally tried to emulate them and practiced on my younger brother and sister. One of my earliest memories is the delight I took from my power to bring them to tears with a story about the sinking of the Titanic. How they wept and howled. How I poured it on.

Did this inspire me to become a writer?

No. My passion was drawing and I was determined to become an artist or an architect. Since I was born in Bellefontaine, Ohio, it seemed eminently sensible to go to school there. I did and graduated from high school in 1931 (which feat my father predicted would cause a Great Economic Depression).

After two years at Urbana (Ohio) University, art defeated architecture and I transferred to the Art Academy of Cincin-

James Flora

nati. There I studied drawing, painting and printmaking for five years. There I met Carl Zimmerman, an instructor and a complete joy of a man. He taught me everything I needed to know about the practices of art plus the even finer art of finding delight in life. Carl was also a busy mural painter and I spent several summers as his assistant. I have such admiration and affection for this man that I've spent the rest of my life trying to stretch to his stature.

In 1938 I met a young writer, Robert Lowry. We pooled our resources and bought an old Chandler & Price treadle press. We founded The Little Man Press on the spot and proceeded to explore and savor the delights of writing, illustrating, printing and selling whatever pleased us.

In 1941 I married Jane Sinnickson, a student at the Art Academy, an excellent painter and an utter darling (still is).

In 1942 Columbia Records offered me a job in their art department. I took it and moved to Connecticut. With hard work and a lavish use of flattery I became Art Director, then Advertising Manager and then Sales Promotion Manager.

In 1950 it suddenly occurred to me that I didn't like office work so I quit and went to Mexico with my wife and two children. We stayed for a year and a half. Had a marvelous enriching time.

Returned in 1951 and set up shop in New York as a free-lance designer and illustrator. One day in 1954 Gerry Gross, then art director for Harcourt Brace, introduced me to Margaret McElderry the juvenile editor. Since she is a perspicacious gambler she said,

"You're full of Mexican lore. Why don't you write something for us?"

"That's a great idea," I laughed dazedly. "But wouldn't you rather have a really rousing tale about the sinking of the Titanic?"

"No! Mexico!" she smiled efficiently.

So I wrote my first book *The Fabulous Firework Family*. I was totally flabbergasted when she took it, added a few lost commas and published it.

Needless to say that I was hooked on authoring after that. I've just finished my eleventh book for Margaret and Harcourt Brace. The royalties have helped add three more children to my family, a house on Long Island Sound, a flotilla of leaky boats and numerous more trips to Mexico and other exotic places in the world. I've recently acquired a piece of land on St. Croix and, if book buyers continue to buy books, I hope eventually to put a house on it and divide every year with Connecticut. I'll surely find time there to write a real tearjerker about the sinking of the Titanic.

James Flora also studied at Atelier 17 in New York, under Stanley William Hayter, for two years.

The Flora children are Roussie, Joel, Caroline, Robert, and Julia.

Flora is a member of Authors Guild and the Westport Artists. Under The Little Man Press imprint he designed and illustrated many books by various authors. He did the script and design of the animated films, *The Fabulous Firework Family*, 1959 and *Leopold, the See-Through Crumbpicker*, 1970.

SELECTED WORKS WRITTEN AND ILLUSTRATED: The Fabulous Firework Family, 1955; Charlie

Yup and His Snip-Snap Boys, 1959; Leopold, the See-Through Crumbpicker, 1961; My Friend Charlie, 1964; Grandpa's Farm, 1965; Sherwood Walks Home, 1966; Little Hatchy Hen, 1969.

ABOUT: Contemporary Authors, Vol. 5-6; Kingman, Lee and others, comps. Illustrators of Children's Books: 1957-1966; Something About the Author Vol. 1; Viguers, Ruth Hill and others, comps. Illustrators of Children's Books: 1946-1956; American Artist January 1955.

JAMES FORMAN

November 12, 1932-

AUTHOR OF *Ring the Judas Bell*, etc.

Autobiographical sketch of James Douglas Forman:

I WAS born during the depression on a bright autumn Monday, twelve hours late for Armistice Day, and there was no suggestion in my red and roaring self that I was a writer-to-be. Except for a remote link to James Fenimore Cooper, writing was certainly not in the blood. Law was. However, some dozen years later one of those rare English teachers who do carry keys to important doors convinced me—at least until summer vacation—that I should "make up stories." The subsequent years were hard enough without fiction and I was sufficiently puzzled by them to major in psychology at Princeton. If it weren't for the butcher shop aspects of medical school I would have been a psychiatrist there and then. So, on to Columbia University and its Law School, which never made me think Perry Mason.

To celebrate the fact that I was at last an attorney in the family firm, my wife Marcia and I went on a belated honeymoon. She was a fashion illustrator by vocation and I a self-imagined Cartier-Bresson. Several cameras went along and more film than clothing. All this resulted in a booklet for the American Geographical Society, *Islands of the Eastern Mediterranean*. Though the writing part proved no real pleasure, it revived repressed desires. Failing to find a market for those photographs taken in Spain, I tried a short children's story on that subject. *Fiesta for Josefa* it was called. Marcia

did the illustrations and after much frustration the project was put away for the spiders and the dust. An epic "War and Peace" for the young followed, some four hundred pages to begin with, concerning the Nazi occupation of Crete in 1941. More revisions than I care to remember pruned it down and if nothing else the title was catchy: *The Cucumber Wind*. And so my first book was finally published with very few changes except for the title, which became *The Skies of Crete*.

Two other books having to do with modern Greece followed, largely due to familiarity, fondness for the land and economy with excessive research: *Shield of Achilles* and the second and most popular of my Greek stories, *Ring the Judas Bell*. The latter seemed to disprove the cardinal rule, "write about what you know," for I never saw its Macedonian setting until long after publication and it was a far less lunar land than I described.

By this time I was an infected writer, living where I always have, apart from school and travel, in a weather-gray Sands Point home overlooking Long Island Sound. Included in the homestead are Marcia, gifted typist, proofreader and ego support, and our daughter Karli, who is too absorbed with assorted pets—four-legged, winged, finned, animated and otherwise—to concern herself overmuch with fiction.

But back to writing: Germany, World War II. From a friend's telling me of his boyhood as a flak gunner during that war came the bones of *Horses of Anger*. The fattening process resulted in *The Traitors* as well, and in part, *My Enemy, My Brother*. If there is a common theme in the books I've written and in those yet unhatched, it is the individual responding to the more savage impositions of the larger world—prejudice, war—with the salvation of some dignity and love. If nothing more can be said for such a theme, it is at least inexhaustible.

James Forman adds that he took his B.A. from Princeton in 1954 and his LL.B. from Columbia in 1957. He was married to Marcia Randall Fore September 3, 1956, and their daughter, Karli Elizabeth, was born May 13, 1959.

Mr. Forman has traveled throughout Europe, the West Indies,, Mexico, Egypt, and Morocco.

SELECTED WORKS: The Skies of Crete, 1963; Ring the Judas Bell, 1965; The Shield of Achilles, 1966; Horses of Anger, 1967; The Traitors, 1968; My Enemy, My Brother, 1969; The Cow Neck Rebels, 1969; So Ends This Day, 1970.

ABOUT: Contemporary Authors, Vol. 9-10.

MARIAN CURTIS FOSTER

See *"Mariana"*

ANDRÉ FRANÇOIS
November 9, 1915-

AUTHOR AND ILLUSTRATOR OF *Crocodile Tears*, etc.

Biographical sketch of André François:

ANDRÉ FRANÇOIS was born André Farkas in Timisoara, Rumania, the son of Albert Farkas, a civil servant, and Olga Plon Farkas. He attended the lycée in Timisoara, but left his native land while he was young and settled in Paris where he took classes at l'École des Beaux Arts. He acknowledges

ANDRÉ FRANÇOIS

the influence in particular of the works of George Grosz and Paul Klee, but perhaps the greatest influence on the development of his career was the year he spent (1935-36) in the studio of the famous French poster painter, Cassandre. Becoming a French citizen, he adopted the pseudonym François. In 1939 he married an English girl, Margaret Edmunds, and they have two children, Pierre and Catherine.

It was as a commercial artist that François first made his reputation, doing advertisements for large corporations such as Standard Oil, Olivetti, Perrier, and Dutch Master Cigars. His approach has been called European, and *Fortune Magazine* published a portfolio of his ads entitled *Advertising—a Continental Touch.*

François has also done art work for numerous internationally-known periodicals, including illustrations for *Vogue, Holiday* and *Femina,* covers for *The New Yorker,* and caricatures and political cartoons for *La Tribune des Nations* and *Punch.* Examples of his satiric work are his best-selling book, *The Tatooed Sailor* (1953), his illustrations for Jarry's play, *Ubu Roi* (1958), and his *The Biting Eye* (1960).

In his introduction to *The Biting Eye,* Ronald Searle says that François used to steal scratchy pens from Paris post offices to ensure a barbed line. But there is nothing cruel about his portraits; as Walt Kelly points out in his preface to *The Tatooed Sailor,* when he makes fun of the ridiculous in human nature François is laughing at himself at the same time.

A writer for *Graphis* has called François "an artist of the greatest dexterity" who has perfected his color and line to a "wily awkwardness" in which childlike freshness and candor are expressed with the skills of maturity.

François has also designed sets and costumes for plays and for the ballet, notably the Roland Petit Ballet of Paris. A painter of considerable reputation as well, he has had a number of one-man shows.

His first book illustrations published in the United States were for *Little Boy Brown,* by Isobel Harris, in 1949. Since then several books for which he has done the pictures have been named among the best-illustrated children's books of the year by the New York *Times,* and *Crocodile Tears,* which François wrote and illustrated, was in the New York *Times* list for 1956.

François has been awarded the Gold Medal of the Art Directors Club of New York.

SELECTED WORKS WRITTEN AND ILLUSTRATED: Crocodile Tears, 1956.

SELECTED WORKS ILLUSTRATED: Little Boy Brown, by Isobel Harris, 1949; The Magic Currant Bun, by John Symonds, 1952; Roland, by Nelly Stéphane, 1958; The Adventures of Ulysses, by Jacques Le Marchand, 1959; The Story George Told Me, by John Symonds, 1964; Tom and Tabby, by John Symonds, 1964.

ABOUT: Artist's and Writer's Who's Who, 1963; Hürlimann, Bettina. Picture Book World; Kingman, Lee and others, comps. Illustrators of Children's Books: 1957-1966; Viguers, Ruth Hill and others, comps. Illustrators of Children's Books: 1946-1956; Graphis No. 76, 1958; No. 86, 1959.

ANTONIO FRASCONI

April 28, 1919-

AUTHOR AND ILLUSTRATOR OF *See and Say,* etc.

Autobiographical sketch of Antonio Frasconi:

ESCAPING the fears of the coming war, my parents left Italy in 1914 and wandered

around South America; finally settling down in Montevideo, Uruguay (which my father did not think much of, eventually leaving his wife and three children in a foreign country). All this traveling was done with all of us tagging along. The three children were born in different countries (Florence, Italy; São Paulo, Brazil; Buenos Aires, Argentina) and finally at the insistence of my mother we anchored in Montevideo. Language was always a question (so I felt). At home our parents spoke Italian but outside we stumbled—at the beginning—with Spanish. Montevideo became our home, and Spanish our language, except for my mother who still speaks Italian.

I always thought—because of my own problems—that languages were a vital part of our education. Twenty years later, and after starting to travel myself, and then forming a family of my own, I realized that I could contribute with my work to some of the many questions involved in a child's education.

Pablo—our first child—was the reason and the need for trying to find books in which he could be shown that there are many people in this world and many ways to say: tree, sun, etc. I did not have the pretension to teach another language but only that the language you "were born with" is not the only language in this world. Probably because I was trying to show him why I speak differently.

To my dismay I could not find any books in the local library which dealt with the many ways of this world, even though it was located in a neighborhood where there were many Spanish-speaking people (below West 14th Street, New York).

At that time a letter from Miss McElderry from Harcourt, Brace opened the door for my first book, *See and Say.*

Obviously it was a necessary book and obviously too, I was not the only one in that kind of need. Now more than ever, I believe that children's literature should show a broader panorama: the diversity of other people, their culture, their language, etc. That should be the first step in the making of character—respect for other nationalities and the understanding of their cultures.

I think that contemporary Anglo-Saxon culture has been too imbued with its own greatness and this may be one of the reasons this country now is forcibly—economically and militarily—imposing its "way of life" upon other people.

I am afraid that as an artist there is very little I can contribute—much as I would like to—and my restraint in trying to write "my own books" is because of what I see being published today. Children's literature is a serious enterprise and it is truly appalling what passes for writing.

My only question is why the "established" writers don't write for them; but alas! they certainly write about their lugubrious childhood—for adults.

Probably the solution is to eliminate all categories and age levels and just publish good books from all over the world.

———

Antonio Frasconi began drawing in his childhood. By the time he was a teen-ager he was doing political cartoons and at twenty had a one-man show of his drawings. He studied at the Circulo de Bellas Artes, Montevideo, and came to the United States in 1945 to study with Yasuo Kuniyoshi at the Art Students League on a scholarship. In 1947 he held a scholarship to study mural painting with Camilo Egas at the New School for Social Research, but he had by then already had a one-man show at the Brooklyn Museum of Art, in 1946. He has had more than sixty one-man shows since, on both American continents and in Europe, and is represented in the permanent collections of numerous museums and galleries, including the Metropolitan Museum of Art.

In 1952 Frasconi married Leona Pierce, also an artist, whom he had met when both were students of Kuniyoshi's. They have two sons, Pablo and Miguel.

Among Frasconi's many honors and awards are two Guggenheim Fellowships in graphic arts, 1952-53, a grant from the National Institute of Arts and Letters, 1954, a Grand Prix, Venice Film Festival 1960 for a film *The Neighboring Shore*, incorporating one hundred of his woodcuts, and the commission, won in competition, to design a postage stamp honoring the National Academy of Science, 1963. *The House That Jack Built* was a runner-up for the Caldecott Medal for 1959. Several of Frasconi's books have been named by the New York *Times* as among the ten best-illustrated for the year. His work has been in a number of exhibitions of the American Institute of Graphic Arts.

SELECTED WORKS WRITTEN AND ILLUSTRATED: See and Say, 1955; The Snow and the Sun, 1961; See Again, Say Again, 1964.

SELECTED WORKS ILLUSTRATED: The House That Jack Built (Mother Goose) 1958; Overhead the Sun; Lines from Walt Whitman, 1969.

ABOUT: Contemporary Authors, Vol. 1; Hürlimann, Bettina. Picture Book World; Kingman, Lee and others, comps. Illustrators of Children's Books: 1957-1966; Viguers, Ruth Hill and others, comps. Illustrators of Children's Books: 1946-1956; Who's Who in America, 1970-71; Who's Who in American Art, 1970; Who's Who in Graphic Art, 1962; Americas May 1957; Graphis No. 77, 1958; Horizon March 1961; New Republic February 29, 1964; Newsweek March 17, 1952; April 5, 1954; Print Winter 1950; School Arts May 1966; Time December 20, 1963.

"PAUL FRENCH"

See *Asimov, Isaac*

"BABBIS FRIIS"

See *Friis-Baastad, Babbis*

BABBIS FRIIS-BAASTAD
August 27, 1921-January 11, 1970

AUTHOR OF *Don't Take Teddy*, etc.

Autobiographical sketch of Babbis Ellinor Blauenfeldt Friis-Baastad, who wrote under her own name and under "Babbis Friis" and "Eleanor Babbis":

BORN in Bergen, Norway. Graduated 1940, married 1942 to airline pilot. Four children, all grown up now. Living outside Oslo, Norway.

University education (arts) broken off twice, first because of war, next because of increasing family.

Started, like so many, with stories for own children. Discovered soon that also neighbors and little friends were listening with pointed ears. Got into radio work and became regular contributor to children's programs in the fifties.

"Why don't you write a book?" someone said. It seemed far too much work. I tried to encourage the children. "Let's make a family book," I suggested. "You make up a story and give me the ideas every Saturday and I'll write it down." Oh yes, great fun. Only no story and no idea came, of course. So one had to go to it oneself. And gradually something grew, which it was fun to follow through. And the first book, *Word of Honour*, did win a publisher's competition.

"What did you mean to express through this book?" a journalist asked. "What was your main aim?" My answer, that I did not wish to express anything actually, and that my only aim was to have the excitement of taking part in a competition—this obviously did not sound too promising.

I wrote a couple of other books too, just for my own and my family's pleasure.

Then something happened. The child of some of my friends had serious trouble at school, because of a handicap. Suddenly I felt that here was a challenge for me; I had to do something to try and help. Not help this child, that was already too late, but the many many others who would get into the same painful situation. I did not dare then to write about a permanent handicap, it would have to be something which could happen to any of the readers, a car accident.

Kjersti (Kristy) became another child in our family,—we got very fond of her, as soon as we got acquainted with her. *Kristy's Courage* was published in 1962 and won several prizes.

As soon as that book was ready, some doctor friends pointed out the necessity for a youth book about the mentally retarded child and its family. So then I had another challenge thrust upon me. This subject far exceeded my ability, and I had no personal experience in it. I started reading heavy medical books, visited institutions, hospitals, and those homes with mentally retarded children, whom I could possibly intrude upon and ask questions.

It took two years to finish *Don't Take Teddy* and I remember very clearly the day when I had managed to forget all the other children I had met in this connection, and

Babbis Friis-Baastad: *BAH bis FREEZE BAW stahd*

Teddy suddenly was alive in my mind. Such days are always great for someone who writes. Still, I did not dare to have the book published before it had been read by a well-known psychiatrist. His, and later other experts' judgement, that the book seemed authentic, was more than I could ever have hoped for.

But the next challenge occurred even before the book about Teddy was finished. One of the teachers whose lessons for retarded readers I had attended during the pre-studies for Teddy, said: "Why don't you write a book for these children, not only about them? They are badly in need of something to read which is made specially for them." "Well, goodness, to do such a job, one must be educated and trained in that special field," I objected. "We-ell," the teacher hesitated, and thus another thing was laid upon my conscience.

After having translated some little Swedish books in order to obtain a simple style, and after having read what was to be found about slow readers in Norwegian libraries, I decided again that I had to forget the knowledge, however scarce, I had acquired about the subject and try to find my own way—write the kind of text I would have needed if I had difficulty in having the combination of letters form any understandable word.

The book *Du ma vakne Tor* has been published in the Scandinavian countries and has been much discussed up here. To some it has been useful, for others the text was too difficult. It is an immensely fascinating field to work in, and I wish to go on experimenting in it.

Only it felt necessary, after these three books, first to write something quite problemless. Last year and this year (1969) I have had two books published about a stable and the group of youngsters around it. The boys and girls are from a socially very mixed milieu, and I was not far into the writing before I discovered that it simply is impossible for me to get away from the difficulties and problems that all young people meet in this mixed-up world of ours.

I don't seem to be able to write anything just for the joy of it any longer.

And that is a strange feeling.

———

Babbis Ellinor Blauenfeldt married Kaare Friis-Baastad and had four children, Anne, Winnie, Beth, and Wilhelm. She received a degree from Oslo University in 1948. Her writings won numerous awards and have been translated into twelve languages. *Aeresord* (published in the United States as *Word of Honor*) won the Damm prize in 1959 and the Norwegian government's second prize in 1960. *Kjertsi* (*Kristy's Courage*) won the Damm prize in 1962, the Norwegian government's third prize in 1963 and was on the Hans Christian Andersen honor list in 1964. *Ikke ta Bamse* (*Don't Take Teddy*) won the Norwegian government's first prize in 1965 and the Batchelder Award in 1969.

Mrs. Friis-Baastad was a member of the Norwegian Association of Writers for Young People. Her untimely death, caused by pneumonia, cut short her work on the third book of a trilogy.

SELECTED WORKS: Word of Honor, 1960; Kristy's Courage, 1965; Don't Take Teddy, 1967.

ABOUT: Contemporary Authors, Vol. 19-20; Bookbird no. 1, 1970; Top of the News June 1969.

JEAN FRITZ

November 16, 1915-

AUTHOR OF *Brady*, etc.

Autobiographical sketch of Jean Guttery Fritz:

STORY characters have a way of moving out of their carefully constructed backgrounds and moving into my house, no matter how inappropriate. I explain to them this isn't what their authors intended but it does no good. There they are and there they stay. So when I think back to the big high ceilinged house in Hankow, China, where I spent my childhood, I find Peter Pan perched on the window ledge of the pink bedroom. Bluebeard rules over the attic and

Jean Fritz

Kipling's cat who walked by himself into
our dining room in 1920 is still there.

As an only child, I spent more time with
story characters than with real people and
I learned early that words could get me
where I wanted to go, which was simply
some place else but most especially America. I began then not only to read but to write
stories. Sue and Margery, the twin heroines
of my first story, did all the American things
I wanted to do. They shot off firecrackers
on the Fourth of July; they went to their
grandmother's for Thanksgiving; they drank
water that came straight from the tap.

We came back to America in 1928 when
I was thirteen—too late to make up entirely
for the time lost so perhaps it is not surprising that one of my first books for children was *121 Pudding Street*, a prolonged
and unrestrained daydream. By this time I
had, however, graduated from college
(Wheaton, 1937), had married (Michael
Fritz, 1941), and had two children (David
and Andrea). I had moved from Hartford,
Connecticut, to New York City, to the West
Coast during the war and had come to
Dobbs Ferry, New York, in 1951 where I've
been ever since.

My next book, *The Cabin Faced West*,
was ostensibly about my great-great-grand-

mother, Ann Hamilton, in early pioneer
Pennsylvania, but I discovered later it was
really about me. In the roundabout way that
writers have, I was trying to show that lonely
girl I left behind how to feel the challenge
of her own times. In the process of this book
I began putting down my roots as an American and I've been doing it ever since. Although I have written books of other types
(*Fish Head, The Animals of Dr. Schweitzer,
How to Read a Rabbit, Magic to Burn*), my
greatest joy has been writing historical fiction. I have gone into the nineteenth century for my stories (*Brady, I Adam*), but
my favorite period is the Revolutionary one,
the setting of my two latest books. I'm not
at all sure I am ready to leave it.

———

Jean Fritz has also had articles and stories
published in a number of periodicals including *Horn Book*, the *New Yorker, Atlantic,
McCall's, Redbook,* and *Seventeen.*

SELECTED WORKS: 121 Pudding Street, 1955;
The Animals of Dr. Schweitzer, 1958; The Cabin Faced West, 1958; How to Read a Rabbit,
1959; Brady, 1960; San Francisco, 1962; I,
Adam, 1963; Magic to Burn, 1964; Early Thunder, 1967; George Washington's Breakfast, 1969.

ABOUT: Contemporary Authors, Vol. 4; Something About the Author, Vol. 1; Library Journal
February 15, 1956.

ROSALIE K. FRY

April 22, 1911-

AUTHOR AND ILLUSTRATOR OF *Bumblebuzz,*
etc.

Autobiographical sketch of Rosalie Kings-
mill Fry:

I HAVE always lived in beautiful surroundings, and most of my stories are set in places
I have known and loved.

I was born on Vancouver Island, British
Columbia, but remember little of this, since
the family returned to England on the outbreak of World War I.

We spent the war years in an aunt's home
in Hertfordshire, the loveliest house and
garden I have ever known. The old tim-
bered house had been a paper mill, and a

small river curved around the garden, streaming under the ancient wooden water wheel in a fall that could be heard throughout the house. There were willow trees and raftered barns, in one of which we had a swing that flew out through a doorway hung with rambler roses. A wonderful place in which to play and wander with a younger sister.

After the war we moved to Wales. There were four of us now, and we found ourselves with a garden full of trees to climb, and a house in which there was ample space for the plays we wrote and acted, adapting fairy stories and *Tanglewood Tales*, giving plenty of scope for scenery and costume.

I was eighteen when we moved to our final family home on the shore of a sandy bay with cliffs and rock pools almost on the doorstep.

All through these years I drew and painted with the idea that I would one day illustrate children's books. I was blessed with parents who encouraged this from the first, and my father kept me supplied with artists' materials, *real* artists' materials, not the students' quality usually given to children.

On leaving school I went to a London art school where I specialised in book illustra-tion. It was only when I left this school that it suddenly dawned on me that I did not know a single author, and had no idea how to get in touch with one. There seemed to be nothing for it but to write my own stories.

I chose a bumble bee as the heroine of my first book which I illustrated in full colour on every page. I did not realise what a costly production this would be, and was much cast down when it was rejected by six publishers in turn. My mother suggested trying America, and to my delight it was accepted by the first publisher to whom I sent it— E. P. Dutton of New York, who produced it quite perfectly, with truly exquisite colour reproduction. This was the start of a long and very happy relationship lasting until today.

However, just as Dutton accepted my third book, World War II was upon us, so I dropped my books to join the Women's Royal Naval Service as coder and cypher officer.

My most rewarding posting was to the Orkney Islands north of Scotland. This area later helped to provide the setting for *Child of the Ron Mor Skerry*.

I am at present writing for older children than those who read my *Bumblebuzz*, and when writing for this age group I often do not illustrate the books myself.

I am always particularly conscious of the places in which my stories are set, and like to write on the spot whenever this is possible. I now live among the Welsh hills, and have already started work on a story centred in and around my own small mountain cottage.

———

Rosalie K. Fry attended St. Margaret's School, Swansea, and the Central School of Arts and Crafts, London, 1929-1934. She has said that she feels sure she inherited her love of painting tiny things from relatives on her mother's side, the miniature painters James Dowling and his sister Mary. Besides writing and illustrating books for children, Miss Fry contributes to magazines, designs Christmas cards, and makes toys. She is a member of the Society of Authors.

Child of the Ron Mor Skerry was published in the United States as *Secret of the Ron Mor Skerry*.

SELECTED WORKS WRITTEN AND ILLUSTRATED:
Bumblebuzz, 1938; Deep in the Forest, 1956;
A Bell for Ringleblume, 1957; Secret of the
Ron Mor Skerry, 1959; Fly Home, Colombina,
1960; The Echo Song, 1962.

SELECTED WORKS WRITTEN: Promise of the
Rainbow, 1965; September Island, 1965; The
Castle Family, 1966; Whistler in the Mist, 1968;
Gypsy Princess, 1969; Snowed Up, 1970.

ABOUT: Author's and Writer's Who's Who,
1963; Contemporary Authors, Vol. 9-10; King-
man, Lee and others, comps. Illustrators of
Children's Books: 1957-1966; Viguers, Ruth
Hill and others, comps. Illustrators of Children's
Books: 1946-1956.

"WILSON GAGE"

May 8, 1922-

AUTHOR OF *Big Blue Island,* etc.

Autobiographical sketch of Mary Quintard
Govan Steele, who writes under the
names of Mary Q. Steele and "Wilson
Gage":

I WAS born in Chattanooga, Tennessee,
and I have lived in Chattanooga and its
suburbs ever since. From the beginning
books were an integral part of my life, for
my mother was a writer, my father a bookseller, later librarian at the University of
Chattanooga, and as far back as I can
remember book review editor for the Chattanooga *Times.* I attended schools in Chattanooga, graduating from the University
where I majored, for reasons that seemed
good and sufficient at the time though I
cannot for the life of me recall them now,
in physics. World War II began while I
was in college and before I was graduated
I was married to William O. Steele, who
happened to be stationed at a nearby fort.
Our older daughter was born while he was
in Italy with the Air Corps. When the war
ended he returned to Chattanooga and got
a job. Eventually we had two more children, another daughter and a son, and my
husband quit his job to devote all his time
to writing. When my children were all in
school I too took up writing, as it now
seemed quite impossible to avoid it.

Natural history is my great passion and
I suppose one reason I started writing was
in order to be able to talk about geese and
spiders and goldfinches just as much as I
wanted to. I was, of course, surprised to
find that the disciplines of writing and the
exigencies of fiction made this impossible.
But at least no one interrupts.

Politics and poetry are my other interests,
along with my family—a source of love and
entertainment and endless material.

———

Mary Quintard Govan received her B.S.
in 1943 from the University of Chattanooga,
after marrying William O. Steele the same
year. Their children are Mary Quintard,
Jenifer Susan, and Allerton William. Most
of her books have been written under the
pen name of Wilson Gage, but in 1969 she
published her first book under the name of
Mary Q. Steele, *Journey Outside.*

Big Blue Island won the 1966 Aurianne
Award. *Secret of Fiery Gorge* was a 1960
New York *Herald Tribune* Children's Spring
Book Festival Honor Book. *Journey Outside*
was a 1970 Newbery runner-up.

SELECTED WORKS: Secret of Crossbone Hill,
1959; Secret of Fiery Gorge, 1960; A Wild
Goose Tale, 1961; Dan and the Miranda, 1962;
Miss Osborne-the-Mop, 1963; Big Blue Island,
1964; Journey Outside, 1969.

ABOUT: Contemporary Authors, Vol. 4.

PAUL GALDONE

June 2, 1914-

ILLUSTRATOR OF *Anatole*, etc.

Autobiographical sketch of Paul Galdone:

WHEN I was about fourteen we left Budapest. A kind aunt in New Jersey had arranged affidavits for us and on arrival there I was promptly enrolled in high school. The Hungarian language proved to be not very useful in the United States, so in an effort to get me over the barrier I had to attend three English classes every day along with one in biology. When it came my turn to read from Shakespeare's *A Midsummer Night's Dream* it was highly embarrassing. Not only did I have an accent that amused the whole class but on top of that I failed to understand most of what I was trying to read. In the biology class, however, I felt more successful; when it was discovered that I was proficient in the drawing of grasshoppers I was soon drawing them for all the other pupils.

We soon moved to New York City. To help support my family in the struggle to get started I worked during the day as bus-boy, electrician's helper on unfinished skyscrapers, fur dyer, and so on. At night I attended art schools: the Art Students League and New York School for Industrial Design. Eventually, four years of working in the Art Department of Doubleday & Company determined my direction. I loved everything in the world of book production, the people and the challenges, and there I had a chance to design my first book jacket. That led to free lancing.

I lived in Greenwich Village and while I free-lanced and built up a busy career in book jacket designing I kept up my interest in fine arts by drawing and painting and by long sketching vacations in Vermont. I also became increasingly interested in illustration.

After four years spent in the U.S. Army Engineer Corps, during which I contributed to *Yank* magazine in my spare time, I settled down in Rockland County, New York, with a wife and, eventually, two children and assorted animals—and resumed free-lancing, leaning more and more to illustrating children's books.

Recently I listed all the publishers for whom I have illustrated children's books and was surprised to find the total came to twenty-five. Miss Margaret McElderry of Harcourt, Brace gave me my first real chance by assigning a William O. Steele book. Then I had the good fortune to work with Mrs. Helene Frye of McGraw-Hill Junior Books. With her encouragement I started illustrating the Ellen MacGregor *Miss Pickerell* series, then many classic nursery tales and such children's classics as Hawthorne's *The Golden Touch, Pandora's Box,* etc.; also collaborated with Eve Titus on the *Anatole* books. For Miss Riley of T. Y. Crowell I wrote and illustrated *Paddy the Penguin,* also illustrated such historical classics as *Paul Revere's Ride* and *The Star Spangled Banner* and quite a few *Let's Read and Find Out* books.

I consider myself lucky that I can work at home and that although I am within easy reach of New York City I still have woods around me and homegrown vegetables and the daily pleasure of a refreshing walk along a lovely brook.

Lately, I have enjoyed adapting and

making picture books of favorite old tales. I find this most satisfying and I like to fancy myself in such venerable company as Caldecott, Arthur Rackham, Walter Crane, Doré —real inspirations and a constant challenge.

Paul Galdone, who is a painter as well as an illustrator, studied under George Grosz, Louis Bouché, and Guy Pène du Bois. He has a wife, Jannelise, a daughter Joanna, and a son Paul Ferencz. He divides his time between his farm in Tunbridge, Vermont, and his rambling house in Rockland County, which is surrounded by woods, gardens, an apple orchard, and trout streams. Galdone likes to hike, garden, and go on sketching trips.

Anatole, 1956, and *Anatole and the Cat*, 1957, were both runners-up for the Caldecott Medal.

SELECTED WORKS WRITTEN AND ILLUSTRATED: Paddy the Penguin, 1959; Little Tuppen, 1967; The Monkey and the Crocodile, 1969.

SELECTED WORKS ILLUSTRATED: Anatole, by Eve Titus, 1956; Anatole and the Cat, by Eve Titus, 1957; Grandfather and I, by Helen E. Buckley, 1959; A Gaggle of Geese, by Eve Merriam, 1960; Paul Revere's Ride, by Henry Wadsworth Longfellow, 1963; Two Laughable Lyrics, by Edward Lear, 1966; A Visit from St. Nicholas: Twas the Night before Christmas, by Clement C. Moore, 1968; George Washington's Breakfast, by Jean Fritz, 1969.

ABOUT: Hopkins, Lee Bennett. Books Are by People; Hürlimann, Bettina. Picture Book World; Kingman, Lee and others, comps. Illustrators of Children's Books: 1957-1966; Viguers, Ruth Hill and others, comps. Illustrators of Children's Books: 1946-1956.

ALAN GARNER

1935-

AUTHOR OF *The Owl Service*, etc.

Biographical sketch of Alan Garner:

ALAN GARNER was born and grew up in the English county of Cheshire. He attended a rural primary school and Manchester Grammar School, where he distinguished himself academically and in athletics (sprinting). He disliked school, however, and has said that his happiest memories are of acting in school plays.

As a schoolboy Garner was not a reader,

ALAN GARNER

which he later ascribed to the fact that he had nothing between the required English classics and, during long spells of illness, the comics. From this polarity he excepts Shakespeare, whom he met in the most natural way—through his acting.

After grammar school Garner enlisted, became a 2nd Lieutenant, and spent two years in the Royal Artillery. Toward the end of his army career, chance put into his hands Golding's *Lord of the Flies*, and Garner saw at once what literature could do for a contemporary generation. Two weeks later he started his first novel, *The Weirdstone of Brisingamen*. After his discharge from the army he entered Magdalen College, Oxford University, but left before graduating. Disillusioned by the Anglo-French Suez venture and the crisis in Hungary, he returned to his native village in Cheshire and settled down to writing.

Garner took two years to finish *The Weirdstone of Brisingamen* and a year and a half to find a publisher. Gradually, however, he gained an audience. Each new book was enriched by his increasing knowledge of the vivid history and legend of his region, which has the Irish Sea on the northwest and Wales on the west. But Cheshire is also highly industrialized; Manchester and Liverpool are both there. Garner is as likely to set his story in the crumbling back streets of Manchester as in the woods and rocks of his native Alderley Edge.

In his work ancient legend is juxtaposed

with harsh, present-day reality; experience of the everyday world occurs in a climate of myth, nightmare, magic, and vision.

Garner was particularly influenced by the *Mabinogion,* a collection of twelfth-century Welsh legends somewhat similar to the Arthurian Legends. To understand them fully he learned Welsh. In *The Weirdstone of Brisingamen* and its sequel, *The Moon of Gomrath,* the children meet with mythical characters and much of the action takes place in an abandoned copper mine, with dreamlike falls down shafts and nightmarish struggles through underground tunnels. In *Elidor,* a runner-up for the Carnegie Medal, he again conveyed the magic of the legendary past and its impact on children's humdrum everyday life of tea and television. His next novel, *The Owl Service,* placed in a Welsh village and based on a legend from the *Mabinogion,* won a number of honors, including the Carnegie Medal, 1967, and the Guardian Children's Book Award, 1968. *The Weirdstone of Brisingamen* received a Lewis Carroll Shelf Award, 1970.

Garner restored a fourteenth-century, half-timbered house in Cheshire called Toad Hall, where he lives with his three children.

SELECTED WORKS: The Moon of Gomrath, 1967; Elidor, 1967; The Owl Service, 1968; The Weirdstone of Brisingamen, 1969; The Old Man of Mow, 1970.

ABOUT: Bookbird no. 3, 1968; Times Educational Supplement October 6, 1967.

RANDALL GARRETT

See *Silverberg, Robert*

MADELEINE GEKIERE

May 15, 1919-

AUTHOR AND ILLUSTRATOR OF *The Frilly Lily and the Princess,* etc.

Autobiographical sketch of Madeleine Gekiere:

EVERY artist the world hears about seems to have known his destiny instantly upon

Gekiere: GAY kyair

arising from the cradle, or possibly already long before in his mother's womb. While this makes for charming fables, it discourages young people who fear that without this almost mystical foreknowledge, they stand no chance in a creative field of endeavor.

I know this to be erroneous, both from my own experience and from years of teaching art.

So-called talent is virtually universal and by giving it opportunities for development no one can foretell where it will lead.

If I give here my own story, it is aimed at these young people. Apart from that, why should anyone be interested in the accidents of another's life? Only the work itself matters.

I saw the light of day in Zurich, Switzerland. No one, at that time, had the remotest notion that a future artist had been born. In fact it would then (as it subsequently did) have horrified my fond parents and relatives, who were firmly committed to the notion that science was going to save the world and that the arts were a wonderful device thought up by antiquity to delight and elevate present-day scientists; whereas present-day artists were wastrels.

Anyway, coming from this hardy stock, I entered school an extremely bright little girl with the firm decision of becoming a doctor. At age seven I was an outstanding scholar among my peers, but I couldn't draw and I couldn't sing. Unfortunately, that lovely state of affairs didn't last and as time went on, I became dumber and dumber; meanwhile I still couldn't draw and I still couldn't sing. As a result I lost my faith in the sciences, or at least in my participation in them. My father didn't give up quite that easily and with cram courses in Latin and algebra, neither of which I could then, nor can now, even begin to understand, by hook and mostly by crook, I managed at nineteen to graduate from the Zurich Gymnasium. Finally eligible for the highest of high studies, I had only one desire, to get out of the place and indulge in a bit of living before old age would strike me down. All this time, I still couldn't sing and I still couldn't draw. I thought a career in fashions sounded glamorous and frivolous enough, and I tried out for that in a commercial art school in London. It turned out though that my personal sense of logic would not permit me to learn how to cut out patterns, but I did get fascinated by making sketches and doing drawings from life and while I was astonishingly bad at it, it turned out to be what I liked doing most.

I kicked around art schools in London and Paris and finally in 1940 came to the United States, where I went to the Art Students League and irrevocably decided to become a painter. I was married to an actor in 1948 and we preferred not having children, to be free to devote all our time to our respective work.

My dear friend, the illustrator Helen Sewell, liked my drawings so much (by that time I could draw, while I still couldn't sing) she showed them to Eunice Blake, at that time editor at Oxford, and that is how I got started doing books. The first book of my own was *Who Gave Us?*, which I did for Pantheon.

In the meanwhile I have become a painter. I have had ten one-man shows, eight of them in New York City, the last five at the Babcock galleries, and I have been teaching art at New York University and City College, a fairish success for someone who couldn't draw and, believe me, still can't sing one clear note.

———

Miss Gekiere has traveled in the art centers of Italy and France. She is married to Paul Potter.

The Fisherman and His Wife, 1957, and *The Reason for the Pelican*, 1959, were each named by the New York *Times* as the best-illustrated picture book of the year. Several books illustrated by Miss Gekiere have been in exhibitions of the American Institute of Graphic Arts.

SELECTED WORKS WRITTEN AND ILLUSTRATED: Who Gave Us . . . Peacocks? Planes? and Ferris Wheels? 1953; The Frilly Lily and the Princess, 1966.

SELECTED WORKS ILLUSTRATED: Mrs. Mc-Thing, by Mary Chase (illustrated with Helen Sewell), 1952; Switch on the Night, by Ray Bradbury, 1955; The Fisherman and His Wife, by The Brothers Grimm, 1957; The Reason for the Pelican, by John Ciardi, 1959; John J. Plenty and Fiddler Dan, by John Ciardi, 1963.

ABOUT: Kingman, Lee and others, comps. Illustrators of Children's Books: 1957-1966; Viguers, Ruth Hill and others, comps. Illustrators of Children's Books: 1946-1956; Who's Who in American Art, 1970.

"JOSEPHINE GIBSON"

See *Hine, Al; Joslin, Sesyle*

FRED GIPSON

February 7, 1908-

AUTHOR OF *Old Yeller*, etc.

Autobiographical sketch of Frederick Benjamin Gipson:

WHY the urge to write? Why the driving compulsion to put down on paper what others can see and hear and do as well as you? Why punish yourself with the gruelling nerve-wracking, frustrating effort

Gipson: *GIP sn*

Fred Gipson

that leads toward loneliness and generally speaking, poor financial reward?

Frankly, I don't know. I can only assume that it is something you are born with, comparable to the urge that makes one man a millionaire, another a religious fanatic, and still another a drunk. If the urge is there, you have to live with it and deal with it the best you can.

And with me, almost from the beginning, the urge was there. Not that at the age of seven, I said to myself: "I want to become a writer." At that time, I was just beginning to spell out the words in my first-grade reader that had to do with the insipid, sugar-coated adventures of *May* and *Will*.

But my interest in *story* was there, my interest in the colorful and the dramatic. Partly, I'm quite sure, due to the fact that I had a father who was a natural storyteller.

In the sense of "book-learning," my father was an uneducated man. In fact, he could just barely read and write. On the other hand he was a good hunter, and an astute observer of nature along with being a wonderful storyteller. From him, I am quite sure, I learned more about the art and technique of storytelling than from anybody or anything else.

We lived then on a little "dry-land" farm in the heart of the Hill Country of Texas.

I was born in Mason. I attended school at Mason, walking four miles each way, twice a day. Except in the coldest of weather, I went barefooted.

In those years—when I could get away from school or work in the fields—I prowled the woods. I hunted and fished and just looked to see what I could find. I followed my trail hounds at night after fox, raccoon, and wildcat. That's how and where I learned about boys and dogs and the great outdoors and the wild animals I was later to write about. That's when I often listened to old-timers tell about their adventures in early-day Texas. That's when I read books like *Tom Sawyer, Huckleberry Finn, Kim,* and *Treasure Island*.

As I grew older, I worked on the surrounding ranches.

In 1940, I took up free-lance writing. With a wife and, later, two children, to support, I nearly went under. But it wasn't the first time I'd gone hungry, so I hung with it and eventually lucked out. I've written hundreds of short stories and articles for magazines, had ten books published, four made into movies. My best, I suppose, is *Old Yeller,* known to practically every school child in America. And I sometimes think every one of those school children has written me a fan letter, bless their hearts.

Why write for children? That's easy. You can be honest with them.

In fact, you damn well better be!

———

Fred Gipson was a journalism major at the University of Texas, 1933-37, and a reporter for the Corpus Christi *Caller*, 1938-40. In 1940 he married Tommie Eloise Wynn.

The Trail-Driving Rooster won the Cokesbury Book Store Award in 1955. *Old Yeller,* a story of a Texas farm boy and his dog, set in the pioneering days of the 1860s, won a number of awards, including the Maggie Award, 1958, the William Allen White Children's Book Award, 1959, the first Sequoyah Award, 1959, the Pacific Northwest Award, 1959, and was a runner-up for the Newbery Medal for 1957. It has been translated into numerous foreign languages.

Gipson has contributed to periodicals, including *Liberty* and *Collier's*, has written books for adults, and did the screen plays for *Hound-Dog Man, Old Yeller*, and *Savage Sam*. He is a member of the Headliners Club and of the Texas Institute of Letters, of which he was president in 1960. He operates a small livestock farm near his birthplace and likes to hunt and fish. In 1970 the Texas Institute of Letters awarded Gipson a lifetime Fellowship.

SELECTED WORKS: Hound-Dog Man, 1949; Recollection Creek, 1955; The Trail-Driving Rooster, 1955; Old Yeller, 1956; Savage Sam, 1962.

ABOUT: Contemporary Authors, Vol. 3; Current Biography, 1957; Wilson Library Bulletin October 1957.

SHIRLEY GLUBOK

June 15, 1933-

AUTHOR OF *The Art of Ancient Egypt*, etc.

Autobiographical sketch of Shirley Astor Glubok Tamarin:

I HAVE wanted to write for as long as I can remember, but it was not easy in St. Louis, where I was born and brought up. First of all there were my brothers, one older, one younger. Because of them it was necessary, naturally, for me to spend many hours trying to do all of the things they did. I had to keep up with them in sports: swimming, ice-skating and tennis.

We lived around the corner from the local Y, with its indoor swimming pool, where, once a day and sometimes twice, summer and winter, I practiced, training with the team and winning all the swim races in the area in the hundred-yard backstroke event. Then there were my neighborhood pals, with our various games and projects, which sometimes involved writing stories.

Fortunately for me St. Louis has Washington University, with an outstanding curriculum in art and archaeology, and I was privileged to study under two eminent professors, one an archaeologist and the other an art historian.

On trips to Florida and to Europe I had made friends with young people from New York, and decided to settle there. After graduate school at Columbia I began teaching kindergarten and giving lectures to children at the Metropolitan Museum of Art. Working with children, both in the classroom and the Museum galleries, I observed that they could understand far more than one would expect. I experimented with new approaches to teaching art history to young children. I tried drawing them out, letting them experience a statue or a painting, giving them a chance to feel the beauty of the art and the emotions behind it. I encouraged the children to look at a work of art, sit quietly in front of it, and if it was a statue, to walk all around it, before I told them a single fact about it.

My art books for young children grew naturally from these lectures, to reach children outside the range of big city museums, and to give New York children a chance to see objects from collections in great museums throughout the world. First came *The Art of Ancient Egypt,* quickly followed by others.

As the young children for whom I was writing were growing up I started a series for older children, to revive great archaeological finds and historic events, editing and abridging eye-witness accounts of the conquests of Mexico and Peru. I did *The Fall of the Aztecs* and *The Fall of the Incas,* then turned to Howard Carter's discovery of Tut-Ankh-Amen's tomb and Sir Leonard Woolley's excavations in the Royal Cemetery at Ur.

One of my basic views is that art books should be in themselves works of art. I am fortunate in having Gerard Nook as my designer. My photographer, Alfred Tamarin, is now my husband. He has photographed most of the covers for my books, as well as many of the objects illustrated inside them. Alfred is writing his own books, as well, and we work at home in our New York apartment, when we are not traveling to Japan, Taiwan, Greece, Israel, Peru or Mexico to get material, always loaded down with cameras, tripods, photographic lenses and flashes, notebooks, references, and a minimum of personal luggage. If we keep up our present pace we shall have soon covered the world.

———

Shirley Glubok took an A.B. from Washington University and in 1958 an M.A. from Teachers College, Columbia University. She married Alfred Tamarin in 1968. Among other organizations, she is a member of Authors Guild, Washington University Archaeological Society, and the Association of Teachers of Independent Schools.

The Art of Ancient Egypt won a Lewis Carroll Shelf Award in 1963.

SELECTED WORKS: The Art of Ancient Egypt, 1962; The Art of Lands in the Bible, 1963; The Art of the Eskimo, 1964; The Art of Africa, 1965; The Fall of the Aztecs, 1965; The Art of Ancient Peru, 1966; The Fall of the Incas, 1967; The Art of the Etruscans, 1967.

ABOUT: Contemporary Authors, Vol. 5-6; Who's Who of American Women, 1970-71.

ALICE E. GOUDEY
January 3, 1898-

AUTHOR OF *Houses from the Sea,* etc.

Autobiographical sketch of Alice E. Goudey:

THE sturdy stone house near Junction City, where I was born, defied the Kansas cyclones. But my environment offered me little in the way of playmates my own age. I was the belated last of five children born to my parents, and neighboring children lived at some distance. As a result I spent many hours roaming the hills and the valleys and along the streams of our farm. On one occasion, I am told, my mother asked me what I did when I stayed away for an unusually long time. I replied, "I was listening."

No doubt what I listened to and what I saw in the woods and along the streams is stored in my memory and has resulted in my books being mainly about animals and nature. It is easy for me to envision the movements, and to recall the sounds and the smells in the world of nature.

I started teaching in a one-room country school house when I was seventeen. I taught for three years. During that time I longed for supplementary reading material for the children. There was no available library and nothing for them to read except textbooks. I tried writing pieces to enliven their program but even I soon recognized that what I wrote was not good.

At the end of my third year of teaching I married Wayne Martin, Jr. During the First World War I filled his position doing editorial work for several trade magazines. Later we came to New York where we lived in Bronxville. During the Second World War I did some political writing and had a weekly column on conservation in the local newspaper.

Our marriage ended in a divorce shortly after the war. At that time I began to think more seriously about writing and enrolled in writing classes at Columbia, the New

Goudey: *GOW dee*

I hope my books have, even in a small degree, supplied some of the supplementary reading which I felt was so badly needed when I was teaching in that little one-room country school house.

The original manuscripts of *Houses from the Sea*, 1959, and *The Day We Saw the Sun Come Up*, 1961, are in the Kerlan Collection at the University of Minnesota. These books, both with illustrations by Adrienne Adams, were runners-up for the Caldecott Medal in 1960 and 1962.

SELECTED WORKS: The Good Rain, 1950; Here Come the Bears! 1954; Houses from the Sea, 1959; Here Come the Raccoons! 1959; The Day We Saw the Sun Come Up, 1961; Here Come the Dolphins! 1961; Butterfly Time, 1964; Red Legs, 1966.

ABOUT: Who's Who of American Women, 1968-69.

School for Social Research and New York University.

At the New School I was fortunate in having as instructors Mrs. Hildegarde Swift and Mrs. Frances Sayers, then head of the Children's Department at the New York Public Library. Both were inspiring teachers.

It was during this period that I married Dr. Earl Goudey, Chairman of the Science Department in the Bronxville schools. He encouraged me in my writing and was of tremendous help in the selection of subject matter.

My first book, *The Good Rain*, grew out of my experience with droughts in Kansas. It has sold well over a period of about twenty years. This I attribute to its being based on authentic experience. The *Here Come* series are animal life-cycle books with a slant toward preservation of our wildlife. They are used in the teaching of elementary science. *The Day We Saw the Sun Come Up*, *Houses from the Sea* and *Butterfly Time* are picture books for the very young and are used in the primary grades. Adrienne Adams illustrated these books with sensitivity and imagination. *Houses from the Sea* and *The Day We Saw the Sun Come Up* were runners-up for the Caldecott Award.

ELIZABETH GOUDGE

April 24, 1900-

AUTHOR OF *The Little White Horse*, etc.

Biographical sketch of Elizabeth Goudge:

ELIZABETH GOUDGE was born in the cathedral town of Wells, in Somerset, England, the only child of Dr. Henry Leighton Goudge, Principal of the Theological College at Wells, and Ida de Beauchamp (Collenette) Goudge. When his daughter was eleven Dr. Goudge was made a Canon of Ely Cathedral and the family moved to another beautiful cathedral town, Ely in Cambridgeshire. From there Elizabeth was sent to a boarding school, where she excelled in English and began to dream of becoming a writer. Her family, however, knowing the risks of a writing career, wished her to qualify for a profession, and she spent two years at the Art School at Reading University. When she came home she taught design and handicrafts and continued to do so for ten years, while writing on the side.

In 1923 Dr. Goudge was appointed Regius Professor of Divinity at Oxford, and the family went to live in one of the most interesting of the Oxford quadrangles, Tom

Goudge: *GOOJ*

ELIZABETH GOUDGE

Quad in Christ Church College. During the years in Oxford Miss Goudge enjoyed her first mild success as a writer, when in 1932 a play she wrote, based on the life of the Brontës, was produced at a "Sunday night performance" in London.

In contrast to the life in clerical circles that her father's position entailed were her summers in the Channel Islands. Her mother came from an Anglo-French family in Guernsey, and Miss Goudge spent many holidays with her grandparents there. Guernsey is the scene of her first novel, *Island Magic* (1934). The books that followed reflected previous places where she had lived: *City of Bells* (1936) being set in Wells, and *Towers in the Mist* (1938) in Oxford. By 1938 she was devoting all her time to writing.

Dr. Goudge died in 1939 and Miss Goudge and her mother left Oxford and built themselves a cottage in Devonshire. The hard years of World War II had begun but Elizabeth Goudge concentrated on her writing. She had always had a preference for writing children's stories and produced two juveniles during this period, *Smoky House* (1940), and *The Blue Hills* (1942). At the same time she was struggling, in spite of all the hardships of war from paper shortage to constant air-raid alarms, to write the novel that was at last to bring her fame. With a plot which the author

herself has said "was hardly credible and yet it was true," *Green Dolphin Street* was published in 1944.

The scene of the novel was the Channel Islands, shifting in the middle section to New Zealand in the period of early British colonization. This was perhaps the only time Miss Goudge wrote of a locale with which she was not personally familiar. The book was an immediate best seller in England and the United States, was made into a film and won the Metro-Goldwyn-Mayer Literary Award of $125,000, at the time the largest monetary prize ever awarded a work of fiction.

Local color, especially description of the English countryside, is one of the most striking qualities of Miss Goudge's work. It is characteristic of *The Little White Horse*, for which she won the Carnegie Medal for the best children's book of the year 1946. Another quality of her work is also noticeable in this book—the moralistic. In a charming setting in Devonshire of the last century, the story is almost a parable which ends with good triumphing over evil. A writer for the *New Yorker* has commented that Miss Goudge sometimes fails to "let the moral implications of the story speak for themselves." Considering her background, a moral—in fact a religious—outlook was natural and many of her stories for children as well as her anthologies and other books for adults are on religious subjects.

Over twelve million copies of Miss Goudge's books have been sold and her work has been translated into numerous languages. In 1951 her mother died and Elizabeth Goudge moved to a seventeenth-century cottage in Oxfordshire. There she gardens and continues to write at about the rate of a book a year. She is a member of the P.E.N. Club, a fellow of the Royal Society of Literature, and votes Labour.

SELECTED WORKS: City of Bells, 1937; Smoky House, 1940; The Little White Horse, 1946; White Witch, 1958; Dean's Watch, 1960; Linnets and Valerians, 1964; I Saw Three Ships, 1969; The Child from the Sea, 1970.

ABOUT: Author's and Writer's Who's Who, 1963; Contemporary Authors, Vol. 7-8; Current Biography, 1940; Leasor, James. Author by

Profession; Twentieth Century Authors, 1942; Twentieth Century Authors (First Supplement), 1955; Who's Who, 1968; Who's Who in America, 1970-71; Who's Who of American Women, 1970-71; Christian Science Monitor Magazine June 8, 1940; Horn Book March 1947; Library Association Record May 1947; New York Herald Tribune Book Review October 7, 1951; Publishers' Weekly February 10, 1951; Saturday Review of Literature June 27, 1942; August 26, 1944; April 24, 1948; December 31, 1949; Scholastic March 4, 1939; Time September 4, 1944; January 2, 1950.

JANUSZ GRABIAŃSKI

July 24, 1929-

ILLUSTRATOR OF *The Big Book of Animal Stories,* etc.

Autobiographical sketch of Janusz Grabiański:

I MADE drawings "from the beginning"— at least this is what my parents said. This "beginning" occurred at Szamotuly near Poznań in Poland. I drew from early childhood, but it was flying that I considered a really serious occupation for me. Leisure hours I used to spend on drawing airplanes, making model airplanes and visiting the airport with my father.

I was ten years old when World War II began. Watching the airplanes in the blue sky ceased to be a safe entertainment.

Later, during the dark years of the Nazi occupation, I came across a booklet, printed on a very poor quality of paper by the underground movement, containing the story of the part played by the Polish Fighter Divisions in the Battle of Britain. The book was fascinating and I was tempted to make illustrations for it. It was the first book that I illustrated and I kept it for long years as a sacred memory of those gloomy times.

After the war I was a glider pilot for several years but my career as "knight of the space" ended abruptly to my great regret when a defect in my sight was discovered. From that time on only drawing was left for me, I thought. But after six years of study at the Academy of Fine Arts I came to believe that I found my own way of

life. I graduated from a book illustration department to working for several editorial offices. The beginning was not easy. For many years I have sought for my own way and my own style of expressing myself in drawings.

In 1958 my illustrations were noticed at an International Book Fair in Frankfurt on the Main. From that date began my cooperation with an Austrian publishing office, Ue Berreuter, and through it with a number of other publishing houses including some in the United States. In a dozen years or so I have made illustrations for some scores of books, mainly for children and young people. Some of them appeared in the United States; among other titles are these: *Grimm's Fairy Tales, Perrault's Classic French Tales, Andersen's Fairy Tales, The Big Book of Pets.*

Apart from illustrations I am busy with designing advertisements, posters, stamps, labels, postcards and the like.

I do not feel well being huddled within the walls of the city. I have a little house with a garden in a green suburban district of Warsaw. I have a wife and two daughters. I love to travel and each year I take out my car and set off somewhere. Fast driving, changing places and meeting new people are my passion, but after a month or two I feel homesick and look forward to meeting my dearest, and sitting again in my cosy atelier full of clean illustration boards waiting to be filled in with drawings. My living models, an Alsatian sheep dog and two funny cats, his friends, are also waiting for me.

I have had an ever-present feeling that all the work that I have done is but an introduction to something that is going to happen in the future. A sense of unfulfillment and looking for better ways has always been with me.

———

Grabiański's wife is named Joanna, his daughters, Kate and Ditta.

Grabianski has designed two series of stamps used in Poland. His *The Big Book of Animal Stories* was named among the ten best-illustrated picture books of 1961 by the New York *Times,* and he has won a number of international awards, including the Gold Medal of the Milan Triennale of 1960.

SELECTED WORKS ILLUSTRATED: The Big Book of Animal Stories, edited by Margaret Green, 1961; The Big Book of Wild Animals, edited by Margaret Green, 1964; The Big Book of Fables, edited by Margaret Green, 1965; Grabiański's Cats, 1967; Grabiański's Horses, 1967; Grabiański's Birds, 1968; Grabiański's Dogs, 1968.

ABOUT: Hürlimann, Bettina. Picture Book World; Kingman, Lee and others, comps. Illustrators of Children's Books: 1957-1966.

LORENZ GRAHAM

January 27, 1902-

AUTHOR OF *South Town,* etc.

Autobiographical sketch of Lorenz Bell Graham:

BORN in New Orleans, son of an African Methodist minister, I lived with my three brothers and one sister in a succession of parsonages as our father's assignments were changed. I attended public schools in Tennessee, Illinois, Colorado, and the state of Washington before being graduated from high school in Seattle.

Later while a student at the University of California at Los Angeles, I accepted a teaching position at Monrovia College in Africa.

In Africa my first serious interest in writing developed. I had gone to Africa believing I knew something about the land and its people. I learned that most of what I had read about "the Dark Continent" was not true. Popular writing had described savages, people who were at best stupid, lazy and amusing, at worst vicious, depraved and beastly. I concluded that the world needed books which described Africans honestly. Such books would make readers understand that different though they might be in custom and appearance, and in environment, Africans are people and they share with others around the world the same basic needs and drives and emotions, and the greatest of these is love.

It was some years later, back in the United States, that I realized that other books could speak on the popular level about Negroes in America. Such books could help to remove from American minds the stereotyped concepts. I was convinced that strife between people of different races is due primarily to lack of understanding of the very simple fact that people are people.

How God Fix Jonah is a collection of Bible stories told in the broken English and local idiom of West Africa.

Tales of Momolu is a book of short stories about the life of an African boy. Momolu lives within the culture of his people. He knows nothing of our civilization.

I, Momolu, published in 1966, is the story of the African boy emerging from the tribal culture of his interior village and viewing elements of our civilization.

South Town won the Follett Award with a gold medal and also the annual award of the Child Study Association of America for "a deeply moving story of a southern Negro family told with compassion and restraint."

North Town, sequel to *South Town,* describes problems and struggles toward adjustment of the Williams family after moving out of the South.

Whose Town?, published in 1969, shows David Williams, now eighteen years of age, dealing with sharp questions of duties and loyalties. He is moved by the call for black power. He hears people say, "This is a white man's town." He is asked, "Whose side are you on anyway?"

While raising a family I did educational and social work; my last employment was as a probation officer in Los Angeles with Watts as part of my assignment.

I now live in Los Angeles with my wife Ruth Morris Graham whom I first met in Africa. Mrs. Graham shares my interest in writing. Her book for young children, *The Happy Sound,* a picture of peasant life in Haiti, will be published soon. Both of us still enjoy travel. Together we have been back to Africa and other lands. We plan a round-the-world trip as our next venture.

The Thomas Alva Edison Foundation awarded a special citation for my Classics Illustrated adaptation of The Ten Commandments.

The Los Angeles City Council by resolution gave a beautiful scroll to me in 1966 "for invaluable contributions to advancing the study of Negro history."

The Association for the Study of Negro Life and History presented me the Wright Author's Award in 1967.

The Southern California Council on Literature for Children and Young People gave me an award in 1968 for "significant contribution to the field of literature for young people."

I hold the California teachers credential for English and history, and I am frequently called upon to speak to students and to professional organizations.

———

Lorenz Graham and Ruth Morris were married in 1929. Their children are Lorenz, Jr., Jean (deceased), Joyce (Mrs. Campbell C. Johnson), Ruth (Mrs. Herbert R. May), and Charles. Lorenz Graham attended the University of Washington, Seattle, the University of California, Los Angeles, and received an A.B. from Virginia Union University in 1936. He has also attended the New York School of Social Work, Columbia University, and New York University.

SELECTED WORKS: How God Fix Jonah, 1946; Tales of Momolu, 1946; The Ten Commandments, 1956; South Town, 1958; North Town, 1965; I, Momolu, 1966; Whose Town?, 1969; Every Man Heart Lay Down, 1970.

ABOUT: Contemporary Authors, Vol. 9-10.

ROGER LANCELYN GREEN
November 2, 1918-

AUTHOR OF *Tales of Ancient Egypt,* etc.

Autobiographical sketch of Roger Gilbert Lancelyn Green:

ALTHOUGH born at Norwich, where my father, a regular soldier, was stationed at the end of the First World War, I have lived since I can remember in an old country house in Cheshire on the estate which has belonged to my family since 1093 or earlier.

Poulton Hall, built on the site of the original Norman castle of the Lancelyns, is old and rambling—with dark attics and

Roger Lancelyn Green

mysterious cellars and passages. Here at Poulton-Lancelyn I spent nearly all my childhood as I was often ill and only managed a few terms of boarding school and a few more as a day-boy in Liverpool. In those days the Hall was still quite in the country, with fields and woods all round; there was no electricity; the carts and ploughs were still drawn by horses on the farm, and we were largely self-supporting on farm and garden produce.

This background influenced my earlier books which were adventure stories based on the life I had known at Poulton before 1939. When I returned here to live in 1950, with a wife and family, much of the land had gone, the way of life had changed completely, we were on the edge of a growing town, and we could only live in part of the house—the rest being let off in flats.

During the previous years I had spent most of my time at Oxford, taking a B.A. degree in 1940, M.A. and B. Litt. in 1944, and working as Deputy Librarian at Merton College 1945-50. I had also spent over a year as a professional actor (which included several months as a pirate in a tour of *Peter Pan*) and had worked for a time in an antiquarian bookshop, and tried—and failed—to be a schoolmaster.

On returning to Poulton-Lancelyn in 1950 I held a Research Fellowship for two years at Liverpool University, during which time I edited *The Diaries of Lewis Carroll*. And both before and since then I have varied the writing of children's books with biography and bibliography; authors on whom I have written books include Andrew Lang, A. E. W. Mason, Rudyard Kipling, Lewis Carroll and J. M. Barrie, and I am at present engaged on the official biography of C. S. Lewis, who was a close friend at Oxford and until his death.

My later books for children have mostly been inspired by my love of Greece and its legends and literature. I have visited and explored the country on more than a dozen occasions, and plan to go again this summer. Besides retelling the stories of ancient Greece I have written romances of my own based on them and firmly sited in the places I have visited: *Mystery at Mycenae, The Land Beyond the North* and *The Luck of Troy*.

But I have also entered the world of fantasy—*The Land of the Lord High Tiger* —which I wove for my own children out of fantasies made in my own childhood.

Roger Lancelyn Green, the son of Gilbert Arthur Lancelyn Green, a major in the Royal Field Artillery, and Helena Mary Phyllis Sealy Green, is hereditary Lord of the Manors of Poulton-Lancelyn and Lower Bebington. Like Lewis Carroll, about whom he has written, Roger Lancelyn Green had a stammer as a young man, which he discovered disappeared when talking to children. During his career as an actor the stammer disappeared permanently.

Green married June Burdett in 1948; their children are Scirard Roger Lancelyn, Priscilla June Lancelyn, and Richard Gordon Lancelyn.

Green held the William Noble Research Fellowship in English literature, Liverpool University, 1950-52. He is the author of more than fifty works of verse, fiction, mythology, and biography and has edited and written introductions to books by others. A frequent contributor to periodicals, he is also assistant editor of Dent's *Children's*

Illustrated Classics and editor of the *Kipling Journal*. His extensive travels have included Greece, Egypt, Persia, Iceland, and the United States.

Among the numerous organizations to which Green belongs are the Sherlock Holmes Society and the R. L. Stevenson Club. Green is editor and committee member of the Kipling Society and was secretary of Oxford University Dramatic Society, 1945.

SELECTED WORKS: J. M. Barrie, 1961; Heroes of Greece and Troy, 1961; Lewis Carroll, 1962; C. S. Lewis, 1963; Tellers of Tales, 1965; Tales from Shakespeare, 1965; Tales the Muses Told, 1965; Tales of Ancient Egypt, 1968; Tales of Ancient Israel, 1969; A Cavalcade of Dragons, 1970.

ABOUT: Author's and Writer's Who's Who, 1963; Burke's Landed Gentry, 1952; Contemporary Authors, Vol. 4.

ANN GRIFALCONI

September 22, 1929-

AUTHOR AND ILLUSTRATOR OF *City Rhythms*, etc.

Autobiographical sketch of Ann Grifalconi:

HAVING been a city child going to public schools, I have always naturally played and studied and argued with and sung with all races and all sorts of people, more often poor than rich. We never thought about color as any sort of problem, more as a note of grace, a special sort of beauty. Having been lucky enough to have a mother that saw things the same way, we (my brother and I), were also lucky that she moved us near the schools of our own choice and aptitude (downtown Manhattan, 16 and 17th streets), near Washington Irving, where I studied art, and Stuyvesant High School, where John studied for an eventual architectural and city-planning career. We both went on to colleges in the city, too; I went to Cooper Union Art School and John first went into the Navy, then returned to go to Columbia.

After having lived tightly through the depression, and somehow managing to remain cheerful, healthy and relatively creative, we all left New York the year I graduated from Cooper Union. The three of us, John, mother and I, went to Cincinnati for a while, John to stay for many years and make his home and career there, mother to stay for a few years and return to New York later, and I to return to New York in two years to complete my B.S. at New York University in order to teach art.

Since then, we've all been doing our own thing, which for me was teaching art in the junior and senior high schools of New York, and to adults for two years at night, varied and interesting experiences for me. After four or five years of teaching, I began work as the co-author of a travel book about my experiences camping through Europe by car. Then I began to get back into illustration which had always been my first love (and which I hadn't had the stamina to stick to when I first took my portfolio around after I left Cooper Union). And now I was glad I hadn't begun then, when I was still under the many influences a student carries with him. I still had had a lot of living to do, a lot to learn about other people, about *their* insides, too. Probably teaching was the very best thing—for it changed my point of view, let me deal with

Grifalconi: *GREE fal koh nee*

so many different sizes and sorts of people and problems—gave me a deep appreciation of all the wonder of a child's mind, and the hurts, and ways to begin to heal the hurts. It helped me to deal with difficult situations with a certain calm and directness that is a big help to me in the new educational media business I'm in now. It taught me about the delicacy of relationships that children have with one another, their ability to "sniff out" false attitudes, to correct false assumptions.

Finally, after teaching, my illustration and a bit of writing, I took a leave of absence and have never gone back. But my interest in teaching never quite left, it just changed form. I tried never to illustrate a book that I did not believe in.

I had noticed when I was planning the art for *City Rhythms* that I saw it as a sequence, sort of a movie. It began with a boy looking down over the city from his high apartment window, and following him down into the busy, noisy street, ended with an even more distant view of him, tiny below, and rising up above him all the apartments, the sky above, the flying birds—the total feeling he had now of *all* the city, known as á whole.

This feeling for pictures telling a story as a *related* sequence fascinates me. As I began to use the color camera after a year or so of black and white studies, I realized that no one picture had the interest for me which a natural sequence did not strengthen: groups of pictures ramified, enhanced the story—for after all, it was the story I was trying to build. Since the story was of our time, my own natural interest and concern about integration found its way both into the books I was illustrating and the photographs I took. I began a large project with a writer and friend who is now my partner, on the black and white experience in America, comparing important black and white American contributions to our common past. It was called *Men of Thought, Men of Action* and after traveling and researching it for over two years, we finished a nine-part series of sound and color filmstrips that we felt told at least a part of the story of America in a new and balanced way. Comparing great Americans like Banneker and Franklin, Frederick Douglass and Thoreau as they saw and acted in their time, bringing it all up to date through King, Malcolm X, the Kennedys, we felt we might have begun to change some attitudes about the real and three-dimensional story of America. We felt, being both black and white ourselves, that we could offer a balanced point of view.

After Doubleday agreed to distribute this series (MTMA) we both decided this could be an important new way of reaching students of any age, so we began a number of projects on our own again, this time deciding to distribute the films and multi-media filmstrips ourselves.

Looking back over the books that I have most enjoyed doing, I find they were the ones that had great beauty and style in writing (for I am an old reader from way back; as a kid I spent most of my time reading—sometimes four books a day). I love words and the way they're strung together, the song, the imagery. I love doing woodcuts most of all, and do, whenever the book calls for it. Then I love to do free, loose, line drawings and line and wash, too, as I did for some delightful Chekhov stories. As a person who's been trained in the technical aspects of reproduction, I do get a certain charge out of doing my own separations for two- and three-color books.

The book that really got me into woodcuts as illustrations (I had been doing them before for pleasure) was my mother Mary Hays Weik's *The Jazz Man*. This started from her seeing a woodcut of mine of a piano player, and then my reading her beautifully textured story about the little boy Zeke and the Jazz Man. Much ahead of its time, that book was a loving collaboration by both of us that finally was given its due (runner-up for the 1967 Newbery) and is now, I feel, a classic, in its very own special way.

———

Ann Grifalconi took her B.S. from New York University in 1954. *The Jazz Man* was named by the New York *Times* as one of the ten best-illustrated books of 1966. Miss Grifalconi's work has been exhibited by the American Institute of Graphic Arts.

SELECTED WORKS WRITTEN AND ILLUSTRATED: City Rhythms, 1965; The Toy Trumpet, 1968.

SELECTED WORKS ILLUSTRATED: The Jazz Man, by Mary Hays Weik, 1966; Pepito, by Nathan

Zimelman, 1966; The Africans Knew, by Tillie S. Pine and Joseph Levine, 1967; Special Bravery, by Johanna Johnston, 1967; The Ballad of the Burglar of Babylon, by Elizabeth Bishop, 1968; Don't You Turn Back, poems by Langston Hughes, edited by Lee Bennett Hopkins, 1969.

ABOUT: Contemporary Authors, Vol. 7-8; Hopkins, Lee Bennett. Books Are by People; Kingman, Lee and others, comps. Illustrators of Children's Books: 1957-1966.

MARIA GRIPE

1923-

AUTHOR OF *Pappa Pellerin's Daughter,* etc.

Autobiographical sketch of Maria Gripe:

I MUST confess that I have always felt reluctant to be in the limelight and to report about myself as a writer. To my way of thinking a writer is a person with a special need for expressing himself and communicating with others anonymously. In writing mainly for children as I have been doing, the feeling of anonymity is of even greater value since children, unless diversely influenced by some adult, will rarely be spontaneously curious concerning the person who wrote their books. Authors don't mean anything to them, only books do, a great advantage to the writer. As a child I considered it tactless when a grown-up showed me a newspaper picture of the author of one of my favorite books. I looked at the picture with distrust and displeasure. I did not want to know how books were written—just to think that *ordinary* women and men were sitting there *dreaming up* stories. How terrible: it took away the enigma of the written word, killed the whole mystery of the book.

On the other hand I was never disturbed by the author's name on the book, not even by pictures or introductions on the back cover. I interpreted them as some kind of label belonging to the makeup of the book, just as license plates belong on cars, without any connection at all with the creation of the book. At that time I did not know of any authors except Hans Christian Andersen. Hans Christian Andersen was a continuing subject in our family. In my father's opinion nobody else was worthy of being called an

author. Thus I could never think of becoming an author. In spite of all that, I did write quite often, I am sorry to say.

As a rule I was very careful to hide my writings, but one day coming home from school, I saw my father—1.97 meters (six feet five) in his stocking feet—bent over the blue composition book in which I had written my latest deep thoughts. I was filled with a mixture of shame and expectation. Calmly he looked at me with his big, square, blue eyes, shook his head and said seriously: "This is horrible, Maria!" Then he told me that if I wanted to write, I would have to have something to write about, and that it would probably take a long time before that happened, but that, in the meantime, I could always learn how to use my Swedish. From then on I wrote occasionally—mostly in order to improve my Swedish. In the meantime I finished high school and studied at the university for a couple of years—philosophy and history of religion—but did not graduate. Instead I got married and had a daughter, who by and by wanted books read aloud to her. It turned out to be expensive, so I started making up stories for her, and, quite naturally, my husband, who is an artist, made the sketches for them. Life's little ironies! I, who had firmly insisted

Gripe: *GREE puh*

that the author should be anonymous to the reader! My daughter never thought of me as a real author, though.

Another thing: people want to believe that you are identical with your characters. When I tell about Josephine (in the series of *Hugo and Josephine*) they think I am indulging in memories of my childhood. Wrong. I am neither Josephine nor Loella (in *Pappa Pellerin's Daughter*) nor Julia (in *The Night Daddy*) nor anybody else. But I cannot deny that some part of me has to be in all of my characters. There is as much of myself in the horrible nurse Nana (in *The Glassblower's Children*) as there is in Josephine. My presence in the books has a function different from identifying with any of the principal characters. And probably, up to now, *The Glassblower's Children* has been the book with which I have felt most at home. Also, illustrating this book gave more pleasure to my husband than any of the others, and it shows! The illustrations follow the changing mood of the text, but also succeed in giving the book that extra dimension, always aimed at but very rarely reached.

Maria Gripe's books have been translated into nine languages and have won a number of awards, among which were the Nils Holgersson Plaque for her two Hugo and Josephine books, 1963, the "Heffalump" awarded by the Swedish newspaper *Expressen* for *Hugo*, 1966, and a Lewis Carroll Shelf Award for *Pappa Pellerin's Daughter*, 1966.

She is married to Harald Gripe, the artist, who has illustrated fourteen of her books.

SELECTED WORKS: Pappa Pellerin's Daughter, 1966; Hugo and Josephine, 1969; Hugo, 1970; Josephine, 1970; The Night Daddy, 1971.

LEO GURKO

LEO GURKO

January 4, 1914-

AUTHOR OF *Tom Paine, Freedom's Apostle,* etc.

Autobiographical sketch of Leo Gurko:

I WAS born in Warsaw, Poland. My mother brought me to New York in the summer of 1917; the train we took from Poland was the last allowed by the Germans to leave Eastern Europe. When my father joined us after the war, we moved to Hamtramck, Michigan, where I went to the public schools and graduated from Hamtramck High School. As a boy, I was studious, lonely, and bored, and developed a mad passion for baseball. My first ambition was to be a first-baseman for the Detroit Tigers. Then I read the novels of E. Phillips Oppenheim and longed to be first a diplomat, then an espionage agent, then a foreign correspondent.

Instead I went to the College of the City of Detroit where I got a B.A. in 1931 and to the University of Wisconsin where I received a Ph.D. in comparative literature in 1934. At Madison, I met my wife. We had a campus romance and were married in 1934.

We came East at the bottom of the depression. I free-lanced as an editor, reviewer, and translator for five years before returning to academic life as an instructor in English at Hunter College. I am now a professor of English there, with a special interest in twentieth-century literature. In the 1950s, during the early years of television, I was a regular guest on a TV show called The Author Meets the Critics. In 1953-54, I spent a year in Europe with my wife and two children, on a Ford Foundation grant. From 1954-1960 I served as chairman of the English department. My career as a writer for younger readers began at the invitation of a former student who invited me in 1956 to do a life of Tom Paine. I have written three books of literary criticism for adults as well as three biographies for younger readers.

We live in a Riverside Drive apartment during the winter and in a country house fifty miles from New York in the summer. My avocations, unchanged over the years, are tennis, bridge, and professional sports.

Leo Gurko was on the editorial staff of G. P. Putnam's Sons, 1934-36, and was a publisher's reader for Macmillan, 1936-62. He had a Dodd, Mead faculty fellowship in 1946. His Ford Foundation fellowship was from the Fund for the Advancement of Education.

Gurko is a member of the Modern Language Association, the National Council of Teachers of English, and the American Association of University Professors. His book *Tom Paine* was a runner-up for the Newbery Medal for 1958.

SELECTED WORKS: Tom Paine, Freedom's Apostle, 1957; The Two Lives of Joseph Conrad, 1965; Ernest Hemingway and the Pursuit of Heroism, 1968.

ABOUT: Contemporary Authors, Vol. 5-6; Directory of American Scholars, Vol. II, 5th edition; Who's Who in America, 1970-71.

MIRIAM GURKO

AUTHOR OF *The Lives and Times of Peter Cooper*, etc.

Autobiographical sketch of Miriam Berwitz Gurko:

I SUPPOSE in the back of my mind there was always the feeling that I would someday become a writer; when I finally did begin to write, it seemed the most natural thing in the world. There were some typical preliminaries: an essay in the fourth or fifth grade on the assigned subject of "what I would like to be when I grow up" contained my reasons (long since forgotten) for planning to be a writer; I contributed the usual poems, essays, and short stories to my high school and college publications.

The high school was in Union Hill (now Union City), New Jersey, where I was born.

MIRIAM GURKO

College was first New York University, then after a year as a regular student I switched to an evening program, with a full-time job in the Dean's office during the day. The following year I quit college altogether and went to work for the Institute of Persian Art and Archaeology. After a year (my experience divides itself neatly into year-sized packages), I went back to college, this time to the University of Wisconsin, where I majored in history and anthropology. It was at Wisconsin that I met and married a graduate student, Leo Gurko.

After graduation we came to New York, where I had a series of jobs doing various editorial, research, and promotional chores. I worked, in turn, for a publishing house which specialized in books on American history, a magazine on economics, on the publications of Phi Beta Kappa, and finally on a research and publishing project studying the family. After a year at this last job, I "retired" in order to raise my own family—two children, Steve and Jane. Steve is now practicing law in Denver, Jane is teaching English at San Francisco State.

I soon found, however, that the domestic life was not quite enough and decided to do a bit of free-lance writing. After publishing several articles, mostly on children and homemaking, I became dissatisfied with this form of writing. I enjoyed the process of composition but felt that I had not found the form or subject which would suit me best. I began experimenting with other fields. Then one day my husband, who had just finished his first book for younger readers, suggested that I might enjoy writing for that age group. He was right. The whole process of presenting a subject—no matter how complex—to younger readers is one that I find thoroughly pleasurable. In doing the research for my books, I find myself constantly seeing even the most familiar subject or historical period through the fresh eyes of a young person. I find myself taking nothing for granted, but asking why? or how? Even the style in which I believe such books should be written—clear, straightforward, carefully organized—is one in which I most prefer to work.

Miriam Berwitz married Leo Gurko in 1934 and took her B.A. from the University of Wisconsin the same year. She is a member of Phi Beta Kappa and of the Authors Guild of the Authors League of America. *Restless Spirit* was named by the New York *Times* in 1966 as one of the fifty best children's books of the preceding five years.

SELECTED WORKS: The Lives and Times of Peter Cooper, 1959; Restless Spirit: The Life of Edna St. Vincent Millay, 1962; Clarence Darrow, 1965; Indian America: The Black Hawk War, 1970.

ABOUT: Contemporary Authors, Vol. 4.

IRENE HAAS

June 5, 1929-

ILLUSTRATOR OF *Zeee*, etc.

Autobiographical sketch of Irene Haas Clark:

WHEN I grew up in a New York suburb, in the 1930s and 40s, there was always plenty of time to think, to be lazy, to dream, and to be alone. There were long days of imaginative play, free from adult supervision. We had a kind of theater, with a big cast of neighborhood children playing complicated roles in long adventures. You could be someone else, somewhere else, for hours and hours. What nourishment for a young imagination to grow on!

In high school, I worked hard at being the class "longhair," and jealously ruled over all

artistic projects, like the school magazines. Then I went to Pratt Institute and after that, inevitably, to what was the finishing school for most young New York artists, the Art Students League. While there, I worked at etching and lithography and discovered my affinity for linear graphic work.

Later, there were some interesting years doing theater design, in the summers, and decorative design work for fabrics and wallpaper and china. Then as a free-lance illustrator I had some success working for magazines, designing record album covers and posters and making advertising illustrations.

One day my work was shown to Margaret McElderry at Harcourt, Brace & World, and I was happily where I belonged, making books for children and sharing my pleasure.

I like to work closely with the authors of my books and have some precious associations to remember, but the ones I recall with most joy were the two books I did with Elizabeth Enright, *Tatsinda* and *Zeee*. It was an exciting challenge to try to match in pictures, as faithfully as I could, some of the loveliest images ever written for children.

Having always illustrated books written by others, I tried recently to write one for myself. Illustrating is a natural thing to me after so many years, but writing requires a differ-

Haas: *HAHS*

ent kind of involvement and concentration. I had a hard time.

Then I remembered something from my childhood—a story I made for myself when I was about eight years old. It was such a good, satisfying tale then that I wrote it out, illustrated it, and bound it into a book. I let my friends share my pleasure in it for a penny a reading. Now thirty years later, the story still seems good.

In remembering the story from my childhood, I regained the longing that makes artists of all ages want to make up stories and tell them to others. I realized that all my life I had had it in my heart to make books.

This kind of remembering is a special quality belonging to artists who work for children. They have a tenderness and respect for themselves as children. They remember old feelings and can feel them all over again.

I now have two very young children, and since their arrival there has not been much time to work. But I've discovered that I've been drawing my children accurately in most of my books for years before I'd even met them! It will be interesting to see if the busy, protected lives these children lead, in a world so changed from the one I knew as a child, will give them time to develop their own special gifts, as mine did.

We now live in an apartment in Manhattan. My husband, Philip Clark, is a partner in a banking firm and he supplies the essential balance for our children, James and Jo Ann. We hope they will love "the way things might be" and also "the way things really are."

_____

Irene Haas's work has been in the New York *Herald Tribune* Children's Spring Book Festival and in a number of exhibitions of the American Institute of Graphic Arts. Two of her books have been named among the ten best-illustrated of the year by the New York *Times Book Review*: *A Little House of Your Own*, in 1955 and *Was It a Good Trade?* in 1956.

SELECTED WORKS ILLUSTRATED: The Mysterious Leaf, by Richard Banks, 1954; A Little House of Your Own, by Beatrice Schenk de Regniers, 1955; Was It a Good Trade? by Beatrice Schenk de Regniers, 1956; There Is a Dragon in my Bed, by Sesyle Joslin, 1961; Tatsinda, by Elizabeth Enright, 1963; Zeee, by Elizabeth Enright, 1965.

ABOUT: Kingman, Lee and others, comps. Illustrators of Children's Books: 1957-1966; Viguers, Ruth Hill and others, comps. Illustrators of Children's Books: 1946-1956.

GAIL E. HALEY

November 4, 1939-

AUTHOR AND ILLUSTRATOR OF *A Story, A Story*, etc.

Autobiographical sketch of Gail Einhart Haley Arnold:

I WAS born in Charlotte, North Carolina. When I was two years old, we moved to Shuffletown, an old-time rural village "just down the road a piece from Mole Hill." Our neighbors ploughed with mules, and drew their drinking water by hand from wells. The women held quilting bees, wore poke bonnets, and saved feed sacks for making dresses, curtains, or children's stuffed toys. The way of life I saw there was simple and beautiful, if difficult.

There were no children my age for miles, so I spent much of my time wandering barefoot through woods and fields. Fantasy and reality were interchangeable in my world, largely because I was alone most of the time. There was time for dreaming, exploring, reading and drawing.

Nature, the abundant wildlife around me, and the fairies, heroes and villains of my books were equally real to me.

My father, then art director of the Charlotte *Observer*, used to let me visit him at the newspaper. In the art department and pressrooms I soaked up the exciting smells and sounds of the graphic arts. I've had printer's ink and rubber cement in my veins ever since.

All my time (even sometimes in class) was spent writing or drawing. I was fascinated by the idea of making the two work together. After graduating from high school, I attended art courses at Richmond Professional Institute. Next I studied graphics and painting at the University of Virginia. Here the artist, Charles Smith, was my teacher. I owe him a great debt of gratitude. He encouraged my first serious attempt to write and illustrate a children's book. It was called *My Kingdom*

for a Dragon and was printed from my wood blocks. I bound and sold most of the limited edition of 1,000 myself. It was the first fulfillment of my lifelong desire to write and illustrate children's books. But I still had a period of apprenticeship before me. I illustrated books by six authors before I was able to sell my own first manuscript.

I prefer to write and illustrate my own books. I work back and forth between text and design until they complement one another. Even the type must work as part of the interrelated whole. I see each page as a highlight in a sequence of events. Not everything is pictured or described, so that the reader is stimulated to fill in the gaps out of his own imagination and experience, losing himself, entering story and pictures as a participant.

I am not committed to any particular style of illustration, preferring to let the technique emerge from the character of the story. For example, I chose woodcuts as the most appropriate medium for *A Story, A Story*, because this more than any other technique captures the spirit of African artifacts. I cut the blocks myself, and printed them in my print shop—one block for each color. I spent about a year researching the story, absorbing

African culture—art, music and dance—before beginning the finished art, which took me another year.

I am married to a very talented man, Arnold Arnold. He writes books for and about children, and a nationally syndicated column, "Parents and Children." He is also an artist and designer, and once had a show of his toys at New York's Museum of Modern Art. We are interested in all facets of child lore and culture. We also collect old children's books and toys; our collection is now housed in Jacksonville (Florida) Children's Museum. We love boats, the sea, and traveling, and plan some day to live on a large sailboat. Our two children, Marguerite and Geoffrey, come along wherever we go, and share our enthusiasms.

I consider myself most fortunate to have the opportunity to write and illustrate children's books—to be permitted to live in the special world of childhood even as an adult. I am surrounded by children: my own and their friends, and those I create for my books and stories. I observe them, listen to them, talk to them, play with them, and help them make things. Sometimes I make presents for them.

My books, especially, are intended as presents to awaken my own children, and others whom I shall never meet, to reality and fantasy. I also address my books to all adults who recall and cherish their childhood.

Gail E. Haley is the daughter of George C. and P. Louise (Bell) Einhart. In 1959, she married Joseph A. Haley, a mathematician. She married her second husband, Arnold F. Arnold, in 1966. They live and work in New York City.

Gail E. Haley received the Caldecott Medal for *A Story, A Story* in 1971.

SELECTED WORKS WRITTEN AND ILLUSTRATED: The Wonderful Magical World of Marguerite, 1964; Round Stories About Things That Live on Land, 1966; Round Stories About Things That Live in Water, 1966; Round Stories About Things That Grow, 1966; Round Stories About Our World, 1966; A Story, A Story, 1970; Noah's Ark, 1971.

ABOUT: Contemporary Authors, Vol. 21-22; Horn Book August 1971; Top of the News April 1971.

CYNTHIA HARNETT
June 22, 1893-

AUTHOR AND ILLUSTRATOR OF *Nicholas and the Woolpack*, etc.

Autobiographical sketch of Cynthia Mary Harnett:

IN this swiftly changing world to have lived one's childhood in Queen Victoria's reign makes one almost a part of history. I was born in Kensington, London, when the old Queen had still some years to live. She too had been born in Kensington, at Kensington Palace, and in her old age sometimes enjoyed an afternoon drive in that direction—a little old lady all in black in a carriage and pair escorted only by a couple of mounted policemen. I saw her often and loved her possessively, weeping genuine tears when, shortly before my eighth birthday, they told me she was dead.

History for me in those days was a magic word. Even before that eighth birthday I had been permitted to tag along behind a much older brother who had a passion for anything historical. He told me endless stories as we explored ruined castles and old churches, making rubbings of the brasses of mediaeval people and taking note of the coats of arms on the tombs of knights and their ladies. My brother wrote historical stories and so of course I had to write stories too. I remember that I received sixpence for any which were actually finished.

But childhood passes. A polite Edwardian boarding school reduced history to the dullest of subjects and the war of 1914-1918 finally wiped out all childish games. After the war I took to painting and worked at the Chelsea School of Art. But the need for honest pennies which art did not provide led back to writing —magazine stories with modern settings—as history was out of fashion. Then I joined an artist cousin, G. Vernon Stokes, in producing children's books for which we jointly concocted the story and jointly drew the pictures. This was fun but still it was not history.

It was not until after the Second World War that I was moved by a consuming desire to make other children enjoy what had been such a joy to me. But how? The average historical thriller left me cold, but what else was there? Then one day a friend said casually, "Why are there so few historical novels about *ordinary* people, people like you and me; how they lived and how they coped with their problems?"

That settled it. I knew what to do. I would write historical stories about ordinary children. I would return, sketch book in hand, to the old game of exploring to find how they had lived and what adventures they could have had.

The first was *The Great House*, about the children of an architect who, in 1690, was pulling down old timber houses to build modern brick ones. Next came *The Wool-Pack*, about a wool merchant of the fifteenth century whose young son unearths a trade plot to ruin his father.

So it went on and still goes on. I live in a thatched cottage old enough to be useful for illustrations, and the three strands of my life have at long last intertwined—writing, drawing and history.

———

Cynthia Harnett was awarded the Carnegie Medal for *The Wool-Pack*, 1951 (published in the United States as *Nicholas and the Woolpack*). She served in British Censorship during both world wars. Her hobbies include painting, music, gardening, heraldry, and exploring historic places and tombs.

SELECTED WORKS WRITTEN AND ILLUSTRATED: Nicholas and the Woolpack, 1953; The Drawbridge Gate, 1954; Stars of Fortune, 1956; Caxton's Challenge, 1960; A Fifteenth Century Wool Merchant, 1962; The Great House, 1968 (publication in England, 1949).

ABOUT: Author's and Writer's Who's Who, 1963; Contemporary Authors, Vol. 9-10; Viguers, Ruth Hill and others, comps. Illustrators of Children's Books: 1946-1956; Library Association Record April 1952.

ERIK CHRISTIAN HAUGAARD

April 13, 1923-

AUTHOR OF *The Rider and His Horse*, etc.

Autobiographical sketch of Erik Christian Haugaard:

MY birth certificate tells that I was born on April 13th (It was a Friday!), in Copenhagen, Denmark. It is hearsay which I won't vouch for since I cannot remember anything about the event. I prefer to think that I was born in that castle which lies east of the sun and west of the moon. As playmates, I had the winds who told me stories of the real world: of kings and wizards, witches and trolls.

I moved from this castle made of solid substance, like dreams and that part of the night which hides in the day, to a flimsy brick house in the suburbs of Copenhagen, when I was six and started school. It had a garden too small for imagination and just right for pretension. Like every other middle-class child in Denmark, I went to dancing school, dressed as a sailor; I have never danced since. Ordinary school I hated with such a passion that it was rewarded with my being allowed to leave when I was fifteen. Then I set out to search for my castle; the directions seemed quite clear. For two years I worked trying to learn farming; from this I gained a knowledge of the sunrise and the ways of horses. My parents, in the meantime, had sold their brick house and moved to America. I followed them, thinking that America was, if not east

of the sun, at least west of the moon. I spent three months bicycling from California to Montana, which taught me something about the nature of the stars, when you are alone in the night. I was in the South for two years, in a place called Black Mountain. It was a peculiar college. In the center of the campus there was a lake called Lake Eden; it was filled with snakes and toads, and we used to swim in it. I was taught something there about the nature of knowledge and the dustiness of roads.

World War II, during which I was an air gunner in the Royal Canadian Air Force, repeated lessons which I already knew. A war is a school for dunces, where the headmaster carries a whip. After the war, I continued the study of the useless things that a poet must know. I married to find out whether love could survive intimacy—it can. I have two children and have bought an old brick house with a garden just big enough for a few birds' nests. Still I travel, both east and west, and feel sad when the wind tells stories to my children that I can no longer hear.

I know that I shall never return to the castle I was born in, before the ghosts of age and time are dead. I write my books because birds must sing, as dogs are meant to bark. I write for children who were born east of the

Haugaard: *HOW gard*

sun and west of the moon, to comfort them for they are lonely and cannot find their way home.

Haugaard became a flight sergeant during the war and received a War Service Medal from Christian X of Denmark. He studied at the New School for Social Research, 1947-1948. In 1949 he married Myrna Seld, now a writer, and their children are Mikka Anja and Mark. He has translated Eskimo poetry collected by Knud Rasmussen, for *American-Scandinavian Review.* For his play *The Heroes,* he received a John Golden Fund fellowship in 1958, and his *Hakon of Rogen's Saga* was an Honor Book in the New York *Herald Tribune* Children's Spring Book Festival, 1963. *The Little Fishes* won the Boston *Globe-Horn Book* Award and a *Book World* Children's Spring Book Festival Award, both in 1967, and the Jane Addams Book Award in 1968.

SELECTED WORKS: Hakon of Rogen's Saga, 1963; A Slave's Tale, 1965; Orphans of the Wind, 1966; The Little Fishes, 1967; The Rider and His Horse, 1968.

ABOUT: Contemporary Authors, Vol. 7-8.

ESTHER HAUTZIG

October 18, 1930-

AUTHOR OF *The Endless Steppe,* etc.

Autobiographical sketch of Esther Rudomin Hautzig:

I ALWAYS dreamt of becoming a writer, the way many children want to become movie stars or ballerinas, sports heroes or firemen. My dreams began in Vilna, a beautiful city which frequently changed "hands" but which was Polish when I was born in 1930. Though an only child I never felt lonely. We lived in what would now be called a family compound, since all of my father's large family lived in one house, in separate apartments surrounding an inner garden. It was a perfect childhood in every way, until the Second World War broke out. In 1941 the Russians, who had by then occupied Vilna, deported us to Siberia as capitalists and "enemies of the people." After some five and a half difficult years in Rubtsovsk, where I nevertheless went

to school, found friends and even laughter, we were allowed to return to Poland. Nine months later we went to Sweden to await entry visas to the United States. I arrived alone in New York in 1947, to live with an uncle whom I did not know. My parents followed later.

Even during all these upheavals I dreamt of becoming a writer and sometimes, almost miraculously, my dreams became reality. I contributed to and then edited the school paper in Siberia; during my year at Madison High School in New York, from which I graduated in 1948, I wrote a story on Siberia for the school literary magazine; and at Hunter College I contributed articles to the college paper.

In 1950, after two years of college, I married Walter Hautzig, a concert pianist, whom I met on the boat when I was emigrating and he was returning from his first concert tour of Europe. After our marriage I decided not to return to Hunter in favor of a job. I was dead sure that such a job had to be in some way

Hautzig: *HOW tzig*

connected with books. In a subconscious way, perhaps, I felt that by being around people who wrote books, or published them, I would be closer to becoming a writer. The good Lord was with me—I landed a job as a secretary in a publishing house. I was a miserable typist, and an even worse stenographer, but I had a kind boss and I worked hard. After two years there I moved on to the Children's Book Council, where I ended up doing promotion and believed myself in heaven. Subsequently I became director of promotion of children's books in a publishing house, which was exciting, stimulating, and time-consuming. But despite, or perhaps because of, the rigors of my job I got an idea for a book. One hot July evening on the bus, I thought "If only there was a book with recipes which needed no cooking. . ." Bingo! That was the subject of my first book, *Let's Cook Without Cooking* (written under my maiden name, Rudomin). My next two books reflected my interest and pleasure in working with my hands *Let's Make Presents* and *Redecorating Your Room for Practically Nothing*. For some nine years I also worked, on and off, on *The Endless Steppe*, the story of our Siberian years. Three quadrilingual picture books, *In the Park, At Home* and *In School*, for which I wrote the texts have given me particular pleasure.

All in all I feel that my dreams have come true, though there were many times when I wanted instead to become a theater projectionist (I love movies) or a laundress (I love ironing) or a pastry chef (I love baking—on a cool day!)

We have two children, Debbie and David, who love books. My husband's profession provides us with endless opportunities to hear good music, and to be armchair travelers as we follow on maps all the places where he plays. We live in a big apartment house in New York, from which we can see slivers of the Hudson River. We also have a house in upper New York state, with a birch grove in the front yard and a pond which reflects it— and where we reflect and relax, too.

———

Esther Hautzig's *The Endless Steppe,* which was nominated for the National Book Awards for 1969, received the Jane Addams Book Award, 1970 and a Lewis Carroll Shelf Award, 1971.

SELECTED WORKS: Let's Cook Without Cooking, 1955; Let's Make Presents: 100 Easy-to-Make Gifts under $1.00, 1962; Redecorating Your Room for Practically Nothing, 1967; The Endless Steppe, 1968; At Home: A Visit in Four Languages, 1968; In the Park, 1968; In School, 1969.

ABOUT: Contemporary Authors, Vol. 2; Publishers' Weekly February 17, 1969; Horn Book October 1970.

WILMA PITCHFORD HAYS

November 22, 1909-

AUTHOR OF *Pilgrim Thanksgiving*, etc.

Autobiographical sketch of Wilma Pitchford Hays:

A LONG time ago my Celtic ancestors must have been bards, for I came of a family of storytellers. Imagination played its part, yet the true facts and adventures of early members of our family who first settled young America were always intensely interesting to me. I grew up with a strong sense of being a part of history. When I began to research and to write books for children, historians provided accuracy. The *feeling* for the times, and the people who lived in them, was already a part of me.

In my cradle I heard the folk songs of the Britons: English, Irish, Scotch and Welsh. Before I went to school I knew the Daniel Boone and Abraham Lincoln families. A grandfather, way back, had served in the Revolutionary War with Daniel, and my grandmother had been named in memory of two of Daniel's daughters. A great uncle was part of a twelve-man militia with Tom Lincoln, in Hardin County, Kentucky, when Abe was born.

As a child, when I visited Grandma Pitchford, I waked early to run and climb in bed with her and beg for a *real* story. She was extravagant with affection, could make any garden grow, would own only spirited thoroughbred horses, and loved kin and God, in that order. Grandma had lived, as a girl, on the border between the South and North during the Civil War, and her father often had to hide in the woods from bushwhackers. Parts of her true stories are in *The Scarlet Badge* and *Abe Lincoln's Birthday*.

Wilma Pitchford Hays

My other grandmother, Grandma Lull, was part French with the French frugality, love of knowledge and of beauty. She lived with us, and was always ready to improve our minds by reading aloud an article if we were trapped by a chore like ironing. She had saved pictures, newspaper clippings and letters telling of her great-grandfather, twelve-year-old Peter Demo, drummer boy at the battle for Quebec in 1759. My *Drummer Boy for Montcalm* is Peter's story.

In 1955, *Pilgrim Thanksgiving*, the first of my eleven holiday books, was published. Previously I had written perhaps a hundred fiction and nonfiction stories for adult magazines. I have written nothing but books for children since my husband, R. Vernon Hays, a superintendent of schools, asked me to write a book which would give children the feel of having been at the Thanksgiving celebration. After months of reading/original sources, Bradford's own journal, Winslow's letters, I found the Pilgrims were young people and very human. I have written four books about them.

In *Rebel Pilgrim*, a recent biography of William Bradford, I stressed the hardships, courage and unwavering leadership which helped the Pilgrims survive. In books for younger children, fear and deprivation were

tempered by the adventure, excitement and day-by-day pleasures which the Pilgrims enjoyed (*Christmas on the Mayflower, Naughty Little Pilgrim*).

As the oldest of six children, I tried to pass along to my sisters and brothers the family stories and genuine love for this country and its people. I have lived in many parts of the United States; born in Nance County, Nebraska, lived a year in South Dakota near the Rosebud Indian Reservation (my mother says I spoke Sioux before I spoke English), was graduated from the high school at Fullerton, Nebraska, attended the University of Nebraska, taught rural school, lived at Cambridge, Massachusetts, while my husband earned a degree at the Harvard Graduate School, lived on Cape Cod, in Connecticut and Florida. I have visited all the states of the union except Alaska. This interest in places and people went into my seven regional books based on true experiences: *Little Horse That Raced a Train, The Pup Who Became a Police Dog, That Burro Pinto Jack* and others.

To date several different publishers have brought out thirty-one of my books, three of which have been Junior Literary Guild choices. I am writing a book about the circus since I now live in Venice, Florida, the winter headquarters of the Ringling Brothers Circus.

Each summer my husband and I return to Connecticut where I research at Yale Sterling and the New Haven libraries, talk with editors about future books, and very important, visit our daughter and three grandchildren; David, four, Stephen, three, and Susanna, one year old. At bedtime they ask for books to be read to them and *real* stories told, so I may soon be writing picture books!

Whether in Florida, Connecticut or Cape Cod, I love to walk along the seashore. The sound of the waves relaxes me and also stimulates my thoughts. Some of my best books are planned while I pick up shells and, if no one is near, sing songs I make up myself for the fun of it.

———

Wilma Pitchford Hays has lectured frequently at book fairs in New York, Boston and elsewhere, and at many conferences of teachers and librarians. She has also taught the Juvenile Writing Course at Cape Cod Writers Conference.

SELECTED WORKS: Pilgrim Thanksgiving 1955; Christmas on the Mayflower, 1956; Drummer Boy for Montcalm, 1959; Little Horse That Raced a Train, 1959; The Scarlet Badge, 1963; The Pup Who Became a Police Dog, 1963; Pontiac: Lion in the Forest, 1965; The Apricot Tree, 1968; Rebel Pilgrim, 1969; Naughty Little Pilgrim, 1969; Patrick of Ireland, 1970; Circus Girl Without a Name, 1970.

ABOUT: Contemporary Authors, Vol. 1; Something About the Author, Vol. 1; Who's Who of American Women, 1961-62.

NAT HENTOFF

June 10, 1925-

AUTHOR OF *Jazz Country,* etc.

Autobiographical sketch of Nathan Irving Hentoff:

I WAS born in Boston, and if I had to associate one word with my childhood instantly, I suppose it would be "books." The trip to the public library every Friday was really quite on a par with the weekly trip to the movies the next day. (McLuhan notwithstanding, one experience does not supplant the other.) The concept, however, of being an author of a book—of having my name on one of those index cards—seemed as fanciful as my being a sideman in Duke Ellington's band, another dream of those years. It was jazz though which led me to become a writer. After being graduated from Boston Latin School and Northeastern University, with some graduate work at Harvard and the Sorbonne, I went into radio in Boston and started to write on jazz after hours for *Down Beat*. In 1953, I became New York editor of that publication but left four years later to free-lance. My first books were about jazz, and they have been succeeded by works on civil rights (*The New Equality*), radical pacifism (*Peace Agitator: The Story of A. J. Muste*), urban education (*Our Children Are Dying*) and addiction (*A Doctor Among the Addicts*), among other subjects. There have also been two novels for adults (*Call the Keeper* and *Onwards!*).

It had never occurred to me to write for young readers until Ursula Nordstrom of

Harper & Row suggested the idea to me. The result was *Jazz Country*, and the experience was so satisfying and challenging that I wrote another, *I'm Really Dragged but Nothing Gets Me Down*, for Janet Chenery at Simon and Schuster. Many more young readers, I've discovered, write to authors than adults do, and what they have to say is often acutely perceptive. I've also found out, in correspondence and in many talk sessions at junior high and high schools, that young readers are, to say the least, intensely interested in and better informed about a far wider range of political and social trends than was my generation in its teens. Accordingly they're a demanding audience—perhaps more so than the mass "adult" audience.

But then I know this from my own children. There are four, ranging from a four-year-old to a girl of thirteen. The youngest doesn't read yet but he can't be conned or easily put off with euphemisms either. With my own children I have no choice but to try to be consistently honest if I'm to have any credibility—and from the contacts I've had with young readers of my books, the same is true of them. I expect I shall be writing more novels for the young. They are readers who are difficult to win, but very much worth having if you do.

I should add that my wife, Margot Goodman Hentoff, is a writer, appearing frequently in the *New York Review of Books.*

Incidentally, I still go into libraries on occasion to see my name on one of those index cards. The pleasure—and surprise—have not diminished.

Nat Hentoff received the Nancy Bloch Memorial Award and the New York *Herald Tribune* Spring Book Festival Award, both in 1966, for *Jazz Country.*

SELECTED WORKS: Jazz Country, 1965; I'm Really Dragged but Nothing Gets Me Down, 1968; Journey into Jazz, 1968.

ABOUT: Contemporary Authors, Vol. 2; Who's Who in America, 1970-71; New York Times Book Review August 21, 1966; Newsweek December 21, 1964; Publishers' Weekly September 2, 1968.

KATHLEEN HERALD

See *Peyton, K. M.*

FLORENCE HIGHTOWER

June 9, 1916-

AUTHOR OF *Dark Horse of Woodfield,* etc.

Autobiographical sketch of Florence Cole Hightower:

I WAS born in Boston, Massachusetts, the only child of my parents. When I was five, my father died. For several years, I was looked after by my grandmothers while my mother went out teaching school. During this time, I came to rely on books, rather than playmates for amusement. One of my earliest memories is of going visiting with a grandmother and taking a book along in the hope of finding a kindly adult who would read it to me. As soon as I'd learned to read, I read constantly and with great enjoyment. My enjoyment was enhanced if I could share it by reading my favorite books aloud, over and over, to anyone who would listen, for as long as they would listen. The grandmothers bore the brunt of this literary sharing, and it was one of them who, in an effort to shut me up, suggested

Florence C. Hightower

that I write a book myself. I barely knew how to join letters in words or string words in sentences—spelling and punctuation were mysteries—but the idea appealed to me, and I set to work. My book was largely borrowed from *Alice in Wonderland,* but it contained one original touch—a scepter which turned into a snake at will and stuck its tongue out at people in authority. Through that scepter, I see now, I satisfied a desire very close to my heart and to the hearts of all children, and it must have been that satisfaction of flouting authority and not getting scolded that gave me strength to pit myself against the English language and hold my own, more or less, for ten whole pages.

This first attempt at writing illustrates what writing has been like for me ever since. I long to give a separate, coherent life to experiences, thoughts, and feelings which, whether borrowed or original, acceptable or egregious, are important to me. I want to be known through my plots and characters, and I certainly don't want to be scolded for them. I set out to apply what knowledge and craftsmanship I have to my material, and am appalled by the difficulty of my task and my inadequacy to perform it. It is only when I can drive myself to work very hard at the words and the sentences that I come up with a book.

When I was eight, my mother and I moved to Concord, Massachusetts, where my mother had a job teaching at Concord Academy, a small girls' school. I attended that school until I graduated and went to Vassar College. Concord was my home until I married. I was very happy growing up in Concord. I had lots of friends, a bicycle, and a dog, and the surrounding country provided fields, woods, ponds, and a river. My years in Concord have provided me with quantities of material for stories.

When I was in college, I gave story writing a try and was so overwhelmed by the demands of serious adult writing (as opposed to adolescent outpouring) that I gave up. Fifteen years later, when I was thirty-seven years old, married, and the mother of three children, I got up the courage to write again. My first book, *Mrs. Wappinger's Secret,* was successful because by now I had the sense to write about something I really knew and cared for—my own children and the island in Maine where we spend our summers. My husband helped me a great deal by criticizing my work as I went along and encouraging me to keep at it. Each book I've written since has posed new problems which have nearly floored me. Writing never gets easier. Neither does it get tedious.

My husband, James Robert Hightower, is Professor of Chinese Literature at Harvard University. His sabbatical leaves have taken us to Europe and the Far East, but, for the most part, since 1951, I have lived in Auburndale, Massachusetts. Our two eldest boys are grown up and married. Our daughter is in college. At home, we have our youngest son, Thomas, who is still a schoolboy.

———

Florence Cole took her A.B. from Vassar College in 1937. She married James Robert Hightower in 1940. Their children are James Robert, Jr., Samuel Cole, Josephine, and Thomas Denzil.

SELECTED WORKS: Mrs. Wappinger's Secret, 1956; The Ghost of Follonsbee's Folly, 1958; Dark Horse of Woodfield, 1962; Fayerweather Forecast, 1967.

ABOUT: Contemporary Authors, Vol. 4.

AL HINE
December 11, 1915-

AUTHOR OF *Where in the World Do You Live?* etc.

Autobiographical sketch of Al Hine who also writes with Sesyle Joslin Hine under the pen names "Josephine Gibson" and "G. B. Kirtland":

I CAN'T remember when I first became interested in books, but, from whatever time that was, I can't ever remember not being interested and having the fatal ambition to become a writer.

I was born in Pittsburgh, Pennsylvania. My first vague memory B.B. (before books) is of being held up to a front window of our house to watch a World War I victory parade featuring the visiting French hero, Marshal Foch. Not too long after came the combined magic of reading and of attending the Saturday movie serials—*Robin Hood, The Green Archer* and so on. In those pre-sound, captioned days, one had to read, at least minimally, to enjoy the movies. These serials became mixed with books—*Ivanhoe,* all the Howard Pyle pirate and knighthood volumes, the adventure novels of Jeffrey Farnol, Edgar Rice Burroughs—to become part of the games I and my friends played in backyards, vacant lots and the nearby Frick Park woods. For weeks we would race about, leaping in ambush from garage roofs, intent in reenacting sagas of Sherwood Forest and then, quite suddenly, shift to being Tarzan of the Apes or John Carter, Warlord of Mars.

I graduated from Shady Side Academy in 1934, went on to graduate from Princeton in 1937, but part of me has always stayed in that not-quite-lost world of innocence and imagination.

I worked for an advertising agency, was a dutiful draftee, found a dream job as an editor of *Yank,* the army weekly, in World War II. I was managing editor by the time of my discharge and moved into editorial work for Curtis Publishing Company which led to an associate editorship on *Holiday* magazine. I left *Holiday* in 1952, on publication of my first novel, to free-lance in books, magazine work and films.

My writing of books for children was the result of a combination of circumstances, an interest awakened by the arrival of children of my own (Victoria 1952, Alexandra 1954, Julia 1957) and an admiration for the work of my wife, Sesyle Joslin. Together, we worked on several books before I was moved to strike out on my own with *Where in the World Do You Live?* An old, continuing interest in history and verse came together in my first anthology, *This Land Is Mine*, and its sister volume, *From Other Lands*.

I continue to write adult fiction as well as juveniles and hope always to be interested in and able to do both. The only difference I find in the two types is a dangerous tendency to "write down" to adults.

We have been living in Rome for the past several years and will probably remain under its spell for a few more, but home and roots are still in the Connecticut farmhouse we bought in 1952.

———

Al Hine spent a year and a half in Iran as correspondent for the local edition of *Yank* before he became overseas news editor and managing editor. He was associate producer of the film, *Lord of the Flies*. His short stories have appeared in *Collier's* and *Esquire*, and he has edited anthologies of verse. Hine mar-

ried Sesyle Joslin in 1949. They collaborated on *One Day in Elizabethan England* and other books under the pen name "G. B. Kirtland" and on *Is There a Mouse in the House?* under the name "Josephine Gibson".

SELECTED WORKS: Where in the World Do You Live? 1962; Money 'Round the World, 1963; A Letter to Anywhere, 1965.

ABOUT: Contemporary Authors, Vol. 1; Library Journal October 1, 1951.

SESYLE JOSLIN HINE

See *Joslin, Sesyle*

"EUGENE H. HIPPOPOTAMUS"

See *Kraus, Robert*

S. CARL HIRSCH
November 29, 1913-

AUTHOR OF *The Globe for the Space Age*, etc.

Autobiographical sketch of S. Carl Hirsch:

A FEW years ago, I met a retired newspaper editor who remembered me as "an eager, interested, skinny little guy who haunted our newsroom like some kids hang around a baseball sandlot."

His remembrance went back to the mid-1920s, when I was moving into my teens. My hopes for a writing career soared on the day I lugged home a handful of new books. The literary editor of the Chicago *Evening Post* was struck with the idea of having a youngster review the juvenile books. That's how I became the children's book editor of a metropolitan newspaper at age thirteen.

By the time I completed my education, the depression had struck full force. I was an unemployed writer before I had my first fulltime writing job. It took me thirty years to get back around to children's books—as an author.

My first book was published in 1963 by Viking Press. I was then deeply involved in the lithography of maps and globes. Understandably, my first book was on the subject of globes, inspired by the fact that astronaut John Glenn had carried a globe with him on his first historic space flight. *The Globe for*

S. Carl Hirsch (signature)

the Space Age won the Thomas Alva Edison award as the best Children's Science Book of 1963.

In 1966, Viking brought out *The Living Community*. This book won for me another Edison Award. *The Living Community* also won the Clara Ingram Judson Memorial Award, presented by the Society of Midland Authors. *Printing from a Stone* was published in 1968 and was chosen as one of its Notable Books by the American Library Association.

Chicago-born and raised, I followed my World War II service with a move into small town life. We are now living in suburban Evanston, Illinois, where I spent my college years at Northwestern University.

My wife, Stina, is a close coworker, taking over most of the technical chores and the important business of creating a writing environment. My two sons, Peter and Bruce, have been a major source of book ideas, flowing directly from their own youthful curiosities.

The subject matter of many successful nonfiction authors reflects their professional specialties. However, I prefer to move into fields in which I have little preparation other than my writing skills. I find that my approach is somewhat fresher that way, unhindered by easy assumptions, language short-

hand or concept shortcuts. In particular, I am drawn to those areas where science and the humanities intersect.

Writing for children, hardly the most lucrative profession, has its own rich, secret rewards. Research, and especially travel research, is my own satisfying way of pursuing "a lifetime of learning." And a child's appreciative letter can "pay off" a year of labor.

In January 1968 my wife and I wandered through the vast steaming, aromatic open marketplace of Accra, Ghana. In its midst we found a small low building, a branch of the United States Information Agency. Inside was a tiny library where youngsters were reading and borrowing books. What an exciting experience to find my own books listed in the card catalog—and checked out to African children!

S. Carl Hirsch married Stina Leander in 1940. He served in the United States Army 1940-44 and has held various positions in advertising and printing, including that of map lithographer. He lives in Evanston, Illinois, and is president of the Children's Reading Round Table.

SELECTED WORKS: The Globe for the Space Age, 1963; This Is Automation, 1964; Fourscore ... and More: The Life Span of Man, 1965; The Living Community: A Venture into Ecology, 1966; Printing from a Stone: The Story of Lithography, 1967; On Course: Navigating in Sea, Air, and Space, 1967; Cities Are People, 1968; Mapmakers of America, 1970.

ABOUT: Contemporary Authors, Vol. 7-8.

LILLIAN HOBAN
May 18, 1925-

ILLUSTRATOR OF *The Mouse and His Child*, etc.

Autobiographical sketch of Lillian Aberman Hoban:

I WAS born in Philadelphia. I was the youngest of three sisters, and we moved so many times and lived in so many different parts of the city that I never had many friends until adolescence. I spent most of what for other kids would be playtime at the various public libraries. Philadelphia had a great many of

LILLIAN HOBAN

them, some of them storefront libraries almost, in shabby neighborhoods. The one that made a lasting impression on me was the Rittenhouse Square Library. There was a tremendous collection of children's books there, and I keep half-remembering titles and authors that I still look for and never find. We couldn't even find that library the last time we were in Philadelphia. There was a long, low, bench that ran around the walls under the shelves so that you could stand on it to get a book and then sit on it to read. The children's room was usually empty except for me, and the librarian's desk was in another room, so it was the coziest kind of private time for looking at books. I used to spend a lot of time drawing too, and designing rooms, especially nurseries. They all had murals I painted on the walls.

I went to the Philadelphia High School for Girls and took classes at the Graphic Sketch Club, where I met Russ. I started at the Philadelphia Museum School the year after he did, left soon after we were married, and came to New York. While he was in the Army I was taking modern dance classes with Hanya Holm and working at MacLevy Slenderizing Salons. Later I taught modern dance —children's classes mostly, first in New York and then in Connecticut. I did some commercial art too, and always wanted to illustrate children's books.

Russ and I have completely different feelings about illustration. It was always a heavy thing for him—he used to sit at the easel groaning and yawning, and he was glad to give it up when he did. But for me it's completely satisfying and cozy. I have just as good a time as a kid with a coloring book. I'm not a strong draughtsman but I don't worry about it—I concentrate on getting the right feeling in the pictures. I sometimes go mad with color separations, but most of the time I'm doing what I like best.

I don't exactly use our children as models, but whether I'm drawing kids or animals I have them in mind, and the expressions on the face of Frances the badger have appeared on various small Hoban faces in our house.

SELECTED WORKS ILLUSTRATED: The Sorely Trying Day, by Russell Hoban, 1964; The Little Brute Family, by Russell Hoban, 1966; The Mouse and His Child, by Russell Hoban, 1967; Will I Have a Friend? by Miriam Cohen, 1967; A Wolf of My Own, by Jan Wahl, 1969; Best Friends for Frances, by Russell Hoban, 1969.

ABOUT: Kingman, Lee and others, comps. Illustrators of Children's Books: 1957-1966.

RUSSELL HOBAN

February 4, 1925-

AUTHOR OF *The Mouse and His Child,* etc.

Autobiographical sketch of Russell Conwell Hoban:

I WAS born in Lansdale, Pennsylvania, and grew up there with my two older sisters. We lived about a mile outside of the town, with the house right next to the school and a lot of good trees to read in. My mother bred pigeons and gardened. My father was advertising manager of the *Jewish Daily Forward* in Philadelphia. He took me hiking, handed out nickels for clever remarks at the dinner table, directed amateur productions of Russian and Yiddish classics and protest plays of the thirties—I had one-line parts in a couple of them—and voted for Norman Thomas. The first two rules of etiquette I learned were never to cross a picket line and always to eat the union label on the pumpernickel for good luck. As a child I drew very well and was expected to be a great artist when I grew up.

RUSSELL HOBAN

My father died in 1936. My mother opened a store and stayed in business until shortly before her death in 1966.

After high school I entered Temple University on a partial scholarship, dropped out after five weeks, went to the Philadelphia Museum School of Industrial Art for a year and a half, then into the Army in 1943. I had met Lillian Aberman at the Graphic Sketch Club in 1942, and we were married in 1944 before I went overseas. I was a messenger (always a private) with the 339th Infantry, 85th Division, in Italy, and in 1945 came home to the apartment Lil had found for us in New York.

There followed a succession of up-and-down jobs. I was a packing clerk, a Western Union messenger, a freight handler, worked in display factories, silk-screen shops, magazines, and art studios. Then five years with Batten, Barton, Durstine & Osborn as a TV art director. We moved to Norwalk, Connecticut, in 1955, and in 1956 I left BBDO to be a free-lance illustrator for the next eight years, with assignments from *Sports Illustrated, Fortune,* and other magazines, some advertising work, and some *Time* covers.

In 1958 Ursula Nordstrom at Harper bought my first book, *What Does It Do and How Does It Work?* Being a published author, I went on writing, and found that writing was what I liked best. Since *Herman the Loser,* in 1961, Lil has illustrated all my

books. In 1965 I dropped illustration altogether, and was a copywriter at Doyle Dane Bernbach for two years. Since 1967 I've been a fulltime writer working at home.

We live in Wilton, Connecticut, now, in a big barn overlooking a pond. Our four children, Phoebe, Brom, Esmé, and Julia, are sixteen, fourteen, eleven, and six. Being with them as much as I have since they were very small has made me pay attention to the details of life close to the ground, and that is the point of view I generally write from. Of my twenty-six published books, *The Mouse and His Child,* my only novel so far, is my favorite.

SELECTED WORKS WRITTEN AND ILLUSTRATED: What Does It Do and How Does It Work? 1959; The Atomic Submarine, 1960.

SELECTED WORKS WRITTEN: Bedtime for Frances, 1960; Herman the Loser, 1961; A Baby Sister for Frances, 1964; The Little Brute Family, 1966; The Mouse and His Child, 1967; The Pedaling Man and Other Poems, 1968.

ABOUT: Contemporary Authors, Vol. 7-8; Something About the Author, Vol. 1; American Artist October 1961.

C. WALTER HODGES

March 18, 1909-

AUTHOR AND ILLUSTRATOR OF *Shakespeare's Theatre,* etc.

Autobiographical sketch of Cyril Walter Hodges:

I WAS born in Beckenham, Kent, and passed the ensuing sixteen years in a manner increasingly disappointing to those who had the care of me. It was not that I was ill-natured or troublesome; far from it. But I was abnormally inept and joyless at all those normally-considered joyful team games, and I was wholly unresponsive to the usual processes of education. In the opinion of my teachers nobody had ever made a longer or more dedicated study of the bottom rung of the academic ladder than I, and our rather early parting brought relief, if not actual pleasure, to us all. At my own request I was then sent—one might almost say consigned—to an art school (Goldsmith's, in London), and so my

C. Walter Hodges.

life began, sixteen years late and myself a little discouraged by the delay. I picked myself up, made friends, read books and plays, developed some (though insufficient) artistic skill, and some idea of what I wanted to do in life. I wanted to be a stage designer. Unfortunately it was a profession that hardly existed at that time—not, at any rate, in terms of money—and after working for a pleasant but unrewarding season or two at a studio theater in London I was obliged to bow my head before the facts of economic life and take a job in the studio of an advertising agency. Alas, advertising is a profession for which I have no vocation. After six—no, five— months they told me so. Rarely has rejection made me so glad. Thereupon I had to accept that the truest fact of my life is that I am basically unsuited to any employment but my own, and so at twenty-one years I settled down to do the best I could as a free-lance illustrator, not expecting much. But somehow I managed to keep going. My work improved a little. I married. I found I was real.

In 1937 my wife and I were staying in New York, and here I complained to a publisher for whom I was doing a bookjacket that the subjects I was given to illustrate were all too rarely the ones I most wanted to do. "Then why," asked this excellent publisher,

"do you not make your own books, with pictures to suit yourself?" Thus encouraged I planned a little picture book about Columbus; but when I started to write its little text, this spun itself out into 65,000 words. I found I enjoyed a sort of talent for writing. However, like so much else in my life (this article, for instance) it all took longer to do than I expected, and by the time *Columbus Sails* was published it was overtaken by the Second World War. So then I spent five years in the British Army (I went as a camouflage officer on the D-Day invasion of Normandy) and when I came out of it I had to pick up the threads again as an illustrator before I could return to writing. Also in the meanwhile I had developed a passionate interest (the adjective is careful and exact) in Shakespeare and his theater; I therefore began to write articles about it for various specialist papers; and when the actor Bernard Miles announced a plan to build an "Elizabethan" theater for a festival season I joined him in this. I worked on his productions of *The Tempest* and *Macbeth*, and helped to design the theater which later developed into what is now London's Mermaid Theater. At this time I was also painting mural decorations and designing exhibitions for Lloyd's and other insurance institutions in the City of London, as well as illustrating many books and continuing when I could to write my own. I published a book of research on the Elizabethan theater (*The Globe Restored*) and this led on to a new field as script writer and art director in educational films for *Encyclopaedia Britannica*. It was therefore not until 1964 that I was able to publish another full-length novel for children, *The Namesake*, which is about England's King Alfred the Great, and which had been lying in my desk drawer waiting to be finished for many years. I followed this with its sequel, *The Marsh King*, three years later.

And so on. I am at present writing scripts and making drawings for a series of filmstrips on the history of Europe in the nineteenth century, and I am planning the interior decoration for a chain of Elizabethan-style restaurants. I have synopses in hand for five more books, and another, *The Overland Launch*, is about to be published. And in all the meanwhile my wife has been raising our two sons ("bringing them up by hand," as Dickens's Mrs. Joe put it) one of whom is now a doctor, the other a lawyer. Too quickly the time passes. I am not surprised that my wife could do this, but I do wonder where on earth she found the time, considering that she has had me on her hands as well.

C. Walter Hodges attended Dulwich College and studied book illustration under Edmund J. Sullivan at Goldsmith's College School of Art, London. He married Margaret Becker in 1936. Their sons are Nicholas Adam and Crispin James. In World War II, Hodges served in the British Army, 1940-1946, and became a captain.

Besides his many activities as painter, designer, writer, and art director, Hodges has regularly contributed drawings to BBC's *Radio Times* magazine. He has also contributed articles to the annual Shakespeare Survey. In addition to his own books for children, he has illustrated more than seventy works by other authors.

He is a Fellow of the Society of Industrial Artists.

Shakespeare's Theatre won the Kate Greenaway Medal for 1964. *The Namesake* was a runner-up for the Carnegie Medal and received the British place on the Honor List of the Hans Christian Andersen Award for 1966. *The Overland Launch* won *The Elizabethan* Children's Books Silver Medal for 1969.

SELECTED WORKS WRITTEN AND ILLUSTRATED: Columbus Sails, 1939; Shakespeare's Theatre, 1964; The Namesake, 1964; The Norman Conquest, 1966; The Marsh King, 1967; The Spanish Armada, 1968; The Overland Launch, 1970.

SELECTED WORKS ILLUSTRATED: The Little White Horse, by Elizabeth Goudge, 1946; Eagle of the Ninth, by Rosemary Sutcliff, 1954; A Swarm in May, by William Mayne, 1956; Silver Sword, by Ian Serraillier, 1959; Red Indian Folk and Fairy Tales, edited by Ruth Manning-Sanders, 1962; Growing Up in 13th Century England, by Alfred Duggan, 1962; Hannibal and the Bears, by Margaret Joyce Baker, 1966.

ABOUT: Author's and Writer's Who's Who, 1963; Contemporary Authors, Vol. 15-16; Kingman, Lee and others, comps. Illustrators of Children's Books; 1957-1966; Mahony, Bertha E. and others, comps. Illustrators of Children's Books:

1744-1945; Viguers, Ruth Hill and others, comps. Illustrators of Children's Books: 1946-1956; Who's Who in Art, 1970; American Artist October 1957; Library Association Record May 1965.

SYD HOFF

September 4, 1912-

AUTHOR AND ILLUSTRATOR OF *Danny and the Dinosaur*, etc.

Autobiographical sketch of Sydney Hoff:

I SUPPOSE I was born three years after the date of my birth. The family had gone for a ride in the subway and when we came home I drew a picture of the conductor. The shape of his cap fascinated me. Anyway, my mother said, "Sydney is an artist," and I've been trying to live up to her words ever since.

When I was a child, my father used to bring home the New York *Evening Journal* and I found myself fascinated with Tad, Opper, Herriman and other great cartoonists. Vowed to follow in their inkprints until I entered the National Academy of Design at fifteen to study fine art. Now new gods impressed themselves on me—Rembrandt, Manet, Da Vinci. Now I would be a painter!

But alas, my most serious efforts evoked only dismay from my instructors. In despair, I submitted a sketch to *The New Yorker*, and they bought it. The die was cast. I was a cartoonist!

From eighteen on, I sold to *The New Yorker, Esquire*, and other leading magazines and newspapers. In 1939, I began a daily comic strip for King Features Syndicate, starring a little girl named Tuffy. Did this for ten years until Tuffy died from tired blood, or insufficient client papers. In between, though, I had tried to do a children's book—*Muscles and Brains*. This one was a catastrophe and nearly destroyed the publisher. However, he fought back gamely with a collection of my adult cartoons, entitled *Feeling No Pain*. Since then I have had a half-dozen other collections of adult cartoons published.

In 1958, still licking my wounds from *Muscles and Brains*, I tried another children's

book. It must have been Ursula Nordstrom, my editor at Harper, or my astrology chart— anyway, *Danny and the Dinosaur* was a decided smash hit and the royalties are still rolling in. I followed this with a number of others at Harper's.

In 1967 I did a book without drawings, just words, a juvenile novel, *Irving and Me*, also for Harper. This is autobiographical in a way, although Artie Granick, the hero, is thirteen when he moves to Florida, and I was substantially older when I picked up and left New York. But Artie expresses most of my ideas (at that age) on such assorted subjects as religion, segregation, bullies and girls.

Other picture books of mine have been published by G. P. Putnam's and by McGraw-Hill. I have also illustrated the books of other writers.

Since 1958 I have been doing a daily newspaper cartoon which appears in about a hundred papers here and abroad, called "Laugh It Off." Every day, except during hurricanes, I ride a bike, swim and play handball. My wife and two daughters look

on this with growing concern and I suppose so will my grandson when he hears about it.

———

Syd Hoff married Dora Berman in 1937; their children are Susan Hoff Gross and Bonnie Joy and their grandchildren, Barry Joel and Shelli Meryl Gross. Hoff is a member of the Authors Guild and the Magazine Cartoonists Guild.

SELECTED WORKS WRITTEN AND ILLUSTRATED: Danny and the Dinosaur, 1958; Julius, 1959; Sammy the Seal, 1959; Who Will Be My Friends? 1960; Oliver, 1960; Where's Prancer? 1960; Albert the Albatross, 1961; Chester, 1961; Little Chief, 1961; Stanley, 1962; Grizzwold, 1963; Lengthy, 1964; Mrs. Switch, 1966; Irving and Me, 1967; Jeffrey at Camp, 1968; Slithers, 1968; Baseball Mouse, 1968; The Horse in Harry's Room, 1970.

SELECTED WORKS ILLUSTRATED: Hello, Mudder, Hello Fadder, by Allan Sherman, 1964; I Should Have Stayed in Bed, by Joan M. Lexau, 1965; The Homework Caper, by Joan M. Lexau, 1966; Rooftop Mystery, by Joan M. Lexau, 1968.

ABOUT: Author's and Writer's Who's Who, 1963; Contemporary Authors, Vol. 5-6; Kingman, Lee and others, comps. Illustrators of Children's Books: 1957-1966; Who's Who in America, 1970-71; Who's Who in American Art, 1970.

FELIX HOFFMANN

April 18, 1911-

ILLUSTRATOR OF *The Seven Ravens*, etc.

Autobiographical sketch of Felix Hoffmann:

I WAS born in Aarau, a small Swiss city, the son of a musician and the third of four children. As far back as I can remember I made drawings. That was a good way for a very shy and quiet child to communicate. Consequently, after I graduated from the *Gymnasium* and after I had given up trying to study archeology, there was no question of any other calling than that of a painter or graphic artist. My training I received in academies in Germany, in Karlsruhe and Berlin.

I came back to Aarau in 1935 as a freelance artist and established residence there, although I have always been on the go on extensive trips. At first I just about managed to make ends meet with illustrations for mag-

Felix Hoffmann (signature)

azines and juveniles. Later I was, and still am, most successful with paintings for stained glass and frescoes and with bibliophilic works for publishers in Germany and America.

How did I happen to paint fairy-tale picture books?

Through my four children to whom I had always told fairy tales, mostly on Sunday mornings in bed, in a whisper, so that their mother could keep on sleeping. I had married in 1936 and we had four children: Sabine (1937), Christine (1940), Susanne (1943) and Dieter (1945).

When my wife was confined with our youngest child, the two older ones stayed with the grandparents and little Susanne (aged two and a half) lay quarantined in her room with the measles. She could not read yet and had looked and looked endlessly at the few picture books. So then, during my work on the Jesaja-window for the Cathedral in Berne, I painted for her *The Wolf and the Seven Little Kids*, doing two or three pages every day. She then sat up expectantly, always starting with special relish each time from the very beginning, and when the last new picture came her eyes shone in her inflamed and swollen face. And when the very last picture came with the rescued seven little kids in the same bed and the mother

standing there, little Susanne was reunited with her brother and sisters and their mother was with them again. Exactly the same situation!

For Christine I painted *Sleeping Beauty* when she had to go to the hospital. The kitten which accompanies the princess wherever she goes was *her* kitten and, because she was so very fond of eating, the monumental wedding cake comes at the end. Sabine got *Rapunzel* as a special reward for something she did and Dieter *The Seven Ravens*. Time passes quickly: *The Four Clever Brothers* are already for Klaus, the first grandchild, (1964) and the second one, Matthias, got *King Thrushbeard*. I thought of the little nursery rhyme "A Boy Went Out to Gather Pears" when the workmen failed to put in an appearance again and again while my studio was being rebuilt, and I took pleasure in doing the little book.

The books had no text, were picture books pure and simple and were made for home consumption without any intention of publishing them. Through a series of unexpected events they chanced to be published after all some twelve years later, one after the other, in Switzerland, Germany, England, America, Japan, and South Africa. It surprised me very much that these books, each of which was made for a particular child, appeal to the children of half the world.

Felix Hoffmann is married to Gretel Kienscherf and still lives in Aarau. He received the Swiss Children's Book Award in 1957 and was on the Hans Christian Andersen Award honor list regularly from 1960 through 1964. In 1963 he won a New York *Herald Tribune* Children's Spring Book Festival Award for his illustrations for *The Seven Ravens*.

SELECTED WORKS ILLUSTRATED: The Wolf and the Seven Little Kids, by The Brothers Grimm, 1959; The Sleeping Beauty, by The Brothers Grimm, 1960; Rapunzel, by The Brothers Grimm, 1961; Prince of Hindustan, by Max Voegli, 1961; He Served Two Masters, by Adolf Haller, 1962; The Seven Ravens, by The Brothers Grimm, 1963; Favorite Fairy Tales Told in Poland, edited by Virginia Haviland, 1963; The Four Clever Brothers, by The Brothers Grimm, 1967.

ABOUT: Hürlimann, Bettina. Picture Book
World; Kingman, Lee and others, comps. Illus-
trators of Children's Books: 1957-1966; Viguers,
Ruth Hill and others, comps. Illustrators of Chil-
dren's Books: 1946-1956; Texas Quarterly
Spring 1962.

ROBERT HOFSINDE

December 10, 1902-

AUTHOR AND ILLUSTRATOR OF *Indian Picture
Writing*, etc.

Autobiographical sketch of Robert Hofsinde
(Gray-Wolf):

I WAS born in Denmark and there had my
formal education, including six years of art
school.

Arriving in this country in 1922, making
my home in Minneapolis, I was engaged to
make a collection of scientific drawings for
the Minnesota Academy of Science.

When that commission ended, I took a
trip into the north woods, planning to spend
a month or so, making paintings of the winter forest. This move changed my entire life,
for it was here that I came in contact with
the Ojibwa Indians, a meeting that eventually guided me to my life's work.

It all started when I happened upon a
young Indian boy who had fallen into a pit
trap, the fall resulting in a compound frac-
ture of his left leg. After getting the boy out,
and setting the break, I placed him on my
sled and took him back to his village. During
his convalescence I often visited him, and
when spring arrived I was adopted into his
family and was given the name Gray-Wolf.

To an artist these people made wonderful
subjects, but as time passed I also found myself drawn to their culture. The result was
that what had started as a sketching trip of
but a few weeks turned out to be a stay with
these Indians for more than three years.

After returning to Minneapolis I began
writing articles for several magazines, including one in Canada, and one in Holland.

The urge to know more about the Indians
drove me on, and eventually I visited other
tribes throughout the west and southwest in
a "research trip" that spanned nearly 16
years.

On these extended tours I was able to earn
my living by stopping from time to time to
work in lumber camps, on farms, and on
ranches.

Then in 1937 in Chicago, I met and married my wife Geraldine, and for some time
we conducted our own daily radio program,
called "Gray-Wolf's Ti-pi" over WAAF.

In 1940 we were invited to join "Junior
Programs" in New York, and through their
management were booked throughout the
country for school assemblies where we gave
a costumed program of Indian lore and
dances. In between I still wrote articles, sold
some paintings, and executed three large
murals.

Then in 1944 it was my good fortune to
meet Elisabeth Hamilton, then editor for
Morrow Junior Books. I had come to see her
in the hope of doing some book illustrations,
but at the end of a two-hour visit, Mrs. Hamilton suggested that I write and illustrate a
book of my own.

The result was *The Indian's Secret World*,
followed by *Indian Sign Language*, followed
by an eventual twelve more titles. After the
retirement of Mrs. Hamilton, the editorial
work has been carried out under the able
direction of Mrs. Connie Epstein.

Hofsinde: *HUFF sin duh*

My wife and I now live and work in a spacious ranch home in the woods some fifty miles from New York where the walls of my studio are hung with old Indian costumes and artifacts, most of which have been seen in my illustrations.

Robert Hofsinde was born next door to Hans Christian Andersen's house in Odense. From the age of fourteen until he came to the United States at twenty he studied art at night at the Royal Academy of Copenhagen and days under the scenic artist Waldemar Kjelgaard, working at his studies from 7:00 A.M. until 6:00 P.M. six days a week. In this country he continued his studies at the Minneapolis School of Art.

Robert Hofsinde says he was puzzled by the warm reception he received from Indians while on a horseback trip from Montana to Arizona, but could not ask how the Indians knew so much about him because they consider any direct question rude. Later he found out from an Indian graduate of an American university that the "moccasin telegraph" had spread the news about him while he was still living with the Ojibwas.

Robert Hofsinde's wife, who has been with him on many visits to the Indians, has been given the Indian name of Morning Star.

SELECTED WORKS WRITTEN AND ILLUSTRATED: The Indian's Secret World, 1955; Indian Sign Language, 1956; Indian Picture Writing, 1959; The Indian and the Buffalo, 1961; Indian Warriors and Their Weapons, 1965; Indian Music Makers, 1967; Indian Costumes, 1968.

ABOUT: Viguers, Ruth Hill and others, comps. Illustrators of Children's Books: 1946-56; Horn Book February 1960.

NONNY HOGROGIAN

May 7, 1932-

AUTHOR AND ILLUSTRATOR OF *One Fine Day*, etc.

Autobiographical sketch of Nonny Hogrogian Kherdian:

I WAS born right in the middle of the depression and right in the middle of the homeliest castle in the world—and there it sat—in the middle of the Bronx.

Nonny Hogrogian: *NONN ee*
ha GROH gee an

It was built by what was probably the first Armenian architect in New York, and it was, without question, the first house he ever built anywhere.

Two crooked flights above the street level and through the stone archways was the door that led to the cellar and basement of the house. I know that it is difficult to visualize but that is how it was. Believe it! It was our playground when it rained. There were five rooms in that cellar and if there was a brain in Mr. Exerjian's head he had to have designed them for a good game of *hide and seek*. That stone monster that he built for my grandparents was a child's paradise. One could hunt there for thieves or be a princess or play *follow the leader* for an hour without coming upon the same scene twice.

There were hours spent in Pop's library in the basement reading the wonderful children's books from among his collection while he read an Armenian newspaper. (It was addressed to Reupen Hrahad Hoghgroghian. That was my grandfather and I adored him.) I'd yell "Shesh-Besh" at him (because I liked the sound of it) over his backgammon board or watch him gently finger his amber beads as he spoke of running messages to his brothers in the Turkish prison.

Visions of sugarplums never danced in my head as I raced up the stairs (one more flight) to the "first" floor where we lived. In the door and through the pantry to that enormous kitchen that was never quite big enough to hold all the delectables that my grandmother made.

By the way, I was born in the middle of that big house because my grandmother was not about to chance the possibility of having babies switched in the confusion of a hospital.

The leanest years were the nicest ones for Gloria (my sister) and me. Those were the years when we all squeezed into the attic— that is the little three-room apartment over the "second" floor where the Farrells lived. Gloria had her own room for the only time in her life. It was the kitchen of course, and it wasn't any bigger than the downstairs pantry but after dinner and until breakfast the next day, it was all hers. For me, the attic years were an adventure in an ivory tower.

There is so much to tell and so little space but they were the special years that formed my life when I learned to read from Pop, and to tell my right hand from my left and to think and dream because he was a dreamer, too. From Memma (my grandmother) I learned to cook and to enjoy a good meal. I also got her temper, her eccentricities and her beautiful little Sarouk rug. My mother was better at almost everything than anyone I knew, and I tried very hard to fashion myself after her. I never really knew what I wanted to be but I knew that I would do something that had to do with art. And that was my father's gift to me—his talent and his stubbornness. On Sundays my father painted and on Mondays while he was away at work, I did. I picked up his brushes and dabbed away at *his* paintings, and he enjoyed every noticeable stroke. And that was where it all began.

Nonny Hogrogian was art editor of her high school magazine and attended Saturday art classes at Pratt Institute. She majored in art at Hunter College, graduating in 1953. In spite of her background, she did not at first think of making her living as an artist, but went to work in a publisher's advertising department. When she took a course in wood-cutting under Antonio Frasconi at the New School for Social Research, he told her, "Stop wasting your time in an office and get to your real business." Leaving her job, she labored over woodcuts for two years. She also studied Japanese methods of cutting and printing with Hodaka Yoshida in his summer classes in Maine.

In 1958, Miss Hogrogian became production assistant in the children's book department at Crowell and there Elizabeth Riley, editor, gave her her first opportunity to illustrate a book for children, *King of the Kerry Fair.*

Later, while she was art director of children's books for Holt, her editor there, Ann Durell, assigned her the illustrations for *Gaelic Ghosts,* which began a fruitful relationship between Miss Hogrogian and the author, Sorche Nic Leodhas, culminating in a Caldecott Award for *Always Room for One More,* for 1966. Miss Hogrogian received a second Caldecott in 1972 for *One Fine Day,* which she wrote and illustrated.

Nonny Hogrogian has designed many books, including nearly all of those she has illustrated herself. She has been represented as designer and/or illustrator in many exhibitions of children's books by the American Institute of Graphic Arts.

She married David Kherdian, a poet, in 1971.

SELECTED WORKS ILLUSTRATED: King of the Kerry Fair, by Nicolete Meredith, 1960; Gaelic Ghosts, by Sorche Nic Leodhas, 1964; Always Room for One More, by Sorche Nic Leodhas, 1965; The White Palace, by Mary O'Neill, 1966; Once There Was and Was Not, by Virginia A. Tashjian, 1966; The Fearsome Inn, by Isaac Bashevis Singer, 1967; Bears Are Sleeping, by Yulya, 1967; The Thirteen Days of Yule, 1968; Vasilisa the Beautiful, translated from the Russian by Thomas P. Whitney, 1970.

ABOUT: Hopkins, Lee Bennett. Books Are by People; Kingman, Lee and others, comps. Illustrators of Children's Books: 1957-66; Who's Who in America, 1970-71; Who's Who of American Women, 1969; American Artist October 1966; Horn Book August 1966; Library Journal November 15, 1964; March 15, 1966; Publishers' Weekly February 21; March 14, 1966; School Library Journal March 1966; Top of the News April 1966.

STEWART HOLBROOK
August 22, 1893-September 3, 1964

AUTHOR OF *Swamp Fox of the Revolution,* etc.

Biographical sketch of Stewart Hall Holbrook:

STEWART HOLBROOK was born and grew up in northern Vermont, the son of Jesse William and Kate (Stewart) Holbrook, and a descendant of nine generations of New England Yankees. He attended Colebrook Academy, but did not go to college.

Since his father was in the lumber business, the first powerful influence in young Stewart's life was logging, and it became a recurrent theme in his writing. As he said in *Yankee Loggers,* "Few of us boys wanted to be soldiers or cowboys. To be a riverman and go down with the drive was the stated or secret ambition of most of us. . . . Logging camps had all the magic of the Land of Oz."

In 1911 Holbrook went to Winnipeg, worked on a newspaper, played semi-professional baseball and toured western Canada in what he described for *Twentieth Century Authors* (*First Supplement*) as "one of the worst repertoire companies" ever seen in those parts. In 1914 he returned to New England and worked in logging camps until 1917.

When the United States entered World War I in 1917, Holbrook joined the American Artillery and served in France. Within a week after his discharge in 1919, he went on a log-drive down the Connecticut River. In 1920 he bought a round-trip ticket to Vancouver, British Columbia, and without definite plan became part of a movement he wrote about later in *The Yankee Exodus.* He scaled timber in the Douglas fir region of Canada for the next few years and there began to write.

He had long since sold the return portion of his ticket. Now he knew what he wanted: to live in the Pacific Northwest and to be a writer. His work won immediate acceptance from national magazines.

He was, however, above all an American and in 1923 he moved to Portland, Oregon, choosing the city which he heard had the best library in the West. He joined the staff

STEWART HOLBROOK

and later became editor of *Lumber News.* He covered forest fires, logging and sawmill strikes, and more than one riot of the I.W.W. In 1934 he left *Lumber News* to become a full time writer.

His first book, *Holy Old Mackinaw,* tells the story of the American lumberjack, whom Holbrook regarded as the greatest of the pioneers, because "before houses could be built . . . there had to be logs and boards." The second strong influence on his writing was American history, which he called, in *Lost Men of American History,* "a tremendous drama arranged with scenery such as no director could visualize and with a cast of characters superbly beyond imagination."

This "cast", usually local rather than national, appeared in some of Holbrook's best-known writing. In particular he liked Ethan Allen and had already written a biography of Allen when he was asked to do a children's book about him. In 1949 *America's Ethan Allen* appeared, illustrated by Lynd Ward; it was a runner-up for the 1950 Caldecott Medal. Other children's books followed. *Swamp Fox of the Revolution,* the story of Francis Marion, won the Young Readers' Choice Award in 1962.

In 1957 Holbrook was awarded a D.H.L. from Pacific University and in 1959 a D. Litt. from Willamette University.

Holbrook spent two years in Cambridge, Massachusetts, where he lectured on American history at Harvard and Boston Universities. He was elected to the American Antiquarian Society, which he said made him very proud. He participated in writers' conferences throughout the country, including those at Boulder, Colorado, and the California Western University Conference at San Diego. Liking to paint, he turned out what have been called "primitive-modern" pictures, which he exhibited in New York in 1958 under the pseudonym of Mr. Otis, simultaneously with the publication of *Mr. Otis*, his satire on modern art.

Holbrook married Katherine Stanton Gill in 1924. After his first wife's death, he married a great-granddaughter of Oregon pioneers, Sibyl Walker, in 1948. They had two children, Sibyl Morningstar and Bonnie Stewart, to whom he dedicated his last two children's books.

SELECTED WORKS: Holy Old Mackinaw, 1938, 1956; Lost Men of American History, 1946; America's Ethan Allen, 1949; The Yankee Exodus, 1950; Wild Bill Hickok Tames the West, 1952; Swamp Fox of the Revolution, 1959; Yankee Loggers, 1961.

ABOUT: Contemporary Authors, Vol. 9-10; Twentieth Century Authors (First Supplement), 1955; Who's Who in America, 1964-65; American Forests October 1964; November 1964; American Heritage April 1959; New York Herald Tribune Book Review June 25, 1950; New York Times September 4, 1964; Newsweek September 14, 1964; Publishers' Weekly September 21, 1964; Time September 11, 1964.

IRENE HUNT

May 18, 1907-

AUTHOR OF *Up a Road Slowly*, etc.

Biographical sketch of Irene Hunt:

IRENE HUNT was born near Newton, in southern Illinois, the daughter of Franklin P. and Sarah (Land) Hunt. She spent her childhood on a farm that had been in the family for generations.

Miss Hunt received her A.B. degree from the University of Illinois in 1939, her M.A. from the University of Minnesota in 1946, and attended the University of Colorado for advanced graduate work in psychology.

IRENE HUNT

She taught French and English in the Oak Park, Illinois, public schools from 1930 to 1945. Between 1946 and 1950 she taught psychology at the University of South Dakota. She returned to her native Illinois to teach junior high school students in Cicero until 1965, when she became Director of Language Arts in the Cicero schools, a post she only recently relinquished. She brought to the children and young teachers her own excitement about great books and the understanding that can be gained from them. She feels strongly that "books bring new dimensions of happiness, of confidence and enlightenment, to young people from the age of three on up." She also believes that the troubled child will often receive the message in a good book that he cannot accept from an adult.

According to her nephew, Wendell Bruce Beem, Irene Hunt worked for many years at her kitchen table, pounding the typewriter until late at night, accumulating rejection slips but learning with every manuscript. Her first novel was not published until she was fifty-seven, but it received great critical acclaim. Miss Hunt used her family farm as the setting for the novel, *Across Five Aprils*, a Civil War story. The historical facts in the book have been painstakingly researched, but the story of the Creighton family was suggested by family letters and records, and by the stories her grandfather told. A boy of nine when war broke out, her grandfather could vividly recall "the anxiety and sorrows of the times as well as the moments of happiness in a closely knit family." The book may be dedicated to his great-grandchildren, the author says, but the story is his.

This first novel won a Lewis Carroll Shelf Award, 1966, the Dorothy Canfield Fisher Award, the Clara Ingram Judson Memorial Award, 1965, the Charles W. Follett Award, 1964, and was sole runner-up for the Newbery Medal for 1965.

Irene Hunt's father died when she was a small child. When another little girl said to her, "You're not going to live here anymore, are you?" the bewildered and grieving little Irene hid in a closet. Her reactions, vividly recalled, are the opening scene of her second novel, *Up a Road Slowly*, albeit in the book it is Julie's mother who has died. The tragic story of Aggie Kilpin is also based upon childhood memories, but the rest of the book is fiction, despite the fact that the characters are so real the whole book is often mistaken for personal reminiscence.

Up a Road Slowly won the Newbery Medal for 1967, and was one of seven juveniles given by the American Booksellers' Association in 1970 (a quadrennial gift of 250 books) to the White House for its home library.

Irene Hunt now lives in North Riverside, Illinois, when she is not traveling. She loves "beautiful, well-written books and beautiful very loud music," refinishes old furniture, and has a flair for cooking. She is slim, chic, and attractive, with curly, graying brown hair.

SELECTED WORKS: Across Five Aprils, 1964; Up a Road Slowly, 1966; A Trail of Apple Blossoms, 1968; No Promises in the Wind, 1970.

ABOUT: Contemporary Authors, Vol. 19-20; Who's Who in America, 1970-71; Who's Who of American Women, 1970-71; Horn Book August 1967; Library Journal March 15, 1967; Publishers' Weekly March 13, 1967; School Library Journal March 1965; March 1967; Top of the News April 1967.

MOLLIE HUNTER
June 30, 1922-

AUTHOR OF *The Kelpie's Pearls*, etc.

Autobiographical sketch of Maureen Mollie Hunter McVeigh McIlwraith:

I AM a mixture of races, owing the Mollie of my pen name to my Irish father, and the Hunter to the Border ancestry of my Scottish mother, but my heart and upbringing are all Scots. I like children, and enjoy writing for them, and here in this old land it is not difficult to do so, for the very stones of Scotland speak of history, of folklore and of magic. My books for younger readers, *The Kelpie's Pearls*, *Thomas and the Warlock*, and others, are based on the last two of these subjects. Those for teen-age readers are drawn from the tremendous pageant of Scottish history which first began to fill my mind as a child in the Lowland village of Longniddry.

I was born there, third among five children of a very happy marriage, and named Maureen Mollie Hunter McVeigh. My father was merry and fiery by nature; my mother, merry and gentle. His tongue had a charm to it that could coax a bird out of a bush. She was, like many a Borderer before her, a born storyteller. Together they set the standards that have been the main formative influence on my life, opened a door into imagination for me, and made my childhood a gloriously happy time till I was nine years old. Then suddenly my father died, and the happy time seemed lost for ever.

We were very poor then also. At fourteen I had to leave home and school for office work in Edinburgh, but I wanted to be a writer and I was a determined thief of learning. I plundered words from every book I could lay hands on, and spent my pirate's treasure recklessly in my own stories and poems. I was lonely, with only characters in books for friends, but I was learning to write.

At eighteen, I fell in love. I married and became McIlwraith—a name from the Highlands of Scotland where I live now with my husband, Michael and two sons, Quentin and Brian, but World War II separated me from my husband then, and for six years

most of my writing was in the form of letters to him. When we settled eventually in the little house near Inverness where we live now, I wrote feature articles for newspapers, plays to express my life-long interest in the theatre, and told stories to my sons. At their demand I made "proper books" from these stories, and at the same time began working on my first historical novel, *The Spanish Letters*. I followed this with *A Pistol in Greenyards*, and others. My husband explored the terrain of these books with me, drew maps, and advised me on the technical detail of many incidents in the stories. The boys grew to share this interest, and the planning of each new "historical" became a family affair.

I count myself a very fortunate person. My original ambition is fulfilled, and my family knit closer because of it. Even greater reward is the knowledge that, for a new generation, I have opened the very door of imagination my parents opened for me, and in the process have found at last again that lost happy time of my own childhood.

SELECTED WORKS: The Kelpie's Pearls, 1966; Thomas and the Warlock, 1967; The Spanish Letters, 1967; A Pistol in Greenyards, 1968; The Lothian Run, 1970; The Walking Stones, 1970.

BETTINA HÜRLIMANN
June 19, 1909-

AUTHOR OF *William Tell and His Son*, etc.

Autobiographical sketch of Bettina Hürlimann-Kiepenheuer:

MY biography is in no way special, except that I have had the luck to meet many special people. My parents were publishers in Germany. Though I was interested in their profession, I really longed to become a writer. I went to the Academy of Arts in Leipzig after I had finished high school and majored in typography. After that I spent a year in England studying art and literature at the University of Bristol and doing typographical work for the Monotype Corporation. I became a publisher for many reasons and in 1933 married the publisher and photographer Martin Hürlimann. We have now spent more than thirty-five years together, publishing, editing a magazine about geography and traveling, and writing for our own magazine and others as well.

When World War II broke out, we left Germany where I was born in Weimar, and went to my husband's country, Switzerland, the country of the great pedagogue, Pestalozzi, the country also of Heidi and the Swiss Family Robinson. In those years I began again to write—articles for newspapers, a novel, stories. Most of these concerned children, their life, their social history and their books. My first serious study in this field was a book about *Five Centuries of Children's Portraits* (Zurich, 1949). Working on this, I realized also that children's books of all times were a sort of mirror of the social situation of children. Eagerly collecting old children's books, I started to write my book *Three Centuries of European Children's Books* (*Europäische Kinderbücher in drei Jahrhunderten*, 1959), and a few years later *Picture Book World* (*Die Welt im Bilderbuch*, 1965).

Meanwhile, as most of our children had left home and the first grandchild started to enjoy picture books, I returned to publishing and worked with modern illustrators. Most

Bettina Hürlimann [signature]

of them, delightful people, were no writers and my work as an editor consisted largely in correcting or rewriting their picture-book stories. As I had always written stories for my own children I had no difficulty in doing this. Among my illustrators was a wonderful bearded young man who came from the lake of Lucerne and was called Paul Nussbaumer. He had lots of ideas, but he was no writer. We worked together on the two books *William Tell and His Son* (Zurich, 1965) and *Barry* (Zurich, 1967). It was a very good collaboration, and I enormously enjoyed being for once a writer for children myself instead of correcting the texts of others. The books, especially the *Tell* book, have been read by many children in many countries. For me it was an interesting task to change two more or less historical stories with a touch of legend into subjects for picture books. I hope I can do more books like that. But at the moment I am much too involved in my theoretical work about children and children's books. Both my books in this field have been translated into English, and the *Three Centuries of European Children's Books* into Spanish and Japanese also. Many new contacts all over the world were the result, and at the moment I am studying the history of Japanese children and their books, which is tremendously fascinating. Some-

times I wish I could write about all these subjects for children too.

Bettina Hürlimann's children are Barbara, Regine, Christoph, and Ulrich. She writes that all are married and she has eleven grandchildren, who are a great inspiration in her work.

William Tell and His Son, with illustrations by Paul Nussbaumer, won the BIB silver medal at Bratislava in 1967, and was nominated for the Mildred L. Batchelder Award in 1969.

SELECTED WORKS: William Tell and His Son, 1967; Barry, the Story of a Brave St. Bernard, 1968.

ROSS E. HUTCHINS
April 30, 1906-

AUTHOR OF *The Amazing Seeds*, etc.

Autobiographical sketch of Ross Elliott Hutchins:

ON many roadmaps of Montana you will find, just west of Yellowstone National Park, a place called Hutchins Ranch. At this location my grandfather and his family settled in 1885 and it soon became the center of activity for that remote region. Trappers and sourdoughs came down out of the mountains at uncertain intervals to pick up mail, news and free meals. In many ways life there resembled the TV versions of western cattle ranches. It was into this setting that I came in 1908, having been born in the gold mining town of Ruby, Montana, where my father, for a time, ran a store. It was at Hutchins Ranch that my life really began. It was, and is, a wild area of mountains, rivers and deep green canyons where wildlife was abundant. In winter game came down out of the high mountains to feed in the sheltered valleys. On cold winter nights the eerie howls of coyotes echoed across the snowy land that glistened under the moon. Mountain lions prowled the forests and I once watched from the kitchen window when my father shot one on a cold Christmas Eve.

As a boy, I roamed the surrounding mountains on foot and on horseback and my play-

As time passed I became more and more interested in photographing and writing about the plants and animals I saw. At first I wrote for magazines such as *Nature Magazine*, *Natural History*, and *National Geographic*. Later, I turned to writing books for both young people and adults. These, I am happy to say, have done well and I am most gratified at their modest success. Most of my books—there are at present twenty—are illustrated with my own photographs.

In June 1968 I resigned from my position at the University to devote full time to travel, photographing plants and animals and in writing books about them.

Looking back down the years, I think that, more than anything else, I owe much to my early years in the Montana wilds. That was the formative period, the time when my interests became oriented in the direction they were to follow in later years.

———

ground was twenty miles across. I reveled in the sense of isolation and often at evening watched from concealment as deer, elk and other game came down to drink at the margins of streams and lakes. I listened to the drumming of grouse and marveled at their clusters of eggs hidden in nests beneath the quaking aspens. Few boys have had the privilege of growing up under such thought-stimulating and soul-satisfying conditions.

In time, I discovered the wonderful world of books that informed me about the things I saw. When about ten years old I became especially interested in insects and decided to make their study my life's work. Later, I enrolled at Montana State College (now Montana State University) and, in 1929, graduated with a B.S. in Zoology and Entomology. In 1932 I received an M.S. from Mississippi State University and in 1935 my Ph.D. from Iowa State University. In 1931 I married Annie Laurie McClanahan of Columbus, Mississippi. My wife holds a master's degree in entomology.

The South, I soon discovered, was truly a biologist's paradise and I found much of interest. Although I was by training an entomologist, there were too many fascinating things about plants and animals and so my interests fanned out and I became a naturalist, or student of wild nature in general.

From 1942-1945, Ross E. Hutchins served in the U.S. Navy as epidemic disease officer attaining the rank of lieutenant commander. In 1951, he became executive officer of the Mississippi Plant Board, and until his resignation in June 1968, he was professor of entomology at Mississippi State College. A member of Sigma Xi and Phi Kappa Phi, he is now a full-time writer.

SELECTED WORKS: Wild Ways, 1961; This Is a Tree, 1964; The Amazing Seeds, 1965; The Travels of Monarch X, 1966; Plants Without Leaves, 1966; Insects, 1966; The Ant Realm, 1967; Island of Adventure, 1968.

ABOUT: American Men of Science: The Physical and Biological Sciences, 11th edition; Contemporary Authors, Vol. 9-10; Who's Who in America, 1970-71.

MARGARET O. HYDE

February 18, 1917-

AUTHOR OF *Animal Clocks and Compasses*, etc.

Autobiographical sketch of Margaret Oldroyd Hyde:

A PREMEDICAL course and graduate work in science led me to writing even though I never had any desire to write a book. While

Margaret O. Hyde

learning more about the exciting challenges of scientific research, I was invited to be a coauthor with Dr. Gerald S. Craig for a sixth-grade science textbook. From the time I began to work on *New Ideas in Science* until now, about twenty books and two television scripts later, science has become increasingly exciting and still challenges me to explore further.

Plans for vacations with novels between writing nonfiction for others seldom materialize because there are always several new science areas that I want to learn more about by writing. Being an author gives me a wonderful chance to talk with experts in a field, to visit their laboratories and to learn about what they are doing firsthand.

From watching heart operations to learning about new theories before their publication, the life of a science writer is interesting. Perhaps one of the most exciting times I have had was working on a script for a television series on the human brain. A young monkey had to be kept alive for twelve hours in a bathtub in the home of two scientists in Princeton, New Jersey, while a television crew came from New York City to photograph it. The monkey had been removed from its mother's uterus, was operated on and returned to the mother.

My family found the many animals which I dissected and cared for less exciting than the television program about the scientists who patiently cared for the monkey mentioned above. But I was always interested in animals and in science generally. I was born in Philadelphia, Pennsylvania. Suburban Philadelphia was my home after graduating from Beaver College and doing graduate work at Columbia University and Temple University. Although I completed the course requirement for a doctor of philosophy degree, I never wrote the dissertation for I was too busy writing books by that time. I was married to Lieutenant Colonel Edwin Y. Hyde, Jr. in 1941, and have two sons, Lawrence Edwin and Bruce Geoffrey, who are now in college. Bruce is majoring in science and coauthoring the revision of *Atoms Today and Tomorrow*.

Our family hobbies include skiing, sailing, and traveling. I am especially interested in mental health after having been involved with the growth of a community mental health center in Philadelphia. This interest led to my latest book, *Mind Drugs,* on which I worked with such interesting people as Dr. David Smith who founded the clinic to help the sick in the Haight-Ashbury section of California. Dr. Duke Fisher, who is one of the world's leading authorities on LSD and who has done much work with young people who have had trouble as a result of experimenting with this drug, and Dr. Kenneth Appel, who is a world-famous psychiatrist, are among the contributors.

At present, I am working on the American adaptation of a book about the deserts of the world which was written in Italian by a photographer who visited all of the great deserts and captured their strange beauty in color.

Animal Clocks and Compasses won the Edison Award for the Best Children's Science Book, 1960. More than sixty foreign editions of various books by Margaret O. Hyde have been published, many in exotic languages, for the United States Information Agency.

SELECTED WORKS: Animal Clocks and Compasses, 1960; Where Speed Is King (with Edwin Hyde, revised edition) 1961; Your Brain, Master

Computer, 1964; Psychology in Action (with Edward S. Marks) 1967; Mind Drugs, 1968; Atoms Today and Tomorrow (fourth revised edition with Bruce Hyde) 1969; Off into Space (third revised edition) 1969; Earth in Action, 1969; Your Skin, 1970; Exploring Earth and Space (fifth revised edition) 1970.

ABOUT: Contemporary Authors, Vol. 1; Something About the Author, Vol. 1; Who's Who of American Women, 1961-62.

DAHLOV IPCAR

November 12, 1917-

AUTHOR AND ILLUSTRATOR OF *I Love My Anteater with an A*, etc.

Autobiographical sketch of Dahlov Zorach Ipcar:

MY parents were both artists, and I grew up in an atmosphere of creative activity. Art was as natural to me as the air I breathed. It never occurred to me that anyone could lead a life without art. I started drawing when I was three, and wrote and illustrated my first "book" (no, not published!) when I was seven. My parents were among the forerunners of the modern art movement, and they had a genuine appreciation of the quality of children's art work. Because they felt that their own art had been hampered by the academic training they had received, they resolved to let me develop in my own way without art instruction—but with plenty of encouragement. The progressive schools I attended also encouraged me to express myself, in creative writing as well as art.

During my childhood, winters were spent in New York City and summers at our farm in Maine, where I still live. I love farm life and animals. The beauty and variety of animal life has always fascinated me. When I was little I collected butterflies and salamanders, and raised wild rabbits and tame guinea pigs. In New York I spent many long afternoons at the Natural History Museum and the Bronx Zoo.

The first winter I was married, I began to consider illustrating children's books. A friend asked me to do some pictures for a story she had written. I also had ideas of my

own, but nothing came of this effort. Publishers were not interested, and I gave up the idea. I can see now that these early ideas were not very saleable.

That summer my husband and I decided to stay on the farm in Maine year round. We both did the farm work, and I painted. We had two babies and lived on very little money —fifty dollars a month!

Then in 1944 one of my former teachers asked me to illustrate a book of Margaret Wise Brown's, *The Little Fisherman*, for William R. Scott Company. This was my first published work, and I have been doing books ever since. After illustrating three for other authors, I began writing my own stories, and I have not illustrated for anyone else since.

I still consider myself primarily an artist. I devote at least half my time to painting, mostly in oils, mostly imaginative animal subjects. I have had nine one-man shows in New York City and many in Maine. My works are in the permanent collections of the Metropolitan and Whitney Museums and other museums throughout the country.

Although, as I said, I am first of all an artist, writing is becoming more and more important to me. I have started writing for older children and for adults. I have had

Dahlov Ipcar: *DAHL iv IP car*

short stories published in *Argosy, The Texas Quarterly*, and *Yankee Magazine. General Felice* was my first published book for older children. It is a wild and whacky tale, derived remotely from my own experiences as a twelve-year-old. I would love to do more of this sort of writing, but find good ideas for stories hard to come by. I have endless ideas for pictures, and my writing for younger children generally develops around some subject I would like to make pictures of. I still remember vividly the things that interested me when I was little. It seems that today's children have many of the same enthusiasms. I enjoy doing my books for children and try to keep a high artistic standard. I feel that only really good art and writing are good enough for the young.

Dahlov Zorach was born in Windsor, Vermont, the daughter of Marguerite Thompson and William Zorach. She attended City and Country School, Walden School, and Lincoln School in New York, and Oberlin College. In 1936 she married Adolph Ipcar and their sons, now grown, are Robert and Charles.

Mrs. Ipcar received the Clara A. Haas Award of Silvermine Guild in 1957.

SELECTED WORKS WRITTEN: General Felice, 1967.

SELECTED WORKS WRITTEN AND ILLUSTRATED: World Full of Horses, 1955; Ten Big Farms, 1958; I Love My Anteater with an A, 1964; Whisperings and Other Things, 1967; The Warlock of Night, 1969; Sir Addlepate and the Unicorn, 1971.

SELECTED WORKS ILLUSTRATED: The Little Fisherman, by Margaret Wise Brown, 1945; Just Like You, by Evelyn Beyer, 1946; Good Work! by John G. McCullough, 1948.

ABOUT: Contemporary Authors, Vol. 19-20; Hopkins, Lee Bennett. Books Are by People; Kingman, Lee and others, comps. Illustrators of Children's Books: 1957-1966; Something About the Author, Vol. 1; Viguers, Ruth Hill and others, comps. Illustrators of Children's Books: 1946-1956; Who's Who in American Art, 1962; Who's Who of American Women, 1961-62; Horn Book October 1961.

"ROBERT IRVING"

See *Adler, Irving*

ROBIN JACQUES
March 27, 1920-

ILLUSTRATOR OF *A Book of Mermaids*, etc.

Autobiographical sketch of Robin Jacques:

MY early childhood was spent in central London, near the river, which was the centre of my interest at that time. My father having died when I was only two years of age, my sister and I were thrown on our own resources as to entertaining ourselves and most of our time was spent playing under and around old Chelsea Bridge. When I was ten years of age I was sent away to boarding school in the country near London and here I stayed until I was fifteen years of age. A serious illness at this time led to a six-month spell in hospital where I began to draw in earnest and the enforced leisure gave much time for reading. I devoured a strange mixture of authors, these reflecting in some ways a typical adolescent confusion of interests. There were, among others, Zane Grey, Oscar Wilde, Sapper, Dornford Yates, Dumas, Anatole France and George Moore.

On leaving hospital, it became necessary to earn my living and on about my sixteenth birthday I joined an advertising agency as a very junior designer and did my best to learn this trade until the outbreak of war, when I was "called up" into the British Army. War service lasted until June 1945 and I was fortunate enough to be offered the chance to illustrate books on a full-time basis for a new publishing house. Here I cut my teeth on children's versions of *Don Quixote, Arabian Nights*, Washington Irving's *Alhambra Tales* and many others. Since those days I have worked for many publishers in the United States, the United Kingdom and France, where I now live, and divide my time between graphic design and book illustration though with the latter as my main concern.

I count myself particularly fortunate in my choice of profession since this allows me to travel very extensively and at different periods in my life I have made my home in Africa, Mexico and now France.

My particular interests, apart from travel, extend to modern painting and music, to early and recent jazz and to poetry. In addi-

ROBIN JACQUES

tion, I try to make a special study of the habits and background of the various people in whose countries I have lived and this has led to a marked sympathy for such gifted but often under-privileged races as the Africans and Mexicans.

The sources of my drawing style are found, I believe, in the English and American draughtsmen of the last century with a marked preference for the romantic illustrators of the last part of that period. More recent masters whose work I particularly admire are Klimt, Forain and Dana Gibson.

Robin Jacques was born in Chelsea, London, to a family which he has said "seemed always on the move, a pattern that has persisted until now." He attended the Royal Masonic Junior and Senior Schools in Hertfordshire. Without formal art training, he practiced drawing nights and weekends in the Victoria and Albert Museum while working for an advertising agency. After four years in the Royal Artillery and Engineers, he was invalided out in 1945, and then worked as an illustrator of children's books for the publisher John Westhouse, as art editor for *Strand Magazine* and as principal art editor for the Central Office of Information. Married twice (both wives deceased), he has a son, John Paul, born in 1948.

Robin Jacques is a Fellow of the Society of Industrial Artists and author of *Illustrators*

at Work. His illustrations, mostly pen and ink, have been in exhibitions of the American Institute of Graphic Arts. He received a gold plaque at the Biennale of Illustrations Bratislava, 1969.

SELECTED WORKS ILLUSTRATED: A Book of Giants, by Ruth Manning-Sanders, 1962; Promise of the Rainbow, by Rosalie K. Fry, 1965; A Book of Witches, by Ruth Manning-Sanders, 1966; Nightbirds on Nantucket, by Joan Aiken, 1966; A Book of Mermaids, by Ruth Manning-Sanders, 1967; The Sea, Ships and Sailors, by William Cole, 1967; Snowed Up, by Rosalie K. Fry, 1970.

ABOUT: Kingman, Lee and others, comps. Illustrators of Children's Books: 1957-1966; Ryder, John. Artists of a Certain Line; Viguers, Ruth Hill and others, comps. Illustrators of Children's Books: 1946-1956; Who's Who in Art, 1970.

"DYNELY JAMES"

See *Mayne, William*

TOVE JANSSON

August 9, 1914-

AUTHOR AND ILLUSTRATOR OF *Tales from Moomin Valley*, etc.

Autobiographical sketch of Tove Marika Jansson:

WE lived in a large, dilapidated studio, and through the windows one could see the whole harbour and the roofs of Helsinki. I pitied other children who had to live in ordinary flats, who had living rooms without staircases and sleeping compartments up close to the ceiling, nothing like the mysterious jumble of turntables, sacks with plaster and cases with clay, pieces of wood and iron constructions where one could hide and build in peace. A home without sculptures seemed as naked to me as one without books.

My mother made illustrations and dust covers for books all day long and well into the night. Every book she had contributed to she got free when it was published, our bookcases grew all over the walls and I read without restriction, anything and anywhere, with pocket flashlights under the bedcovers

Tove Jansson: *TOH VAY YAN son*

Tove Jansson.

and on the dustbins down in the yard if I was told to get some fresh air. If any book was really unsuitable for a child my mother only had to say "that one you should read, it is very instructive" to ensure that I didn't.

Sometimes she told me stories in front of the fire in the Dutch-tile stove. The studio was in darkness, there were only the fire and we and our unreal, completely safe world.

But it was my father who gave the necessary background of excitement to this idyll. When there was a fire in town he would wake us up in the middle of the night and hurry us along dark streets to look, he played the balalaika at our parties which lasted for several days, parties where absolutely anything could happen. Summers he took the whole family along to a desolate island in the Gulf of Finland where we rented a fisherman's cabin, he took us out sailing whenever the weather was bad enough, walked with us into the huge forests to pick mushrooms that only he was able to find, salvaged smuggled canisters of liquor and driftwood from the bays, and loved thunderstorms above anything else.

The happiest childhood is, I think, the one which offers both security and excitement. In my books I have tried to describe both, to find my way back to that early world which keeps the balance between the excite-

ment of the commonplace and the safety of the fantastic, the child's taken-for-granted world of kindness and cruelty, colourful light and impenetrable darkness. If there are any greys they are not the colour of gloom but rather those half tones necessary for the unspoken, the hidden. In a book for children I think there should always be something left unexplained and without any illustration. There should be a path at which the writer respectfully stops to let the child continue alone.

Actually I am a painter, but writing has by and by come to mean as much to me as painting. I was born in Helsinki in 1914, studied book design in Stockholm 1930-33, painting in Helsinki 1933-36 and in Paris 1938, started to write in 1939, did some murals in the forties and for seven years did the Moomin strip for the London *Evening News* in the fifties.

And during all this time, every spring, I have returned to the islands for five or six months, only now I live farther out, on the last skerry of the archipelago where nothing grows but wild flowers and knee-high juniper. In the middle of the islet there is a deep lagoon, the cabin has one single room, it is a place which perfectly combines security and excitement. And it is a good place to work— or leave it undone.

———

Tove Jansson is the daughter of sculptor Viktor Jansson and designer Signe Hammarsten Jansson. An author, artist, and illustrator, Miss Jansson has won awards for painting and numerous literary prizes, including the Stockholm Award for best children's book, 1952, the Selma Lagerlöf Award, 1953, and the Elsa Beskow Award (Malmo) 1958. Her books have been on the Hans Christian Andersen honor list four times and she won the Hans Christian Andersen Medal in 1966. As a member of the Swedish-speaking minority in Finland, she writes in Swedish, but her children's books have all been published in English as well. Her books have also been translated into seventeen other languages.

SELECTED WORKS WRITTEN AND ILLUSTRATED: Moomin Summer Madness, 1961; Moominland Mid-Winter, 1962; Tales from Moomin Valley,

1964; Finn Family Moomintroll, 1965; Moomin-pappa at Sea, 1967; Comet in Moominland, 1968.

ABOUT: Author's and Writer's Who's Who, 1963; Contemporary Authors, Vol. 17-18; Jansson, Tove. Sculptor's Daughter; Kingman, Lee and others, comps. Illustrators of Children's Books: 1957-1966; Bookbird no. 4, 1966; Top of the News April 1967.

RANDALL JARRELL

May 6, 1914-October 14, 1965

AUTHOR OF *The Animal Family*, etc.

Biographical sketch by Mary von Schrader Jarrell:

"RANDALL talked at seven months," his mother liked to tell other mothers. His first words, though, were not "Ma-ma" or "Da-da," but "Bow-wow-wow-wow," to imitate—or maybe answer—a little barking dog who was left alone all day in the room next to theirs in a hotel in Los Angeles. Born in Nashville, Tennessee, where the language of the home and the environment was pure Southern, Randall Jarrell spoke with hardly any of this accent. When people remarked on this, he told them, "That's right. I was born in the South, but I learned to talk in the West."

Words, their sounds, the look of them on a page, and their vivid and lyrical possibilities were what absorbed my husband from his first years to his last. He learned to read before he went to school and he said he had a library card before he had a wallet to put it in. *Stalky and Co., Huckleberry Finn,* and *The Three Musketeers* were grade-school favorites he never outgrew. Shakespeare, Shaw, Ibsen, the Bible and *The Odyssey* were high-school favorites he never outgrew. As a man he added many "grown-up" favorites; but always nearby and often reread were *Kim, The Wind in the Willows* and Grimm's fairy tales.

Randall Jarrell liked to say he only joined two things, Phi Beta Kappa and the Army. He received his B.A. and M.A. from Vanderbilt University, where he was a member of Phi Beta Kappa. And during World War II he enlisted in the Army and became a Celes-

RANDALL JARRELL

tial Navigation Tower Operator. During peacetime he taught literature and creative writing at various universities. He had hobbies such as sports cars, hi-fi, tennis, pro football, zoos; and serious interests such as opera, painting, anthropology and psychology. With it all—war or peace—every day he read or wrote for several hours. He wrote eight books of poetry, three books of essays, and a novel. He translated Chekhov's play *The Three Sisters* from Russian and Goethe's *Faust: Part I* from German. Then, at forty-eight, he discovered he could write for children.

His first and last children's books, *The Gingerbread Rabbit* and *Fly by Night,* are possibly the most congenial to the pre-reader. The third book, *The Animal Family,* is something of a fantasy about a bearded hunter (not unlike the author) who lives by the sea in a house with fur rugs, a hunting horn, a glass window seat and a huge fireplace, and in a house not unlike the Jarrells' own home in Greensboro, North Carolina.

The Bat-Poet is fantasy-and-real too. It can be enjoyed simply for its story, but if a deeper meaning is sought it might be interpreted as the poet-author speaking through the poet-bat about some of the difficulties that go with artistic creativity. For instance, the Bat-Poet wakes up in the daylight instead of at night like his fellows, and he finds a new world that he tells them about

Jarrell: *juh RELL*

in his poetry and hopes they will enjoy with him. But they don't. They don't know what he is talking about and they won't even try to learn. The Mockingbird is such a superb and imaginative singer that he can't think of anything but his art. Through the Bat's admiring encounters with him, we learn something about the sensitivity and irritability, and even the helpless vanity, that often go with creativity and drive it onward. In the Bat's friendship with the unrivalling Chipmunk we begin to understand an artist's touching need for a welcoming audience and his touching dependence upon someone he can trust to arrange details and be a link between him and his public. In the Bat's failed effort to write a poem about the Cardinal, even though he very much wanted to, we are shown that the artist cannot create at will or coerce his gifts.

Randall Jarrell was teaching at the University of North Carolina at Greensboro when he wrote these books. Much of the writing was done outdoors in a hammock in the woods. Chipmunks, squirrels, owls, cardinals and a mockingbird still flourish there. In midsummer a few little brown bats still come to hang from the porch beams of the house where he lived before he was killed in a traffic accident.

———

Randall Jarrell married Mary von Schrader in 1952. Besides his active career as a teacher of poetry and creative writing in various institutions and, from 1958, as professor of English at the University of North Carolina at Greensboro, Jarrell served as the Poetry Consultant at the Library of Congress (1956-58), poetry critic of *Partisan Review* (1949-51) and the *Yale Review* (1955-57); was a member of the editorial board of *American Scholar* beginning in 1957, and contributed to numerous leading periodicals. He was a chancellor of the Academy of American Poets and a member of the National Institute of Arts and Letters. Among his many honors and awards were a Guggenheim fellowship in poetry in 1946, the Levinson prize in 1948, the Oscar Blumenthal prize in 1951, a grant from the National Institute of Arts and Letters in 1951 and the National Book Award for poetry for *The Woman at the Washington Zoo*, in 1961. *The Animal*

Family was a runner-up for the Newbery Medal for 1966 and received a Lewis Carroll Shelf Award in 1970. Before his death, Jarrell finished *Fly by Night*, for which illustrations are being prepared by Maurice Sendak.

SELECTED WORKS: The Gingerbread Rabbit, 1964; The Bat-Poet, 1964; The Animal Family, 1965.

SELECTED WORKS TRANSLATED AND EDITED: The Golden Bird and Other Fairy Tales of The Brothers Grimm, 1962; The Rabbit Catcher and Other Fairy Tales of Ludwig Bechstein, 1962.

ABOUT: Arendt, Hannah. Men in Darkness; Contemporary Authors, Vol. 7-8; Harte, Barbara and Carolyn Riley. 200 Contemporary Authors; Hoffman Frederick J. The Achievement of Randall Jarrell; Lowell, Robert and others, eds. Randall Jarrell, 1914-1965; Shapiro, Karl. Randall Jarrell: a lecture . . . Library of Congress, 1967; Twentieth Century Authors (First Supplement), 1955; University of North Carolina Library. North Carolina Authors; Who's Who in America, 1966-67; Who Was Who in America, 1961-1968; Atlantic Monthly September 1967; Commentary February 1966; Harper's April 1967; Nation June 30, 1955; National Review November 2, 1965; New Republic December 26, 1960; New York Times Book Review May 2, 1954; February 2, 1969; January 4, 1970; New Yorker June 19, 1954; Newsweek September 17, 1956; March 17, 1958; October 25, 1965; Poetry March 1952; December 1964; Publishers' Weekly October 25, 1965; Reporter September 8, 1966; Saturday Review May 8, 1954; June 3, 1954; January 28, 1961; September 2, 1967; Time November 9, 1962; October 22, 1965; September 15, 1967.

ANNABEL JOHNSON

June 18, 1921-

and

EDGAR JOHNSON

October 24, 1912-

AUTHORS OF *The Grizzly*, etc.

Autobiographical sketch of Annabel Jones Johnson and Edgar Raymond Johnson by Annabel Johnson:

THE question most often asked by our young readers, I think, is this: How did you come to write books? The best answer we can give is that, in our two lives, we have run across so many stories worth the telling.

ANNABEL JOHNSON

EDGAR JOHNSON

Edgar especially has bridged a strange span of time and space. Born in a coal-mining town in Montana, he can still remember stagecoach days. After working as a railroad section hand, a semi-pro baseball player, fiddler in a dance band and in a number of other odd-jobs, he studied art in Kansas City and New York, where he went on to become one of the country's leading ceramists.

I was born in St. Louis to a much more conventional world, but broke away to go to New York myself in the years after the second war. It was still a wonderful free place then, where people weren't so self-conscious about poverty. We were all blissfully poor, but having a wonderful time. I'd always wanted to be a writer, so lost no time in getting a job in a publishing house—several of them. I found no golden key to success, though, until I married Edgar.

Together we began to write books for young people in the 1950s, largely because we had both always loved the history and challenge of the West and wanted to pass along our feelings to the boys and girls growing up in big cities, far from any wilderness.

Working at temporary or part-time jobs to make ends meet whenever the cash ran low, we spent twelve years roaming the country in a small camp-trailer, living outdoors year-around—the desert in wintertime, the high mountain country in summer. We poked around museums, reading the diaries and newspapers of long years past, talking to old-timers who could still remember panning for gold or breaking new trails across the land. When we had our material in hand, we would hide out deep in the national forest to write the books, with no other neighbors but the wild animals. And from one of them came the idea for our best-known story, *The Grizzly*.

That was a tale of the present, and so have our more recent stories been. It seems to us particularly important to young people for authors to examine the confusing world that is turning so swiftly today. But sometimes the past can throw light on the present, too, so we hope to do more historical novels as well.

———

Annabel Johnson attended William and Mary College and has worked as a librarian. Edgar Johnson studied at Billings Polytechnic Institute and graduated from the Kansas City Art Institute. He has also attended the Art Students League and New York State College of Ceramics at Alfred University. He is a wood carver and jeweler as well as a ceramist and has had his work in an exhibition of American handcrafts at the Museum of Modern Art. At one time he did restorations of antique musical instruments for the Smithsonian Institution.

The Johnsons were married in 1949. Occasionally they use the pen name of A. E. Johnson for adult books. For one of their adult books, *The Secret Gift,* they received the $1,000 Friends of American Writers Award, in 1962. They have won awards for juveniles as well, including a Golden Spur from the Western Writers of America for *The Burning Glass,* in 1966, and the William Allen White Award for *The Grizzly,* in 1967. *The Black Symbol* and *Torrie* were Honor Books in New York *Herald Tribune* Children's Spring Book Festivals, in 1959 and 1960, respectively.

Annabel Johnson enjoys hand weaving and trout-fly tying, Edgar Johnson seventeenth-century music and fishing.

SELECTED WORKS: The Black Symbol, 1959; Wilderness Bride, 1962; A Golden Touch, 1963; The Grizzly, 1964; The Burning Glass, 1966; Count Me Gone, 1968; A Blues I Can Whistle, 1969; The Last Knife, 1971.

ABOUT: Author's and Writer's Who's Who, 1963; Contemporary Authors, Vol. 9-10; Library Journal February 1, 1957.

"CROCKETT JOHNSON"

October 20, 1906-

AUTHOR AND ILLUSTRATOR OF *Barnaby,* etc.

Biographical sketch of David Johnson Leisk, who writes under the pen name "Crockett Johnson":

CROCKETT JOHNSON, whose real name is David Johnson Leisk, is of Scottish descent, the son of David and Mary (Burg) Leisk. Crockett is a nickname from his childhood and he uses Johnson, his middle name, because he says Leisk is too hard to pronounce.

Born in mid-Manhattan, on East 58th Street, Johnson grew up on Long Island, near the southern edge of Long Island Sound, where he enjoyed sailing and kept a small boat of his own.

Johnson studied art at Cooper Union in 1924 and at New York University in 1925. A man of varied occupational background, he worked in an ice plant, played professional football, and was employed by Macy's in the advertising department. He has been an adaptor and consultant for television and for animated films and was art editor of several magazines. Most recently he has been a cartoonist for children and adults, a de-

"CROCKETT JOHNSON"

signer, a book illustrator, and the author of more than twenty juveniles.

In 1940, Johnson married Ruth Krauss, the well-known writer for children.

From 1938-1941, Johnson drew a weekly cartoon, *The Little Man with the Eyes,* for *Collier's,* and in 1955 did a syndicated newspaper panel, *Barkis.* His comic strip *Barnaby,* created in 1941 and featuring a small boy and his fairy godfather Mr. O'Malley, appeared every day for years, although after 1946 it was ghost written, with Johnson as story consultant. As a feature of the Chicago Sun syndicate, it ran in fifty-two American newspapers, having a total circulation of nearly 5,600,000. *Barnaby* was in a dozen foreign newspapers as well, and was translated into Italian and Japanese. It has been adapted for television and in Japan it was broadcast as a weekly half-hour radio program. With Jerome Chodorov, Johnson wrote a play based on the strip, called *Barnaby and Mr. O'Malley. Barnaby's* publication as a book in 1943 was hailed as a literary event, with blurbs supplied by important people in the arts and literature, including William Rose Benét, Louis Untermeyer, and Rockwell Kent. Dorothy Parker, claiming she was trying to talk calmly, called the characters in *Barnaby* "the most important additions to American Arts and Letters in Lord knows how many years."

In 1955 *Harold and the Purple Crayon* appeared and was followed by a series of much-admired books about Harold, whose adventures range from his circus, to the North Pole, to the sky.

Johnson has said that ideas come hard to him, but that his characters, once created, often make their own plots. He claims never to have written down to children; when his adult characters speak in big words, he believes children accept it as parent talk, even though they don't understand it.

Johnson designs and illustrates all the books he writes, and has illustrated a number of books by others, including several by his wife. He describes his illustrations as "simplified, almost diagrammatic, for clear storytelling, avoiding all arbitrary decoration."

A serious painter as well, Johnson has had work exhibited in a gallery in New York City. He does large, vivid canvasses, concentrating on geometric painting which requires the help of a computer.

Johnson is a member of Authors Guild of Authors League of America and of the Society of Authors (England). He is six feet tall, tan, husky, and blue-eyed. Like some of the characters in his cartoons, he is completely bald.

The Johnsons live in Rowayton, Connecticut, a small town near the north shore of Long Island Sound, where they like to sail.

SELECTED WORKS WRITTEN AND ILLUSTRATED: Barnaby, 1943; Harold and the Purple Crayon, 1955; Will Spring Be Early or Will Spring Be Late? 1959; A Picture for Harold's Room, 1960; We Wonder What Will Walter Be! When He Grows Up, 1964; Castles in the Sand, 1965; Upside Down, 1969.

SELECTED WORKS ILLUSTRATED: The Carrot Seed, by Ruth Krauss, 1945; How to Make an Earthquake, by Ruth Krauss, 1954; Is This You? by Ruth Krauss, 1955; Mickey's Magnet, by Franklin Branley, 1956.

ABOUT: Contemporary Authors, Vol. 9-10; Hopkins, Lee Bennett. Books Are by People; Kingman, Lee and others, comps. Illustrators of Children's Books: 1957-1966; Something About the Author, Vol. 1; Viguers, Ruth Hill and others, comps. Illustrators of Children's Books: 1946-1956; Editor and Publisher July 16, 1960; Time September 2, 1946.

GERALD W. JOHNSON
August 6, 1890-

AUTHOR OF *America, a History for Peter,* etc.

Biographical sketch of Gerald White Johnson:

GERALD W. JOHNSON was born in Riverton, North Carolina, a village so small that he has jokingly claimed the whole population was related to him. His grandfather was the postmaster and his father, Archibald Johnson, the editor of a small country newspaper. His mother, Flora Caroline (McNeill) was an aunt of the North Carolina poet, John Charles McNeill.

Archibald Johnson was a versatile musician, and in this as well as in his interest in newspaper writing, his son resembled him. Gerald was already editing his own newspaper (*The Thomasville Davidsonian,* combining the names of two small North Carolina towns) before he graduated from Wake Forest College in 1911. His newspaper, however, was not a profitable venture and after graduation he went to work for the Lexington (N. C.) *Dispatch.* Two years later he got a chance to combine his interests when he was appointed music critic on the Greensboro (N.C.) *Daily News.*

World War I intervened and he served in the Army for two years, including a year with the American Expeditionary Force in France. Afterwards he returned to the *Daily News,* and in 1922 he married Kathryn Hayward.

During the twenties, when he was still with the *Daily News,* he attracted the attention of H. L. Mencken, then on the staff of the Baltimore *Sun.* Mencken described Johnson as "the best editorial writer in the South, a very excellent critic, and a highly civilized man." Johnson began to contribute to the "Sunpapers" (the Baltimore *Sun* and the Baltimore *Evening Sun*). In 1924 he left the *Daily News* to teach journalism at the University of North Carolina. By 1926 he was a regular editorial writer for the Baltimore *Evening Sun* and he and his wife and two small daughters went to live in Baltimore. They lived first in the suburbs, then moved to Bolton Street, into one of the famous

GERALD W. JOHNSON

Baltimore red brick houses with the four white marble steps leading to the front door.

While writing for the Sunpapers Johnson was also beginning to write books, and his third, *Andrew Jackson, an Epic in Homespun* (1927) brought him fame and established him as an authority on American history and government. In successive books (for instance, *The Secession of the Southern States,* 1933, and *America's Silver Age,* 1937) he developed a knack for making complex subjects clear without oversimplification or distortion. His easy, witty, ironic, yet down-to-earth style lifted history above the dull category of schoolbooks and made it immensely readable. He has never claimed to be a scholar although he was notoriously knowledgeable. "Ask Gerald" was a catchphrase at the Sun.

In 1943 Johnson severed his connection with the Sunpapers. He says that political differences made the move necessary and that it was done in a friendly manner. He continued to write and to comment on the news as a free lance.

In 1950 one of his two married daughters gave birth to a son. The responsibility of being a grandfather turned his mind to writing a book for his grandson which would make him aware of his American heritage. *America, a History for Peter,* was written as a trilogy: *America Is Born,* which was runner-up for the Newbery Medal, 1960, *Amer-*

ica Grows Up, and *America Moves Forward,* also a runner-up for the Newbery, 1961. Critics agreed, when the work appeared, that Johnson took it for granted that boys and girls wanted to think and were capable of doing so.

The success of his first work for children encouraged Johnson to start a second trilogy, this time on the three branches of the United States government, *The Presidency, The Supreme Court* and *The Congress.* Johnson describes the growth as well as the present state of these institutions, showing the system of checks and balances, and enlivening the whole with sketches of the men who made these institutions great—in *The Presidency,* a chapter on strong presidents, and in *The Supreme Court,* a glowing account of how two great chief justices were able to give the Court power and prestige without the use of force. The books have been translated into more than thirty languages. In 1966 Johnson added a fourth volume, *The Cabinet.*

In 1964 Johnson embarked on a more controversial subject with *Communism, an American's View.* Clarity and justice are outstanding in this account of the history of the Communist ideal, and make it an intelligent antidote to both excessive fear and awe of the subject. Above everything, the book emphasizes the tremendous responsibilities of the citizen of a democratic nation.

Gerald W. Johnson has written more than twenty books for children and adults, in addition to his many journalistic activities.

For his "scholarly commentary on the news" as a broadcaster for WAAM-TV, Baltimore, Johnson received a Peabody award in 1954.

SELECTED WORKS: America, a History for Peter (America Is Born, 1959; America Grows Up, 1960; America Moves Forward, 1960); The Presidency, 1962; The Supreme Court, 1962; The Congress, 1963; Communism, an American's View, 1964; The Cabinet, 1966.

ABOUT: Twentieth Century Authors (First Supplement), 1955; University of North Carolina Library. North Carolina Authors; Who's Who in America, 1970-71; New York Herald Tribune Book Review September 4, 1949; October 7, 1951; March 5, 1961; New York Times March 7, 1961; Saturday Review of Literature June 3, 1950.

HAROLD JONES
February 22, 1904-

ILLUSTRATOR OF *Lavender's Blue*, etc.

Autobiographical sketch of Harold Jones:

I ATTENDED my first illustration class at Goldsmith's College, New Cross. It was conducted by a venerable old gentleman, with long white hair, who wore a large black cloak and pince-nez spectacles secured by a black band. He was an imposing and lovable person and his name was Edmund Sullivan —he had some years previously taught Arthur Rackham. We, his students, used to keep and cherish the exquisite drawings he made for our instruction on the margins of our paper.

Some years later I won a scholarship to the Royal College of Art, South Kensington, where I studied the graphic arts.

I liked to tell little stories to my two daughters at bedtime, and one day it occurred to me it might be fun to try and make from these a book for each little girl. So I set to and moulded the books into shape and drew my pictures. Each daughter was to be the heroine of her own book. The first I called *The Visit to the Farm* and the second *The Enchanted Night*.

About this time I collaborated with Walter de la Mare and we produced *This Year, Next Year* (1937), a book of rhymes and pictures descriptive of the seasons of the year. There were illustrations to each page and I lithographed these on both stone and slate. The book was in full color throughout.

But now war loomed on the horizon and I had to lay my brush and pen aside for many years.

I was fortunate to join a map reproduction section of the Royal Engineers. Fortunate, because I was able to use my skill as a draughtsman in this important wartime work —the compilation of maps. The unit to which I belonged drew the maps for the invasion of Europe, D Day.

My first big commission after the war was to design and work out a large book of nursery rhymes for the Oxford University Press. This work was to take me a year or two to complete—from first draught to final

drawings. Many of the backgrounds to the pictures were recollections of the countryside remembered so well from a year spent in the country, when I was very young. I hummed aloud the rhymes as I drew. This helped me a great deal in trying to get the spirit of them, and what wonderful subject matter these rhymes are—at times pure surrealism. The book, when completed, was entitled *Lavender's Blue*.

Many books followed and one of them, *The Pied Piper of Hamelin*, took me to Germany, where I made drawings of the medieval architecture and landscape for background and atmosphere, and of course innumerable drawings of the children as they played.

I live at Putney—where we enjoy both river and heath and my studio window overlooks my garden—an ever-changing picture of tree and shrub, birds and sunshine, light and shade and flowers and raindrops. And of course, there's the sundial—which tells me that time is passing.

Harold Jones married Mollie Merry in 1933 and their daughters are Stephanie Angela and Gabrielle Pamela. Jones has received a number of honors and awards, including honorable mention for the Hans Christian Andersen Medal for *Lavender's*

Blue. His work is in collections of the Tate Gallery, the Victoria and Albert Museum, and in the Lillian H. Smith Collection of the Toronto Public Library. There is a Harold Jones collection at the University of Southern Mississippi.

SELECTED WORKS ILLUSTRATED: This Year, Next Year, by Walter de la Mare, 1937; Lavender's Blue, compiled by Kathleen Lines, 1954; Once in Royal David's City, by Kathleen Lines, 1956; Bless This Day, compiled by Elfrida Vipont, pseud., 1958; Songs of Innocence, by William Blake, 1961; The Pied Piper of Hamelin, by Robert Browning, 1962; The Complete Greek Stories of Nathaniel Hawthorne, 1963.

ABOUT: Hürlimann, Bettina. Picture Book World; Kingman, Lee and others, comps. Illustrators of Children's Books: 1957-1966; Mahony, Bertha E. and others, comps. Illustrators of Children's Books: 1744-1945; Viguers, Ruth Hill and others, comps. Illustrators of Children's Books: 1946-1956; Who's Who in Art, 1970; The Junior Bookshelf December 1948.

"IVAR JORGENSON"

See *Silverberg, Robert*

SESYLE JOSLIN

August 30, 1929-

AUTHOR OF *What Do You Say, Dear?* etc.

Autobiographical sketch of Sesyle Joslin Hine who also writes with Al Hine under the pen names "Josephine Gibson" and "G. B. Kirtland":

I WAS born in Providence, Rhode Island, and remained there until I was high enough —with a little help on the side—to reach the counter of the corner drugstore and buy a Sunday afternoon cigar. My father's, that is.

We then moved to Hyannis, Massachusetts: site of the next memory; sitting in a winter's sun-beamed attic playroom and being patiently taught to write the alphabet and my name by a determined trio of older sisters and brother. One day I learned, and once become the young mistress of these skills never let go them for a moment after but began at once to fashion small stories and sign them with a large name, a habit I am happy to say that eventually reversed itself.

Was it learning the alphabet thus—in a half-lit, dust-beamed attic corner that left me always with the impression of having been secretly initiated into language—having been given at once the mystery and the key to the mystery? I do not know, but surely from that beginning to write and to read became my work, my treasure.

So I grew and went to schools and worked in bookshops and acted in little theaters, attended the University of Miami, Goddard College and Antioch College, and became an editorial assistant for a national magazine and a publishing firm.

In 1949 I was married to Al Hine, the novelist. We moved into an old farmhouse in New Milford, Connecticut, and proceeded to fill it with three daughters, Victoria, Alexandra and Julia, and an assortment of pets ranging from cats and dogs to African geese. Although we've been living in Rome for the past several years, this white and blue colonial house is home and from this busy household have stemmed our various writings; including collaboration in some children's books under the pen names of Josephine Gibson and G. B. Kirtland.

My own children have been the reason, I suppose, as well as often the inspiration for the children's books I've written. *What Do You Say, Dear?*, my first book, grew from a game I had hopefully invented to put them on easy friendly terms with politesse. The *Baby Elephant* books are perhaps more autobiographical than one might suppose at first glance.

As my daughters grow, so seemingly do my books. My first full-length book for older children, *The Night They Stole the Alphabet,* was published last fall and perhaps in some way also reflects that long-ago child learning her letters in the attic, thus completing a certain circle of time.

What Do You Say, Dear? with illustrations by Maurice Sendak, was a runner-up for the Caldecott Medal for 1959. *Spaghetti for Breakfast* with illustrations by Katharine Barry, was an honor book in the New York *Herald Tribune* Children's Spring Book Festival, 1965. *Please Share That Peanut,* with illustrations by Simms Taback, was named by the New York *Times* as among the best-illustrated books for children, 1965.

Under the pen name "G. B. Kirtland" Sesyle Joslin and her husband, Al Hine, collaborated on *One Day in Ancient Rome,* 1961, *One Day in Elizabethan England,* 1962, and *One Day in Aztec Mexico,* 1963. Under the pen name "Josephine Gibson" they wrote *Is There a Mouse in the House?* 1965.

SELECTED WORKS: What Do You Say, Dear? 1958; Baby Elephant's Trunk, 1961; There Is a Dragon in My Bed, 1961; Dear Dragon . . . and Other Useful Letter Forms, 1962; La Petite Famille, 1964; Please Share That Peanut, 1965; Spaghetti for Breakfast, 1965; The Night They Stole the Alphabet, 1968; Doctor George Owl, 1970.

ABOUT: Contemporary Authors, Vol. 15-16.

ERICH KÄSTNER

February 23, 1899-

AUTHOR OF *Emil and the Detectives,* etc.

Biographical sketch of Erich Kästner:

AN only child, Erich Kästner was born in the German city of Dresden. His father Emil

Kästner: *KEST ner*

ERICH KÄSTNER

was a harness maker who lost his workshop to machine age progress and took a job in a luggage factory before his son was born. His mother, Ida Amalia (Augustin) Kästner, supplemented the family income by sewing and working as a hairdresser. She also boarded a teacher and Erich's close contact with members of the profession influenced him to decide that teaching would be his career.

After completing elementary school in 1913 he entered a teacher-training institute in Dresden, which he attended until he was drafted into the Imperial army in 1917. Discharged about a year later with a heart ailment, he was hospitalized for a time, then continued his training at an institute in Stehlen. However, by this time he had lost his enthusiasm for the profession. He began attending the King George Gymnasium in Dresden, and after a semester there, passed with distinction the entrance examination for the University of Leipzig, and with a stipend from the city of Dresden, took up the study of German and French literature, history, and philosophy. He continued his studies to the graduate level, taking some courses at the universities of Rostock and Berlin and finishing his doctorate at Leipzig while he worked at various jobs—as bookkeeper, publicist, researcher, and journalist.

After receiving his Ph.D. in 1925, Kästner took his first foreign trip (to Italy and Switzerland) in the company of his mother. Back in Leipzig again, he was employed as drama critic and associate feuilleton editor of the *Neue Leipziger Zeitung* but was dismissed in 1927 because of public objection to his satire. He then moved to Berlin where he supported himself as a free-lance journalist. The year 1928 was one of the most notable in his career. He published his first two volumes of poetry, *Herz auf Taille*, and *Lärm in Spiegel*, and his first children's book, *Emil und die Detektive (Emil and the Detectives)*. A humorous story of a boy's first trip to the big city, where he captures a thief with the aid of new friends, *Emil* was adapted for radio, TV, and stage, made into films in German, English, and Spanish, translated into nearly thirty languages and was soon considered a children's classic. At this time also, Kästner met the cartoonist Walter Trier, whose illustrations considerably enhanced the popularity of many of Kästner's books. Kästner made his first trip to Paris during this period, as well.

In the next few years Kästner published his semi-autobiographical novel, *Fabian*, four more books of poetry, and several children's stories. When Hitler came to power in 1933, Kästner was branded "undesirable and politically unreliable" because of his declared pacifism and his uncomplimentary remarks about Nazism. His books were banned from Germany and publicly burned by the Nazis, but he continued to publish abroad until 1942, when he was forced to cease publication altogether.

After World War II, Kästner settled in Munich. There he worked from 1945 to 1947 as feuilleton editor of the *Neue Zeitung* and also edited a children's magazine, *Pinguin*, which he started in 1946. He shared in the founding of the literary cabaret, *Schaubude*, in 1945 and its successor, *Die Kleine Freiheit*, founded in 1951 and named after a song he had written. New books by him began to appear, the most notable of his postwar works being his satire, *Die Konferenz die Tiere (The Animals' Conference)*; his children's book, *Das doppelte Lottchen* (published in America as *Lisa and Lottie*), which was made into a prize-winning film; his autobiographical account of his boyhood, *Als ich ein kleiner Junge war (When I Was*

a Boy), which received a Lewis Carroll Shelf Award in 1961; and his *Der kleine Mann (The Little Man)*, which won the Mildred L. Batchelder Award in 1968.

Kästner won the literature prize of Munich in 1956, the Büchner prize in 1957, and the Hans Christian Andersen Medal in 1960. He has served as president of the German P.E.N. center and vice president of the international P.E.N. club. A bachelor, he lives with several cats. He does much of his writing in a café.

SELECTED WORKS: Emil and the Detectives, 1930; Lisa and Lottie, 1951; The Animals' Conference, 1953; Puss in Boots, 1957; When I Was a Boy, 1961; The Little Man, 1966; The Little Man and the Big Thief, 1970.

ABOUT: Columbia Dictionary of Modern European Literature; Current Biography, 1964; International Who's Who, 1963-64; Kästner, Erich. When I Was a Boy; Penguin Companion to Literature Vol. 2, Winkelman, J. The Poetic Style of Erich Kästner; Winkelman, J. Social Criticism in the Early Works of Erich Kästner; Who's Who, 1964; Who's Who in Germany, 1960; Bookbird no. 1, 1969; Hudson Review Winter 1957-1958; South Atlantic Quarterly April 1951; Times Literary Supplement June 19, 1959; December 1, 1966; Top of the News June 1968.

CHARLES KEEPING

September 22, 1924-

AUTHOR AND ILLUSTRATOR OF *Charlie, Charlotte and the Golden Canary*, etc.

Autobiographical sketch of Charles William James Keeping:

I WAS born in Lambeth, South London, right near the river Thames. My family were not Cockneys of long standing. I lived in my grandparent's house and they were seafaring people from Hampshire and Dorset. My grandfather had retired from the sea to London and never tired of telling me of his life around the world in sailing ships, reciting rhymes and singing sea songs and hating the city. My father, a well-known local professional boxer, was also a great storyteller, singer, and reciter of every poem or parody that came his way. I never knew his parents, but they were street traders, as was most of

his family. My Uncle Charley used to come around the streets with a horsedrawn fruit cart. We were a large family, Gramp, uncles, aunts and cousins, although I had only one sister, four years older than I.

Next door to our house was a stableyard and because my parents never allowed us to play in the streets my sister and I spent our time in the little garden watching the activities of the yard or looking out of the front window at the busy street. Our main interest was making stories and pictures of all that we saw. The local people became our heroes and villains and lovers.

Our own world was never intruded on by the family. It was greatly encouraged but never understood. They were a simple people, with their parties, singing, and dancing and acting. Births, deaths and weddings were all rich affairs and great material for a child's mind. Then, when I was ten, my father and grandfather died, and somehow that idyllic childhood was over. At fourteen I was apprenticed into the printing trade because my mother couldn't afford to keep me at school. As an apprentice I spent most of my time behind a horsedrawn van delivering

books around the publishing houses of the City of London, writing and drawing all the time from these new experiences.

The war came and printing died so I went into a war work factory in Bermondsey. This got bombed during the blitz and I went on to demolition work. Then for a time I worked as a rent collector and in 1942, at eighteen, I joined the Royal Navy as a wireless operator.

After the war and a couple of years back at rent collecting (a wonderful job for a writer or illustrator) I finally got a grant to study art full time. In 1952 I gained my National Diploma, married Renate Meyer, a fellow art student, and set about putting all my private world of creativity into public.

From 1956 until 1966 I illustrated over one hundred books by other writers and then at long last came the chance to do my own. I joined B. L. Kearley Ltd., my present agents, to whom I owe so much for their belief in my work, also Miss Mabel George of Oxford University Press, who gave me my first book and in 1966 encouraged me to write and illustrate my own books. There was so much material by this time that I hardly knew where to begin.

My first book, *Shaun and the Carthorse*, gained me a certificate of merit from the British Library Association. *The Black Dolly* gained a further certificate of merit at Leipzig. I followed this with *Charley, Charlotte, and the Golden Canary*, and for this received the Kate Greenaway Medal for 1967. Now I have followed with *Alfie and the Ferryboat* and *Tinker Tailor*, a collection of folk tales. Recently I have completed two films for television which will also be books. My wife also has completed her first book for children, called *Vicki*.

We have four children, Jonathan, Vicki, Sean and Frank, and live in a large rambling old house in Bromley. We like to think our children have a childhood that is nice for creativity. Drawing, writing and singing are encouraged to the full. I hope it works because it's understood. I'm not sure that the old families with their simple rich folklore and traditions were not the best for a small child, of whom nothing was expected and who could drink his fill and privately consume, digest, and then use for his own fantasies.

———

Charles Keeping attended the School of Art, the Polytechnic, London. His lithographs have been exhibited in London, the United States, Australia, and Italy, and are in the Victoria and Albert Museum, London, and in many other galleries and museums. He has taught at the Polytechnic and at Croydon College of Art.

SELECTED WORKS WRITTEN AND ILLUSTRATED: Shaun and the Carthorse, 1966; Black Dolly, 1966; Charley, Charlotte, and the Golden Canary, 1967; Alfie and the Ferryboat, 1968; Tinker Tailor, 1968.

SELECTED WORKS ILLUSTRATED: Three Trumpets, by Ruth Chandler, 1962; Lost John, by Barbara Leonie Picard, 1963; The Knights of the Golden Table, by Martha Edith Almedingen, 1964; Heroes and History, by Rosemary Sutcliff, 1965; Splintered Sword, by Henry Treece, 1966; The Sky-Eater, by James Holding, 1966.

ABOUT: Contemporary Authors, Vol. 21-22; Hürlimann, Bettina. Picture Book World; Kingman, Lee and others, comps. Illustrators of Children's Books: 1957-1966; Ryder, John. Artists of a Certain Line.

CAROL KENDALL

September 13, 1917-

AUTHOR OF *The Gammage Cup*, etc.

Autobiographical sketch of Carol Seeger Kendall:

FORTUNATELY for my parents' hopes, I was born a girl. That was in Bucyrus, Ohio. Being a girl child at the end of a long line of brothers was marvelous. I played baseball and football, built snowforts, scrambled up trees and over the garage roof. One hot summer's day I had my hair sheared short, and my mother thenceforth gave up buying me dolls. Rainy days I rummaged in the attic and read the dusty books piled on the floor. I remember especially a fat book of rebuses and other puzzles, and a thin book of French stories which I blissfully read by looking up

Carol Kendall

the vocabulary in the back of the book. I still enjoy puzzly things, like codes and foreign languages, and they often sift into my writing.

By the fourth grade I had decided to be a writer, and started my first novel immediately. It was a lurid tale of cruel stepfathers and pickpockets in the slums of Chicago, but I ran out of material after nineteen pages. Although I continued to write—mostly feature stories and columns for school newspapers—I didn't start another novel until I had finished college (Ohio University), married Paul Kendall (an English professor), and bought a secondhand typewriter, all in the same month. The first two novels I had published were mysteries for adults, but the hero was a twelve-year-old boy. I was working on a third when I discovered I was bored with the plot and the grown-up characters, and really only enjoyed the children. It finally came to me that I was meant to write about children *for* children.

The Other Side of the Tunnel, a mystery, was my trial run into the new territory. Then I found the Minnipins kicking around in my head, especially that untidy Muggles, and they became the fantasy, *The Gammage*

Cup. In some fright because I began to think and talk like a Minnipin myself, I came back to the real world with Huggins Pindar in *The Big Splash.* But the Minnipins kept nagging at me until I wrote *The Whisper of Glocken,* a story of how heroes get to be that way even when they start out as cowards.

I don't draw characters whole from life, but I do admit to using our elder daughter's nickname and general characteristics for Curley Green in *The Gammage Cup,* and I wrote our younger daughter Gillian into *The Whisper of Glocken* under the name she wished we had given her—Silky. Other characters' names stem from my fascination with the sounds and meanings in words: Mingy (stingy, but nicer); Muggles (muddle); Glocken ("bells" in German); Scumble (humble with a bit of Scat! thrown in).

As a family we spend every third or fourth year in Europe so that my husband can do research for the biographies he writes, but our next trip will be to Africa, where Curley (the real one, grown up) and her husband Kerry are teaching for the Peace Corps. I long to go to China to practice the Chinese I am now learning. In the meantime I find some very Chinesey-looking picture-writing elbowing its way into my next book!

———

Carol Seeger took her A.B. in 1939 from Ohio University, where she was elected to Phi Beta Kappa and was a member of Phi Mu Sorority. She married Paul Murray Kendall in 1939 and they have two children, Carol Seeger and Gillian Murray. *The Gammage Cup* won the Ohioana Award and was a runner-up for the Newbery Medal in 1960.

In addition to the Chinese she mentions, Mrs. Kendall speaks French, German, and Russian, and says she enjoys music, exploratory walking, and stamp collecting.

SELECTED WORKS: The Other Side of the Tunnel, 1957; The Gammage Cup, 1959; The Big Splash, 1960; The Whisper of Glocken, 1965.

ABOUT: Contemporary Authors, Vol. 5-6; Who's Who of American Women, 1968-69.

"LACE KENDALL"

See *Stoutenberg, Adrien*

JULIET KEPES
June 29, 1919-

AUTHOR AND ILLUSTRATOR OF *Lady Bird, Quickly,* etc.

Autobiographical sketch of Juliet Appleby Kepes:

I WAS born in London, England, the fourth in a family of six children. In spite of growing up in a large city, there was always ample opportunity to be in touch with nature because of the many parks and heaths within reach of every district. There were ponds with boating, ducks and swans, tennis courts, evening band concerts, rivers, rolling hills, flowers, trees, herds of fallow or red deer, in one park or another. The memories of the wonderful hours I spent wandering, observing and soaking in all of the nuances of light, colors, perfumes and changes in these surroundings, and our summers spent at the seaside, where I was confronted with the vastness and changing moods of the ocean, made deep impressions on me.

I began to draw when I was very small. It was as much a need for me as eating and drinking. I became one with the creatures I was producing on paper. Sometimes, in an elated mood, I would fill a notebook with rhymes, limericks and poetry. I loved to listen to stories; the *Blue, Yellow* and *Red Fairy Books,* Lear, Aesop, myths, *Alice in Wonderland;* and so many of the others we are all so familiar with.

By continuously watching those animals that were within my orbit, I absorbed a knowledge of their anatomy, movement, different natures and reactions, without being conscious of it. The wild creatures from the "mysterious" jungles, deserts, mountains and plains in other parts of the world I had to imagine, making use of the only clues I had to them through books and word of mouth. The incredible variety of fish, birds, animals, insects and plants were wonders that have never lost their fascination for me. The stories, fables, myths gave me an insight into the joys, sorrows, conflicts, courage, foolishness and intelligence of man.

Kepes: *KAY pash*

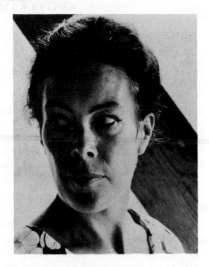

JULIET KEPES

It is with this general background that my children's books emerge. The sounds of words and the ways of putting them together to make sense, nonsense, rhymes, rhythms, moods, etc. are as important as the illustrations and the complete design of the book, and that is why I prefer to do the text, illustrations, layout and jacket design myself.

I cannot say exactly how an idea for a story develops for me, there are so many unexpected sources. *The Five Little Monkeys* came rather naturally, with the underlying realization that children do identify themselves with the characters in a story. The monkeys, like children, loved to play tricks, but were basically good. When another animal was in trouble, they did not think twice about coming to his aid, with the resulting resounding approval of all the other beasts, including those they had teased. *The Seed That Peacock Planted* is a fantasy about the way the different birds acquired their songs. The voicing of the joy of life. *Lady Bird, Quickly* came from the delight I had upon learning that the ladybird was a harmless bug, through the rhyme of "Lady Bird, Lady Bird . . ." and on blowing her off on her journey you could have a wish.

It is my hope that in my books I am able to give children something that they will enjoy, learn from and look at.

I respond to various pronunciations of my surname, but correctly it is similar to Kapash.

My husband is Hungarian by birth. Our married daughter was born in Chicago, Illinois, and our college-age son, in Cambridge, Massachusetts, where we have been living for the past twenty years.

Juliet Appleby attended the Askes Hatcham School in London and the Brighton School of Art. She came to the United States in 1937, entered the Chicago School of Design, and the same year married Gyorgy Kepes, Hungarian author and painter, later professor of visual design at the Massachusetts Institute of Technology.

Juliet Kepes's drawings and paintings have been exhibited in a number of galleries and museums, including the Art Institute of Chicago, the Baltimore Museum, and the Gropper Gallery in Cambridge, and she has received prizes for her work from the Museum of Modern Art.

Two Little Birds and Three, Five Little Monkeys, and *Beasts from a Brush* were all named by the New York *Times* as among the ten best picture books of their year of publication. *Five Little Monkeys* was also a runner-up for the Caldecott Medal for 1953. *Lady Bird, Quickly* was an Honor Book in the New York *Herald Tribune* Spring Book Festival, 1964. *Give a Guess* received a Certificate of Excellence from the American Institute of Graphic Arts and *Frogs Merry* a Citation of Merit from the Society of Illustrators.

Juliet Kepes has collaborated with her husband on several architectural murals and on a design for a children's room, which was published in *Interiors.*

Selected Works Written and Illustrated: Five Little Monkeys, 1952; Beasts from a Brush, 1955; Two Little Birds and Three, 1960; Frogs Merry, 1961; Lady Bird, Quickly, 1964; The Seed That Peacock Planted, 1967; Birds, 1968.

Selected Works Illustrated: Give a Guess, by Mary Britton Miller, 1957; Puptents and Pebbles, by William Jay Smith, 1959.

About: Kingman, Lee and others, comps. Illustrators of Children's Books: 1957-1966; Viguers, Ruth Hill and others, comps. Illustrators of Children's Books: 1946-1956.

LARRY KETTELKAMP

April 25, 1933-

AUTHOR AND ILLUSTRATOR OF *Puzzle Patterns*, etc.

Autobiographical sketch of Larry Dale Kettelkamp:

I WAS born in Harvey, Illinois. As early as I can remember I liked art and music, and I was always curious about how things worked. The art interest seemed the strongest so later I studied painting at the University of Illinois and illustration at Pratt Institute in Brooklyn, New York. I started a career in art by illustrating some junior science books for Herbert Zim. At the same time I had been studying music since I was five, first piano, then flute and all kinds of guitars. Starting in the fifth grade I drove my family crazy by practicing magic tricks on them. I did magic shows to earn money later during my college years, and this led to an unusual opportunity.

I had started my first book illustration work for William Morrow. Elizabeth Hamilton, the juvenile editor, became interested in some of my hobbies, including magic. She suggested that I try writing a beginning book on the subject. I did and to my surprise, *Magic Made Easy* was published. Since then I have written and illustrated one informational book each year on the average. The subjects have included kites and gliders, puzzles, spinning tops, and a series on the instruments of the orchestra. I like to build things and so almost all of my books have included experiments with what you have around the house. The musical instrument series was followed by a book on the most amazing instrument of all, the human voice. It was called, *Song, Speech and Ventriloquism*.

Your voice is really controlled by your thoughts, hopes and fears, and I became interested in this strange world of the mind. Just how amazing it was I could only guess as I started work on a book called *Dreams*. I visited sleep laboratories and was astounded. In one lab they were finding that thoughts in the mind of one person could be picked up by a sleeping person and made into a part of his dreams.

I experimented with my own dreams and kept a dream notebook. I told myself I would dream of the future and sometimes I did. I studied the lives of people who were very good at predicting the future. And I studied the equally surprising idea that some people could remember the past so well that they reported having lived many times before. And sometimes their memories could be checked and were correct. So I told myself I would remember my own past lives, and I am beginning to remember. I find that things I do well without much practice are those I seem to have learned in earlier lifetimes as other people. And I feel that my wife and I and our four children have all met before in earlier times and places.

These studies have already led to two junior books, the first called *Haunted Houses* and the second called *Sixth Sense*, which is about the mysterious "invisible eye" which we all have if we care to practice using it. I am beginning to understand what I somehow already knew as a child—that true life is much more than can be quickly seen, and that it extends farther back and farther forward than we had ever dared to hope.

Larry Kettelkamp illustrated his first book at the age of nineteen—*The Sun,* by Herbert S. Zim. Kettelkamp received a B.F.A. from the University of Illinois in 1953, served for two years as a lieutenant in the Army Security Agency, and after his discharge in 1956 worked for Spencer Press, Urbana, Illinois, on visual educational materials. Later he was art director for Garrard Publishing Company, Champaign, Illinois, and then worked as layout and staff artist for *Highlights for Children* magazine, Honesdale, Pennsylvania.

Kettelkamp is married to the former Florence Goy, and their four children are Lauren, Keith, Karl, and Marianne.

SELECTED WORKS WRITTEN AND ILLUSTRATED: Magic Made Easy, 1954; Flutes, Whistles and Reeds, 1962; Puzzle Patterns, 1963; Spinning Tops, 1966; Song, Speech and Ventriloquism, 1967; Dreams, 1968; Haunted Houses, 1969; Sixth Sense, 1970.

SELECTED WORKS ILLUSTRATED: The Sun, by Herbert S. Zim, 1953; Parrakeets, by Herbert S. Zim, 1953.

ABOUT: Kingman, Lee and others, comps. Illustrators of Children's Books: 1957-1966.

"G. B. KIRTLAND"

See *Hine, Al; Joslin, Sesyle*

"CALVIN M. KNOX"

See *Silverberg, Robert*

E. L. KONIGSBURG
February 10, 1930-

AUTHOR AND ILLUSTRATOR OF *From the Mixed-up Files of Mrs. Basil E. Frankweiler,* etc.

Autobiographical sketch of Elaine Lobl Konigsburg:

ALTHOUGH I was born in New York City, I did most of my growing up in small towns in Pennsylvania. My mother and father were

E. L. Konigsburg

business people, and I am the middle of three daughters.

Passing courses was the thing I did best as a child. I'm convinced that doing so has been compensation for being tone deaf and for never getting past twosies in jacks. I graduated as valedictorian from Farrell High School and then worked as a bookkeeper in a wholesale meat plant. One of the owners had a brother, David Konigsburg, who would sometimes visit the office.

Having saved enough money to start college, I entered Carnegie Institute of Technology in Pittsburgh. At that time David was a graduate student of psychology at the University of Pittsburgh and taking courses in testing. I was subject #14 for the Stanford-Binet and subject #8 for the Wechsler I.Q. Tests. I continued being good at course passing; Tech gave me a scholarship to supplement my part-time income; I graduated with honors; and David Konigsburg married me. (I had played it safe and refused to take the Rorschach.)

I worked and attended graduate school at the University of Pittsburgh being a chemist. After two years there, I had passed all those courses with flying colors; unfortunately, that is also the way I passed the lab courses. There the colors flew because of a few explosions in the lab sink. Those malachite green stains were the worst. The University of Pittsburgh moved their Graduate School of Chemistry the year after I left.

After David received his doctorate and moved us to Jacksonville, Florida, and I was teaching at a private girls' school, I began to suspect that chemistry was not my field. Not only did I always ask my students to light my Bunsen burner, having become match-shy, but I became more interested in what was going on inside of them than what was going on inside the test tubes. I finished teaching a few weeks before Paul was born. Then Laurie, and then Ross.

After Laurie was born I began to paint and after Ross was a year old, I returned to teaching, briefly and part time. Those same kinds of kids, softly comfortable on the outside and solidly uncomfortable on the inside. Then we moved into the metropolitan New York area, first to suburbs in New Jersey, and I took art lessons on Saturdays at the Art Students League.

We moved to Westchester, Ross started kindergarten, and I started writing. Being a firm believer in Parkinson's Law that work, especially housework, expands to fill the time available, I decided that I would compress the time since I couldn't compress the work. So when all three children left for school in the mornings, I sat down to write amidst dust and unmade beds. I wanted to tell about suburban kids, comfortable/uncomfortable kids, that I had taught once and that I was raising now.

Jennifer, Hecate, Macbeth, William Mc-Kinley, and Me, Elizabeth came from our being newcomers in an apartment house in Port Chester, New York. *From the Mixed-up Files of Mrs. Basil E. Frankweiler* grew from watching the fussiness and tidiness of my children and their friends and realizing that they needed adventure and would have to find a suburban kind of it. *About the B'nai Bagels* also came from watching; I had begun it while we still lived in New York, and I carried it with me throughout two moves, one to an apartment in Jacksonville and another to a new house. We moved into that new house on the day that I received the call telling me that *The Mixed-up Files* had won the 1968 Newbery Award and that *Jennifer* was runner-up.

I shall probably not return to the lab, but all those years in chemistry were not wasted; I learned useful things: to use the materials at hand, to have a point of view, to distill. And I obviously learned how to handle messy sinks—move.

———

Mrs. Konigsburg is the first author in the history of the Newbery Medal to place first and runner-up in the same year. *From the Mixed-up Files of Mrs. Basil E. Frankweiler* also won a Lewis Carroll Shelf Award in 1968 and the William Allen White Children's Book Award in 1970.

SELECTED WORKS WRITTEN AND ILLUSTRATED: From the Mixed-up Files of Mrs. Basil E. Frankweiler, 1967; Jennifer, Hecate, Macbeth, William McKinley and Me, Elizabeth, 1967; About the B'Nai Bagels, 1968; (George), 1970.

ABOUT: Contemporary Authors, Vol. 21-22; Who's Who in America, 1970-71; Horn Book August 1968; Library Journal March 15, 1968; New York Times Book Review February 25, 1968; Publishers' Weekly February 26, 1968; School Library Journal March 1968; Top of the News April 1968.

ROBERT KRAUS

June 21, 1925-

AUTHOR AND ILLUSTRATOR OF *Miranda's Beautiful Dream*, etc.

Autobiographical sketch of Robert Kraus, who writes under his own name and the pen name "Eugene H. Hippopotamus":

I WAS born in Milwaukee, Wisconsin, and I have always liked to draw. When I was eleven my first cartoon was published on the children's page of the Milwaukee *Journal*. I did many cartoons for the children's page, and a few years later began selling cartoons to the *Saturday Evening Post, Esquire*, and other magazines.

After finishing high school, I attended an art school in New York, where I met my wife, Pamela. I soon began to do cartoons and covers for the *New Yorker* magazine. We moved to Connecticut where we live with our two sons, Bruce and Billy. It was also at this time that my first children's book, *Junior, the Spoiled Cat* was published. I liked to

draw talking animals, giants, and Mother Goose characters in my cartoons so it seemed natural to do talking animals, giants, etc., in children's books. I have always written my own cartoon ideas and found I enjoyed writing stories. I write and think the pictures at the same time and my first drafts include pictures and text.

For some time I had felt that there were many fine cartoonists and artists who had not done children's books, who could make important contributions to the field, and so in 1965, after twenty years with the *New Yorker* and twenty children's books, I started a publishing company, Windmill Books, Inc. We have published fifteen books so far, including *The Charles Addams Mother Goose, Roland the Minstrel Pig* and *CDB!* by William Steig, *Harriet and the Promised Land* by Jacob Lawrence, and *The Norman Rockwell Storybook.* I keep very busy as publisher, editor, and designer of Windmill Books and I also write some of the stories, under my own name and under the pen name of Eugene H. Hippopotamus.

Robert Kraus studied at the Layton School of Art in Milwaukee and at the Art Students League, where he had a scholarship in 1946. He has created a series of animated cartoons

for movies and television. Under the pen name of Eugene H. Hippopotamus he wrote *Hello, Hippopotamus.*

SELECTED WORKS WRITTEN AND ILLUSTRATED: All the Mice Came, 1955; Mouse at Sea, 1959; The Littlest Rabbit, 1961; The Trouble with Spider, 1962; Miranda's Beautiful Dream, 1964; Amanda Remembers, 1965; The Bunny's Nutshell Library, 1965; How Spider Saved Christmas, 1970.

SELECTED WORKS ILLUSTRATED: Red Fox and the Hungry Tiger, by Paul Anderson, 1962; Rabbit and Skunk and the Scary Rock, by Carla Stevens, 1962.

ABOUT: Kingman, Lee and others, comps. Illustrators of Children's Books: 1957-1966; Who's Who in America, 1970-71; Who's Who in American Art, 1966.

JAMES KRÜSS
May 31, 1926-

AUTHOR OF *My Great-Grandfather and I,* etc.

Autobiographical sketch of James Krüss:

ON a sunny May day I was born between the white sails of yachts and the smell of flowers; for the yachts were racing around the island of my birth and the only midwife of the island was the owner of a small flower shop.

I grew up on a small island, surrounded by the North Sea. Today I live on a somewhat larger island, surrounded by the Atlantic Ocean. Between these two islands there are some thousand kilometers and about forty years of life. During this time I have been scholar, soldier, student, teacher, journalist and, at the same time, writer and passionate traveler. I know most parts of Europe and some parts of Africa, and I hope to see Japan and America, the two countries in which the majority of my books have been translated and printed.

My special talent, to write and to rhyme for children, I discovered in 1950, when I was without money in Munich, the capital of Bavaria. In that year I took some children's poems, which I had made for my own fun, to a radio station and to a famous newspaper. To my great surprise the poems were both

gasoline." "And what damned kind of gasoline is that?" "Fantasy, uncle."

I really think that is it: fantasy. It helps me, as in *My Great-Grandfather and I*, to write a book about my small island, in which I encircle the whole world. It helps me, as in *The Happy Islands*, to build a world, which —though not real—is imaginable. It helps me, as in my last book *In Aunt Julie's House*, to find out if a relationship exists between the sounds of letters and their meaning.

And it helps me—last but not least—to keep my childhood as long as I want to.

James Krüss was born on Helgoland, a German island in the North Sea. He studied at the teachers' training school in Lüneburg but never taught. He served for a year in the Air Force and edited a periodical in Hamburg before going to live on Gran Canaria, one of the Canary Islands. His books, of which there are more than seventy, including many picture books, have been translated into many languages. Among his numerous honors are German juvenile book awards in 1960 and 1964. In 1968 he tied for the Hans Christian Andersen Medal. An elementary school in Berlin is named after him. Krüss is not married but claims seventeen godchildren.

SELECTED WORKS: My Great-Grandfather and I, 1964; Eagle and Dove, 1965; The Happy Islands Behind the Winds, 1966; Pauline and the Prince in the Wind, 1966; Return to the Happy Islands, 1967; The Lighthouse on the Lobster Cliffs, 1969; Coming Home from the War, 1970.

ABOUT: Bookbird no. 4, 1968; Top of the News January 1969.

broadcast and printed. From that moment began the success of which I myself at least had dreamed. I wrote for radio and theater with Eric Kästner and wrote my own radio plays. Later I collected my children's poems, which had been printed in many newspapers, weeklies and monthlies. At the same time I wrote several children's books and texts for picture books. All this yielded me a house, a name and some prizes, among which is the international Hans Christian Andersen Award.

Today I get letters—not only from children —from both Germanies, America, Japan, Russia, Holland and some other countries. The last letter from America, written by Janet Burke of Birmingham, Michigan: "I liked it (meaning *The Happy Islands*) because it is imaginary without being so far out it is really quite impossible."

When my uncle, a lobster-fisherman, visited me on the Canary Islands and saw my house, he asked, unbelieving, "All that stuff made with a pencil?"

When I nodded, he shook his head and said, "To make money for a house, I need a motorboat for 40,000 marks, and ropes and nets and wicker-traps and oil and gasoline. . . ." "Well," I interrupted, "I also need

KARLA KUSKIN

July 17, 1932-

AUTHOR AND ILLUSTRATOR OF *Watson, the Smartest Dog in the U.S.A.*, etc.

Autobiographical sketch of Karla Seidman Kuskin, who writes under her own name and under the pen name "Nicholas Charles":

I WAS born in New York City and except for vacations and college years that is where I have spent my life.

Karla Kuskin

I began my schooling at the age of two, attended the Little Red School House and graduated from Elisabeth Irwin High School. These schools are in Greenwich Village where I lived on a gingko-tree-lined block with my parents.

Growing up in the city was always rewarding. We played king ball on sidewalk squares, lounged in Washington Square's circle, ice-skated, went to museums, galleries, movies and plays. Yet of all childhood pastimes I think that my favorite was reading. At times books took the place of people for me. Maybe only children have a more distinct feeling of aloneness than others. At any rate I lived in the stories I read. I still do. My parents were great readers and they liked to read aloud. My mother, who had been both a photographer and an actress, especially loved poetry. I became a reading-aloud addict early, captured by the swing and color of words. I made up stories and verses long before I could write and would dictate my works to my mother.

Drawing was another way of having a private world; one of my own making. The parents of my best friends were artists and we children were constantly posing or painting. I illustrated my own stories and poems and scenes from favorite books. My father is a writer and instant versifier who wrote letters to me in verse. Rhyming and scansion came almost too easily. I have to fight them now or I can destroy a verse with the clop, clop, clop of tiny metric feet.

I attended Antioch College and graduated from the School of Fine Arts at Yale University. As a class project I wrote, printed and bound a book about animal noises called *Roar and More*. Harper & Bros., now Harper & Row, published it in 1956. I have been writing and illustrating, mostly for children, since then.

In 1955 I married Charles Kuskin who is the oboist with the Dorian Quintet. We have two children: Nicholas who is eight and Julia who is four and a Siamese cat named Rosalie Katskin. We live in an old red brick town house in Brooklyn Heights. The windows of my studio are filled with treetops and housetops. A perfect city view.

Perhaps because I never wanted to grow up my memories of childhood are still very close. A great deal of the writing I do now comes from those memories plus the ramblings of an itinerant imagination rather than specific happenings. A picture in my mind of a dog riding a tricycle was the beginning of *Which Horse Is William?*. Both *James and the Rain* and *Alexander Soames: His Poems* grew from rhymes that refused to leave me alone. The latter book is about a child who is only able to speak in verse. It is as close to autobiography as I have come so far.

Karla Kuskin took her B.F.A. from the Yale School of Design in 1955. Under the pen name of Nicholas Charles, she wrote and illustrated *How Do You Get from Here to There?*, 1962, and *Jane Anne June Spoon and Her Very Adventurous Search for the Moon*, 1966.

Karla Kuskin's work has been in several exhibitions of the Amercan Institute of Graphic Arts.

SELECTED WORKS WRITTEN AND ILLUSTRATED: Roar and More, 1956; James and the Rain, 1957; In the Middle of the Trees, 1958; Which Horse Is William? 1959; Alexander Soames: His Poems, 1962; Watson, the Smartest Dog in the U.S.A., 1968.

SELECTED WORKS ILLUSTRATED: Harrison Loved His Umbrella, by Rhoda Levine, 1964;

Boris the Lopsided Bear, by Gladys Schmitt, 1965; Look at Me, by Marguerita Rudolph, 1967.

ABOUT: Contemporary Authors, Vol. 3; Hürlimann, Bettina. Picture Book World; Kingman, Lee and others, comps. Illustrators of Children's Books: 1957-1966.

JANET LAMBERT

December 17, 1894-

AUTHOR OF *Star-Spangled Summer*, etc.

Autobiographical sketch of Janet Maude Snyder Lambert:

CRAWFORDSVILLE, in my day, was often referred to as "the Athens of Indiana," because it had provided so many authors. Knowing a few made me yearn to become one. Mary Hannah Krout, best known for her poem, "Little Brown Hands," would invite me to tea and read her poetry to me; Maurice Thompson, author of *Alice of Old Vincennes*, inspired me; General Lew Wallace often let me sit with him under the beech tree where he had written much of *Ben Hur*, and I knew many others.

All well-known actors took their plays on tour in those days, stopping for one night in my town. My father, who thoroughly enjoyed his dreamy daughter, not only took me to the theater, but also backstage. The actors and actresses were as kind to me as the authors were.

Having now a choice of two careers, acting first, writing second, I was so eager to start the first that I hurried through high school in three years. Then I chose Ferry Hall, a junior college in Lake Forest, because it was near Chicago and I could go in to see plays. I saw only one during my freshman year. That made me abandon my formal education.

I enrolled with a dramatics teacher in Indianapolis, and had professors tutor me in German and French.

My fondest dream was to play with Walker Whitside, a brilliant actor of that time. When Mr. Whitside brought his current play to Indianapolis, I found the ingenue inadequate, and with the confidence my father had given me, hurried backstage

to tell him that I could do much better. Three weeks later I received a telegram requesting me to join the company in Minneapolis, and off I went, chaperoned by an older sister.

The following fall I went to New York to do a small but good part, this time chaperoned by a friend of my mother's. When the play closed after a short run, I joined a stock company in Northhampton, Massachusetts, where friends of my family agreed to take me in.

I had two and a half wonderful years in the theater. Back in New York rehearsing for another play, the boy from home appeared, Captain Kent Craig Lambert, resplendent in an army uniform, polished boots and cavalry insignia. We were married at Fort Ethan Allen, Vermont, on January 1, 1918. Three months later my bridegroom sailed for France. I was sure I could continue my career, unchaperoned at last, but eight months later my daughter Jeanne Ann was born, and my career in the theater ended.

A delightful life in the army followed. The years were contented ones as we moved about the world. Then, as Jeanne Ann grew older, I took up my second career, writing: short stories for a little girl, later for an older one, and still later, family stories about teen-agers. They were all lost during one of our many moves.

In 1938 the War Department ordered us to New York City. There I learned that no modern novels were being written for teen-agers. I promptly began one. It was difficult to do as our penthouse apartment was constantly filled with girls and West Point cadets. It was not until the fall of 1940, after Jeannie had married her West Pointer, 2nd Lt. Dean Titus Vanderhoef, that I could stay at my typewriter.

In December I finished *Star-Spangled Summer*. It was a timely book because America had become war-conscious, and it had a catchy title. I finished it on a Thursday and E. P. Dutton bought it the following day. My second career began as suddenly as my first had and has extended through fifty-four books for girls, with number fifty-five now in the making.

In 1951 my husband was retired as a colonel, and we moved to our summer home on Long Beach Island, off the New Jersey coast. Here we lived for eighteen years, with the ocean rolling up to our dune—twice, during hurricanes, sweeping it away. For the last two years we have lived on the bay side of the island, safely bulkheaded against storms, and with a dock and slip for a boat.

My three grandchildren love the island, and my grandson, Craig Titus Vanderhoef, now serving in Vietnam, is looking forward to coming home and relaxing here.

Whenever my husband and I have a disagreement, as all husbands and wives should have now and then, he usually ends it by saying in despair, "You still have a teen-age mind!" To which I gratefully reply, "Thank goodness."

SELECTED WORKS: Star-Spangled Summer, 1941; Summer for Seven, 1952; Don't Cry, Little Girl, 1952; Rainbow after Rain, 1953; Welcome Home, Mrs. Jordan, 1953; Fly Away, Cinda, 1956; Extra Special, 1963; Bright Tomorrow, 1965; Sweet as Sugar, 1967; My Davy, 1968; The Odd Ones, 1969.

ABOUT: Current Biography 1954; Who's Who of American Women, 1961-62.

SHEENA PORTER LANE

See *Porter, Sheena*

JOHN LANGSTAFF
December 24, 1920-

AUTHOR OF *Frog Went A-Courtin'*, etc.

Biographical sketch of John Meredith Langstaff:

JOHN LANGSTAFF was born in Brooklyn on Christmas Eve. In childhood he began singing publicly, as a soprano soloist at Manhattan's Grace Church and as one of the Bretton Woods Boy Singers. After graduating from the Choate School, Langstaff studied voice and music at the Curtis Institute of Music and the Juilliard School of Music. He became interested in traditional singing through hearing the folk songs of Southern Appalachia, and he pursued his interest under the guidance of John Powell in Virginia and Douglas Kennedy, director of the English Folk Dance and Song Society, in Great Britain.

After finishing his studies, Langstaff embarked on a professional career in music with many facets, not the least of them involving work with or for children. He became head of the department of music at the Potomac School in McLean, Virginia; began to give recitals and to appear as guest baritone in children's concerts given by major international symphony orchestras, with a repertoire stressing American music from traditional ballads to poetry scored by such composers as Charles Ives and Ernst Bacon; recorded for His Master's Voice in Europe and for Odeon-Capitol in the United States. He started to translate the folk songs he was collecting and singing to the pages of children's books. Such translation involved two difficulties: putting oral tradition into writing, and selecting the best of numerous versions of each song.

His first retelling of a folk song in picture-book form for children was *Frog Went A-Courtin'*, winner of the 1956 Caldecott Medal. Feodor Rojankovsky, who humorously illustrated that book, also did the pic-

JOHN LANGSTAFF

tures for Langstaff's *Over in the Meadow,* a counting song. Beth and Joe Krush illustrated Langstaff's *The Swapping Boy,* and Joe Krush did the art work for his *Ol' Dan Tucker.*

Langstaff's retelling of *On Christmas Day in the Morning!* was illustrated by Antony Groves-Raines, and Robin Jacques drew the pictures for *Hi! Ho! The Rattlin' Bog,* a collection of forty-nine songs, from sea chanteys to folk hymns, with guitar arrangements suggested by Happy Traum.

In 1966 Langstaff did a program of Christmas carols for NBC television, and for several years he did the school series *Making Music* for BBC television in England. He moderated the NBC weekly series *Children Explore Books* and did programs of music participation for Channel 13 in New York. He sang in and trained the children for more than twenty performances throughout this country of Benjamin Britten's opera *Noye's Fludde.* After thirteen years at the Potomac School, Langstaff assumed his present position as director of music at the Shady Hill School in Cambridge, Massachusetts. In 1948 he married Nancy Woodbridge, who is also a music teacher. They live in Lexington, Massachusetts. Their three children are John Elliot, Peter Gerry, and Deborah Graydon. By a previous marriage Langstaff has another daughter, Carol. His favorite recreations are camping, hiking and Morris danc-

ing. He belongs to a number of organizations, including Actors Equity, International Folk Music Council, and English Folk Song Society and is a member of the executive board of the Country Dance Society of America.

SELECTED WORKS RETOLD AND/OR EDITED: Frog Went A-Courtin', 1955; Over in the Meadow, 1957; On Christmas Day in the Morning! 1959; The Swapping Boy, 1960; Ol' Dan Tucker, 1963; Hi! Ho! the Rattlin' Bog, 1969.

ABOUT: Contemporary Authors, Vol. 2: Who's Who in America, 1970-71; Washington Post December 24, 1966.

JANINA DOMANSKA LASKOWSKI

See *Domanska, Janina*

JERZY LASKOWSKI

April 12, 1919-

AUTHOR OF *Master of the Royal Cats,* etc.

Autobiographical sketch of Jerzy Laskowski:

I WAS born in Poland.

I have always wanted to write. At the age of ten, I was creating small stories, sentimental poems, and plays on which I collaborated with my brother. In spite of the problem of having no actresses to take the female parts, we produced our plays anyway, for the most charitable of audiences—our parents. But even charity has its bounds. I recall how my father would usually walk out during the twelfth act, with half the play yet to be performed.

In high school I was writing more professionally and won some prizes for my work. Among these was an award from an abstinence league for a novel about a drunken railroad man. The first real success came when at the University for a faculty-assigned paper on geography, I subsequently wrote a story of a beautiful Syrian princess whose hand in marriage was sought by seven handsome men. To resolve this septempartite dilemma, the princess ordered the suitors to duel to the finish; she would marry the victor. Unfortunately, the victor was so wound-ridden that he died too. When I read my dissertation to the student body, they re-

sponded with a tremendous bravo. This was to be some consolation when I was resoundingly flunked by the faculty on the grounds that I had deviated from the topic.

At this same time I was thinking only of how to acquire a motorcycle. So, to get the money, I decided to write a musical comedy. The play opened and scathing denunciations emanated from virtually every pulpit in Warsaw. Needless to say, the play's success was guaranteed, and I got my motorcycle. The majority of Warsaw went to see the play, only to see an innocuous drama about a mayor's daughter who makes her bid for the legitimate stage via the burlesque circuit—and found the part of the daughter played by the Mayor of Warsaw's own daughter.

While I was working as a foreign correspondent in Czechoslovakia, war broke out. I returned to Poland, enlisted in 1939 and was wounded in the legs and hospitalized in Budapest. Because I was not yet able to walk, I was assigned to a post in the consulate. In 1940, dismayed because this had nothing to do with the war, I traveled incognito and without a passport to Syria, to the country of a beautiful princess, and as soon as my

legs healed enlisted in the French Foreign Legion. The Legion was a potpourri of nationalities and religions. It was a no-questions-asked outfit; a chain was strapped around a man's wrist and the man became a number. When the French colony capitulated to the Vichy, the Poles in the Legion revolted, formed their own brigade and moved to Palestine.

During this time, I was writing articles for the American press from different countries under different names. I received no money for these contributions because of the passport problem and the fact that they could never have found me anyway. During this period were published a volume of poetry, a drama *Case No. 113* which was translated into Hebrew and French. I was then appointed editor of a daily paper published in Iraq and Palestine for which the Army footed the bill.

One of my poems, "Thank You"—which was translated into French and Russian—provides a quaint insight into the art of subtle propaganda. In Baghdad, a Russian troupe was performing at one of the theaters. An actor announced that he would read a poem by a Russian soldier recently killed in action. The poem was "Thank You," and sitting in the audience was the poet, very much alive and definitely not a Russian.

After the war, I lived in England where I wrote a drama, *The End of Adventure*, produced in 1948, and a musical comedy, *Beautiful Helen*, 1949, both of which enjoyed commercial success.

Since coming to the United States, I have published a slender volume of poetry and two children's books. A third book for children is to be released soon.

My preference in writing is nonfiction. To date I have put in five years' research and have traveled the route taken by Abraham according to the Bible in preparation for my yet unfinished book about the Friend of God.

Jerzy Laskowski was born in the city of Cracow. He was only in his mid-teens in 1934 when his first play was performed and his first book, *Scandal*, was published. He studied law and philosophy at Lwow University. From 1936 to 1939 he was a staff correspondent for several Polish newspapers.

During World War II he was wounded twice, became a lieutenant in the Second Polish Corps and served 1942-1945 in the Middle East and in Italy.

Laskowski came to the United States in 1952 and married the artist, Janina Domanska, in 1953. His wife has illustrated his children's books.

SELECTED WORKS: Master of the Royal Cats, 1965; The Dragon Liked Smoked Fish, 1967.

PATRICIA LAUBER
February 2, 1924-

AUTHOR OF *Clarence Goes to Town*, etc.

Autobiographical sketch of Patricia Grace Lauber:

"ONCE upon a time"—when I was a little girl I thought those the most wonderful words I had ever heard. In them was all the promise and magic of the story that would follow. Fortunately for me, my mother also loved stories and enjoyed reading aloud. Even so, I wanted more stories than my mother had time to read me, and it occurred to me fairly early that the way to get these stories was to learn to read myself. In learning to read, I learned to spell, after a fashion, and to print. At that point I made the great discovery of a second magic world. This was one I could create myself by making up stories and poems and putting them on paper. From that time on I have never really wanted to be anything except a writer. And I became a writer in the way that I suppose all writers do: I wrote . . . and wrote and wrote.

I was born in New York City. When I was about four years old, my family moved to Connecticut, where I went to school; learned to climb trees, ride, and sail; and owned a number of dogs and one cat. After graduating from Wellesley College, I went to work in New York on the staff of a magazine for adults. I was still not sure just what kind of writer I wanted to be, but I was working on short stories and light essays and selling a few. More or less by chance, I left my first job and went to a new one on *Junior Scholas-*

tic magazine. This was the first time I had tried writing for children, and I discovered that I liked it very much.

One day at lunch I happened to be telling a fellow editor about my dog Clarence. She enjoyed the stories I had to tell and suggested that I write a book about him. Clarence and I both thought this was a fine idea, and I got to work putting down things that had happened and almost happened, but changing them so that they took the form of stories instead of anecdotes. The result was my first book: *Clarence the TV Dog*.

Since then, I have been editor of a science magazine, science editor of an encyclopedia for young people, and editor of various books. I have traveled a lot in Europe and the United States. And I have written more than forty books. Most of my fiction is based on dogs and horses that I have known. My nonfiction deals with animals, countries I have visited, astronomy, and some of the many other things that interest me to the point where I want to learn about them and then share what I have learned. But whatever I write, whether fact or fiction, I try to keep alive the magic worlds I discovered as a child. Even though I do not write fairy tales, I hope that some of my books mean to my readers what the words "Once upon a time" meant to me.

———

Patricia Lauber received her B.A. from Wellesley in 1945. She has been on the staff of *Look* magazine, editor of *Junior Scholastic,* editor-in-chief of *Science World,* and chief science editor of the *Book of Knowledge.* She likes travel, the theater, music, animals and sailing.

SELECTED WORKS: Clarence the TV Dog, 1955; Clarence Goes to Town, 1957, 1967; The Friendly Dolphins, 1963; The Look-It-Up Book of Mammals, 1967; The Look-It-Up Book of Stars and Planets, 1967; Bats: Wings in the Night, 1968; Curious Critters, 1969; This Restless Earth, 1970.

ABOUT: Contemporary Authors, Vol. 9-10; Something About the Author, Vol. 1; Who's Who of American Women, 1958-59.

MILDRED LEE

February 19, 1908-

AUTHOR OF *The Rock and the Willow,* etc.

Autobiographical sketch of Mildred Lee Scudder:

I WAS born in Blockton, Alabama, next to the eldest of four children. Our father was a Baptist minister in the days when his profession brought a lower living wage—even relatively—than it does today. Still, we did not think of ourselves as "poor." We had advantages most of our friends had not—among them the example of good vocabularies and books. There must always have been a shortage of cash but our ingenious mother saw to it that we had notable birthdays and Christmases as well as many small luxuries in between.

We always lived in small towns in the south, moving to Georgia from Alabama, but rural life was close by and intertwined from time to time with our town existence. This was mainly due to my father's serving small country churches to provide them with a minister and to supplement his small salary. He frequently took one or more of us children along with him on these missions and

the little wooden churches, country graveyards and simple farm homes must have made an everlasting impression upon me. They are what I like best to write about (*and* read about), having long since passed the stage of more sophisticated writing.

When I was seven I had scarlet fever. My mother was expecting her last child soon and the doctor said she must under no circumstances be exposed to me. There was no hospital, not even a trained nurse in our little town, so my father took over the nursing, isolating himself along with me in his study. As I began to recover he invented a game for my amusement: we took turns making up stories of the pictures on the walls.

I don't know whether or not that was the beginning of my creativeness. It was later, though not very much later, that I began to "make up" stories on my own. My chief duty in the home was entertaining my younger brother and sister and as soon as I could read well enough I spent a lot of time reading to them. I was only ten or eleven, I think, when I began to "read" to them from any randomly selected book, imagining characters and events as if I had written them—as not too long afterward I began to do.

I was thirty years old before I had the reward of seeing one of my short stories in

Redbook Magazine. I had written many thousands of words before then, most of them for the love of doing so, but a few stories I had tried to place. I was by this time married and the mother of two children. Instead of "growing out of" writing I had grown into it, forsaking other moderate talents I had nurtured in my youth.

I believe that reading, or the love of it, more than anything else gave me the desire to write. It was and is my favorite thing, though I like to travel. Not by air or water, but through the countryside I love. I love strange cities too and seeing little houses sitting lonely in a twilight and knowing they are homes with people living lives in them. It is people, in the last analysis, who are most interesting, but of course one has to ration them in order to have writing time.

I lived for many years in the North: New York and vicinity and New England. In 1955 my husband, our (then) four-year-old daughter and I came to Florida and made our home in St. Petersburg.

———

Mildred Lee attended Bessie Tift College and has taken courses at Troy Normal College, Columbia University, New York University, and the University of New Hampshire. She married James Henry Hurstwood Scudder in 1947. Her children are Barbara Lee Schimpff DuLac, Robert Donald Schimpff, and Jane Powell Scudder. She is a member of the St. Petersburg Council on Human Relations. Besides books for children, Mrs. Scudder has written a novel for adults and has contributed short stories to periodicals including *Ladies' Home Journal* and *Redbook*. She won a Child Study Association Children's Book Award, 1963, for *The Rock and the Willow*.

SELECTED WORKS: The Rock and the Willow, 1963; Honor Sands, 1966; The Skating Rink, 1969.

ABOUT: Contemporary Authors, Vol. 9-10.

DAVID JOHNSON LEISK

See *"Johnson, Crockett"*

BLAIR LENT

January 22, 1930-

AUTHOR AND ILLUSTRATOR OF *John Tabor's Ride,* etc.

Autobiographical sketch of Blair Lent, who also writes under the name "Ernest Small":

ALL my life I've been trying to suppress the awful memories I have of the town where I grew up. I couldn't fit into the suburban atmosphere because I was fat, and clumsy at sports, and my family was poor. In this particular town, money, appearance, and athletic prowess were considered one's most important attributes. At the time I believed that the whole world was like that, until I read *Babbitt* and *Main Street* and realized I wasn't mad. What did get me through my childhood was the books my father would bring me from the secondhand bookstore, books I got out of the library, and books I made myself, as presents for my parents and my grandmother. Summers my parents and I would go to a small cottage on a New Hampshire lake, which was a wonderful escape; but it was years and years after I left the town before I grew away from the identity it had left upon me.

One of the aspects of living there, however, was the importance that books had for me as a child. All my life I have wanted to write and illustrate books for children. After I graduated from the Boston Museum School I traveled and studied in Europe for a year on a fellowship from the Boston Museum of Fine Arts. When I returned to Boston I designed tin can labels and advertisements for bank loans. I also painted—enough for two one-man shows, until finally Emilie McLeod, juvenile editor at Atlantic Monthly Press, saw something she liked in one of my stories and encouraged me to do more work on it. I did, and it became *Pistachio*, my first book. The idea for *Pistachio* came from an experience I had in Paris. The circus in the story is like circuses I enjoyed there, and circuses I saw on a later trip to Southern Germany.

As a child, the Russian hag Baba Yaga was always my favorite witch, and so writing my picture book about her, *Baba Yaga* (un-

BLAIR LENT

der the pseudonym Ernest Small), was a fascinating experience. This was true not only because of all the lore about the old woman, but also because of the many weird, unexplainable things that happened while the book was in progress—the old witch didn't want to be exposed! A strange black cat jumped through my studio window and ran across my sketches, I almost died of turpentine poisoning while I was making the prints, and a phone conversation between Walter Lorraine, the art director and myself was interrupted by a cackling voice telling us to get off the line.

My favorite of all the books I have done is *John Tabor's Ride*, another book based on legend, this time from New England. In making this book I tried to get the rolling feeling of the sea into both the words and the pictures.

I don't always write my own stories. *Why the Sun and the Moon Live in the Sky* is an African folk tale recorded many years ago by Elphinstone Dayrell. I prefer to do my own writing, but this story was beautifully written and suggested a unique idea to me: to depict the elements as costumed natives. In this way the words and the pictures tell different stories, yet work together to produce a unified whole. I also chose to illustrate *The Little Matchgirl* because I wanted to try to illustrate one of my favorite sentimental stories in a not too sentimental way.

Presently I am developing stories and pictures from ideas I gathered when I was in the Soviet Union last year. My trip there was made possible by another traveling scholarship from the Boston Museum of Fine Arts.

When I look back at my childhood, I realize that although I was unhappy growing up in that atmosphere, it was partly the reaction against it that gave me the determination to stick to what I really wanted to do. And without this determination, I might not be writing and illustrating today.

———

Blair Lent graduated with honors from the Boston Museum School in 1953. He received the Amos Cummings Memorial Traveling Scholarship in 1954 and studied in Europe. In 1967 he traveled through the U.S.S.R. on a Bartlett scholarship.

Lent often designs his own books. His work has been in several exhibitions of the American Institute of Graphic Arts. Twice he was a runner-up for the Caldecott Medal, for *The Wave*, 1965, and for *Why the Sun and the Moon Live in the Sky*, 1969. For *The Wave* he also received a Silver Medal at the São Paulo Bienal in Brazil. *Tikki Tikki Tembo* won the Boston *Globe-Horn Book* Award for illustrations, 1968. *From King Boggen's Hall to Nothing-At-All* won the Bronze Medal at the Biennale of Illustrations, Bratislava, Czechoslovakia, 1969.

SELECTED WORKS WRITTEN AND ILLUSTRATED: Pistachio, 1964; John Tabor's Ride, 1966; Baba Yaga, 1966; From King Boggen's Hall to Nothing-At-All, 1967.

SELECTED WORKS ILLUSTRATED: The Wave, by Margaret Hodges, 1964; The Little Matchgirl, by Hans Christian Andersen, 1968; Tikki Tikki Tembo, by Arlene Mosel, 1968; Why the Sun and the Moon Live in the Sky, retold by Elphinstone Dayrell, 1968; The Angry Moon, by William Sleator, 1970.

ABOUT: Contemporary Authors, Vol. 20-22; Hopkins, Lee Bennett. Books Are by People; Kingman, Lee and others, comps. Illustrators of Children's Books: 1957-1966; Who's Who in American Art, 1970; Horn Book August 1965; Publishers' Weekly February 17, 1969.

SORCHE NIC LEODHAS

See *"Nic Leodhas, Sorche"*

WILLY LEY

October 2, 1906–June 24, 1969

AUTHOR OF *Engineers' Dreams*, etc.

Biographical sketch of Willy Ley:

WILLY LEY

WILLY LEY was born in Berlin, the son of Julius Otto Ley, a wine merchant, and Frida (May) Ley. He demonstrated an early penchant for science by visiting the Berlin Museum of Natural History when he played hookey from Sunday School. His scientific interests were broad, ranging from astronomy, to zoology, to botany, to paleontology and by the time he finished his secondary education he had decided to make geology his career. Between 1920 and 1927, he studied at the University of Berlin and the University of Königsberg, but his attendance was somewhat irregular because of financial problems connected with the postwar inflation in Germany and the failure of his father's business. Later in his academic career, another distraction interrupted his studies: in 1925 he came across Herman Oberth's writings on rocketry and became an enthusiast of space travel. His first book, published in 1926, was *Trip in Space*, and in 1927, he joined with nine other young German scientists to found the Society for Space Travel.

Ley was the Society's vice president and was very successful in recruiting new members, including Wernher von Braun. His ability to communicate in English, French, Dutch, Russian, and Italian, as well as German, made it possible for him to correspond with rocket pioneers throughout Europe and America, and he thus established the first clearinghouse for rocket news and information. Meanwhile, he worked in an industrial firm, wrote a biography of Konrad Gesner von Zürich, began a history of rockets, and collaborated with Fritz Lang on several science fiction films.

After the Nazis took power they forced the Society to disband, and Ley soon found himself in trouble with the Gestapo when some of his articles on rocket research appeared in foreign journals. In 1935 he left Germany and came to the United States, where he supported himself precariously for several years by writing articles on scientific subjects. He did not write on rocketry, however,

since few Americans were interested in the field at that time. Between 1940 and 1944, he was science editor for the newspaper *PM*. Meanwhile, he met and married (in 1941) Olga Feldman, a Russian-born ballet dancer and artist who later illustrated some of his books and articles. In 1941 he also published his first American book, *The Lungfish and the Unicorn*.

Late in 1944, Germany began sending V-2 rockets against England, and Ley, who had just become a U.S. citizen, suddenly found himself in great demand as a rocket expert. From 1944 to 1947 he worked as research engineer for the Washington Institute of Technology, and in 1947, he began his long service as a consultant to the office of technical services of the U.S. Department of Commerce. Meanwhile, he continued to write books and articles, and many of them now concerned rockets and space travel. Most were directed to an adult audience (although they were often recommended for interested teen-agers), but some were written for older children. His first juvenile book, *Engineers' Dreams*, won the 1954 New York *Herald Tribune* Children's Spring Book Festival Award for older children and in the later 1950s he wrote a special "Adventures in Space" series of books for children.

Willy Ley, who predicted back in 1949 that a manned rocket trip to the moon would be made by 1974, died on June 24, 1969,

Ley: *LAY*

less than a month before the first manned rocket landed on the moon. He is survived by his wife and two daughters, Sandra and Xenia.

SELECTED WORKS: Engineers' Dreams, 1954; Space Travel, 1958; Our Work in Space, 1964; Inside the Orbit of the Earth, 1968; Dawn of Zoology, 1968; The Drifting Continents, 1969.

ABOUT: Author's and Writer's Who's Who, 1963; Contemporary Authors, Vol. 9-10; Twentieth Century Authors (First Supplement), 1955; Who Knows—and What (1949); Who's Who in America, 1968-69; Who's Who in Engineering, 1948; Current Biography February 1953; September, 1969; New Outlook October 1934; New York Herald Tribune Book Review May 16, 1954; New York Times June 25, 1969; New York Times Book Review July 22, 1951; Newsweek May 22, 1944; July 7, 1969; Publishers' Weekly July 14, 1969; This Week November 16, 1952; Time July 4, 1969.

BETTY JEAN LIFTON

June 11, 1926-

AUTHOR OF *Kap the Kappa*, etc.

Autobiographical sketch of Betty Jean Kirschner Lifton:

"MORE dogs should travel and the world would be a better place" is the philosophy of the canine narrator in *Taka-chan and I*, and I should confess that it is also mine. During the time I was growing up in Cincinnati, Ohio, I was also in the Isles of Greece with Byron, sharing some corner that is forever England with Rupert Brooke, and perhaps dying a little with Keats in Italy. I was physically bound to the Middle West, but like Sherwood Anderson, whom I also admired, I was looking out toward some world beyond my own.

I began to find this world when I went to Barnard College in New York, and during the following years when I worked in television there. At that time I wanted to be a playwright. But my marriage took me out into another world previously undreamed of —the Far East.

In Japan I often felt much like Alice, for everything had a way of seeming upside down and the perceptions one had accepted as reality were continually being shaken into new patterns. Like my river elf in *Kap the Kappa* who was to discover his true self deep in his native rivers after living for a while on land with humans, I was constantly uncovering the wellsprings of my own background there in the exotic setting of Asia.

I became a journalist then, covering the end of the American occupation of Japan, the last days of the Korean War, the post-Geneva-Accords period in Vietnam. I also made a documentary film on the children of Hiroshima while my husband was studying the psychological effects of the bomb on the survivors there. But at the same time another part of me, one I had not known too well until now, was busily collecting tales and folk lore.

As my articles began to appear in magazines and newspapers, so did strange folk creatures—kappas, tengus, amanojakus and ghost cats—begin to inhabit the children's books I found myself writing. Gradually the journalism became something perfunctory that allowed me to travel, while the children's books became a form of symbolic expression that I found I could not do without.

Most of my writing has been influenced by those years in Asia—Joji espouses nonviolence as a working philosophy in all of my Joji books; the gentle spirit of the Buddha is diffused through *The Dwarf Pine Tree*; and the theme of metamorphosis is dealt with playfully in *The Many Lives of Chio and Goro*.

My husband's research still takes us back and forth across the Pacific. Now he is a research professor of psychiatry at Yale University, and home is an old former inn in Woodbridge, Connecticut. Here with our two small children, Kenneth (who was the little boy in *The Secret Seller*) and Karen, we raise talking ducks, and flying mice and writing dogs. Our animals, like those mischievous folk creatures, have a way of intruding themselves into my books. Jumblie, our silver poodle, has just finished *A Dog's Guide to Tokyo*, a must for any dog planning a trip to Japan.

Which brings us full circle to dogs and travel again. With the confession that my Pekin duck, who cannot fly, says in *The Silver Crane*: "The greatest traveler stays at home."

And perhaps that is part of my philosophy too.

———

Betty Jean Kirschner received her B.A. from Barnard College in 1948 and married Robert Jay Lifton in 1952.

Kap the Kappa was an honor book in the New York *Herald Tribune* Children's Spring Book Festival of 1960. A multi-media space fantasy by Betty Jean Lifton was produced three weekends in November 1970 at City Center, New York.

SELECTED WORKS: Kap the Kappa, 1960; The Dwarf Pine Tree, 1963; The Cock and the Ghost Cat, 1965; Joji and the Amanojaku, 1965; Takachan and I, 1967; The Many Lives of Chio and Goro, 1968; The Secret Seller, 1968; A Dog's Guide to Tokyo, 1969.

ABOUT: Contemporary Authors, Vol. 5-6.

LEO LIONNI

May 5, 1910-

AUTHOR AND ILLUSTRATOR OF *Swimmy*, etc.

Biographical sketch of Leo Lionni:

LEO LIONNI was born in Amsterdam. He started to paint as a child and spent the first twelve years of his life near two of Europe's best museums. He spent the rest of his childhood traveling with his family throughout Belgium, France, Switzerland, and Italy.

From 1928 to 1930 he attended the University of Zurich and then worked for the Motta Panettoni baking company. In 1931

LEO LIONNI

he married Nora Maffi. During the next few years he opened his own advertising agency, contributed articles on art and the cinema to European art journals, and in 1935 received a doctorate in economics from the University of Genoa.

Lionni left Italy in 1939 for the United States, where he took a job as a designer for the Federal Housing Administration and the Office for Emergency Management. Later, from 1939-1947, he worked for N. W. Ayer & Sons, an advertising agency in Philadelphia. His work for Ayer won him the Art Directors Club Medal. He was naturalized in 1945. In 1947 he turned to serious painting, staging a one-man show of oils and watercolors at the Norlyst Gallery in New York. He bought a house on the Riviera, and from 1947 to 1949 he painted and exhibited throughout Europe. Returning to the United States in 1949, he became the design director for Olivetti, art director for *Fortune*, chairman of the Graphic Design Department of Parsons School of Design, and coeditor of *Print*. He also served as president of the American Institute of Graphic Arts.

In 1953 Lionni had a one-man show at the Museum of Modern Art in New York. He was the chairman that year of the International Design Conference in Aspen, Colorado.

His "Resurgent India," a photographic portfolio for *Fortune*, was the result of his three-month stay in India in 1956. In 1957 he had a one-man show at the American

Institute of Graphic Arts and was designer for the "Unfinished Business" pavilion at the Brussels Fair. In 1959 he had one-man shows in Worcester, Portland, San Francisco, and Philadelphia.

In the midst of this diversified career, in 1959, Leo Lionni wrote and illustrated his first children's book, *Little Blue and Little Yellow*, a story of two blotches of color who hug each other and become one green blotch. A number of books and many awards followed. *Inch by Inch* was named by the New York *Times* as one of the ten best-illustrated children's books of 1960, was a runner-up for the Caldecott Medal for 1961, received a 1962 Lewis Carroll Shelf Award and was a 1963 Honor Book (German Youth Book Award). *Swimmy* was a Caldecott runner-up for 1964, received the German Youth Book Award, picture book category, in 1965 and a "Golden Apple" from the 1967 Biennale of Illustrations, Bratislava, Czechoslovakia. It was among the *Times* ten best-illustrated children's books in 1963 and the "fifty books of the past five years" in 1966. *Frederick* was a 1968 Caldecott runner-up and on the Honor List for the 1968 German Juvenile Book Award. *Alexander and the Wind-up Mouse* was a 1970 Caldecott runner-up.

Asked if his books have sociological undertones, Lionni replied that all works of art, no matter how simple in scope, must have more than one level of meaning.

A big house of his own design overlooking the Gulf of Genoa is now the place Lionni calls home, although he visits the United States often. He continues painting, designing, and writing and still finds time to play the flamenco guitar for his wife, his two sons, Louis and Paul, and his two grandchildren.

SELECTED WORKS WRITTEN AND ILLUSTRATED: Little Blue and Little Yellow, 1959; Inch by Inch, 1960; Swimmy, 1963; Tico and the Golden Wings, 1964; Frederick, 1967; Alexander and the Wind-up Mouse, 1969; Fish Is Fish, 1970.

ABOUT: Hopkins, Lee Bennett. Books Are by People; Kingman, Lee and others, comps. Illustrators of Children's Books: 1957-1966; Who's Who in America, 1970-71; Who's Who in American Art, 1970; Who's Who in Graphic Art, 1962; American Artist April 1953; Library Journal March 15, 1964; Time December 22, 1958; Top of the News October 1962; Wilson Library Bulletin October 1964.

ANITA LOBEL
June 2, 1934-

AUTHOR AND ILLUSTRATOR OF *Sven's Bridge*, etc.

Autobiographical sketch of Anita Kempler Lobel:

I WAS pampered and overprotected as a child in Cracow, Poland, until it all came to an abrupt end with the Nazi invasion. During the war years, my younger brother and I were taken care of by the "nannie" who had raised us since we had been born. She was devoutly religious and we spent a good deal of time at church. This became our only entertainment, our shelter from the cold and often refuge from the Nazis. The drama and ceremony made a great and lasting impression, leaving me with a sense of theatre which I believe helps me in my work today. After having successfully evaded the Nazis for four and a half years, my brother and I were captured and sent to a concentration camp in Germany. We managed to survive and were rescued in April 1945 by the Swedish Red Cross. Much later in Sweden, we were miraculously reunited with our parents. While attending school in Sweden, I was encouraged by many people to become an artist.

After seven years, my parents decided to move to the United States. Having lived in Stockholm, which had seemed to me to be a large city, New York was overpowering, frightening and dirty. However, I have grown to love it and now I won't dream of living anywhere else—almost!

I completed my education at Washington Irving High School and then went on to Pratt Institute to continue my studies in art. For a time, I considered acting as a career, but discovered that I still preferred the privacy and immediacy of painting and drawing. Meanwhile, I met and married Arnold Lobel, who was also a student at Pratt. Presently, we have two children, Adrianne and Adam.

After leaving Pratt, I worked as a freelance textile designer. While hard and exacting work, it was during this time I acquired most of the techniques and skills that I now use in my books.

Lobel: *LO bel*

I feel my work is also influenced by contemporary forms in film and drama, particularly in the "staging" of my stories.

———

Anita Kempler married Arnold Lobel in 1955. *Sven's Bridge* was named among the best-illustrated picture books of 1965 by the New York *Times*. This and other books of hers have been in exhibitions of the American Institute of Graphic Arts.

SELECTED WORKS WRITTEN AND ILLUSTRATED: Sven's Bridge, 1965; The Troll Music, 1966; Potatoes, Potatoes, 1967; The Seamstress of Salzburg, 1970.

SELECTED WORKS ILLUSTRATED: Puppy Summer, by Meindert De Jong, 1966; Cock-A-Doodle-Doo! Cock-A-Doodle Dandy! by Paul Kapp, 1966; Indian Summer, by F. N. Monjo, 1968.

ABOUT: Hopkins, Lee Bennett. Books Are by People. Kingman, Lee and others, comps. Illustrators of Children's Books: 1957-1966; Publishers' Weekly May 17, 1971.

When in 1964 I was given the opportunity to write and illustrate a book for children, I was utterly delighted . . . and also a bit scared. But after designing textiles for seven years, I was eager to do something new and this seemed to me to be just the thing. Here was the chance to merge my interest in pageantry and the theatre with my experience as a designer. The result was *Sven's Bridge,* a deliberately nostalgic and affectionate tribute to the folk designs of Sweden which I love. This was followed by *The Troll Music,* a story told in a folk tale manner. In these two books, the illustrative approach was a decorative one, while in *Potatoes, Potatoes,* my third book, I concentrated on the emotional content and pathos of the story.

Sometimes the germ of an idea for a story occurs first with the visual aspect and sometimes with words. For instance, *Sven's Bridge* started with pictures and the words followed. In the case of *The Seamstress of Salzburg,* however, the writing of the story was completed before I began drawing the illustrations.

Although the technique I use is very traditional, inspired by medieval tapestries and eighteenth and nineteenth century paintings,

ARNOLD LOBEL

May 22, 1933-

AUTHOR AND ILLUSTRATOR OF A *Holiday for Mister Muster,* etc.

Autobiographical sketch of Arnold Stark Lobel:

SHORTLY after their wedding ceremony, my father and mother got on a train heading west to California. They had both grown up in Schenectady, New York, but my father had decided that his particular "pot of gold" lay somewhere on the sunny shores of that far state. Of course, in the early thirties, there were very few "pots of gold" anywhere. Several years later, they arrived back in Schenectady and, along with their disappointment, they carried with them a screaming, red-faced, ill-tempered infant of six months. That was me!

The house in which I grew up in Schenectady was large and ramshackle. The wide front lawn sloped down to a pleasant tree-lined street and, for the most part, my very early childhood was quite happy. Later, however, a series of illnesses kept me hospitalized for long periods of time. I can remember

Lobel: *LO bel*

sitting on the sundeck of the hospital look-ing out at the school playground across the street and feeling isolated and separate from the children I saw playing there.

With adolescence came improved health, as well as the knowledge that I wanted to be an artist. After high school with this end in mind, I applied for admission and was ac-cepted at Pratt Institute in Brooklyn. The sense of independence and the excitement of the Big City was a heady combination for a young man fresh from a quiet town in up-state New York. In settling down to my studies at Pratt, I discovered that book il-lustration was the special branch of art that intrigued me the most.

It is a prevailing truism that Pratt students marry Pratt students, and I was no exception. I met my wife, Anita, there and married her shortly after my graduation in 1955. Find-ing Brooklyn an agreeable place in which to live, we discover ourselves, fourteen years later, still happily living there in a charming apartment in the Park Slope section with our two children, Adrianne and Adam. My wife is also an author and illustrator of children's books and we work side by side in the same studio every day. Our styles are very dis-similar so, up to now, we work separately and have never collaborated on the same

book. Of course, as critics, we are by turns mutually irritating and helpful to each other.

Most of the ideas for my books I find have really not come from observing my own chil-dren as much as from my own childhood. I find that the majority of my books have as their central characters "child substitutes" rather than real children. My first book was *A Zoo for Mister Muster* and the gentleman of the title would most certainly fit into that description. A portly and friendly little man with a passion for zoo animals and a general distrust of adult institutions, he has all the attributes of a child but moves through the story with the independence of an adult.

In *Giant John,* we meet an enormous young man of unspecified age who, while be-ing devoted to his mother in a manner with which children may identify, goes forth to achieve fame and some fortune through his own efforts and cleverness.

Small Pig, one of my newest heroes, is a "child" in every way but physical form. His momentary burst of independence brings him adventure and some misery, but in the end, he is a richer pig for it.

I never like to use the same illustrative technique over and over, but rather use a repertory of styles as they suit the mood of the manuscript.

I cannot think of any work that could be more agreeable and fun than making books for children.

———

A Holiday for Mister Muster was named one of the ten best-illustrated children's books of 1963 by the New York *Times* and was exhibited by the American Institute of Graphic Arts.

SELECTED WORKS WRITTEN AND ILLUSTRATED: A Zoo for Mister Muster, 1962; A Holiday for Mister Muster, 1963; Giant John, 1964; Martha, the Movie Mouse, 1966; Small Pig, 1969.

SELECTED WORKS ILLUSTRATED: Little Run-ner of the Longhouse, by Betty Baker, 1962; The Quarreling Book, by Charlotte Zolotow, 1963; Dudley Pippin, by Phil Ressner, 1965; Oscar Otter, by Nathaniel Benchley, 1966.

ABOUT: Contemporary Authors, Vol. 4; Hop-kins, Lee Bennett. Books Are by People; Hürli-mann, Bettina. Picture Book World; Kingman, Lee and others, comps. Illustrators of Children's Books: 1957-1966; Publishers' Weekly May 17, 1971.

"NANCY LORD"

See *Titus, Eve*

JOSEPH LOW
August 11, 1911-

AUTHOR AND ILLUSTRATOR OF *There Was a Wise Crow*, etc.

Autobiographical sketch of Joseph Low:

THE small town where I was born was just down the Ohio from Pittsburgh. Its name is Coraopolis—Greek for "City of Maidens"— a nineteenth century affectation said to reflect either the pride or the problem of its founder, who thus drew attention to the seven daughters he placed upon the marriage market.

We left there when I was seven and I have never been back, but the lovely, rural quality of the place must have left its impression. My strongest memories of that short interval are the fascination of the woods and hills just beyond our house, the implication of the Indian arrowheads we sometimes found, and the riverboats then still active on the Ohio. Even though my father's work was with a steel foundry in the town, the flavor of life there was still very much that of the unpressured nineteenth century. He could and did walk to his work, kept dogs, loved hunting and the woods.

What a wrench, then, to be taken away and, for most of my growing up, compelled to live in the barren flatness of the towns just outside of Chicago! I accepted it, as a child does, but there was always a submerged longing for the rich mysteries of nature. Finding nothing in the countryside, I was drawn into sailing when I was about fifteen. Life on the water again brought me close to what I lacked and needed. I took to it with an adolescent's passion and couldn't decide whether I wanted to be an artist or a sailor.

In somewhat the same way, I was seldom able to find what I wanted in school classrooms. In those days the academic teaching of art—even more than other subjects—was

more deadly dull than anyone who has grown up since can imagine. In time, searching on my own, I found voices here and there in the art of the past, and among a few of the moderns, speaking a visual language I could recognize as my own. So began a long process of learning and development which still continues and will, I hope, last as long as I do.

From the beginning, for whatever reason, I had a strong interest in books and their illustrations. When the depression made art school impossible, I managed to get a small press, some type and occasional encouragement from a few professionals in the field and thus educate myself. This interest persists: in addition to my work in children's books and more-or-less fine editions, I have produced a number of publications and a great deal of ephemera with my private venture, the Eden Hill Press. The old dilemma of artist-or-sailor? has happily been resolved. A small racing cruiser lies at anchor a few minutes' walk from my home and studio. Early rising and diligent application allow me to sail or "mess about with boats" most late afternoons and every weekend during the season, to return refreshed for the next day's work.

———

Joseph Low attended the University of Illinois as an art major, 1930-1932, and later studied drawing under George Grosz at the Art Students League in New York. He married Ruth Hull in 1940, and has two daughters, Damaris and Jennifer.

Low taught design and graphic art at Indiana University, there setting up the Corydon Press. A large commission from World Publishing Company finally enabled him to free lance.

In 1959, Low became proprietor of the Eden Hill Press, and published his own material, while continuing to illustrate books and to design book jackets and record and magazine covers. In collaboration with his wife, he wrote and illustrated *The Mother Goose Riddle Rhymes*, published in 1952.

Joseph Low's work has been shown in the United States, Europe and South America and is represented in the collections of a number of universities and museums. His book illustrations have often been in exhibitions of the American Institute of Graphic Arts. He has received awards from the American Institute of Graphic Arts, the Society of Illustrators and the Art Directors Club. *Adam's Book of Odd Creatures* won the New York *Herald Tribune* Children's Spring Book Festival Award in 1962.

SELECTED WORKS WRITTEN AND ILLUSTRATED: Adam's Book of Odd Creatures, 1962; Smiling Duke, 1963; There Was a Wise Crow, 1969.

SELECTED WORKS ILLUSTRATED: The Big Cheese, by Miriam Schlein, 1958; Jack and the Beanstalk, by Walter de la Mare, 1959; How a Seed Grows, by Helene Jordan, 1960; The Cat and the Mouse, by Maria Elena de la Iglesia, 1966; Telephones, by Bernice Kohn, 1967; The Legend of the Willow Plate, by Alvin R. Tresselt and Nancy Cleaver, 1968; The Lost Zoo, by Countee Cullen, 1969.

ABOUT: Kingman, Lee and others, comps. Illustrators of Children's Books, 1957-1966; Viguers, Ruth Hill and others, comps. Illustrators of Children's Books: 1946-1956; Who's Who in America, 1970-71; Who's Who in American Art, 1970; Who's Who in Graphic Art, 1962; American Artist October 1951; Graphis No. 41, 1952; Print Winter 1950.

DAVID McCORD
November 15, 1897-

AUTHOR OF *Far and Few*, etc.

Biographical sketch of David Thompson Watson McCord:

DAVID McCORD likes to introduce himself as "born in New York, raised in Oregon, and educated at Harvard." The only child of Joseph Alexander and Eleanore Baynton (Reed) McCord, he spent his early years in Long Island, when it was "still woods and fields." At twelve he moved with his parents to what was then pioneer country, a ranch in Oregon. He had no further schooling till he was fifteen, but learned to live in the wilderness and acquired his characteristic self-reliance.

Recurrent fevers from malaria he had contracted as a child often kept McCord from classes, but did not prevent his writing for the school paper at Lincoln High School in Portland, and his graduation with high honors. He served as a 2nd Lieutenant, F.A., U.S. Army, in 1918. He went on to Harvard, became president of the *Lampoon*, and took his B.A. in physics in 1921 and his M.A. in Romance Languages in 1922. The next five years he spent as music and drama critic on the Boston *Transcript*. Then he returned to his Alma Mater, to devote the rest of his career to serving her in many capacities, including those of fund raiser and alumni editor.

Seriously as McCord approached the craft of writing (setting himself the goal of a book a year and almost achieving it), he has been happy in keeping his writing a hobby rather than a vocation. The charm of his occasional essays on such subjects as the woods of New Hampshire or the landmarks of Boston lies in this quality. He contributed to such leading magazines as the *New Yorker, Harper's*, and the *Yale Review*, and wrote special pieces for special occasions in what has become his hometown: a short history of the Boston Public Library, an account of the founding and growth of Radcliffe College, and a book on Peter Bent Brigham Hospital. Most of all, perhaps, he has used his hobby to enrich and enhance his vocation: no

DAVID McCORD

Harvard alumnus could resist reading the annual appeal for contributions, so literate and so versatile was its author. Money flowed in—over the years it reached a total of $15,319,872.26.

It is as a poet that McCord has become a writer for children. His earliest and most deeply felt influences were Edward Lear and Robert Louis Stevenson. He ascribes his sense of rhythm and his predilection for rhyme to his having learned Lear's *The Owl and the Pussycat* when he was five. It is a debt he has repaid with interest. When he gave the Lowell Lectures in 1950 he used Lear as his subject; he assigned a prominent place to Lear in three anthologies of humorous verse he has edited, *What Cheer*, the *Pocket Book of Humorous Verse*, and the *Modern Treasury of Humorous Verse*; and his first volume of children's verse had as title a quotation from Edward Lear, *Far and Few*. The debt to Stevenson is less obvious but can be felt whenever he writes of a child alone and especially alone with nature.

McCord is a man of varied and rich interests. He holds a first-grade amateur wireless operator's license from 1915. A talented water-colorist, he has had several one-man shows of his landscapes. He has served at the Bread Loaf Writers Conference and is a trustee of a number of institutions and an overseer of the Perkins Institute for the

Blind. He belongs to numerous organizations, including International P.E.N., Phi Beta Kappa, and Authors' League of America, and he is a Fellow of the American Academy of Arts and Sciences. Among his many distinctions are several honorary degrees, including the first L.H.D. ever awarded by Harvard. Harvard also established a scholarship in his name and made him honorary curator of the Poetry and Farnsworth Rooms, Harvard College Library. He was Phi Beta Kappa poet at Harvard, Tufts, and William and Mary, and has received grants from the Guggenheim Foundation and from the National Institute of Arts and Letters. He received the William Rose Benét Award in 1952 and the Sarah Josepha Hale Medal for distinguished service to education in 1962, the year of his retirement.

SELECTED WORKS: Far and Few, 1952; Take Sky, 1962; All Day Long, 1966; Every Time I Climb a Tree, 1967; For Me to Say, 1970.

ABOUT: Hopkins, Lee Bennett. Books Are by People; Who's Who in America, 1970-71; Time June 29, 1962.

MAUREEN MOLLIE HUNTER McVEIGH McILWRAITH

See *Hunter, Mollie*

ROBIN McKOWN

AUTHOR OF *Janine*, etc.

Autobiographical sketch of Robin Clason McKown:

AFTER World War II, I quit a pleasant job writing radio scripts and newspaper columns on books for the Book-of-the-Month Club and went to live in a small mining town in the north of France called Avion. I had this fixed idea of writing about these exceptionally brave and hardy mining people and their lives under Nazi occupation, a much too ambitious project since I'd never written a book before. What emerged, some years later, were two teen-age books—*Janine*, which won the 1960 Child Study Association Award and was a Junior Literary Guild selection, and a boys' story, *Patriot of the Underground*.

Robin McKown

This French experience set a pattern for my writing which, while I would not recommend it to anyone else, has proved rewarding for me. Having always been told that one should write only about what one knows, I have found it far more exciting to decide on a topic on which I know next to nothing, so that each book becomes an adventure in self-education. This was true of *The Fabulous Isotopes* and several scientific biographies, of *Seven Famous Trials*, which taught me something about law, and *Heroic Nurses* (also a Junior Literary Guild selection), which required considerable homework on nursing skills.

Exotic backgrounds have a great lure for me; I have used books as an excuse for more foreign travel. *The Story of the Incas* required a stay in Peru. To gather material for *Foreign Service Girl*, I visited Rome, Paris, London and five North African countries, staying longest in Benghazi, Libya. I went to Ireland for *The Ordeal of Anne Devlin*. One night several years ago I dreamed of Madagascar and the next day started to arrange transportation to what most travel agencies seem to consider the end of the world. Three books came out of that venture: *Rakoto and the Drongo Bird*, based on a Madagascar legend; *The Boy Who Woke Up in Mada-*

gascar, and *Girl of Madagascar*, the story of a Malagasy nurse.

I accepted with delight an assignment to write *The Congo, River of Mystery*, which gave me a chance to get acquainted with a land and a people totally strange to me. That voyage also led to my most recent book, a biography of Patrice Lumumba (Doubleday, 1969).

Regarding my own background, I was born in Denver, Colorado, spent my childhood vacations with my grandparents in a tiny ghost mining town high in the Rocky Mountains, graduated from the University of Colorado, spent an extra six months at Northwestern University School of Drama, and took courses at New York University in interior decorating and radio script writing. My first literary acceptance, and the one that thrilled me most, came while I was at the University of Colorado. A Boston magazine called *Poet Lore* agreed to publish a one-act play I had sent them, promising me eight copies in payment. Months later I tumbled out of the clouds when I received a printed notice that the magazine had stopped publication.

After my first marriage, in college, New York City became my home and home base until 1969. Our present, and I hope permanent residence is a ninety-seven-acre farm, mostly wooded hills, in western New York State.

SELECTED WORKS: Janine, 1960; The Fabulous Isotopes, 1962; Seven Famous Trials in History, 1963; Patriot of the Underground, 1964; Eleanor Roosevelt's World, 1964; Heroic Nurses, 1966; Rakoto and the Drongo Bird, 1966; The Boy Who Woke Up in Madagascar, 1967; Girl of Madagascar, 1968.

ABOUT: Contemporary Authors, Vol. 3.

RUTH MANNING-SANDERS

1895-

AUTHOR OF *Story of Hans Andersen: Swan of Denmark*, etc.

Biographical sketch of Ruth Manning-Sanders:

RUTH MANNING-SANDERS was born in Swansea, Wales, the youngest daughter of a

RUTH MANNING-SANDERS

minister. When she was three the family moved to Cheshire, and it was there that she grew up. She has very happy memories of childhood—a home full of books, where she wrote and performed plays with her two older sisters, and summers spent in the Highlands of Scotland where the children were free to run wild. When she grew up she went to Manchester University where she read English and specialized in Shakespearean studies.

It was at the university that she met and married George Manning-Sanders, a Cornish artist and writer. They spent the early years of their marriage touring the British Isles in a horse-drawn caravan. For two of those years Mrs. Manning-Sanders worked regularly with a circus.

The arrival of children changed this way of life. At some time between the births of their children Joan and David, the caravan was abandoned, but the nomadic life continued. The children's schooling was no problem: they had found the perfect governess, who went with them everywhere and became a part of the family.

Both Ruth Manning-Sanders and her husband continued to write, he novels and short stories, she mostly novels and poetry. Several of her books had the circus as a setting; one was a history of the English circus. In 1926 she won the Blindman International Poetry Prize for a long narrative poem, "The City."

Their daughter Joan developed into a talented artist and by sixteen was exhibiting at the Royal Academy. Her parents settled down at Senner Cove, Cornwall, so that she might have her own studio on the rocky coast.

Then came a long hiatus in the career of Ruth Manning-Sanders. World War II intervened with all its demands on the British people. Her husband died and she went to live with Joan, now married, in Bristol. When she began to write again it was no longer for adults but for children. In 1950 she wrote a life of Hans Christian Andersen. Since then, in addition to other books for children and young people, she has written a number of volumes in the popular *A Book of . . .* series, based on the folklore of many countries.

Ruth Manning-Sanders writes in a lively, colloquial style, particularly suitable to reading aloud. The *New Yorker* said of *A Bundle of Ballads* that the original dialect was so well retained that you could "almost hear the twang of the harp." William Stobbs's illustrations for this book won the Kate Greenaway Medal, 1959.

Ruth Manning-Sanders now lives in Penzance, Cornwall. She has two grandsons.

SELECTED WORKS: A Bundle of Ballads, 1961; A Book of Dwarfs, 1964; The Story of Hans Andersen: Swan of Denmark, 1966; A Book of Witches, 1966; A Book of Mermaids, 1968; A Book of Ghosts and Goblins, 1969; The Spaniards Are Coming! 1970; Gianni and the Ogre, 1971.

"MARIANA"

1896-

AUTHOR AND ILLUSTRATOR OF *Miss Flora McFlimsey's Christmas Eve*, etc.

Autobiographical sketch of Marian Curtis Foster, who writes under the pen name "Mariana":

LIKE the happy nations which have least history, my early years were so peaceful as to be quite uneventful.

I was born in Cleveland, Ohio, but we moved to Georgia when I was six months old.

Marian Foster

I grew up in the country near Atlanta—which was really the country then. My brother and sister and I could ride our bikes along red clay roads meeting with only an occasional mule-drawn wagon, and pick blackberries and wild persimmons along the way.

We didn't have much money; but then nobody we knew had very much money either—so there wasn't any pressure about status or keeping up with the Joneses.

I very early rebelled against piano practice—the alternative being drawing lessons—I chose what seemed the lesser of two evils.

I soon grew to love it, however, and I found one young friend who shared my interest. Together we pooled our finances and sent off for a book on anatomy which we'd seen advertised.

It was a good idea inasmuch as the art course in our school consisted mostly of copying the teacher's rather awful landscapes, which she made during summer vacations, or the covers on the *Ladies' Home Journal* and the *Saturday Evening Post*.

We could, too, make charcoal drawings of plaster casts of the head of Julius Ceasar or the death mask of Voltaire or the wounded lion of Lucerne. Armed with our anatomy book my friend and I aspired to portraits—mostly of our unwilling and rebellious playmates.

The books I read and cared most for were the Kipling stories, *Wind in the Willows*, *Alice* and of course *Uncle Remus*.

After high school I studied art at Sophie Newcomb College in New Orleans and then at the Art Students League in New York—and, much later, one winter in Paris at the Grande Chaumière.

I loved New York in those days—even the precarious business of trying to sell my first drawings seemed an exciting adventure.

One of my first jobs after art school was to make small pen and ink headings for the woman's page of the New York *Herald Tribune*. They paid for each drawing separately when it was published in the paper on Sundays and only then.

I'd look anxiously through the woman's section of the Sunday *Tribune* to see if my drawing appeared. If it did, I could pay my room rent and eat besides.

When the Great Depression hit I got a job on the "American Index Project of the W.P.A." We made factual drawings of "Early Americana" at the museums and here I discovered the fine craftsmanship and beauty of pre-mass-production days.

It was the old toys which charmed me most—the little soldiers, the tiny wooden horses and especially the old dolls in their faded elegance. They all seemed held like the figures on the Grecian Urn in a world of timelessness and eternal childhood.

I kept my interest in things of earlier days long after the project was dissolved.

It was Herman Wechster of the F.A.R. Gallery who suggested that I try to do a book. I didn't think I could but I followed his advice. I'd come across an old book titled *Child Life in Colonial Days*. In it was the picture of a rag doll called Bangwell Putt, which had belonged to a child in Deerfield, Massachusetts, in the early nineteenth century.

I took it as a sort of basis and wrote a story called *The Journey of Bangwell Putt*.

After that I discovered another old doll in the New York Historical Society named for the heroine of the nineteenth-century poem—"Miss Flora McFlimsey of Madison Square"—a young lady who had silks and velvets galore but nothing to wear.

Since the first book, *Miss Flora McFlimsey's Christmas Eve,* I have done a whole series of stories about my doll heroine Miss Flora McFlimsey.

I've lived in East Hampton on Long Island for the last two years—where I have a small house and where all is peace.

Before that I lived for many years in New York—and even now, ever and anon I feel the lure of it and go back for a spell.

Here on nice days my problem is to stay put in my workroom and not to look too long at the rabbits hopping about in the garden and the blue jays, and sternly suppress all desire to go out and join them or to listen to the ocean roaring two miles away.

I remember a review I read once of an interview with an author—whose name I've forgotten—who when asked whether he found it easier to work in the city or the country—replied, "In the city in a small room"—and he added, "preferably with the wolf scratching at the door." I think I know what he meant.

———

The Hockessin Elementary School Library in Wilmington, Delaware, has a Mariana Room which houses many of Miss Foster's original drawings. *The Journey of Bangwell Putt* was in the Fifty Books exhibition of the American Institute of Graphic Arts, 1966.

SELECTED WORKS WRITTEN AND ILLUSTRATED: Miss Flora McFlimsey's Christmas Eve, 1949; Miss Flora McFlimsey's Easter Bonnet, 1951; Doki, the Lonely Papoose, 1955; Miss Flora McFlimsey's Valentine, 1962; The Journey of Bangwell Putt, 1965.

SELECTED WORKS ILLUSTRATED: Little Bear's Christmas, by Janice Brustlein, 1964; Little Bear's Thanksgiving, by Janice Brustlein, 1967; Little Bear Marches in St. Patrick's Day Parade, by Janice Brustlein, 1967.

ABOUT: Kingman, Lee and others, comps. Illustrators of Children's Books: 1957-1966; Viguers, Ruth Hill and others, comps. Illustrators of Children's Books: 1946-1956; Life September 22, 1952.

WILLIAM MAYNE
March 16, 1928-

AUTHOR OF *A Grass Rope,* etc.

Autobiographical sketch of William James Carter Mayne:

I LIKE writing books because it is private and comfortable. Outside it may be raining, snowing or sunny, but indoors, between me and the typewriter any sort of weather may be happening. If I go out in the cold winter shivering I can come back to cozy scenes of the mind whenever I like. If nothing is happening outside in the world, the sky is grey, life is grey, there is nothing to do, I can get out a piece of paper and make things happen. The difference between ordinary day-dreaming and what I do is quite small. I write the dreams down, dreamers dream. I don't know why I should be different from others in this way, though I am happy to be as I am.

Perhaps when I was young it never occurred to me that people have to work, go to offices, dig holes in the ground, drive buses. My father is a doctor, and it did not seem to me that he worked. He went out visiting because he liked it, I thought. Perhaps that was true, because though he has retired now he still works, if it is work, and visits patients. I thought he just liked going to see people. I like going to see people too, and hearing what they have to say and finding what they are like. It's a help for writers to know that, because books are about people. Books are about places and things too, and I like all sorts of things and every kind of place. If I were not a writer I think I would have to dig holes in the ground, in the hope of finding things, like treasure.

I began to want to write when I was eight or nine. I knew nothing about it, but it seemed to be the proper thing to do. I had never met a writer, and I hated taking up a pen and making marks on the paper. I still hate writing with a pen, and I have very scrawly handwriting that I can't read. I think I knew it would be a good excuse for hiding among my own thoughts, away from

William Mayne

the rest of the family—I have three sisters and a brother. I think it is important for everybody to be able to get away from others. It is certainly important for me to be able to, but since I like being with other people too, and want them to know it, what I do when I am alone is think about other times and places, and write books about them. It shows me that when I am in my own withdrawn world I am still in the real one. And, of course, it doesn't feel like work. I suppose work is necessary to the world, but it seems an unhappy state of affairs, and I hope that the people who do it like it.

For a long time now I have lived in a very small village in a small stone house, with a cat for company. I have plenty of visitors, and plenty of time for sitting and doing nothing (I call it thinking). I am quite happy and the cat is generally asleep. I do all my own housework, even the washing, and I am a good cook. I don't like gardening, so I don't do much, just cut the grass, which is all I have in the garden. I cut the grass on the village green as well, because if I don't no one does. I look after all the affairs of the village, and call Public Meetings, because it is important to be part of the community one lives in, and if I did not have a family

of some sort to withdraw from at times I would be very lost.

———

William Mayne was born at Kingston-upon-Hull, Yorkshire. He entered the Choir School at Canterbury on a scholarship when he was nine, and remained five years. During this period the school moved to Cornwall to escape German air raids, and William Mayne sang cathedral services in various Cornwall churches. He left the school in 1942 when his voice broke, attended a Yorkshire school for another three years, after which he has said he spent seven years teaching himself to write. *Follow the Footprints*, his first novel for children, was published in 1953.

His interests include speech habits, vintage cars (both he and his father drive 1924 Bentleys), composing music, and building, by slow stages, additions to his Yorkshire cottage. He also represents his village, Thornton Rust, in the Rural District Council.

William Mayne received the Carnegie Medal in 1957 for *A Grass Rope*. With R. D. Caesar, under the joint pseudonym of Dynely James, he wrote *Gobbling Billy*.

SELECTED WORKS: A Swarm in May, 1957; Chorister's Cake, 1958; A Grass Rope, 1962; The Changeling, 1963; Earthfasts, 1967; The Hill Road, 1968; Ravensgill, 1970.

ABOUT: Contemporary Authors, Vol. 11-12; Wilson Library Bulletin April 1963.

MILTON MELTZER

May 8, 1915-

AUTHOR OF *Langston Hughes: A Biography*, etc.

Autobiographical sketch of Milton Meltzer:

I DID my growing up in Worcester, Massachusetts, where I was born. My parents came young from Europe, and worked in factories until my father achieved a shaky independence hiring himself out to wash windows at fifteen cents apiece. Uneducated themselves, my mother and father had a great respect for learning. They felt the future was assured when they saw me reading—no matter what. It was more often a

Nick Carter or a Tom Swift than something uplifting, but so long as it was words on paper I loved them.

My older brother took me crying to school the first day, but the tears soon stopped. For here there were books, far more than I had seen in one place before, and adults who were paid to read to us. I think I must have decided that day to be a teacher. Then I discovered the public library, and began reading from one wall to the other. Soon I found that I liked to make words on paper, too. By high school, I was working on student magazines.

I went off to Columbia University in 1932, at the lowest point of the Great Depression, just making it on five dollars a week from home, a scholarship, and a waiter's job for my meals. I was preparing to teach school, a job that seemed doubly important because it was one of the few ways to survive those terrible times.

But towards the end of college I knew teaching wasn't for me. I wanted instead what I thought of as the more active life of a journalist in the swiftly-changing world outside. Apart from service in World War II, many years went into writing jobs of all kinds —for the WPA Federal Theater, for trade

unions, for political campaigns, for community organizations, for public relations agencies, for industrial corporations, for a medical newspaper. Meanwhile, I married Hilda Balinky and helped raise our two daughters, Jane and Amy.

Not until the 1950s did I learn that what I liked most was digging into American history, and writing about it. The desire to write a book came out of the sad realization that nothing I had ever written would last, or would be worth keeping. Happily for me, Langston Hughes agreed to collaborate on my first idea, *A Pictorial History of the Negro in America* (1956). Then came book after book, worked on in early morning hours before going off to the daily job. Finally, with some 20 books published I was able to quit the job and give all my time to the books waiting to be written.

Perhaps because of what I learned coming of age in the thirties, I have found the greatest meaning and the greatest joy in telling of the struggle to win freedom and equality and justice for all. All my books are somehow connected to this theme. I hope they help readers to understand the truth about our past and to want to take part in making the life of man more human.

———

Milton Meltzer won the Thomas Alva Edison Foundation Mass Media Award for excellence in portraying America's past in 1965 for *In Their Own Words.* He was nominated for the National Book Award in 1969 for *Langston Hughes: a Biography* and won the Christopher Award in 1970 for *Brother, Can You Spare a Dime?*

SELECTED WORKS: Tongue of Flame: the Life of Lydia Maria Child, 1965; Bread and Roses: the Struggle of American Labor, 1865-1915, 1967; Thaddeus Stevens and the Fight for Negro Rights, 1967; In Their Own Words: a History of the American Negro (3 vols.) 1967; A Pictorial History of the Negro in America (with Langston Hughes) third revised edition, 1968; Langston Hughes: A Biography, 1968; Brother, Can You Spare a Dime? the Great Depression, 1929-1933, 1969.

ABOUT: Contemporary Authors, Vol. 13-14; Directory of American Scholars, Vol. 1: History; Something About the Author, Vol. 1.

GEORGE MENDOZA

June 2, 1934-

AUTHOR OF *The Hunter I Might Have Been,*
etc.

Biographical sketch of George Mendoza:

GEORGE MENDOZA is a native and perhaps typical New Yorker in that he comes
from diverse stock: His mother, Elizabeth,
was Irish (born in Dublin) and his father,
George, Spanish. When he was a boy his
parents moved the family, consisting of himself and three younger sisters, to Long Island.
There he attended a preparatory school at
Stony Brook and acquired his passion for
sailing.

When he was fourteen he set off one day
to sail from Stony Brook to Block Island in
his little sloop. The second day out he was
beyond Montauk Point on the tip of Long
Island, when the rudder of his sloop came
loose, the center board broke and the jib was
lost. His boat was being carried helplessly
out to sea. He tied his red sweater to the
mast as a signal of distress and was sighted
by a yacht and towed home. He claims his
birth as a writer took place on that home-
ward voyage. Then he first felt the rhythm of
the sea "when it hits below the keel," a
rhythm which he believes was to be trans-
muted into that of language and style.

His interest in writing led him to major
in English and creative writing at Columbia
University, where he took his B.A. in 1953.
Because of his interest in sailing, he attended
the State Maritime College at Fort Schuyler,
1954-1956. He also trained as a navy fighter
pilot.

He has twice sailed alone across the Atlantic, from Stony Brook to Southampton, and
on each voyage has produced a book. He
finds that writing at sea not only frees him
from interruptions but enables him to write
more naturally and more easily plumb the
depth of his imagination.

The first book, which he worked on inter-
mittently for eight years and finished during
his voyage of 1959, was an allegory entitled
*And Amedeo Asked, How Does One Become
a Man?* The story was based on his early
attempt to sail to Block Island. He has said,

GEORGE MENDOZA

"It was when the hero was caught in the
midst of a terrible storm in his little sailboat that he actually understood what it
meant to be a man."

His next book, *The Puma and the Pearl*
(1962), was also an allegory but was written on land, in collaboration with Wendy
Sanford.

In the summer of 1962 he undertook his
second solo voyage, during which he wrote
The Hawk Is Humming (1964). This book
is not a sea story, although the sea plays a
role in it. Mendoza says he does not aim to
write about the sea ("What could a writer
do after Conrad?"). What he likes are the
conditions created by being alone at sea.
"You set sail, take barometric and compass
readings, keep an ear for the wind while
you're below, and set to work." Despite these
precautions the notes for his novel were
whipped overboard by the wind when he
was a few days out, and he had to start again
from the beginning. Nevertheless, the manuscript was ready to mail to his publisher when
he reached England. The story concerns a
man alienated from society by his guilt feelings over a war incident, in which he was
powerless to prevent a crime, but he finds
his way back through a fatherless little boy's
faith in him, and need of him.

George Mendoza is also a poet, in fact
always a poet, and in 1968 he won a Lewis
Carroll Shelf Award for *The Hunter I Might*

Have Been, a poem illustrated with photographs by DeWayne Dalrymple. Recently he has turned more and more to writing books for children. These fall into two categories: ghost or witch stories with a Halloween atmosphere (*The Crack in the Wall and Other Terribly Weird Tales,* 1968) and natural history, either imaginary (as in *The Gillygoofang,* 1968, the story of a fish who swam backward to keep the water out of his eyes) or realistic (as in *The Digger Wasp,* 1969). The effect of these stories is achieved largely by the success with which the writer and his various illustrators have worked together. Sometimes, however, especially in the "weird" stories, the sophisticated humor and almost surrealist quality is such that, as the *School Library Journal* points out, "children old enough to enjoy them would not be seen *near* a picture book."

A quality of Mendoza's work which has emerged in his children's books is his "commitment to issues"—to use his own words; his horror at injustice and sympathy for the underprivileged. In 1968 he edited *The World from My Window,* a collection of poems and drawings of children from seven to seventeen who live in poverty in the United States. Critics have felt that he overemphasized the lonely; but loneliness is a theme in much of Mendoza's writing.

Loneliness, sympathy for the poor, love of the sea, and belief in the power of the imagination, all these qualities of his find expression in Mendoza's picture book *And I Must Hurry for the Sea Is Coming In.* Once more photos by DeWayne Dalrymple illustrate the poem, giving a sense of the limitless and everchanging ocean on which the little black boy sails his *Intrepid* with such skill and in such obvious bliss. Only at the end, before the reader has had time to wonder what the boy is doing in command of such a ship, does the whole dwindle down to his toy boat and an open hydrant on an abandoned city block. The book typifies the allegorical nature of much of Mendoza's work.

In the same year he created a much more controversial picture book, *The Inspector,* about law, order, and the public. Again Mendoza's theme is social, told entirely in pictures by Peter Parnall. It shocked some readers because the violence of the story seemed excessive for a book addressed to children.

Mendoza married Nicole Sekora in 1967. He has one daughter, Ashley.

SELECTED WORKS: And Amedeo Asked, How Does One Become a Man? 1962; The Puma and the Pearl, 1962; The Hawk Is Humming, 1964; Gwot, Horribly Funny Hairtickles, 1967; The Hunter I Might Have Been, 1968; The Crack in the Wall and Other Terribly Weird Tales, 1968; And I Must Hurry for the Sea Is Coming In, 1969; Herman's Hat, 1969; The Inspector, 1970; The Good Luck Spider and Other Bad Luck Stories, 1970.

ABOUT: New York Post August 12, 1964; New York Times June 21, 1964; New York Times Book Review May 2, 1971.

EVE MERRIAM

July 19, 1916-

AUTHOR OF *A Gaggle of Geese,* etc.

Autobiographical sketch of Eve Merriam:

AS far back as I can remember, I have been intrigued by words: their sound, sight, taste, smell, touch, for it has always seemed to me that they appeal to all the senses. It pleased me mightily that my home state meant William Penn's woods; I was born and brought up in Philadelphia and could see the statue of great Billy in the city center, while out in the suburbs where I spent most of my childhood there were woodlands where I climbed and lolled. Puns and rhymes and alliteration were games for me along with skipping rope, playing hopscotch, tag, swimming, dancing, beachcombing.

I found it amusing that Germantown High School which I attended was located at the corners of Germantown Avenue and High Street. The University of Pennsylvania from which I graduated had no special magic in its name, but the library there had books by poets whose work I admired: MacLeish, Auden, Eliot, Spender, Gerard Manley Hopkins. Hopkins especially was an influence on my early poems: his condensed, weighted line struck me as the essence of what poetry tries to accomplish in its economy of language.

Eve Merriam

After college I came to New York and worked at a variety of writing jobs: advertising agencies, magazines, radio stations. My poems began to appear in various "little" magazines, and in 1946 my first collection *Family Circle* was awarded the Yale Younger Poets Prize and was published by the Yale University Press. For awhile I conducted a weekly program on modern poetry for Station WQXR in Manhattan, and also wrote short stories and articles for various magazines.

It never occurred to me to try writing for children, but when I was asked to attempt a biography for young people of the life of Franklin D. Roosevelt, I couldn't refuse. He had been a hero to me and to my family; one of my most vivid childhood memories was sitting around all together, my father, mother, two sisters, brother and myself listening to the President's "Fireside Chats." Then when my own two sons, Guy and Dee, were born, I started writing picture books and poetry for children and more biographies. My first picture book, *A Gaggle of Geese*, went back to my original and continuing delight: the pleasures of wordmongering. It depicted group words for animals, birds and fish, such exotic but true images as "a shrewdness of apes" and "a labor of moles." Almost all my books have dealt with

some special aspects of language: *Small Fry* is a sequel to *A Gaggle of Geese*, illustrating the unusual and charming words for animal young (a "joey," for instance, is a baby kangaroo). *Miss Tibbett's Typewriter* fools around with keyboard arrangements of letters; the books of poetry *Catch a Little Rhyme, There Is No Rhyme for Silver, It Doesn't Always Have to Rhyme*, and *Independent Voices*, all skip around with syllable play. Perhaps some day I'll write a book that hasn't a single pun in it, but I won't promise. (The more the merriam?)

For some years now I have lived with my two sons and husband, Leonard C. Lewin who is also a writer, on Riverside Drive in New York City. We have a very fat cat named Towel, not enough bookshelves for all our books, a view of the Palisades across the Hudson River, and wild winter winds. Two mornings a week I teach writing courses at the College of the City of New York, and am lucky enough to live so nearby that I can walk to work instead of crowding into the subway.

Eve Merriam received her B.A. degree from the University of Pennsylvania in 1937 and did graduate work at the University of Wisconsin and Columbia University. After the Yale Younger Poets Prize in 1946, she won the *Collier's* Star Fiction Award in 1949, the William Newman Poetry Award in 1957 and a grant to write poetic drama for the Columbia Broadcasting System in 1959. She writes fiction and nonfiction for adults as well as children and has contributed to magazines, including *Nation* and *New Republic*. Her favorite nonwriting activities include frequenting libraries and secondhand book shops, travel, bike-riding, swimming "in temperate water," and walking.

SELECTED WORKS: The Real Book about Franklin D. Roosevelt, 1952; A Gaggle of Geese, 1960; Mommies at Work, 1961; There Is No Rhyme for Silver, 1962; It Doesn't Always Have to Rhyme, 1964; Small Fry, 1965; Miss Tibbett's Typewriter, 1966; Catch a Little Rhyme, 1966; Independent Voices, 1968; Finding a Poem, 1970.

ABOUT: Contemporary Authors, Vol. 5-6; Hopkins, Lee Bennett. Books Are by People; Who's Who in America, 1970-71; Who's Who of American Women, 1970-1971.

JEAN MERRILL

January 27, 1923-

AUTHOR OF *The Superlative Horse*, etc.

Autobiographical sketch of Jean Fairbanks Merrill:

"NOW as I was young and easy under the apple boughs/ About the lilting house and happy as the grass was green . . . ."

Dylan Thomas's celebration of his boyhood in Wales always evokes powerfully my own country childhood on an apple and dairy farm on Lake Ontario in upstate New York. I, too, remember feeling "famous among the barns" and "prince of the apple towns."

My family moved to the country from Rochester, New York, where I was born, when I was eight. From then on, my two younger sisters and I spent most of our waking hours, when we were not in school, out-of-doors. My memory of this time is a kaleidoscope of strenuous physical activity: building huts, dams, rafts, forts, making barrel-stave skis, bows and arrows, inner-tube guns, roller-skate scooters, collecting wild flowers and fossil rocks, swimming, tobogganing, climbing silos, riding hay wagons, tumbling in haylofts.

The impulse to write came directly from books and the intense pleasure they gave me from my earliest years. And then there was a school librarian. I was about eleven and still happily hooked on *The Little Maid* series and the innumerable adventures of Jeeves, when she stopped me one day at the checkout desk as I was departing with an armful of P. G. Wodehouse and Little Maids. She added an anthology of Emily Dickinson to the stack and said matter-of-factly, "I think you might like this, too."

I sat up half the night, awestruck. The terse charged lines I was reading were so totally unlike the prettily phrased and cleverly rhymed stuff that is usually presented to children as poetry. This was my first awareness that writing might be more than a diversion—for both reader and writer—that it could also be a centering on the most deeply felt of our experiences as human beings.

Jean F. Merrill

My formal education began in a one-room country school and ended at the University of Madras, to which I had a Fulbright grant for the study of Indian folk stories (an interest that led to the several adaptations I have done of stories from the Far East—*The Superlative Horse, Shan's Lucky Knife,* and *High, Wide and Handsome*). In between I studied English and drama at Allegheny College and did graduate work in English at Wellesley.

After college I worked for five years as a writer and editor for *Scholastic* magazines. This first job brought me to New York City, which provided the settings for *The Pushcart War, The Travels of Marco, Boxes,* and *Henry, the Hand-Painted Mouse.* My country childhood contributed in various ways to the moods and scenes of *Tell About the Cowbarn, Daddy, A Song for Gar, The Tree House of Jimmy Domino,* and *The Black Sheep.*

I now manage to combine the best of both worlds by living half the year in New York City and half on a hill farm in Washington, Vermont.

Jean Merrill took her B.A. from Allegheny College in 1944 and her M.A. from Wellesley in 1945. She won a Lewis Carroll Shelf Award in 1963 for *The Superlative Horse.*

She won the Boys Clubs of America Junior Book Award and a Lewis Carroll Shelf Award, both in 1965, for *The Pushcart War*.

SELECTED WORKS: Henry, the Hand-Painted Mouse, 1951; The Tree House of Jimmy Domino, 1955; The Travels of Marco, 1956; A Song for Gar, 1957; The Very Nice Things, 1959; Shan's Lucky Knife, 1960; The Superlative Horse, 1961; The Pushcart War, 1964; High, Wide and Handsome, 1964; The Black Sheep, 1969.

ABOUT: Contemporary Authors, Vol. 1; Something About the Author, Vol. 1. Who's Who of American Women, 1970-1971.

"SUZANNE METCALF"

See *Baum, L. Frank*

"MANFRED MICHAEL"

See *Winterfeld, Henry*

EARL SCHENCK MIERS

May 27, 1910-

AUTHOR OF *Billy Yank and Johnny Reb*, etc.

Autobiographical sketch of Earl Schenck Miers:

ALTHOUGH I had written books for junior adults before I left as director of the Rutgers University Press to become an editor for Alfred A. Knopf, Inc., it seemed to me that there was no more worthy enterprise than writing for young adults. Most of all, I wanted to do books about America and why youngsters growing up in this country should be happy in their heritage.

Eighty percent of the books that I have written in the past fifteen years have concentrated on this subject. The themes have covered such items as what is a child's right to freedom under the United States Constitution, what is the history of Black Americans, what is the obligation of Congress to protect the rights of an American under the Constitution and the Bill of Rights. I have written *America and Its Presidents, Our Fifty States,* and *Freedom*. These books have all been published by Grosset & Dunlap, Inc.; another series of books on American history has been written for Rand McNally covering such periods in our history as the American Revolution, the Civil War, the Exploration of the West, and World War II. *The Rainbow Book of American History* which I did for World covers the entire period from the arrival of the Norsemen to the astronauts who circled the moon.

I was born in Brooklyn, New York, but raised in New Jersey, where I graduated from the Hackensack High School in 1928. I attended Rutgers University where in 1933 I received the degree of Bachelor of Letters in Journalism; since then I have been given two honorary degrees by Rutgers—M.A., 1943 and D.Litt. in 1963. I received the degree of L.H.D. from Lincoln College in Lincoln, Illinois, in 1962.

I write books particularly for teen-agers because I do not believe that a "generation gap" exists. When Thomas Jefferson and George Mason combined to create the Declaration of Independence and the Bill of Rights, they believed that all persons were created with inalienable rights that made them free. I do not believe that the pledge of allegiance to the flag should now end "with liberty and justice for all who can afford it"—and neither would Mason or Jefferson.

It is very difficult writing books for teen-agers on subjects like the Bill of Rights, the Emancipation Proclamation and due process

Miers: *MY ers*

of law, but unless we try honestly to emphasize these subjects, the true meaning of American freedom will be lost.

———

As a victim of cerebral palsy before much was known or done about the disease, Earl Schenck Miers had a difficult childhood. His parents never despaired of his future, however, and insisted that he be allowed to enroll in Public School 72 in Brooklyn against the wishes of the principal, who said he should be institutionalized. The boy continued in public schools after his family moved to Hackensack. Though unable to use a pencil, he did well in studies, even arithmetic, with the aid of a heavy typewriter he carried from class to class.

Always an avid reader, he decided early to be a writer and his first stories turned out on the old typewriter were published in papers of the Lone Scouts of America. Before the age of fifteen he was selling short pieces to magazines. While still in junior high he became a reporter for the Bergen *Evening Record* and after high school he worked for the Bergen *Weekly Democrat.* He was editor of the campus newspaper at Rutgers University and served as campus correspondent for several city newspapers, including the New York *Times.* After graduating, Miers wrote a number of sports books for boys. He returned to work at Rutgers and in 1935 became assistant editor of university publications and in 1945 was made the first director of the newly organized Rutgers University Press, where his notable achievements included works published in cooperation with the Abraham Lincoln Association of Springfield, Illinois. In 1949, Miers left Rutgers and became an editor for Knopf. Since 1951 he has devoted himself to freelance work.

Miers married Starling Wyckoff in 1934. They have two sons, David Wyckoff and William Holmes, and a daughter, Meredith. Miers is a member of Phi Beta Kappa and a member of the board of trustees of the National Society for Crippled Children and Adults. He is the author of numerous books, fiction and nonfiction, for young people and adults. He enjoys stamp collecting and going to horse races.

SELECTED WORKS: The Rainbow Book of American History, 1955; Mark Twain on the Mississippi, 1957; Billy Yank and Johnny Reb, 1959; We Were There When Grant Met Lee at Appomattox, 1959; America and Its Presidents, 1959 rev. 1962; The Story of John F. Kennedy, 1964; Story of the American Negro, 1965; Freedom, 1965; That Lincoln Boy, 1968; That Jefferson Boy, 1971.

ABOUT: Contemporary Authors, Vol. 3; Miers, E. S. Why Did This Have to Happen; The Trouble Bush; Something About the Author, Vol. 1; Who's Who in America, 1970-71; Current Biography September 1967.

ELSE MINARIK

September 13, 1920-

AUTHOR OF *Little Bear,* etc.

Autobiographical sketch of Else Holmelund Minarik:

LADIES in my family have lived to be a hundred. Should I follow this pattern, I can now say that I find myself at the midpoint, looking back, and wondering ahead. If the second part of my life can mirror the first, I shall have no complaints.

I am particularly pleased that there have been enough challenging problems. One of my first was language—the American language. My parents brought me to this country from Denmark when I was four years old. I hated the language immediately. Father coped by introducing me to cowboy movies. Mother took me almost daily to the park where she taught me to communicate with playmates. In time I became American. Now, at the risk of appearing chauvinistic, I wish to affirm that I consider the American language one of the most vigorous and colorful to be found on this planet. Even in its simplest form, the form I use in my reader-picture books for children, it is a wonderful tool for a writer.

Although I have degrees in psychology and education, and have used them, I think I can safely say that my principal work has taken place in my garden. I am garden-oriented, primarily. Gardening helps me think—helps, as my husband used to quote, to let the fancy "ever roam." A tomato plant can be as inspiring as a rose, for me, and

Minarik: *MIN ah rik*

Else H Minarik

few things can thrill me more than the bursting of the lilacs, or the plumping of the apples, or the remembrance of gooseberry bushes we used to have in Denmark, yet can't have here.

Teaching children to read presented another problem. My little daughter Brooke wanted to read at a very early age, and so I wrote books for her. Then followed my first graders, with their special needs. I considered one day, while setting out the spring garden, that plants and children are alike in this respect—they flower beautifully if placed in the right setting, and subjected to no gaps of neglect, either by us, or by nature. I thought of my first graders, all as willing and marvelous as the plants I was tucking into the earth. They had learned the elementals of reading, and yet would, almost to a one, spend the summer without using this fine new skill, and would return in September to astonish their second grade teacher with a seemingly complete lack of memory. Here was a gap that needed mending! I submitted my books to Miss Ursula Nordstrom of Harper and Row, who said this was just what she had been looking for, and promptly began the *I Can Read* series with my first book, *Little Bear*—so superbly illustrated by Maurice Sendak.

Now I have moved to a farm in New Hampshire, and am looking forward hopefully to grandchildren. Fortunately there is no shortage of children in New Hampshire. I have found many who will listen to my stories. And I have started a new garden.

Else Holmelund married Walter Minarik, who died in 1963. She has one child, Brooke. Her degree in psychology was from Queens College and her degree in education from New Paltz College of the State University of New York. Else Minarik was married to Homer Bigart in 1970.

Little Bear's Visit, with illustrations by Maurice Sendak, was a runner-up for the Caldecott Medal for 1962.

SELECTED WORKS: Little Bear, 1957; No Fighting, No Biting, 1958; Father Bear Comes Home, 1959; Little Bear's Friend, 1960; Little Bear's Visit, 1961; The Little Giant Girl and the Elf Boy, 1963; A Kiss for Little Bear, 1968.

ABOUT: Hopkins, Lee Bennett. Books Are by People.

"NELSON MINIER"

See *Stoutenberg, Adrien*

KAZUE MIZUMURA

AUTHOR AND ILLUSTRATOR OF *I See the Winds*, etc.

Autobiographical sketch of Kazue Mizumura:

FOR as long as I can remember, I have always liked to draw, and that was the thing I could do best among all the things I had to learn throughout my school years. Thus it was quite natural for me to enter the Art Institute even though I did not particularly want to be an artist. I guess my parents and I always wanted me to be just an ordinary happy wife. So, for a short time, until World War II ended my dreams, I was a wife and mother. During the war years, when there were no books to be bought, I made by hand a picture book for my daughter. And that was the only book she ever had for the three years of her life. It was my first children's book, and of course I did not realize at that time that it was the beginning of a career for me.

After I lost my husband and daughter and had to make my own living, I taught traditional Japanese sumi-e painting and worked

Kazue Mizumura

in commercial art. Since the United States was the best place to learn this medium, I was encouraged by my American friends in my art class to try to come to the United States. At that time, I was told that Pratt Institute was one of the best schools for commercial art. I applied for an exchange teachership to teach Japanese sumi-e, but instead I was given a scholarship. I came to the United States in 1955.

After Pratt Institute, while I tried to get into the field of book illustration, I worked as textile designer for four years. In 1959, I was asked to illustrate Elizabeth G. Vining's *The Cheerful Heart* for Viking Press. Until recently, my illustration assignments seemed to have been limited to books with Japanese themes. I believe that most publishers felt that since I was Japanese they could expect authenticity for the Japanese background text from me. In doing the illustrations for the Japanese background stories, there was little I could do with my technique since the publishers expected authentic representational illustrations.

Luckily, Miss Elizabeth Riley of Thomas Y. Crowell understood my problems and encouraged me to write my own text. The result was *I See the Winds* in 1966 and *If I Were*

a Mother in 1967. Since I started as an illustrator, I prefer to draw the pictures first and then write my text.

I like to work with different mediums. And I do believe the mediums should differ according to the theme of the text. In illustrating my own books, I hope that I can develop my technique and style without restraint.

———

Kazue Mizumura was born and spent her childhood in Kamakura, Japan. She attended the Gakushuin School before entering the Woman's Art Institute in Tokyo, from which she holds a Teacher's Certificate.

If I Were a Mother was named by the New York *Times* as one of the outstanding picture books of 1968.

SELECTED WORKS WRITTEN AND ILLUSTRATED: I See the Winds, 1966; If I Were a Mother, 1968; The Emperor Penguins, 1969.

SELECTED WORKS ILLUSTRATED: The Cheerful Heart, by Elizabeth Vining, 1959; A Pair of Red Clogs, by Masako Matsuno, 1960; Rokubei and the Thousand Rice Bowls, by Yoshiko Uchida, 1962; The Greedy One, by Patricia Miles Martin, 1964; Mystery in Little Tokyo, by Frank Bonham, 1966; My Mother and I, by Aileen Fisher, 1967.

ABOUT: Kingman, Lee and others, comps. Illustrators of Children's Books: 1957-1966.

BENI MONTRESOR
March 31, 1926-

ILLUSTRATOR OF *May I Bring a Friend?* etc.

Autobiographical sketch of Beni Montresor:

"I WAS born with a pencil in my hand." This is usually how I start to tell about my life. The place was near Verona, the town of Romeo and Juliet. I remember, around the age of three, when my grandfather would come to visit me I would say to him, "Grandpa, next time instead of candies please bring me pencils."

In 1960—on my first visit to this country—someone asked me if I would like to do a children's book. "Yes," was my quick reply. I didn't know exactly what a children's book was. As a child I had never owned one. Be-

Beni Montresor: *BAY nee MOHN tre sor*

Beni Montresor

sides, in Italy there is only one book for children, *Pinocchio*. But . . .

Having had the good fortune to be born in Italy, I grew up looking at church and palace walls covered with medieval and Renaissance frescoes. They were all visual stories done for people that didn't know how to read, telling about heroes and their adventures and saints and their miracles. . . . Those walls were my picture books. I spent hours and hours looking at them, living with them, intrigued by everything I saw. . . . I was caught by the magic of a three-headed dragon, a whirling heavenly body and a mysterious regal character. . . . I make my books thinking of those walls of my childhood.

But all the rest, what I did and what I am doing, came also from that childhood experience—when I am writing or when I am designing sets and costumes for an opera. Now, I am making my debut as a movie director. Even though it is a story set in today's New York City I know the look the movie will have—mysterious. . . .

After Verona, I moved through many other places. I went to Venice, where I attended painting school and wrote plays for Italian radio. Then, to Rome, Paris, Berlin, Madrid and Africa where I worked as a set and costume designer for about thirty movies directed by Rossellini, Fellini, Germi, etc.

Finally came New York and the working on children's books and operas began. I designed operas for the Metropolitan of New York, The Royal Opera House of London, La Scala of Milano, etc.

I have illustrated over twenty children's books, among them my own *House of Flowers, House of Stars, The Witches of Venice, Cinderella, I Saw a Ship A-Sailing* and *A for Angel*. In 1965 I won the Caldecott Medal for the illustrations I did for Beatrice Schenk de Regniers's *May I Bring a Friend* and in 1968 the Society of Illustrators Gold Medal for *I Saw a Ship A-Sailing*.

Often people ask me why I like New York. "Because it is mysterious," I answer. Today it is the only place where one can see a three-headed dragon or a whirling heavenly body . . . the only place in the world.

———

Beni Montresor studied at the Verona Art School and at the Academy of Fine Arts in Venice. In 1950, in competition with two hundred others, he won a two-year scholarship to study design for the movies at the Centro Sperimentale di Cinematografia in Rome. He worked on more than twenty-five important films, in association with Fellini, de Sica, Rossellini, and others. He has also designed sets and costumes for music festivals in Europe and for stage plays such as Giraudoux's *La Folle de Chaillot* and Moravia's *Beatrice Cenci*.

In the United States, Montresor designed sets and costumes for Rodgers' *Do I Hear a Waltz?* on Broadway and for productions by the Metropolitan Opera Company, including Menotti's *The Last Savage*, in 1964, and *La Gioconda*, in 1966. In 1966 also he designed and was stage director of *The Magic Flute* for the New York City Opera.

Beni Montresor was knighted by the Italian government in 1966 for services to the arts, and he bears the title of Cavaliere.

Montresor's birth date has been reported as March 21 and March 30. The correct date is March 31, 1926.

SELECTED WORKS WRITTEN AND ILLUSTRATED: House of Flowers, House of Stars, 1962; The Witches of Venice, 1963; Cinderella, 1965; I Saw a Ship A-Sailing, 1967; A for Angel, 1969.

SELECTED WORKS ILLUSTRATED: On Christmas Eve, by Margaret Wise Brown, 1961; Belling the Tiger, by Mary Stolz, 1961; May I Bring a Friend? by Beatrice Schenk de Regniers, 1964; Willy O'Dwyer Jumped in the Fire, by Beatrice Schenk de Regniers, 1968.

ABOUT: Current Biography Yearbook 1967; Hopkins, Lee Bennett. Books Are by People; Hürlimann, Bettina. Picture Book World. Kingman, Lee, ed. Newbery and Caldecott Medal Books; Kingman, Lee and others, comps. Illustrators of Children's Books, 1957-1966; Who's Who in America, 1970-71; Horn Book August 1965; Library Journal March 15, 1965; Opera News February 8, 1964; Publishers' Weekly March 8, 1965; School Library Journal March 1965; Show March 1962; This Week March 3, 1968.

"CAROLINE MORE"

See Cone, Molly

WALT MOREY

February 3, 1907-

AUTHOR OF Gentle Ben, etc.

Autobiographical sketch of Walt Morey:

PEOPLE who have read Gentle Ben, Home Is the North, and Kavik the Wolf Dog, and who, I hope, will read Angry Waters will learn quite a bit about Walt Morey. There is a little bit of me in each of these books. I was born in Hoquiam, Washington, the heart of the Olympic Mountains, and like Mark in Gentle Ben, was a sickly kid. I met my first bears there. A man kept three black bears chained in a shed at the opposite end of our block.

We moved from Hoquiam to Jasper, Oregon, where my brother and I got our first few years of schooling. Then back to Hoquiam for awhile, on to Great Falls, Montana (my dad worked in construction), and then to Canada. We homesteaded in Northern Alberta in the Battle River country. Then we moved to Portland, Oregon.

I had been a nonreader until I was tricked into reading my first book, Chip of the Flying U by B. M. Bower. I was told it was the life story of Charles M. Russell, the famous cowboy artist. Mr. Russell was a next-door neighbor in Great Falls, Montana. I dis-

covered reading and it became one of the greatest pleasures I have ever known.

After grade school, high school, and a short term at business college, I decided I would become a writer. I wrote ten years on one book, rewriting it thirteen times. I never did sell it, and would love to forget the whole thing.

Finally, during the depths of the depression, I met another writer who was selling to the pulps. He put me on my feet by showing me what was wrong with my work. During those years I worked in sawmills, veneer plants, did construction work, managed a theater—and wrote nights and weekends on the side—selling a number of short stories and novelettes to the pulps for from one-half to one cent a word. Fortunately for me, my wife Rosalind was a schoolteacher and she corrected my many mistakes and acted, as she still does, as my good right hand.

During World War II, I was a foreman for the Kaiser Company building ships in Vancouver, Washington. I also operated a fifty-acre farm and was writing when I could find time. I wrote my first full-length novel then —No Cheers No Glory, published in Blue Book Magazine in 1945.

Shortly after the war ended television burst on the scene and literally thousands of writers had no market as hundreds of pulp magazines folded up. Some writers turned to promotion, to advertising, or to local radio and TV scriptwriting. Others went into the business world into stores, offices and such. I kept on working on the farm caring for a fifty-acre filbert orchard. Rosalind continued to teach in an elementary school some twelve miles away.

Eventually I met Virgil Burford. He'd been adventuring in Alaska for years as a miner, a construction worker on the DEW Line, a deep-sea diver, a fisherman and a hunter. I began writing and selling his true adventures. He invited me to go north with him in 1952. I did, and went up as a deep-sea diver to inspect the underwater sections of the fish traps in Prince William Sound. While there I studied the country, the wildlife and the people. From all this came our book *North to Danger*, published by John Day in 1954.

Rosalind kept "nagging" me to do a children's book on my adventures. I finally decided to try one, and from my experiences and knowledge of the north came *Gentle Ben, Home Is the North* and *Kavik the Wolf Dog*. The latest book, *Angry Waters*, is the story of a flood on the Columbia River. Everything I write is based on facts that are fictionalized. The backgrounds and people are true. I don't just research a story in books. I go there, see it, feel it, smell it and live it. I get to know the people so I can portray them as I find them.

I hope to write more books along the lines of the last four.

We now live on a sixty-acre filbert orchard at Wilsonville, Oregon. Rosalind has quit teaching and acts as my secretary. We love it here and hope never to leave, except to hunt for new material. We both enjoy writing, hard as it is. The hundreds of letters we receive from readers are just added rewards.

———

Walt Morey first met his wife Rosalind in the third grade in Hoquiam, but he did not pay much attention to her until they met again some years later and she helped him with his studies in high school. They were married in 1934.

Morey's attempts to write had no success until he met John Hawkins, whose help led to the sale of a short story to the magazine *Knockout,* in 1937. Morey sold more than a hundred stories to pulp magazines and wrote two adult novels before doing his first book for children, *Gentle Ben,* which immediately brought him fame. *Gentle Ben* won the Dutton Junior Animal Book Award in 1965, the Sequoyah Children's Book Award, was runner-up for the Yippee Award of Iowa, for the William Allen White Award, and for the Pacific Northwest Young Readers Award. It was made into a movie, purchased for a television series and has been translated into French, Japanese, German, Swedish, Norwegian, and Spanish. In 1968, Morey won the Dutton Junior Animal Book Award again for *Kavik the Wolf Dog,* which that year also won the Pacific Northwest Booksellers award. It won the Dorothy Canfield Fisher Award in 1970.

SELECTED WORKS: Gentle Ben, 1965; Home Is the North, 1967; Kavik the Wolf Dog, 1968; Angry Waters, 1969; Gloomy Gus, 1970; Deep Trouble, 1971.

FARLEY MOWAT
May 12, 1921-

AUTHOR OF *Lost in the Barrens,* etc.

Biographical sketch of Farley McGill Mowat:

FARLEY MOWAT was born in Belleville, Ontario, the son of Angus McGill Mowat, a librarian, and Helen Elizabeth (Thomson) Mowat. Until the age of nine, Farley lived in Trenton and in Belleville. In the following years he lived in several Canadian communities where his father had various library responsibilities.

During these years Farley became increasingly interested in nature, birds, and photography and kept many animal pets. In 1935 he became the youngest person in Canada to hold a bird-bander's permit. Summers the family spent traveling across Canada. Young Mowat's first introduction to the Arctic Barrenlands, so prominent in his later writing, occurred when he was fourteen, when he

FARLEY MOWAT

and his great-uncle Frank Farley, a well-known ornithologist, traveled to Churchill, Manitoba, to study Arctic birds.

In 1937, when Angus Mowat was appointed Director of Public Libraries for Ontario, the family moved to Toronto.

In 1940 Farley Mowat joined the Reserve Battalion of the Hastings and Prince Edward Regiment. Later he attended the Officers' Training Course at Brockville, was posted overseas, and eventually attained the rank of captain. He participated in the invasion of Sicily, was present during the capitulation of the German forces in Holland, and was made an Intelligence Officer assigned to German 25th Army Headquarters until the end of the war.

After he was demobilized in May 1946, Mowat bought a jeep and set out to collect birds in Saskatchewan. It was at this time that he began to consider a writing career, but his efforts to write about the war proved futile. In the fall of that year he enrolled at the University of Toronto to "give myself a breathing spell while I considered what I wanted to do."

In the summer of 1947 he went on a biology field trip to central Keewatin, but after a few weeks he gave up biology for good. With a young halfbreed he set out on a canoe trip from Nueltin to Brochet, Manitoba, and back. It was on this trip that he met Eskimos

and Indians and became outraged at their degradation.

Mowat spent the winter of 1947 again studying at the University of Toronto. There he met and married Frances Elizabeth Thornhill. The next spring he returned to the Arctic as a government biologist, but found that his real interest lay with the Eskimos and Indians. He began work on his first book, *People of the Deer*, the story of the dying Ihalmiut Indian tribe. The Mowats returned to Toronto in January 1949, and he received his A.B. from the University that spring.

After graduation Mowat bought ten acres of sand hills near Palgrave, Ontario, built a log house with his own hands, and began writing for a living. He published a number of short stories and articles in popular periodicals such as *Saturday Evening Post, Argosy,* and *Maclean's.* His *People of the Deer,* published in 1952, won the Anisfield-Wolfe Award but reaction to it was highly varied. Some called the book inspired, others accused Mowat of making misleading statements about the Ihalmiut tribe.

Commissioned by the Hastings and Prince Edward Regimental Association to write the story of the regiment, Mowat and his wife went to Europe in the spring of 1953 to do the necessary research. *The Regiment* was published in 1955.

Mowat's *Lost in the Barrens,* an adventure story for ages twelve to sixteen, published in 1956, won the Governor General's Award for juvenile literature, the Book of the Year Medal of the Canadian Association of Children's Librarians, and was on the Honours List for the Hans Christian Andersen Award.

The Desperate People, a further book about the Ihalmiut Indians, 1959, was highly praised and settled any question about Mowat's accuracy in describing the condition of the Indians.

The Mowats' first son, Robert Alexander, was born in April 1954, and they adopted a second son, David Peter, in 1957.

The next years of Mowat's life were spent in extensive travel throughout Canada, England, Scotland, Wales, and Russia, in sailing in his schooner "Happy Adventure," in prolific writing and in appearances on radio and television, often on behalf of the Eskimos.

Farley Mowat was married a second time, to Claire Wheeler. He is five feet, eight inches tall, bearded, has blue eyes and what he calls mouse-colored hair. He claims no political, religious or club affiliations.

SELECTED WORKS: Lost in the Barrens, 1956; Dog Who Wouldn't Be, 1957; Grey Seas Under, 1958; Owls in the Family, 1961; Never Cry Wolf, 1963; The Boat Who Wouldn't Float, 1970.

ABOUT: Author's and Writer's Who's Who, 1963; Contemporary Authors, Vol. 3; Who's Who in America, 1970-71; Saturday Evening Post July 29, 1950; April 13, 1957; Wilson Library Bulletin February 1961.

BRUNO MUNARI

October 24, 1907-

AUTHOR AND ILLUSTRATOR OF *Bruno Munari's ABC*, etc.

Autobiographical sketch of Bruno Munari:

ALTHOUGH I have a good visual memory, I don't remember the features of the midwife who helped me into the world at Milan, on a morning in October 1907. My father was a waiter in a big cafe in the center of the Galleria of Milan, in the heart of the city, the famous cafe Gambrinus. This cafe, which was near the Teatro della Scala, was frequented by personalities of the cultural world of Milan, famous opera singers, well-known authors, and my father used to tell me that once he spoke with Toscanini: "Would you like more coffee, maestro?" and always courteous Toscanini answered, "No, thank you."

After about one year my father got the idea of turning the ancient house of the Dukes d'Este, which was in a town near Verona, into an inn and thus I spent my childhood in Badia Polesine.

The small town was very beautiful. With my young friends I used to play on the banks of the Grande Fiume Adige despite the danger of falling into the whirling currents. The skies were immense, the summers were felt in the bare legs. The work at the inn took up all of my parents' time and my mother

could not embroider her precious fans with multicolored paillettes. The inn also had a big space for horses and many mysterious rooms and some immense garrets full of material fascinating in form and smell. Until I was nineteen I remained in this small town; and the brightness of summer, the winter fogs, the bells at dusk, the bamboo in my friends' gardens, linden and tamarind trees that absorb all the humidity of the night, the tiniest windows of the lofts, the warmth of the marble benches in August, the mud full of many surprises when the river dried up—all left imprints in my mind.

At twenty I was in Milan and I wanted to be a futurist painter. I met Marinetti and others of his group; I exhibited with them in the most important exhibitions. I did paintings and constructed "useless machines" and after about a year I exhibited abroad and lost all of my works. An art critic at that time comforted me: "Too bad this talented young man wastes his time with the futurists, he should start painting reality as everybody sees it and not do things no one understands."

At twenty-six, on a summer evening during a festival with fireworks in Milan, I found my wife sitting on the grass of a meadow. She didn't know she was my wife, but I told her and we are still together in the same house. My wife's relatives are from Emilia, there are so many and they are all so nice. One day we went to visit them in their fields where they cultivate lambrusco (from which is made a type of Coca-Cola Italian style) and I counted fifty-three. The people of Emilia have unusual names, but my wife's name is almost normal: her name is Dilma (they all call her Wilma). Our son's name is Alberto. We only have this son who was born during the war. We are very pleased with him and also with his wife Lucy (they live in Ginevra) and you can't imagine how happy we are with our nice Valeria, born on Christmas day two—as a matter of fact three —(how time flies) years ago.

I started to think about and to do children's books when my son Alberto was five years old. Today Alberto is a graduate in psychology and teaches at the University of Ginevra. At that time there were (according to me) no good books for children and I decided to make some. I prepared handmade models since I wanted to express myself with images, with paper, with the dimensions of the pages, with imagination, with anything, even with words. And Alberto was my first supervisor. Then Mondadori saw them and wanted to publish them. But in time of war it was not an easy undertaking, many things were lacking and only a few books were printed. I continued planning others and the latest one dedicated to Valeria is also published in the United States with the title *The Circus in the Mist* (World). Besides books for children I have also published books for designers, *The Discovery of the Square* (Wittenborn) and, with the same publisher, *The Discovery of the Circle*. As you can imagine, I'm now gathering material for *The Discovery of the Triangle* (equilateral). These are the three basic forms of geometry. Another book published by Laterza of Bari is *Arte come Mestiere* (Art As a Profession) in which I tell in a cheerful but precise manner the secrets of my trade as a designer.

I have been to the United States many times. I have exhibited in various galleries in New York. The Museum of Modern Art has some of my works and has published one of my *Libro Illeggibile* (Illegible Books), a book without words but with a red string crossing the pages. Two years ago I had the great satisfaction of being invited by Har-

vard University of Cambridge to teach "Basic Design" and "Advanced Explorations in Visual Communication." The experience for me was fundamental since I was able to experiment with a new method of teaching design to about eighty students from different nations. I completed the method in Italy and Laterza published it in a book *Design e Comunicazione Visiva* (Design and Visual Communication) which is becoming a textbook in the new art schools.

In 1965 I was invited to hold a large, complete, one-man show in Tokyo (books, objects of design, programmed art, research films, light-polarized objects). About three thousand people a day visited the exhibit. The newspapers wrote that my spirit was very Zen. So then I returned to Milan where I live, and while crossing the North Pole in flight I discovered that the sunset and dawn are the same when seen from two different points.

In Milan I have a small house in a neighborhood with many trees. The prevailing wind of the city enters exactly from this place. My terrace faces west and I cultivate small Bonsai trees. The cat at times is a little annoying.

———

Bruno Munari attended the Technical Institute of Naples but had no formal art training. Besides being a writer, illustrator and designer of children's books, Munari is a graphic artist, painter, sculptor, photographer, designer of toys and a constructor of mobiles, which he calls "useless machines." One of his large, colorful "useless machines" was displayed outdoors at the Milan Fair of 1950 and, set in motion by every breeze, it attracted much attention. Munari has done others for subsequent fairs.

Munari has received a number of awards, including a Gold Medal of the Triennale of Milan and several Golden Compasses for his industrial designs. *Bruno Munari's ABC* was named among the ten best-illustrated children's books of 1960 by the New York *Times Book Review* and was exhibited by the American Institute of Graphic Arts. *Circus in the Mist* was named one of the ten best-illustrated children's books of 1969 by the New York *Times Book Review*.

SELECTED WORKS WRITTEN AND ILLUSTRATED:
Animals for Sale, 1957; Tic, Tac and Toe, 1957;
Jimmy Has Lost His Cap, 1959; Bruno Munari's
ABC, 1960; Bruno Munari's Zoo, 1963; Circus
in the Mist, 1969.

ABOUT: Hürlimann, Bettina. Picture Book
World; Kingman, Lee and others, comps. Illustrators of Children's Books: 1957-1966; Viguers,
Ruth Hill and others, comps. Illustrators of Children's Books: 1946-1956; Graphis No. 61, 1955.

EVALINE NESS

April 24, 1911-

AUTHOR AND ILLUSTRATOR OF *Sam, Bangs
& Moonshine,* etc.

Autobiographical sketch of Evaline Ness:

AS an author and illustrator, I was late-
blooming. But a critic I was, from the
beginning.

As soon as I was able to read and write, I
copied down my favorite stories on the hundred-yard rolls of white paper that backs
ribbons. (My grown-up sister was a milliner.)
And with that same critical industry, I
searched through magazines to find appropriate pictures to illustrate stories which another creative sister turned out daily. (She
was twelve; I was seven.) It never occurred
to me to compete with ready-made words
and pictures. Anyway, I was too busy sewing
clothes for my family of dolls, of which the
smallest measured two inches.

It wasn't until my first year at Ball State
Teachers College in Muncie, Indiana, that
my muse appeared in the form of an elderly
gentle alcoholic man who had slipped from
being a top illustrator in Chicago to retouch-
ing photographs. He told me a story more
stimulating than any I had ever read. He told
me about a woman he knew who illustrated
shoes and was paid five dollars per drawing.
In 1930 that was, to me, unheard-of wealth!
My anxiety about my future was over! All I
had to do was to enroll in the Chicago Art
Institute, study art and come out a shoe artist. And so I did, and I didn't.

I enrolled and I studied art, but not knowing the difference between commercial art
and fine art, I found myself in the fine arts
department and was never, never taught
how to draw shoes.

But I did draw and paint everything else:
fashions for Saks Fifth Avenue, illustrations
for *Ladies' Home Journal, Good Housekeeping, Seventeen, Sports Illustrated* and, as the
raconteur always says, "a host of others."

It was Mary Cosgrave, children's book editor for Houghton Mifflin & Co. in 1957, who
started my book-illustration career. She gave
me the manuscript of *The Bridge* by Charlton Ogburn, Jr. and I closed myself up or in
or whatever an artist has to do, to illustrate it
and discovered that I had never been hap-
pier. I was seven years old again "finding"
appropriate pictures to correlate magic
words, but this time I had no need for
magazines.

After *The Bridge,* I stopped other kinds of
illustrating altogether and concentrated on
books. About fifteen books later, I was runner-up for the Caldecott Award for three
consecutive years for *All in the Morning
Early* by Sorche Nic Leodhas, *Pocketful of
Cricket* by Rebecca Caudill, and *Tom Tit*

Tot (no author). The fourth year (1967) I actually got the medal for *Sam, Bangs & Moonshine*. It was all mine! I had written the story too. It was the fifth book that I had written as well as illustrated. The first four were *Josefina February, Sula Sula, Exactly Alike,* and *A Double Discovery*.

I am still surprised and very pleased when someone calls me an author. I like to think I owe it all to ribbon paper.

———

Evaline (Michelow) Ness was born in Union City, Ohio. In addition to Ball State Teachers College and the Art Institute of Chicago, she has studied at the Corcoran Gallery Art School, Washington, D.C., the Art Students League, New York, and the Academia de Belles Artes, in Rome. *Josefina February*, the first book she both wrote and illustrated, grew out of a year's stay in Haiti. It was selected as a Notable Book by the American Library Association and an Honor Book by the New York *Herald Tribune*. Several of her books have been cited as among the best illustrated of the year by the New York *Times Book Review* Children's Books section, and a number have been included in exhibitions of the American Institute of Graphic Arts. She married Elliot Ness in 1938 (deceased), and Arnold A. Bayard in 1959.

SELECTED WORKS WRITTEN AND ILLUSTRATED: Josefina February, 1963; A Gift for Sula Sula, 1963; Exactly Alike, 1964; A Double Discovery, 1965; Sam, Bangs & Moonshine, 1966; The Girl and the Goatherd, 1970.

SELECTED WORKS ILLUSTRATED: The Bridge, by Charlton Ogburn, Jr., 1957; All in the Morning Early, by Sorche Nic Leodhas, 1963; A Pocketful of Cricket, by Rebecca Caudill, 1964; Tom Tit Tot, 1965; The Truthful Harp, by Lloyd Alexander, 1967.

ABOUT: Contemporary Authors, Vol. 7-8; Hopkins, Lee Bennett. Books Are by People; Kingman, Lee and others, comps. Illustrators of Children's Books: 1957-66; Something About the Author, Vol. 1; Who's Who in America, 1970-71; Who's Who of American Women, 1970-1971; American Artist January 1956; August 1967; Horn Book October 1964; August 1967; Library Journal March 15, 1964; School Library Journal March 1967; Top of the News April 1967.

EMILY NEVILLE
December 28, 1919-

AUTHOR OF *It's Like This, Cat*, etc.

Autobiographical sketch of Emily Cheney Neville:

I AM one of a dwindling number of living authors born at home. This was in Manchester, Connecticut, in a large comfortable brick house, complete with cook and nursemaids, and I was the youngest of seven children. My mother did not believe in doctors and hospitals. She loved wild flowers, reading aloud, and serenity at any price. My father and his brothers ran the family business, a silk mill, and we children played and went to school with only our Cheney cousins.

I was ten years old before I went to a public school, had a best friend outside the family, or even went to a movie for fun. I had pets and trees to climb and a bike to ride, and I read a great deal, books good and bad without any discrimination. My favorites concerned loyal-to-the-death dogs and knights in armor. This safe little world, and its ending, was the subject of my fourth book, *Traveler from a Small Kingdom*, published in 1968.

My teen-age years and twenties were spent in vigorous efforts to flee the Manchester cocoon and join the mob. It was still a rather select mob, at school in Hartford and at college in Bryn Mawr. I studied economics, graduating in 1940. I like to read books in social science, biography and religion, but I don't ever expect to write one, as I am too much in love with written conversation. After college, I went to work for the New York *Daily News* as an errand girl. I moved on to the New York *Mirror*, where I wrote a casual profile column during World War II, and married Glenn Neville, the executive editor, in 1943. We had five children, who grew up around Stuyvesant and Gramercy Parks, and while they were little I did no regular writing.

My first book, *It's Like This, Cat*, was published in 1963, when I was forty-three years old, and I was amazed and delighted. It had started in my head as a colloquial, irritated argument between a boy and his father. In

Emily Cheney Neville

reaction to the sentimental dog books of my youth, I had them argue over whether the boy could get a cat. This was published as a short story in the *Mirror,* and with the encouragement of Ursula Nordstrom, juvenile editor of Harper & Row, it grew into a book and won the John Newbery Medal for 1964.

Berries Goodman, published in 1965, was longer and harder to write and won the Jane Addams award in 1966. *The Seventeenth-Street Gang,* published in 1966, won no prizes, but I love the children in it and I was happy when I wrote it. All were published by Harpers.

In 1964, the *Mirror* ceased publication, and we left New York City for the little mountain village of Keene Valley, New York, where my husband died the following June. Once death happens to you, instead of being an accident in others' lives, you are forced to upend your values: getting and spending become accidental, and only life, death, and love matter.

The *Ramayana,* as told by Aubrey Menen, says: "There are three things which are real: God, human folly, and laughter. Since the first two pass our comprehension, we must do what we can with the third. . . . We have work to do." Producing even a little laughter is a meticulous job, and I have been at work

for two years on a small book, tentatively entitled *Local Boy Makes Good.*

———

Emily Neville is the daughter of Anne Bunce and Howell Cheney. The memory of her father, a pioneer in industrial education, is honored in the Howell Cheney High School, in Manchester, Connecticut. Critics who have compared Mrs. Neville's work to that of Mark Twain may not know that when he lived in Hartford, Mark Twain was a friend of both the Bunce and Cheney families. It has been said that Emily Neville plays erratic golf, fair tennis, is an excellent swimmer, preferably in icy water, and is one of the country's best fly-casters. Her children are Emily Tam, 1945; Glenn, Jr., 1947; Dessie, 1949; Marcy Ann, 1953; and Alexander, 1956. *It's Like This, Cat* also won the Nancy Bloch Memorial Award. *Local Boy Makes Good* was published as *Fogarty.*

SELECTED WORKS: It's Like This, Cat, 1963; Berries Goodman, 1965; The Seventeenth-Street Gang, 1966; Traveler from a Small Kingdom, 1968; Fogarty, 1969.

ABOUT: Contemporary Authors, Vol. 7-8; Something About the Author, Vol. 1; Who's Who in America, 1970-71; Who's Who of American Women, 1970-1971; Library Journal March 15, 1964.

CROSBY NEWELL

See *Bonsall, Crosby Newell*

"SORCHE NIC LEODHAS"

May 20, 1898-November 14, 1969

AUTHOR OF *Always Room for One More,* etc.

Autobiographical sketch of Leclaire Gowans Alger, who wrote under her own name and under the pen name of "Sorche Nic Leodhas":

WHEN I was a child I was often ill and missed so much school that my family finally decided to have me taught at home. Later, when I compared notes with children who went to school, I discovered that they seemed to have a much easier time of it than I did because I had to study a number of

Sorche Nic Leodhas: *SORE kuh nik lee OH das*

subjects they had never heard of, and my lessons were much harder than theirs. Besides, I had lessons six days a week instead of five, and I was given no holidays at all. However, when I thought it over I realized that my school day ended at one o'clock when they were just settling down on their hard little wooden seats for the long afternoon, while I could take an apple or two in my pocket, and a book or two under my arm, and, if it was summer, find a cool green hillside, or if it was winter, curl up before the fire at my ease, all through the long pleasant afternoon with no one to say "Do this!" or "Do that!" On the whole I liked my life better than theirs, so I made no complaint.

I learned to read very early, long before I was old enough to go to school. My family, I suspect, taught me in self-defense so as to relieve themselves of the burden of amusing me when I was ill and had to stay in bed. When I had once learned how to read, I began to read everything I could lay my hands on, and as I was given the freedom of my father's bookshelves, I found enough to keep me busy and happy as a lark.

It was only a step from reading to writing. My father and my sister did free-lance writing for fun. I was as imitative as a monkey so I soon began to copy them. My early attempts at writing were nothing to brag about, and thank heaven, none of my family were ever so misguided as to save any of them. My father, though loving, was a harsh critic and when he had examined my effort, word for word, and pointed out what was wrong with it, I was only too happy to tear it up and start out again. I began to write when I was six years old but I was twelve before I had written anything that won even a grudging approval from my family. My mother insisted that I should try again, but my father and my sister decided that I might as well send my endeavor out. Of course they expected it would never be accepted, but it was. After a while I got a check for eight dollars, and that was the beginning of my writing career.

The collecting of old Scottish stories, superstitions, songs and poems is a traditional occupation in our family. It goes back for generations on both my mother's and my father's side. None of us has ever bothered

with stories that have been published, preferring to keep only those which have come down by oral tradition. When we find a printed version of a story we have been told, unless ours differs greatly in the telling, we discard the tale.

Gathering stories is a lot of fun. You can't just step up to a person who you think knows one, and ask him pointblank to tell you a tale about the old days or the old beliefs. You have to be wily as a fox, sliding up to the story by bypaths of casual conversation, until by and by you have your storyteller thinking that he is the one who brought the subject up, while you are only the polite (but willing) listener to the tale.

We have found stories in all sorts of places. Of course there are hundreds that have come down to us through our own family. They may be found at big clan gatherings where a number of clans may have representatives, at the outings of separate clans, at Gaelic Club meetings, at ceilidhs, big and little. I've found stories along the docks of the East River, in New York; along the edge of a soccer field, with the game over and folk ready to talk; in the engine room of an old coastwise liner; in a cabin on a Pennsylvania hillside; in the kitchen of a Nova Scotia farmhouse over a plate of scones and a cup of tea, and more places than you could find time to name. Anywhere you find a tongue with a real Scottish burr to it, you're likely to find an old Scottish tale there, too.

———

Leclaire Gowans was born in Youngstown, Ohio, the daughter of Louis Peter Gowans. She attended Brushton Public School and Peabody High School, both in Pittsburgh, although her attendance at the latter, 1911-1915, was irregular, and she studied at home under the tutelage of her father. Her long association with the Carnegie Library of Pittsburgh began in 1915, when she started as a page. In 1916 she married Amos Risser Hoffman, who died two years later, leaving her with a son, Louis. She married for the second time several years later. From 1921-1925 she worked for the New York Public Library, and in 1926 she returned to Pittsburgh to prepare for entrance to the Carnegie Library School. Without previous college training, Mrs. Alger entered the Library

School by examination and received her certificate in 1929. As a librarian and a children's librarian she worked in various branches of the Carnegie Library of Pittsburgh until her retirement in 1966, when she devoted full time to writing. She died in Wilkinsburg, Pennsylvania, survived by her son, Louis R. Hoffman.

Among the books she wrote under her own name, Leclaire Alger, was *Jan and The Wonderful Mouth Organ*, 1939. Her pen name, "Sorche Nic Leodhas," she has said means Claire, daughter of Louis, in Gaelic.

The story of *All in the Morning Early* was handed down for three generations or more in the Gowans family, and in its original form may be a century older. The East River docks gave Mrs. Alger the story which became *The Man Who Helped Carry the Coffin*.

Thistle and Thyme received a Lewis Carroll Shelf Award in 1962, and was a runner-up for the Newbery Medal in 1963. *All in the Morning Early*, illustrated by Evaline Ness, was a Caldecott runner-up in 1964. *Always Room for One More*, illustrated by Nonny Hogrogian, won the Caldecott Medal in 1966.

SELECTED WORKS: Thistle and Thyme, 1962; All in the Morning Early, 1963; Gaelic Ghosts, 1964; Ghosts Go Haunting, 1965; Always Room for One More, 1965; Claymore and Kilt, 1967; The Laird of Cockpen, 1969.

ABOUT: Digby, Jenifer Jill. "Sorche Nic Leodhas: A remembrance," in Nic Leodhas, Sorche. Twelve Great Black Cats and Other Eerie Scottish Tales.

STERLING NORTH

STERLING NORTH

November 4, 1906-

AUTHOR OF *Rascal*, etc.

Biographical sketch of Sterling North:

STERLING NORTH was born in a farmhouse on the shore of Lake Koshkonong, near Edgerton, Wisconsin. His father, David Willard North, whom the son has called a dreamer, was not as successful at farming as he was at digging for Indian artifacts and exploring nature. His mother, Elizabeth Nelson North, who had entered college at four-

teen and graduated at the head of her class at eighteen, taught all of her children to read and write at early ages. She died when Sterling North was seven and he was reared by his sister, Jessica Nelson North, who later became a well-known poet. Like his older sisters and brother, Sterling wrote verse, and his first published work was a poem that appeared in *St. Nicholas* magazine when he was seven.

As a student at the University of Chicago, North edited the campus literary magazine, wrote lyrics for student musicals, and began publishing poetry and short stories in *Dial* and other national magazines. The University of Chicago published a small volume of his poems when he was nineteen. In his sophomore year he married Gladys Delores Buchanan, whom he had known in high school. After the birth of his first child, David Sterling, in February 1929, and the simultaneous publication of *The Pedro Gorino*, he quit college to become a feature writer for the Chicago *Daily News*.

North was literary editor of the Chicago *Daily News* from 1932 to 1943, when he became literary editor of the New York *Post*. After moving east with his wife and two children, David and Arielle, he bought twenty-seven acres of sylvan land on a small lake south of Morristown, New Jersey, and on that site he had built, according to his own design, the house in which he and his wife still live. "We have deer, foxes, raccoons, and all sorts of birds on the property," he once reported, "but some murderer shot the only bear."

In 1947 Doubleday published North's *So Dear to My Heart,* a homespun story of a boy and a lamb in rural Indiana at the turn of the century. North moved from the *Post* to the literary editor's desk at the New York *World Telegram and Sun* in 1949. After seven years there he gave up book reviewing to devote more time to his farm and his books. Since 1957 he has been general editor of Houghton Mifflin's North Star Books, a series on American history for young adults. His own contributions to that series include biographies of Thomas Edison, Henry David Thoreau, and Mark Twain.

In *Rascal,* published in 1963, Sterling North tells, in his usual clear, simple style, how as a boy he adopted and finally freed a raccoon.

The book received the Dutton Animal Book Award as well as the Aurianne, Dorothy Canfield Fisher, Lewis Carroll Shelf, William Allen White and Pacific Northwest Library Association Young Readers' Choice awards. Like *So Dear to My Heart,* it was translated into many languages, sold more than a million copies, and was made into a motion picture by Walt Disney. *The Wolfling,* winner of the 1969 Dutton Animal Book Award, is a novel based on the boyhood of North's father, who learned from naturalist Thure Kumelien the ways of nature and how to befriend and partly tame a wolf. North has written some thirty books, edited about thirty others, contributed to anthologies, and had poems, short stories, and articles published in leading periodicals such as *Saturday Review, Dial, Atlantic* and *Harper's.* He has received awards for poetry including the Witter Bynner Award, and his books have been translated into more than fifty languages.

Although he belongs to Authors League, Sterling North eschews membership in churches, political parties, clubs, or "any other type of pressure group." He has explained: "If a man cannot stand alone on his two feet and be judged by his own work he is not a very strong man. I study nature, converse, correspond, write my books and try to live by the Golden Rule—not always with success."

SELECTED WORKS: Midnight and Jeremiah, 1943; So Dear to My Heart, 1947; Abe Lincoln, 1956; George Washington, 1957; Mark Twain and the River, 1961; Rascal, 1963; Hurry Spring, 1966; Raccoons Are the Brightest People, 1966; The Wolfling, 1969.

ABOUT: Author's and Writer's Who's Who, 1963; Contemporary Authors, Vol. 5-6; North, Sterling. Rascal, 1963; Something About the Author, Vol. 1; Twentieth Century Authors, 1942; Twentieth Century Authors (First Supplement), 1955; Warfel, Harry P. American Novelists of Today, 1951; Who's Who in America, 1970-71; Editor and Publisher September 24, 1949; Library Journal March 15, 1964; Publishers' Weekly December 31, 1956.

MARY NORTON
December 10, 1903-

AUTHOR OF *The Borrowers,* etc.

Autobiographical sketch of Mary Pearson Norton:

MY first love (and perhaps, still, my last) was the theatre. As a little girl with four brothers I was a tireless impresario, enlisting them and such friends who came to play with us into enacting scene after scene from well-loved and much-read books—or in less conventional (but more melodramatic) improvisations of our own. These performances would take place in the more remote parts of the garden or, in winter or wet weather, in various unoccupied bedrooms of the house. It was a house very like that around which the Borrowers' story was written, rambling enough to escape for hours on end from grown-up supervision. Privacy for some reason had to be assured; we never acted our plays to adult audiences, we never rehearsed them—nor, in those days had we ever seen a professional performance. Our theatre was indeed the "living theatre," an added dimension born of moment.

Deserted bedrooms were enchanting places—away from the watchful eyes of those supposed to be in charge of us—they seemed to us like "foreign parts." Those were the days of "airing" mattresses. Small figures, flitting secretly along dark passages, would

Mary Norton

pause with stealth and open a closed door and there—oh joy of joys!—would be a sudden warmth, shadows of firelight on the ceiling, and the whisper of living coals.

Round the fire, propped up against chairs, dragged-up desks or ottomans, great sagging mattresses stood on their sides like screens, cooking gently in the steady glow; there would be a smell of hot flock and warm horsehair—a cave of heat and light amid the alien shadows. In no time at all pillows, bereft now of their linen covers, would be gathered into a nest and there we would sit, our backs to the hot ticking, telling our stories and arranging our plays. Sometimes, if we were lucky, there would be biscuits in a canister on a table beside the bed, leftovers from a previous guest. Many a stirring drama was acted out within that charmed half-circle, with a coal fire for footlights and shadows for the wings. On fine days, in the garden, we had yew hedges for a backdrop, and dark, shrubbery tunnels for our exits and our entrances.

Later, after seven years in a strict convent and a short course at art school, I did join the Old Vic Shakespeare Company, first as a student, then as a paid member. It still seems, looking back, two of the happiest

years of one's life. Not always carefree, but entirely satisfying: we were privileged to act with great stars and to understudy them. I remember the first time I "played my understudy" (Bianca to Edith Evans' Katherine in *The Taming of the Shrew*)—the terror and the triumph! Then "Beauty" in *Everyman* (a piece of casting which, in one's humble teens, seemed at the time to be peculiarly eccentric); then "The Young Girl" in *Thirty Minutes in the Street* . . . And so on, gradually finding one's feet and emerging from that nameless, background group called "Ladies of the Court."

How keen we were! Above the wash basin in our dressing room, someone had pinned the inspiring slogan: "If the sacred fire burns in you, you will succeed. Sarah Bernhardt." And the sacred fire, at that time, burned quite as brightly as those remembered fires in the bedrooms back at home.

In spite of this, it seemed hardly to have occurred to me that marriage into a family which had been domiciled in Portugal for several generations might mean the end of a stage career. But so it, of course, proved. The house stood remotely in its own grounds, cut off from Lisbon and surrounding villages by well-nigh impassable roads. No government had stayed in power long enough to repair them: it was the era of yearly revolutions until, at last, the coming of Salazar. There were long days of great peace and, sometimes, of loneliness. It was there I began to write—partly for my children.

———

Mary Pearson was born in London and reared in Leighton Buzzard, then a country market town. She is the daughter of Mary Savile Hughes and Reginald Spenser Pearson, a descendant of the poet Edmund Spenser. She married Robert Charles Norton, of a well-known ship-owning family, in 1927, and their children are Ann Mary, Robert George, Guy, and Caroline. Their life in Portugal ended with the outbreak of the Second World War. Norton joined the staff of the British Embassy in Portugal and later enlisted in the British Navy as a gunner and Mrs. Norton and the children returned to England, where Mrs. Norton worked for the War Office. Following this she worked for two years in New York as a member of the

British Purchasing Commission. She has said that it was then she began writing "in grim earnest" to help support her children and to pay the rent on their house in Connecticut.

Back in England near the end of the war, Mrs. Norton's eyes were injured by the explosion of a V-2 bomb, but her sight was restored by an operation.

Mary Norton has written plays for stage and radio. *The Magic Bed-knob* and its sequel, *Bonfires and Broomsticks* (published together in the United States as *Bed-knob and Broomstick*), were both dramatized on the BBC's Children's Hour. *The Borrowers* was first published in the United States as a serial in *Woman's Day* magazine. *The Borrowers* won the Carnegie Medal in 1952 and a Lewis Carroll Shelf Award in 1960.

Mary Norton is a member of P.E.N.

SELECTED WORKS: The Magic Bed-knob, 1944; The Borrowers, 1953; The Borrowers Afield, 1955; Bed-knob and Broomstick, 1957; The Borrowers Afloat, 1959; The Borrowers Aloft, 1961; The Complete Adventures of the Borrowers, 1967; Poor Stainless, 1971.

ABOUT: Author's and Writer's Who's Who, 1963; Ontario Library Record November 1958; Wilson Library Bulletin May 1962.

EILÍS DILLON O'CUILLEANAIN

See *Dillon, Eilís*

IB SPANG OLSEN

June 11, 1921-

AUTHOR AND ILLUSTRATOR OF *The Marsh Crone's Brew*, etc.

Autobiographical sketch of Ib Spang Olsen:

I WAS born in Copenhagen, Denmark, was educated as a teacher, and after graduation (1943) discovered I had certain abilities in drawing. So I went to the Royal Academy of Art and studied graphic art for several years. Part of the time I taught children—which I liked very much—and illustrated stories in the Sunday editions of the newspapers, which I also liked very much. So I went on for many years as two persons, teacher and illustrator, the latter always for a grown-up audience. Besides short stories

I did illustrations for longer works, some twenty books, including Melville's *Benito Cereno*, some Chaucer, *Life on the Mississippi* by Mark Twain, and *The Smelling Garden*, to name some books known abroad.

All this time I continued having an interest in the classic graphic technics, and for years I had an old lithographic handpress, so old that it might have been owned by Seenefelder himself. This led to a series of lithographies and research into the possibility of getting some of the values of the handgraphic into mass-printed newspapers and books. I never liked reproduction, the translating of art work into something very similar, sometimes even more beautiful, but always a surrogate, never the thing itself. I tried to make original graphics for mass-printing to use the wonderful modern technic of the huge presses and still have the touch of the artist's hand in print no. 100,000. This resulted in the so-called Zinkografi—a sort of etching, useful in book-printing for newspapers, etc., also in color. For offset I developed (I did not say invented) the so-called direct copy, which is drawing directly on the copy-film. This method will perhaps be of greater use; it has consequence and beauty and is also very cheap to use. All my own books are done in that technique. I was always interested in folk tales and illustrated some of them, and contemporary children's books, too, before I had children of my own. Then I had to tell bedside stories, and a number of our own occurred. At that time it was not easy to have a children's book published. Denmark is a little country, and just then, in the early fifties, a phenomenon called "Golden Books"—American low-quality children's books—was dumping lots of cheap editions here. Then I did some folding books for the newspapers, which could be cut out, folded and made into little primitive children's books. So it began. So far I have made a dozen real books and a number of smaller, folding books, not yet published in the usual form.

Five of my books have had awards in my country, four of them as the year's best children's books (for text). The last three times the international Hans Christian Andersen award was presented I was among the runners-up (as illustrator). One book got a diploma at the biennale in Bratislava, 1967. For publication in Denmark, I translated and re-illustrated Meindert de Jong's *Nobody Plays with a Cabbage*. I have worked for TV, mostly drawing "directly on the screen" while telling a story, but also making real animated films, and for the broadcast telling bedside stories. I do not think I could go on telling stories in this way without having contact with children of the age I am addressing; when I no longer have that, I stop being a children's book specialist. Now I am regarded as one, but I do not feel so myself. There are so many things to draw and to illustrate, and working with industry and therefore under a discipline very similar to being tied hand and foot, you must change subjects when you feel it necessary. So I make children's stuff half the time and devote the rest to whatever else there is to do.

Personally, I find it much more difficult to illustrate than to write a book for children. If any justice was found the illustrator should be paid four times as much as the poet. Much of the attitude of an author of children's books must be pedagogical, intended or not; you must think more about what happens within the reader if he is a child than if he is a thoroughly developed and regression-proof grown-up, similar to yourself, who can take it or leave it. You must try not to lie, not to make life seem more idyllic and distant than it is, and yet have it as wonderful and capricious as it can be; not hurt the reader, and yet not be afraid of being yourself. You must not believe you can teach fantasy. Your hope is to keep some of what is not yet destroyed in them. You must be contemporary and not spread too much nostalgia, but it is your duty to represent the time that is really your own.

You must be clear and understandable, but your language must be rich, musical, neither a speaking-language nor a reading-language, but one which can come through the boring reading aloud of an uninterested babysitter. In a time which leaves less and less space for the child's free development the mass media become of greater and greater importance, and you must find your way between empty entertainment and manipulation.

I have never known enough about the mind of the child; I can only tell the story that occurs to me as I sit before the children, in the presence of one important person in addition—the child in me.

SELECTED WORKS WRITTEN AND ILLUSTRATED: The Marsh Crone's Brew, 1960; The Boy in the Moon, 1963.

SELECTED WORKS ILLUSTRATED: Lars-Peter's Birthday, by Virginia Allen Jensen, 1959; Tobias, the Magic Mouse, by Jacob Bech Nygaard, 1968.

ABOUT: Hürlimann, Bettina. Picture Book World; Kingman, Lee and others, comps. Illustrators of Children's Books: 1957-1966.

MARY O'NEILL

February 16, 1908-

AUTHOR OF *The White Palace*, etc.

Autobiographical sketch of Mary le Duc O'Neill:

"THEY'LL never raise that poor little scrawny thing." This was the opinion commonly held by all adults who viewed me as an infant. All, except my parents, to whom I was a first experience.

I was born in New York City. And, in the summertime of that year, whenever my mother pushed the carriage containing me along the sidewalks on the warm summer

Mary L. O'Neill

afternoons, children would gather, and after their latest look at what the carriage contained, they would offer her their honest and direct sympathy. "She's yella yet, ain't she, Mrs. le Duc. But don't worry. Maybe she'll stop crying sometime. Maybe she'll even be all right, someday."

What a good thing it was that I happened to my parents first: a jaundiced, colicky, premature and beloved bundle of misery. For, following me into the family there were four more, a brother and three sisters, all strong, healthy, beautiful. We left New York in my infancy and moved to Ohio. There my lovely mother died when I was almost twelve years old. My father then moved us into the home of his mother and sister in Berea, Ohio, which was then a small suburb of Cleveland. We lived in a great big white barn of a Victorian house set into an immense yard. Our childhood was busy and exciting and happy.

I cannot remember when I first noticed books, or began to read them. They were always around, always a part of life. But I do know that I wanted to write books before I could read them, for I would tell this to my mother every time she read to me, or told me one of her own made-up stories. And I began to try to do this in about second grade. These first stories were very short and dull, for they contained only the words I could spell. My brothers and sisters did not think

much of them, and told me so indirectly, by asking me not to bother trying to write stories, but just to make them up and say them out loud. What a wonderful difference between the painfully written ones and the easily told ones. For one could use all the words one knew, change voice tones and gestures in the telling of a story.

Nevertheless, I kept on trying to write. This meant learning to spell words. And finally, after many years I wrote a story that pleased the most critical audience I have ever known: my brother and sisters and their friends.

As I grew I thought the stories should grow up, too. And I wrote many adult stories and articles that were published in national magazines. And I wrote advertising for a while.

But none of this writing was quite as satisfying to me as the earlier, unpublished stories a child once wrote for children.

When my own children were born the old, made-up stories began again, a second and more elaborate cycle. And another audience that quickly gave approval or showed boredom or disappointment.

Finally, when these children were in high school and college, I began to write books for children. There was time to do it, then, and I had learned to spell.

Mary le Duc attended St. Joseph Academy in Cleveland, Cleveland College of Western Reserve University, and the University of Michigan. She married John Arthus O'Neill and their children are Erin Gibbons Kelly, Abigail Gibbons and John R. Mrs. O'Neill's short stories and articles have appeared in a number of periodicals, including *McCall's*, *Good Housekeeping*, *Woman's Day* and *Scholastic*, and her verses have appeared in school books. She is a member of New York Women's Advertising Club and of Authors Guild. She enjoys travel, music, and the theater.

SELECTED WORKS: Hailstones and Halibut Bones, 1961; Saints: Adventures in Courage, 1963; People I'd Like to Keep, 1964; The White Palace, 1966; Words, Words, Words, 1966; Poor Merlo, 1967; Take a Number, 1968; Ali, 1969; Winds, 1971.

ABOUT: Contemporary Authors, Vol. 5-6.

EDWARD ORMONDROYD
October 8, 1925-

AUTHOR OF *Michael the Upstairs Dog*, etc.

Autobiographical sketch of Edward Ormondroyd:

I WAS born in Wilkinsburg, Pennsylvania. When I was about four or five my family moved east to Swarthmore. It was an ideal place to grow up in, with a creek, woods and fields all around, almost every street a tunnel through trees, rabbits and squirrels and birds everywhere. For ten cents you could ride on a little four-wheeled trolley through the woods for miles. On weekends my father took me on long walks through the blissful countryside, to a Colonial house, or a duck pond, or an Indian millstone, or an abandoned quarry. With my friends I made rollerskate scooters, collected and swapped bubble-gum cards, engaged in enormous wars with rubber-band guns; on the Fourth of July we set off boxes of fireworks (they were allowed then), in the fall we made bonfires by the curbs and roasted hickory nuts, in winter we sledded and skated and caught perpetual runny-nosed colds. I read or had read to me the Pooh books, all of Dr. Doolittle, Seton's *Two Little Savages*, the Jungle Books. My cousin John and I invented our own countries: drew maps, issued currency, wrote newspapers. My first book came out in a limited edition of one copy, written, illustrated and bound by the author.

My family moved to Ann Arbor, Michigan, when I was twelve. More beautiful countryside, only now there was a river instead of a creek. We lived on the edge of town next to miles of open country. With the boys across the street I roamed the fields, dabbled in photography, made bows and arrows and model airplanes, caught snakes and mice. We read P. G. Wodehouse to each other, laughing so much that we could hardly get the words out. I discovered *Wind in the Willows*, H. G. Wells, and that blessed man Arthur Ransome, whose books about the Swallows and Amazons so inspired me and my friend that we built a thirteen-foot sailboat forthwith.

Edward Ormondroyd

During World War II I sailed aboard a destroyer-escort in the Pacific. Afterwards I attended the University of California at Berkeley, graduating in 1950 with an A.B. degree in English. While I was going to college I wrote *David and the Phoenix* for my own amusement, and discovered I had something children might like. It took seven years to find a publisher, but children did like it, and I still get letters from them saying so twelve years later.

I live in Berkeley. In ten minutes I can walk to my publishers at Parnassus Press to consult about our next book. I have a son, Evan (he block-printed the cloth in the background of my portrait), and two daughters, Kitt and Beth. I work as a librarian. My interests are music, birds, cooking and wine, poetry and walking. My name, by the way, is not as hard as it looks. It is pronounced just as spelled, with the accent on the first syllable. It comes from Yorkshire.

Edward Ormondroyd plays the recorder, shawm and flute. *David and the Phoenix* won the Commonwealth Club of California Juvenile Book Award.

SELECTED WORKS: David and the Phoenix, 1957; Time at the Top, 1963; Theodore, 1966; Michael the Upstairs Dog, 1967; Broderick, 1969.

Ormondroyd: *OR mon droyd*

"DAVID OSBORNE"

See *Silverberg, Robert*

HELEN OXENBURY

June 2, 1938-

ILLUSTRATOR OF *The Dragon of an Ordinary Family*, etc.

Autobiographical sketch of Helen Oxenbury Burningham:

I WAS born in Ipswich in Suffolk in the middle of World War II. Some of my earliest memories are the drone of doodlebugs, the whine of sirens, and being snatched from my bed and rushed down the garden shelter where we had delicious cups of tea and over-jolly games until the "all clear." Not understanding the danger, I thoroughly enjoyed these lively interludes, and nights spent quietly in bed were a great disappointment. In the daytime my brother and I searched for shrapnel and jumped into old bomb craters on the heath behind our garden.

During these years I can't remember even looking at a children's book, and any bedtime stories my father made up. I think these were potentially very good, but he had the maddening habit of dropping off to sleep before the end. In fact the only children's books I can remember were the Babar and Rupert books, both of which I still love dearly.

When I was about eight years old my parents moved to Felixstowe, a small seaside town, but I continued my schooling in Ipswich near by. I loathed school, and my great passion at this time was sport of any kind, but especially tennis which I played from morning till night during the holidays and at weekends. When I was eventually released from school I began a two-year general art course at the Ipswich School of Art, and my tennis days were over.

During the vacations I worked at the Ipswich Repertory Theatre helping to paint sets and this decided me to specialize in theatre design at the Central School of Art in London. Although I thoroughly enjoyed these two years I don't think they had much im-

pression on me careerwise. The only outstanding development at this time was my meeting John Burningham, who became my husband some years later.

After the Central School I worked for a short time in Repertory, and then joined John in Israel, where he was working. Some months passed before I became assistant to a designer in the Habimah Theatre, and eventually I designed several sets for this theatre myself.

When I returned to England I tried working in television and films, but I felt it a terrible anticlimax after the theatre. Sitting at a drawing board almost all day was not my idea of fun.

After my marriage I spent two desperate years wondering what on earth I could do. However I realize now that was an extremely useful time. Watching my husband through every stage of his books was as good if not better than a two-year course in book illustration, and I was "studying" under one of the best author's illustrators in the country.

When I actually began to illustrate, with *Numbers of Things*, I found it enormously satisfying, and seven books—among them *The Great Big Enormous Turnip* and *The Hunt-*

ing of the Snark—four years, two children later, I still find it so.

Helen Oxenbury was awarded the Kate Greenaway Medal in 1970 for *The Dragon of an Ordinary Family* and *The Quangle Wangle's Hat*.

SELECTED WORKS WRITTEN AND ILLUSTRATED: Numbers of Things, 1968.

SELECTED WORKS ILLUSTRATED: The Great Big Enormous Turnip, by Alexsei Tolstoy, 1968; Letters of Thanks, by Manghanita Kempadoo, 1969; The Dragon of an Ordinary Family, by Margaret Mahy, 1969; The Quangle Wangle's Hat, by Edward Lear, 1970.

TONY PALAZZO

April 7, 1905-September 10, 1970

AUTHOR AND ILLUSTRATOR OF *Bianco and the New World*, etc.

Autobiographical sketch of Tony Palazzo:

BORN in Manhattan more than six decades ago and educated in New York City schools and colleges. No formal art training—just picked it up when art wasn't quite as elusive and many-faceted. Started in the gray flannel set, (though at that time I wore hand-me-downs) and only comparatively recently devoted all my time to the writing and/or illustration of books for children. Between stints of being art director of many publications, among them *Esquire, Coronet, Collier's, Look,* I exhibited oils and drawings at various galleries and museums throughout the United States—Pennsylvania Academy of Fine Arts, Chicago Art Institute, San Diego Museum, Albright Gallery of Buffalo, Museum of Modern Art in New York.

Between *those* times I wrote and illustrated children's books which had been an underlying hobby. Thus, since starting in the gentle and soft-spoken world of children's literature, I have had to do with more than sixty-five books in one way or another, broken down this way: Most were original illustrated stories, some were adapted, retold, or edited and illustrated, and a few were illustrated only. Of the entire group seven were Junior

Literary Guild selections, four of which were originals.

Fortunately for me, my principal hobby still is the imagery of books for children, though I still occasionally ride horses, do some gardening and, when Mrs. Palazzo is too tired, act as handyman around our house in Hastings-on-Hudson. We have no children, though the youngsters in the neighborhood call me Uncle Tony—and we have always had animal pets of various species, breeds and numbers. Occasionally when things get dull I talk to groups of children in libraries, schools and hospitals, giving them sugar-coated lectures on illustrating and writing.

After studying at the High School of Commerce, Tony Palazzo became a bookkeeper. He soon began work as a commercial artist, however, and at the same time attended classes at Columbia and New York Universities. In 1928 he married Philomena de Beaumont. Palazzo taught advertising design at Pratt Institute and the School of Visual Arts. His work has been in exhibitions of the American Institute of Graphic Arts and he won a number of awards for advertising and editorial illustrations. He was a member of

Palazzo: *Pah LAHT zoh*

the Art Directors Club of New York. *Timothy Turtle* was a runner-up for the Caldecott Medal in 1947. Tony Palazzo died at his home in Hastings-on-Hudson, New York, September 10, 1970.

SELECTED WORKS WRITTEN AND ILLUSTRATED: Susie the Cat, 1949; Aesop's Fables (adapted) 1954; Bianco and the New World, 1957; Peter and the Wolf (adapted) 1961; Jan and the Reindeer, 1963; Magic Crayon, 1967; Charley, the Horse, 1967.

SELECTED WORKS ILLUSTRATED: Timothy Turtle, by Al Graham, 1946; Hubbub in the Hollow, by Irene Smith, 1952; Beagle Named Bertram, by Amalie Sharfman, 1954; Old Bet, by Anne Colver, 1957: The Rhymes of Squire O'Squirrel, by Al Graham, 1963.

ABOUT: Contemporary Authors, Vol. 7-8; Kingman, Lee and others, comps. Illustrators of Children's Books: 1957-1966; Viguers, Ruth Hill and others, comps. Illustrators of Children's Books: 1946-1956; Coronet July 1937; Publishers' Weekly October 10, 1970.

EDGAR PARKER

August 12, 1925-

AUTHOR AND ILLUSTRATOR OF *The Duke of Sycamore,* etc.

Autobiographical sketch of James Edgar Parker, Jr.:

BORN in Meridian, Mississippi . . . two sisters, no brothers. . . . Father was a lawyer; mother a former school teacher . . . holidays on the Gulf Coast and in the countryside . . . animals always about.

Early drawn to illustrated books in the small family library—Waverly novels, sets of Irving, Dickens, Shakespeare (Stothard's gossamer steel engravings), but most of all to Ridpath's *History of the World,* brimming with wood engravings (Nevins, Doré, etc.) of besieged castles, massacres, coronations, decapitations, brooding kings, skulking assassins—plumes, armor . . . I suppose I entered the realm of literature through the keyhole of picture captions. ("It is a common rose. Preserve it, however," says Scott's Black Dwarf, and I would shiver at the talismanic intrigue long before I could fathom the

story.) Another early interest was making marionettes, puppets, jumping jacks.

After graduation from Meridian Junior College, I studied art under Richard Zoellner at the University of Alabama, then came to New York (1946) and studied under Amédée Ozenfant and later under Gabor Peterdi. Much of my work differs in character from my children's book illustration.

Since 1947 I have lived in Brooklyn's Park Slope. Unmarried . . . sort of retiring . . . sort of lazy . . . not at all (as may be evident) autobiographically disposed.

_____

Edgar Parker studied etching, engraving, and painting in New York. Besides writing and illustrating books, he has painted murals and designed record album covers and book jackets. His works have been in several exhibitions of the American Institute of Graphic Arts.

SELECTED WORKS WRITTEN AND ILLUSTRATED: The Duke of Sycamore, 1959; The Enchantress, 1960; Stuff and Nonsense, 1961; The Dream of the Dormouse, 1963; The Question of a Dragon, 1964; The Flower of the Realm, 1966; Rogue's Gallery, 1969.

ABOUT: Kingman, Lee and others, comps. Illustrators of Children's Books: 1957-1966.

PETER PARNALL
May 23, 1936-

ILLUSTRATOR OF A *Dog's Book of Bugs*, etc.

Autobiographical sketch of Peter Parnall:

WHERE and when was I a little boy? It was a hundred and ten years ago in the Big Bend area of Texas. It SEEMED like 1860. All us kids had old retired Indian ponies and spent a lot of our time chasing each other around old Fort Davis, an abandoned army post of the Civil War era. Trouble was, the Indian kids insisted on being the soldiers and us few white-eyes who lived there were always on the losing end of those historical battles! There were many adventures during those years I like to call my impressionable ones. Animals abounded, the young of every wild creature in the desert found their way into our home. At one time I harbored twenty-seven different kinds of animals!

We moved back East after the war. After various schooling I went to Cornell with the idea of becoming a veterinarian. Fortunately I was a rotten student. All my life I devoured all printed matter, but when it came to formal education I simply endured. I left college soon after entering and set out to "find my thing," and mostly found that talk was cheap and answers were mighty hard to come by. I went West to find some of those good old times again. I pumped gas, swept out a department store basement, worked as a day laborer, parked cars, and finally found a job around horses. It was at the bottom; I cleaned twenty-four stalls a day. I drifted from Denver to Albuquerque, to Tucson and on to California. I ended my itchy foot in Las Vegas, and found that lively town a pretty dull place to live. I drew a picture of a dog while there, and sent it to my father for his birthday. He had been following my travels with some apprehension and thought it a good idea if I came back and went to Pratt. I came and I did, but didn't stay long. I left Pratt after a year and got a job as art director of a little travel magazine. Soon I started to do some free-lance advertising design and left the magazine to devote full time to making some of that confidence money. Several years passed during which I devel-

oped the beginnings of an illustrative style, and also developed a disgusted opinion of many idiotic clients and the advertising geniuses who sold their self-respect for a price. I quit.

I bought a copy of *Literary Market Place*, made twenty appointments in two weeks with juvenile editors, and a week later did my first book. I met Jean Karl at Atheneum and found that there were indeed publishers to whom quality is important. She encouraged me and I have found others. The publishing people are a most pleasant and civilized group on the whole and it's a pleasure working with them. I have been very fortunate. Have received various awards and good publicity. Our business has been kind to me and I have been kind to it by working like a slave trying to improve the fare we publish for our children. Seeing my little neighbors smile at a drawing makes me feel I could make the rain fall up.

———

Peter Parnall now does his work at home on a farm beside the Delaware River, where he lives with his wife and son and enjoys frequent long walks to watch deer and other wild creatures. *A Dog's Book of Bugs*, *Knee Deep in Thunder*, and *Malachi Mudge* were all named by the New York *Times* as among the best-illustrated children's books for the year of publication. Parnall's work has been exhibited by the American Institute of Graphic Arts and the Society of Illustrators, New York.

SELECTED WORKS ILLUSTRATED: A Tale of Middle Length, by Mary Francis Shura, 1966; Knee Deep in Thunder, by Sheila Moon, 1967; A Dog's Book of Bugs, by Elizabeth Griffen, 1967; Malachi Mudge, by Edward Cecil, 1968; Kavik the Wolf Dog, by Walt Morey, 1968; Tall Tales of the Catskills, by Frank Lee DuMond, 1968; Apricot ABC, by Miska Miles, 1969; The Inspector, by George Mendoza, 1970; Annie and the Old One, by Miska Miles, 1971.

ABOUT: Kingman, Lee and others, comps. Illustrators of Children's Books: 1957-1966.

PHILIPPA PEARCE

1920-

AUTHOR OF *Tom's Midnight Garden*, etc.

Autobiographical sketch of Ann Philippa Pearce Christie:

THE only place I remember living in, until I was quite grown up, was the mill-house in the village of Great Shelford, five miles south of Cambridge. The only reason I wasn't born in the mill-house was that my grandfather was living there at the time: he was the miller, and my father, who lived with his family in another house in the village, worked under him in the mill. My grandfather died when I was about two, my grandmother moved out of the mill-house, and our family—my parents, my sister, my two brothers, and myself—moved in.

We had a wonderful place to grow up in, to love. Our house stood next to my father's mill, which was partly water-powered. The river ran beside our garden, and we had a canoe on it. The river and the canoe are really those of my first published book, *The Minnow Leads to Treasure*. We fished—with worms—and bathed; and, in a hard winter, we skated on the flooded water-meadows. None of us ever skated from Cambridge to Ely, but my father did, when he was a young man; and I put some of his experience into my second book, *Tom's Midnight Garden* (Carnegie Medal winner 1958). Anyone can see what the outside of our house looked

like, from Susan Einzig's illustrations for that book; but you must take away the extra story—that was put in only to accommodate Mrs. Bartholomew. The garden of our house was almost exactly the Midnight Garden— or, at least, the garden as my father described it from his boyhood. He had been born in the mill-house.

I went to school in Cambridge, and then to Cambridge University; I moved to London to earn a living. Almost my first job was as a scriptwriter and producer in the School Broadcasting Department of the BBC. This was *sound* radio, of course. I worked there for thirteen years, enjoyed it a great deal, and learnt a great deal. Above all, I learnt to write for speaking, or at least for reading aloud. This is an all-important part of writing, especially in the writing of stories.

My first book was published while I was still in the BBC; and perhaps I got the idea of publishing rather on the brain. For in 1958 I left for a job as editor in a publishing house. From about that time onwards I have earned my living with a mixture of editing, radio scriptwriting and production, reviewing, lecturing, and so on—all in the field of children's literature. At first I was sure that, as a free lance, my writing would dry up and I would starve; but I wrote *A Dog So Small,* and after that several short stories. One of them, *Mrs. Cockle's Cat,* was made into a picture book, and Anthony Maitland's illustrations for it won the Kate Greenaway Award. My most recent book (1968) was *The Children of the House,* in collaboration with Sir Brian Fairfax-Lucy.

I have written less since my marriage, and especially since the birth of my daughter. On the other hand, I have done more story-*telling*—to begin with, stories about teddy bears and pussy-cats; later, fairy stories. For me, story-telling has turned out to be interestingly different from story-writing. Yet probably one kind of story-making helps with the other kind. I shall see.

Philippa Pearce won a scholarship to Girton College, Cambridge University, and received her M.A. with honors in 1942. She married Martin Christie in 1963. They have one daughter, Sarah Gertrude Isabella, always known as Sally.

Besides winning the Carnegie Medal, *Tom's Midnight Garden* was on the Honor List for the Hans Christian Andersen Award in 1960 and won a Lewis Carroll Shelf Award in 1963. *The Minnow Leads to Treasure* won a Lewis Carroll Shelf Award in 1958. *A Dog So Small* won a New York *Herald Tribune* Children's Spring Book Festival Award in 1963.

SELECTED WORKS: The Minnow Leads to Treasure, 1958; Tom's Midnight Garden, 1959; Mrs. Cockle's Cat, 1961; A Dog So Small, 1963; The Children of the House, with Brian Fairfax-Lucy, 1968.

ABOUT: Author's and Writer's Who's Who, 1963; Contemporary Authors, Vol. 7-8; Something About the Author, Vol. 1; Who's Who in America, 1970-71; Library Association Record May 1959; Wilson Library Bulletin April 1964.

BILL PEET

January 29, 1915-

AUTHOR OF *Fly Homer Fly*, etc.

Biographical sketch of William Bartlett Peed:

BILL PEET was born William Bartlett Peed in Grandview, Indiana, the son of Orion Peed, a traveling salesman who saw little of

BILL PEET

his children, and Emma Thorpe Peed, a handwriting teacher and supervisor in Indianapolis schools for more than thirty-five years. Though he has not changed it legally, Peed has used the surname Peet since 1947. When Peet was three, the family moved to Indianapolis, where he spent his childhood. Peet has said that one of his favorite memories is of a visit to his grandfather's farm in southern Indiana, where, to his delight, many kinds of small wildlife could be found in nearby uncultivated fields. "Animals have always been of special interest to me," he says. "My first visit to a zoo was on a trip to Cincinnati . . . I spent all the money I had saved from selling newspapers to buy film for a small box camera, hoping to get a picture of every animal there." Not a picture turned out. From that time on he took along a sketch pad instead, and drew his animals.

Drawing had been Peet's main interest from early childhood, and since his mother taught handwriting, he always had paper. In high school he decided that drawing was the only thing he liked that could become a career. In 1933 Peet's decision was reinforced when he received a scholarship to the John Herron Art Institute in Indianapolis. There he studied drawing, painting, and design for three years.

In addition to his studies, Peet devoted his free time to sketching and painting, and he received a number of prizes. His subjects were often farm, circus, and zoo animals.

He met Margaret Brunst at art school. Anticipating marriage, he decided that he had better begin earning a living. After working briefly as a greeting card artist, he went to Hollywood to become a continuity illustrator for motion pictures. When he felt secure enough financially, he married Miss Brunst, on November 30, 1937. After his two sons, Bill and Steve, were born, he would make up bedtime stories for them, and through the telling of stories he became interested in writing fiction. Along with his job making continuity drawings for the movies, he began to write movie scenarios. When his boys outgrew his storytelling at home, he sought a wider juvenile audience through the writing of books—in his words—"as a hobby."

His first book, published in 1959, was *Hubert's Hair-Raising Adventure,* the story of a silly, proud lion, which has been translated into five languages and reproduced in Braille. He has since written and illustrated a number of books and has received awards from the Indiana University Writers Conference and the Southern California Council on Literature for Young People, among other honors. In 1967, Peet was named outstanding Hoosier author of books for children.

Peet lives and works in Studio City, California.

SELECTED WORKS WRITTEN AND ILLUSTRATED: Hubert's Hair-Raising Adventure, 1959; Smokey, 1962; Randy's Dandy Lions, 1964; Chester, the Worldly Pig, 1965; Farewell to Shady Glade, 1966; Buford the Little Bighorn, 1967; Fly Homer Fly, 1969; The Wump World, 1970.

ABOUT: Contemporary Authors, Vol. 19-20; Kingman, Lee and others, comps. Illustrators of Children's Books: 1957-1966.

ANN PETRY

October 12, 1912-

AUTHOR OF *Harriet Tubman: Conductor on the Underground Railroad,* etc.

Autobiographical sketch of Ann Lane Petry:

PERHAPS because I was born in the morning (upstairs over my father's drugstore

ANN PETRY

in Old Saybrook, Connecticut) I think the morning is the most beautiful part of the day. About five A.M. I begin my daily stint of writing. At that hour the telephone does not ring, there are no peremptory knocks at the front door; and there are no visitors.

I always wanted to be a writer. When I was in high school I wrote poetry and one-act plays. It was in high school, too, that I first encountered textbook descriptions of slaves in the United States. The history books we used said that slaves were happy, mindless savages who thrived in the deadly heat of the cotton fields and the rice paddies of the South. I found this impossible to believe.

Despite my interest in writing as a career I studied pharmacy at the Connecticut College of Pharmacy (now the School of Pharmacy at the University of Connecticut). After I received my degree I worked in the drugstores that my family owned. I married and went to New York City to live. While I was living in New York I wrote my first novel, a book for adults—*The Street*—which deals with life and death in the Harlem ghetto.

I was still living in New York City when I wrote my first book for children, entitled *The Drugstore Cat.* It is about a cat who lived in a drugstore. It was a perfectly logical book for me to write for I know a great deal about drugstores and I am very fond of cats.

The cat who lives with me now is named Tobermory after the cat in Saki's story of that name. We call him Mister Toby. Visitors are always surprised when I say, "Oh, here comes Mister Toby." They usually turn around expecting to see a person and they see instead a slow-moving, majestic black cat.

Not too long after *The Drugstore Cat* was published, I came across some references to Harriet Tubman, an escaped slave, who led other slaves to freedom before the Civil War. She seemed to me the epitome of everything that is indomitable in the human spirit and the exact antithesis of the textbook image of the slave as stupid, docile, and pleased with his lot in life. And so I wrote a book about her: *Harriet Tubman: Conductor on the Underground Railroad.*

My next book, *Tituba of Salem Village,* was about Tituba, a slave who was involved in the witchcraft trials in Salem, Massachusetts, in the late seventeenth century.

In addition to these books for children and young people, I have written novels and short stories for adults.

Though I plan to write more books about the African slave trade and slavery in the United States, I dislike doing the necessary research for books that involve the history of another era. It seems to me that the necessity for accuracy of details, the constant checking of the facts, serves as a kind of cage which holds the imagination captive.

Fortunately I live in a very old house. And the house itself with its fireplaces, and Dutch oven, and small-paned windows, is a constant reminder of another way of life. It is like a realistic stage set designed for a time when candles were the only source of light and fireplaces were the only source of heat —and it helps me recapture the past.

———

Ann Lane married George D. Petry in 1938 and they have a daughter, Elisabeth Ann.

During the year she lived in New York following her marriage, Ann Petry worked as advertising salesman and writer for *Amsterdam News* and as a reporter and woman's page editor for *People's Voice.* She is a member of P.E.N., of Screen Writers Guild, of Writers Guild of America West, and of Authors Guild, Authors League of America, for which she served as secretary in 1960.

Mrs. Petry received a Houghton Mifflin literary fellowship in 1945, for her first novel, *The Street.*

SELECTED WORKS: The Drugstore Cat, 1949; Harriet Tubman; Conductor on the Underground Railroad, 1955; Tituba of Salem Village, 1964.

ABOUT: Author's and Writer's Who's Who, 1963; Cherry, Gwendolyn and others. Portraits in Color; Contemporary Authors, Vol. 7-8; Current Biography Yearbook 1946; Richardson, Ben Albert. Great American Negroes; Twentieth Century Authors (First Supplement), 1955; Warfel, Harry Redcay. American Novelists of Today; Who's Who in America, 1970-71; Who's Who of American Women, 1970-71; Horn Book April 1965; New York Herald Tribune Book Review August 16, 1953; Opportunity Spring 1946; PM March 3, 1946; The Writer July 1948.

K. M. PEYTON
August 2, 1929-

AUTHOR OF *Thunder in the Sky,* etc.

Autobiographical sketch of Kathleen Wendy Herald Peyton:

I NEVER came to the point of deciding to be a writer, because I have always written books since I was physically able to push a pen. I had written six or seven full-length books before I had the first one published at the age of fifteen. But it never occurred to me that writing was a profession: I wanted to be a painter, and went to art school (in Manchester) and took my teacher's diploma. My first job was teaching art at Northampton High School.

I had married a fellow art student who had the wanderlust, but no money. We set out on our honeymoon in a canoe down the Thames estuary and slept out on the beaches and seawalls. Before the honeymoon was over we had lived in Paris, walked through Switzerland, lived in a cave in Cannes, a convent and monastery respectively in Siena and Rome, been to Innsbruck, Venice and Paris again, hitchhiking or walking all the way.

Later we spent a year in Canada, working until we made enough money to be independent, when we made a canoe trip in Ontario, paddling and portaging without seeing

K. Peyton

a living soul for days, and drove across to the Rockies to do a climbing trip. We drove back through the States and got jobs worm-picking, baby-sitting and working in a bowling alley and sausage factory before we sold the car and went home, via New York. In New York we stayed ten days on a hundred and fifty dollars and saw everything a good tourist should, although it meant walking everywhere and half starving.

Home again and having to work within reach of London, we decided to live on the Essex coast and try sailing. This led to many adventures, through inexperience in difficult sailing waters, which were later to provide plenty of material for books. On one occasion we were taken off our disabled gaff-cutter by a steamer. It was midnight with a full gale blowing, and we had our two daughters with us, then aged three and four. On another occasion in mid-Channel, becalmed thirty miles from land, we were all but run down by a Dutch coaster.

Fortunately writing, for me, has always been my favourite way of enjoying myself, and my husband being what he is I have never lacked for material to draw on. We now, five boats since our first dinghy, own an eleven-ton yawl in which we go abroad every summer and sail quite often in the winter—on the last occasion having to break the ice the last two hundred yards in our home creek to get her back in her mud-berth.

Windfall, The Maplin Bird, The Plan for Birdsmarsh and *Thunder in the Sky* are all based on our home area and sailing grounds. The story of the lifesaving suit in *The Plan for Birdsmarsh* is based on the experiences of a friend who invented a similar suit and tested it from our boat. He actually swam to France and back in his, without a boat to accompany him, but when the tide turned off Dover and he couldn't make shore he had to take refuge on one of the buoys marking the Goodwin Sands, where he had to sit for six hours being seasick.

Thunder in the Sky was written after we had listened to the old barge skippers chatting in the local pub. They had carried supplies over to France in the 1914-18 war in the barges, several of which are still sailing off Essex and Kent. We sailed the same route for our next holiday and did the necessary research for the story.

The books about riding are also based on our own interests, as we have three ponies, a New Forest, a Welsh and a half Arab. A good deal of the material for *Fly-by-Night* was provided by our own efforts to break in Cracker, the New Forest pony, and what has happened since is more than enough to provide a sequel, should I ever get around to writing it! Our eldest daughter, Hilary, now twelve, goes hunting on the Welsh pony, Jacko, who is a terrific goer, and when she comes home I, like Russell in *Flambards,* want to know all about it.

We live in an old farm cottage in a village forty miles from London, our boat moored in a creek ten minutes walk away, the ponies grazing in a field next door. We draw, write, charter our boat and take photographs for a living—and feel that it is a very good arrangement!

———

Kathleen Herald Peyton was born in Birmingham and lived in the suburbs of London until she was seventeen. She studied for a year at Kingston-upon-Thames School of Art and then for four years at Manchester School of Art, when her father, director of an engineering firm, moved north in his job. She received her Art Teachers Diploma in 1952 and taught at Northampton High School, 1952-1955.

Before her marriage in 1950, Mrs. Peyton had published several books under her maiden name of Kathleen Herald. One of these, *Sabre the Horse from the Sea,* she wrote when she was fifteen.

K. M. Peyton was originally the pseudonym for Kathleen Peyton and her husband and coauthor Michael Peyton, but Michael Peyton has not collaborated since *Sea Fever.*

The Plan for Birdsmarsh was a runner-up for the Carnegie Medal in 1965. *Thunder in the Sky* and *Flambards* were recommended for the Carnegie Medal in 1966 and 1967 respectively. *The Maplin Bird* was an Honor Book in the New York *Herald Tribune* Children's Spring Book Festival in 1965. *The Edge of the Cloud* won the Carnegie Medal for 1969 and *Flambards in Summer* was a runner-up.

SELECTED WORKS: Sea Fever (Windfall), 1963; The Maplin Bird, 1965; The Plan for Birdsmarsh, 1966; Thunder in the Sky, 1967; Flambards, 1968; The Edge of the Cloud, 1970; Flambards in Summer, 1970.

"JOAN PHIPSON"

November 16, 1912-

AUTHOR OF *The Family Conspiracy,* etc.

Autobiographical sketch of Joan Margaret Fitzhardinge, who writes under the pen name of "Joan Phipson":

PERHAPS reading and writing are two sides of the same coin, especially for an only child never long enough in one place for her first ten years of life to send down roots or make lasting friends. I was born in Sydney, Australia, christened in England, went to my first school in India, my second in England, and my third and last back in Australia. During the last lap I was twice plucked away from beneficial school routine to go romping 'round Europe with my mother. My constants were reading and, for some unexplained reason, a devotion to animals and the countryside. The devotion remains. The reading, stimulated by a more than usual variety of experiences, tended to drift with fantasy and imagined stories which, in time, got themselves put into words. Perhaps this was how I began. Animals and children somehow go together, and when I wrote my first book, *Good Luck to the Rider,* I tried to pass on my delight in horses by describing what I thought would be the loveliest thing that could happen to a small girl with the same inclinations as my own. By the time I wrote it I was already married with two children, a girl and a boy. In the meantime I had been a typist (mainly in London), a school librarian and painter in a very small way, and an advertising copywriter.

I began living in the country from this time on, and doing the usual things that a country housewife does, but with rather less than normal skill. And my husband raised sheep and sold the wool, and raised cattle and sold the beef (on the hoof, as they say). This pleasant way of life we still pursue, though the children are grown up and at home rather less than they used to be. The background that I have known for so long has been the setting for most of my books. The children in them are not my own, but a lot of their thoughts and feelings and wishes were once mine.

When I had written all I wanted to about children living on what you call a ranch and we call a station, or property, I wrote about the children living in a little country town like ours. This book was *Birkin*. The first incident in the book was a true one.

When we bought a small sailing boat to sail about the coast of New South Wales, I wrote the book called *Cross Currents*. And in this way I have tried, as far as I am able, to transform the experiences I have had into something that children will enjoy. I have tried to be a middleman, turning the raw material on one side of me into something that will give pleasure, and perhaps occasionally more than pleasure, on the other. It seems that I am really trying to be a silkworm.

———

"Joan Phipson" is married to Colin Fitzhardinge. They have a daughter, Anna, and a son, Guy.

She has twice received the Children's Book Council of Australia Book of the Year Award: in 1953 for *Good Luck to the Rider* and in 1963 for *The Family Conspiracy*, which also received the New York *Herald Tribune* Children's Spring Book Festival Award in 1964. *The Boundary Riders* received the Boys' Clubs of America Junior Book Award for 1964.

SELECTED WORKS: The Boundary Riders, 1963; The Family Conspiracy, 1964; Threat to the Barkers, 1965; Birkin, 1966; Cross Currents, 1966; Good Luck to the Rider, 1968; The Haunted Night, 1970.

ABOUT: Contemporary Authors, Vol. 15-16; Who's Who of American Women, 1970-71.

CELESTINO PIATTI

January 5, 1922-

AUTHOR AND ILLUSTRATOR OF *The Happy Owls*, etc.

Biographical sketch of Celestino Piatti:

CELESTINO PIATTI was born in Switzerland in a small village near Zurich. In 1937 he attended the School for Industrial Arts in Zurich and was apprenticed in the graphic arts from 1938 to 1942, teaching commercial

Celestino Piatti: *sel les TEE noh pee AH tee*

CELESTINO PIATTI

art with Gebrueder Fretz AG. After military service and four years doing commercial art for Fritz Bühler in Basel, he opened his own studio, specializing in posters for competitions, cultural activities, commerce, and industry. He entered exhibits all over the world, winning the poster competition for the Foire Internationale de Lyon in 1959 and the Kieler Woche in Germany in 1961.

In 1961 he began to do paperback covers for Deutscher Taschenbuch Verlag in Munich, designing more than six hundred covers for them. He decided, after two years of designing covers, to illustrate children's books, beginning with *The Happy Owls*. It was so successful that it was published in Germany, the United States, Sweden, Denmark, Japan, Greece, France, and Italy. In 1964 a television film, "Piatti-Owls" was produced, and is now in the collection of films in the Museum of Modern Art in New York. After *Celestino Piatti's Animal ABC*, Piatti illustrated *The Nock Family Circus*, written by Ursula Huber, a Swiss journalist who had traveled with the Nock circus as a tutor for the children of the family. He then illustrated *Christmas Eve* and *The Golden Apple*.

Celestino Piatti is married and lives in Basel.

SELECTED WORKS WRITTEN AND ILLUSTRATED: The Happy Owls, 1964; Celestino Piatti's Animal ABC, 1966.

SELECTED WORKS ILLUSTRATED: The Nock Family Circus, by Ursula Huber, 1968; The Holy Night, by Aurel von Jacken, 1968; The Golden Apple by Max Bolliger, 1970.

ABOUT: Hürlimann, Bettina. Picture Book World; Kingman, Lee and others, comps. Illustrators of Children's Books, 1957-1966; Advertising Production Journal April 1968; Graphis No. 66, 1956; No. 115, 1964.

BARBARA LEONIE PICARD
December 4, 1917-

AUTHOR OF *One Is One,* etc.

Autobiographical sketch of Barbara Leonie Picard:

I WAS born of mixed German-Venezuelan and French parentage, at Richmond, Surrey, England, leaving there at the age of three for Sussex. Since then my home has been in one part or another of Sussex. I was educated at boarding school, at St. Katherine's School, Wantage, Berkshire. I am unmarried and my life has been uneventful—which is as I would wish it to be.

I believe I have always wanted to write. I remember, when I was about nine or ten, editing—and inflicting on my long-suffering family—several issues of a weekly magazine. Each issue was limited to a single copy written in an exercise book; and every feature in the magazine—including a readers' competition, a serial, and the illustrations—were solely the work of the editor.

I may always have wanted to write, but I never intended to write children's books, and I became a children's author only by accident. I have always been interested in language, mythology, and all manifestations of folk culture; and in modern literature I have a particular affection for the original fairy tale, whether written after the style of the old traditional models or not, so long as it is of high literary merit, as typified by the masterpieces of Hans Andersen and Oscar Wilde.

To my regret, I had never been able to find enough stories of this genre, and towards the end of the 1939-1945 war, it occurred to me to try my hand at writing a few for my own amusement and as a means of passing the time between air raid alarms on my weekly "fire-watching" night. I decided upon four stories, each based on some theme connected with one of the four elements, fire, water, earth and air.

These first stories more than served their purpose. They not only occupied the pauses between air raid warnings very satisfactorily; they also gave me a great deal of pleasure in the writing, and I was even able to enjoy reading them back, as though they had been the work of someone else.

My original intention of only four stories was soon abandoned, and even when the war was over and fire-watching was no longer a necessity, I still found entertainment in writing a story now and then. Eventually it occurred to me that others might like to share in this entertainment. In 1947 I had a story broadcast for the first time: it was followed by others. I sent a number of stories to the Oxford University Press, and in 1949 my first collection of fairy tales, *The Mermaid and the Simpleton,* was published.

It was reviewed with astonishing kindness, and the Oxford University Press asked me to make a retelling of the *Odyssey* for their collection of Children's Classics. This also was well received, and to my great surprise I found myself a children's author. Two further collections of fairy tales followed the first, and *The Odyssey of Homer* was succeeded by a number of retellings of myths and legends of many lands; and then, in 1956, my first full-length novel for children, *Ransom for a Knight,* appeared.

———

Barbara Leonie Picard's many other interests include comparative religion, archaeology, history, primitive and Oriental music, languages, all kinds of animals not even excluding slugs and mosquitoes, the theater, opera, embroidery, and Japanese prints. She claims one serious dislike: intolerance.

One Is One was a runner-up for the Carnegie Medal in 1965.

SELECTED WORKS: Ransom for a Knight, 1956; The Lady of the Linden Tree, 1962; Lost John, 1963; The Faun and the Woodcutter's Daughter, 1964; The Goldfinch Garden, 1965; Celtic Tales, 1965; The Young Pretenders, 1966; One Is One, 1966.

ABOUT: Author's and Writer's Who's Who, 1963: Contemporary Authors, Vol. 7-8.

Picard: *PIC ard*

MADELEINE POLLAND
May 31, 1918-

AUTHOR OF *Children of the Red King*, etc.

Autobiographical sketch of Madeleine Angela Cahill Polland:

IT always pleases me when people ask me what type of books I write, to say that I specialise in ghost stories. This naturally causes raised eyebrows, as none of my books appear to be conventionally of this type.

What I am really referring to is my preoccupation, since I was a very small child, with the feet that have walked before mine—in effect with history from the angle that it is concerned exactly as is the present, simply with people. When I could little more than read, I could be found weeping over tombstones whose legends told of tragedy or early death, my mind weaving the details of some long-gone loss. As I grew older, and began to read more, and to study history for myself, this obsession grew, and with it some faculty to sense the past in certain places or concerning certain people.

It is this obsession that has written all of my historical books, although some of them may have taken a great many years to creep from my first interest to the moment at which they have turned themselves into words.

Often, I think, it is a disappointment to people who ask me when I started to write that I cannot tell them of any fierce early enthusiasm or youthful efforts with the pen. It seems almost as if I spent my childhood and my youth absorbing all the material that was one day, on the smallest provocation, to burst out into years of writing.

I had arrived in my life at the restless stage when my two children were at school, and I had begun to feel the need of something to do, both to express myself and occupy my time. Quite by chance I happened on a friend I had not seen for some years, and she had entered publishing. I spoke to her of my urge to do something, and "Go home," she said, and "write a book."

When I had stopped laughing, I did exactly that, and *The Children of the Red King* was published. It was as if some damned-up stream was loosed, and all these characters

of history who had lain bothering my brain for years came marching forth, with such certainty that often I would feel a rooted belief that I was more than writing a book as the result of much research. I *knew* the things that had occurred.

All this may possibly be due to my Celtic blood, for although I live in England and have done for the greater part of my life, I am Irish born, and my family is recorded in the same piece of land in the west of Ireland as far back as the times when the Vikings raided up along that coast.

My family came to England when I was four, and I grew up in the same county in which I am living now, until the war came, and my three brothers and I all joined the Services. I was in Ground Control Radar on the south coast of England, and it was while I was still a WAAF, towards the end of the war, that I met my husband, who is also Irish.

We married just after the war was over, and lived first in London, where we had a son and a daughter. A few years back, we moved out into the country in Hertfordshire, some miles across the country from where I grew up, and where as a child I wept above my tombstones.

Mr. Polland is a Chartered Accountant, and has also written in his own field, Charlotte my daughter is nineteen and married, with a very very small son called Christian, and my own son Fergus is seventeen, somewhere far above my head, and already far more clever with words than I have ever been.

Madeleine Cahill married Arthur Joseph Polland in 1946. Mrs. Polland has been an assistant librarian in the public library at Letchworth, England. Two of her works, *Children of the Red King* and *Beorn the Proud*, were honor books in the New York *Herald Tribune* Children's Spring Book Festivals, in 1961 and 1962 respectively.

SELECTED WORKS: Children of the Red King, 1961; Beorn the Proud, 1962; The White Twilight, 1962; The Queen's Blessing, 1964; Deirdre, 1967; To Tell My People, 1968; Stranger in the Hills, 1969; Shattered Summer, 1970.

ABOUT: Contemporary Authors, Vol. 5-6.

SHEENA PORTER

September 19, 1935-

AUTHOR OF *Nordy Bank*, etc.

Autobiographical sketch of Sheena Porter Lane:

SHEENA, spelt so, is a Scottish name, but I am plain Midlands English; I was named after the daughter of the Scottish doctor who brought me into the world, simply because I was meant to be a boy. There was no girl's name in readiness for me, and all the little garments were blue!

So I grew up wild: short hair, trousers, climbing trees, tramping the countryside, very much more at home outdoors than in, certainly more boyish than girlish, anyway. But I found to my dismay that I couldn't be a farmer and I couldn't be a forestry worker, and so began work in a public library, for the peculiar reason that I liked reading! That was in 1954, and I soon found that the only books that I had time to read thereafter, were textbooks on librarianship.

By 1958 I had discovered that library work with children was what pleased me

SHEENA PORTER

most, and was very happy in it, but 1960 was my truly fortunate year.

Although an avid reader of children's literature, I had never thought of writing a book myself. In 1960, I met a well-known children's author and the editor of the Children's Books Department of the Oxford University Press, quite by chance, while on holiday in the north of England. I was rather overfull of ideas as to how I thought children's books *ought* to be written, and they tactfully suggested that I might try to put my ideas into practice, instead of merely criticising the work of others.

I did try, very hard, with *The Bronze Chrysanthemum,* and found that it wasn't quite as easy as I had thought it was! No one was more surprised than I when it was accepted for publication, in 1961.

For the next three years and three books, I continued to work full time: for six months on the editorial side of the Children's Books Department of the Oxford University Press, the rest of the time in children's library work. Then, feeling the need for more leisure I retired myself, tried to live on my earnings as a writer, and almost starved to death! I began to drift a little, doing various part-time jobs, and gradually losing something of my sense of purpose. So that when I heard that *Nordy Bank* had been awarded the Carnegie Medal for 1964, it was several weeks before I could believe that it was true.

Steadied by this, and also by my marriage to an artist in 1966, I began to feel that I could make some progress again, and wrote *Deerfold* and *The Scapegoat*, with both of which I was reasonably satisfied.

I am settled now in Shrewsbury, a town facing towards the countryside I love, the borderlands of Wales, and with the birth of our daughter, Katharine, in 1968, look forward very much to that process usually described as "having one's sympathies enlarged!" I feel sure that better books should be the result of it.

SELECTED WORKS: Nordy Bank, 1964; The Bronze Chrysanthemum, 1965.

ABOUT: The Library Association Record May 1965.

ALICE PROVENSEN

ALICE PROVENSEN
August 14, 1918-
and
MARTIN PROVENSEN
July 10, 1916-

ILLUSTRATORS OF *The Charge of the Light Brigade*, etc.

Biographical sketch of Alice and Martin Provensen:

THE lives of Alice and Martin Provensen almost touched at many points before they finally met. Both were born in Chicago and grew up loving books and book illustration. Each decided at an early age to make beautiful books. They both won scholarships to the Art Institute of Chicago. Later they both transferred to the University of California and spent a year there, Alice in Los Angeles and Martin in Berkeley. Alice went to New York and studied for a while at the Art Students League. Returning to California, she began to work for Walter Lantz Studios. Martin worked for five years for Walt Disney on such films as *Fantasia* and *Dumbo*. During his three and a half years in the Navy he worked on training movies. While working on a film for the Navy on the Universal lot with Lantz he and Alice discovered each other. They were married in Washington, D.C., in 1944.

MARTIN PROVENSEN

In 1945 the Provensens moved to New York and began to illustrate children's books together. Their first book was *The Fireside Book of Folk Songs*, with five hundred illustrations. Following it were *The Fireside Cookbook, The Golden Mother Goose*, and then *Animal Fair*, which they wrote as well as illustrated.

After traveling throughout Europe in 1950 collecting material for illustrations, they returned to the United States, bought a farm near Staatsburg, New York, and converted the barn into a studio. In 1952 they illustrated *The Golden Bible: The New*

Testament, taking their models from color photographs of the Holy Land and from illuminated manuscripts. Many books followed, including their own favorite, *The Iliad and the Odyssey.* For this they traveled to Greece for three months in 1954, filling sketchbook after sketchbook with what the eye could see and the camera could not.

Karen's Opposites, published in 1963, was both written and illustrated by them. Their own daughter Karen, then four years old, is the Karen of the story about two little girls, one dark and one light, one shouting and one whispering, doing exactly opposite things. The book won honorable mention in the New York *Herald Tribune* Children's Spring Book Festival.

The Provensens work together on all their illustrations, much as the medieval scribes and scriveners did, passing the drawings back and forth between them, adding this and taking out that, until each is satisfied. They discard sketch after sketch, until they finally obtain the effect they feel will most delight the young eye. They completed a set of illustrations for *The Charge of the Light Brigade* and then, unhappy with its complexity, redid the whole book. This stern self-criticism results in a deceptively easy, spontaneous-looking style that has spawned a host of imitators in art school circles. Their work has received many awards, including honors from the American Institute of Graphic Arts and the Society of Illustrators. They won a National Offset Lithography Competition prize and their books have appeared frequently on the New York *Times* lists of best-illustrated books.

The farm supplies many models for their work: cows, cats, horses, lambs. Their daughter, who shares their art enthusiasm, contributes her criticism to their work and her drawings hang in the Provensen studio among those of her parents.

"Our profession is drawing and painting," say the Provensens. "Our hobbies are drawing and painting. Our enthusiasms are drawing and painting. Outside of that, our interests are doing it better."

SELECTED WORKS ILLUSTRATED: The Fireside Book of Folk Songs, by Margaret Bradford Boni, 1947; The Golden Mother Goose, 1948; The Golden Bible for Children: New Testament, 1953; The Golden Treasury of Myths and Legends, by Ann Terry White, 1959; Ten Great Plays, by William Shakespeare, 1962; The Charge of the Light Brigade, by Alfred Tennyson, 1964; Aesop's Fables, 1965; Tales from the Ballet, by Louis Untermeyer, 1968; The Golden Book of Fun and Nonsense, by Louis Untermeyer, 1970.

SELECTED WORKS WRITTEN AND ILLUSTRATED: Animal Fair, 1952; Karen's Curiosity, 1963; Karen's Opposites, 1963; What Is a Color? 1967; Who's in the Egg? 1970.

ABOUT: Hürlimann, Bettina. Picture Book World; Kingman, Lee and others, comps. Illustrators of Children's Books: 1957-1966; Viguers, Ruth Hill and others, comps. Illustrators of Children's Books: 1946-1956; Who's Who in Graphic Art, 1962; American Artist December 1959; Famous Artists Magazine, 1961; Publishers' Weekly July 13, 1964.

ABOUT ALICE PROVENSEN: Who's Who of American Women, 1970-71.

ANNE RAND

AUTHOR OF *Did a Bear Just Walk There?* etc.

Autobiographical sketch of Anne Binkley Rand Ozbekhan:

THE Skokie marsh and my daughter, Catherine, are probably what started me writing children's books. The Skokie (an Indian name for marsh) lies about twenty miles north of Chicago and bordered what, in those days, was the village I grew up in. Today that village is a total suburb, and the swamp has been invaded by subdivision developments or appropriated by park districts which have largely tamed its former wildness. When I was a child the Skokie was a splendid place for escaping "civilization" and for finding things, so I spent a lot of time there. A marsh is always full of mysteries: small, furtive animals, strange plants, wild birds, and little ponds hidden among reeds that change dramatically with the season—tadpoles become frogs, eggs turn into fish, and the ponds that are soupy warm in the summer glaze with ice in late fall and finally freeze so solid in winter that you are amazed when the spring thaw reveals them to be once again bustling with insect and animal life. A swamp also spices discovery with danger such as snakes—in this case

Ann Rand

rattlers—and bogs. The combination is irresistible.

Through my daughter I relived the wonder and excitement of a child's finding out about the world. Most of the children's books I've written have to do with this experience, one of course that all children have. And even animals. Today I watch our puppy suddenly and excitedly discover the existence of butterflies, and last week he found out that round objects roll. The first children's book I wrote is about the child's discovery of "things" and the pride he takes in what he knows. The book was also, in another sense, a discovery for me, a visual or graphic one, thanks to the beauty and originality of the illustrations that Catherine's father made for it. After the initial awareness and identification of things, you inevitably become concerned with the child's experience of the relation among things and the association, both actual and poetic, that he perceives between various kinds of objects and events. I know "an ant can carry a load on his back as big as a berry." It seems to me that children begin quite early to think metaphorically and to understand by analogy as well as by descriptive definition. If you drop a ball of string "perhaps it will crawl like a snake through the grass" or "some words are gay and bright and full of light like tinsel and silver and sparkle and spin." In this area

the writer of children's books hopes to serve as a stimulus to the child's imagination and to his enthusiasm for discovery—an enthusiasm one wishes could, in all of us, be perpetually renewed.

Of course it's also fun to tell stories. I have written about the adventures of a mouse, of a river, a city child who wants to keep a horse in his apartment, and a lonely little number which, naturally, had to be 1.

Catherine is now fifteen, the remains of the marsh are some two thousand miles away, and I am writing adult novels, yet I also continue to write children's books and hope that I always will.

————

Anne Rand studied at the University of Chicago, the University of California and took her B.S. from the Illinois Institute of Technology in 1946, while Mies van der Rohe was the head of the Department of Architecture. She married Paul Rand in 1949. They were later divorced, and in 1960 she married Hasan Ozbekhan. She likes to travel and has had long stays in Mexico and Europe. The recipient of a number of awards, she has written articles about architecture and design, and novels for adults. In some of her children's books she spells her name Ann.

SELECTED WORKS: I Know a Lot of Things, 1956; Sparkle and Spin, 1957; Umbrellas, Hats, and Wheels, 1961; Edward and the Horse, 1961; Little I, 1962; So Small, 1962; Did a Bear Just Walk There? 1966; Listen, Listen, 1970.

ABOUT: Who's Who of American Women, 1968-69; Library Journal February 1, 1968.

PAUL RAND
August 15, 1914-

ILLUSTRATOR OF *I Know a Lot of Things*, etc.

Autobiographical sketch of Paul Rand:

I WAS born, an identical twin, in Brooklyn, New York. My brother and I were interested in both music and art—but he more in music and I more in art. I can never remember a time when I didn't draw. My earliest improvised drawing board was a kitchen chair, after which I graduated to a low shelf under the fish counter in my father's grocery store.

There I also lettered amateurish signs advertising his wares and even tried to design for his front window a monogram that would equal, or excel, that of the A & P. Mostly, however, I spent my time copying whatever paintings or illustrations came my way. The Sunday color gravure section of the old New York *World* was a particularly rich source and my favorite subjects were pretty girls with "the skin you love to touch," the cowboys and Indians of Frederic Remington and Walter Ufer, and the illustrations of J. C. Leyendecker. I also have vivid memories of the Cavalier of Frans Hals, which I discovered reproduced in a local hat store window.

The most exciting presents I received as a child were pens, papers, crayons, paints—and, eventually, a small drafting table.

I studied art nights at Pratt Institute in Brooklyn, while commuting days to high school in Manhattan. There I won the three art awards offered in the public schools: the Alexander Medal, the St. Gaudens Medal and the School Art League Scholarship to Parsons School of Design. Later I also studied at the Art Students League, under George Grosz.

While the art training available in the USA in the 1930s was pretty much limited to the academic styles of drawing and the me-chanics of rendering and airbrushing, the art that really excited me was the work being done in Europe, as an outgrowth of the German Bauhaus. So, I spent weekends in the New York Public Library studying foreign magazines, and used what little money I had to buy books and prints and periodicals (particularly *Gebrauchsgraphik*) from Europe.

There were very few jobs available during those depression years, but I managed to get into one of the better small design studios (George Switzer) for fifteen dollars a week. When there was not enough money to pay me that, I worked there for nothing.

At twenty-three I became art director of *Esquire Magazine's* New York office and also of *Apparel Arts Magazine*, and a few years later, art director of an advertising agency.

Since 1954, I have had my own studio, designing everything from printed material, trademarks, packaging and signs to exhibitions, furniture and fabrics. I also paint and have written books and articles on design. I've taught at Pratt Institute and since 1954, have been a professor at Yale University's School of Art and Architecture.

In 1956, I illustrated my first children's book, *I Know a Lot of Things*. I found this a wonderful change from so-called commercial work, and yet I approach book illustration in exactly the same way as graphic design or painting. I am interested in designing the total page, as a unit, rather than in doing "illustrations," per se. Typography is as important to me as drawing, or form, or color or space. It seems to me that the book designer's job is to complement the text, by adding another dimension to the author's words through the use of humor and the visually unexpected. But, most of all, I think it is his responsibility to design pages that are beautiful and exciting in themselves—and fun to look at—with or without the text.

Paul Rand has received numerous awards, including the Gold Medal of the American Institute of Graphic Arts (1966) and a citation from the Philadelphia College of Art (1962). Among other organizations, he is a member of Alliance Graphique International, Paris, and a Fellow of the Royal

Society of Arts, London. He is a former Ful-
bright scholarship juror and an Honorary
Professor of Tama University, Tokyo. In
May of 1970 a one-man show of his work
was held at the IBM Gallery in New York.
His books have twice been named among
the ten best-illustrated of the year by the
New York *Times Book Review*, children's
section: *I Know a Lot of Things*, in 1956 and
Sparkle and Spin, in 1957. *I Know a Lot of
Things* was featured in the short film, *The
Lively Art of Picture Books*.

Paul Rand's books and articles on design
for adults have been published in the United
States and in England. He was formerly married to Anne Rand, with whom he collaborated on picture books. They have a daughter, Catherine.

SELECTED WORKS ILLUSTRATED: I Know a
Lot of Things, by Ann Rand 1956; Sparkle and
Spin, by Ann Rand 1957; Little 1, by Ann Rand,
1962; Listen, Listen, by Ann Rand, 1970.

ABOUT: Contemporary Authors, Vol. 23-24;
Hürlimann, Bettina. Picture Book World; Kame-
kura, Yusaku. Paul Rand; His Work from 1946
to 1958; Kingman, Lee and others, comps. Illustrators of Children's Books: 1957-1966; Viguers,
Ruth Hill and others, comps. Illustrators of Children's Books, 1946-1956; Who's Who in America, 1970-71; Who's Who in American Art, 1970;
Print January 1969.

"ROBERT RANDALL"

See *Silverberg, Robert*

ELLEN RASKIN

March 13, 1928-

AUTHOR AND ILLUSTRATOR OF *Nothing Ever
Happens on My Block*, etc.

Autobiographical sketch of Ellen Raskin:

AT age four I decided to become a musician. I practised hours a day for the next
five years until the finance company came
for the piano. Then, determined to become
a writer, I filled composition book after book
with a labored hand. During this time I was
drawing, but that was too much fun to take
seriously. Not until my second year at the
University of Wisconsin did I consider becoming an artist. Now I have a book of songs

behind me which was a delight to do. I've
also written five books. That, too, was fun.
It is the illustrations that are hard work.

I was born in Milwaukee, Wisconsin, spent
my college years at Madison and in 1949
moved to New York City where I took a
paste-up job in a small art studio to learn
the mechanics of art production. With an
optimism given only to youth I prepared a
portfolio of art samples, quit my job with
only a week's salary in the bank, and tried
my luck as a free-lance illustrator. The first
day was spent making appointments with
art directors. The second day I started on
my rounds and picked up five assignments:
three book jackets and two record album
covers.

Ten years later, after completing my one-
thousandth book jacket, I again questioned
my position. All my efforts were spent inter-
preting other writers' ideas, never my own.
I made a hurried sketch for a book I called
Nothing Ever Happens on My Block and
submitted it to Jean Karl of Atheneum. At
the same time Alex Gotfryd, art director of
Doubleday, heard that I was writing music
and asked to see it. I notated four of my
melodies with piano accompaniment and
added a few illustrations. Within a week I
received contracts for my first two children's
books. *Nothing Ever Happens on My Block*

won the *Herald Tribune* Spring Book Festival Award for the best picture book of 1966, and *Songs of Innocence* was chosen by the American Institute of Graphic Arts as one of the Fifty Books of the Year 1966.

I have given up free-lance illustration entirely now, and devote myself only to children's books (and my husband Dennis Flanagan, editor of *Scientific American* magazine, and my daughter Susan Kuhlman). I write one book a year and illustrate several others. My book jacket experience has taught me the many various illustrative techniques I use to make each book a special one unto itself. I'm not quite sure where my story ideas come from. I begin with a definite idea to teach: stop feeling sorry for yourself and look about you (*Nothing Ever Happens on My Block*), wearing glasses can be an advantage (*Spectacles*), family relationships (*Ghost in a Four-Room Apartment*), elementary logic (*And It Rained*). Somehow, by the time my book is completed, the message has become secondary and I end up with a humorous book. Which pleases me, really. Perhaps my true ambition is to be a comedienne. After all, when one loses a piano at age nine nothing can be very tragic after that.

Ellen Raskin writes, illustrates, designs, and does the mechanical preparation for most of her books. She found a happy combination for her talents in Blake's *Songs of Innocence*, setting the poems to music and illustrating them with woodcuts. In addition to those she mentions, Ellen Raskin has received awards from the Society of Illustrators, the American Institute of Graphic Arts, the Art Directors Clubs of New York and Detroit, and the Type Directors Club.

SELECTED WORKS WRITTEN AND ILLUSTRATED: Nothing Ever Happens on My Block, 1966; Silly Songs and Sad, 1967; Spectacles, 1968; Ghost in a Four-Room Apartment, 1969; And It Rained, 1969; A & The, 1970.

SELECTED WORKS ILLUSTRATED: Songs of Innocence, by William Blake, 1966; A Paper Zoo, by Renée Karol Weiss, 1968; Come Along! by Rebecca Caudill, 1969; Goblin Market, by Christina Rossetti, 1970.

ABOUT: Contemporary Authors, Vol. 23-24; Hopkins, Lee Bennett. Books Are by People; Kingman, Lee and others, comps. Illustrators of Children's Books: 1957-1966.

ANTHONY RAVIELLI

July 1, 1916-

AUTHOR AND ILLUSTRATOR OF *Wonders of the Human Body,* etc.

Autobiographical sketch of Anthony Ravielli:

MY first artistic works were rendered, literally, on the sidewalks of New York. Long before I was old enough to go to school, I remember covering the streets with chalk-drawings of fiery dragons, brave knights and vivid battle scenes to the amused amazement of gathering crowds.

As I look back, expressing myself artistically has always been a way of life. I was fortunate to be born into a family that regarded drawing as the natural thing to do. My father, a marine engineer by training and a wood carver by inclination, created an artistic aura that deeply influenced my brothers, my sisters and me. So it was more by design than by accident that we all chose art as a career.

Although I now make my home in Connecticut, I was born, raised and educated in New York City. After attending Textile High School, I continued my art studies at Cooper Union and the Art Students League. My professional career began while I was still attending school. Starting as a part-time commercial artist and portrait painter, I became, upon graduation, a full-time illustrator and art director. World War II interrupted my career only in a formal sense, for during three years of service I was assigned to paint instructional murals and visual training aids at various army posts.

When I returned to civilian life, I launched a new career as a science and medical illustrator, a field which has always fascinated me. And it was this specialty that led to, what is to me, the most satisfying of pursuits —writing and illustrating children's books.

My first book, *Wonders of the Human Body,* for example, was originally planned as a conventional anatomy book for adults. For years I had been compiling data which included, among other specimens, an articulated skeleton. As a consequence, my studio became a mecca for my assorted nieces and nephews and their little friends who found

SELECTED WORKS WRITTEN AND ILLUSTRATED: Wonders of the Human Body, 1954; An Adventure in Geometry, 1957; The World Is Round, 1963; The Rise and Fall of the Dinosaurs, 1963; Elephants, the Last of the Land Giants, 1965; From Fins to Hands, 1968.

SELECTED WORKS ILLUSTRATED: Men, Ants & Elephants, by Peter K. Weyl, 1959; Relativity for the Million, by Martin Gardner, 1962; The Human Body, by Isaac Asimov, 1963; The Shape of Intelligence, by H. Chandler Elliott, 1969.

ABOUT: Author's and Writer's Who's Who, 1963; Kingman, Lee and others, comps. Illustrators of Children's Books: 1957-1966; Viguers, Ruth Hill and others, comps. Illustrators of Children's Books: 1946-1956; Who's Who in the East, 1968-69.

MARJORIE KINNAN RAWLINGS

August 8, 1896-December 14, 1953

AUTHOR OF *The Yearling*, etc.

Biographical sketch of Marjorie Kinnan Rawlings Baskin:

MARJORIE KINNAN was born in Washington, D. C., the daughter of Frank R. Kinnan, an attorney in the United States Patent Office, and Ida May (Traphagen) Kinnan. She had happy childhood memories of summers on the family farm in Maryland and of rambles in the country with her father, with whom she was very close.

As a little girl, Marjorie was certain that someday she would be an author. When she was eleven, a two-dollar prize for a short story published in the Washington *Post* confirmed her belief.

When Marjorie Kinnan was seventeen, just after her graduation from Western High School in Washington, D. C., her father died, which she felt as a great loss. Shortly afterwards, her mother moved the family to Madison, Wisconsin. There Marjorie Kinnan spent summers on her grandfather Traphagen's farm and, along with her younger brother, attended the University of Wisconsin. She majored in English, wrote for and helped edit the university literary magazine, and was elected to Phi Beta Kappa in her junior year.

When she graduated, in 1918, she headed for New York City with hopes of a literary career. After typical adventures of a small-

the skeleton exciting yet somewhat mystifying. It was impossible for them to conceive the idea that a similar structure existed within their bodies. I answered their questions about this culprit, the skeleton, that was hiding inside of them, with drawing after drawing and analogy after analogy. Eventually, a picture book evolved. And, it occurred to me, why not for children? They not only have an insatiable curiosity about themselves but are even more inquisitive than adults about the mysteries of nature.

Subsequent books were similarly inspired. *An Adventure in Geometry, The World Is Round, From Fins to Hands,* etc., were the outgrowth of provocative inquiries by children about the wonders of the world around them.

Anthony Ravielli married Georgia Ann Weber in 1954. They have three children, Jane Letizia, Ellen Toni and Anthony Peter. Ravielli's work has been in exhibitions held by the American Institute of Graphic Arts, the National Litho and Offset Printers, and the Society of Illustrators, among others. He has used his facility for drawing the human body in action in a great deal of work for the magazine *Sports Illustrated.*

MARJORIE KINNAN RAWLINGS

town girl in a big city, such as having her money stolen, she went to work on the editorial staff of the National Board of the YWCA.

In 1919, she and her college sweetheart, Charles Rawlings, were married. Not long after, they moved to his home town of Rochester, New York, where she wrote newspaper features and syndicated poetry for housewives. She later expressed the belief that this newspaper experience had taught her the invaluable lesson of writing simply.

Neither she nor her husband was happy with city life and newspaper work. In 1928, they left it behind and bought an orange grove in Cross Creek, in the backwoods of Florida. Here Marjorie Kinnan Rawlings was inspired by the simple people and the natural setting.

"Cracker Chidlings," her first short story from Cross Creek, was sold to *Scribner's Magazine*. Several months later Scribner's bought "Jacob's Ladder." In 1933 another story, "Gal Young Un" won the O. Henry Memorial Award. In the same year, her first novel, *South Moon Under*, was published, a story about the life a man made for himself and his family hiding out in the scrub country to evade revenuers.

So began Marjorie Rawlings's career, which reached its peak with the publication of *The Yearling* in 1938. The idea for a story

about a boy's adventure in the scrub was suggested by Maxwell Perkins, chief editor at Charles Scribner's Sons.

To gather material for her books on the scrub country, Marjorie went into the heart of it and learned to know the families. She gathered material from oldtimers' tales, and was taken along on bear hunts. When she was planning *The Yearling*, the story seemed to grow naturally as she gathered material in the very setting she wanted for the boy's home. At last she took her notes to a cabin in Banner Elk, North Carolina, where, free of interruptions, she set to writing this book with her characteristic care, but with steadily mounting delight. It went well from the beginning, and needed little revision.

The Yearling was published by Scribner's in 1938, with drawings by Edward Shenton. The reset edition of 1961 has color illustrations by N. C. Wyeth. Although basically regional, the story and its central characters, Jody and his pet deer, have universal appeal. The book has been translated into thirteen languages, was a Book-of-the-Month Club selection, and was bought for the movies by Metro-Goldwyn-Mayer. Its author was elected to the National Academy of Arts and Letters in 1938 and received the Pulitzer Prize for it in 1939.

The success of *The Yearling* opened a new life for its author. Her first marriage had ended in divorce, and in 1941 she married Norton Sanford Baskin and moved to St. Augustine with him. Another successful book, *Cross Creek*, published in 1942, was an account of her love of this part of Florida, and told of its real-life people.

Two other books followed, and Marjorie Kinnan Rawlings was working on a biography of the novelist Ellen Glasgow when she died in St. Augustine, in 1953, of a cerebral hemorrhage. She is buried in Antioch Cemetery, near the Florida backcountry she loved so well.

Marjorie Kinnan Rawlings has continued to receive awards posthumously. *The Secret River* was a runner-up for the Newbery Medal for 1956 and *The Yearling* received a Lewis Carroll Shelf Award in 1963.

SELECTED WORKS: The Yearling, 1938; The Secret River, 1955.

ABOUT: Americana Annual 1954; Bigelow, Gordon E. Frontier Eden; the Literary Career of Marjorie Kinnan Rawlings; Current Biography Yearbook 1942; 1954; Gray, James. On Second Thought; Magill, Frank, ed. Cyclopedia of World Authors; Montgomery, Elizabeth Rider. Story Behind Modern Books; Rawlings, Marjorie Kinnan. Cross Creek; Scherman, David Edward and Redlich, Rosemarie. Literary America; Twentieth Century Authors, 1942; Twentieth Century Authors (First Supplement), 1955; Warfel, Harry Redcay. American Novelists of Today; Who's Who in America, 1954-55; Land Winter 1953; New York Times December 16, 1953; New York Times Book Review February 1, 1953; Publishers' Weekly June 29, 1946; October 2, 1948; December 26, 1953; Saturday Review January 3, 1953; Sewanee Review Spring 1965; Wilson Library Bulletin February 1954.

PHILIP REED

January 17, 1908-

ILLUSTRATOR OF *Mother Goose and Nursery Rhymes,* etc.

Biographical sketch of Philip Reed:

PHILIP REED was born in Park Ridge, Illinois, into a family with a high regard for fine books and book production. As a boy he served as a printer's devil for his father, who operated a hand press in the basement of the Reed home, and he soon became familiar with the tools and techniques of printing. Later he studied book design and illustration at the Art Institute of Chicago under Ernst Detterer, one of the most eminent teachers of graphic techniques.

After four years of training at the Institute Reed set up his own printing shop near Barrington, Illinois, in 1930. Because it was his original intention to produce woodcut broadsides, he called his shop the Broadside Press, a name that proved to be inappropriate since few people knew what it meant and since Reed had few opportunities to print broadsides anyway. In fact, most of the jobs that came to the shop in its first years were hack work and privately issued Christmas books, and even such work was

scarce enough to leave him with plenty of time for studying and experimenting.

In 1936 Reed moved his press to Katonah, New York, where he attracted a number of clients with a taste for fine printing. During his three years in the East he produced several quality pieces and also began work on three large woodcut prints to be offered for sale as well as a fine edition of *The Seven Voyages of Sindbad the Sailor.* The Sindbad book, which was illustrated with his woodcuts, was completed after he moved back to Illinois in 1939. The type was set by his brother, John, one of the best compositors and pressmen in the country, who joined him in business during this period.

Back in Illinois the Reed brothers at first operated their press in an abandoned post office building in Park Ridge but moved before the end of 1939 into the Monastery Hill Bindery in Chicago's North Side. At the time of the move the name of the shop was changed from Broadside to Monastery Hill Press, the name it still bears. Closed for a few years in the 1940s while the two brothers went to war—John to the Air Force and Philip to the Graphic Section of Fort Belvoir Engineer School in Virginia, it reopened after the war and attracted clients interested in fine quality work. In 1955 the firm became associated with the A. & R. Roe Company of St. Joseph, Michigan, where the shop is now located.

Reed's *Mother Goose and Nursery Rhymes* was a runner-up for the Caldecott Award in 1964. Many of his books have been listed among the Fifty Books of the Year by the American Institute of Graphic Arts, and his work also has been honored by the Society of Typographic Arts, the Chicago Book Clinic, and other organizations. His woodcuts place him among the foremost living masters of the engraving art, and his works can be seen in collections at the Library of Congress, the Art Institute of Chicago, the Victoria and Albert Museum of London, and at other museums and libraries throughout the world.

Reed is married and the father of three children.

SELECTED WORKS ILLUSTRATED: The Seven Voyages of Sindbad the Sailor, 1939, 1963; A

Christmas Carol, by Charles Dickens, 1941;
Many Moons, by James Thurber, 1958; Mother
Goose and Nursery Rhymes, 1963.

ABOUT: Kingman, Lee and others, comps. Illustrators of Children's Books: 1957-1966; Mahony, Bertha E. and others, comps. Illustrators
of Children's Books: 1744-1945; American Artist May 1948; September 1949; Library Journal
March 15, 1964.

JAMES REEVES

July 1, 1909-

AUTHOR OF *The Cold Flame*, etc.

Autobiographical sketch of James Reeves:

I WAS born at Harrow-on-the-Hill on the
outskirts of London. During World War I my
parents moved to the wooded hills of Buck-
inghamshire, whose scenery filled my imagination from then on. I have always lived
in the south of England and travelled from
time to time in Europe. I married in 1936 and
have three children and two grandchildren.
My life has not been externally eventful. I
was deeply influenced by the books my
mother chose to read to me in childhood,
especially Beatrix Potter, *Alice in Wonderland,* Kipling's *Just So Stories* and Arthur
Ransome's masterpiece, *Old Peter's Russian
Tales.*

I began writing poems about 1920, and
the habit has never left me. I have written
many books of poems and stories for children.
The most important influence here was my
bad eyesight. With the onset of glaucoma
about 1946 I have read nothing myself for
over twenty years. All my reading has been
done for me by others. My own writing has
been done by means of touch-typing, and I
have never read anything I have written, but
I have listened to every word of it. Any
appeal my writing has for children, therefore, is to some extent due to its being written
as much for the ear as for the eye. Everything that does not *sound* right is changed.
My first book of poems for children, *The
Wandering Moon,* was written in 1948, when
I had little to do but sit at the typewriter
and compose verses in my head. After that
followed folk tales and other stories. My job
at that time was that of lecturer at a training college for teachers, following about four-

teen years as a teacher in schools. This work
helped me to find out what appeals to children.

In choosing subjects for stories and poems
I have followed my own interests, which are
largely centred on folklore and folk poetry.
I have edited the uncensored manuscripts of
Cecil Sharp and other folk song collectors,
by which means I have got in touch with the
folk mind of the English-speaking world—
that is, the ordinary people in their childhood state. Real folklore is the property of
both adults and children. It occurs, like all
good literature for children, at the point
where childhood and adulthood meet. I write
for the adult in children and the child in
adults.

I have been much influenced by the
Household Tales of The Brothers Grimm, in
editing a selection from which I came across
the remarkable though brief story, *The Blue
Light.* I wrote a full-length story based on
this, intended for adults. It came out in an
edition for children under the title of *The
Cold Flame.* No publisher would take it on
as an adult novel, but that is what it is.

———

James Reeves attended Stowe School and
Jesus College, Cambridge. He is a critic,
reviewer, and anthologist as well as a poet,

and has contributed to many leading newspapers and magazines. *The Cold Flame* was a runner-up for the Carnegie Medal in 1967.

SELECTED WORKS: The Blackbird in the Lilac, 1959; Exploits of Don Quixote (retold), 1960; The Wandering Moon, 1960; Fables from Aesop, 1961; Sailor Rumbelow and other stories, 1962; The Strange Light, 1966; The Secret Shoemakers and Other Stories (retold), 1967; The Cold Flame, 1969; The Angel and the Donkey, 1970.

ABOUT: Author's and Writer's Who's Who, 1963; Orr, Peter, editor. Poet Speaks.

LESTER DEL REY

See *del Rey, Lester*

RUTH ROBBINS

December 29, 1917-

AUTHOR OF *Baboushka and the Three Kings,* etc.

Biographical sketch of Ruth Robbins Schein:

RUTH ROBBINS was born in Newark, New Jersey, and spent her childhood in that state. She began her professional training at the Pratt Institute in Brooklyn, New York, from which she graduated in 1939, and continued it at the School of Design in Chicago for two years. In 1941 she married Herman Schein, completed her training at the Institute, and took a job as art director for the Public Health Service. In 1944 she moved from there to the Office of Price Administration, where she worked until 1946 when she became a design consultant for the United States Army. She left government work in 1948, and in 1949 moved with her husband to the San Francisco Bay area. During the next several years she worked as a free-lance art director and design consultant for private advertising and industrial clients. Then, in 1957, she and her husband started the Parnassus Press, a children's book publishing house in which she became vice president with particular responsibility for book production, including supervision of design and illustration for each book, selection of paper, and supervision of printing and binding. She also has illustrated many of the books published by Parnassus, and she says

RUTH ROBBINS

that her illustrating and design work has been helped by the fact that she is familiar with all aspects of publishing, including the editorial, and by her experience in rearing her own son, Steven, who taught her that "children respond in many surprising and uninhibited ways to art and drawing in books, giving the artist great freedom and the opportunity to think creatively."

Ruth Robbins's first venture into story writing was an adaptation of the old Russian folk tale, *Baboushka and the Three Kings,* which she prepared because she and her husband were dissatisfied with all available versions of the story. Illustrated by Nicolas Sidjakov, the book won the Caldecott Medal for 1961 and was on the Honor List for the Hans Christian Andersen Medal, 1962. Miss Robbins has since written adaptations of two more stories, *The Emperor and the Drummer Boy,* which is based on an incident in Napoleon's life, and *Harlequin and Mother Goose,* inspired by an early nineteenth-century pantomime. Both were illustrated by Nicholas Sidjakov.

SELECTED WORKS: Baboushka and the Three Kings, 1960; The Emperor and the Drummer Boy, 1962; Harlequin and Mother Goose, 1965.

SELECTED WORKS ILLUSTRATED: Stories California Indians Told, by Anne B. Fisher, 1957; Wild Animals of the Far West, by Adrien Stoutenburg, 1958; A Penny and a Periwinkle, by Josephine Haskell Aldridge, 1961; Ishi, Last of

His Tribe, by Theodora Kroeber, 1964; A Wizard of Earthsea, by Ursula K. Le Guin, 1968.

ABOUT: Kingman, Lee and others, comps. Illustrators of Children's Books: 1957-1966; Who's Who of American Women, 1961-62.

ELIZABETH ROSE

June 30, 1933-

and

GERALD ROSE

July 27, 1935-

AUTHOR AND ILLUSTRATOR OF *Old Winkle and the Seagulls,* etc.

Biographical sketch of Gerald and Elizabeth Jane Pretty Rose, by Elizabeth Rose:

GERALD was born in Hong Kong. His mother was Chinese, his father English. When the Japanese invaded Hong Kong he was interned with his mother and sister at Stanley Camp, a civilian camp peopled by all nationalities. There he stayed for four years.

In 1945 he returned to England and lived in Lowestoft, a fishing town, where he later attended the School of Art. It was there that I met him as I was a student there too.

I decided that I would like to teach young children and went to Saffron Walden College, in Essex. By the time I had finished my training Gerald had moved to London and was studying painting at the Royal Academy Schools, Piccadilly. I was teaching six-year-olds in Tottenham and after a year we were married.

It was while I was teaching that I searched for good picture books to read to the children. I borrowed the best I could find from the library. Gerald was rather rude about some of the illustrations. I asked if he thought he could do any better and he said that he would try if I wrote a story. It was a challenge and had to be accepted.

I wrote *How St. Francis Tamed the Wolf* and the drawings were begun. Every evening and weekend Gerald worked on them. When they were finished he took them to Faber and Faber's himself—they were painted on very large sheets of card and were quite a

Elizabeth Rose.

Gerald Rose.

problem to carry around. The publisher promised to let us know and we waited impatiently for the decision. When the letter of acceptance finally arrived we could hardly contain ourselves. We started working out ideas for our second book.

Later we moved north to Blackpool, with our young son, Martin, and we continued to write and illustrate books while Gerald taught drawing and painting at Blackpool School of Art.

Wuffles Goes to Town was the story of a country dog's adventures in London.

Old Winkle and the Seagulls, which was awarded the Kate Greenaway Medal in 1960, had Lowestoft as its background. Gerald had filled many sketchbooks with drawings and notes of fishermen, trawlers and the fishmarket.

While we were living near Blackpool we were excited by the seaside and the holidaymakers. One stall on the seafront shouted "Hats hats hats!" and another "Jellied eels! Cockles! Whelks!" Hoardings proclaimed "Rock" in letters five feet high. Horse-drawn carriages carried visitors along the seafront and a huge funfair blazed at one end of the promenade. It was a wonderful setting for a story. Eventually *Punch and Judy Carry On* was written in which Punch runs away and tries out all the holiday attractions in the course of his adventures.

Gerald is a keen fisherman and used to go fishing for trout in a river nearby while I sat by the river and watched the water swirling by or walked along the bank to where the river broadened and slowed down. I wondered, as many others have done, where the river had come from and where it was going. Soon we had produced *The Big River* —the story of a river's journey to the sea.

Since then we have produced other books together. Among them are *The Sorcerer's Apprentice, Alexander's Flycycle* and *The Great Oak.* Gerald also illustrates books written by other authors.

Martin is twelve now and we have two other children; Richard is seven and Louise is five. They are our stern critics and see our books in all their early stages.

We live in Maidstone, where Gerald teaches graphic design at Maidstone College of Art. In the garden we keep ducks, geese and white fantail doves. We enjoy trips to the seaside, fishing, swimming and lazing in the garden.

SELECTED WORKS ILLUSTRATED BY GERALD ROSE AND WRITTEN BY ELIZABETH ROSE: How St. Francis Tamed the Wolf, 1959; Wuffles Goes to Town, 1960; Old Winkle and the Seagulls, 1960; The Big River, 1964; St. George and the Fiery Dragon, 1964.

SELECTED WORKS ILLUSTRATED BY GERALD ROSE: Seven Thieves and Seven Stars, by Barbara Ireson, 1961; The Emperor's Oblong Pancake, by Peter Hughes, 1962; The Giant Who Drank from His Shoe, by Léonce Bourliaguet, 1966.

ABOUT GERALD ROSE: Author's and Writer's Who's Who, 1963; Hürlimann, Bettina. Picture Book World; Kingman, Lee and others, comps. Illustrators of Children's Books: 1957-1966.

ABOUT ELIZABETH ROSE: Author's and Writer's Who's Who, 1963; Contemporary Authors, Vol. 7-8.

ABOUT GERALD AND ELIZABETH ROSE: Library Association Record May 1961.

BELLE DORMAN RUGH

June 8, 1908-

AUTHOR OF *Crystal Mountain,* etc.

Autobiographical sketch of Belle Dorman Rugh:

IT WAS over one hundred years ago that my great-grandparents sailed from Boston on a small sailing ship to be missionaries in Lebanon. Their children and grandchildren also became missionaries; thus it was that my five brothers and I, though Americans, were born in the Middle East and spoke baby Arabic before we spoke English.

Life in Lebanon in those days was about fifty years behind life in the United States. I remember the magic of the first electric lights in our Beirut house, the excitement of my first ride in a car, at the invitation of a British colonel, hurtling up the street at twenty miles an hour.

Winters we spent in the Beirut house, with its semi-tropical garden, the jasmine and roses often beaten by the heavy winter rains blowing in from the sea, while clouds rolled over the snow-capped mountains behind us. Our friends were Americans and Lebanese. When the hot, dry summer began, we moved to the mountain house on the first ridge of Lebanon. There my brothers and I were free to wander over the high cliffs and rocky mountainsides, exploring ancient sarcophagi and picnicking under the pines.

After an interim at college and post-graduate studies in America (B.A., Vassar, M.A.,

Belle Dorman Rugh

Columbia) I returned to Lebanon as a teacher. There I met a young instructor at the American University, one Douglas Rugh who had grown up in China, the son of missionary parents. Romance ensued; we were married one summer day, in the shadow of Crystal Mountain; and two weeks later we embarked on a honeymoon voyage to China. For two years we lived in a Manchu garden outside Peking, at the time the campus of Yenching University, where my husband was teaching.

Years later, when we were living in Connecticut, my daughter Molly asked me one day, "What was so great about living in Lebanon?" My attempts to describe it only baffled myself and Molly too. Finally it dawned on me that the only way to share that experience was to take her there; if not physically, at least in a story. And this is how my first book, *Crystal Mountain*, was begun.

Our home is still in Connecticut, where my husband is on the faculty of Central Connecticut State College. We have three daughters, a son-in-law and a grandson. Twice we have been back to Lebanon for extended visits, and each visit has inspired another book: *The Path Above the Pines*, and *The Lost Waters*. The old Beirut I knew as a girl has vanished, disappearing into the ground

along with Phoenician Berytus; and I realize that *Crystal Mountain* is now a period piece. But high in the mountains of Lebanon there are villages like Roumani in *The Lost Waters* which still hold some of the savor and the tranquillity of days gone by, lending a rich background to the stir of young life there in this new jet-space age.

Belle Dorman graduated from Vassar in 1929 and took her M.A. from Teachers College, Columbia University, in 1932. She has taught in Beirut in the Ahliah School and at the Beirut College for Women, at Yenching University, Peking, and at Central Connecticut State College. She married Douglas Rugh in 1934. At the time of his death in December, 1969, he was professor of psychology at Central Connecticut State College. Their three daughters are Elizabeth Patricia, Mary Dorman, and June Caroline.

Crystal Mountain won a New York *Herald Tribune* Children's Spring Book Festival Award in 1955.

SELECTED WORKS: Crystal Mountain, 1955; The Path Above the Pines, 1962; The Lost Waters, 1967.

ABOUT: Author's and Writer's Who's Who, 1963; Contemporary Authors, Vol. 15-16; Who's Who in America, 1970-71; Who's Who of American Women, 1970-71.

JOSÉ SÁNCHEZ-SILVA
November 11, 1911-

AUTHOR OF *The Boy and the Whale*, etc.

Biographical sketch of José María Sánchez-Silva:

BORN in Madrid, José María Sánchez-Silva came from a literary background. His father, Lorenzo Sánchez-Silva, was a journalist, and his mother, born Adoración Garcia-Morales, wrote poetry. His early life was a time of hardship. Before he was ten years old his mother died and his father disappeared, leaving him to fend for himself. For a time he lived with his godmother while working at various jobs—as errand boy in a drugstore, kitchen worker in a hotel, and helper in a

JOSÉ SÁNCHEZ-SILVA

tailoring shop. When his godmother emigrated from Spain to Mexico he was placed in an orphanage, and in 1926 he began attending an educational institute in Madrid, where he received a general education and training in stenography and typing—skills that enabled him to obtain a temporary job at the town hall in Madrid. In 1932 he took a course at a school of journalism, El Dabate, which gave him a scholarship, and then obtained an editorial position. During the next year he married a judge's daughter, María del Carmen Delgado (who was to bear him six children) and made his first trip abroad, visiting France, Cuba, Mexico, and the United States.

Sánchez-Silva's first book, *El Hombre y la Bufanda* (The Man and the Neckcloth), a collection of short stories, was published in Madrid in 1934. During the mid-thirties he worked for various newspapers and in the sales department of Renault, the French automobile firm. In 1939 he joined the staff of the daily newspaper, *Arriba,* and became editor-in-chief. Over the next few years he also worked on a number of other periodicals. In 1942 he received his first professional award, the Francisco de Sales prize, and other honors followed: Spain's National Prize for Literature in 1944; the first prize for children's stories from the publishing house of Boris Bureba and the National Prize for Journalism in 1945; the Mariano de Cavia

prize in 1947; and the Rodriguez Santamaria prize in 1948. Meanwhile he had been promoted to the position of assistant director of *Arriba* in 1944 and appointed editor of the *Revista de las Artes y los Oficios* (Review of Arts and Crafts) in 1946.

After World War II, Sánchez-Silva began to travel extensively—to Italy on assignment for *Arriba* in 1946, to England where he covered the winter Olympic games in 1948, on a round-the-world pilgrimage (commemorating the four hundredth anniversary of St. Francis Xavier's arrival in Japan) in 1949, to Brazil for the world championship football games in 1950, and to France, Belgium, Holland, and Sweden as a sports reporter in 1951. Besides his other activities, he continued to turn out books, published at the rate of one about every two years, and he also wrote the script for a motion picture, *Ronda Española,* which was released in 1952.

During the mid-fifties, Sánchez-Silva retired temporarily from his newspaper job to devote more time to his personal writing and to travel, and his output of books increased. As the list of them lengthened, so also did the list of his honors. In 1957 he had an audience with Pope Pius XII. He received another National Prize for Literature in 1957. In 1959 the Spanish Government conferred on him the Grand Cross of the Order of Cisneros. He received the Virgen del Carmen prize for the best book of the year in 1960, and an award for special services from the Peruvian government in 1962. Appointed to the Council of the General Society of Spanish Authors in 1963, he received the Spanish government's Grand Cross of Merit in 1964 and Grand Cross of the Order of Alfonso X in 1968.

Sánchez-Silva is widely regarded in the Spanish-speaking world as its greatest contemporary juvenile writer. He has written more than twenty books for children and young people, avoiding violence and morbidity and stressing the values of gentleness and imaginative realism. Some of his outstanding books are centered around the family and human relations—for example, his quartet consisting of *Marcelino, Historias Menores* (Little Stories), *Aventura en el cielo* (Adventures in Heaven), and *Adán y el*

Señor Dios (Adán and the Lord), and his
Luiso, the story of a little boy in a family of
merchant marines. Others deal with children's love for animals—for example, *La
Burrita Non* (Little Donkey Odd), *Un Gran
Pequeño* (A Great Little One), and *Segundo
Verano* (Second Summer). Another of his
favorite themes is the magic that lies within
reality, which is developed in his *Adiós,
Josefina* (Goodbye, Josefina), a story about
a boy who has an imaginary whale, and his
El Espejo Habitado (The Lived-in Mirror),
about dreams that happen within a mirror.
Books by Sánchez-Silva have been translated
into twenty-six languages, and some of them
have been used as texts for students of
Spanish in Europe and North America.

In 1968 he tied for first place for the Hans
Christian Andersen Award.

SELECTED WORKS IN ENGLISH TRANSLATION:
The Boy and the Whale, 1964; Ladis and the
Ant, 1969.

ABOUT: Bookbird no. 4, 1968; Bookbird no. 1,
1969.

INGER SANDBERG
August 2, 1930-

and

LASSE SANDBERG
February 17, 1924-

AUTHOR AND ILLUSTRATOR OF *Little Ghost
Godfrey,* etc.

Autobiographical sketch of Karin Inger Erikson Sandberg and Lasse Erik Mathias
Sandberg:

INGER ERIKSON was born in Karlstad,
Sweden. She was studying until she married
Lasse Sandberg. He was born in Stockholm.
Lasse was working as a press photographer
until he started studying arts at Anders Beck-
man's Art School, 1948-49.

In spring 1950 we got married and moved
to a red cottage in the country. We had a
dog and went on skis in the forest, lived very
far away from the city life that we were both
accustomed to. We were working for magazines and papers: Lasse with satiric cartoons,
Inger with stories illustrated by Lasse.

In 1952 we moved to a small town, and
Inger started her education as a teacher. At
this time our daughter Lena was born. When
Inger had finished her education as a teacher, our son Niklas was born, in 1955.

We moved to a tall house in Karlstad and
found out that for city children there were
very few stories with identification possibil-

ities. We started looking for stories among cars, tall houses and elevators. Thus the ideas for books like *At My Place, Lena Stories, Filuren on Adventures, Nicholas' Favorite Pet* were born.

Simultaneously, in 1962, little brother Mathias was born and Inger was awarded the Swedish State's working scholarship, finished working as a teacher and became a full-time author. Compared to Lena and Niklas, little brother Mathias seemed incredibly small. He should have small books, too! This was the beginning of the five books about *Little Anna.* Mathias has meant very much to our production. He was sitting on Lasse's drawing table when *Little Ghost Godfrey* was created. He cried bitterly when the drawings were sent to the publisher in Stockholm. Mathias is also portrayed in *The Boy with 100 Cars* and *The Boy with Many Houses.*

We feel it is something that is most important, most responsible and most funny in the world to do books for little human beings, to try teaching them facts without their noticing it, as for example in *Nicholas' Favorite Pet.* Perhaps we look so positively upon the creation of children's books because Lasse is illustrating only Inger's text, and Inger is always writing her texts with Lasse's pictures before her eyes.

Today we are living in a modern one-family house by the shore of Sweden's biggest lake. Lena and Niklas are rather grown-up now and Mathias has started school. But we are still childishly fond of working for small people.

_____

Inger and Lasse Sandberg have won numerous scholarships, prizes, and awards, among which are the Elsa Beskow Plaque in 1965 for *Lilla Spöket Laban* (published in the United States as *Little Ghost Godfrey*), a silver plaque from the Biennale of Illustrations, Bratislava, in 1967 for *The Boy with 100 Cars*, and an honorable mention for the Hans Christian Andersen Award in 1966 for *Niklas Röda Dag (Nicholas' Red Day).* Their books have been published in a number of countries, including the Scandinavian, the United States, Germany, England, and Japan. The Sandbergs have also collaborated on children's programs for Swedish television. In 1969 *Daddy, Come Out!*

received the Heffalump Award given by the newspaper *Expressen,* for the best children's book of the year.

SELECTED WORKS WRITTEN AND ILLUSTRATED: What Anna Saw, 1964; Little Anna and the Magic Hat, 1965; Little Anna's Mamma Has a Birthday, 1966; What Little Anna Saved, 1966; Nicholas' Red Day, 1967; The Boy with 100 Cars, 1968; Little Ghost Godfrey, 1968; The Boy with Many Houses, 1970; Daddy, Come Out! 1970.

ABOUT: Kingman, Lee and others, comps. Illustrators of Children's Books: 1957-1966; Bookbird no. 3, 1969.

HELGA SANDBURG

November 24, 1918-

AUTHOR OF *Joel and the Wild Goose,* etc.

Biographical sketch of Helga Sandburg Crile:

HELGA SANDBURG was born in Maywood, Illinois, third daughter of Carl and Lillian (Steichen) Sandburg. Her father was the noted poet and historian of Lincoln. Her mother, known in her own right for raising world champion goats, was the sister of Edward Steichen, the photographer.

Young Helga's request for farm animals started the Sandburgs' famous goat herd. When the family moved from Illinois to the sand dunes on the lake at Harbert, Michigan, Helga was seven, and numbered among her pets goats, calves, colts, dogs, cats, chickens, rabbits. This love for animals is evident in her children's books, which are all set in the dunelands.

The three sisters attended rural schools. In those years, Helga roamed the semi-wild countryside, gathering flower and leaf collections and a comprehensive collection of moths and butterflies. She went on to Michigan State College in 1939, then to the University of Chicago in 1940.

The Sandburg family moved once more. Helga was with her mother and grandmother when they found beautiful Connemara Farm, with its two hundred and forty acres, in Flat Rock, North Carolina. There, from 1945 to 1952, Helga worked with her mother as dairy-goat breeder, and with her father as personal secretary.

HELGA SANDBURG

During 1952-1956 she was on the staff of the Library of Congress. Later, 1958-1959, she was administrative assistant at the Woodrow Wilson Foundation in New York. The Finnish American Society and Svenska Institutet awarded her a grant for travel in Finland and Sweden in 1961, and in the same year she lectured and conducted seminars in Great Britain and Europe as an American specialist for the State Department's Bureau of Cultural and Educational Affairs. Since 1964 she has been an independent lecturer.

Helga Sandburg had written poetry and kept notebooks and diaries all her life, but it was not until 1957, when she was nearing forty, that she began to write with the determination she believes she inherited from her maternal grandmother, "a tornado of a woman." (She doubts that the ability to write is inherited.) Within five years she produced three novels and a number of poems, short stories, and juveniles. The family sings around their father's guitar inspired her to play that instrument, which in turn inspired her first nonfiction, *Sweet Music: A Book of Family Reminiscence and Song*, published in 1963. *Joel and the Wild Goose*, Helga Sandburg's most outstanding book for children, was published in the same year. *Blueberry*, a novel for young adults about a girl's first horse, was also published that year, and *Gingerbread*, its sequel about Blueberry's foal, came out in 1964.

John Carl Steichen, born in 1941, and Karlen Paula Steichen, 1943, are children of Helga Sandburg's first marriage, which ended in divorce in 1945. Her second marriage ended in 1962. She married George Crile, Jr., a surgeon, in 1963. Dr. Crile is also a naturalist and they have collaborated on a McGraw-Hill American Wilderness Series book, *Above and Below*. They live in Cleveland, Ohio, and have a country home in the environs.

This auburn-haired, blue-eyed daughter of Carl Sandburg has become a prolific writer, and has earned her own place in American literature. She enjoys cooking, especially baking bread from her grandmother's recipe, and is an amateur painter and gardener and an accomplished guitarist. She belongs to a number of organizations, including Poetry Society of America, American Folklore Society, P.E.N., American Luxembourg Society, and American Milk Goat Record Association. She is an honorary fellow of American-Scandinavian Foundation.

Among other awards, she has received the Emily Clark Balch Award for her short story "Witch Chickens." In 1965 she received a Lewis Carroll Shelf Award for *Joel and the Wild Goose.*

SELECTED WORKS: Blueberry, 1963; Joel and the Wild Goose, 1963; Gingerbread, 1964; Bo and the Old Donkey, 1965.

ABOUT: Contemporary Authors, Vol. 4; Golden, Harry. Carl Sandburg; Sandburg, Helga. Sweet Music; A Book of Family Reminiscence and Song; Who's Who in America, 1970-71; Who's Who of American Women, 1970-71; Saturday Review April 26, 1958.

MARI SANDOZ
1901-March 10, 1966

AUTHOR OF *The Horsecatcher*, etc.

Biographical sketch of Mari Susette Sandoz:

MARI SANDOZ, born at the Sandoz post office, Sheridan County, Nebraska, was the eldest of six children of Jules Ami Sandoz and Mary Elizabeth (Fehr) Sandoz, both immigrants from Switzerland. Her father, the son of an upper-class family, abandoned the study of medicine at the end of his fourth

Mari Sandoz: *MAH ree san DAHS*

MARI SANDOZ

year and came to America, emigrating to the sparsely settled sand hills of Nebraska where he could live as he chose.

It was there that Mari Sandoz faced many of the hardships later described in her novels. At the age of ten she lost the sight in her left eye as the result of snow blindness from a late spring blizzard which she and her younger brother braved to rescue their lost cattle. Before she was fourteen she was shot twice in hunting accidents. She learned to tend her father's trapline, knew how to catch a mink or coyote and how to remove the pelt and cure it. Her mother spent most of her time in the field and garden, and so the care of the house and children usually fell to Mari. Because of these many demands and because her father scorned American teachers, her school attendance was irregular.

In school Mari was introduced to Hawthorne, Shakespeare, Conrad, Hardy, and others. Her father disapproved of reading fiction, so she borrowed books and brought them into the house hidden in the front of her low-belted dresses. Almost as soon as she learned to read she began to write. This also had to be done in secret and under a pen name since writers, according to her father, were the "maggots of society." At the age of sixteen, after finishing four and a half years of school, Mari Sandoz passed a teacher's certification examination and found a job in a rural school. When she was twenty-

one she decided to go on to college and enrolled at the University of Nebraska, where she studied off and on for eight years. She never graduated, chiefly because she did not have a high school diploma.

To support herself in college, she worked in a laboratory and as an English assistant at the University. During this period she wrote seventy-eight short stories (all unpublished), but in 1926 she won honorable mention in a Harper's intercollegiate contest. She sold a number of articles on such subjects as prairie fires and Indians, under the pen name of Marie Macumber. From 1927 to 1929 she was associate editor of *School Executive Magazine*.

Early in November 1928, Mari Sandoz was called to the bedside of her dying father and there heard his last request that she write his life story. Five years of extensive research went into the writing of *Old Jules*, her tribute to her father. During this period she was a proofreader for the *Lincoln Star* and *Nebraska State Journal*. *Old Jules* was published in 1935 and won that year's Atlantic Monthly nonfiction award of five thousand dollars.

In 1934-35 she was director of research for the Nebraska State Historical Society and associate editor of the *Nebraska History Magazine*. From 1947 to 1956 Miss Sandoz was in charge of the course in advanced novel writing at the Writer's Institute at the University of Wisconsin (summer sessions). She was also on the staff of writers' conferences at the universities of Colorado and Indiana, served as a judge in several writing contests and often lectured (her subjects were Indians, pioneers, and writing).

Additional honors awarded to Miss Sandoz include: Honorary Doctor of Literature, University of Nebraska, 1950; Award for Distinguished Service, Native Sons and Daughters of Nebraska, 1954; National Achievement Award, The Westerners Chicago Corral (more books [four] than any other author on the list of 100 Best Books of the West) 1955; Headliner Award, Theta Sigma Phi, 1957; The Buffalo (the award of The Westerners, New York Posse), for *The Cattlemen*, 1960; Oppie Award for *These Were the Sioux*, 1962; Western Heritage Award for

"*The Look of the Last Frontier,*" in *American Heritage,* 1962; and the CAR Plaque (Children of American Revolution) for writings on Indian and Nebraska pioneer life, 1963.

The Horsecatcher was a runner-up for the Newbery Medal for 1958. *The Story Catcher* received the Western Writers of America Spur Award, 1963.

Miss Sandoz's later life was spent in Greenwich Village, New York City, but she made annual trips back to the plains looking for first-hand material. She died of cancer March 10, 1966.

SELECTED WORKS: Old Jules, 1955; The Horsecatcher, 1957; Love-song of the Plains, 1961; These Were the Sioux, 1961; The Story Catcher, 1963; Battle of the Little Bighorn, 1966.

ABOUT: Contemporary Authors, Vol. 2; Sandoz, Mari Susette. The Christmas of the Phonograph Records, 1966; Twentieth Century Authors, 1942; Twentieth Century Authors (First Supplement), 1955; Who's Who in America, 1966-67; Who's Who of American Women, 1958-59; American West Spring 1965; Baltimore Bulletin of Education May 1958; New York Times March 11, 1966; New York Times Book Review June 22, 1958; Newsweek November 2, 1935; Publishers' Weekly August 7, 1954; March 21, 1966; Saturday Evening Post March 4, 1939; Saturday Review August 21, 1954; Saturday Review of Literature November 27, 1937; Time November 4, 1935; March 18, 1966; Wilson Library Bulletin February 1938.

MIROSLAV SASEK

MIROSLAV SASEK

November 18, 1916-

AUTHOR AND ILLUSTRATOR OF *This Is New York,* etc.

Biographical sketch of Miroslav Sasek:

MIROSLAV SASEK was born in Prague, Czechoslovakia, and educated there, specializing in art and architecture. When the Communists came into power in 1946, he left the country and went to Paris where he continued his studies at l'Ecole des Beaux Arts. Much as he loved Paris and felt at home there, he did not become a French citizen but has preferred to remain stateless.

From 1947 to 1951 he traveled and studied in England, Holland, Belgium, Italy, Spain, and North Africa. In 1951 he settled

in Munich, Germany, where he worked for Radio Free Europe for six years. There he met a Czech girl, also working for the radio station, and they married. They have one son, Dusan Pedro.

Sasek first had the idea of writing travel books for children when he was on a three-week vacation in Paris, and *This Is Paris* appeared in 1959. He noticed that children traveling with their parents were never told what they were seeing and stood around bored while the grown-ups studied their *Baedekers.* He decided to show Paris to the children and teach them what to look for in a guidebook with a minimum of text and a maximum of pictures. His skill as an architectural draughtsman shows in the beautiful delicate sketches of the buildings and monuments and bridges of Paris, his eye for telling detail in the vignettes of pavement artists, mailboxes, or the open bookstalls along the Seine. He specializes in signs, as he feels they give authenticity ("Direction Neuilly" "Direction Vincennes" in the Metro for instance).

Sasek's original idea was to do three *This Is* books, Paris, London, and Rome, and then quit. However, their success led to an invitation from his American publisher to come over and do a book about New York. *This Is New York* appeared in 1960, was named by the New York *Times* among the best-illustrated children's books that year

Miroslav Sasek: *MEER oh slahf SAH sek*

and won a Boys' Clubs of America Junior Book Award in 1961. The same wit in the text, and style and color in the pictures prevails, with a final little sketch of the artist himself, portfolio under arm, staggering home permanently bent backward from so much looking up.

More European cities followed (Edinburgh, Munich, Venice) and another American one (San Francisco). Then Sasek began to think in terms of whole countries, and added Israel, Ireland, and Greece. Between these he wedged in delightful studies of Cape Kennedy and Hong Kong.

In 1969 he returned to the United States to do a book about Washington, D.C. He could not have chosen a worse time to visit the capital. The riots that followed the assassination of Martin Luther King, Jr., were tearing the city. He was still there when the assassination of Robert Kennedy took place, and was working on a sketch of John Kennedy's grave when the guards asked him to leave; they were about to dig the grave of Robert Kennedy. Perhaps these events explain why *This Is Washington, D.C.* was less well received by the critics. There is more text, which they felt was rather dull and derivative; the pictures seemed more ponderous and as though taken from photographs. Only the occasional sketch, of the balloon man or the little Black boy on his paper route, retain the true Sasek spirit.

Above everything Sasek remains European and when he looks at an American city it is through the eyes of a European. This is partly what makes his work so fresh and exhilarating. Nor does he ever talk down to children. He will use such words as "baroque" and "rococo" to describe German churches, without explanation, leaving his pictures to illustrate the meaning. This is why grown-ups as well as children can enjoy his work.

When he is not traveling, writing, and painting (and even designing his own books) he returns to his home in Munich, where Mrs. Sasek still works for Radio Free Europe. There he relaxes in the beautiful Bavarian woods, picking mushrooms.

SELECTED WORKS WRITTEN AND ILLUSTRATED: This Is Paris, 1959; This Is London, 1959; This Is Rome, 1960; This Is New York, 1960; This Is Israel, 1962; This Is Hong Kong, 1965; This Is Greece, 1966; This Is the United Nations, 1968; This Is Washington, D.C., 1969.

ABOUT: Author's and Writer's Who's Who, 1963; Hopkins, Lee Bennett. Books Are by People; Kingman, Lee and others, comps. Illustrators of Children's Books: 1957-1966.

RICHARD SCARRY

June 5, 1919-

AUTHOR AND ILLUSTRATOR OF *Richard Scarry's Great Big Schoolhouse*, etc.

Autobiographical sketch of Richard McClure Scarry:

BORN in Boston, Massachusetts.

Went to school but didn't learn much. No college would have me. Went to Boston Museum School of Fine Arts instead.

World War II came along and they needed me. I had a bit of a problem getting in. Because I wore glasses they wouldn't accept me as a volunteer but preferred to draft me instead.

They thought that I would make a good radio repair man. My exam mark was minus thirteen so they decided to make me a corporal. An ex-bunk mate turned officer told me that I should become an officer and then I would have someone shine my shoes every night.

I applied for Officer Candidate School before a board of officers. The interview consisted of one question. "How many men in the waiting room outside?" I replied, "Ten, sir. Two sergeants, three corporals and five privates." I was right so they accepted me.

Shortly after graduation I was sent to be art director for the Troop Information Section Headquarters of North African Theater of Operations where I learned how to tell the troops what the war was all about. Moved on to Italy and eventually Paris.

Returned to the United States and moved to New York with the idea of becoming some sort of artist. Did a bit of magazine work and about 1946 did my first book for Golden Press. For a number of years I illustrated stories written by others. Then I had an idea for a book of my own. Golden Press liked it

Scarry: *rhymes with "carry"*

Richard Scarry .

and the result was, *Richard Scarry's Best Word Book Ever.*

I married Patricia Murphy in 1949. She was born in Vancouver, British Columbia. She writes children's books too, but she can't draw. We have a sixteen-year-old son, Huck, who draws all the time. We have lived in New York, Ridgefield and Westport, Connecticut, but have recently moved to Lausanne, Switzerland. We're living down by the Lake of Geneva and I commute to my studio in the center of the old town by the shortest subway in the world.

When I'm not working, which is almost always, I am in the mountains, an hour or so away. In the winter I ski. In the summer I hike. I am a very slow skier but a very fast hiker.

———

Richard Scarry served in the United States Army, 1941-1946, and became a captain. With his son, Richard McClure II (Huck), and his wife Patricia, he moved to Switzerland in 1968.

Scarry has illustrated more than eighty books since 1947, estimating that their total sales in the United States alone had reached twenty-five million by 1969.

SELECTED WORKS WRITTEN AND ILLUSTRATED: Tinker and Tanker, 1960; The Rooster Struts,

1963; Busy, Busy World, 1965; Is This the House of Mistress Mouse? 1966; Richard Scarry's Storybook Dictionary, 1966; What Do People Do All Day? 1968; Richard Scarry's Great Big Air Book, 1971.

SELECTED WORKS ILLUSTRATED: Let's Go Fishing, by Kathryn Jackson, 1949; The Animals' Merry Chistmas, by Kathryn Jackson, 1950; Little Indian, by Margaret Wise Brown, 1954; Pierre Bear, by Patricia Scarry, 1954; Rudolph the Red-nosed Reindeer, by Barbara Shook Hazen, 1964.

ABOUT: Contemporary Authors, Vol. 19-20; Kingman, Lee and others, comps. Illustrators of Children's Books: 1957-1966; Publishers' Weekly October 20, 1969.

JACK SCHAEFER

November 19, 1907-

AUTHOR OF *Shane,* etc.

Biographical sketch of Jack Warner Schaefer:

JACK SCHAEFER was born in Cleveland, Ohio, one of four children of Carl Walter Schaefer, a lawyer, and Minnie Louella (Hively) Schaefer. He grew up in Cleveland, went to Oberlin College for his undergraduate work, majoring in English literature, and received his A.B. degree in 1929. He went to Columbia University for graduate studies in 1931. He married Eugenia Hammond Ives in 1931 and has four children, Carl, Christopher, Susan, and Jonathan.

He became a newspaperman and, except for some intervals in more or less related work, spent the next twenty years in journalism: with the United Press from 1930 to 1931, the New Haven (Connecticut) *Journal-Courier* from 1932 to 1939, the Baltimore *Sun* from 1942 to 1944, and the Norfolk *Virginian-Pilot* from 1944 to 1948. He also served, 1931-1938, as assistant director of education at the Connecticut State Reformatory. He has been a free-lance writer since 1948.

In 1948 Schaefer's first marriage terminated in divorce and a year and a half later he remarried. His second wife is the former Louise Wilhide Deans and by her he acquired three step-daughters, Sharon, Stephani, and Claudia.

JACK SCHAEFER

Schaefer has claimed that newspaper writing is bad training for a "real writer." Nonetheless his first novel, *Shane* (1949), was not only a best seller and made into a film, but has become a minor American classic. It is a Western, but not in the conventional sense associated with movie previews, stampeding cattle, whizzing bullets, and so on. Schaefer had a real sense of the West, for both scenery and character. He had been influenced by Frederick Jackson Turner's idea in *The Significance of the Frontier in American History*, that the ever-receding frontier, with cheap land, was the dominant factor in creating the American national character, and more than anything else made Americans different from Europeans.

The West Schaefer wrote about in a series of successful novels (*First Blood*, 1953, etc.) and in short stories (*The Pioneers*, 1954, etc.) was no longer a country of sheer frontier, where men could avoid the consequences of their actions simply by moving on. It was now fully settled and Schaefer's heroes encounter situations which they have to resolve. Their frontier environment, however, makes them able to act independently of convention and in accordance with their own sense of what is right, often taking the law into their own hands. The tradition of violence and self-sufficiency is still there: Shane resorts to the action of a gunfighter when he is unable in any other way to pro-tect the family who had befriended him when he was alone and unknown.

Old Ramon, which appeared in 1960, is regarded as a juvenile although it has great attraction for older people too. A powerful story about sheepherding in the semi-arid plains of the Southwest, it was an Honor Book in the New York *Herald Tribune* Children's Spring Book Festival in 1960 and a runner-up for the Newbery Medal, 1961. In it the boy hero (he is never named) is put under the tutelage of Old Ramon who has already taught the boy's father and grandfather the art of sheepherding. The old man has a deep and humble respect for book learning, which he lacks, but as the story proceeds the boy comes to realize that Old Ramon's kind of knowledge could never find its way into a book. The friendship grows; the old man recognizes that his younger dog has shifted his allegiance to the boy and must now be regarded as his dog. A wolf threatens the herd and the younger dog sacrifices his life; the older dog saves the whole herd by refusing to fight the wolf. An indication of the boy's growing maturity is his realization, gently prodded by Old Ramon, that the older dog is the more heroic.

Another of Schaefer's mature juveniles, *The Plainsmen*, a collection of short stories about the west, was an Honor Book in the New York *Herald Tribune* Children's Spring Book Festival, 1963.

Schaefer and his family live in New Mexico, near Santa Fe.

SELECTED WORKS: Shane, 1949; Canyon, 1953; Old Ramon, 1960; The Plainsmen, 1963; Stubby Pringle's Christmas, 1964; Mavericks, 1967; New Mexico, 1967.

ABOUT: Contemporary Authors, Vol. 11-12; Who's Who in America, 1970-71; Top of the News May 1962; Wilson Library Bulletin February 1961.

WILLIAM E. SCHEELE

April 14, 1920-

AUTHOR AND ILLUSTRATOR OF *Prehistoric Man and the Primates*, etc.

Biographical sketch of William Earl Scheele:

BORN in Cleveland, Ohio, the son of William Carl and Pauline (Karl) Scheele, Wil-

WILLIAM E. SCHEELE

liam Earl Scheele attended the special junior and senior high schools for talented students in the Cleveland Public School System.

He won scholarships in both art and biology to Western Reserve University. In the fall of 1939 when he won the first annual Bird Art Contest sponsored by the Cleveland Museum of Natural History, he was invited to join the staff of the Museum and worked there summers and after school while attending the School of Art.

World War II interrupted his studies and he was inducted into the army in 1942. The same year, at Fort Belvoir, Virginia, where he was stationed, he met and married Joann Marjorie Seubert, an art major from Kent State University, who was working as a draftsman for the Engineering Board. Scheele went through Officers' Candidate School and upon graduation in March, 1943, went overseas to serve in England and other parts of Europe. Returning in 1945 and discharged in 1946, he went back to work for the Cleveland Museum of Natural History and continued his studies in art. He graduated from Adelbert College, Western Reserve University, in 1947. In the same year he was appointed chief of preparation and exhibition at the Museum and in 1949 was made director, being then the youngest museum director in the United States. In 1953 he conducted a weekly television program for the Museum.

Scheele's special work at the Museum was the preparation of exhibition material, for which he was highly qualified by his training in both art and biology. Trips to different sections of the country and, while he was overseas, to different European countries, had widened and deepened his experience. At the Museum, it had been found that the fossil exhibits drew more attention than any others, both from the general public and from school classes. Displaying the reconstructed skeletons against a contrasting background, giving a clear and not too technical description and adding drawings to show how the animals looked greatly increased attendance and heightened interest.

Scheele and his staff found while working on these exhibits that there was almost no descriptive literature to draw on. It was this that inspired Scheele to bring out a book on the subject aimed particularly at young people whose interest was awakening. His *Prehistoric Animals* won the Ohioana Book Award for 1955. Besides clearcut descriptions and black-and-white brush drawings of the animals who inhabited the earth during the first five hundred million years of life, the book contains excellent and helpful charts of geologic time, comparative size (with a six-foot man as a measure) and the evolution of the different groups.

In his next book, *The First Mammals*, Scheele covered the most recent sixty million years of the earth's history. One of his aims in writing was to stimulate interest in the search for fossils, as the finds of amateurs as well as those of the experts have played an important role in the expansion of the comparatively recent science of paleontology. The same accurate descriptions and drawings are there, as well as the charts. In this case the comparative size charts use today's mammals and measure them against their ancient ancestors.

Men and apes were not included, as the author felt the story of their evolution could be better told separately. This he did in *Prehistoric Man and the Primates*, which won a medal from the Boys' Clubs of America in 1958. From then on a series of anthropological and archeological picture books have followed on the same pattern. Scheele especially emphasizes in each the methods by which the search for remains is undertaken and how these precious remains can be preserved when they are discovered.

Scheele himself enjoys fossil hunting. He also does gem cutting and his paintings of natural history subjects have been exhibited in museums throughout the country.

Scheele and his wife and three sons live on a seventy-two acre tree farm near Chardon, Ohio. Mrs. Scheele's help with the picture books is acknowledged in the preface to each.

SELECTED WORKS WRITTEN AND ILLUSTRATED: Prehistoric Animals, 1954; First Mammals, 1955; Prehistoric Man and the Primates, 1957; Ancient Elephants, 1958; Cave Hunters, 1959; The Mound Builders, 1960; The Earliest Americans, 1963.

ABOUT: Kingman, Lee and others, comps. Illustrators of Children's Books: 1957-1966; Viguers, Ruth Hill and others, comps. Illustrators of Children's Books: 1946-1956; Who's Who in America, 1970-71.

JOSEPH SCHINDELMAN

July 4, 1923-

ILLUSTRATOR OF *The Great Picture Robbery*, etc.

Autobiographical sketch of Joseph Schindelman:

I BEGAN illustrating children's books by accident.

I'd sent one of my Christmas cards to Joseph Low who showed it to a friend at Atheneum and it all led to Eve Merriam's *There Is No Rhyme for Silver*, which is probably my favorite if only because it came first.

William Gropper, political cartoonist for *Freiheit*, (a Yiddish newspaper in New York) was a very early influence on my work. Persian rugs were, too. Thereafter the more I learned about the masters, the more my style would change. Right now I imagine I can be placed somewhere in the vicinity of Cruikshank, Tenniel, Walt Kelly, very early Picasso and Rembrandt—among others. When it comes to style, I'm very catholic.

Another institution I regularly attended was the New York *Times Magazine* cover. I

JOSEPH SCHINDELMAN

used to copy them when the *Times* employed illustrators. (But now that they employ photographers, I try to do the crossword.)

This is not to say that photography doesn't have its place: as a nose gunner with the 15th Air Force, I was pressed into service as an aerial photographer and dropped a big lens over Germany. Maybe it hit something.

I've been an advertising art director for the last ten years and have had to work very closely with copy writers in coming up with our ads and promotion pieces. This is almost completely opposite to the way I've worked with my authors. Among Eve Merriam, Leon Harris, Padraic Colum, Roald Dahl, John Raymond and J. Allan Bosworth, I've only met one. And that was for a convivial rather than a business purpose.

I'm not sure what this proves except that perhaps when you have to sell to adults, you want help. But when you want to reach a child, you don't need anyone else around.

My wife, three daughters, one son and I live on Long Island. They think we moved there to be nearer our relatives. I think we moved there to be closer to the beach. I fish. More exactly, I surf cast for striped bass. The world record is a seventy-three-pounder and my record is thirty-five. So I have a long way to go. I think if I had a chance to illustrate *The Old Man and the Sea*, the sharks never would have gotten to the marlin. And the fisherman would have lived happily ever after.

Joseph Schindelman was born in New York and attended the Art Students League, WPA art classes, and City College. He married Ida Zager in 1944 and their children are Dale, Laurel, Maxine, and Michael.

The Great Picture Robbery was named by the New York *Times Book Review* among the best-illustrated children's books of 1963. Schindelman's work has been in several exhibitions of the American Institute of Graphic Arts.

SELECTED WORKS ILLUSTRATED: There Is No Rhyme for Silver, by Eve Merriam, 1962; The Great Picture Robbery, by Leon A. Harris, 1963; Charlie and the Chocolate Factory, by Roald Dahl, 1964; The Six Who Were Left in a Shoe, by Padraic Colum, 1968; Maurice Goes to Sea, by Leon A. Harris, 1968.

ABOUT: Kingman, Lee and others, comps. Illustrators of Children's Books: 1957-1966.

CHARLES SCHULZ

November 26, 1922-

AUTHOR AND ILLUSTRATOR OF *Happiness Is a Warm Puppy*, etc.

Biographical sketch of Charles Monroe Schulz:

CHARLES SCHULZ was born in Minneapolis, Minnesota, of Norwegian and German ancestry, the only child of Dena Halverson and Carl Schulz, a barber. From infancy Schulz has been called "Sparky," after the horse in the Barney Google cartoon. In the first grade, when he found he could draw Popeye, he decided to become a cartoonist.

Except for drawing, school was difficult for Schulz. Having skipped two and a half grades in elementary school, he found himself the youngest and smallest in his room, ignored and rebuffed by the other children much as Charlie Brown, of the *Peanuts* comic strip, was to be.

Schulz's scholastic difficulties continued throughout high school. Failing at least one subject every year, he was sustained only by his desire to draw. After graduation from high school in 1940, Schulz was too discour-

CHARLES SCHULZ

aged to go to college, and enrolled for courses at Art Instruction, Inc., in Minneapolis. He took the entire two-year course by mail rather than face instructors in person.

In 1943 Schulz was drafted and served in the United States Army in France and Germany, becoming staff sergeant of a light machine-gun squad.

After the war, Schulz took a job lettering comic pages for a religious magazine in St. Paul, and later, to his surprise, was offered a position on the staff of Art Instruction, Inc. He met and married Joyce Halverson, sister of another staff member.

Schulz sold his first cartoons to *Saturday Evening Post* in 1948. Two years later United Feature Syndicate bought his idea for a comic strip and named it *Peanuts*. In 1956, within eight years of his first cartoon sale, Schulz received the Reuben Award, highest of his profession, when the National Cartoonist Society chose him Cartoonist of the Year. He was named Humorist of the Year (1957) by Yale undergraduates, and received the School Bell Award (1960) from the National Education Association.

In 1963 Schulz's inexpensive little book about the characters in the *Peanuts* cartoon, *Happiness Is a Warm Puppy*, sold more copies in the United States than any other hardcover book for children or adults, followed closely by his *Security Is a Thumb and a Blanket*. By the end of 1963, these two combined had sold more than 1,350,000 copies. His later books have also sold in enormous quantities.

One writer for *Time* magazine has said that the appeal of *Peanuts* is "its sophisticated melding of wry wisdom and sly one-upmanship." According to an article in *Current Biography*, "the astuteness with which Charles Schulz has dealt with human foibles . . . has given him a reputation as a semanticist, psychologist, and even as an existentialist." To this might be added theologian, in view of Robert L. Short's serious studies of the religious ideas in Schulz's work. (*The Gospel According to Peanuts*, 1965, and *The Parables of Peanuts*, 1968).

Charles and Joyce Schulz live in Sebastopol, California, with their children, Meredith, Charles, Jr., Craig, Amy, and Jill. Schulz enjoys tennis, golf, and bridge and teaches Sunday School. According to *Current Biography*, he does not smoke or drink and uses as his only expletives the familiar "good grief" and "rats", of the *Peanuts* characters.

SELECTED WORKS WRITTEN AND ILLUSTRATED: More Peanuts, 1954; Happiness Is a Warm Puppy, 1962; Security Is a Thumb and a Blanket, 1963; Home Is on Top of a Dog House, 1966; Happiness Is a Sad Song, 1967; You're in Love, Charlie Brown, 1968.

ABOUT: Contemporary Authors, Vol. 9-10; Current Biography Yearbook 1960; Richards, Carmen, ed. Minnesota Writers; Who's Who in America, 1970-71; Life March 17, 1967; Look July 22, 1958; New York Times Book Review March 12, 1967; New York Times Magazine April 16, 1967; Newsweek March 6, 1961; Psychology Today January 1968; Reader's Digest July 1967; Redbook December 1967; Saturday Evening Post January 12, 1957; April 25, 1964; Saturday Review April 12, 1969; Seventeen January 1962; Time March 3, 1958; April 9, 1965.

MILDRED LEE SCUDDER

See *Lee, Mildred*

"LEE SEBASTIAN"

See *Silverberg, Robert*

IAN SERRAILLIER

September 24, 1912-

AUTHOR OF *The Silver Sword*, etc.

Autobiographical sketch of Ian Serraillier:

I WAS born in London and first went to school near Hampstead Heath, where my family was then living. Later I went to a boarding prep school in Sussex and then to Brighton College. I never liked being a boarder. University life appealed to me much more. Soon after leaving school I won an exhibition in classics to St. Edmund Hall, Oxford, but took my final degree in English Literature and became a schoolmaster. For many years teaching was my livelihood, and most of my writing was done in school vacations. Much as I enjoyed teaching, I had always wanted to be a writer, and I was glad when I was able to make it a full-time occupation.

My best known book is, I suppose, *The Silver Sword* (entitled *Escape from Warsaw* in the American paperback edition published by Scholastic). It is the story of a group of Polish children caught up in the Second World War, and of their trek across Europe in search of their parents. It has been translated into many languages and also serialised on television and radio. I wrote the book out of a concern for the fate of the thousands of refugee children stranded in Europe, and before embarking on it I studied many case histories as well as the background. In one or two places—the canoe episode, for instance—I drew on personal experience. Two other novels of mine (*There's No Escape, Flight to Adventure*) reflect my liking for mountains. As a boy I spent many holidays in the Alps, which made a strong impression on me. I have returned to them many times since to climb and walk and ski.

On the whole, though, I don't make much use of direct personal experience in my writing. The best stories are the old ones that have stood the test of time—Greek legends, folk tales, fairy tales. They need reinterpreting for each generation, and I enjoy retelling them whether in prose or in verse. Verse writing has sometimes brought me into collaboration with composers. Richard Rod-

IAN SERRAILLIER

ney Bennett, Gordon Crosse and Malcolm Arnold have composed the music for the musical stories I have written for the BBC TV service for schools. I also enjoy my editorial work, which keeps me in touch with children and teachers. My wife and I together edit a series of widely varied fiction, travel and biography for use in schools.

We have four children: a married daughter Helen, Jane, (at Cambridge University), Christine Anne and Andrew (both at school). Our home is a charming flint house over three hundred years old, in the South Downs in West Sussex, within easy reach of the sea. We have a beach hut, which we use whenever we can, usually in the summer and autumn.

My name, Serraillier, is pronounced: SER (as in *ser*pent), and if you rhyme the rest with *Australia* you won't go far wrong.

Ian Serraillier took an M.A. from Oxford University in 1935. He was a schoolmaster at Wycliffe College, Stonehouse, then at Dudley Grammar School, Dudley, and finally at Midhurst Grammar School, Midhurst. In 1944 he married Anne Margaret Rogers. With his wife he is coeditor of the "New Windmill" series published by Heinemann Educational Books, Ltd. Serraillier's poems have been broadcast widely in the English-speaking world. In 1960, he re-

ceived a Boys' Clubs of America Junior Book Award for *The Silver Sword*.

SELECTED WORKS: The Silver Sword, 1959; Beowulf the Warrior, 1961; The Gorgon's Head, 1962; The Way of Danger, 1963; The Enchanted Island, 1964; The Challenge of the Green Knight, 1967; Robin in the Greenwood, 1968; Heracles the Strong, 1970; The Tale of Three Landlubbers, 1971.

ABOUT: Author's and Writer's Who's Who, 1963; Contemporary Authors, Vol. 1; Something About the Author, Vol. 1.

MARGERY SHARP

1905-

AUTHOR OF *Miss Bianca*, etc.

Biographical sketch of Margery Sharp Castle:

MARGERY SHARP, born to British parents, grew up on the island of Malta, about which she retains "a deep pool of amiable memories." Growing up, she liked to paint as well as to write. "The fact that I had to earn a living probably turned me into a writer rather than a painter," she once told an interviewer. "I think I obtain something of the tactile pleasure a painter gets from slamming paint on canvas. I write everything in longhand two or three times, and I quite enjoy the physical sensations of dealing with pen and ink and paper."

Before her graduation from Streatham Hill High School, in England, Margery Sharp began contributing verse fillers to magazines, and soon her work was appearing in *Punch*. She took her B.A. in French from London University, although she says her time there was devoted "almost entirely to journalism and campus activities." As a member of the British University Women's Debating Team in 1929 she made the first of several visits to the United States, for which she has said she has an abiding affection.

Beginning in 1930, Miss Sharp wrote a score of popular adult novels in which unconventional but charming heroines bring humor to commonplace situations. The most successful were *The Nutmeg Tree, Cluny Brown*, and *Brittania Mews*, all of which were made into motion pictures. Also well known are *Martha in Paris* and her other

MARGERY SHARP

"Martha" novels, about a headstrong young woman intent on becoming a painter.

In 1938 Miss Sharp was married in New York to Lloyd Castle, from London. During World War II, while her husband served as a major in the British army, she worked in England in Armed Forces Education. After the war the couple took up residence in an apartment near Piccadilly Circus in London.

After three decades devoted to the writing of adult fiction, Miss Sharp turned to children's books for "complete release of the imagination." Between 1959 and 1966 she published four stories illustrated by Garth Williams—*The Rescuers, Miss Bianca, The Turret,* and *Miss Bianca in the Salt Mines*—all of them about a mouse which heads an international society of mice dedicated to bringing cheer to prisoners. Her juveniles have been translated into several languages.

Meanwhile Miss Sharp continued to write adult novels, and also has contributed to a number of British and American periodicals, including *Strand, Punch, Collier's, Harper's* and *Saturday Evening Post.* Her dramatization of *Lady in Waiting* had a short run in New York, with Gladys George in a leading role.

Miss Sharp lives in London, and says she enjoys skating, swimming and sailing, gardening, painting, and embroidering her own designs in gros point.

"You must learn to write rather than be a writer," is her advice to young writers. "Don't think of what is . . . popular, what will sell. Write what you want, and write as well as you can."

SELECTED WORKS: The Rescuers, 1959; Miss Bianca, 1962; The Turret, 1963; Miss Bianca in the Salt Mines, 1967.

ABOUT: Author's and Writer's Who's Who, 1963; Contemporary Authors, Vol. 21-22; Newquist, Roy. Counterpoint; Something About the Author, Vol. 1; Twentieth Century Authors, 1942; Twentieth Century Authors (First Supplement), 1955; Who's Who in America, 1970-71; Who's Who of American Women, 1970-71; New York Herald Tribune Book Review October 7, 1951.

BEN SHECTER

April 28, 1935-

AUTHOR AND ILLUSTRATOR OF *Partouche Plants a Seed,* etc.

Autobiographical sketch of Ben Shecter:

IT all began with a great big chicken little in Brooklyn. That's where I was born, in Brooklyn, and the chicken little I'm referring to was one that I had drawn over a work table in back of my father's picture frame shop. I suppose this was my first attempt at illustrating. I was about four years old at the time.

My father bought me a paint set soon after. It was either to discourage my wall decorations or to encourage my future artistic expression. The transition from wall to a large watercolor pad was an easy one, and an exciting one. I did a really stupendous chicken little with bright yellow feathers, and a red, red comb. The introduction of color, glorious color, mixing them and discovering what I thought were new colors, and more important using them. That big chicken little has since led me to two careers, designing scenery and costumes for the theater, and writing and illustrating children's books.

There seems to be a dominant theme in the books that I have written; believe in what you're doing and do it. I think it's very important for children to realize this because so many young people are copping out. I

know from my own experiences that the moment I lost faith in myself, everything about me crumbled. I grew up in New York City, a good-bad place to grow up. Bad because there aren't any fields for a child to run through. Good, because at an early age one can be exposed to culturally stimulating events.

I remember seeing the original production of Tennessee Williams's *A Streetcar Named Desire;* I was then twelve years old. I came out of the theater at intermission and told my father that I wanted to be a set designer. It was always a dream of mine. My father was very understanding about it, but my mother . . . well, she was a very sensible lady. She said, "Who grows up to be an artist? It just doesn't happen."

Things began to happen for me when I met Franco Zeffirelli at a party and saw his production of *Romeo and Juliet* at the New York City Center.

At that time I was working in the field of window display. I still hadn't given up my dream of scene design, and when I went to the theater, I would go home and redesign the sets. Zeffirelli introduced me to Gian Carlo Menotti, and as a result of that introduction I went to Spoleto in the summer of

1962 to design scenery. I gave up my job and left everything behind.

At this same time enjoying the freedom away from a routine type job, I did a series of illustrations about a little girl in a haunted house. These illustrations eventually inspired Joan Lexau to write the book *Millicent's Ghost.* I find that the fields of theatrical design and book illustration work together for me. When illustrating I think in terms of the theatrical, close-ups, surprises, and visually dramatic montages.

These two fields give me the opportunity to create and explore new worlds, and that's the fun of it all.

———

Ben Shecter attended City College of New York, served in the United States Army from 1958 to 1960, then studied at the Yale School of Drama. He has designed the scenery and costumes for the Harkness Ballet, for theater, and numerous television shows. For a year he designed *Camera Three* for CBS. He has designed several productions for the Washington Opera Society: *Vanessa, Beatrice and Benedict* and *Le Compte Ory. The Hating Book* was named by *House Beautiful* in its list of ten best children's books for 1969. Shecter's work has been exhibited by the American Institute of Graphic Arts.

SELECTED WORKS WRITTEN AND ILLUSTRATED: Emily, Girl Witch of New York, 1963; Jonathan and the Bank Robbers, 1964; Partouche Plants a Seed, 1966; Conrad's Castle, 1968; Ben, 1969; Inspector Rose, 1969.

SELECTED WORKS ILLUSTRATED: Millicent's Ghost, by Joan M. Lexau, 1962; If It Weren't for You, by Charlotte Zolotow, 1966; Every Day a Dragon, by Joan M. Lexau, 1967; A Ghost Named Fred, by Nathaniel Benchley, 1968; My Friend John, by Charlotte Zolotow, 1968; The Hating Book, by Charlotte Zolotow, 1969.

ABOUT: Kingman, Lee and others, comps. Illustrators of Children's Books: 1957-1966.

SYMEON SHIMIN
November 1, 1902-

ILLUSTRATOR OF *Onion John,* etc.

Autobiographical sketch of Symeon Shimin:

SYMEON SHIMIN was born in Astrakhan, on the Caspian Sea, in Russia. His father,

Symeon Shimin: *SIM ee un SHIH min*

a cabinet maker and dealer in antiques, brought the family to this country in 1912. The family's economic struggle dated from this period, and continued while Shimin was in grade school. The family of six lived in two small rooms back of their delicatessen, where Symeon worked after school and summers. He also delivered the bundles of sweaters on which his mother sewed buttons at three cents a sweater.

Shimin had wanted to become a musician, but when his uncle objected, he turned to drawing and has said he never stopped. In order to contribute to the family's support, Shimin at sixteen worked as an apprentice to a commercial artist, and attended art classes in Cooper Union at night. At eighteen he began to free-lance in the commercial field with his one object to be able to paint. At this time he painted for about six months in George Luks's studio. When he was twenty, he contracted tuberculosis and could work only an hour or two a day, but within a short period he made a full recovery. Primarily self-taught, Shimin found his schooling in the museums and galleries. His search for greater understanding of painting

at this time led him to France and Spain, where he stayed for one and a half years, and where the work of El Greco, Cézanne and Picasso had particular meaning for him.

On his return from Europe in 1930, he continued to paint. In 1938 he won the award for the mural painting in the Department of Justice building at Washington. Mural painting presented him with new problems of technique and organization. The work on this painting involved hundreds of drawings, and experimenting with new mediums. The mural was executed in casein tempera on canvas prepared with a silica gypsum ground. He has been invited to exhibit in many museums. His paintings are in public and private collections.

In 1958—in a national competition—Shimin received second purchase award in the First Provincetown Arts Festival, the painting going into the permanent collection of Walter Chrysler Arts Museum, Provincetown, Massachusetts.

Shimin's work on children's books started when his friends Herman and Nina Schneider asked him to illustrate a new edition of their *How Big Is Big?* originally published in 1950. Since then he has illustrated some thirty-seven books, including the Newbery winner, *Onion John,* and his work has been represented in several shows of the American Institute of Graphic Arts.

Shimin has two daughters, Tonia, a dancer, and Toby.

SELECTED WORKS ILLUSTRATED: Onion John, by Joseph Krumgold, 1959; Listen Rabbit, by Aileen L. Fisher, 1964; One Small Blue Bead, by Byrd Baylor Schweitzer, 1965; Sam, by Ann Herbert Scott, 1967; Zeely, by Virginia Hamilton, 1967; Dance in a Desert, by Madeleine L'Engle, 1969; A Pair of Shoes, by Aline Glasgow, 1970; Joseph and Koza, by Isaac Bashevis Singer, 1970.

ABOUT: Hopkins, Lee Bennett. Books Are by People; Kingman, Lee and others, comps. Illustrators of Children's Books: 1957-1966; Viguers, Ruth Hill and others, comps. Illustrators of Children's Books: 1946-1956; Who's Who in American Art, 1962.

LOUISA R. SHOTWELL
May 1, 1902-

AUTHOR OF *Roosevelt Grady*, etc.

Autobiographical sketch of Louisa Rossiter
Shotwell:

ONE day in the course of collecting material
for an adult book on migrant farm labor, I
visited a summer school for migrant children
in upstate New York. The room was very
noisy, but I noticed one small boy who paid
no heed to the bedlam. He sat off by himself at an ancient double desk, the kind that
turns up now and then in antique shops and
used to be standard equipment in one-room
rural schools. I peered over his shoulder.
With a stubby pencil he was working his way
steadily down a huge sheet of paper covered
with what looked to be exercises in subtrac-
tion. I sat down beside him and asked, "What
are you doing?" He raised neither eyes nor
pencil as he told me with bored courtesy,
"I'm takin' away."

I have the mind of a pack rat. Four years
later "Taking Away" became the opening
chapter of *Roosevelt Grady*, my first book
for children. The rest of Roosevelt's story
developed out of similar remembered sights
and sounds and people, from echoes of casual
talk with migrant fathers, mothers, and children in farm labor camps in Florida, on the
Eastern Shore of the Chesapeake, in New
Jersey and New York, and in California,
where I encountered the cotton-chopping
geese of Manowar's story.

I was born in Chicago. We lived in Des
Moines and Philadelphia, too, and I have
sharp recollections of my life in all three
cities, but when I was nine, my parents moved
to Skaneateles, New York, a village in the
Finger Lakes region and my father's boyhood home. This became my symbol of "a
satisfactory stay-put place," as Matthew
Grady would say. I grew up there and taught
English in the high school after my graduation from Wellesley. Through the years, as
I've taught and traveled and studied and
done a variety of things in a variety of places,
I've always managed to get back there at
least once a year. Now I spend my summers

in a cottage on Skaneateles Lake, elastic summers that begin in early May and end only
when late October brings killing frosts. Winters I live in an apartment in Brooklyn
Heights, and that is why *Adam Bookout*
takes place mainly in Brooklyn. Like Adam,
I am an only child.

A while ago I made a memorable expedition to Thailand, India, and Indonesia, out
of which came *Beyond the Sugar Cane Field*.

Most things I do rather fast, but I am a
slow writer, especially of fiction, which is
what I like best to write. I am always working on a story and I think about it all the
time, even when I'm busy at something else.
After a while, and it takes a long time for
this to happen, the characters begin to talk
back to me, and when they wake me up in
the morning, I know the time has come to
get them down on paper and see what
happens.

———

Louisa R. Shotwell took an M.A. from
Stanford University, 1928. Her book *Roosevelt Grady* won the Nancy Bloch Memorial
Award, the Woodward School Award, and
a Lewis Carroll Shelf Award, all in 1964.
Roosevelt Grady and *Adam Bookout* have
been published also in German editions, and

Roosevelt Grady and *Beyond the Sugar Cane Field* in Danish.

SELECTED WORKS: Roosevelt Grady, 1963; Beyond the Sugar Cane Field, 1964; Adam Bookout, 1967.

ABOUT: Contemporary Authors, Vol. 3; Who's Who of American Women, 1958-59; Horn Book June 1965.

URI SHULEVITZ

February 27, 1935-

ILLUSTRATOR OF *The Fool of the World and the Flying Ship*, etc.

Autobiographical sketch of Uri Shulevitz:

I WAS born in Warsaw. When the Warsaw blitz occurred, I was four. I still remember streets caving in, buildings burning, people carrying water from the Vistula. We fled Warsaw. Years of wandering followed. In 1947 we arrived in Paris. I was fascinated by the city, especially by the Quais de la Seine, where I spent countless hours browsing in the bookstalls. At that time I also developed a passion for films and comic books. I began drawing my own and a friend wrote the words. At the age of twelve I won first prize in a drawing competition held among all the grammar schools in my district.

In 1949 my parents, my baby brother, and I settled in Israel. From the age of fifteen to seventeen I went to high school at night and worked during the day at various jobs. I was apprentice to a rubber stamp maker, a house painter, and a carpenter, and I issued dog licenses at Tel Aviv City Hall (where I also had time to read, and for my first attempts at writing).

From 1952 to 1956 I studied at the Teachers' Institute near Tel Aviv, my first systematic education. I did especially well in literature, but purposely took courses in natural sciences to balance my natural inclination to fantasy.

At the same time I was studying art at night at the Art Institute of Tel Aviv. Previously the painter Ezekiel Streichman had been giving me private lessons in painting. After basic training in the Israeli Army, I joined the Ein Geddi kibbutz by the Dead

Sea, founded by a group of my friends, where I stayed for over a year.

In 1959 I came to New York to study painting at the Brooklyn Museum Art School. In 1963 *The Moon in My Room,* my first book—it was preceded by many unsatisfactory attempts—was published by Harper & Row; I contributed both words and pictures. More books, with text by other writers and my illustrations, followed. In 1969 I won the Caldecott Medal for my illustrations for *The Fool of the World and the Flying Ship,* a Russian folk tale retold by Arthur Ransome (Farrar, Straus & Giroux).

When it was suggested to me that I write my own book, my first reaction was that this was impossible, since I was not a writer and furthermore my English left a lot to be desired. "Writing," I later came to realize, has less to do with language than one might think. First, one has to have something to say. This may appear in one's mind in pictures, not necessarily in words, very much as in a film or comic strip. As I was to discover, the picture book is a medium in which words and pictures complement each other without repetition.

I have been fascinated by the concept of traveling, having covered many miles myself.

Uri Shulevitz: *OO ree SHOOL uh vitz*

In *The Moon in My Room,* a little boy "travels" in his room, discovering the different worlds that make up his own. And I have traveled in the course of my books, from total fantasy in *The Moon in My Room,* to a confrontation between fantasy and reality in *One Monday Morning* (Scribner's, 1967), to a total reality in *Rain Rain Rivers* (Farrar, Straus & Giroux, 1969). It was a long trip. But the real trip, I found, had little to do with mileage, but rather with experience and discovery; and this may happen anywhere around or within us.

———

Uri Shulevitz served in the Israeli Army from 1956-1959, during part of which time he worked as art director of a magazine for teen-agers. Shulevitz is interested in music and old tales and parables of eastern tradition, studies tai-chi-chuan, which is a form of Chinese calisthenics, and has studied Chinese calligraphy in New York's Chinatown, both under Professor Cheng.

A designer of books as well as author and illustrator, Shulevitz has received a citation from the Society of Illustrators and has been represented in a number of exhibitions of the American Institute of Graphic Arts and in the Biennale of Illustrations, Bratislava, Czechoslovakia, 1969. He collaborated with Tom Spain on a film version of his book *One Monday Morning.*

Uri Shulevitz is now a United States citizen.

SELECTED WORKS WRITTEN AND ILLUSTRATED: The Moon in My Room, 1963; One Monday Morning, 1967; Rain Rain Rivers, 1969.

SELECTED WORKS ILLUSTRATED: Charley Sang a Song, by H. R. Hays and Daniel Hays, 1964; The Second Witch, by Jack Sendak, 1965; The Carpet of Solomon, by Sulamith Ish-Kishor, 1966; The Twelve Dancing Princesses, by The Brothers Grimm, 1966; The Silkspinners, by Jean Russell Larson, 1967; The Fool of the World and the Flying Ship, adapted by Arthur Ransome, 1968; Runaway Jonah, by Jan Wahl, 1968.

ABOUT: Contemporary Authors, Vol. 11-12; Hopkins, Lee Bennett. Books Are by People; Kingman, Lee and others, comps. Illustrators of Children's Books: 1957-1966; Horn Book August 1969; New York Times Book Review May 4, 1969; School Library Journal May 1969.

MARY FRANCIS SHURA

February 27, 1923-

AUTHOR OF *The Nearsighted Knight,* etc.

Autobiographical sketch of Mary Francis Shura Craig:

THERE has to be some place for the extra energy of life to spill into. For me, that place is a sentence or a brushed line.

"Remember" was the order I always gave myself, knowing that to delineate, you must see, and to describe, you must feel. I must have always known that the world of words is not life, but only the place it spills into, blessed with order, spiced with human frailty, and haunted, hopefully, by the flavor that is more viable than the substance.

Although I was born in Pratt, Kansas, (near Dodge City) I never lived there, but grew up in Portland, Oregon, and Spokane, Washington. High school and college years (Maryville State College) in Missouri and subsequent marriage and widowhood in that area imbued me with the truculent strength of the midwest.

As the tagalong to three older sisters, I was encouraged to go off by myself. Ever since I have been grateful for time alone.

Who would create a fantasy world they didn't like? Not I. I write of things that I enjoy—gay families with lots of room for people to be individuals. I like animals, the out-of-doors, games and great terrifying storms and all those half-magic things that stir in mists and come to you alone. Also I like chuckles hidden so carefully that you have to listen twice.

My own four children, Minka, Dan, Alice and Shay, do not live in my books but give gifts to them—the loneliness of leaving friends, those transient fears, the helplessness of growing, the pain of being different, and most of all the joy of untangling a problem so that it lies smooth on the lap of your life and is named success.

Now we are gypsies of that special American sort. My husband is in college textbook sales and we move our children and books and chessmen about until we have literally changed the map of America into one vast friendly smile. Omaha, Atlanta, Chicago,

Boston. You name the city and we have lived near that zoo.

Now we are in the San Francisco Bay area where the ghosts jingle silver Spanish spurs and the brown pelicans all have degrees in physics. (How else could they dive from so high and predict where the fish will be when they hit the bay?)

But books are born where you are. At first a fragrance stirs in the mind, then it shapes into someone likeable but less than perfect. A child looks for you and the other one shrugs, "Mother? At her desk. Where else?"

———

Mary Francis Shura, whose maiden name was Young, married Daniel C. Shura in 1943 and by this marriage had three children, Marianne, Daniel C., and Alice Barrett. Her husband died in 1959. She married Raymond Craig in 1961, and Mary Forsha Craig was born in 1964. In a letter accompanying her autobiographical sketch, she says, "When faced with any biographical request, I am confounded by how very unexciting an extremely fun life can read when set down in trimly lettered lines. If I were to do this again, I would most assuredly have the wit to be a changeling in a Welsh hayfield and be abducted by pirates or at least be cast adrift at the age of two in a Chinese junk.

Instead I managed to make do and enjoy every minute. This is perverse, isn't it?"

A collection of Mary Francis Shura's poetry, stories, letters, galleys and other materials is in the library of the University of Oregon.

SELECTED WORKS: Simple Spigott, 1960; Garret of Greta McGraw, 1961; Mary's Marvelous Mouse, 1962; The Nearsighted Knight, 1964; Run Away Home, 1965; Shoefull of Shamrock, 1965; A Tale of Middle Length, 1966; Backwards for Luck, 1967; Por Nada, 1968.

ABOUT: Contemporary Authors, Vol. 3; Who's Who of American Women, 1970-1971.

ROBERT SILVERBERG

AUTHOR OF *The Lost Race of Mars*, etc.

Autobiographical sketch of Robert Silverberg, who writes under his own name and under the pen names "Walker Chapman," "Walter Drummond," "Ivar Jorgenson," "Calvin M. Knox," "David Osborne," "Lee Sebastian" and with Randall Garrett under the name "Robert Randall":

I WAS born in New York City during FDR's first Administration and had the customary unhappy childhood, spending too much of my time reading, going to museums, and scribbling stories, and too little of it learning how to outrun the oversized classmates who wanted to help adjust me to contemporary social norms. But I survived all that and lived happily ever after.

The fantastic, the grotesque, the improbable, and the imaginary attracted me early: as a reader I had gone through the local library's shelf of mythology and fantasy by the time I was nine, and shortly graduated to the science fiction pulps. When I began trying seriously to write—at about the age of thirteen—it was natural for me to create the sort of visionary stuff I preferred to read, and by the time I entered Columbia College in 1952 I was writing science fiction at a near-professional level. Short story sales quickly followed, and, when I was eighteen or nineteen I placed my first s-f novel, *Revolt on Alpha C*, with Thomas Y. Crowell. (It came out in 1955 and is still in print.) Upon my graduation from Columbia in 1956 I immediately became a full-time free-lance writer, and have been ever since, so I can list no long string of unlikely occupations. Writer is what I set out to be, writer is what I very quickly became, with (I now see) amazingly little difficulty along the way.

After writing s-f and some miscellaneous things for a few years, I slipped into nonfiction—first with a book on archaeology called *Lost Cities and Vanished Civilizations* (Chilton, 1962). As the title indicates, my original plan in doing nonfiction was to choose subjects that had much the same sort of romantic appeal for me, much the same sense of distance, color, and strangeness, as science fiction. In the main I kept to this, writing about extinct animals, living fossils, prehistoric men, unusual parts of the planet, and so forth. But I also let my editors occasionally seduce me into more mundane topics, which is how I happened to write books about bridges, great battles, nuclear physics, ghost towns, and some other subjects far from my original orientation toward fantasy.

After a decade of expository writing, my interest in nonfiction has about spent itself, and I'm seeking very few new commitments for such books. Instead I've returned to my old home base of science-fiction, where I've found a whole new universe of creative possibilities. My favorites, among my s-f books for younger readers, are *The Gate of Worlds* (Holt) and *Across a Billion Years* (Dial), but I've written many others and will write more. I also write science fiction for adult readers and have collected an assortment of awards and honors for it that I prize more highly than any other literary tribute.

In 1956 I married Barbara Brown, whom I met one night in the Columbia University observatory while trying to find Saturn. She's a physicist by education and an engineer by profession, and helps me no end with my books, quarreling with style and content, checking galleys, even doing indexes sometimes. We live in a vast old house in New York that once belonged to Fiorello LaGuardia, but spend much of our time traveling in the United States and overseas. We have no children but a whole platoon of cats, the offspring of which have been liberally dis-tributed through the New York publishing industry.

Robert Silverberg is the son of Michael and Helen (Baim) Silverberg. His wife, a designer of medical research equipment, is his technical advisor on the futuristic machines in his science fiction. The Silverbergs have devoted two floors of their home to a research library which was nearly destroyed by fire in 1968, but since restored. Making a list of all the books he has written would be impossible, Silverberg has said, because of their great number and because he no longer has complete records on the earlier titles. However he has more than a hundred books in print and has published about six hundred stories and articles.

In 1956 Silverberg received the Hugo trophy of the World Science Fiction Society. He received a second Hugo in 1969 and in 1970 his short story "Passengers" was awarded the Nebula trophy of the Science Fiction Writers of America. He has been chairman of the Hydra Club and president of Science Fiction Writers of America.

SELECTED WORKS: Revolt on Alpha C, 1955; Lost Race of Mars, 1960; Lost Cities and Vanished Civilizations, 1962; Man before Adam, 1964; The World of Coral, 1965; Forgotten by Time, 1966; The Morning of Mankind, 1967; The Gate of Worlds, 1967; The Auk, the Dodo, and the Oryx, 1967; The World of the Ocean Depths, 1968; Across a Billion Years, 1969.

ABOUT: Contemporary Authors, Vol. 3; New York Times Book Review May 4, 1969.

ISAAC BASHEVIS SINGER

July 14, 1904-

AUTHOR OF: *A Day of Pleasure*, etc.

Autobiographical sketch of Isaac Bashevis Singer:

I HAVE been writing for forty years and it never occurred to me that I would ever write for children. My adult works are full of demons, imps, dybbuks, haunted houses, and somehow I never thought that children might be interested in the supernatural the way I see it. But my friend Elizabeth Shub, who was then an editor of juvenile books at Har-

dren's stories first in Yiddish and then I translate them together with Mrs. Shub, who is also my editor. A day hardly passes without my getting letters from young readers. Their words, often written with many errors in spelling and grammar, are highly refreshing and encouraging to an old writer.

I am married and have a son and two grandchildren who are going to read me in Hebrew translation because this is their mother tongue.

In our times storytelling has almost become a forgotten art. It is only in juvenile books that a writer still has to tell a story, not discuss social changes or psychological motivations. The writers for children don't suffer from literary amnesia, they know that the story is *the thing*. There is a good chance that even adults will sooner or later begin to read juvenile books because they still tell a story.

———

Isaac Bashevis Singer was born in Radzymin, Poland, the son of Pinchos Menachem, a rabbi, and Bathsheba (Zylberman) Singer. His grandfathers on both sides were rabbis and he himself studied at the Tachkemoni Rabbinical Seminary in Warsaw, but gave up a religious career against his parents' wishes to follow the example of his elder brother, the writer Israel Joshua Singer. Isaac Bashevis Singer parted from his first wife, Rachel, and their son, Israel, who settled finally in Israel, where the son became a teacher at Beth Alfa Kibbutz and is now the father of three children.

Coming to New York in 1935, Isaac Bashevis Singer began writing for the Yiddish newspaper, *Jewish Daily Forward*. In 1940 he married his second wife, Alma Haimann, and in 1943 he became a United States citizen.

It has been estimated that between fifteen and twenty thousand people read Singer's stories in Yiddish newspapers around the world. His works have appeared in English in numerous American periodicals, including *The New Yorker, Saturday Evening Post, Esquire,* and *Harper's Magazine.* His books have been translated into fifteen languages and have won him a number of awards. His adult books have twice won the Louis Lamed Prize, in 1950 and 1956, and the Harry and

per, had different ideas. For a long time she tried to persuade me that this is the very stuff that children might love and that I was, at least potentially, a writer for children. My first book *Zlateh the Goat* was illustrated by Maurice Sendak. It came out in 1966, and it has in a way changed my life. I am now as interested in books for children as in those for adults.

As a matter of fact I think that children are the best readers in our time. They are not influenced by critics and names. If they don't like a book they just put it away no matter how famous the author might be. Also, children have a healthy approach to literature. They know that it is to entertain, not to bring about sociological revolutions. I have just finished a new story which I call *The Topsy Turvy Emperor of China* and I'm at work on a number of others. My publishers for adult books, Farrar, Straus & Giroux, were at first skeptical of my ability to write for children, but they have changed their minds completely. In the fall of 1969, a new juvenile book of mine was published by them; *A Day of Pleasure, Stories of a Boy Growing Up in Warsaw.* Besides Mr. Sendak, the illustrators of my books were Nonny Hogrogian and Margot Zemach. As in the case of books for adults, I write my chil-

Ethel Daroff Memorial Fiction Award for 1962. His children's books were runners-up three times for the Newbery Medal, *Zlateh the Goat* for 1967, *The Fearsome Inn* for 1968, and *When Shlemiel Went to Warsaw* for 1969. In 1970, *A Day of Pleasure* won the National Book Award for children's books in prose.

Singer is a member of the I. L. Peretz Writers Union and P.E.N. of New York City, and a fellow of the Jewish Academy of Arts and Sciences, and the Polish Institute of Arts and Sciences in America. He has been a member of the National Institute of Arts and Letters since 1965, and of the American Academy of Arts and Sciences since 1969. He received a grant from the American Institute of Arts and Letters in 1959 and an honorary degree, the L.H.D., from Hebrew Union College, Cincinnati, in 1963, and in 1970 the Medal of Achievement from Brandeis University.

SELECTED WORKS: Zlateh the Goat and Other Stories, 1966; Mazel and Schlimazel; or, The Milk of a Lioness, 1967; The Fearsome Inn, 1967; When Shlemiel Went to Warsaw and Other Stories, 1968; A Day of Pleasure, Stories of a Boy Growing Up in Warsaw, 1969; Joseph and Koza, 1970.

ABOUT: Author's and Writer's Who's Who, 1963; Buchen, Irving H. Isaac Bashevis Singer and the Eternal Past; Contemporary Authors, Vol. 1; Harte, Barbara and Carolyn Riley. 200 Contemporary Authors; Singer, Isaac Bashevis. In my Father's Court; Who's Who in America, 1968-69; Commentary November 1963; Contemporary Literature Winter 1969; Current Biography January 1969; Paris Review Fall 1968; Publishers' Weekly October 16, 1967; Saturday Review June 16, 1962; Time October 20, 1967; Vogue April 1, 1966; Wilson Library Bulletin December 1962.

ESPHYR SLOBODKINA

AUTHOR AND ILLUSTRATOR OF *Caps for Sale,* etc.

Autobiographical sketch of Esphyr Slobodkina:

I WAS born in the small Siberian town of Cheliabinsk at the foot of the Ural Mountains, the first sizable stop on the Asiatic side of the Trans-Siberian Railway. The town it-

Esphyr Slobodkina: *ess FEER sloh BOD keen ah*

self did not play a very large part in our lives. The railroad did—we lived within a few hundred feet of the station, and a spur track to bring in the tanker cars of crude oil, kerosene, and benzine passed within a few feet of our garden fence.

It may not seem very exciting to have been born a daughter of an oil yard manager in a small Siberian town, but it was. Perhaps it was so because of the kind of parents we happened to have been blessed with, because of their attitude towards us, and because of the variety of people who came to buy oil products from Father, to work for him, or to seek his advice.

There were clumsy peasants in sheepskin coats and felt boots who stood uneasily in the doorway until Father began to talk to them in their own singsong dialect. There were Chinese peddlers with huge bundles of raw silk, pongee and even occasionally a game of little lacquered bowls under which they hid tiny white mice. Once a Palestinian Jew with the unforgettable name of Karabajak came to sell religious relics from the Holy Land and stayed to help to nurse me through scarlet fever, while my older brother was dying of rheumatic heart. I'll never forget his dark, kindly, sad face, though I was only five at that time. There were Kirghiz nomads suddenly appearing in our yard mounted upon, of all things, camels! And then there was the unforgettable day when we saw our first automobile!

The yard itself was a constant beehive of activities. There was the cooper's shop where they made barrels for the oil. There was a pungent-smelling "raslivnaya" where they filled the barrels. There were the workers' children, a goodly number. My special friend, Vera, had eight sisters and brothers. There were the horses, and the cows, and the geese, the ducks, the turkeys. Then, one day, Rosalia, complete with a stack of papers and her own trained groom arrived. She was a thoroughbred mare, all black with only a white star on her forehead, given to my father by a wealthy Tartar friend. As a special mark of regard, he chose a mare which was about to foal. And, in the evenings, if the parents were out, there were the maids with their ignorant, fascinating and always hair-raising stories and folk tales.

The house was a different matter, simple, genteel, and rather elegant. Besides sweet aunts, entertaining uncles, a dear grandmother, and numerous cousins, there were always some interesting people visiting us. Later on, when Father was promoted and we moved to a bigger town in Russia proper, we lived in an eleven-room apartment. By that time the Russian Civil War had begun in earnest, and hordes of refugees came to our remote province. There was hardly a room in our apartment where somebody did not sleep either on the couch or on a folding cot or on some other ingeniously constructed contraption.

The refugees were a very interesting lot. Some were simply rich or politically prominent, some knew that their liberalism, egalitarianism, nihilism, or what have you, simply did not have a chance in the life-and-death class struggle. There were conscientious objectors, and there were those who would have fought willingly for their cause, but refused to be drafted on the wrong side. There were swashbuckling, empty-headed young "White" officers, and Talmud-learned, earnest believers in the Revolution as the "final solution" to the Jewish question in Russia. We children had a grand and I suspect highly educational time listening to their endless, heated discussions.

In the meantime life went on as usual, only more so. "Pelmeni" or "blini" parties, moonlight rides in troika-drawn sleighs, charity balls, and endless, fleeting flirtations. . . .

My people were always interested in the arts (Mother had a stunning mezzo, and sang at home and for worthy causes), so some evenings turned into improvised concerts, poetry recitals, and others were given over to well-organized children's theater performances. Perhaps the high standards set in those early years account for my complete lack of tolerance for "amateurism."

I am so glad that I can, most of the time, illustrate my own stories. I research endlessly, and unless it is an obviously fantastic folk tale, without specific time and/or place, I try to give authentic knowledge of the way the animals, the people, and their surroundings look.

But to come back to the story of my life, when things became too uncomfortable, we left Russia. Years of semi-nomadic existence followed. They were years of hard work, close family alliance, and hilarious laughter through tears of fatigue, hunger, and despair. These years took us to the Far Eastern Provinces of Russia (Vladivostok), Manchuria (Harbin) and, finally, to the United States.

During the Great Depression of the 1930s a friend of mine introduced me to Margaret Wise Brown. To Margaret with her childlike appreciation of the direct, simple and honest in art, my work had great appeal. *The Little Fireman* was the first in the series of books I illustrated for her. She was a wonderful person to work for—appreciative and encouraging. Because she was so encouraging, I dared to write my first story, *The Wonderful Feast*, later *Caps for Sale* and some fifteen other published stories, and endless numbers of unpublished ones.

In the meantime, even though I had to give up my first love, architecture, I did manage to become a rather well-known painter, with paintings in several art museums and important collections. In my "spare time" I also sculpt, do interior designing and decorating, design anything from clothes to lampshades, print scarves with my special silk-print process, and above all, constantly design and build on to my lovely, unique house in Great Neck which stands on the hill overlooking—guess what?—the tail end of Manhasset Bay with its array of oil tanks, and within the sight and sound of slithering oil barges.

———

Esphyr Slobodkina married William Lester Urquhart in 1960. As a student at the National Academy of Design, she received several prizes for composition, and later had repeated fellowships to Yaddo and to Mac-Dowell Colony. She is a founding member of the American Abstract Artists and of the American Federation of Modern Painters and Sculptors, with which groups she shows annually. She has had a number of one-man shows. Her work is represented in numerous collections, including those of the Whitney Museum of American Art, the Corcoran Gallery and the Philadelphia Museum of Art. *Caps for Sale* won a Lewis Carroll Shelf Award in 1958.

SELECTED WORKS WRITTEN AND ILLUSTRATED: Caps for Sale, 1938; The Wonderful Feast, 1955; The Clock, 1956; Pinky and the Petunias, 1959; The Long Island Ducklings, 1961; Pezzo the Peddler and the Circus Elephant, 1967; Pezzo the Peddler and the Thirteen Silly Thieves, 1970.

SELECTED WORKS ILLUSTRATED: The Little Fireman, by Margaret Wise Brown, 1938; The Little Cowboy, by Margaret Wise Brown, 1948; Sleepy ABC, by Margaret Wise Brown, 1953.

ABOUT: Artist's and Writer's Who's Who, 1963; Contemporary Authors, Vol. 1; Something About the Author, Vol. 1; Viguers, Ruth Hill and others, comps. Illustrators of Children's Books: 1946-1956; Who's Who in American Art, 1962; Who's Who of American Women, 1961-62.

"ERNEST SMALL"

See *Lent, Blair*

ZILPHA KEATLEY SNYDER

May 11, 1928-

AUTHOR OF *The Egypt Game,* etc.

Autobiographical sketch of Zilpha Keatley Snyder:

I WAS born and grew up in the country in rural southern California. The depression was

a harsh daily reality in the community where I lived, and the richness and variety of my life centered almost entirely around books and animals. My two sisters and I had lots of both.

I read early and constantly. My mother tells about my throwing myself on a surprised librarian and hugging and kissing her when, after learning that I could read, she offered to let me have my own library card, although I wasn't really old enough, according to the rules. All through school I averaged seven or eight library books a week, when they were available.

At the age of eight I decided that I was cut out to be a writer, but it was a long time before anyone shared my conviction. I wasn't easily discouraged, however, and I went on writing for about thirteen years, poems, short stories, and unfinished novels. I can comfort myself for my lack of early recognition by thinking that it was at least partly due to the fact that I had no typewriter. Looking at samples of my handwriting in those days, I'm sure that it would have been almost impossible for anyone to find out what I was doing.

I had always assumed that when I graduated from college, and stopped living on scholarships, college part-time jobs, and summer work as a waitress, that I would retire to an attic somewhere and write and/or starve. But I hadn't reckoned with growing up and becoming a victim of adult weaknesses, such as financial responsibility and romance. And so I found myself preparing to teach school and then getting married. My husband, Larry Snyder, was a music major at Whittier College in Whittier, California, where we both graduated. After our marriage we went to New York, where I taught school while he acquired a master's degree at Eastman School of Music. There followed several years of travel, four of them while Larry was in the Air Force, teaching, having babies and more graduate school for Larry.

It was the year that my husband got out of—and my youngest child into—school, that I decided to take up writing again. We had moved to Marin County, just across the Golden Gate Bridge from San Francisco, and one of the most beautiful places in the world. It was a natural time and place to write, and after having taught school for nine years and produced children of my own, writing for children seemed the natural thing to do. So I did, and the final result after much rewriting, was *Season of Ponies*, my first book.

My other books have been *The Velvet Room*, full of ghosts of my own childhood, *Black and Blue Magic*, written for my son who was having a little "black and blue" trouble of his own at the time, *The Egypt Game*, inspired by kids I taught in Berkeley, California, and a game my daughter was playing that year, and *Eyes in the Fishbowl*, the story of a kind of haunting that forced its way into my head and haunted me until it was written. A book of poetry, *Today Is Saturday*, is out, and I am working now on another prose book. My husband is now dean at the San Francisco Conservatory of Music, our daughter, Susan, is in ninth grade and Doug and Ben are in seventh.

Mrs. Snyder's book *The Egypt Game* was a runner-up for the Newbery Medal in 1968, received a New York *Herald Tribune* Children's Spring Book Festival Award in 1967, and a Lewis Carroll Shelf Award in 1970.

SELECTED WORKS: Season of Ponies, 1964; The Velvet Room, 1965; Black and Blue Magic, 1966; The Egypt Game, 1967; Eyes in the Fishbowl, 1968; Today Is Saturday, 1969; The Changeling, 1970.

ABOUT: Contemporary Authors, Vol. 11-12; Something About the Author, Vol. 1.

AIMÉE SOMMERFELT
April 2, 1892-

AUTHOR OF *The Road to Agra*, etc.

Autobiographical sketch of Aimée Dedichen Sommerfelt:

I WAS born into a very happy family living out in the country near Oslo. And as good authors usually have a gloomy background I shouldn't have much chance to compete at all.

In the early days of my life children had to entertain themselves as there was neither television nor radio. We acted all the books we read from romantic Norwegian fairy tales about captured princesses to the bloodiest Fenimore Cooper. I believe that this kind of activity is stimulating to children's imagination and that my mind was turned towards fiction at a very early age. At any rate when in the evening the lights were out and we were all in bed, my younger sister and brother and friends visiting us, came creeping up in the largest bed, saying: "Now let's have a story!" And we invented the most romantic or nerve-racking stories until we heard the staircase creak under parental steps. Then there were tap, taps of bare feet across the floor, everybody rushing into their own beds and happily asleep when my parents put their heads in for inspection.

I never quite stopped inventing tales, and some of my "invented" children became very real to me. I felt that they had something on their minds. They forced themselves onto paper, and from the papers they crept into books. That is how it started.

My education at home finished, my father, the head doctor of a mental hospital, sent me abroad to learn languages. This was for many reasons a good decision, particularly as I later married a linguist, professor Alf Sommerfelt at Oslo University. During World

Aimée Sommerfelt (signature)

War II it so happened that he, then in London, was asked to cooperate at the foundation of UNESCO. And when the war was over we traveled a good deal together and I met children in many countries.

When I started writing, my one and only intention was to make children laugh and have a good time. And I still think that juvenile books should be entertaining, not gloomy. But the war, the occupation of my country and later the visits to underdeveloped parts of the world have been an eye-opener to me. Traveling with UNESCO, one is shown more than most tourists. Coming to India and Mexico, for instance, seeing those colorful countries from the inside, made a deep impression on me. Even slum children who are so happy when they get proper food and so lucky when they get education, are full of possibilities. It struck me how children all over the world are alike. In a mystic way they have more in common than adults. Even those speaking different languages are able to play together.

I believe that what children read in the most formative, open-minded years of their lives is of great importance. They are the most wonderful audience for any writer who can stir their imagination. Not that they are angels, far from it, but prejudices do not block the way to understanding, to identification. Not yet. Not until they are planted into them. I sometimes wonder if one has to be grown up to start misunderstanding one another for good.

My husband and I passed a wonderful year in California at the Center for Behavioral Sciences, Palo Alto, and we were also invited to a most stimulating term at the Ossabaw Island Project. These were our last adventurous and fruitful journeys together. Three years ago he was killed in a car accident.

Life will never be the same after that. But I still live and work in our home, not far from where I told my first silly little stories in late evenings, and children, grandchildren and friends do their best to make my life as good and happy as they can.

———

Aimée Sommerfelt has two married daughters, Wenche Werring and Anne Louise Ziesler, and a son, Axel, who is an associate professor at the University of Oslo.

The Road to Agra won the Norwegian State Prize in 1960, was on the Honor List for the Hans Christian Andersen Award in 1962, won a Child Study Association Children's Book Award in 1961, the Jane Addams Book Award in 1962 and a Boys' Clubs of America Junior Book Award in 1962.

White Bungalow won a Thomas Alva Edison Foundation National Mass Media Award in 1964.

Pablo won the Norwegian State Prize, 1965, and was on the Honor List for the Hans Christian Andersen Award in 1966.

Mrs. Sommerfelt's books have been published in about twenty countries in addition to Norway and the United States.

SELECTED WORKS: The Road to Agra, 1961; Miriam, 1963; The White Bungalow, 1964; My Name Is Pablo, 1965; No Easy Way, 1967.

IVAN SOUTHALL

June 8, 1921-

AUTHOR OF *Ash Road*, etc.

Autobiographical sketch of Ivan Francis Southall:

I'M an Australian country-dweller, a big, wide, booming, beautiful country, so I write

Ivan Southall.

is true. I think you might guess if you read *Ash Road* that the enormous forest fire that begins at the beginning and ends fourteen chapters later happened to us. And if you read *The Fox Hole* I wonder whether you will recognize that it is set in exactly the same place? And would you decide from *Hills End* that the writer knew the children very well? He did, I assure you. He tucked some of them into their real-life beds every night!

And what about *Let the Balloon Go?* Where does John Clement Sumner come from, the spastic boy who wants to be an ordinary person like everyone else? I suppose John is a little bit of all of us, a little bit of me, and of my wife (she had fire when I met her and she's got it still), a little bit of each of my children and a little bit of you. John is my favorite hero, overcoming every obstacle, fighting like mad to be right. In a way it's the story of everyone's life.

I was born in Melbourne and grew up in a pleasant suburb called Surrey Hills. I lived on top of a hill, even then, with my father and mother and brother, and went to state schools until the eighth grade. Then I won a modest scholarship to a small college—Box Hill Grammar School—where my father hoped I would gain the background a writer should have. It was not to be. My father died and I was the elder son. Just fourteen I had to leave that school and go to work, to be educated by life.

about Australia. I'm a person as well, once a boy, now father of a son and three daughters and forever in trouble with one of them or another, so I write about people. I was also a pilot in the Second World War, quaking under my helmet, trying to dodge the other fellow before he caught me, so I know what it is like to be in danger. If you mix those ingredients, remembering that since you were twelve years of age you had longed to be nothing but a writer, something like my books for boys and girls begins to happen.

I met a girl in England, you see, during the war (she was a stunner) and took her home to Australia as my wife. I don't suppose she's a "girl" now, really, but she was then. We lived restlessly in the city for a year or two but then went "bush" to a little run-down farm with a tumbledown house high in the hills. With our own hands we pulled the house down and built another; we planted acres of garden; we grew our own food; and we raised our kids.

They were rugged years—we don't live there now—but so many of the things that happened then, so many of the people I came to know, so many of the scenes I came to love, have found a way into books like *Hills End, Ash Road* and *To the Wild Sky*. In a way all those books have much in them that

Ivan Southall married Joyce Blackburn in 1945. Their children are Andrew John, Roberta Joy, Elizabeth Rose, and Melissa Frances. Ivan Southall's books have been translated into Norwegian, Swedish, French, and Dutch. He received the Australian Children's Book of the Year Award in 1966 for *Ash Road* and in 1968 for *To the Wild Sky*.

SELECTED WORKS: Hills End, 1963; Ash Road, 1966; To the Wild Sky, 1967; The Fox Hole, 1967; Let the Balloon Go, 1968; Finn's Folly, 1969; Chinaman's Reef Is Ours, 1970; Walk a Mile and Get Nowhere, 1970.

ABOUT: Contemporary Authors, Vol. 9-10; Hetherington, John. Forty-two Faces; Horn Book June 1968; Publishers' Weekly October 28, 1968; Top of the News June 1969.

IB SPANG OLSEN

See *Olsen, Ib Spang*

PETER SPIER
June 6, 1927-

ILLUSTRATOR OF *London Bridge Is Falling Down!* etc.

Autobiographical sketch of Peter Edward Spier:

I WAS born in Amsterdam, the Netherlands, but grew up in Broek in Waterland, a small romantic village which Americans know as the birthplace of Hans Brinker. Don't ever ask the Broekers for details, they'll tell you: "Eh, what? Hans Brinker . . . silver skates? Never heard of him. There are no Brinkers in the county. But wait! Let me ask Neighbor, just in case." He'll call across the fence and the subject will be pursued endlessly. I guarantee that you will learn absolutely nothing about Hans Brinker, but it is at any rate good for a cup of coffee and a long conversation.

We went to school in Amsterdam, a trip in an ancient swaying train filled with the smoke of cigars and clay pipes, Volendam fishermen wearing huge wooden shoes and baggy pants, and the unforgettable aroma of herring and smoked eel, stacked in baskets in the aisles as they were taken to market. After the train a short boatride, some walking and the city streetcar. It was a varied and wonderful trip, offering us a multitude of plausible and implausible excuses for being late. All this to the intense envy of our friends. Weekends and vacations were spent sailing the old Zuyderzee, great sections of which have now been reclaimed, and it is a strange and nostalgic sensation to drive past freshly-plowed fields on the old sea-bottom, when you sailed only eighteen years ago where the swallows fly now.

I cannot remember a time when I did not dabble with clay, draw, or see someone draw, for my father, the illustrator and journalist Jo Spier, worked at home. So I grew up with it all. But it was not till I was eighteen that I decided to make it my career, and went to the Rijksacademie voor Beeldende

Kunsten in Amsterdam. Following that I was drafted and became an officer in the Royal Netherlands Navy, serving part of that time in the West Indies and South America. Once that was out of the way I went to work for *Elsevier's Weekly*, the largest Dutch weekly newspaper, and was stationed in Paris for the first year. In 1952 I came to the United States where Elsevier Publishing then had a branch in Houston, Texas. Soon I moved to the New York area and have lived there ever since. It was then that I began illustrating magazines and children's books, almost a hundred of them. Later I began doing my own books.

There is very little I can say about "how I draw" beyond the mystery of putting a nice, white piece of paper on my table, picking up a pen (Gillot 192), dipping it in India ink and making a start. And the last, alas, I often find the most difficult. But before I get to that point a great deal of work has already been done. Since most of my picture books have some sort of historical setting—as in the case of *London Bridge Is Falling Down*—or a very defined local setting like New England in *The Fox Went Out on a Chilly Night*, I first find out as much as possible about subject or region. Then I go there, sketchbook in hand, to collect the hundreds of details that go into the making of these books. The result of these trips is a stack of hundreds of sketches with notes on the color. It is then that the actual work of combining those sketches and details begins. Since I like to retain the effect of a colored pen drawing, I first make the black key and then use only blue, red and yellow watercolors on non-photo blues of the black key. In this way there is no black halftone in the books at all, which I believe helps the impression of crispness. I am often asked whether I think of my own children or of the reaction of children in general while working on a book. I do hope that I am not offending anyone by admitting that I do it initially for only one person in the world, namely myself. The worry about what others will think comes soon enough after the work is done!

I am married to the former Kathryn Pallister and we have two children, Tom and Kathryn. I am one of those few fortunate people who earn their living with their hobby. My pleasures away from the drawing table are still sailing and, in winter, the building of old-time ship models.

———

Peter Spier married Kathryn M. Pallister in 1958, and is now a United States citizen. He is a member of the Netherland Club (New York).

Spier has won a number of awards for his illustrations, including the Diploma di Triennale di Milano and several certificates from the American Institute of Graphic Arts. *The Fox Went Out on a Chilly Night* was a runner-up for the Caldecott Medal for 1962 and *London Bridge Is Falling Down!* won the Boston *Globe-Horn Book* Award for 1967.

In 1967, Spier originated The Mother Goose Library, a series of books he designs and illustrates and for which he selects and adapts the rhymes.

SELECTED WORKS WRITTEN AND ILLUSTRATED: Of Dikes and Windmills, 1969; The Erie Canal, 1970.

SELECTED WORKS ILLUSTRATED: The Cow Who Fell in the Canal, by Phyllis Krasilovsky, 1957; The Fox Went Out on a Chilly Night (folk song), .1961; London Bridge Is Falling Down (Mother Goose), 1967; To Market! To Market! (Mother Goose), 1967; Hurrah, We're

Outward Bound! (Mother Goose), 1968; And So My Garden Grows (Mother Goose), 1969.

ABOUT: Contemporary Authors, Vol. 7-8; Hopkins, Lee Bennett. Books Are by People; Kingman, Lee and others, comps. Illustrators of Children's Books: 1957-1966; Viguers, Ruth Hill and others, comps. Illustrators of Children's Books: 1946-1956.

ARNOLD SPILKA
November 13, 1917-

AUTHOR AND ILLUSTRATOR OF *Paint All Kinds of Pictures*, etc.

Autobiographical sketch of Arnold Spilka:

IF Wordsworth was right when he wrote, "The world is too much with us," then I guess we're justified in saying that nonsense is its own reward. Which is a sneaky way of mentioning the fact that I've written two books of nonsense poems for no other reason than that they might make the world a little less with us. I suppose we all have a more or less hidden desire to be comedians at some time and I'm no exception. And so my *A Lion I Can Do Without* and *Once upon a Horse*. Another book, my tiny *Little Birds Don't Cry* just happened along in the midst of my writing other nonsense.

Being a sculptor and painter of sorts, it was natural that one of my first books was *Paint All Kinds of Pictures*, an attempt at putting over the idea of the importance of self-expression in art. We all know that all children have this natural urge for self-expression. But we also know that for some reason they too often lose this as they grow up. My hope was to help prolong this natural urge for creativity.

I seem to be going back in time but before any others I did a book called *Aloha from Bobby*. Having spent some time in Oahu, Hawaii, a number of years before, the urge to reminisce about some of my memories there was logical. At this point I must say that my brother Michael (who writes under the name of Michael Sage) has been my good right arm. Four of his books for children that I've illustrated are his *Words inside Words* and *If You Talked to a Boar*, fun books that are educational as well, and the

ARNOLD SPILKA

two tiny books *Deep in a Haystack* and *Dippy Dos and Don'ts.*

Going back in time being a common practice among people in the children's book field, I now go back again and here I put first things last. The fact that I was born to a father who was a respected creative designer, a mother who bragged about my early attempts at art, and to a family where, despite the usual frictions, the feeling of family love was part of everyday breathing . . . well, this hasn't hurt a bit.

———

Arnold Spilka, a native New Yorker, studied sculpture and drawing at the Art Students League.

SELECTED WORKS WRITTEN AND ILLUSTRATED: Aloha from Bobby, 1962; Paint All Kinds of Pictures, 1963; A Lion I Can Do Without, 1964; Little Birds Don't Cry, 1965; Once upon a Horse, 1966; A Rumbudgin of Nonsense, 1970.

SELECTED WORKS ILLUSTRATED: If You Talked to a Boar, by Michael Sage, 1960; Words Inside Words, by Michael Sage, 1961; Lines and Shapes, by Solveig Paulson Russell, 1965; You Better Come Home with Me, by John Lawson, 1966; Best Little House, by Aileen Fisher, 1966; Deep in a Haystack, by Michael Sage, 1966; Dippy Dos and Don'ts, by Michael Sage, 1967; The Tree and Me, by Michael Sage, 1970.

ABOUT: Kingman, Lee and others, comps. Illustrators of Children's Books: 1957-1966.

"SCHUYLER STANTON"

See *Baum, L. Frank*

MARY Q. STEELE

See *"Gage, Wilson"*

WILLIAM STEIG
November 14, 1907-

AUTHOR AND ILLUSTRATOR OF *Sylvester and the Magic Pebble,* etc.

Biographical sketch of William Steig:

WILLIAM STEIG, author, artist, cartoonist, and sculptor, was born in New York City, son of Joseph and Laura (Ebel) Steig. Both parents were painters, and his three brothers are artists. Irwin is also a writer, Henry a musician and writer, and Arthur a poet. It was Irwin, the eldest brother, who first gave William lessons in painting and drawing when the little boy showed his interest.

He recalls being deeply affected by *Grimms' Fairy Tales,* Charlie Chaplin movies, *Hansel and Gretel,* the Katzenjammer Kids, and *Pinocchio*—especially *Pinocchio.* In his Caldecott Award acceptance speech of 1970, for the book *Sylvester and the Magic Pebble,* Steig said, "It is very likely that Sylvester became a rock and then again a live donkey because I had once been so deeply impressed with Pinocchio's longing to have his spirit encased in flesh instead of in wood."

Early schooldays at P.S. 53, in the Bronx, are vivid memories, now immortalized in Steig's "Small-Fry" drawings, which first appeared in the *New Yorker,* and later in book form. High school years are mainly remembered for all-around athletics, and his two years at the City College of New York for his membership on the All-American Water Polo Team. He attended the National School of Design in New York from 1925 to 1929, but even in these years, Steig remembers that he "got all his fun playing football in the back yard."

At twenty-three he began his career as a cartoonist, working for the old *Life* and

WILLIAM STEIG

Judge magazines, and later for the *New Yorker, Vanity Fair, Collier's,* and others. Many of these cartoons have been collected and published in book form.

On January 2, 1936, he married Elizabeth Mead, who is the mother of his two older children, Lucy and Jeremy. They moved to Connecticut, where he and his brother Henry pruned trees and stacked a woodpile. One day Steig began whittling a chunk of wood and so began his career as sculptor. All his male carvings are known in the family as Jason, all the female as Tessie. The stark wood sculptures are less than a foot high. He touched up his later sculpture with bits of rope for hair, mesh for veiling, or a few beads. New York City's Downtown Gallery held a one-man showing of fourteen of these figures in 1939, the same year in which Steig's first book of one hundred and five symbolic drawings *About People* appeared. In 1940 he exhibited drawings and sculpture at Smith College. His works are in the collections of the Rhode Island Museum, Providence, in the Smith College Museum, Northampton, Massachusetts, and in the Brooklyn Museum, New York City.

His first marriage having ended in divorce, William Steig married Laura Homestead in 1950. His third child, Margit Laura, was born of this marriage, which ended in divorce in 1963. In December, 1964, he and

Stephanie Healey were married, and they were divorced in December, 1966.

He was inspired to write and illustrate children's books by his good friend and publisher, Robert Kraus, of Windmill Books, "who had the insight that I—and others like me—could make a contribution in this field." Steig says that he takes books for children very seriously, and that his work is a large part of him.

An apartment in Greenwich Village off Washington Square is Steig's home and workshop now. He draws with his left hand at "an almost incredible speed." He is a night person who prefers to work in the evening, and seldom rises before noon. It is said that he is also a very private person who rarely sees anyone but old friends and members of his family. A devoted father, he is often with his married son and daughter who live in the neighborhood, and he even helps Lucy with her baby, his first grandchild. Lucy paints, and Jeremy is an artist as well as a distinguished jazz flautist. His youngest daughter, Margit Laura, Maggie, is already showing signs of artistic ability. Steig's three children seem to be carrying on the tradition of the talented Steig family.

SELECTED WORKS WRITTEN AND ILLUSTRATED: Roland the Minstrel Pig, 1968; CDB! 1968; Sylvester and the Magic Pebble, 1969; The Bad Island, 1969; The Bad Speller, 1970; An Eye for Elephants, 1970.

ABOUT: Current Biography, 1944; Who's Who in America, 1970-71; Who's Who in American Art, 1970; American Artist March 1943; Horn Book August 1970; Magazine of Art January 1943; PM Magazine June 18, 1944; Publishers' Weekly August 17, 1970; Time April 3, 1939; Top of the News April 1970.

DOROTHY STERLING
November 23, 1913-

AUTHOR OF *Freedom Train: the Story of Harriet Tubman,* etc.

Autobiographical sketch of Dorothy Sterling:

IF you're born in New York City and you're no good at sports, you spend your free time picking violets on Riverside Drive, planting gardens in vacant lots, and feeding

Dorothy Sterling

ducks in Central Park. At least, that's what I did in those bygone years when urban blight had not yet destroyed the city's wildlife. Summers in camps in Maine where I was conspicuously *not* chosen for the baseball team gave me a further chance to explore the natural world. I had a thousand questions to ask about trees, flowers, insects—and no way to find the answers. Perhaps there were children's books on these subjects. If so, I never encountered them. Further, no one I knew was interested in nature and I was already marked as a "nut" because I preferred bugs to baseball.

Finishing high school, I spent two years at Wellesley College and was graduated from Barnard at the height of the Great Depression. With millions unemployed, there were no jobs for a young woman who vaguely knew that she wanted to write—or edit—or work on a magazine—and had no training in these fields. After more than a year of job-hunting the Federal Writers Project rescued me from my private depression. The Writers Project was a significant learning experience. For the first time I met people who had not shared my sheltered middle-class background. I was still living at home while most of the writers on the project were supporting grandparents, parents, children on the

$23.86 that Uncle Sam paid us each week. When Congress threatened to abolish the arts projects, I too marched on picket lines, shouting "Give the bankers Home Relief. We want jobs!". This was The Movement of our day. I'm glad that I had the chance to be part of it.

On the Writers Project, I also met my husband, Philip Sterling. We married in 1937 and had two children, Peter and Anne. Meanwhile I continued to work, learning my trade during twelve years at Time Inc. As a researcher and in *Life's* news bureau, I learned how to collect facts, assemble them in readable form, and check them for accuracy. When I left *Life* in 1949 I was at last ready to become a writer.

There was no question of what to write about. We lived in the suburbs and Peter and Anne brought home caterpillars, snakes, leaves, mushrooms. Digging out the answers to their questions resulted in books like *Insects and the Homes They Build, Caterpillars, The Story of Mosses, Ferns and Mushrooms* and *The Outer Lands. The Cub Scout Mystery, Brownie Scout Mystery* and others also grew out of their interests and experiences.

While looking for a subject for a biography, I read about Harriet Tubman, that remarkable and courageous woman who led more than three hundred slaves to freedom. Research for *Freedom Train,* my biography of her, made me realize how ignorant I was about the lives of Black people. Appalled by the omissions and distortions in history books, I turned to old newspapers, letters, convention minutes to write *Captain of the Planter, Forever Free* and *Tear Down the Walls!* After the Supreme Court declared that separate schools were *per se* unequal, I traveled through the South to interview Black youngsters entering "white" schools for the first time. Out of this came *Tender Warriors* (for adults) and *Mary Jane,* my best-selling book which has been translated into seven languages.

Recently my husband traded in his public relations job for a typewriter at home. He has written several excellent books for young people, including *Four Took Freedom, The Quiet Rebels* and *Sea and Earth, the Life of*

Rachel Carson. Both Peter and Anne are scientists and this summer I plan to take my granddaughter, Emily, on her first nature walk.

In more than twenty-eight books since 1951, Dorothy Sterling has written on a number of subjects, but her main interests are biology and American history, particularly Black history. Seven of her works have been book club selections and six have been published in foreign countries. She received the Nancy Bloch Award in 1958 for *Captain of the Planter,* a biography of Robert Smalls, and again in 1959, for *Mary Jane,* which also won the Community-Woodward School's award for promotion of "one-worldness" among children, and an honorable mention from The Child Study Association of America. She has been Consulting Editor for the multi-racial Firebird Books, published by Scholastic Book Services, as well as editorial consultant for Perspective Books, a series of Black biographies published by Doubleday.

SELECTED WORKS: Insects and the Homes They Build, 1954; Freedom Train: The Story of Harriet Tubman, 1954; The Story of Mosses, Ferns and Mushrooms, 1955; Captain of the Planter: The Story of Robert Smalls, 1958; Mary Jane, 1959; Caterpillars, 1961; Forever Free: The Story of the Emancipation Proclamation, 1963; Lucretia Mott: Gentle Warrior, 1964; Lift Every Voice (with Benjamin Quarles), 1965; The Outer Lands, 1967; Tear Down the Walls: A History of the American Civil Rights Movement, 1968.

ABOUT: Contemporary Authors, Vol. 9-10; Something About the Author, Vol. 1; Negro History Bulletin, December 1958.

WILLIAM STOBBS

June 27, 1914-

ILLUSTRATOR OF *A Bundle of Ballads,* etc.

Autobiographical sketch of William Stobbs:

WHEN illustrating books I never use the text as something to be translated into pictures, but more as a companion who is seeing and talking one way, while I look around, listening to the author, but seeing other things which he has apparently missed, like the carp at the bottom of the pond, or the

cat yawning his head off. If the author has already described something in detail with words, it seems pointless to repeat these facts in pictures. The illustrator must find some other way of making the book wider, deeper and richer. Words and images should complement rather than produce reflections of each other, and grow in the process, after which they can be fused by good typography and book production into something alive. Of course there are some authors who prefer to do without pictures, like Dylan Thomas, who once told me with a voice like a tuba that if his poems needed propping up with pictures he would burn them as useless.

The technology of book production and colour reproduction has been accelerating during the last twenty years. As Head of the Faculty of Graphic Design at the London College of Printing (1948-58) I was concerned with the new developments and learned during that period a great deal from the staff of the College, who are all specialists in various fields connected with printing and methods of reproduction. It is essential for all illustrators to know something of this technology because their work is not complete until the finished book appears.

My work is divided into two kinds. First there are the educational books, like the series on explorers written by Ronald Syme and published by William Morrow of New York, and the six volume *Life in England,* by Amabel Williams-Ellis and myself, published by Blackie of London. Then there are books for younger children, like the series of traditional folk tales, published by Bodley Head, McGraw Hill and Follett. I like working in both of these fields.

The folk and fairy tales come to me very fresh because as a child I had no time for them at all. My eight seafaring uncles were always coming to stay with my parents between voyages, and their stories, it seemed to me, were incomparably better. Stories about Hong Kong, Shanghai, Valparaiso, Naples, Istanbul, Cape Horn, the Persian Gulf, fog off the west coast of Scotland and engine failure off the coast of Peru. I still see these seafaring uncles, now retired, and they can effortlessly continue where they left off.

Then there was my grandfather William, who used to disappear for long periods and then send postcards from unpredictable places. He reached most of them on foot, including Rome. His anecdotes were almost as hypnotic as those of the uncles. Neither the eight uncles nor my grandfather ever wrote books or made drawings. They just enjoyed or deplored everything as it came, making comments, but not in writing.

Transforming life into words or images is not easy. It means withdrawing from existence from time to time in order to concentrate on producing something which will be as vital as the living world outside. For the last ten years I have been living with my family in a sixteenth-century house on a high hill overlooking the Weald of Kent. The family, the house and the landscape have all influenced my work.

William Stobbs was born in South Shields, England. He attended the King Edward VI School of Art, 1933-1938, and received a First Class Honours Degree (B.A.) in History of Art in 1938 and an M.A. in 1945, both from Durham University. He and his wife Brenda were married in 1938 and they have two sons. In 1958, Stobbs became Principal of the Maidstone College of Art, Kent.

He is a Member of the Society of Industrial Artists.

Stobbs's illustrations for Ronald Welch's book, *Knight Crusader,* won commendation when Welch received the Carnegie Medal in 1954. In 1959, Stobbs won the Kate Greenaway Medal for his illustrations for *Kashtanka* and *A Bundle of Ballads.*

SELECTED WORKS ILLUSTRATED: Balboa, Finder of the Pacific, by Ronald Syme, 1956; A Bundle of Ballads, edited by Ruth Manning-Sanders, 1961; Kashtanka, by Anton Pavlovich Chekov, 1961; King Arthur and His Knights, retold by Ronald Derek Storer, 1962; Round the World Fairy Tales, retold by Amabel Williams-Ellis, 1966; Three Billy Goats Gruff, 1968; Amerigo Vespucci, by Ronald Syme, 1969; Gianni and the Ogre, by Ruth Manning Sanders, 1971.

ABOUT: Hürlimann, Bettina. Picture Book World 1969; Kingman, Lee and others, comps. Illustrators of Children's Books: 1957-1966; Ryder, John. Artists of a Certain Line; Viguers, Ruth Hill and others, comps. Illustrators of Children's Books, 1946-1956; Library Association Record May 1960.

ADRIEN STOUTENBURG
December 1, 1916-

AUTHOR OF *American Tall Tales,* etc.

Autobiographical sketch of Adrien Pearl Stoutenburg, who writes under her own name and under the pen names of "Barbie Arden," "Lace Kendall," and "Nelson Minier":

AS a young child, walking through the twilight of my small home town in Minnesota farming country, I remember my awe at the beauty of an evening star. Deeply moved, I silently promised that star something, as children will. The promise was associated with the star's splendor and with a vague sense of dedication to that beauty. This may sound lofty, but I mention it because that experience, and others in my childhood, make me know that children often have keen, long-remembered aesthetic responses even though they may never be able to articulate them.

My desire even then, I believe, was to be a poet. With two published books of poetry for adults, and one for children, I think I can say that I have made a beginning. I have also

Adrien Stoutenburg (signature)

done some thirty-eight books of other kinds for young readers—picture books, mysteries, biographies, folk tales, and books emphasizing the need to conserve our wildlife.

I was born in Minnesota prairie land, at Darfur, and my father died when I was two years old. My young, hard-pressed mother let my paternal grandmother take me into her home in the town first mentioned, Hanley Falls. So I grew up with her, and a step-grandfather, both doting, but still it was a rather lonely childhood—though one with room for clouds, crickets, rainbows, and rambles through the pines in the Minnesota lake country where we stayed for a time and where I went to a one-room, country schoolhouse. There was much that was grim about that, but there were also the sound of loons, the freshly gleaming lakes.

I had a talent for drawing—and art was long a major hobby—but a teacher in my sixth grade class stimulated· literary ambitions with her praise of an essay I did. So, for awhile, I rode twin horses, art and poetry. In high school, in Minneapolis, where I went to live with my mother after my grandmother's death, I was an introverted dreamer on a cloudy peak of Parnassus. The dreams ended swiftly when I graduated into the depression. I managed to find scrubby little jobs—filing, typing (I had taught myself to type on the borrowed machine of a neighbor), dime-store clerking, and the like.

I scribbled worthless poetry, went to art school and to adult extension courses, and eventually met a man who was earning a living writing stories for Sunday School weeklies. This was a revelation—one could actually earn money by writing! He taught me much about the mechanics of plotting fiction, and after a studious apprenticeship I sold my first short story about, of all things, a bush flyer in Alaska. When a $30 check arrived just before Christmas, it was a high point of my life.

After publishing in many magazines, I seriously settled down to writing books in 1951. Five have been Junior Literary Guild selections, others have been translated into foreign languages, and three have seen publication in England. Recent titles are *American Tall-Tale Animals* (to be recorded by Caedmon Records), *Listen America*, a biography of Whitman done in collaboration with my housemate, Laura Nelson Baker, and *Animals at Bay; Rare and Rescued American Animal Species.* One of my favorite books is *Rain Boat*, under the pseudonym Lace Kendall.

I have lived in Iowa, Colorado, New York, and Mexico, and now reside on a Lagunitas, California, hillside thirty miles from San Francisco, surrounded by tall firs, and visited by deer and almost tame humming birds. The stars are bright here, too!

Adrien Stoutenburg has written under the pen names of Barbie Arden and Nelson Minier, as well as under Lace Kendall and her own name. She won the Lamont Poetry Award in 1964, for her first volume of poems, *Heroes, Advise Us.* In 1961 she won two Poetry Society of America Awards and she has had poems in the last six Borestone Mountain Award volumes. Miss Stoutenburg collects driftwood, loves cats and camping trips, is an amateur artist and sculptor, and plays the piano, guitar, and harmonica. The first part of her last name, she says, is pronounced simply like the word "stout".

SELECTED WORKS: Dear, Dear Livy (with Laura Nelson Baker) 1963; Explorer of the Unconscious (with Laura Nelson Baker) 1965;

Rain Boat, 1965; The Crocodile's Mouth, 1966; American Tall Tales, 1966; Listen America (with Laura Nelson Baker), 1968; Animals at Bay, 1968; Out There, 1971.

ABOUT: Contemporary Authors, Vol. 7-8; Who's Who in America, 1968-69; Who's Who in the West; Who's Who of American Women, 1970-1971.

EDWIN WAY TEALE
June 2, 1899-

AUTHOR OF *The Junior Book of Insects,* etc.

Autobiographical sketch of Edwin Way Teale:

I WROTE my first book when I was nine years old. It was called *Tales of Lone Oak.* But in the manuscript, in which each chapter was held together with a safety pin, I spelled it "Tails." Lone Oak was my grandfather's farm in the dune country of northern Indiana. It was the great and wonderful influence in my early life. Born in Joliet, Illinois, I spent my winters in school in a city. In summers I lived a life of freedom, racing over my grandfather's acres, hunting for Indian arrowheads on an island in a swamp, watching sandhill cranes and bald eagles among the dunes along the Lake Michigan shore, fascinated by all the natural history of an exceptionally interesting region.

I remembered it all, years later, in *Dune Boy; the Early Years of a Naturalist.* That book has been transcribed into Braille for the blind, been published in an Armed Services edition during the war and has appeared in a Spanish edition in South America and an Arabic edition in the Near East, and recently, a quarter of a century after its original publication, was issued in a Bantam paperback. Other memories of those early days appear in *The Junior Book of Insects,* which has now been in print for thirty years.

After graduating from Earlham College, where I met Nellie Imogene Donovan, who became my wife, I taught English and public speaking at Friends University, in Wichita, Kansas; obtained a master's degree in English literature from Columbia University; acted as editorial assistant to Dr. Frank Crane, the newspaper columnist; and for

thirteen years was staff feature writer on *Popular Science* magazine. In gathering material for articles, I flew with a test pilot, went down in a submarine, attended a scientific crime detection school, and in general acquired the foundation of a wide variety of information which has been of aid in producing my twenty-five books.

During this period, I was living on Long Island with my wife and son, David. Nature —birds, animals, plants, insects—remained my main interest. For years, in an old orchard beside a swamp, I maintained a garden of wildflowers and shrubs especially attractive to insects. In this "insect garden," I studied and photographed butterflies and bees, beetles and ant lions. Out of this avocation came such books as *Grassroots Jungles, Near Horizons, Insect Friends* and *The Strange Lives of Familiar Insects.*

In the fall of 1941, I quit my magazine job to become a free-lance writer of books on nature. Over a period of twenty years, I worked on a series of four books on the American seasons, gathering material from the Atlantic to the Pacific and from Mexico to Canada.

In 1945, two months before the end of the war in Europe, our son, David, was killed on

Teale: *TEEL*

the Moselle River, in Germany, at the age of nineteen.

My wife and I now live in the northeastern corner of Connecticut, near the village of Hampton, in a house built in 1806, on a hundred and thirty acres of woods and fields, with two brooks, three miles of trails through our own woods, a pond that spreads out below the house and a log writing cabin among aspen trees on the slope beyond. Out of this close-to-nature life, my books develop. They have now appeared in more than sixty-five editions, have been translated into more than a dozen foreign languages, including Finnish, Hindi and Japanese, and have been awarded the John Burroughs Medal, the Sarah Chapman Francis Medal and the Pulitzer Prize.

At the age of twelve, Teale changed his middle name from Alfred to Way, his mother's maiden name, since he thought this more distinguished for the naturalist and writer he had already decided to become.

Since 1941, Teale has contributed to more than a hundred periodicals, written or edited many books, and developed a growing file of about 30,000 nature photographs. His photographs have been shown, among other places, at the Royal Photographic Society Salon in London and at the American Museum of Natural History in New York.

Teale has been president of a number of societies, including the Thoreau Society, the New York Entomological Society and the American Nature Study Society. He is a fellow of the New York Academy of Sciences and of the American Association for the Advancement of Science, and an associate of the Royal Photographic Society. He also belongs to other organizations, including the Explorer's Club. In 1957 Teale received an honorary LL.D. from Earlham College. His Pulitzer Prize, received in 1966, was for *Wandering through Winter,* the last of his books on the four American seasons.

SELECTED WORKS: Grassroots Jungles, 1937; Near Horizons, 1942; Dune Boy; the Early Years of a Naturalist, 1943; The Junior Book of Insects, 1953; Insect Friends, 1955; Strange Lives of Familiar Insects, 1962.

ABOUT: Author's and Writer's Who's Who, 1963; Contemporary Authors, Vol. 2; Current Biography Yearbook 1961; Dodd, Edward Howard. Of Nature, Time and Teale; Dunaway, Philip and Evans, Melvin, eds. Treasury of the World's Great Diaries; Poole, Lynn and Poole, Gray. Scientists Who Work Outdoors; Teale, Edwin Way. Dune Boy; the Early Years of a Naturalist; Twentieth Century Authors (First Supplement), 1955; Who's Who in America, 1970-71; Audubon Magazine May 1952; May 1962; May 1965; Collier's February 26, 1949; New York Herald Tribune Book Review October 7, 1951; December 2, 1951; New York Times Book Review October 9, 1960; August 1, 1965; June 26, 1966.

"PETER THAYER"

See *Ames, Rose Wyler*

EVE TITUS
July 16, 1922-

AUTHOR OF *Anatole,* etc.

Autobiographical sketch of Eve Titus, who has also written under the pen name of "Nancy Lord":

I WAS born in New York City, of wonderfully wise and witty parents, who loved books and music greatly. And all my life I've been engaged in combat with myself—shall it be writing or music? I can't bear to give up either one—both are my true loves!

From age seven on, I wrote poetry madly, then prose. Also, at seven, I began to study the piano, soon winning scholarships from teachers who foresaw my concert career.

My musical self appears in my books—I'm highly conscious of rhythmic flow and melodic prose. I lay out my books line for line, *as I hear them.* Also, I see pages as scenes in a play, and write down descriptions of the drawings *as I see them.* My goal? Read-aloud qualities and balanced blending of text and illustrations.

Vividly I recall being begged to make up bedtime stories for my brothers and sister. Remembering helps now, for projecting back to one's childhood means one can write on the child's own level.

Anatole, my first book, was a bedtime story for my son Ricky. To answer his endless

EVE TITUS

questions about the mysterious world of business into which Daddy vanished every day, I made up a story about a business mouse. At first he was an American mouse, then a Britisher named Dwight. Intrigued, I put on my writer's cloak, and made my mouse French, gallant, and sensitive. I gave him warm family background, a friend, a bicycle, and a secret. Yesterday I completed Anatole's eighth adventure, in which wife and children are held prisoner in a toy-shop window! (I wonder who'll dash to the rescue!)

Basil of Baker Street lives in Sherlock Holmes's cellar and takes notes abovestairs, in shortpaw. I read Sherlock Holmes when I was too young to understand all the difficult words. As an author, I *had* to do Holmes in miniature, to lead children toward him later, rather than to sex-cum-sadism detectives. I am an honorary Baker Street Irregular because of the Basil books.

I used a pen name, "Nancy Lord," on a rhymed book for the very young, *My Dog and I*, a Junior Literary Guild choice.

My most serious book, *The Two Stonecutters*, is a free, free adaptation of a Japanese folk tale. I worked lovingly to flesh out what I consider just a skeleton of a story, and plan to write an article on why I liked but never loved the original.

The Mouse and the Lion, an original fable, one of my favorites, is a modern satire on animals and people.

When I cruised the Caribbean as concert pianist, *Mr. Shaw's Shipshape Shoeshop* grew out of my love for the sea. The tongue-twisting title came to me under the beauty shop dryer. My best ideas come under hair dryers, showers, on planes, buses, etc.

In 1964 I originated the first workshop devoted entirely to writing for children, Storybook Writing Seminar. I've lectured and given workshops in the United States, Canada, and Mexico. My original manuscripts and notes are now part of the Case Collection at Wayne State University, Detroit.

Fame, foreign editions, films—but alas, I lack the degree of Bachelor of Mousology! Can't some kind soul arrange it?

———

Two of Eve Titus's books have been made into color-and-sound films, available to schools and libraries in 16-mm. She often closes her lectures at schools and libraries with a brief piano program.

Anatole, 1956, and *Anatole and the Cat,* 1957, illustrated by Paul Galdone, were both runners-up for the Caldecott Medal.

SELECTED WORKS: Anatole, 1956; Anatole and the Cat, 1957; My Dog and I, 1958; Basil of Baker Street, 1958; The Mouse and the Lion, 1962; Mr. Shaw's Shipshape Shoeshop, 1969; Anatole and the Toy Shop, 1970.

ALAIN and DENISE TREDEZ

See *"Trez, Alain"* and *"Trez, Denise"*

ELIZABETH BORTON DE TREVIÑO

September 2, 1904-

AUTHOR OF *I, Juan de Pareja*, etc.

Autobiographical sketch of Elizabeth Borton de Treviño:

I WAS born in Bakersfield, California. My parents were both native-born Californians, which gives me a distinction not shared by many Californians. I was, though stout, a somewhat sickly child; I had contracted

malaria at six, and so I was sent, every summer, to spend the school vacations at the shore with my grandmother. After setting me a "task," which I had to finish before leaving the house, every day she set me free to go to the library, where I think I read every book on the shelves. It started a reading habit which I have never got over, and very soon, that started a writing habit, too. At eight, I wrote a poem, which was published in the Monterey Peninsula *Herald*. I was then vaccinated with printer's ink, and I looked upon myself, despite a steady flood of rejection slips, as a writer, from that glorious day of publication, forward.

My father had published stories and poems in his younger days, before turning all his energies to the law. He constantly encouraged me to write and he and my mother gave me a love and respect for words. Wonderful teachers, in high school Mr. Mark Willcox, and at Stanford University, Professor Philip Grey, taught me valuable lessons about form, writing discipline, and the marshalling of ideas. After I graduated from the University, I went to Boston to study music, later took a job as a music reviewer, and in time, because of a knowledge of Spanish, I was taken over to the City Room and given work as a staff reporter. The training in factual writing

and in accuracy, was invaluable, as were the many friends who helped me and inspired me in those days.

In the depression years my dear father brought me home, took an office for me, gave me a typewriter, and paid me a salary to *write*. I wrote seven hours a day, keeping the same office hours he did. I produced a great deal, none of it saleable, but that year in the office near my father, taught me the two most important concepts about a writer's profession. It is *work*, and it must be done every day.

It is a lonely profession, but rewarding in wonderful ways.

Best of all the many splendid things my life as a professional writer has given me are letters from children who read my books. I answer them all, and I treasure and trust their judgment.

Like all other writers, I have had many disappointments, but I would not have lived my life any other way, and I hope to continue writing for many years more.

All of my books enclose a little kernel of truth . . . something that really happened. *Nacar the White Deer* enlarges upon a note in history that a great Spanish vessel carried across the Pacific a beautiful albino deer as a gift for the king. *I, Juan de Pareja* retells the story of the friendship of Velazquez for his Negro slave, Juan, who taught himself to paint in secret; later, Velazquez freed him and made him his assistant. *Casilda of the Rising Moon* recounts the story of a young Moorish princess of the eleventh century who became a Christian saint. *Turi's Poppa* is the tale of a small boy and his father who walked halfway across Europe so that the father could take up a position as a violin-maker in Cremona, Italy.

Each of these stories required travel, research, and study, and each attempts to paint a true picture of the countryside described and of the century in which the characters lived.

At the same time, each of my stories tries to show some phase of love, that powerful emotion "which makes the world go round."

Elizabeth Borton took her B.A. in Latin American history from Stanford University in 1925. She studied violin at the Boston

Conservatory of Music and worked on the Boston *Herald*. Among the eight children's books published under her maiden name are five which continued Eleanor Porter's *Polly-anna* series.

In 1934 the *Herald* sent her to Mexico to do a series of interviews and there she met Luis Treviño Gomez, assigned to be her guide. A year later she married him, thereby adding "de Treviño" meaning "wife of Tre-viño," to her name. Their children are Luis Federico and Enrique Ricardo.

Elizabeth Borton de Treviño lives and works in Cuernavaca, takes an interest in art, plays violin with several chamber music groups and travels frequently to lecture in Mexico and the United States. The author of books for adults as well as for children, she has been made an honorary citizen of Texas. *I, Juan de Pareja* won the Newbery Medal for 1966.

SELECTED WORKS: Our Little Aztec Cousin, 1934; About Bellamy, 1940; A Carpet of Flowers, 1955; Nacar, the White Deer, 1963; I, Juan de Pareja, 1965; Casilda of the Rising Moon, 1967; Turi's Poppa, 1968; Here Is Mexico, 1970.

ABOUT: Contemporary Authors, Vol. 17-18; Something About the Author, Vol. 1; Who's Who in America, 1970-71; Who's Who of American Women, 1970-71; Horn Book August 1966; Library Journal March 15, 1966; Publishers' Weekly March 14, 1966; School Library Journal March 1966; Top of the News April 1966.

"ALAIN TREZ"

February 2, 1929-

and

"DENISE TREZ"

June 22, 1930-

ILLUSTRATOR AND AUTHOR OF *Sophie*, etc.

Biographical sketch of Alain and Denise Laugier Tredez, who work under the pen names of "Alain and Denise Trez," by Denise Tredez:

ALTHOUGH we live with our three daughters in Paris, we own an old mill on the Cote d'Azur, where we spend all of our holidays.

What both of us enjoy most is creating books for children. After working out the story line together, Alain does the illustrations while I am writing the text. Thus, each of our works is a joint effort.

Alain and I are very different in character, but I believe that I was fated from the beginning to marry a man full of comic ideas, for I always appreciated humor in others. When I was small, I loved *Alice in Wonderland* and *The Pickwick Papers*. I myself am incapable of drawing a line, but our three daughters are full of talent.

Alain is the seventh child in a family of eight and was born in the north of France. Like all children, he drew cartoons of his schoolteachers. These early works must have shown promise, for his parents, who were perceptive (both were teachers), wished him to enter the Ecole des Beaux-Arts to concentrate on painting. Their ambition was not so unreasonable as it may sound, since he was also producing some very fine water colors.

Being of a somewhat contrary nature, he decided that he would study law instead, with the idea of entering diplomatic service. During his military service, however, he discovered that he had little talent for diplomacy. As a parachutist, he spent more time in the guardhouse than he did in jumping. Thinking to get out of the guardhouse, he volunteered to decorate the officers' mess. His idea of appropriate art for a military installation was not at all appreciated, and he found himself back in his cell.

Oddly enough, it was in such experiences that he found his vocation, and he determined to become a humorist. As soon as he was demobilized, he began to publish his first cartoons in the magazine *Paris-Match,* and since then his works have appeared in many publications throughout the world.

As for myself, I was born in Marseille in the south of France. My father was a doctor, and I have two elder brothers and a sister. During my girlhood, I wrote frequent letters to one brother who had become a journalist in Paris. Because he found them well-written, he had me come to Paris as soon as I finished school, thinking that I would find a career in journalism too.

Very soon thereafter, I met and married Alain. Because I had already published some stories for children, the two of us were asked to create a children's magazine to be distributed in France by the Caisses d'Epargne. It was when our first child Isabelle (now aged fifteen) was a little girl that the idea came to us of making a book just for her. This was our first, *Circus in the Jungle,* published by the World Publishing Company in 1958. The following year we did another for our second daughter Corinne. Since then, we have produced at least one book every year, one of which was for our third daughter Florence, born in 1961.

My share in the books springs from a profound attachment to my own childhood, which was a remarkably happy one in spite of World War II, whereas for Alain, it is the future that counts. He is always enthusiastic about new ideas, new projects. It is the reason for his extremely varied career as an artist, including cartooning, book illustration, advertising, and serious painting. In 1968, the first major exhibition of his works was held in Paris. In spite of all these activities, he shares my love of creating books for children, and we enjoy more than anything else the fan mail from those whom we have amused and entertained.

Alain Tredez was born in Berck-sur-Mer, Pas-de-Calais, attended the local Ecole d'Artois, and later the Ecole des Sciences-Politiques in Paris. His military service, 1949-1950, was with the 25th Airborne Division of the French Army. Denise Laugier studied at Notre-Dame-de-France in Marseilles. They were married in 1950.

Sophie received Honorable Mention, Picture Books, in the New York *Herald Tribune* Children's Spring Book Festival, 1964.

SELECTED WORKS: Circus in the Jungle, 1958; The Magic Paintbox, 1962; The Little Knight's Dragon, 1963; Sophie, 1964; The Royal Hiccups, 1965; Rabbit Country, 1966; Good Night, Veronica, 1968; Maila and the Flying Carpet, 1969.

ABOUT ALAIN TREDEZ: Kingman, Lee and others, comps. Illustrators of Children's Books: 1957-1966.

ABOUT DENISE TREDEZ: Contemporary Authors, Vol. 5-6.

JIŘÍ TRNKA
February 24, 1912-December 30, 1969

ILLUSTRATOR OF *The Fireflies,* etc.

Biographical sketch of Jiří Trnka:

THE son of a plumber and a seamstress, Jiří Trnka was born in the city of Pilsen in what is now western Czechoslovakia. His parents and grandmother all made toys in their spare time, and Trnka became familiar with the art of dollmaking at an early age. In the school he attended, drawing classes were taught by a famous puppeteer, Josef Skupa, who recognized Trnka's artistic talent and gave him an opportunity to work backstage in the Pilsen puppet theater which Skupa ran. When Trnka was about fifteen, his family had financial difficulties and decided he would have to quit school and take up a trade. Trnka was apprenticed to a baker but

Jiří Trnka: *JEER ee TRINK a*

JIŘÍ TRNKA

quit after only two months and became an apprentice mechanic in the Pilsen Skoda works. Then Josef Skupa came to his rescue by finding him a job in an art supplies store that left him with enough time to resume his work in Skupa's theater.

Two years later, in 1928, Trnka's family was persuaded by Skupa to send their son to the Prague Academy of Art. While attending school he continued to design costumes for Skupa and also worked as an illustrator for a Prague children's magazine, and by the time he graduated in 1935 he was becoming known as a designer and illustrator. For a time he worked with Skupa, who successfully produced his play *The Waterman*, then, in 1936 he opened his own *Wooden Theater*, so named because he used wooden puppets. However, his productions failed to attract audiences, and the theater was closed in less than a year. During the next several years Trnka concentrated primarily on book illustrating, and from the beginning was very successful. His first major work, the illustration of *Tygr pana Boška* (Mr. Boschka's *Tiger*), by V. Šmejc, was highly praised, and his illustrations for the series on "Miša Kulicka" (Misha Roly-Poly), by Josef Menzel, made him famous. Besides book illustration, Trnka also designed tapestries, worked at the Prague National Theater as costume and stage designer, and painted still lifes, portraits, and landscapes.

After World War II, Trnka collaborated with a group called "the brothers in leotards" in producing cartoon and trick films, using techniques developed by Disney but with an entirely different spirit. The making of these films reinforced an old ambition of his to create puppet films, and at the end of 1946 he opened his own studio in Prague. There over the next quarter century he produced about thirty films, of which the best known in the United States are *The Emperor's Nightingale,* made in 1948, and *A Midsummer Night's Dream,* made in 1959, for which he used a new kind of rubbery lifelike puppet.

Trnka received many awards for his work, including the biennial prize of Venice, the Czechoslovakian peace prize, and in 1968 the Hans Christian Andersen Medal. The Czechoslovakian government named him a "national artist," the highest honor it could confer.

Trnka died in Prague of a chronic heart ailment on December 30, 1969. He was married and the father of five children.

SELECTED WORK: The Fireflies, adapted by Max Bolliger from the original story in Czech by Jan Karafiát, 1970.

ABOUT: Hürlimann, Bettina. Picture Book World; Kingman, Lee and others, comps. Illustrators of Children's Books: 1957-1966; Bookbird no. 4, 1968; no. 1, no. 3, 1970; New York Herald Tribune December 17, 1961; New York Times May 20, 1962; December 30, 1969; Newsweek March 28, 1966.

BRINTON TURKLE

August 15, 1915-

AUTHOR AND ILLUSTRATOR OF *The Fiddler of High Lonesome,* etc.

Autobiographical sketch of Brinton Cassaday Turkle:

GROWING UP in Alliance, Ohio, was not always happy for an odd boy who liked drawing pictures, reading books, playing the piano or building model theaters better than playing baseball. Fortunately, Gertrude Alice Kay, a successful author and illustrator of children's books and a former student of Howard Pyle, was a family friend. She

Brinton Turkle

helped convince my parents that I had artistic ability worth encouraging.

After high school, there was a sojourn in the drama department of Carnegie Tech, where I discovered that starving actors outnumbered starving artists. At the school of the Boston Museum of Fine Arts, I developed skill in drawing; and in my last year there, I worked up an idea for a children's book that I brought to New York for one purpose: to allow the Viking Press to publish it. May Massee let the opportunity slip through her fingers; but she did say she felt sure that I would be doing children's books one day.

That day dawned about ten years later when I fled from the Chicago advertising world to the piñon-covered hills of New Mexico with my new wife. There, I began to earn a precarious living illustrating books. Never quite recovered from being stagestruck, I also worked with the Santa Fe Community Theatre and was an extra and bit-player in a couple of movies shot nearby on location. The arrival of two sons and a daughter, Jonathan, Haynes and Matilda, made living even more precarious, and I was obliged to move to New York to find more work.

All the time I had been illustrating other people's books, I had been trying to write stories of my own. Recently, a little girl wrote me plaintively that she liked to write stories but that she had more beginnings than endings. That was my problem, too. One beginning was just a valentine I made for the small daughter of friends. It was a drawing of a shy, red-headed Quaker lad who looked as if he had a story in him. He had, but it took me two years to find it. This was my first book, *Obadiah the Bold,* and the Viking Press published it—alas, after May Massee had retired. I have written three more books, am presently working on a fourth and hope the end is not yet in sight.

I find the combination of words and pictures that is possible today only in children's books very exciting. It is a heady experience steering one's own magic carpet. It is also a privilege and a challenge trying to engage the attention of children, who must never be offered less than the very best. In my books are things I am very serious about: indestructibility of the human spirit, respect for truth, reverence for life and sensitivity to mutual needs. But I don't write sermons. My first aim is to delight. If, along the way, I help the younger generation dream of a better world, . . . well, they just might fashion one. I, for one, could use it.

———

Although he has illustrated more than fifty text and trade books, Brinton Turkle says he is still better known in his home town as the son of an eminent funeral director than as an author-illustrator. *The Fiddler of High Lonesome* won a Lewis Carroll Shelf award in 1968. *Thy Friend, Obadiah* won a *Book World* Children's Spring Book Festival Award in 1969 and was a runner-up for the Caldecott Medal in 1970.

SELECTED WORKS WRITTEN AND ILLUSTRATED: Obadiah the Bold, 1965; The Magic of Millicent Musgrave, 1967; The Fiddler of High Lonesome, 1968; Thy Friend, Obadiah, 1969; The Sky Dog, 1969; Mooncoin Castle, 1970.

SELECTED WORKS ILLUSTRATED: Mr. Blue, by Margaret Embry, 1963; War Cry of the West, by Nathaniel Burt, 1964; The Doll in the Bakeshop, by Carol Beach York, 1965; Four Paws into Adventure, by Claude Cenac, 1965; Catch a Little Fox, by Beatrice Schenk De Regniers, 1970.

ABOUT: Hopkins, Lee Bennett. Books Are by People; Kingman, Lee and others, comps. Illustrators of Children's Books: 1957-1966; Publishers' Weekly July 14, 1969.

JANICE UDRY
June 14, 1928-

AUTHOR OF *A Tree Is Nice*, etc.

Autobiographical sketch of Janice May Udry:

WHEN I was a child, a new book or a new box of crayons were my favorite gifts. As soon as I learned to read and write, making up poems and stories, drawing pictures, and reading became favorite pastimes. They still are.

I was born in Jacksonville, Illinois. I rarely left that state until I was eighteen years old. I had no brothers or sisters but there were always playmates on my street and cousins that I visited on farms near town. Aunts and grandparents were not far away. Several of my teachers had also taught my mother or father. It was a small midwestern world. The yards where we played were large and un-fenced, shaded by old elm trees. There were grape arbors, peony bushes, lilacs, and vege-table gardens in the backyards. All of the houses had big front porches with porch swings where we often played during the long summer days waiting for the ice truck to stop. Passenger trains came regularly to the station then and going to meet an out-of-town visitor was a common but exciting event. Children always reminded visitors that Jacksonville was said to be the only place in the world where ferris wheels were made. That was great enough claim to fame for us.

While I was going to college I worked part time in the library. I was graduated from Northwestern University and married Rich-ard Udry in 1950. I was an assistant in a Chicago nursery school for awhile and began to notice wonderful new picture books for small children.

After we moved to southern California we lived near the ocean and hiked in the moun-tains. It was beautiful but I saw how rapidly the trees, especially orange groves and euca-lyptus wind-rows, were being cut down for housing developments. It looked as if there wouldn't be a tree left in a few years. I wrote *A Tree Is Nice* for children and it was pub-lished with Marc Simont's fine illustrations.

As soon as my first daughter, Leslie, was old enough to look at books, we began to visit the children's room of whatever library

Janice May Udry

we were living near. And it has been the same with my second daughter, Susan. Leslie is now thirteen and Susan is seven.

After fourteen years in California, we moved to Chapel Hill, North Carolina, where my husband is a sociologist at the university.

The idea for many of the books I have written began when something one of my daughters did or said reminded me of an incident or a feeling from my own childhood. *The Mean Mouse & Other Mean Stories* is a little collection written for Leslie when she was small. I was remembering the joy of being allowed to play out after dark on a hot summer night in Illinois when I wrote *The Moon Jumpers*.

———

A Tree Is Nice, with Marc Simont's illus-trations, won the Caldecott Medal for 1957. *Let's Be Enemies* was an Honor Book in the New York *Herald Tribune* Children's Spring Book Festival, 1961. *The Moon Jumpers*, illustrated by Maurice Sendak, was a runner-up for the Caldecott Medal for 1960.

SELECTED WORKS: A Tree Is Nice, 1956; The Moon Jumpers, 1959; Let's Be Enemies, 1961; The Mean Mouse & Other Mean Stories, 1962; What Mary Jo Shared, 1966; Mary Ann's Mud Day, 1967; What Mary Jo Wanted, 1968; Glenda, 1969.

ABOUT: Contemporary Authors, Vol. 5-6; Who's Who of American Women, 1964-65.

TOMI UNGERER
November 28, 1931-

AUTHOR AND ILLUSTRATOR OF *The Mellops Go Flying*, etc.

Autobiographical sketch of Jean Thomas Ungerer:

I WAS born in Strasbourg in Alsace. My father died when I was three. Still, through my older brother and sisters, he became a great influence in my work. He was a painter, a historian, an inventor, builder of astronomical clocks which were the specialty of my family's factory. After his death we moved to my grandmother's house in Colmar. There I was to grow up and witness the war and its effects from every angle. I became German for the length of the Second World War and as a child was thoroughly marked by the Nazi's indoctrination. Across the street there was a prison camp where Russian prisoners were left to die. The Gestapo, terror, daily propaganda, were for four years a way of living. The front came nearer and we were in the pocket of Colmar for three months—in the winter of 1944-45. It was living in a battle. Through all that my family life with two sisters and one brother stayed close, warm, and tight as could be.

I did not graduate from high school but left on my own. I traveled a lot for eight, nine years, seeking adventure and finding it. From Lapland to Greece, skipping borders without passport, picking up jobs, studying what I felt like studying.

Serious illness in Africa where I had joined the Camel Corps put a stop to my vagrancies.

I came to New York in 1956. I was still very sick and poor. I met Ursula Nordstrom at Harper's, who advanced me five hundred dollars on a book I did not have. I had always drawn, painted, and written. The book was *The Mellops Go Flying*, and became an Honor Book in the Children's Spring Book Festival. From there all went well. I soon was published in *Esquire, Charm, Harper's Magazine* and *Sports Illustrated*. My ads and posters appeared everywhere; awards flew in.

I have made many more books since, some for children, some for adults, over fifty by

now. My hobbies are many: old books, old toys, mineralogy, botany, kites and so on. I live in New York. I must love that city, for it seems that I need its absurdities and contrasts. My studio is on the worst block of 42nd Street. I spend most of my time up there, now concocting more new books than I ever have.

I love my work and consider myself a lucky man.

———

Besides writing and illustrating for children, Tomi Ungerer is a cartoonist, caricaturist, advertising artist, and designer.

In his book *Close-up*, John Gruen said that Ungerer's particular genius is for transforming human cruelty into "blackest, sickest laughter," and that Ungerer's drawings in *The Underground Sketchbook* and *The Party* may make even a strong stomach go weak. He adds, however, that as in all first-rate black humor, the result is first-rate morality.

Ungerer's books for children have been exhibited by the American Institute of Graphic Arts. He has received a number of awards, including a gold medal from the Society of Illustrators in 1960. *Crictor* won a New York *Herald Tribune* Children's Spring Book

Tomi Ungerer: *TOH me UNG ger er*

Festival Award in 1958 and *Moon Man* won one in 1967. *The Three Robbers* was named by the New York *Times* as one of the ten best-illustrated books of 1962.

Tomi Ungerer has a daughter, Phoebe Alexis.

SELECTED WORKS WRITTEN AND ILLUSTRATED: The Mellops Go Flying, 1957; Crictor, 1958; Emile, 1960; Snail, Where Are you?, 1962; The Three Robbers, 1962; One, Two, Where's My Shoe? 1964; Moon Man, 1967; Zeralda's Ogre, 1967; Ask Me a Question, 1968; The Hat, 1970.

SELECTED WORKS ILLUSTRATED: Warwick's 3 Bottles, by André Hodeir, 1966; Mr. Tall & Mr. Small, by Barbara Brenner, 1966; The Donkey Ride, by Jean B. Showalter, 1967; Lear's Nonsense, by Edward Lear, 1967; Oh, What Nonsense, by William Cole, 1967.

ABOUT: Gruen, John. Close-up; Hopkins, Lee Bennett. Books Are by People; Hürlimann, Bettina. Picture Book World; Kingman, Lee and others, comps. Illustrators of Children's Books: 1957-1966; Who's Who in America, 1970-71; Art in America December 1965; Coronet September 1960; Graphis no. 82, 1959; no. 120, 1965; Horizon January 1961; Print July 1959; January 1966.

EDITH UNNERSTAD

July 28, 1900-

AUTHOR OF *The Spettecake Holiday,* etc.

Autobiographical sketch of Edith Totterman Unnerstad:

I WAS born in Helsinki, Finland, of Swedish parents. In 1910 we moved to Sweden.

One day when I was eleven I had a letter from one of my sisters who was in hospital with scarlet fever. She asked me to send her some of our books. The letter was badly singed by the disinfection oven. I could hardly read it. All of us seven children were great bookworms. Every volume in the house meant to us a dear treasure. No doubt if she got the books, they would have to pass through that awful oven before we could get them back. That would never do. Then I made up my mind. "We can't do it," I said. "Instead I'll write her one."

Making up fairy tales and rhymes and telling long stories to myself and anybody who cared to listen was a habit I had practised

since I was very small. But I had never before put any of it on paper. I started at once. For three weeks I carried on, almost every day writing a chapter. Before going to bed I used to read my new opus aloud to my breathlessly listening sisters and brothers, and on my way to school in the morning I dropped it in the hospital box.

The "book," if I remember right, turned out to be a horrifying mixture, evidently inspired by my idols: Cooper, Jules Verne, Captain Marryat, and Swedish Finland's great old story teller, Topelius. But my listeners and the little reader in the hospital highly appreciated my concoction and wanted more, more.

After that there was no turning back. I knew I wanted to be a writer. At fourteen I got a short story and two sentimental poems published in a magazine. Oh joy and pride, I already *was* a writer! The fee was spent on a long-desired pair of patent-leather pumps, a giant bag of toffee, and a copy of *Atala* with pictures by Doré. The shoes pinched my toes and had to be given to a younger sister. The toffee disappeared in a twinkling into seven sweet-peckish tummies. But *Atala* is still in my possession.

Needless to say my pride had been a bit too early. Much could be told about my thorny path to authorship, for as a matter of fact my début didn't happen before I was thirty-two. During the years I had never given up the thought of being a writer, but life had had too many different things in store for me, blocking my way to the goal. School, art studies, public service, love, marriage (1924), a baby (1928), travels. But I know now that the main reason for my shortcoming was that I hadn't yet got my eyes opened and found my own right field. This didn't happen before my daughter Lena was big enough to ask for stories.

My first book was a children's book. After that came a long row of volumes. Not all of them are children's books, but in my nine novels and my book of poetry the favorite theme has been the same: *childhood.*

Though my first real success-books in Sweden and abroad were novels, the children's books soon passed them. The four Peep-Larsson Books (*The Saucepan Journey, The Peep-Larssons Go Sailing, Pysen,* and *Little O*) are the most translated, followed closely by *The Spettecake Holiday, The Journey with Grandmother, Journey to England,* etc.

My grandmother, born in 1839, was a good story teller. So is my mother. What they have told me about childhood in olden days has meant a lot to my books. My own memories and experiences as mother and grandmother have of course influenced my writing. But above all the plain truth is: I was once a child, and the child I was, in many respects, I still am. That's why I know, and that's why I love to write about it.

———

Edith Totterman Unnerstad studied at Detthow College and attended art school in Stockholm. She married Arvid B. Unnerstad in 1924 and they have one daughter, Madeleine (Lena). Mrs. Unnerstad won the Children's Book Prize in 1949, the Nils Holgersson Award in 1957, and was awarded Swedish government fellowships in 1956 and 1959. She has published twenty-one children's books, eleven novels and a collection of poetry, in addition to writing for motion pictures, television, radio, magazines, and newspapers. Her books have been published in Norwegian, Danish, Finnish, Dutch, German, French, Spanish, Italian, Polish, Japa-

nese, Hebrew, and Afrikaans, as well as in English.

SELECTED WORKS: The Saucepan Journey, 1951; Pysen, 1955; Little O, 1957; The Spettecake Holiday, 1958; The Journey with Grandmother, 1960; Journey to England, 1961; The Pip-Larssons Go Sailing, 1963; The Ditch Picnic, 1965; Two Little Gigglers, 1968.

ABOUT: Author's and Writer's Who's Who, 1963; Contemporary Authors, Vol. 5-6.

"EDITH VAN DYNE"

See *Baum, L. Frank*

BETTY LOU BAKER VENTURO

See *Baker, Betty*

BERNARD WABER

September 27, 1924-

AUTHOR AND ILLUSTRATOR OF *The House on East 88th Street,* etc.

Autobiographical sketch of Bernard Waber:

WE changed addresses frequently during my childhood in Philadelphia, Pennsylvania. The prospect of moving loomed continually during the depression years as one or another of our family's business ventures folded. Each time a move was considered, I sought assurance from my parents that the new neighborhood would be bountiful with prospective playmates, and that a public library and motion picture theater would exist within easy roller-skating distance. Like food and drink, I considered the library and movies life-giving staples, and could not conceive of survival without them. The library, with its great store of unrequired reading, was a banquet to which I brought a ravenous appetite. And the movies; western, thriller, adventure-story—it never mattered—I was a willing transportee to whatever cinematic never-never-land Saturday's marquee hailed.

The youngest of four children, I was accustomed to all manner of hand-me-downs from an older brother. Luckily, my brother also handed down his great interest in drawing. My own early efforts were confined to the laborious copying of photographs of film stars and other heroes of the day. Appreciation

Bernard Waber

for the beauty of landscape, still-life, figure drawing and abstract design came later in life when I enrolled at the Philadelphia College of Art. Sometime during those years, I discovered I could win attention and modest approval by giving my art assignments a humorous twist. It must have been then that I drew my first comic crocodile.

In 1951, I came to New York to work, subsequently to marry and raise a family. My first employment was with the art department of Conde Nast publications, followed by a stint at *Seventeen* magazine. My employment for the past fourteen years in the art department of *Life* magazine has afforded me opportunity for expression in design, graphics and typography.

My interest in picture books had natural development through read-aloud sessions with my children. At first, it was on a sometimes basis, but with the realization I was enjoying it as much if not more than they, my reading to them became a joyous nightly ritual. I am afraid my enthusiasm for their books began, in fact, to cause my children occasional discomfort. "Daddy, why don't you look at the grown-ups' books?" they once chided, as I trailed after them into the children's room of our local library. I understood. It wasn't easy to explain a father squeezed into a junior-sized chair, happily absorbed in picture books. What impressed

me most was the great and unlimited variety of expression afforded to writers and illustrators of children's books. Before long, I was writing and submitting. With the publication of *Lorenzo*, I was launched on a new and exciting road.

Strangely, writing seems to come easier for me while I am in transit. I commute daily to Manhattan. As the train rattles onward, the rhythm of the wheels and the rocking motion somehow give my thoughts a fresh release. The ride is all too short, as frequently I discover myself totally absorbed and still writing past arrival time in a vacant car at Pennsylvania Station. I also enjoy think-walks. Walking tours along Manhattan's Upper East Side were most beneficial during the planning stages of *The House on East 88th Street* and other Lyle the Crocodile stories. *Rich Cat, Poor Cat* took me through the Lower East Side, Fulton Fish Market, Wall Street and even for a ride on the Staten Island Ferry. In soaking up atmosphere, I was particularly attracted to old billboards of political campaigns, sporting events and forgotten theatrical engagements, and made use of them in the artwork for *Rich Cat.*

I enjoy very much the periods when I am between books. These are times when my mind is open to adventurous thought and the hope that my next will be the best ever. Most ideas for books come about with struggle, but occasionally one will fall, gift-wrapped, out of the blue. It was on a family picnic that the concept, pictures and words for *How to Go About Laying an Egg* struck unexpectedly, and all at once. I don't know what relationship it had to the picnic, but there it was, nevertheless, asking to be written. "Did you pack a pencil?" I asked my wife, whom I rate as the world's most efficient picnic-basket-packer. She may have answered that she had not anticipated we would be eating pencils, I don't remember. I do recall that my "Egg" book came desperately close to being the first modern children's book scratched out on rock.

In earlier days, my studio was the kitchen table of a small apartment. I was an island surrounded by traffic, and everyone, from neighbors dropping in for a chat to the milkman collecting his bill, offered advice and thought on the work in progress. Often, I had to remind my children not to rock the table while I drew in delicate areas. Still, wriggly, swiggly lines that were not necessarily my style, found their way into my work. And very often, I would return to a drawing only to discover that someone, obviously enthralled by my art, had dropped crumbs upon it from an after-school snack.

We have since moved to our present home in Baldwin, Long Island, where I have a quiet place to do my illustrations. There are times when I find myself, somehow, missing those earlier years of noise and confusion.

———

Bernard Waber studied at the Philadelphia College of Art four years and also attended the Pennsylvania Academy of Fine Arts and the University of Pennsylvania. He served in the United States Army, 1942-1945, becoming a staff sergeant. In 1952 he married Ethel Bernstein and they have three children, Paulis, Kim and Jan Gary.

The House on East 88th Street was an Honor Book in the New York *Herald Tribune* Children's Spring Book Festival, 1962, and appeared on the New York *Times* list of Best Sellers for Children the same year. This and other work of his has been in exhibitions of the American Institute of Graphic Arts.

SELECTED WORKS WRITTEN AND ILLUSTRATED: Lorenzo, 1961; The House on East 88th Street, 1962; Rich Cat, Poor Cat, 1963; How to Go About Laying an Egg, 1963; Lyle, Lyle, Crocodile, 1965; You Look Ridiculous, Said the Rhinoceros to the Hippopotamus, 1966; An Anteater Named Arthur, 1967; A Firefly Named Torchy, 1970.

ABOUT: Contemporary Authors, Vol. 3; Kingman, Lee and others, comps. Illustrators of Children's Books: 1957-1966.

JAN WAHL

April 1, 1933-

AUTHOR OF *Hello Elephant*, etc.

Autobiographical sketch of Jan Wahl:

I WAS born in Columbus, Ohio. My father was a medical student and next a struggling doctor during the depression, and I was sent to my grandparents in the northwest Ohio

farmlands for intervals and so, I believe, learned to make up stories to amuse myself. Later I had five small brothers to entertain. I did this by a number of means, one of them being a puppet show which I took around to schools in Toledo, where my family had settled. I also had a traveling magic act and a shadow-play theater in the fourth and fifth grades. Music attracted me, too, and I appeared on a radio program called The Kiddies Karnival.

A re-issue in 1943 of Charlie Chaplin's masterpiece *The Gold Rush* electrified me. I wanted to learn immediately all about silent movies, so I started collecting them, and I am sure this has helped me to think visually. Several artists have agreed with me that fundamentally planning a picture book is like planning a kind of film. When I was at Cornell University, I had no piano or movie projector, and I turned to the typewriter instead. A friend handed me a copy of Isak Dinesen's *Seven Gothic Tales* and I decided that writing must be the most magical experience of all. A few months later I won a Fulbright scholarship to study folk literature and film in Denmark. The eleven-day trip across the Atlantic on the old and slow-moving Oslofjord was the greatest experience of my life till that time. What lay at the other end? Something wonderful or terrible?

After receiving a graduate school certificate from the University of Copenhagen, I returned to this country to begin work on my Master's Degree at the University of Michigan. That work was interrupted by a surprise message from Isak Dinesen herself, suggesting I return to Denmark to act as her secretary! I borrowed money quickly, hocking my car! I remember taking the great lady two dozen yellow roses. The *next* thing I remember is that she fired me one gray day for mis-spelling two words. She grumbled, "You have no feeling WHATSOEVER for literature. Will you please go?" Finally, after I had dusted myself off and managed passage back home again, I completed the work for the M.A. and began publishing short stories and poems, then started a novel. And to keep my spirits high tried my hand at fables and fairy tales.

One morning like a white thunderbolt it struck me that this was actually what I loved doing. I feel it *is* important and fulfilling to write for children. That is, to begin at the roots and growing of Life itself; that is, also, to write for the child still alive in oneself. I love not only writing but working closely, if possible, with the artist, shaping the final book. Uri Shulevitz, Garth Williams, Feodor Rojankovsky, Adrienne Adams, Edward Ardizzone, Blair Lent have been some of my illustrators, and each book has been a special joy to me. My first published book, *Pleasant Fieldmouse*, was accepted by Harper's editor Ursula Nordstrom, who took me to lunch and wistfully asked, "I wonder if Maurice would illustrate it?" Maurice was Maurice Sendak. And he did—some very memorable drawings indeed. Seeing the first bound copy was the second great experience of my life.

I agree with Hans Christian Andersen that life, at its best and worst, is a fairy tale, and it is this message that I try to convey in my books.

———

Jan Wahl won the Young Critics Award, International Children's Book Fair—Bologna, Italy, in 1969, for *Pocahontas in London*, and the Ohioana Book Award for *The Norman Rockwell Storybook*, in 1970.

SELECTED WORKS: Pleasant Fieldmouse, 1964; Hello Elephant, 1964; Cabbage Moon, 1965; The Muffletumps, 1966; Pocahontas in London, 1967; The Furious Flycycle, 1968; Cobweb Castle, 1968; A Wolf of My Own, 1969; How the Children Stopped the Wars, 1969; The Prince Who Was a Fish, 1970.

DENYS JAMES WATKINS-PITCHFORD

See *"BB"*

HARVEY WEISS

April 10, 1922-

AUTHOR AND ILLUSTRATOR OF *Pencil, Pen & Brush*, etc.

Autobiographical sketch of Harvey Weiss:

I WAS about eleven or twelve years old before I really became aware of books. It happened when a friend told me of a place not too far from where I lived that was called a "library," and, by gosh, there was an entire section upstairs filled with books for children. This was a revelation. At home and at school, books were always rather purposeful things— geography books, dictionaries, history books and (horror of horrors) grammar books! At the library, books were something else again. I was on my own. I could choose what I wanted. And what I wanted at that age, I remember, was fiction, the novel, tales of young people in all kinds of likely and unlikely predicaments. It was many years before I realized there was a very large part of that dusty upstairs children's library that contained nonfiction.

I write of these early experiences with my local library because I feel that it had a great deal to do with the sort of person I grew up to be. It provided a fund of experience— second-hand experience perhaps—but nevertheless experience.

It was in library books that I first encountered sculpture, and began my first hesitant experiments with this medium. And I'm afraid I've been continuing these same hesitant experiments for the last thirty-five years or so.

Sculpture remains a major interest and occupation of mine to this day. I spend ap-

proximately half my time working at sculpture. In fact, I will often come into my studio and spend the morning working at my typewriter or at my drawing board on a book in progress. Then, after lunch, I will take off my literary hat and pick up modeling tools or welding torch or stone-cutting chisels and work at current sculpture projects.

I have an enormous skylighted studio on the top floor of an ancient factory building in Westport, Connecticut. I keep one part of the studio reasonably neat and clean for the literary half of my life, and the other half is a shambles, ankle-deep in plaster dust, chips and bits and pieces of half-finished or abandoned statues.

I find that this double life suits me just fine, because I'm afraid I'm a creature of limited patience and easily frustrated. The advantage of my dual profession is that when I get bored with what I am doing I can simply shift to a fresh activity and come to it with a fresh mind and some enthusiasm.

It's odd, but for some reason all of the things I'm seriously interested in seem to affect one another. In fact, they seem at times to be almost growing together into some kind of composite literary-art form. For example, I have been working off and on for some time on a series of terra cotta reliefs which incorporate a text which is printed into the still-soft clay with printer's type. I have sat at my typewriter and "written" a statue before actually starting work with the clay.

And other interests have determined what I write. There is, needless to say, a book on sculpture (*Clay, Wood and Wire*). I have always found print making interesting. So I have done a book on this subject (*Paper, Ink and Roller*). I am fascinated by sailboats and spend much of my time during the summer months sailing on Long Island Sound in my twenty-six foot sloop. So there is a book called *Sailing Small Boats*, which, like all my books was tremendous fun both to write and illustrate.

My introduction to children's books (as producer rather than consumer) was through my wife, Miriam Schlein, who had some twenty or so books in print when we were married in 1956. At this time I was working at a very exasperating and monotonous job with an advertising agency, and working at sculpture in my spare time. I suppose it was inevitable that I eventually illustrate some of my wife's books and then, some time later, try writing one myself. I had at various times in college and at different jobs done some writing, so it wasn't a completely new area for me.

My first few books were fiction, published by G. P. Putnam's Sons. My first nonfiction book was the one on sculpture and this developed into the *Beginning Artists Library* series published by Young Scott Books. There are now six books in this series covering drawing, ceramics, printing, crafts and sculpture. It has been enormously satisfying to find that these books have served and continue to serve a real purpose both in school and library. I am at the time of this writing in the middle of the seventh of this series which is about collage and construction.

I still write fiction from time to time—often humorous or tongue-in-cheek books like *How to Be a Hero*, or, a favorite title of mine,

How to Ooze, and Other Ways of Travelling.
But the bulk of my work nowadays seems to
be nonfiction. I have just completed a book
for T. Y. Crowell called *Motors and Engines
and How They Work,* and I have a few other
plans for books not entirely unrelated to
mechanical and handicraft projects.

I enjoy the multiplicity of my activities,
and I like the way things are going. I hope
I'll be able to continue in ever-increasing
and more varied activities.

———

Harvey Weiss studied at the University of
Missouri, New York University, Rutgers, the
Art Students League, and the National
Academy School of Fine Arts. In Paris he
studied sculpture with Ossipe Zadkine. He
served in the United States Air Force, and
has worked in the fields of advertising, printing, and photography. His sculpture is in
permanent collections of several museums
and he has exhibited in New York at the
Paul Rosenberg Gallery and the Sculpture
Center Gallery. During 1964-65, three of his
works were purchased by the Ford Foundation. He won a citation in the Museum of
Modern Art's Playground Sculpture Competition. In 1970, he won a major award from
the National Institute of Arts and Letters.
Three of his books, *A Gondola for Fun, Paul's
Horse, Herman,* and *Pencil, Pen and Brush*
have been Honor Books in New York *Herald
Tribune* Children's Spring Book Festivals.

Weiss is a member of Authors Guild and
Silvermine Guild, and was president of the
Sculptors Guild, 1969-70. He and his former
wife, Miriam Schlein, have two children,
Elizabeth and John. The Weisses were di-
vorced in 1970.

SELECTED WORKS WRITTEN AND ILLUSTRATED:
Clay, Wood & Wire, 1956; A Gondola for Fun,
1957; Paul's Horse, Herman, 1958; Paper, Ink &
Roller, 1958; Horse in No Hurry, 1961; Pencil,
Pen & Brush, 1961; How to Be a Hero, 1967;
Sailing Small Boats, 1967; Motors and Engines
and How They Work, 1968; Collage and Con-
struction, 1969.

SELECTED WORKS ILLUSTRATED: Big Talk, by
Miriam Schlein, 1955; Amazing Mr. Pelgrew,
by Miriam Schlein, 1957; The Raggle-Taggle
Fellow, by Miriam Schlein, 1959; Looking for
Alexander, by David Cornel De Jong, 1963.

ABOUT: Contemporary Authors, Vol. 5-6;
Illinois University. College of Fine and Applied

Arts. Contemporary American Painting and
Sculpture; Kingman, Lee and others, comps.
Illustrators of Children's Books, 1957-1966;
Something About the Author, Vol. 1; Viguers,
Ruth Hill and others, comps. Illustrators of Chil-
dren's Books, 1946-56.

BARBARA WERSBA

August 19, 1932-

AUTHOR OF *The Dream Watcher,* etc.

Autobiographical sketch of Barbara Wersba:

PEOPLE ask me questions. Do you have
children of your own? (No) Do you like
children? (Not always) Then why do you
write for them? The answer is easy. I write
for children because my own childhood is
still within me—and if one feels the connection, it is natural to express it. A writer is a
person who is obsessed with rearranging his
life, clarifying it, putting the pieces together
differently—and the pieces that concern me
are my earliest years.

I was an only child, solitary, and extremely self-conscious. And though I wrote
stories from the time I could hold a pencil, I
never planned to be a writer. I wanted to be
an actress, and began my career at the age of
twelve in a community theater. Born in Illinois, I grew up in California, spent my adolescence in New York—and never stopped
acting. I acted off-Broadway, in summer
stock, television and radio. I took acting
classes during high school and majored in
drama at Bard College. I played every part
offered me—from the voice of a rabbit in a
cartoon, to Camille—and was miserable the
entire time. Since I was a good actress, I
could not understand my misery; but the
reason was simple enough. I was in the
wrong profession. As the years passed and
I graduated from college, took an apartment
in the East Village, and "made the rounds,"
I continued to write in the manner of a person conducting a secret love affair. Poems,
stories, plays and fairy tales filled dozens of
notebooks which I kept hidden in the closet.
The only odd thing is that I never thought
it odd.

Then, in 1960, everything changed. A theater group I was working with and had

Barbara Wersba (signature)

helped to create, broke up. I caught hepatitis and was put to bed for three months. I became terribly depressed. To while away the time, I wrote a children's story called *The Boy Who Loved the Sea*—and twelve months later it was published. A friend of a friend had taken the manuscript to Coward-McCann, and they had liked it. Somewhat dazed, I wrote a second book called *The Brave Balloon of Benjamin Buckley*, which was published by Atheneum. I was asked to review children's books for the New York *Times*. I wrote more books for Atheneum, and as though it had been a mirage, the theater faded away. Those first years of writing professionally were like a religious conversion—though the truth had not come in a blaze of light. It had simply been there all the while.

With my sixth book, *The Dream Watcher*, I entered the world of adolescence. The hero of this story, a fourteen-year-old misfit, is more personal to me than any character I have created, and I want to explore the teenage experience in future books. I now live in an old house overlooking the Hudson River, outside New York City, and have not seen a play in years. I don't even recite Shakespeare in the bathtub anymore.

SELECTED WORKS: The Boy Who Loved the Sea, 1961; The Brave Balloon of Benjamin Buckley, 1963; A Song for Clowns, 1965; Do Tigers

Ever Bite Kings? 1966; The Dream Watcher, 1968; Let Me Fall Before I Fly, 1971.

ABOUT: Something About the Author, Vol. 1; Top of the News June 1971.

ESTER WIER

October 17, 1910-

AUTHOR OF *The Loner*, etc.

Autobiographical sketch of Ester Alberti Wier:

IT took many years and many roads to bring me to the juvenile writing field. I started with poetry early in life, some of which was published when I was ten years old, and stayed with it throughout my schooling, dreaming of becoming another Millay or Dickinson. That career however was postponed by my marriage. I traveled to Hankow, China, in 1934, to become the wife of Henry Robert Wier, a lieutenant in the U.S. Navy. From then until 1953 I kept very busy raising two children while traveling to join my husband whenever and wherever I could. We lived on the west coast, the east coast, and in Florida through those years.

In the 1950s Captain Wier was on duty at the Pentagon and our children were well along in school so I began to pick up the pieces of that writing career I had planned so long before, starting with books for service wives on social customs and general information on how to be a military wife. These kept me busy for the next five years, until my husband retired from the navy. Then, while he earned a Master's degree at Purdue University, I tackled the job I had had in mind for a long time, writing a book about a boy on a sheep ranch. Indiana was a fine place for research on farm animals, and the result was *The Loner*.

In the five years since then, I have written and had published eleven books for boys, with time out to visit Israel, Greece, Italy, France, Spain, Morocco, and islands along the way. To date I haven't used these travels as background but I feel they widened my understanding of people and excited my imagination. Since my husband began teaching, we have lived in Arizona, which I have used

Ester Wier

as background for two books, and settled in Florida, which has already provided the setting for several books.

Our children have become travelers too. David followed in his father's footsteps, graduating from the Naval Academy and seeing a fair share of the world before resigning to study law. He is now a practicing attorney in New York City and happily married. Susan took degrees from Duke and Brown Universities, with time out for undergraduate study at the University of Munich, Germany. She spent two years in Beirut, Lebanon, teaching, before marrying a professor and settling in Gainesville, Florida.

Having two granddaughters and a grandson, I should now be writing for both girls and boys I suppose but recently I have started doing books whose characters are members of the animal world. I find this is a field in which I feel very much at home and completely happy so shall no doubt continue along this line for a time.

———

Ester Wier was born in Seattle, Washington. Her book *The Loner* was a runner-up for the Newbery Medal, 1964. Her papers have become part of the Kerlan Collection at the University of Minnesota.

SELECTED WORKS: The Loner, 1963; Gift of the Mountains, 1963; The Rumptydoolers, 1964; Easy Does It, 1965; The Barrel, 1966; The Wind Chasers, 1967; Action at Paradise Marsh, 1968; Winners, 1968; The Long Year, 1969; The Straggler, 1970; The White Oak, 1971.

ABOUT: Contemporary Authors, Vol. 11-12; Library Journal March 15, 1964.

BRIAN WILDSMITH

January 22, 1930-

ILLUSTRATOR OF *Brian Wildsmith's ABC*, etc.

Biographical sketch of Brian Lawrence Wildsmith:

BRIAN WILDSMITH was born in the small mining town of Penistone in Yorkshire, England. At the age of ten he was given a scholarship to attend De La Salle College in nearby Sheffield, where he centered his interest on chemistry with the intention of making a career in that field. One day in October six years later he happened to put some paint on paper and was overwhelmed by what he calls a "moment of truth." He decided that what he wanted to do was to express himself through painting, and the next day he left De La Salle for the Barnsley School of Art. Three years later, in 1949, he was awarded a scholarship to the University of London's Slade School of Fine Art, where he studied until he was called up for National (military) Service in 1952. He spent the greater part of the next two years teaching mathematics at the Royal Military School of Music. When he was discharged from the army in 1954 he took a position as an art teacher and taught full time until 1957 when he decided to resign and try his luck as a free-lance illustrator.

Among the commissions of his early free-lancing days were his work on *The Story of Jesus*, by Eleanor Graham, and on *High Sang the Sword*, by Eileen O'Faolain, both published in 1959. All his early commissions were for line illustrations of the text with color used only for jacket designs. His first chance to do full color illustrations was offered him by editor Mabel George, of Oxford University Press, who commissioned him to work on a new edition of *Tales from the*

BRIAN WILDSMITH

Arabian Nights, published in 1961. Another opportunity to branch out in his work was offered him by Helen Hoke Watts, of the American publishing firm of Franklin Watts, who contracted for *Brian Wildsmith's ABC,* a radiantly colored alphabet picture book which was entirely Wildsmith's creation. Published in 1962, it won the Kate Greenaway Award for distinguished illustration in that year and was later one of the few works by contemporary artists to be included in the Library of Congress Showcase Exhibit, "Three Centuries of ABC Books."

Since the ABC book, Wildsmith has created several more picture books, and has produced his own illustrated versions of a number of La Fontaine fables, a collection of Bible stories, and classic anthologies of children's poetry. His illustrations have appeared in books published in at least seven countries (including England, the United States, Switzerland, Sweden, Holland, Germany, and South Africa), and Christmas cards illustrated by him for UNESCO in 1965 sold nearly seven million copies around the world. In 1964 and 1967 he was runner-up for Kate Greenaway Awards. His *Brian Wildsmith's Birds* was named by the New York *Times* among the best-illustrated children's books for 1967. In 1968, he was a runner-up for the Hans Christian Andersen Award for illustrators.

Wildsmith, his wife Aurelie, and their four children, Clare, Rebecca, Anna, and Simon, live in London. He paints large abstract pictures for his own pleasure, is an accomplished pianist, and enjoys playing cricket and squash.

SELECTED WORKS ILLUSTRATED: Brian Wildsmith's ABC, 1962; The Secret Friends, by Nan Chauncy, 1962; The Lion and the Rat, by Jean de La Fontaine, 1964; The North Wind and the Sun, by Jean de La Fontaine, 1964; Brian Wildsmith's 1,2,3's, 1965; Havelok the Dane, by Kevin Crossley-Holland, 1965; Brian Wildsmith's Mother Goose, 1965; A Child's Garden of Verses, by Robert Louis Stevenson, 1966; Brian Wildsmith's Birds, 1967; Brian Wildsmith's Fishes, 1968; The Miller, the Boy and the Donkey, by Jean de La Fontaine, 1969.

ABOUT: Hopkins, Lee Bennett. Books Are by People; Hürlimann, Bettina. Picture Book World; Kingman, Lee and others, comps. Illustrators of Children's Books: 1957-1966; Ryder, John. Artists of a Certain Line; Chicago Tribune Books Today May 8, 1966; Junior Bookshelf July 1963; Library Association Record May 1963; School Library Journal November 1965.

MARY HUISKAMP CALHOUN WILKINS

See *Calhoun, Mary*

JOANNE S. WILLIAMSON

May 13, 1926-

AUTHOR OF *The Glorious Conspiracy,* etc.

Autobiographical sketch of Joanne Small Williamson:

I WAS born in Arlington, Massachusetts. By the time I was sixteen I had lived in Washington, D.C., Port Washington, Long Island, Syracuse, Forest Hills, New York, briefly in Chicago, and in the states of Delaware and Connecticut.

My home base, however, was always where I live now—Kennebunkport, Maine, a few steps from the Atlantic Ocean, where my nephews and niece are the fifth generation and where I have written all but one of my books. Many other places and things have influenced the writing of them, however—my first sight of the Lincoln Memorial in Washington at the age of three and the first Flag Day, which my father helped publicize; a trip to California at ten with the company of the play "Saint Joan" (my great-aunt was

Joanne S. Williamson

wardrobe mistress); standing with my mother outside a railroad car in Syracuse and listening to the great Paderewski practice for a road tour concert.

Music has always been an important part of my life, as readers of *And Forever Free* can guess. After two years at Barnard College I spent a year at the Diller-Quaile School of Music in New York. The writing urge was stronger, however. (That began when I was seven with a story of a princess with "beautiful golden hair trailing down her spine.")

At twenty I began writing charm and fashion scripts for the Powers Charm School of the Air. At the same time I had the chance to write a series of radio scripts on United Nations problems for the Carnegie Endowment for International Peace. In the course of this I learned some sobering things about what can happen to people in a time of violence and change. Feature writing for the Bridgeport, (Connecticut) *Herald,* where I was fashion editor for a while, taught me a lot more. This gave a deeper impulse to a somewhat romantic interest I had always had in history and the people who make it; and, a few years later, while working as the editor of a men's fashion paper in New York, I wrote my first novel, *Jacobin's Daughter,*

about a Parisian family during the French revolution.

I have not been to all the places I have written about since then. But I have seen the house in Paris that was the setting for *Jacobin's Daughter;* have visited the Rome of *The Iron Charm* and *The Eagles Have Flown;* the England of *To Dream Upon a Crown;* and, of course, the locales of my New York stories *And Forever Free* and *The Glorious Conspiracy.* The people in them—whatever the time in which they lived—are all people I have met in real life, who behave (I hope and believe) as they would behave in the situations I have invented for them. The problems they face are problems I have known, and that people will probably know (and, hopefully, solve) as long as the world lasts.

SELECTED WORKS: Jacobin's Daughter, 1956; Hittite Warrior, 1960; The Glorious Conspiracy, 1961; The Iron Charm, 1964; And Forever Free, 1966; To Dream Upon a Crown, 1967.

ABOUT: Contemporary Authors, Vol. 13-14; Who's Who of American Women, 1968-69.

HENRY WINTERFELD

April 9, 1901-

AUTHOR OF *Detectives in Togas,* etc.

Autobiographical sketch of Henry Winterfeld, who writes under his own name and under the pen name of "Manfred Michael":

I WAS born in Hamburg, Germany. My father, Max Winterfeld, was a composer of operettas. He was popular under the pseudonym Jean Gilbert. In France Jean is a common first name for males. Here in America however some people ask me: "How come your father is a woman?" I try to explain but they still wonder. My brother is a song writer. Not to be left behind I started studying the piano at Stern's Academy of Music in Berlin, together with Claudio Arrau and Frederick Loewe. I couldn't compete with them and switched to the profession of writing.

In 1933 I left Germany and went to Austria. There I wrote *Timpetill.* I wanted somehow to entertain my son Thomas, who was

Henry Winterfeld

sick with scarlet fever. Surprisingly other people liked the story too. Since then I have written only children's books. It's painful but I do it because I love children so much. Most of my best friends are children.

I wrote my next book here in the United States but I had already had the idea for it in Vienna. One morning I read in my newspaper, *Die Freie Presse* (The Free Press), about the excavation of a temple in Pompeii. On the wall was scribbled, in a childish hand, "CAIUS ASINUS EST." "Look here!" I thought. "The boys in Ancient Rome were the same rascals as to-day." And this inspired me to write *Detectives in Togas*. Which shows, don't neglect to read your favorite newspaper.

Later I wrote *Star Girl* and *Castaways in Lilliput*. My books have been published up to now in: America, France, Great Britain, Germany, Spain, Italy, Switzerland, Holland, Sweden, Norway, Yugoslavia and Japan. My latest opus, finished 1967, is *Pimmy Ponytail* —a royal entertainment for young girls. It has been published so far in Germany, Holland, France and Japan.

By the way, I almost forget to say that I'm married. My wife is one of the best-known toy designers in America. She is now retired.

We live in Maine, on the ocean, and even have a little private beach all to ourselves. Each summer we give a Young People's Garden Party for the children of our friends the lobster men, clam diggers and other neighbors. It's great fun!

––––––

Henry Winterfeld wrote for the stage and the movies before he started doing books for children. He says he is most proud of having been voted "man of the month" by the sixth grade classes of the Willets Road School, East Williston, New York. He married Elsbeth Michael in 1923.

Selected Works: Detectives in Togas, 1956; Star Girl, 1957; Castaways in Lilliput, 1960; Trouble at Timpetill, 1965.

MAIA WOJCIECHOWSKA
August 7, 1927-

Author of *Shadow of a Bull*, etc.

Autobiographical sketch of Maia Wojciechowska:

I WAS born in Poland in 1927 and I grew up in Spain in 1957. It was there, at thirty, that I fired a symbolic gun at a target marked: "Be the best Maia you can be and the rest will take care of itself." The bullet hit the outside of the first circle, but ever since then I've been getting closer to the bull's eye. Trying to hit it, I realized, was what life was all about. And that realization made me grown-up but not quite an adult, a thing I don't even try for.

Before Spain there was a lifetime of fumbling around. As a child, I found war very exciting. Together with my older brother I "fought" the Germans as well as the French whose war conduct we both found shameful. Being kicked out of school seemed like a badge of honor, if not courage. We refused to speak French and the French schools refused to understand our silence. Arriving in Portugal in 1942, we felt like deserters, and a few months later, in England, we felt cheated because no bombs fell on our house. With our arrival in the United States our war came to a bloodless end. My brother, at seventeen, volunteered and was accepted by the

Maia Wojciechowska: *MY-a Voi-che-HOV-skah*

Polish Air Force in Canada but he never saw the "action" that we both were itching for. In three and a half years in war-torn Europe the closest I came to *real* fear was for my pride and not my skin and that was when I almost picked up some half-chewed grapes someone spat out. I was hungry but not hungry enough. Later it was the hunger to fear for my life that seemed to guide a lot of my actions. Skiing impossible slopes, bull-fighting, driving a motorcycle, swimming further than I thought I could, were some of the things I did to appease the hunger. But the only way to really get rid of a thing like that was to grow old. And I finally succeeded in that. Last year.

The fumbling around to find not only my-self but what it was that I really wanted to do was both time wasting and energy con-suming. I always wanted to write and I al-ways did. But I wanted more, I wanted to be read. Rupert Hughes, a novelist, was the first to read my first full-length book. He called me, way past midnight, to tell me that he had read my book and that he was moved to tears. Without waiting for further details (and he must have wept because it was so

awful) I took the MS, caught a Greyhound bus in Los Angeles and came to New York, certain of my genius and immediate success. I left the MS with the receptionist at Harper & Bros. and in my best seventeen-year-old voice informed her that I would be back tomorrow. To my great disappointment she handed me my MS the following day. My first try at publication produced not even a rejection slip.

Two years later the next person who read what I wrote was Selden Rodman. I married him and he is the only person, besides myself (not counting my editors, for what do they *really* know?) who realizes that I am improv-ing at the craft we both have in common. From him I learned an awful lot and I owe him more than he will ever know. But our friendship, which continues ten years after our divorce, is an indication that I am still learning.

My books speak of my interests and most of them are with children for they are the only people with the built-in quality of growth. And growing means getting closer to that bull's eye. I know I will make it one day because from my mother I got the tendency of aiming with the heart rather than with the mind, from my father I got the idea of the importance of the target, and from my daughter, Oriana, I got the sense of obliga-tion to keep at it.

———

Maia Wojciechowska is the daughter of Zygmunt Wojciechowski, wartime chief-of-staff of the Polish Air Force. The family left Warsaw following the German invasion of Poland in 1939, and lived in France, Spain, Portugal, and England before settling in Los Angeles in 1942. Miss Wojciechowska grad-uated from the Sacred Heart Academy in Los Angeles in 1945 and attended Immaculate Heart College, Hollywood. She moved to New York, married Selden Rodman in 1950, and the couple spent much time in Haiti, where she wrote her first published book for children, *Market-Day for Ti André*. After her divorce in 1957, Miss Wojciechowska re-turned to Spain, where she conceived the idea for *Shadow of a Bull*, which was awarded the Newbery Medal for 1965 and the Deutscher Jugendbuch-preis in 1968. To pronounce her last name, she writes, say off-handedly "watch your house key."

SELECTED WORKS: Market-Day for Ti André, 1952; Shadow of a Bull, 1964; Odyssey of Courage, 1965; A Kingdom in a Horse, 1965; The Hollywood Kid, 1966; A Single Light, 1968; Tuned Out, 1968; Don't Play Dead Before You Have To, 1970.

ABOUT: Contemporary Authors, Vol. 11-12; Something About the Author, Vol. 1; Who's Who in America, 1970-1971; Who's Who of American Women, 1970-71; Horn Book August 1965; Library Journal March 15, 1964; March 15, 1965; October 15, 1965; New York Times Book Review May 5, 1968; Saturday Review March 27, 1965.

WILLIAM WONDRISKA

WILLIAM WONDRISKA

June 29, 1931-

AUTHOR AND ILLUSTRATOR OF *The Tomato Patch,* etc.

Biographical sketch of William Allen Wondriska:

WILLIAM WONDRISKA was born in Chicago, Illinois, the son of William Charles and Ruth Marie (Zavodsky) Wondriska. His childhood was spent in the Chicago suburb of Oak Park.

He says he was always "visually oriented." A third grade teacher suggested that his parents encourage his talent in art, and so he was sent to Saturday classes at the Chicago Art Institute. Two art scholarships were offered to him after high school, and he attended the University of Chicago for a time.

In 1953 he was graduated from the School of the Art Institute of Chicago. He traveled in central and southern Europe, and returned to graduate studies in the School of Art and Architecture of Yale University. "It was a very exciting time to have been studying there," he says. "Albers had just been there three years, and new people were coming to the Art School." In 1954 Wondriska received his B.F.A. degree.

His first children's book was created in 1955, when he wrote, designed, illustrated, and printed *The Sound of Things* as one of the requirements for his M.F.A. degree from Yale. The book was exhibited by the Amer-

ican Institute of Graphic Arts and was later reprinted by Pantheon.

On August 27, 1955, he married Rebecca Shoemaker in Lake Geneva, Wisconsin. He was drafted and served as a private in Japan and Korea from 1955 to 1957. After his war service he worked with the designer Lester Beale in Brookfield Center, Connecticut, until 1958, when he moved to West Hartford, Connecticut, to be an instructor at the University of Hartford Art School.

In 1961 Wondriska became a full time free-lance designer, having already resumed the writing, designing, and illustrating of children's books with the publication of *One, Two, Three, a Book to See,* 1959, and *Puff,* 1960. He has continued to create new books fairly regularly. One of them, *All By Myself,* 1963, uses photographs of the oldest of his three little daughters, who inspired the book. *The Dove,* 1970, was developed during a two-year period of speaking to school children, PTAs, and Book Fairs in which some two thousand children watched him do the drawings.

Puff was a Junior Literary Guild book in the Fall of 1960. *The Sound of Things, One, Two, Three, a Book to See,* and *Puff* were American Institute of Graphic Arts selections, and *One, Two, Three, a Book to See* was included in their Fifty Books of the Year, 1959, as was *The Tomato Patch* in 1965.

William Wondriska's work has been discussed in several magazines, including *Graphic Design, Graphis Annual,* and *The Penrose Annual.* He is one of a group of illustrators about whom in her book, *The Art of Art for Children's Books,* Diana Klemin writes, "they entertain the youngest children with effects as magic as kaleidoscopes, and introduce them to the beautiful aesthetic experience of a book." Wondriska has said, "The satisfactions of creating a book that is beautiful are overwhelming."

He and his family live in a glass house in West Hartford, Connecticut. He works at home. When asked about his favorite recreation and his hobbies, William Wondriska has one answer—graphic design.

SELECTED WORKS WRITTEN AND ILLUSTRATED: One, Two, Three, a Book to See, 1959; Puff, 1960; Which Way to the Zoo? 1962; A Long Piece of String, 1963; The Tomato Patch, 1964; Mister Brown & Mister Gray, 1968; All the Animals Were Angry, 1970.

ABOUT: Contemporary Authors, Vol. 4; Kingman, Lee and others, comps. Illustrators of Children's Books: 1957-1966.

EVA-LIS WUORIO

AUTHOR OF *Tal and the Magic Barruget,* etc.

Autobiographical sketch of Eva-Lis Wuorio:

I MUST have been nearly seven that particular early morning the foghorn awakened me and I knew the harbour was open, the spring had at last come. That was in the historic Hansa town of Viipuri, in the eastern corner of the Gulf of Finland, which for centuries had been a trading post-harbour town between western lands and the mysterious east. Through most of the long Finnish winter months the harbour would remain icebound in those days, but a foghorn meant the first foreign boat was in. Even before I'd finished my breakfast porridge my cousins Kalevi and Erik came to fetch me. This was the first year we'd be going to see "the first boat" without a nurse or a grown-up with us, because Erik was nearly ten.

We crossed the market squares that separated the more modern city from the old town and climbed through narrow ancient

streets to the high granite promenade built into what once had been the fortress walls. From there the view over the island-speckled bay, the Castle, and the harbour was splendid. The reason I am telling you this is because the ship that had come in brought a cargo of oranges and, in unloading, one of the cases broke. Golden globes spilled prodigally onto the still snow-slushed stone quay. We'd been shouting and waving happily so I suppose what happened was that the captain or whoever said, "Let those children have the oranges." In any case, up to the ramparts came the foreign sailors bearing their gift of blood-oranges, sweet and juicy, with red-veined flesh, the first I had ever seen. We'd only had the ordinary ones before, and as we couldn't understand the strangers, I made a story on the way home about the magic land they'd come from.

So that's how it started, the stretching of one's imagination, the urge to see far places with far-sounding names, many of which I have seen and lived in through the years, all given impetus by the fact that in Finland quite literally everybody loved books. (There is no illiteracy in Finland.) That love stayed with me when I went to live in Canada at the age of eleven, and that's where I wrote my first children's book.

Eva-Lis Wuorio: *AY va lees WOR ee oh*

It started in pique. I was working during college holidays on the Toronto *Evening Telegram* (later I worked on it full time, then moved to the *Globe and Mail* and later still worked as assistant editor on *Maclean's Magazine*). Children of a friend got me annoyed by being very insularly Anglo-Saxon, you know, foreigners were no good. So I wrote a story called *Vikings Return*, which showed how Norwegians, French, Czechs and Poles had all had a part in building Canada. But it wasn't until many years later when I was living on the Balearic Island of Ibiza that I really began to write children's books in earnest and with much pleasure. That was an accident too.

I had gone to visit the tiny island of Formentera then connected to Ibiza only once a day by a fat little boat called Manolito. It carried people and fish and mail and pigs and wasn't very dependable in any weather. (Ultimately it sank, actually, but fortunately on a sand bank.) An English friend had an old farmhouse in Formentera, plus two small daughters, Belinda and Lucy. One morning she wanted to take the Manolito to Ibiza to do shopping and asked me to keep an eye on them during the day, as she intended to return in the evening. Of course that day the wind rose. Manolito couldn't make the straits that day, nor for the next three days. The one thing that kept Belinda and Lucy most amused, and least longing for their mummy was a story about themselves, an imaginary, "so then you went up to the windmills. . ."

It was some years later, during a foggy winter in London, longing for the sun, that I wrote Belinda's and Lucy's adventures. It is called *The Island of Fish in the Trees*. Edward Ardizzone did delightful illustrations for it, and somehow, ever since, I have found it restful to space my other writing with books for children. I have been to all the places described in them, for example, *Kali and the Golden Mirror* stems from the months I spent on the Aegean island of Skyros, *October Treasure* is set on the Channel Island of Jersey where I now live, and so on. Yes, obviously I love seas and islands, and also Boxer dogs and Siamese cats who have a tendency to creep into my stories. In fact I must go and feed them now.

I have not graduated from any school I ever attended, I have never worked at anything else except writing (though for a time I thought I would become a sculptor and a painter,) and Eva-Lis Wuorio is the shortest version of the name under which I was born. Since you ask, it's pronounced A-va-lees, and Wuorio as though it worried you worr-y-oh.

SELECTED WORKS: Return of the Viking, 1955; The Island of Fish in the Trees, 1962; Tal and the Magic Barruget, 1965; Kali and the Golden Mirror, 1967; Save Alice, 1968; Happiness Flower, 1969; The Singing Canoe, 1969; Code: Polonaise, 1970.

ROSE WYLER

See *Ames, Rose Wyler*

MARIANNE YAMAGUCHI
January 10, 1936-

and

TOHR YAMAGUCHI
October 22, 1932-

AUTHOR AND ILLUSTRATOR OF *Two Crabs and the Moonlight*, etc.

Biographical sketch of John Tohr Yamaguchi and Marianne Illenberger Yamaguchi by Marianne Yamaguchi:

IT is July and midwinter here in Canberra, Australia. I have just lit the evening fire to fend off the chill of the late afternoon and as I warm to the feverish crackle of the gum logs I can see grey white smoke beginning to drift from my neighbor's kitchen chimney. The moment itself is a homely metaphor for the domestic simplicity and beauty we have felt during our sojourn in this valley-city, lying exposed to the capricious antics of saucy magpies and ringed round by staid mountain hills of snow eucalypts.

We came to Australia three years ago when Tohr received a fellowship to study for his doctorate in demography at the Australian National University. While he has been writing his thesis I have taught art in one of the local high schools and completed

Marianne Yamaguchi

TOHR YAMAGUCHI

a new picture book about fingerplays. A year ago our second daughter, Kara Elizabeth, was born. In our leisure we raise vegetables and flowers, a duck and a chicken and an Australian Afghan hound who wants to come back to America with us.

My own memories of childhood are buried in the seasons of northern Ohio. I remember the excitement of spongy spring bogs and green meadows blushing with forget-me-nots. Summer ripening in fields of wild straw-

berries. Glowing autumn days strung like lanterns against bleak November. And finally the rapture and whoopee of waking to a winter morning. Snowbound!

From the beginning I always liked to draw and make things but my father's great love for the piano influenced my ambition to become a musician. By the time I graduated from high school, however, I had abandoned this idea and entered Bowling Green State University as a degree candidate in art education. Though a practical solution for my creativity it became a less satisfying one as I became more involved in my studio courses. After two and one half years I transferred to the Rhode Island School of Design where I graduated with a BFA degree in painting three years later.

Tohr's mother and father were both musicians and it was from them that he first listened to the stories recounted in European music. Those early memories of childhood are in sharp contrast to his life when he graduated from high school. Japan was still under the postwar occupation and the country's outlook was no more promising than his own. Three years were spent in recovering from a serious illness before he could hold his first job selling newspapers in a Tokyo hotel which housed some five hundred Americans working for the occupation forces. With the help of some of these friends he began to study English seriously and in 1955 sailed to America with the high hopes of studying journalism at Columbia University.

His travels ended in Vermont, however, and he began his academic studies at Marlboro College, concentrating in math and physics. There was also time for writing, particularly short stories which had held his interest since high school. Eventually he did transfer to Columbia to complete his undergraduate degree in mathematics while working in the statistical office of the United Nations.

It was just about at this point that our lives crossed each other in the tiny town of Chatham on Cape Cod where we were both working in a summer inn. The following winter Tohr wrote an assignment for Ellen Lewis Buell's course in juvenile writing which he later sent to me in Providence. I illustrated some of the episodes in the story for a drawing class, but we both forgot about the manuscript and the drawings until after we were married and living in New York. A friend suggested we show our work to one of the editors at Holt, Rinehart and Winston. A few weeks later the manuscript was accepted and on the eve of the birth of our daughter Esmé I finished the last drawing which happened to be the title page for *The Golden Crane*.

Tohr continued to work for the United Nations until he resigned to accept a fellowship to study demography for one year at Princeton. Bicycling home one night through the tree shadows of a full moon he began to think about another story which was to become *Two Crabs and the Moonlight*. On our last trip to Japan a little boy brought us two river crabs in a pan. They looked just like Ake and his mother and I was delighted to see how long their eyes really were because I didn't have any live models when I made the drawings.

Returning to New York once again Tohr resumed his work with the United Nations and I illustrated two more books by different authors. *The Sea of Gold* by Yoshiko Uchida and *Palace in Bagdad* by Jean Russell Larson, both Scribner books. Then in 1966 Tohr received his fellowship and we packed three suitcases and left for Canberra. This brings me back to where I began except that it is now very late and the fire has almost gone out.

———

Marianne Illenberger was born in Cuyahoga Falls, Ohio, John Tohr Yamaguchi in Tokyo, Japan. They were married in 1960.

Tohr Yamaguchi received his B.S. from Columbia University in 1960 and a Certificate in Advanced Studies in Demography from Princeton in 1963. He is a member of the Population Association of America, and the International Union for the Scientific Study of Population.

SELECTED WORKS WRITTEN BY TOHR YAMA- GUCHI: The Golden Crane, 1963; Two Crabs and the Moonlight, 1965.

SELECTED WORKS ILLUSTRATED BY MARIANNE YAMAGUCHI: The Golden Crane, by Tohr Yamaguchi 1963; Two Crabs and the Moonlight, by Tohr Yamaguchi, 1965; The Sea of Gold, by Yoshiko Uchida, 1965; Palace in Bagdad, by Jean Russell Larson, 1966.

ABOUT MARIANNE YAMAGUCHI: Kingman, Lee and others, comps. Illustrators of Children's Books: 1957-1966.

ABOUT TOHR YAMAGUCHI: Contemporary Authors, Vol. 19-20.

ED YOUNG

November 28, 1931-

ILLUSTRATOR OF *The Emperor and the Kite*, etc.

Autobiographical sketch of Ed Tse-chun Young:

"EDDY, I wonder what is to become of you." This sentence still rings clearly in my ears, when my mother would glance up from my uncomely report card for some ten of my academic years in China. The glance, though concerned, had a touch of warmth and amusement to it. Somehow I knew that she knew my formal schooling was secondary to my dreams and everything would be all right in the end.

I was born, near Peking, in a coal-mining town called Tientsin two months after the Manchurian invasion. Three years later when northern China was under renewed threat, my family moved southward to the mouth of Yangtze River, a metropolis called Shanghai. The city was divided under the jurisdiction of many European countries which, for a while, ironically guarded us against much of the new intruder's insensibility. It was there that I grew up. The war restricted many material things, but my family learned to develop great tenacity and flexibility so as to enjoy life under the most adverse circumstances. At one time my father held three jobs and my mother attempted many small enterprises to keep the household running. We had five children in the family and often it increased to seven or eight when our friends came and decided to stay for a while. We played unceasingly by ourselves, with friends and relatives and occasionally with several families. When I was alone I daydreamed and many of my dreams were manifested in the form of plays or drawings.

They were shown to artistic friends of the family and I knew no matter what I did in life it would have to be first and foremost related to art. Since my father was a structural engineer it was hoped that I might develop into an architect. When the Communists took Shanghai, I went to Hong Kong to continue high school. Two and a half years later I was able to come to the United States and start my schooling as an architect, which took three years to reveal itself as a mistaken profession. In 1954 I entered Art Center College in Los Angeles and graduated in another three years as an illustrator. The forces of opportunity drew me to New York City and there I accepted work in an advertising studio until it folded in 1961. While there I did studies of movements on my own, especially those of animals. Upon the suggestion of friends I showed them to Ursula Nordstrom of Harper & Row, who asked if I would try a book called *The Mean Mouse and Other Mean Stories*. It was then merely fun to bring back for a moment the long-forgotten childhood days when animals behaved like human beings. However, the book took root and it was followed by Holt, Rinehart and Winston's *Poetry for Young Sci-entists;* Follet's *The Yellow Boat;* World's *The Emperor and the Kite,* and *Chinese Mother Goose Rhymes;* Doubleday's *The Tiniest Sounds;* and Funk and Wagnall's *The Bird from the Sea.*

It is to my amusement now to be called a children's book artist. Somehow still, "Eddy, I wonder what is to become of you," rings in my ears.

———

Ed Young has also studied at the City College of San Francisco, the University of Illinois, and Pratt Institute, New York, where he has taught as well. *The Emperor and the Kite* was a Caldecott runner-up for 1968. Illustrations for this work were included in an international exhibition arranged by the Smithsonian Institution and shown in Japan. Several of Ed Young's books have been in exhibitions of the American Institute of Graphic Arts.

SELECTED WORKS ILLUSTRATED: The Mean Mouse and Other Mean Stories, by Janice May Udry, 1962; Poetry for Young Scientists, compiled by Leland B. Jacobs and Sally Nohelty, 1964; The Yellow Boat, by Margaret Hillert, 1967; The Emperor and the Kite, by Jane Yolen, 1967; Chinese Mother Goose Rhymes, edited by Robert Utley Hyndman (Robert Wyndham, pseud.), 1969; The Tiniest Sounds, by Mel Evans, 1969; The Bird from the Sea, by René Weiss, 1970.

ABOUT: Publishers' Weekly September 2, 1968.

HARVE ZEMACH
December 5, 1933-

and

MARGOT ZEMACH
November 30, 1931-

AUTHOR AND ILLUSTRATOR OF *The Judge,* etc.

Biographical sketch of Harvey Fischtrom and Margot Zemach Fischtrom:

IN their work as author and illustrator of children's books, Harve and Margot Zemach, who are Mr. and Mrs. Harvey Fischtrom in private life, use Mrs. Fischtrom's maiden name.

HARVE ZEMACH

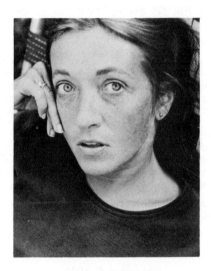

MARGOT ZEMACH

For Margot Zemach, working as a book illustrator is the realization of a childhood ambition. Born in Los Angeles, California, to Benjamin Zemach, a dancer-director, and Elizabeth Dailey, his actress wife, she has early childhood recollections ". . . of looking and feeling my way into pictures in books and of living inside them for hours." When she was a little older and began to draw, she decided upon a career as an artist and, in the course of time, began her professional training at the Los Angeles Institute of Art. After studying there and at the Jepson In-stitute of Art and the Chounard Institute of Art, she received a Fulbright Scholarship to attend the Vienna Academy of Fine Arts in 1955-56.

Harvey Fischtrom was a Fulbright student in Vienna at the same time as Margot Zemach. Born in Newark, New Jersey, the son of Mac and Ida (Rabinowitz) Fischtrom, he had taken his B.A. degree at Wesleyan University before winning a Fulbright to study at the University of Vienna in 1955-56.

Margot Zemach and Harvey Fischtrom were married on January 20, 1957, shortly after they had completed their programs of foreign study. Still intent upon her ambition to illustrate children's books, the new Mrs. Fischtrom persuaded her husband to write one for her. He turned out A Small Boy Is Listening, published in 1958.

During the 1960s, the author-illustrator team of Harve and Margot Zemach produced about a half dozen more children's books, and their three daughters were born—Kaethe, Heidi, and Rachel. Harvey Fischtrom, who received his M.A. degree in the history of ideas in 1959, taught history and social science at Boston University from 1960 to 1965 and later at the University of Massachusetts.

Concentrating on children's books, Margot Zemach has turned out several on her own besides those produced with her husband, and her work has been cited by the American Institute of Graphic Arts and the Society of Typographic Arts. In addition, the Harve and Margot Zemach version of Salt, a Russian Tale, won a first prize at the Book Week Spring Book Festival in 1965, and their book The Judge was a runner-up for the Caldecott Award in 1970 .

In spite of the recognition she has received, Margot Zemach regards most of the work she has done thus far as "preparation and half-realized intentions, with the exception of occasional pages which manage to tell something true about the meaning of the text and how I think and feel about drawing." She prefers to make line drawings, applying color as a wash "that will strengthen rather than negate the drawing," which she says is of primary importance to her. She often draws the same page thirty or forty times.

The Fischtroms have traveled in Italy, spent a year in Denmark, and at present live in England. They now have four children.

SELECTED WORKS WRITTEN OR ADAPTED BY HARVE ZEMACH AND ILLUSTRATED BY MARGOT ZEMACH: A Small Boy Is Listening, 1958; Nail Soup, 1964; Salt, a Russian Tale, 1965; The Speckled Hen, a Russian Nursery Rhyme, 1966; Mommy, Buy Me a China Doll, 1966; The Judge, 1969.

SELECTED WORKS WRITTEN OR ADAPTED AND ILLUSTRATED BY MARGOT ZEMACH: The Three Sillies, 1963; The Little Tiny Woman, a Folktale, 1965; The Fisherman and His Wife, 1966.

SELECTED WORKS ILLUSTRATED BY MARGOT ZEMACH: Take a Giant Step, by Hannelore Hahn, 1960; The Question Box, by Jay Williams, 1965; King of the Hermits and Other Stories, by Jack Sendak, 1966; Mazel and Shlimazel, by Isaac B. Singer, 1967; Harlequin, by Rose L. Mincieli, 1968; When Shlemiel Went to Warsaw and Other Stories, by Isaac B. Singer, 1968.

ABOUT HARVE ZEMACH: Who's Who in America, 1970-71.

ABOUT MARGOT ZEMACH: Kingman, Lee and others, comps. Illustrators of Children's Books: 1957-1966; Who's Who in America, 1970-71; Who's Who of American Women, 1970-71.

ABOUT HARVE AND MARGOT ZEMACH: Top of the News April 1971.

REINER ZIMNIK

December 13, 1930-

AUTHOR AND ILLUSTRATOR OF *The Bear on the Motorcycle*, etc.

Autobiographical sketch of Reiner Zimnik:

I WAS born in Beuthen, in Silesia. (Zimnik is a Slavic word and means "cold man" or "winter man" or also "winter coat.") Together with my brothers and sisters (four in number) and eight to twelve friends, I spent a normal and secure childhood. At the end of the war we had to flee. At that time also my father lost his life in the war and we came to Bavaria. There I learned the trade of cabinetmaker; then I graduated from the Gymnasium and after that I went to the Academy of Art in Munich. I have stayed in that city until the present day and since I do not like to travel there will probably be no change in that respect.

I can remember that when I was still very small an uncle, who was a book restorer, kept giving me books with blank pages which I then always filled with drawings: at first of tigers and lions, later Indians and trappers and knights, and finally submarines and aeroplanes. I was very angry in those days that even when I was only seven I could draw almost everything and all kinds of animals except chickens and cows. I finally made do with "horses with horns." I still cannot do chickens very well and at the Academy no one could teach me how—it is just very hard to do.

Otherwise I am doing quite well and I am content. The only thing is that every Sunday the Catholics in the church across the way from my studio beat with iron hammers on bronze bowls they call bells and in this way make ugly booming noises. That annoys me again and again.

———

While still a student Zimnik was asked to illustrate a story he did not like. He substituted a story of his own and the result was his first book, published in Germany, *Xaver der Ringelstecher*, 1954. *The Bear on the Motorcycle* was an Honor Book in the New York *Herald Tribune* Children's Spring Book Festival, 1963. Zimnik's work has been exhibited by the American Institute of Graphic Arts.

SELECTED WORKS WRITTEN AND ILLUSTRATED: Jonah the Fisherman, 1956; The Proud Circus Horse, 1957; The Little Roaring Tiger, 1961; The Bear on the Motorcycle, 1963; The Crane, 1970; The Bear and the People, 1971.

SELECTED WORKS ILLUSTRATED: The Snow Party, by Beatrice Schenk De Regniers, 1959.

ABOUT: Hürlimann, Bettina. Picture Book World; Kingman, Lee and others, comps. Illustrators of Children's Books: 1957-1966; Viguers, Ruth Hill and others, comps. Illustrators of Children's Books: 1946-1956.

PICTURE CREDITS

Berenice Abbott, Symeon Shimin; *Bachrach, Boston,* Wilma Pitchford Hays; *Bradford Bachrach,* Else Minarik; *Baltimore News-Post,* Gerald W. Johnson; *Bassano & Vandyk,* E. M. Almedingen; *Peter Beckett,* Peter Spier; *Kurt Bethke,* James Krüss; *Margaret Brooks,* Betty Jean Lifton; *photograph by John Campbell,* Lester del Rey; *Mrs. Rose Cole,* Anne Rand; *sketch by Milein Cosman,* Harold Jones; *George Cserna,* Mary O'Neill; *Gene Dauber,* Antonio Frasconi; *Marc Ellidge,* C. Walter Hodges; *Elliotts' Studio,* Mary Francis Shura; *courtesy Milton Esterow, Kennedy Galleries,* Bernarda Bryson; *Faber & Faber,* Eilís Dillon; *Carl Fischer,* Joseph Schindelman; *Mogens Gad,* Jan Wahl; *David Gahr,* Ellen Raskin; *Mark Gerson,* Cynthia Harnett; *Alex Gotfryd,* Joan Aiken; *Bernard Gotfryd,* Nat Hentoff; *H. H. Graham, Inverness,* Mollie Hunter; *T. H. Greville,* Madeleine Polland; *Siegfried Halus,* William Wondriska; *Galen Hall,* Maia Wojciechowska; *Richard Harrington,* Nan Chauncy; *H. Lee Hooper,* Charles Schulz; *HT-Bild,* Inger Sandberg, Lasse Sandberg; *Leon Kotkofsky,* Uri Shulevitz; *Bruce Kraus,* Robert Kraus, William Steig; *Nina Leen, Life Magazine,* © *Time Inc,* "Mariana"; *N. Levering,* Ann Grifalconi; *Rik Levy,* Isaac Asimov; *self-drawing,* Joseph Low; *Mc-Candless of Urbana,* Natalia Maree Belting; *McKnight Studio,* Fred Gipson; *Patt Meara,* Isaac Bashevis Singer; *Mitchell Studio,* Robin McKown; *Karsten Mortensen,* Ib Spang Olsen; *Mossbargers Studio,* Walt Morey; *Clifford Norton,* William E. Scheele; *Ann Oakes,* John L. Anderson; *C. E. Olson,* Sterling North; *P & M Photographic,* Pauline Baynes; *Pach Bros., N.Y.,* Louisa R. Shotwell; *Self-drawing,* Edgar Parker; *Peoples Studio,* "Wilson Gage"; *Barbara Pflaum,* Janusz Grabiánski; *James A. Rackwitz, St. Louis Post-Dispatch,* Emily Neville; *Ramsey & Muspratt,* Lucy Boston; *Francis de Regniers,* Irene Haas; *Henry Ries,* Janet Lambert; *courtesy of Charles Scribner's Sons,* Marjorie Kinnan Rawlings; *Susanne Singer,* Louise Fitzhugh; *Ronni Solbert,* Jean Merrill; *Somerville Photographs,* Crosby Newall Bonsall; *Studio Edmark,* Hester Burton; *Sturlason,* Aimée Sommerfelt; *Jim Theologos,* Joan Walsh Anglund; *self-drawing,* Brinton Turkle; *Walters Studio,* Molly Cone; *Washington Post,* Helga Sandburg; *Ray Webber,* Farley Mowat; *Jerome Weidman,* "Crockett Johnson"; *Welinder,* Edith Unnerstad; *Wells Studio,* Joanne S. Williamson; *Wickman,* Babbis Friis-Baastad; *Weston Woods,* Celestino Piatti; *Chiang Yee,* David McCord.

JUNIOR AUTHORS AND ILLUSTRATORS INCLUDED IN THE SERIES

The following list indicates the volume in which each individual may be found:

J—THE JUNIOR BOOK OF AUTHORS, second edition (1951)

M—MORE JUNIOR AUTHORS (1963)

T—THIRD BOOK OF JUNIOR AUTHORS (1972)

Branley, Franklyn M.–M
Brann, Esther–J
Bransom, Paul–M
"Breck, Vivian" (Vivian Gurney Breckenfield)–M
Breckenfield, Vivian Gurney. See "Breck, Vivian"–M
Brier, Howard M.–M
Briggs, Raymond–T
Bright, Robert–M
Brindze, Ruth–M
Brink, Carol–J
Bro, Margueritte–M
Brock, C. E.–J
Brock, Emma L.–J
Brock, H. M.–J
Bromhall, Winifred–M
"Bronson, Lynn." See Lampman, Evelyn Sibley–M
Bronson, Wilfrid S.–J
Brooke, L. Leslie–J
Brooks, Walter R.–J
Broster, D. K.–J
Brown, Edna A.–J
Brown, Marcia–M
Brown, Margaret Wise ("Golden MacDonald")–J
Brown, Paul–J
Brunhoff, Jean de–J
Brunhoff, Laurent de–M
Bryson, Bernarda–T
Buehr, Walter–T
Buff, Conrad–J
Buff, Mary Marsh–J
Bulla, Clyde Robert–M
Burbank, Addison–J
Burch, Robert–T
Burchard, Peter–T
Burgess, Thornton W.–J
Burglon, Nora–J
Burkert, Nancy Ekholm–T
Burningham, Helen Oxenbury. See Oxenbury, Helen–T
Burningham, John–T
Burton, Hester–T
Burton, Virginia Lee–J
Busoni, Rafaello–J
Byars, Betsy–T

Caldecott, Randolph–J
Calhoun, Mary (Mary Huiskamp Calhoun Wilkins)–T
Cameron, Eleanor–T
Camp, Walter–J
"Campbell, Bruce." See Epstein, Samuel–M
Carigiet, Alois–T
Carlson, Natalie Savage–M
Carpenter, Frances–M
Carr, Harriett H.–M
Carr, Mary Jane–J

Carrick, Valery–J
Carroll, Latrobe–M
Carroll, Ruth–M
Carter, Helene–M
Casserley, Anne–J
Caudill, Rebecca–M
Cavanah, Frances–M
Cavanna, Betty (Elizabeth Headley)–M
Chalmers, Mary–T
"Chapman, Walker." See Silverberg, Robert–T
Chappell, Warren–T
Charlip, Remy–T
Charlot, Jean–M
"Charles, Nicholas." See Kuskin, Karla–T
Chase, Richard–M
Chastain, Madye Lee–M
Chauncy, Nan–T
Chipperfield, Joseph E.–M
Chrisman, Arthur Bowie–J
Church, Alfred J.–J
Church, Richard–M
Chute, B. J.–M
Chute, Marchette–M
Ciardi, John–T
"Clare, Helen." See Clarke, Pauline–T
Clark, Ann Nolan–J
Clarke, Pauline ("Helen Clare")–T
Cleary, Beverly–M
Coatsworth, Elizabeth–J
Coblentz, Catherine Cate–J
Coggins, Jack–M
Colby, Carroll B.–M
"Collodi, C." (Carlo Lorenzini)–J
Colman, Hila ("Teresa Crayder")–T
Colum, Padraic–J
Cone, Molly ("Caroline More")–T
Coolidge, Olivia E.–M
"Cook, John Estes." See Baum, L. Frank–T
Cooney, Barbara–M
Corbin, William (William Corbin McGraw)–M
Cormack, Maribelle–J
Cosgrave, John O'Hara, II–M
Courlander, Harold–M
"Crayder, Teresa." See Colman, Hila–T
Craig, Margaret Maze–M
Craig, Mary Francis. See Shura, Mary Francis–T
Crane, Walter–J
Crawford, Phyllis–J

Credle, Ellis–J
Crew, Fleming H. See Gall, Alice Crew–J
Crew, Helén Coale–J
Crowell, Pers–M
Crownfield, Gertrude–J
Crump, Irving–J
Cunningham, Julia–T

Dahl, Borghild–T
Dahl, Roald–T
Dalgliesh, Alice–J
Daly, Maureen–M
Daniel, Hawthorne–J
Daringer, Helen Fern–M
Darling, Louis–M
Daugherty, James–J
d'Aulaire, Edgar & Ingri Parin. See Aulaire, Edgar & Ingri Parin d'–J
Davis, Julia (Julia Davis Adams)–J
Davis, Lavinia R.–J
Davis, Mary Gould–J
Davis, Robert–J
de Angeli, Marguerite–J
de Brunhoff, Jean. See Brunhoff, Jean de–J
de Brunhoff, Laurent. See Brunhoff, Laurent de–M
de Jong, Dola–M
DeJong, Meindert–M
De La Mare, Walter–J
de Leeuw, Adèle–J
de Leeuw, Cateau. See de Leeuw, Adèle–J
del Rey, Lester–T
de Treviño, Elizabeth Borton. See Treviño, Elizabeth Borton de–T
Dennis, Morgan–M
Dennis, Wesley–M
de Regniers, Beatrice Schenk–M
Deucher, Sybil–M
Deutsch, Babette–M
Dickson, Marguerite–M
Dillon, Eilís (Eilís Dillon O'Cuilleanain)–T
Ditmars, Raymond L.–J
Dix, Beulah Marie–J
Doane, Pelagie–M
Dolbier, Maurice–M
Domanska, Janina (Janina Domanska Laskowski)–T
Drummond, V. H.–T
"Drummond, Walter." See Silverberg, Robert–T
du Bois, William Pène–J
du Jardin, Rosamond–M

J–THE JUNIOR BOOK OF AUTHORS; M–MORE JUNIOR AUTHORS; T–THIRD BOOK OF JUNIOR AUTHORS

Dulac, Edmund—**J**
Duncan, Norman—**J**
Dunlop, Agnes Mary Robertson. See "Kyle, Elisabeth"—**M**
Du Soe, Robert C.—**M**
Duvoisin, Roger—**J**

Eager, Edward—**M**
Earle, Olive L.—**M**
Eastman, Charles A.—**J**
Eaton, Jeanette—**J**
Eberle, Irmengarde—**J**
Edmonds, Walter Dumaux—**M**
Ehrlich, Bettina. See "Bettina" —**M**
Eichenberg, Fritz—**M**
Eipper, Paul—**J**
Ellsberg, Commander Edward —**J**
Elting, Mary ("Campbell Tatham")—**M**
Emberley, Barbara—**T**
Emberley, Ed—**T**
Emery, Anne—**M**
Enright, Elizabeth—**J**
Epstein, Beryl Williams—**M**
Epstein, Samuel ("Adam Allen," and "Bruce Campbell")—**M**
Erdman, Loula Grace—**M**
Estes, Eleanor—**J**
Ets, Marie Hall—**J**
Evans, Eva Knox—**M**
Eyre, Katherine Wigmore—**M**

Fabre, Jean-Henri—**J**
Falls, C. B.—**J**
Farjeon, Eleanor—**J**
Farley, Walter—**J**
Fatio, Louise—**M**
Feelings, Tom—**T**
Felsen, Gregor—**J**
Felton, Harold W.—**M**
Fenton, Carroll Lane—**M**
Fenton, Edward—**T**
Fenton, Mildred Adams—**M**
Ferris, Helen—**J**
Field, Rachel—**J**
Fillmore, Parker—**J**
Fischer, Hans Erich—**M**
Fisher, Aileen—**M**
Fisher, Leonard Everett—**T**
Fitch, Florence Mary—**M**
"Fitzgerald, Captain Hugh." See Baum, L. Frank—**T**
Fitzhardinge, Joan Margaret. See "Phipson, Joan"—**T**
Fitzhugh, Louise—**T**
Flack, Marjorie—**J**
Fleischman, Sid—**T**
Floethe, Richard—**M**

Floherty, John J.—**J**
Flora, James—**T**
Forbes, Esther—**M**
Forman, James—**T**
Foster, Genevieve—**J**
Foster, Marian Curtis. See "Mariana"—**T**
François, André—**T**
"Françoise" (Françoise Seignobosc)—**M**
Franklin, George Cory—**M**
Franklin, Madeleine. See "L'Engle, Madeleine"—**M**
Frasconi, Antonio—**T**
Fraser, Claud Lovat—**J**
Freeman, Don—**M**
Freeman, Ira Maximilian—**M**
Freeman, Lydia—**M**
Freeman, Mae Blacker—**M**
French, Allen—**J**
"French, Paul." See Asimov, Isaac—**T**
Friedman, Frieda—**M**
Friermood, Elisabeth Hamilton —**M**
"Friis, Babbis." See Friis-Baastad, Babbis—**T**
Friis-Baastad, Babbis ("Eleanor Babbis," "Babbis Friis")—**T**
Fritz, Jean—**T**
Frost, Frances—**M**
Fry, Rosalie K.—**T**
Fyleman, Rose—**J**

Gaer, Joseph—**M**
Gág, Flavia—**M**
Gág, Wanda—**J**
"Gage, Wilson" (Mary Q. Steele) —**T**
Galdone, Paul—**T**
Gall, Alice Crew—**J**
Galt, Tom—**M**
Gannett, Ruth Chrisman—**M**
Garner, Alan—**T**
Garrett, Randall. See Silverberg, Robert—**T**
Garst, Shannon—**J**
Gates, Doris—**J**
Gatti, Attilio—**J**
Gay, Zhenya—**M**
Geisel, Theodor Seuss. See "Seuss, Dr."—**M**
Gekiere, Madeleine—**T**
George, Jean Craighead—**M**
"Gibson, Josephine." See Hine, Al and Joslin, Sesyle—**T**
Gibson, Katharine—**J**
Gipson, Fred—**T**
Girvan, Helen—**M**
Glubok, Shirley—**T**
Godden, Rumer—**M**

Gollomb, Joseph—**J**
Goudey, Alice E.—**T**
Goudge, Elizabeth—**T**
Grabiański, Janusz—**T**
Graham, Lorenz—**T**
Graham, Margaret Bloy—**M**
Graham, Shirley—**M**
Gramatky, Hardie—**J**
Gray, Elizabeth Janet (Elizabeth Gray Vining)—**J**
Green, Roger Lancelyn—**T**
Greenaway, Kate—**J**
Grierson, Elizabeth W.—**J**
Grifalconi, Ann—**T**
Grinnell, George Bird—**J**
Gripe, Harald. See Gripe, Maria —**T**
Gripe, Maria—**T**
Guillot, René—**M**
Gurko, Leo—**T**
Gurko, Miriam—**T**

Haas, Irene—**T**
Hader, Berta—**J**
Hader, Elmer—**J**
Haley, Gail E.—**T**
Hall, Rosalys Haskell—**M**
Handforth, Thomas—**J**
Harkins, Philip—**M**
Harnett, Cynthia—**T**
Hartman, Gertrude—**J**
Haskell, Helen Eggleston—**J**
Haugaard, Erik Christian—**T**
Hautzig, Esther—**T**
Havighurst, Marion—**M**
Havighurst, Walter—**M**
Hawthorne, Hildegarde—**J**
Hays, Wilma Pitchford—**T**
Haywood, Carolyn—**J**
Headley, Elizabeth. See Cavanna, Betty—**M**
Heinlein, Robert A.—**M**
Henderson, Le Grand. See "Le Grand"—**J**
Henry, Marguerite—**J**
Hentoff, Nat—**T**
Herald, Kathleen. See Peyton, K. M.—**T**
Hess, Fjeril—**J**
Hewes, Agnes Danforth—**J**
Heyliger, William—**J**
Hightower, Florence—**T**
Hillyer, V. M.—**J**
Hine, Al ("Josephine Gibson," "G. B. Kirtland")—**T**
Hine, Sesyle Joslin. See Joslin, Sesyle—**T**
"Hippopotamus, Eugene H." See Kraus, Robert—**T**
Hirsch, S. Carl—**T**
Hoban, Lillian—**T**

Hoban, Russell—T
Hodges, C. Walter—T
Hoff, Syd—T
Hoffmann, Felix—T
Hofsinde, Robert—T
Hogan, Inez—M
Hogner, Dorothy—J
Hogner, Nils—J
Hogrogian, Nonny—T
Holberg, Richard A.—J
Holberg, Ruth—J
Holbrook, Stewart—T
Holland, Rupert Sargent—J
Holling, H. C.—J
Holling, Lucille W. See Holling,
    H. C.—J
Hosford, Dorothy—M
Howard, Elizabeth—M
Hunt, Clara Whitehill—J
Hunt, Irene—T
Hunt, Mabel Leigh—J
Hunter, Mollie (Maureen Mollie
    Hunter McVeigh McIlwraith)
    —T
Huntington, Harriet E.—M
Hurd, Clement—M
Hurd, Edith Thacher—M
Hürlimann, Bettina—T
Hutchins, Ross E.—T
Hyde, Margaret O.—T

"Ilin, M." (I. Marshak)—J
Ipcar, Dahlov—T
"Irving, Robert." See Adler,
    Irving—T

Jacques, Robin—T
Jagendorf, Moritz Adolf—M
"James, Dynely." See Mayne,
    William—T
James, Will—J
Jansson, Tove—T
Jarrell, Randall—T
Jewett, Eleanore M.—M
Johnson, Annabel—T
"Johnson, Crockett" (David
    Johnson Leisk)—T
Johnson, Edgar—T
Johnson, Gerald W.—T
Johnson, Margaret Sweet—J
Johnson, Siddie Joe—J
Jones, Elizabeth Orton—J
Jones, Harold—T
Jones, Mary Alice—M
"Jorgenson, Ivar." See Silver-
    berg, Robert—T
Joslin, Sesyle ("Josephine Gib-
    son," "G. B. Kirtland")—T
Judson, Clara Ingram—J
Justus, May—J

Kahl, Virginia—M
Kalashnikoff, Nicholas—M
Kaler, James O. See "Otis,
    James"—J
Kästner, Erich—T
Keats, Ezra Jack—M
Keeping, Charles—T
Keith, Harold—M
Kelly, Eric P.—J
Kelsey, Alice Geer—M
Kendall, Carol—T
"Kendall, Lace." See Stouten-
    burg, Adrien—T
Kent, Louise Andrews—J
Kepes, Juliet—T
Kettelkamp, Larry—T
Kingman, Lee—M
"Kirtland, G. B." See Hine, Al
    and Joslin, Sesyle—T
Kjelgaard, Jim—J
Knight, Ruth Adams—M
Knipe, Alden Arthur—J
Knipe, Emilie Benson—J
"Knox, Calvin M." See Silver-
    berg, Robert—T
Knox, Rose B.—J
Koering, Ursula—M
Koffler, Camilla. See "Ylla"—M
Konigsburg, E. L.—T
Krasilovsky, Phyllis—M
Kraus, Robert ("Eugene H.
    Hippopotamus")—T
Krauss, Ruth—M
Kredel, Fritz—M
Krumgold, Joseph—M
Krush, Beth—M
Krush, Joe—M
Krüss, James—T
Kuskin, Karla ("Nicholas
    Charles")—T
Kyle, Anne D.—J
"Kyle, Elisabeth" (Agnes Mary
    Robertson Dunlop)—M

Laboulaye, Édouard—J
La Mare, Walter De. See De
    La Mare, Walter—T
Lamb, Harold—J
Lambert, Janet—T
Lampman, Evelyn Sibley
    ("Lynn Bronson")—M
Lamprey, Louise—J
Lane, Sheena Porter. See Por-
    ter, Sheena—T
Langstaff, John—T
Lansing, Marion Florence—J
Laskowski, Janina Domanska.
    See Domanska, Janina—T
Laskowski, Jerzy—T
Latham, Jean Lee—M
Lathrop, Dorothy P.—J

Lattimore, Eleanor Frances—J
Lauber, Patricia—T
Laut, Agnes C.—J
Lawrence, Mildred—M
Lawson, Marie Abrams. See
    Lawson, Robert—J
Lawson, Robert—J
Leaf, Munro—J
Lee, Manning de V.—M
Lee, Mildred (Mildred Lee
    Scudder)—T
Lee, Tina—M
Leeming, Joseph—J
Leeuw, Adèle de. See de
    Leeuw, Adèle—J
"Le Grand" (Le Grand Hender-
    son)—J
"Leodhas, Sorche Nic." See
    "Nic Leodhas, Sorche"—T
Leighton, Margaret—M
Leisk, David Johnson. See
    "Johnson, Crockett"—T
"L'Engle, Madeleine" (Made-
    leine Franklin)—M
Lenski, Lois—J
Lent, Blair ("Ernest Small")—T
Lent, Henry B.—J
Le Sueur, Meridel—M
Lewellen, John—M
Lewis, C. S.—M
Lewis, Elizabeth Foreman—J
Lewiton, Mina—M
Ley, Willy—T
Lifton, Betty Jean—T
Linderman, Frank B.—J
Lindgren, Astrid—M
Lindman, Maj—J
Lindquist, Jennie D.—M
Lindquist, Willis—M
Lionni, Leo—T
Lipkind, William—M
Lippincott, Joseph Wharton—
    M
Lobel, Anita—T
Lobel, Arnold—T
Lofting, Hugh—J
Longstreth, T. Morris—M
"Lord, Nancy." See Titus, Eve
    —T
Lorenzini, Carlo. See "Collodi,
    C."—J
Lovelace, Maud Hart—J
Low, Joseph—T
Lownsbery, Eloise—J
Lucas, Jannette May—J

McCloskey, Robert—J
McClung, Robert M.—M
McCord, David—T
McCracken, Harold—J
"MacDonald, Golden." See
    Brown, Margaret Wise—J

Sandberg, Lasse—**T**
Sandburg, Helga—**T**
Sandoz, Mari—**T**
Sarg, Tony—**J**
Sasek, Miroslav—**T**
Sauer, Julia L.—**M**
Savery, Constance—**J**
Sawyer, Ruth—**J**
Sayers, Frances Clarke—**J**
Scarry, Richard—**T**
Schaefer, Jack—**T**
Scheele, William E.—**T**
Schindelman, Joseph—**T**
Schlein, Miriam—**M**
Schlick, Pamela. See Bianco, Margery Williams—**J**
Schneider, Herman—**M**
Schneider, Nina—**M**
Scholz, Jackson V.—**M**
Schoonover, Frank—**M**
Schultz, James Willard—**J**
Schulz, Charles—**T**
Scoville, Samuel Jr.—**J**
Scudder, Mildred Lee. See Lee, Mildred—**T**
Seaman, Augusta Huiell—**J**
"Sebastian, Lee." See Silverberg, Robert—**T**
Seignobosc, Françoise. See "Françoise"—**M**
Selsam, Millicent E.—**M**
Sendak, Maurice—**M**
Seredy, Kate—**J**
Serraillier, Ian—**T**
"Seuss, Dr." (Theodor Seuss Geisel)—**M**
Sewell, Helen—**J**
Shannon, Monica—**J**
Shapiro, Irwin—**J**
Sharp, Margery—**T**
Sheahan, Henry Beston. See Beston, Henry—**T**
Shecter, Ben—**T**
Shepard, Ernest—**M**
Shimin, Symeon—**T**
Shippen, Katherine B.—**M**
Shotwell, Louisa R.—**T**
Shulevitz, Uri—**T**
Shura, Mary Francis (Mary Francis Craig)—**T**
Sidjakov, Nicolas—**M**
Silverberg, Robert ("Walker Chapman," "Walter Drummond," "Ivar Jorgenson," "Calvin M. Knox," "David Osborne," "Robert Randall," "Lee Sebastian")—**T**
Simon, Charlie May—**J**
Simon, Howard—**M**
Simont, Marc—**M**
Singer, Isaac Bashevis—**T**

Skinner, Constance Lindsay—**M**
Slobodkin, Louis—**J**
Slobodkina, Esphyr—**T**
"Small, Ernest." See Lent, Blair—**T**
Smith, Jessie Willcox—**J**
Snedeker, Caroline Dale—**J**
Snyder, Zilpha Keatley—**T**
Sommerfelt, Aimée—**T**
Sorensen, Virginia—**M**
Southall, Ivan—**T**
Spang Olsen, Ib. See Olsen, Ib Spang
Speare, Elizabeth George—**M**
"Spencer, Cornelia" (Grace S. Yaukey)—**J**
Sperry, Armstrong—**J**
Spier, Peter—**T**
Spilka, Arnold—**T**
Spykman, Elizabeth C.—**M**
Spyri, Johanna—**J**
"Stanton, Schuyler." See L. Frank Baum—**T**
Stapp, Arthur D.—**M**
Steele, Mary Q. See "Gage, Wilson"—**T**
Steele, William O.—**M**
Steig, William—**T**
Stein, Evaleen—**J**
Sterling, Dorothy—**T**
Sterne, Emma Gelders—**M**
Stevenson, Augusta—**M**
Stobbs, William—**T**
Stolz, Mary—**M**
Stone, Helen—**M**
Stong, Phil—**M**
Stoutenburg, Adrien ("Barbie Arden," "Lace Kendall," "Nelson Minier")—**T**
Streatfeild, Noel—**J**
Suba, Susanne—**M**
Sublette, C. M.—**J**
Summers, James L.—**M**
Sutcliff, Rosemary—**M**
Swift, Hildegarde Hoyt—**J**
Syme, Ronald—**M**

"Tatham, Campbell." See Elting, Mary—**M**
Taylor, Sydney—**M**
Teale, Edwin Way—**T**
Tenggren, Gustaf—**M**
Tenniel, Sir John—**J**
Tharp, Louise Hall—**M**
"Thayer, Jane." See Woolley, Catherine—**M**
"Thayer, Peter." See Ames, Rose Wyler—**T**
Thorne-Thomsen, Gudrun—**J**
Thurber, James—**M**

Titus, Eve ("Nancy Lord")—**T**
Todd, Ruthven—**M**
Tolkien, J. R. R.—**M**
Torrey, Marjorie—**M**
Tousey, Sanford—**J**
Travers, Pamela—**J**
Trease, Geoffrey—**M**
Tredez, Alain. See "Trez, Alain"—**T**
Tredez, Denise. See "Trez, Denise"—**T**
Treece, Henry—**M**
Tresselt, Alvin—**M**
Treviño, Elizabeth Borton de (Elizabeth Borton)—**T**
"Trez, Alain" (Alain Tredez)—**T**
"Trez, Denise" (Denise Tredez)—**T**
Trnka, Jiří—**T**
Tudor, Tasha—**J**
Tunis, Edwin—**M**
Tunis, John R.—**M**
Turkle, Brinton—**T**
Turngren, Annette—**M**

Uchida, Yoshiko—**M**
Udry, Janice—**T**
Ungerer, Tomi—**T**
Unnerstad, Edith—**T**
Unwin, Nora S.—**M**
Urmston, Mary—**M**

Vance, Marguerite—**M**
"Van Dyne, Edith." See Baum, L. Frank—**T**
van Stockum, Hilda—**J**
Venturo, Betty Lou Baker (Betty Baker)—**T**
Verne, Jules—**J**
Vining, Elizabeth Gray. See Gray, Elizabeth Janet—**J**
Voight, Virginia Frances—**M**

Waber, Bernard—**T**
Wahl, Jan—**T**
Waldeck, Jo Besse McElveen—**J**
Waldeck, Theodore J.—**J**
Walden, Amelia Elizabeth—**M**
Wallace, Dillon—**J**
Ward, Lynd. See McNeer, May—**J**
Watkins-Pitchford, Denys James. See "BB"—**T**
Weber, Lenora Mattingly—**M**
Weisgard, Leonard—**J**
Weiss, Harvey—**T**
Wellman, Manly Wade—**M**
Wells, Rhea—**J**

J—The Junior Book of Authors; **M**—More Junior Authors; **T**—Third Book of Junior Authors

Wersba, Barbara—**T**
Werth, Kurt—**M**
Wheeler, Francis Rolt-. See Rolt-Wheeler, Francis—**J**
Wheeler, Opal—**M**
White, Anne Terry—**M**
White, E. B.—**M**
White, Eliza Orne—**J**
White, Robb—**J**
Whitney, Elinor—**J**
Whitney, Phyllis A.—**J**
Wibberley, Leonard—**M**
Wier, Ester—**T**
Wiese, Kurt—**J**
Wilder, Laura Ingalls—**J**
Wildsmith, Brian—**T**
Wilkins, Mary Huiskamp Calhoun. See Calhoun, Mary—**T**
Williams, Garth—**M**

Williamson, Joanne S.—**T**
Winterfeld, Henry ("Manfred Michael")—**T**
Wojciechowska, Maia—**T**
Wondriska, William—**T**
Wood, Esther—**J**
Woody, Regina J.—**M**
Woolley, Catherine ("Jane Thayer")—**M**
Worth, Kathryn—**J**
Wuorio, Eva-Lis—**T**
Wyeth, N. C.—**J**
Wyler, Rose. See Ames, Rose Wyler—**T**
Wyndham, Lee—**M**

Yamaguchi, Marianne—**T**
Yamaguchi, Tohr—**T**

Yashima, Taro—**M**
Yates, Elizabeth—**J**
Yates, Raymond F.—**M**
Yaukey, Grace S. See "Spencer, Cornelia"—**J**
"Ylla" (Camilla Koffler)—**M**
Young, Ed—**T**
Young, Ella—**J**

Zarchy, Harry—**M**
Zemach, Harve—**T**
Zemach, Margot—**T**
Zim, Herbert S.—**J**
Zimnik, Reiner—**T**
Zion, Gene—**M**
Zollinger, Gulielma—**J**
Zolotow, Charlotte—**M**
Zwilgmeyer, Dikken—**J**

J—The Junior Book of Authors; **M**—More Junior Authors; **T**—Third Book of Junior Authors